W9-CBP-845

The
Southern Baptist Convention
and Its People
1607-1972

The Southern Baptist Convention
and Its People
1607·1972

Robert A. Baker

BROADMAN PRESS · NASHVILLE, TENNESSEE

Library of Congress Catalog Card Number: 73-91614
Dewey Decimal Classification: 286.06
Printed in the United States of America

CONTENTS

PREFACE

There has been nothing available for use as a text for Southern Baptist history since the fine work of W. W. Barnes, *The Southern Baptist Convention,* went out of print several years ago. It is inconceivable that without some instruction young Southern Baptist ministers should be expected to mature rapidly enough to work effectively without delay in a denominational structure whose proceedings sometimes are complex and whose history forms such a vital link with the present. The material in this book has been used for the past several years in manuscript to inform Southern Baptist students how their denomination has developed to its present proportions and to assist them in understanding how the huge and sometimes intricate Convention structure operates. Most of the important documents referred to in this book are found in my *Source Book* (Nashville: Broadman Press, 1966), which follows almost the same outline as this book.

A history of the Southern Baptist Convention demands a larger perspective than simply a study of the organization itself. A holistic approach to the Convention, its constituency, and its historical context is necessary to make the story intelligible. The constantly shifting political, economic, social, and religious milieu must always form a part of the picture if the Convention is to be interpreted accurately. For example, there was no "religious" reason to explain why Baptists in practically every state in the South reported a decrease in baptisms in the late 1920's. The answer is found in economics: fewer missionaries were employed because of the financial crisis and there were fewer conversions as a result. "Secular" factors constantly spill over into Baptist development, and the scene on the canvas is deficient without them.

Furthermore, a study of the Convention structure without surveying the constituency (who actually make up the Convention) ignores a principal part of the story. The advances of the Convention have always resulted from the interaction between the constituency (people, churches, associations, and state bodies) and the Convention itself. **IX**

Only through the recognition of the structural relationships that extend from the people to the Convention can the fragile "rope of straw" binding together all cooperating Southern Baptists be understood and strengthened.

In addition, for the first time in such a history an attempt has been made in this account to secure accurate statistics and use them in interpreting Southern Baptists. It is true, of course, that the improper manipulation of statistics is one of the classic forms of lying, but the proper use of statistics can provide answers to be found nowhere else. Did Southern Baptists grow or decline in a given period? How rapid was the growth in that period, and how does it compare with the rate of growth experienced in other chronological periods? How does the growth in one region of the nation compare with the growth in others, and of what significance is this? Did Southern Baptists increase at a rate faster or slower than that of the population about them? Was this growth achieved at such a time and under such circumstances that it revealed the priorities of the people? Statistics can often answer these and other questions that reflect the character as well as the zeal of the people. Statistical analysis, of course, requires reliable statistics, and no little effort was made to secure accurate and consistent sources for this information. In the Appendix will be found a description of the sources used for the various statistical data and an evaluation of their reliability.

It was necessary to utilize smaller geographical divisions than the entire Convention territory in order to describe and compare the advance of the constituency in the various chronological periods of this study. State divisions were impracticable, particularly in the modern period when fifty subdivisions would be required. It was decided to adapt the regional demarcations utilized by the United States Census Bureau, which were developed by them on the basis of natural physiographic features. These regional divisions were both applicable and relevant to Southern Baptist development during the 128 years of Southern Baptist life, so they were adapted with slight modifications for this story.

The population growth reflected in the statistics of the Census Bureau is very significant. The number of people in each region and state, the rate of their increase, and the mobility of the population substantially affect the history of Southern Baptists. For example, the principal reason for Southern Baptist expansion from work in eighteen states in 1917 to activity in all fifty states of the Union in 1972 was the mobility of the population. For the purpose of making comparative statistics useful, an effort has been made to translate percentages of growth into easily identifiable common denominators. Thus, both for population and for Baptists, the method that was chosen to put the statistics into comparative form was to note the increase in number at the end of a period over the number at the beginning of the period. This increase was translated into a percentage for the total number of years in the period, then divided by the number of years in the period to give the average annual percentage of increase over the original figure. While this method does not reflect the cumulative annual percentage of increase as the original number grew year by year, it does give an accurate means of computing the average annual growth over an entire period in such fashion that the rate of advance can quickly be compared from region to region and from chronological period to chronological period.

The question of naming important leadership in the various regions and chronological divisions has been a perplexing one. It was felt that the naming of leaders chosen by the states and by historians for inclusion in the three volumes of the *Encyclopedia of Southern Baptists* (which included all deceased leaders up to 1970) would be a proper procedure. This was done in the earlier divisions of the story, but in the modern period, in particular, the list became so long and so obviously artificial that it was not felt advisable to include it. Consequently, an attempt was made to summarize the leadership in the modern period in terms of their service as editors, authors, laymen, women, etc. Even these summaries must be recognized as typical or representative rather than completely accurate, because of the contingent factors just mentioned.

Another problem that developed from dealing with so many different elements had to do with documentation. The first draft of several early chapters turned up over a hundred references in each chapter, particularly in those cases where state histories were reviewed. It was felt that in the earlier state stories, where there have been few questions about the facts, the most accurate and up-to-date material is to be found in the three-volume *Encyclopedia of Southern Baptists* edited by Norman W. Cox and Davis C. Woolley, so unless the documentation specifically shows some other source, it can be understood that the summary story of the early state material has come from the *Encyclopedia* under the title of the particular state being discussed. Of course, in some of the later chapters, where specific references are necessary to identify the more recent history, the documentation must of necessity be more complete.

This book has been divided into seven major periods, each one forming a logical and chronological unit. Such a strictly chronological treatment sometimes weakens the organizational continuity that is found in a semi-topical outline, but it also avoids the redundancy and loss of context that inevitably takes place when chronology is ignored. In one chapter in each of the seven periods there is a brief summary of the rapidly changing context in which Southern Baptists lived and worked during that period. The story of the constituency and the events leading to the formation of the Southern Baptist Convention are covered in the first three periods. With the organization of the Convention in 1845, a dual approach to each period will become evident—one section describing the Convention itself, while the other section examines the constituency. These two facets are treated in the same chapters in periods four and five, but periods six and seven have specific chapters on the constituency (chapters 14 and 15), while the Convention is dealt with in chapters 12, 13, and 16.

No one can be more conscious of the inadequacies of this account than the writer. Many details of importance have been passed over for lack of space. Most of these details can be found in the three volumes of the *Encyclopedia of Southern Baptists* prepared by the Historical Commission. Sometimes it appears that there has been a prodigal use of wordage for raw facts or tedious and mechanical description, when something more exciting would have had much more appeal. This, of course, is one of the problems of trying to write into a single volume the story that should be told in no less than a dozen volumes, each providing rich details and plentiful illustrations. For a brief summary like this one, such literary luxuries are not permitted. As it is, the title to this volume notes that the story was limited only to those southern Baptists related to the Southern Baptist Convention. There are many other significant and substantial southern Baptist groups whose story cannot be told here.

Most of the quoted materials in this story are in the public domain. Appreciation is due to several publishers for permission to quote from their current publications. Thanks to Baylor University, Waco, Texas, for permission to include substantial portions of my article published in *The Teacher's Yoke: Studies in Memory of Henry Trantham* (Waco: 1964); to Broadman Press for permission to quote from Robert A. Baker, *A Baptist Source Book* (Nashville: 1966), from W. W. Barnes, *The Southern Baptist Convention 1845-1953* (Nashville: 1954), from *Encyclopedia of Southern Baptists,* Vols. I and II (Nashville: 1958) and Vol. III (Nashville: 1971), from William L. Lumpkin, *Baptist Foundations in the South* (Nashville: 1961), and from William A. Mueller, *A History of Southern Baptist Theological Seminary* (Nashville: 1959); to Convention Press for permission to quote from Robert A. Baker, *The Story of the Sunday School Board* (Nashville: 1966); to the Historical Commission of the Convention for permission to use substantial portions of my article in *Baptist History and Heritage* (Nashville: July, 1973); to the Sunday School Board of the Southern Baptist Convention for permission to quote from *The Quarterly Review*

(Nashville: issued quarterly each year); to the American Baptist Historical Society for permission to quote from *Foundations* (Rochester, New York; published quarterly each year); to Oxford University Press for permission to quote from David M. Reimers, *White Protestantism and the Negro* (New York: 1965); to the General Board, South Carolina Baptist Convention for permission to quote from Joe M. King, *History of South Carolina Baptists* (Columbia: 1964); to James E. Tull for permission to quote from his excellent work, *A Study of Southern Baptist Landmarkism in the Light of Historical Baptist Ecclesiology* (Ph.D. dissertation, Columbia University, New York, 1960: privately published); to the University of Tennessee Press for permission to quote from John Lee Eighmy, *Churches in Cultural Captivity* (Knoxville: 1972); and to the Virginia Baptist Board of Missions and Education for permission to quote from Garnett Ryland, *The Baptists of Virginia 1699-1926* (Richmond: 1955).

Appreciation is expressed also to Lynn E. May, Jr., and his staff at the Historical Commission of the Southern Baptist Convention for their helpful cooperation and to the staff of Fleming Library, Southwestern Baptist Theological Seminary, Fort Worth, Texas, for numerous services. William L. Lumpkin read a portion of the manuscript and caught some of my mistakes.

My sincere thanks to my secretary, Sue Rainey, who not only typed the manuscript but read it carefully and suggested many changes that greatly improved the story. Despite this assistance, the errors that have undoubtedly crept into a manuscript that deals with so many names, dates, statistics, percentages, and summary interpretations are my own responsibility. I am grateful to my helpmeet at home for understanding the spending of much time in this "after hours" ministry of research and writing. Most of all, I am grateful to a gracious God who permitted me to complete this manuscript after a severe illness.

Robert A. Baker

Fort Worth, Texas, 1973

BAPTIST BEGINNINGS IN THE SOUTH
1607-1740
From the First Permanent Settlement in the South
to the First Great Awakening

1 The First Southern Baptists

The first Baptists in America originated principally with the emigration of General and Particular Baptists from Great Britain in the
seventeenth and eighteenth centuries. Such a statement, of course,
needs amplifying. Why did these Baptists come from Britain? Why
were some called General and some called Particular Baptists, and
what distinguished one group from the other? Why did they leave
their comfortable homes and make the perilous trip to crude hamlets
in the American wilderness?

The British Cradle

To understand Baptist beginnings in America, one must plant his
feet firmly on the soil of Great Britain. It is true that the stage for
this drama was the American wilderness, yet the script was written
in Britain; the players were British; their thoughts, attitudes, and
reactions were British; all of the stagehands were British; and the
theater belonged to a British proprietor. The British background
explains the presence of Baptists in America, the doctrinal differences
that existed among them, and the kind of people they were.

Great Britain created the world for early American Baptists. What
a world it was! A millennium of history focused on seventeenth-century **15**

Britain, the very century that brought British Baptist people to American shores. The Council of Whitby in A.D. 664 had introduced Roman Catholic domination into England. Open dissent followed. From these dissenters at Whitby runs a direct road through Hastings, Wycliffe, Lollardy, Mortmain, Premunire, Provisors, and Reformation that finally led to complete alienation between Canterbury and Rome. Under Henry VIII (1509-47) England severed her relationship with Rome, and Henry was declared to be both secular sovereign of England and head of the church in England. The monarch now became both the political head of a nation and the religious leader of all his people. The two medieval swords, symbols of secular and spiritual sovereignty once shared by emperor and pope, now belonged to the king of England in his realm. He demanded loyalty and conformity in religious matters as well as secular. To differ with him religiously was more than heresy; it was treason.

It is not difficult to understand why this state of affairs would create religious dissent. Many Englishmen who would gladly bow the knee to their secular sovereign were unwilling to shackle their consciences to submit to his religious convictions. This was especially true when religious convictions might change radically from sovereign to sovereign. Henry himself wavered in his doctrinal ideas between a strict Roman Catholicism and a tendency toward reform; his daughter Mary (1553-58) was completely Roman Catholic, and forced legislation through Parliament that returned the English church to the control of the pope; her half-sister Elizabeth (1558-1603) wrenched the English church back into Protestantism. Since the king or queen was head of the church, an overnight change from Protestantism to complete Catholicism (which took place when Mary assumed the throne) or from Catholicism to Protestantism (which took place when Elizabeth gained control) demanded that the consciences of all the people of England promptly oscillate in this same fashion. This was a monstrous dilemma for any person who really believed something, for he could not discard true doctrinal convictions simply because a new occupant had come to the palace. Orthodoxy and heresy exchanged places so rapidly at times and so often that conformity was more important than conviction. It was more needful to please the king or queen than it was to please God.

Dissent from this unfortunate situation was already taking place before the death of Queen Elizabeth I in 1603. The tension was increased when a distant cousin of Elizabeth, James VI of Scotland, came to England as James I. He brusquely bellowed that anyone who did not agree with him religiously would be harried out of the land. To compound the problem, his subjects did not know at first what his religious convictions would be. He was the son of a pious

Roman Catholic mother but for many years had been king in Scotland where Presbyterianism was dominant. Before long he developed anti-Catholic and anti-Presbyterian feelings, and demanded that the Church of England, which was halfway between Roman Catholicism and Protestantism, become the religious standard for every one of his subjects. Dissenters of many kinds were severely persecuted during the remainder of his rule. His son, Charles, succeeded him in 1625 and continued persecution of dissenters. Civil war sparked by religious differences broke out early in the 1640's, and Charles was defeated and beheaded in 1649. From then until 1660, Protestant dissent was permitted under Oliver Cromwell.

Most severe persecution of dissenters took place during the reign of Charles II from 1660 to 1685. Five acts known as the Clarendon Code were passed. The Corporation Act of 1661 excluded all dissenters from taking part in local government in England. The Act of Uniformity of 1662 banished all pastors from the pulpits and all teachers from public or private schools who did not conform doctrinally to the Church of England. The Conventicle Act of 1664 forbade dissenters from meeting for religious purposes. The Five Mile Act of 1665 prohibited dissenting ministers from coming within five miles of any city or town or of any parish in which they had ministered. The Test Act of 1673 excluded dissenters from all civil and military positions. On his deathbed in 1685, Charles was received into the Roman Catholic Church and was succeeded by his brother James, an active Roman Catholic. This situation gave rise to fears by non-Catholics that additional persecution was in the offing.

Baptists in England

The demand that the consciences of the English people coincide with the religious position taken by the crown and the attempt to enforce conformity by physical persecution brought several types of response from the people in the sixteenth and seventeenth centuries in England. Some followers of John Calvin determined to remain within the established Church of England and attempt to purify it from its corruptions, particularly those copied from the Roman Catholic system. By 1564 these were known as Puritans, and they played an important part in the controversies of the next century.

It was inevitable that some dissenters would be unwilling to remain within the church system which they regarded as unscriptural and unjust. As early as 1567 the authorities apprehended a group in London who had withdrawn from the Church of England and organized a church whose authority was conceived to be in the congregation itself. Several of these Separate or Independent churches can be identified in the early seventeenth century.

It was in this context that English Baptists emerged. The full story of these worthy forebears cannot be told here, but their courageous stand for religious liberty is a matter of record. They were the first Englishmen to reject totally the episcopal government of the established church, its ordinances (baptism and the Supper), and the authority of the secular sovereign to coerce the people in matters of conscience.

Two types of Baptists developed in England: General Baptists and Particular Baptists. The early history of the two is quite dissimilar. General Baptists originated historically from the Smyth-Helwys-Murton separation that formed what is regarded as the first Baptist church on English soil in 1611 or 1612 at Spitalfield, just outside of London. Thomas Helwys, the actual founder of this church, boldly published the doctrine of full religious liberty about 1612, the first time this principle had been advocated in writing in England. A presentation copy addressed to King James I bluntly said that the king was a man, not God, and thus had no authority to bind the souls of men to follow the religious convictions of the crown. For writing this, Helwys died in prison, but the church lived.

These Baptists were called General Baptists because they believed in the doctrine of the general atonement of Christ. Their confession of 1678 clearly enunciated this view in the following words:

> God the father, out of his royal bounty, and fountain of love, when all mankind was fallen by sin, in breaking of the first covenant of works made with them in Adam, did chuse Jesus Christ, and sent him into the world to die for Adam, or fallen man. And God's love is manifest to all mankind, in that he is not willing, as himself hath sworn, and abundantly declared in his word, that mankind should perish eternally, but would have all to be saved, and come to the knowledge of the truth. And Christ died for all men, and there is a sufficiency in his death and merits for the sins of the whole world, and hath appointed the gospel to be preached unto all, and hath sent forth his spirit to accompany the word in order to beget repentance and faith: so that if any do perish, it's not for want of the means of grace manifested by Christ to them, but for the non-improvement of the grace of God, offered freely to them through Christ in the gospel.[1]

General Baptists were probably influenced toward these views by their sojourn in the Amsterdam area to which John Smyth and company had fled from English persecution in 1609. In that very section of the Low Countries, the Mennonite adherents were dominant and were strongly pressing this distinct view of the work of Christ.

By 1626 there were five General Baptist churches in England with about 150 members. They numbered about forty churches by 1644. In 1654 they formed the General Assembly of General Baptists and in 1678 adopted a strong confession of faith, a part of which was quoted above. Many of these General Baptists, holding the distinctive doctrine set out heretofore, emigrated to Carolina and Virginia in the colonial period, and they will be identified when possible.

Another distinctive characteristic of the General Baptists was their centralized ecclesiology. While Particular Baptists magnified the autonomy of their local congregations almost to the point of fault, General Baptists delegated considerable authority to the general body which they organized in 1654. This general body disciplined church members, handled churches rather high-handedly, and in general overwhelmed the authority of the churches in its structure. Article XXXIX of their 1678 confession of faith said:

> General councils, or assemblies, consisting of Bishops, Elders, and Brethren, of the several churches of Christ, and being legally convened, and met together out of all the churches, and the churches appearing there by their representatives, make but one church, and have lawful right, and suffrage in this general meeting, or assembly, to act in the name of Christ; it being of divine authority, and is the best means under heaven to preserve unity, to prevent heresy, and superintendency among, or in any congregation whatsoever within its own limits, or jurisdiction. And to such a meeting or assembly, appeals ought to be made, in case any injustice be done, or heresy, and schism countenanced, in any particular congregation of Christ, and the decisive voice in such general assemblies is the major part, and such general assemblies have lawful power to hear, and determine, as also to excommunicate.[2]

This centralizing tendency of General Baptists appeared among Baptists of this type after they moved to American shores.

Particular Baptists, on the other hand, developed historically from the Jacob-Lathrop-Jessey separation. Probably about 1638 the first Particular Baptist church was organized in England, and this movement grew under the leadership of men like John Spilsbury, Henry Jessey, and William Kiffen.

The name Particular Baptists was applied to them because they believed in a limited or particular atonement; that is, that Christ died only for the elect. Their confession of faith of 1689 was quite specific at this point, as follows:

> 3. By the *decree* of God, for the manifestation of his glory some men and Angels are predestinated, or fore-ordained to Eternal Life, through Jesus Christ, to the praise of his glorious grace; others being left to act in their sin to their just condemnation, to the praise of his glorious justice.
> 4. These Angels and Men thus predestinated, and fore-ordained, are particularly, and unchangeably designed, and their number so certain, and definite, that it cannot be either increased, or diminished.
> 5. Those of mankind that are predestinated to life, God, before the foundation of the world was laid, according to his eternal and immutable purpose, and the secret Council and good pleasure of his will,

hath chosen in Christ unto everlasting glory, out of his meer free grace and love; without any other thing in the creature as a condition or cause moving him thereunto.

6. As God hath appointed the Elect unto glory, so he hath by the eternal and most free purpose of his will, fore-ordained all the means thereunto, wherefore they who are elected, being faln in Adam, are redeemed by Christ, are effectually called unto faith in Christ, by his spirit working in due season, are justifyed, adopted, sanctified, and kept by his power through faith unto salvation; neither are any other redeemed by Christ, or effectually called, justified, adopted, sanctified, and saved, but the Elect only.[3]

Some of the early Baptist people in Carolina and Virginia came from the ranks of these Particular Baptists, as will be described hereafter.

Although these two groups of Baptists did not see eye to eye on all doctrines, they were agreed on the basic interpretation of the Christian faith. In the Particular Baptist confession of faith of 1644, for example, it was made plain that Baptists expected to suffer for their convictions concerning religious liberty. They said:

But if God with-hold the Magistrates allowance and furtherance herein; yet we must notwithstanding proceed together in Christian communion, not daring to give place to suspend our practice, but to walk in obedience to Christ in the profession and holding forth this faith before mentioned, even in the midst of all trialls and afflictions, not accounting our goods, lands, wives, children, fathers, mothers, brethren, sisters, yea, and our own lives dear unto us, so we may finish our course with joy: remembering alwayes we ought to obey God rather than men.[4]

How could one better express the Particular Baptists' view of baptism of the believer than they said it in this same confession?

That Baptisme is an Ordinance of the new Testament, given by Christ, to be dispensed onely upon persons professing faith, or that are Disciples, or taught, who upon a profession of faith, ought to be baptized. The way and manner of the dispensing of this Ordinance the Scripture holds out to be dipping or plunging the whole body under water: it being a signe, must answer the thing signified, which are these: first, the washing the whole soule in the bloud of Christ: Secondly, that interest the Saints have in the death, buriall, and resurrection; thirdly, together with a confirmation of our faith, that as certainly as the body is buried under water, and riseth againe, so certainly shall the bodies of the Saints be raised by the power of Christ, in the day of the resurrection, to reigne with Christ.[5]

Because of their views and particularly their insistence upon religious freedom, Baptists felt the heavy hand of persecution, not only from the Anglicans but from other groups as well during this entire period in English history. It is not surprising, then, that they turned their eyes toward the new world in colonial America.

The American Haven

Many dissenters fled their British homes during these days of persecution. Among them were Baptists. The members who constituted the first Baptist church on English soil, referred to previously as being founded about 1611-12, had first gone to Amsterdam in 1607 to escape their persecutors, but being desirous of bearing witness in their own land, they returned to form the church near London. Other dissenters also sought refuge in the Low Countries.

The principal haven of dissenters, however, was America. In this account, the stories of the first colonies in America cannot be told, but there is evidence that there were Baptist people among some of the earliest settlements in America. The two most famous, of course, were Roger Williams and John Clarke, who founded the settlements that subsequently united to form the Providence Plantations with a charter that granted democratic government and religious liberty. Other Baptist settlements were located in Massachusetts under John Myles and Thomas Gould; in Maine under William Screven; and in Pennsylvania at Pennepek under the pastorate of Elias Keach. Baptist growth in these northern areas was slow. One Baptist historian estimated that by 1740 there were less than a dozen small churches with not more than three hundred total members, most of them by emigration from Britain.

It is curious that with the rather extensive migration to the new world taking place between 1607 and 1660, there is no record of Baptists appearing in the South until after the restoration of Charles II to the throne in 1660. What had deterred Baptists from fleeing in larger numbers to America, and in particular why had not some of them appeared in the southern colonies before 1660?

For one thing, the expense of the journey itself was not inconsiderable. The very poorest accommodations generally cost approximately the equivalent of two years' income of the average worker. Baptists in general were of the lower economic class, and although some may have bound themselves to indentured servitude in America in return for the price of the voyage, the economic factor itself was vital in preventing extensive migration of British Baptists.

Another very basic deterrent was the peril involved in making the long trip in relatively small vessels on the stormy Atlantic Ocean. In his *History of the Welsh Baptists,* J. Davis described the trials of Abel Morgan, an early American Baptist preacher, who left Wales to emigrate to America. Morgan took his family to the seaport of Bristol, and they embarked for the new world on September 28, 1710. Davis continued:

> The next day the wind being contrary, and the ship exceedingly tossed with the tempest, they turned in to Milford haven, where they

were detained three weeks. And when they sailed from that place, they were driven by the tempestuous winds to Cork, in Ireland, where they were obliged to stay five weeks, in very uncomfortable circumstances, as most of the passengers were unwell. From there, however, they all sailed on the 19th of November. On the 14th of December, Abel Morgan's little boy died, and on the 17th of the same month, his dearly beloved wife breathed her last, and both of them were committed to the deep. This was to him a severe trial, indeed. . . . He arrived in America on the 14th of February, 1711.[6]

Added to these perils were the many dangers of the American environment, including unfriendly Indians and unfavorable climate, illustrated vividly by the loss of lives and suffering during the early years at Jamestown and at Plymouth.[7]

Another factor that may have given English Baptists pause was the recognition that dissenters might be jumping from the frying pan into the fire by going to the colonies. The perilous journey to America not only did not take them beyond the strong arm of England, as will be noted shortly, but reports from the several colonies themselves showed that the rude settlements on the virgin continent of America were already highly cultured in the art of persecution. Baptists in England were quite familiar with the tragic situation through the publication there of Roger Williams' *The Bloody Tenet of Persecution* and John Clarke's *Ill News from New England.* These writings described the principles and practice of Congregational intolerance in Massachusetts Bay Colony. Maryland, settled in 1634, tolerated some types of dissent in order to attract needed settlers, but the limited type of toleration and the Roman Catholic character of the colony caused considerable distrust. Providence Plantations was the only northern colony in 1660 that offered complete liberty of conscience, and this colony was under constant attack from its neighbors to eliminate that feature. In the South, Governor William Berkeley of Virginia had been totally intolerant of dissent of any kind from the Church of England after he took office in 1642.

As indicated, it was evident also that the English government was keeping a careful watch on the colonies across the Atlantic. Three types of colonies were developed during this period: corporate colonies, organized under charters granted by the crown to an incorporated body; proprietary colonies, developed under a grant by the crown to individuals, as in the case of Maryland; and royal colonies which were under the direct supervision of the crown. The first two types of colonies were encouraged early as a means of exploiting potentially profitable colonies without the risk to the crown of loss if the colonizing efforts were not successful. Theoretically, under corporate and proprietary colonies, dissenters might be welcome to assist in the arduous task of carving cities out of the wilderness. However, the crown began taking over control of the colonies as soon as they were successful. Virginia, begun as a corporate colony in 1607, became a royal colony in 1624. Both Maryland, a proprietary colony, and Massachusetts Bay, a corporate colony, were brought under royal control before the end of the seventeenth century, although Maryland was later returned to obedient proprietors. Thoughtful dissenters pondered the question of whether or not their situation would be improved in a colony that had local repression and still felt the strength of the English crown.

In addition, it is likely that many who contemplated the journey to America, and particularly to the South, were repelled by the class structures that were developing. There were extreme class diversities in many of the colonies. Virginia in the South, for example, was stocked with many marginal workers who entered into indentured servitude to pay for their journey; and at the same time, at the opposite extreme, a large group of Cavaliers fled to that colony after the beheading of Charles I in 1649. The spector of Negro slavery, introduced in 1619 into Virginia, also raised many moral and economic questions for marginal economic workers like Baptists and was a melancholy harbinger of evil through the centuries to come. Perhaps these hesitating Englishmen remembered that the Virginia House of Burgesses endeavored to eliminate slavery from Virginia but were overruled by the English government on economic grounds.

On the other hand, there were some factors that were encouraging to an Englishman considering emigration. The economic situation in England at the opening of the seventeenth century was deplorable. Peace with Spain in 1604 found many soldiers and sailors without any means of livelihood. American gold and silver had greatly inflated English currency, but an oversupply of labor reduced the average wage to the very minimum amount that would sustain life. The profitable trading enterprises, some large and some small, beckoned for emigrants at every seaport.

In addition, the basic ingredient of success, the land itself, was extremely plentiful and rich in the new world, while in England this was next to impossible for the lower class to secure. Word had also filtered back that the geography of the great coastal plains, which were partitioned from the hinterlands by the Appalachian mountain barrier, along with the numerous sheltered bays and laborsaving rivers and creeks, provided a providential preparation awaiting those that would come.

Added to these favorable ingredients, there were other factors that beckoned British Baptists to the American shores after the middle of the seventeenth century. Some Baptists and other dissenters in the colonies were well satisfied with the risks they had taken and were experiencing relative prosperity in the new world, and they wrote these tidings back to their friends in England. In their desire to secure settlers, several of the colonies were moderating their persecuting tactics and developing a measure of regional stability and local tolerance. Most of all, however, so far as Baptists in the South were concerned, the advertisement of a new colony where complete religious liberty would prevail in a section of the country with rich and abundant land environed by friendly natives proved irresistible to many British Baptists and other dissenters being rigorously persecuted for their religious beliefs, and the story of Baptists in the South was begun.

Baptist Beginnings in the South

South Carolina. Although an English colony was planted in 1607 at Jamestown, Virginia, the first Baptist church in the South appeared in South Carolina. For that reason, the Carolina story will be told first, although this colony was founded over half a century later than Virginia.

At the very height of religious persecution in England (in the reign of Charles II from 1660 to 1685), a great incentive was given for dissenters to journey to America. In 1663 eight proprietors were given a liberal grant along the southern coast of North America by Charles II, and in 1670 they established the first permanent white settlement in the area and called it Carolina. One of the proprietors, writing to another proprietor in 1663, remarked that they could not expect people to live in the colony without the promise of religious liberty. Later in the year the proprietors said, "We will grant, in as ample manner as the inhabitants shall desire, freedom and liberty of conscience in all religious and spiritual things, and to be kept inviolably with them, we having power in the charter to do so." Not only did their second charter of 1665 guarantee religious freedom, but their agents voiced this principle and pamphlets advertising the colony specifically stated that there would be full liberty of conscience granted to all.

It is no wonder that dissenters flocked to the new colony. The city of Charleston was settled about 1670 by colonists under Joseph West, who later became governor and improved the site of the city. "Ship following ship disembarked its human cargo, most of whom were religious dissenters." [8] John Oldmixon, almost a contemporary of the earlier settlers, in discussing the extensive migration of dissenters to Carolina, mentioned the large company led by Humphrey Blake, brother of the famous Admiral Blake, and it is known that in this company was a nephew, Joseph Blake, whose family were Baptists. Oldmixon said that dissenters probably comprised two thirds of the people in South Carolina in the opening years of the eighteenth century.[9] Scottish dissenters appeared under Lord Cardross and William Dunlop. Englishmen in the Barbados and other parts of the British West Indies constantly removed to Carolina. Three successive governors of South Carolina (Thomas Smith, Joseph Blake, and John Archdale) were dissenters, the last being a Quaker, and all urged dissenters to emigrate to this colony. Smith and Blake seem to have been related rather closely to Baptist life. It is true that in 1706 the Church of England was established in South Carolina and in 1719, at the initiative of the people, South Carolina became a royal colony, but liberty of conscience was not impugned.

A study of land warrants, wills, and other legal documents before 1700 reveals that people and families known to be Baptists were in the colony of South Carolina as early as 1681 and 1682. The Blakes, Axtells, Grimballs, Chapmans, Bullens, Caters, Butlers, and other Baptist emigres were familiar names in the early history of this colony. That many came for religious liberty cannot be doubted. In fact, in March, 1706, citizens of South Carolina in a petition to the House of Lords said that "the greatest part of the inhabitants of South Carolina were Protestant Dissenters from the Church of England, who had been induced to leave their native country by hope of enjoying religious liberty." [10]

North Carolina. The colony of Carolina subsequently was divided into two sections: North and South. In the period before a Baptist church was planted in North Carolina, it is undoubtedly true that there were some Baptists in the area.[11] The Albermarle Assembly passed an Act shortly after 1685 which asserted that all Christians had freedom of conscience in religious matters and could freely assemble for religious services.[12] However, the sharp antagonism of Church of England missionaries who began coming to the province after about 1700, coupled with the great turbulence for the first three decades—the Anglican-Quaker confrontation, the Carey Rebellion of 1711 and thereafter, the Tuscarora War of 1711-12, the continuous smuggling and pirating with local official approval—helped discourage an active Christian witness. On the other hand, marginal laborers and indentured servants, seeking to escape from the increasing competition of Negro slavery, fled in great numbers from Virginia to North Carolina in the period. The population was five times as great before 1730 as it was in 1710, says Paschal.

There is a curious confirmation of the presence of Baptists in this province rather early. It is true that several Anglican missionaries from the Society for the Propagation of the Gospel made no mention of the presence of Baptists in their reports on religious conditions in the province at the opening of the eighteenth century.[13] However, some Baptists were evidently soon included in the local structure of the Anglican church. The organization of the several precincts into vestries after 1701 by the Church of England involved the naming of twelve men of the precinct to act as vestrymen. They did not necessarily need to be members of the Church of England, so ofttimes dissenters who had the confidence of the people were named to the office. Their duties were partly civic and partly ecclesiastical. On June 12, 1714, John Urmstone, Anglican missionary in the Chowan Precinct, wrote to the Society in England to say that two of his vestrymen in Chowan Precinct were "Anabaptists." Four years later Urmstone wrote to the Society that in Currituck a very influential "Anabaptist" was "always chosen Burgess for that precinct and a leading man in our Assemblies, a fit man you will say for a vestryman, but we have too many such in other vestries, whence it is we find so little favor among them." [14]

Virginia. Although the first of the southern colonies to be founded in 1607, Virginia records do not show a Baptist church organized until more than a century later. This is not surprising. From the first the colony refused to allow dissent from the Church of England. The Church of England was established in 1619, and a constant watch was kept to prevent Puritan, prelate, or Quaker from neglecting or challenging its canons. The long, intolerant reign of Governor William Berkeley (who served from 1642 to 1679 with only a brief interruption during the Protectorate) guaranteed there would be no relaxing of rigorous laws against recusants. After the Restoration, Berkeley, a strong royalist, led the legislature to tighten even more the rigid laws of the province against dissent. In 1661 the Virginia Assembly passed an Act which said:

> Whereas, many schismatical persons, out of their averseness to the orthodox established religion, or out of the new fangled conceit of their own heretical inventions, do refuse to have their children baptized; Be it therefore enacted by the authority aforesaid, that all persons who in contempt of the divine sacrament of Baptism, shall refuse when he may carry their child to a lawful minister of that county to have them baptized, shall be amerced two thousand pounds of tobacco; half to the informer; half to the public. [15]

When Lord Culpeper succeeded Berkeley as governor in 1679, he was instructed to permit liberty of conscience to all except Papists. It is likely that this relaxation toward dissent brought non-Anglicans to the Virginia colony. There is one obscure reference to Baptists in Virginia in the journal of the English Quaker Thomas Story. He visited Virginia and noted that on January 23, 1699, at York, the Quaker meeting was held at the house of Thomas Bonger, whom he called "a Preacher among the General Baptists." [16] No other word on Bonger or on these General Baptists of Virginia has been found.

Georgia. This proprietary colony was founded pursuant to a charter grant in 1732 to General James Edward Oglethorpe and Lord John Percival. Oglethorpe was a leader in prison reforms in England and desired to plant a colony where poor debtors could make a fresh start. England also wanted a buffer state between South Carolina and the Spanish in Florida and the French in Louisiana; it was hoped that this colony would produce silks and other raw materials, as well as stimulate fur trade with the Indians; and some felt that it would attract persecuted German Protestants.

In 1733, near the end of this period, Oglethorpe and his party settled the colony at Savannah. Despite direct subsidies from England for the purpose of defense, the colony did not prosper during this period. War with Spain from 1739 to 1744 depleted its resources greatly.

Some Baptists were among the first settlers. William Calvert of Lincolnshire, William Slack of Ireland, and Thomas Walker of Northampton have been the Baptists of Georgia mentioned in the literature.

Thus, the first scanty records involving Baptists in the South speak of these British immigrants in South Carolina, North Carolina, Virginia, and Georgia before any formal Baptist church was organized anywhere in the South. The story of the organization of the earliest Baptist churches in the South will be related in the following chapter.

Notes

1. W. J. McGlothlin, *Baptist Confessions of Faith* (Philadelphia: American Baptist Publication Society, 1911), pp. 137-38.

2. *Ibid.*, p. 154.

3. *Ibid.*, pp. 233-34.

4. *Ibid.*, pp. 185, 188.

5. *Ibid.*

6. J. Davis, *History of the Welsh Baptists* (Pittsburg: D. M. Hogan, 1835), p. 69.

7. See Marcus W. Jernegan, *The American Colonies 1492-1750* (New York: F. Unger Pub. Co., 1959), *passim.*

8. Joe M. King, *History of South Carolina Baptists* (Columbia: General Board of the South Carolina Baptist Convention, 1964), p. 7.

9. John Oldmixon, *History of the British Empire in America*, reprinted in Alexander S. Salley, Jr., ed., *Narratives of Early Carolina 1650-1708* (New York: Charles Scribner's Sons, 1911), pp. 354 ff.

10. George W. Paschal, *History of North Carolina Baptists* (Raleigh: General Board, North Carolina Baptist Convention, 1930), I, p. 64. Compare also Robert A. Baker, *The First Southern Baptists* (Nashville: Broadman Press, 1966), pp. 49-51.

11. Paschal, *op. cit.*, I, pp. 65-66, footnote.

12. *Ibid.*, I, p. 127.

13. *Ibid.*, I, pp. 129-30.

14. *Ibid.*, I, p. 131.

15. Robert A. Baker, *A Baptist Source Book with Particular Reference to Southern Baptists* (Nashville: Broadman Press, 1966), p. 7. Hereafter this reference will be shown as Baker, *Source Book.*

16. Quoted in Garnett Ryland, *The Baptists of Virginia 1699-1926* (Richmond: The Virginia Baptist Board of Missions and Education, 1955), p. 1.

2 Earliest Baptist Churches in the South

The earliest Baptist churches of record in the South were planted in South Carolina (1696 or before), Virginia (1715), and North Carolina (1727). By the time the first of these churches was founded, the . character of the southern colonies had undergone considerable change. In the first century of English colonization the colonies were closely related to England, and the Baptist churches in America were quite similar to those at home except for their remote location. The Baptist preachers and people in America for the most part came from England. Very few indigenous Baptist preachers were found in the southern colonies before 1740. English Baptist doctrinal divisions were reproduced in the American colonies, including such groups as the Particular Baptists, the General Baptists, the Seventh-Day Baptists, the Six-Principle Baptists, and Seekers. The colonial environment contained a strong Church of England influence, particularly in the southern colonies. Leaders in the American Anglican church reproduced the attitude of their English counterparts toward dissenters. Practically all dissenters themselves were copies of their English prototypes. Fortunately, the Act of Toleration of 1689 in England worked a considerable improvement in relations between the government and dissenters, although it must be admitted that it required time before the benefits of this Act were widely enjoyed in America.

However, this situation began to change early in the eighteenth century. There is a curious parallel between political developments in England and those in the colonies. Extensive and rapid development of the English parliamentary system began with the coming of the first Hanover, George I, in 1714. In the American colonies, this same period marked the growing encroachment of the colonial assemblies on the powers of the several governors and royal councils. By gradually obtaining control of provincial funds and by contesting practically all of the administrative prerogatives of the governor, most of the provincial assemblies, aided by the dilatory and ineffective support of the governors by Parliament in England, practically wrested control from the hands of the royal officials. The efforts of the Lords Commissioners for Trade and Plantations, brought into existence in 1696 by

William III to supervise the colonies, were directed during the first half of the eighteenth century toward reducing the colonies to a uniform type through establishing royal control. They were indeed successful in asserting royal control over most of the colonies by 1740, but absentee government, combined at times with poor governors and the aggressive demands of the several assemblies, greatly diminished the effectiveness of their policies.

From an economic viewpoint, the American colonies moved toward a new destiny. To show that it is an ill wind that blows nobody good, the efforts by the Lords Commissioners of England to heighten the efficiency of the First Navigation Act of 1660 and its subsequent revisions by increasing restrictions upon colonial enterprises ultimately resulted in diversification of agriculture and even brought industry to the colonies and thus helped make them more self-sustaining. As will be noted, some of the colonies were helped by the English mercantile policies, while others were hurt.

Another factor of change was the increasing immigration of settlers from elsewhere than England, many of whom felt no loyalty toward the English government and would be inclined to resent its authority.

Writers have often noted that from a religious standpoint both the background and the environment of the colonists on the American shores began to develop a different sort of religious climate than had been found in England or on the continent. The several reformations had worked their purifying effects so that even Roman Catholic Christianity, transplanted primarily from England, was of a different character than that developed in pre-Reformation days. Most American colonists knew of the conflict between Parliament and Charles I and gloried in the rights of Englishmen even in opposition to the crown. The avalanche of English tracts and books in the seventeenth century advocating religious toleration and even religious liberty was familiar to colonial America. With this background and the comparative isolation of the American colonies, a new sort of Christianity began to develop in America. It magnified religious individualism, the development of separate denominations, religion by conviction rather than coercion, competition in religion, a sharpened sense of lay obligation, and similar distinctives that are seen in American Christianity. By the close of this period in 1740, there were probably over 350,000 white population in the southern colonies. From 1725 on, an increasing number of non-English immigrants arrived. By 1750 perhaps nine tenths of the people of New England were still of English descent, probably due to the scarcity of land and to religious intolerance. Nearly two thirds of the population in the middle colonies was made up of Dutch, Scotch-Irish, Germans, Irish, Scots, Swedes, and French. In the southern colonies by this time, the English primarily occupied the coast, while the western areas were principally settled by Scotch-Irish and German immigrants.

During this period the social and economic aspects of southern society began to polarize. Large planters emerged and became a favored class. The use of indentured servants declined through the extension of Negro slavery, which had spread rather rapidly in the South due to what amounted to a climatic and geographical determinism. Already questions were being raised about the status of the Negro, his rights, if any, and his treatment. A curious item has been recently discovered involving the Baptist church at Charleston. In 1711 a problem arose in the Charleston church concerning the treatment of a Negro slave who had been severely punished by his master, a church member, for running away. Some in the church wanted to withdraw fellowship from this slaveholder for the severity of his treatment of the slave. William Fry and William Sadler wrote to the Baptist church at South Moulton, Devon, in England asking their judgment in the matter. The reply urged that peace be restored in the church and essentially supported the member in his severity. The South Moulton church took the matter to the Western Baptist Association in England, which subsequently echoed the position of the South Moulton church.[1]

During the period before 1740 in the southern colonies, in addition, relative prosperity had made life much more attractive for the people. The colonies were exporting rice, indigo, tobacco, lumber products, cotton, and tar for Navy purposes. A few semipublic schools and a number of private schools provided education, particularly for the higher social classes. Fox hunts, dinners, dances, and music brought recreation. Even postal service was enjoyed by Virginia in 1732, and newspapers helped keep the colonists abreast of the times.

South Carolina

In the years between the founding of this colony in 1670 and the close of the period in 1740, conditions within the colony changed in many important ways. The European wars between England and Spain and England and France spilled over into this early settlement. In 1686 and again in 1702-04, Charleston was forced to protect itself from Spanish attacks, while in 1706, five Spanish and French ships attempted to reduce Charleston by sea but were driven away. Wars with the Indians also harrassed the colony, the Tuscaroras in 1713 and the Yamassees in 1715. Troublesome pirates were finally subdued in 1718. Added to these hardships were the intermittent epidemics of various sorts, principally of yellow fever induced by the swampy topography.

Problems sparked by a friction between absentee proprietors and local self-interest were partly responsible in 1693 for the colonial house of commons demanding and securing the right to initiate legislation. In 1719 the house of commons in the colony seized control, and the settlement became a royal colony *de jure* in 1729 when the crown purchased South Carolina from the remaining proprietors.

What is now known as North Carolina was included in this grant to the eight proprietors in 1663, but in the following year a separate proprietary governor and an elective legislature were established in Albemarle in what is now North Carolina, and except from 1691 to 1711, this colony maintained separate governance. North Carolina became a separate royal colony in 1729.

Meanwhile, in South Carolina the pace of life increased rapidly during this period. Rice and indigo became principal crops for export. To encourage the application of their mercantile policies, England established bounties in 1705 for the production of indigo, tar, pitch, hemp, turpentine, and wooden masts, and South Carolina received considerable income from this source. The livestock industry (swine in particular) began to flourish, and animal skins were added to the list of exports. Apprenticeship legislation helped increase the supply of artisans, and the utilization of natural resources laid the foundations for milling, meat-packing, textile-manufacturing, shoemaking, etc. A significant factor in the story of the colony was the acquiring of large tracts of good land by the planters as they looked to future needs. By 1730 practically all of the good unoccupied land near the coast and along navigable rivers in South Carolina was claimed. As a result, the frontier began to move toward the west rapidly, creating new opportunities and problems. Into this back country came Germans, Swiss, Huguenots, and other European immigrants. Many of these settled as "squatters," who had no legal title to the lands they occupied. They claimed ownership by reason of occupation and the hazards involved in living on the land. Like other colonial governments, South Carolina was involved during this entire period in the struggle by the people to resist arbitrary government and enlarge their own privileges.

After some controversy, in 1706 the Church of England was established as the official faith in South Carolina. However, neither this event nor the shift in 1719 from proprietary to royal control affected the liberty of conscience in religious matters that had characterized this colony from its beginning.

In this background, five small Baptist churches appeared in South Carolina before 1740. Four of these were organized in Charleston and vicinity, while one was founded in the Peedee section to the north and west.

Charleston Church. The records of the First Baptist Church, Charleston, the earliest Baptist church to be formed in the South, were entirely destroyed in the great Charleston flood of September 15, 1752. As a matter of fact, all denominations in Charleston were deficient in the preservation of their earliest records.

However, authentic legal records make it possible for Southern Baptists to know that their first church actually existed before the opening of the eighteenth century. A legal execution of a deed involving a gift to the Baptist church by William Elliott of Lot No. 62 on Church Street in Charleston dated July 18, 1699, contained a clause, "of which Church he professeth himself a member." Furthermore, a legally recorded deed of sale dated January 20, 1701, described the bounds of certain property to be "to the northward upon the Baptist Meeting House." [2]

Additional collateral records speak of the antiquity of this church. The Baptist historian Morgan Edwards visited Charleston in 1771-72 and secured information which he later put into written form. He conversed with Oliver Hart (whose wife was a Screven), at that time pastor of this Charleston church, who had actually seen the original records of the church before they were destroyed in 1752. Edwards might also have talked with Mrs. Catherine Stoll Screven Pelot, wife of the son of the first pastor of the church, since Mrs. Pelot did not die until 1772. In addition, there were scores of grandchildren of William Screven, the first pastor. Many of them lived in Charleston at this time and could have had authentic knowledge of the early days of the church.

Wood Furman's *History of the Charleston Association* and Morgan Edwards' account were the principal sources of the work of David Benedict, although Benedict in preparing his 1813 history did have correspondence with Richard Furman and other knowledgeable Baptist leaders in South Carolina about the origins of this church.

From all of these collateral records (and Edwards in particular), it is evident that there were two sources for the Charleston church. The first and probably the earliest source consisted of both Particular and General Baptists who had emigrated to South Carolina from England. A study of the land warrants, wills, and similar instruments shows that known Baptists were in the colony quite early. For example, John Raven, a legal trustee of the original Baptist church built at 62 Church Street in Charleston, arrived in the colony in 1672 and secured five land warrants between 1684 and 1702. The Bullen family, also among the trustees of this first church building, had land warrants in the 1670's and 1680's. Similar warrants in the 1680's were issued for other known Baptists like Jonathan Barker, Richard Baker, Thomas Cater, and Benjamin Blake.[3] Morgan Edwards gives over a dozen names of families who were Baptists. Evidently these Baptist families came from England rather early.

Exactly when these Old England Baptists began to worship as a group, it is difficult to know. One might speculate that the spiritual children of Thomas Helwys, the General Baptist who gave his life for freedom of worship, and ·William Kiffen, the Particular Baptist who suffered grievously for his faith, would not likely make the long and perilous journey to America to escape laws forbidding such worship and then not seize the opportunity when it came. As a matter of fact, it is clear from the wills of this period that these known to be Baptists associated together, signing as witnesses to the wills of one another, and giving other evidence of some organic relationship.[4] It is unlikely that many of these who came to the colony as early as 1672 would not engage in some type of worship together. Indeed, it is quite possible that one of the factors that encouraged William Screven, the first pastor of the church, to move to Charleston from Kittery, Maine, may have been information that there were already Baptists worshiping there.[5]

The second source of members of the Charleston church was the party of Particular Baptists with William Screven, who evidently emigrated from Kittery, Maine, to Charleston, South Carolina, between June 28 and December 7, 1696. Screven, who may be the man by that name who signed the Somerset Confession of 1656 in England, first appeared in American records in 1668 when he witnessed a deed at Salisbury, Massachusetts. He was indicted on July 6, 1675, for not attending Puritan services in Kittery, Maine, where he had moved. From 1679 to 1691, while Massachusetts Bay Colony and the crown of England were jousting over their political claims, Screven steadfastly took the royal side of the question. The Puritan leadership persecuted him for dissent after he was baptized in the Boston church on July 21, 1681. He was licensed to preach on January 11, 1682. In that same year a church was organized at Kittery with Screven ordained as pastor, Humphrey Churchwood as deacon, and eight other men and seven women as original members. From 1692 until his departure in 1696, Screven was one of the leaders of the Kittery community, holding the highest elective office of the community for several years.

In the earlier stories of Screven it was asserted that he migrated from Maine to South Carolina in 1682-83, that he left Kittery because he was being persecuted by the Puritan leadership, and that his son William Screven remained in New England until 1696. It is now definitely known that William Screven did not come to South Carolina until 1696. He did not leave Kittery because of persecution for conscience sake but probably for several other reasons. (1) The Indian raids at Kittery were becoming increasingly severe. (2) The timber around Kittery was almost completely depleted, and the possession of the contiguous area by the Indians made it impossible to secure additional timber farther away from town. Since William Screven the preacher was a shipbuilder, this took away his means of livelihood. (3) Several of the children of William Screven were now grown and in the ship business. Samuel, for example, owned a sloop and probably transported his father to South Carolina in it. (4) A number of the close relatives and friends of Screven were related to South Carolina and the Barbadoes, including his mother-in-law, Mrs. Mary Champernowne, the first husband of Screven's wife's sister, Elizabeth Elliott Wetherick, Humphrey Axtell, William Chapman, William Adams, John Green, and William Sadler. (5) The governors of South Carolina (Thomas Smith, Joseph Blake, and John Archdale) at this time were all dissenters. William Screven may have had some connection with Smith in England, some of the Blake family were certainly Baptists, and it is quite possible that Screven knew John Archdale personally from a previous contact in Maine.[6]

It has also been demonstrated by legal documents that William Screven the preacher could not have come to South Carolina to live before 1696, and that the William Screven whose name appears on the records from 1682 to 1696 could not have been his son, but was the preacher himself.[7]

The date to be assigned to the First Baptist Church, Charleston, does not depend upon when Screven came to that city. The church organized on September 25, 1682, in Kittery was evidently moved to Charleston in 1696. Its date of founding was not changed by the removal to Charleston. The original church had as members ten men—Screven, Humphrey Churchwood, Robert Williams, John Morgradge, Richard Cutt, Timothy Davis, Leonard Drown, William Adams, Humphrey Axtell (or Axill), and George Litten—and "seven sisters." These women certainly included Bridget Screven, her mother Mrs. Mary Hole Cutt Champernowne, and Mrs. Sarah Morgradge; and probably two sisters of Bridget Cutt Screven (Elizabeth Cutt Elliott Wetherick and Mary Cutt Churchwood), Mrs. Leonard Drown, and Mrs. Humphrey Axtell. The last four names are conjectural, although there are good grounds for naming each one. Unquestionably added to the membership of the church at Kittery were seven of the eight sons of Screven (Samuel, Robert, Joshua, William, Joseph, Permanus, and Aaron); the five daughters of Screven (Mercy, Sarah, Bridget, Elizabeth, and Patience); the stepson of Humphrey Axtell (John Green) and the five stepdaughters; the adopted son of William Screven (Joseph Atwell) and Atwell's wife; and the two sons of Bridget Screven's sister, Mrs. Elizabeth Cutt Elliott Wetherick, by her first husband (Champernowne Elliott and Robert Elliott). Robert Wetherick, the second husband of Elizabeth, probably joined the group.

Thus, before leaving Kittery the church had added at least 23 members who, with the original 17, brought the membership to at least 40. Of these 40 it is known that 2 died before December 16, 1693 (Churchwood and Litten); 2 moved to the First Baptist Church, Boston, in 1692 (Drown and wife, who became outstanding members there); 6 remained in New England (Richard Cutt, John Morgradge and wife, Robert Williams, Timothy Davis, and Mary Churchwood); and 29 emigrated in the William Screven party to South Carolina (William Screven and Bridget; Bridget's mother, Mrs. Mary Hole Cutt Champernowne; their 7 sons and 5 daughters; Joseph Atwell, Screven's adopted son, and Atwell's wife; Bridget Cutt's sister, Elizabeth Cutt Elliott Wetherick, her husband Robert, and the 2 sons of Elizabeth by her first husband, Champernowne and Robert Elliott; Humphrey Axtell and wife; and John Green and his 5 sisters, stepchildren of Axtell). Evidently one of the original church, William Adams, had preceded the Screven party to South Carolina. With this large party, it is no wonder that William Screven applied for a large grant of 1500 acres of land on December 7, 1696, presumably shortly after he arrived there at Charleston.

Official documents of South Carolina make many references to William Screven between 1696 and his death on October 10, 1713. He purchased land at Somerton about forty to fifty miles northeast of Charleston in 1698 and 1700 and was known to be living there on February 21, 1699. His house burned in Charleston in February, 1700, and he suffered in the epidemic there about that time; he was criticized for his preaching by a Puritan minister in 1702; he sold his land at Kittery in 1704-05; he declined to return to Boston as pastor of the church there in 1707; he sold his Somerton plantation on October 15, 1708; he secured land warrants in Craven County and on Charleston Neck in 1710-11. He probably retired to what is now Georgetown before his death there in 1713.

Screven was a Calvinistic or Particular Baptist in his doctrinal persuasion. Upon his retirement from the active pastorate of the Charleston church, he urged them to secure an able and faithful minister as soon as possible who was "orthodox in the faith, and of blameless life, and does own the confession put forth by our brethren in London, in 1689." [8] This was a Particular Baptist confession. In a controversy about thirty years later, the son of William Elliott, one of the original members of the church and the donor of the lot in Charleston upon which the church was built, said that his father had been a General Baptist at the time he entered into the church relationship. From the acuteness of the controversy between General and Particular Baptists, it is apparent that there were a number of General Baptists in the Charleston church, certainly not won to that persuasion by the preaching of Screven.

The strength of the Charleston church slowly deteriorated during the remainder of this period and sorely needed the enthusiasm of the First Great Awakening to revive it.

There were three offshoots from the Charleston church.

1. Euhaw church. William Screven preached on Edisto Island about 1700, baptizing a number of early influential Baptists who, after some difficulty with the Presbyterians over a meetinghouse, built their own in 1726. One of their members, William Fry, was ordained and preached for them, and in 1731 William Tilly became their minister. About this time the members moved away from Edisto, the main group settling at the Euhaws on Broad River. At the end of this period the members of this body were still considered a branch of the Charleston church.

2. Ashley River. One of the early branches of the Charleston church was the Ashley River congregation, who either went into Charleston for services or requested the minister to come to them to hold meetings. The group built a meetinghouse in 1727, and about 1733 Isaac Chandler became their minister. In 1736 this congregation became a separate church with about twenty-seven charter members.

3. Stono. The Baptist group at Stono had first been a branch of the church of Charleston, erecting a building in 1728, and sharing the minister from Charleston. However, a schism occurred in the Charleston church between the Calvinistic or Particular Baptists and the Arminian or General Baptists. Both the Euhaw and Ashley River group were Calvinistic or Particular Baptists. Some of the General Baptists, who had held these tenets when the original church was formed at Charleston, began to form a party in the 1730's based on their Arminian or General Baptist views. A schism took place in 1735, resulting in the organization in the following year of a separate General Baptist church, which began meeting in the building at Stono and secured Robert Ingram, a General Baptist minister from England. At the close of this period, Henry Heywood became the new pastor of this church and aggressively pressed the claims of the General Baptists.

Welsh Neck Church. The variety of Baptist life in South Carolina was enriched in 1736 with the coming of Baptists from Welsh Tract (now Delaware). Mrs. Leah Townsend remarked that the coming of this group to form the second center of Baptist influence in the province was as important to the religious life of South Carolina as the Screven movement.[9] These Peedee settlers had been a part of or descended from a larger body of Baptists that had emigrated from Wales in 1701 to Welsh Tract. The fertile lands on the Peedee River near present-day Society Hill were secured, and in January, 1738, a Baptist church was formed. Evidently the first pastor was Philip James, who was ordained to this charge on April 4, 1743. The widespread influence of this new Baptist center was significant.

> Its ministers preached or assisted weak congregations up and down the river; its people left it to aid in forming other Baptist groups; its descendants covered the Peedee section with such churches as Catfish, Mars Bluff, Cashaway, Beauty Spot, Lunches Creek, Cheraw Hill, and many others.[10]

Virginia

The first Baptist churches in Virginia were founded during a time of transition in the colony. The population, which had been almost entirely English during the first century of Virginia's history, began to be altered in the western regions by the coming of Scotch-Irish, German, and other immigrants, who were encouraged to settle there as a means of frontier defense. Large land bounties on the frontier were given to companies and individuals for settling immigrants.

There was a rapid increase in Negro slaves: it is estimated that the southern colonies contained 180,000 of them by 1750, with Virginia being the principal participant. In contrast, the remainder of the colonies (in the North) probably had no more than 20,000 at this time. Part of the reason for this was the rapid expansion of the plantation system and the emergence of the large planters as an influential part of Virginia society. Tobacco was Virginia's principal money crop, although cereals, cattle, sheep, hogs, packing products, and lumber were also exported. There was some manufacturing on a small scale because the English Navigation Acts interdicted trade with the continent. The correspondence of this period shows that the debts by Virginia planters to England were increasing at an alarming rate. At the opening of the Revolution these debts, caused by overproduction, low prices, and heavy import duties, amounted to about $10,000,000, an enormous deficit for that day. The best land along the coast was being depleted rapidly by the raising of tobacco. Shrewd planters acquired large tracts for future use; and by 1730 practically all of the land located near the coast or on a navigable river was gone. Many people were leaving the colony to seek lands to cultivate.

Most of the education during this period was conducted by tutors and private schools, although there were a few "endowed free schools" in some parts of the colony. After some discouraging setbacks, William and Mary College was chartered in 1693, primarily for ministerial education.

In this background, during the period between 1715 and 1740, three small Baptist churches were constituted.

Prince George County. The first Baptist church in Virginia was constituted in Prince George County in southeastern Virginia. English records of the General Assembly of General Baptists reveal that in May, 1714, Robert Norden and Thomas White, two outstanding elders of the Assembly, had been appointed to sail to Virginia to propagate the gospel. White died enroute, but Norden ministered effectively there until his death on December 1, 1725. Colonial records show that he took the oath of allegiance required under the Act of Toleration of 1689 in Prince George County on June 14, 1715, and on the same day the house of Matthew Marks, a well-known dissenter of many years, was properly licensed as a Baptist meeting place.[11] In the following month the house of Nicholas Robertson, a long-time resident in another part of the county, was licensed as another Baptist meeting place. Norden preached throughout this and adjacent counties, evidently pastor of a church meeting in one of the licensed houses. After Norden's death, he was succeeded by Richard Jones, who was ordained by the church on April 30, 1727. In 1742 the church had about forty members. A "wasting, pestilential disease" decimated the community in 1742, and evidently in that year William Sojourner emigrated southward with some of the surviving members of the church to Scotland Neck, North Carolina, and constituted the Kehukee church, of which he became pastor.[12]

Isle of Wight and Surrey Counties. Isaac Backus recorded that Robert Norden had held meetings in other places than Prince George County, and evidently from his work two churches were constituted in Isle of Wight and Surrey counties, the latter county joining the former with Prince George County on the south side of the James River in an area approximately fifty miles in length.[13] No more is known of the Surrey church, but on December 27, 1756, the Isle of Wight church at Burleigh wrote for assistance to the Philadelphia Association, evidently confused over the doctrinal differences between the Arminian doctrines of its founder and the Calvinistic or Particular Baptist views that were being propagated by the Association. There is no further record until Issac Backus, over thirty years later, attended a meeting in his travels through Virginia.

> I came . . . to Elder Barrow's meeting-house in Isle of Wight County, to an association of churches partly of Virginia and partly of North Carolina. This association was held amongst the small remains of an Arminian Baptist church which was gathered by Elder Norden who came from London in 1714. They were reduced almost to nothing when Elder Glamore and others came and preached sovereign grace among them and a great reformation has taken place in these parts.[14]

North Carolina

Reference has already been made to the turbulent political and social conditions in North Carolina during the first several decades of the eighteenth century. The flow of a large number of substantial workers from Virginia during these years doubtless helped prepare the way for the introduction of Baptist organized life in this province.

The earliest Baptist churches in North Carolina are related to the work of Paul Palmer, a General Baptist.[15] David Benedict said that Palmer was a native of Maryland, and after his baptism in Delaware and ordination in Connecticut, had returned to Maryland to preach at the house of Henry Sater and baptized nine persons. In 1742, over twenty years later, from this center the first Baptist church in Maryland was constituted.

Palmer is first found in the records of North Carolina in Perquimans Precinct in 1720. Here he had married a wealthy widow and acquired considerable land of his own. By 1726 he was evidently preaching in Chowan County (although he did not secure a license under the Act of Toleration of 1689 until 1738).[16] In 1727 he constituted the first Baptist church in North Carolina in Chowan County. Paschal's analysis of the church roll identified a number of substantial families of the area.[17] Young Joseph Parker, a protege of Palmer, became first pastor of this church, and with the removal of Parker and some of the members to Meherrin about 1730 the church evidently dissolved.

The second church in North Carolina was probably also constituted under the leadership of Palmer at Shiloh in Camden County. It was registered to meet in the house of William Burges on September 5, 1729. This became a very influential and fruitful church, and is the oldest church of the state in existence. Palmer likely gathered another church in Onslow County after 1735, but it was evidently swallowed up in the Separate Baptist movement later on.

Before the close of the period in 1740 one other General Baptist center was constituted in North Carolina. As mentioned in a previous paragraph, Joseph Parker evidently brought some of the membership of the Chowan church to the area east of the Roanoke River along the Virginia line and constituted the Meherrin church. Parker seems to have preached in all of this area, laying Christian foundations and constituting churches or branches until his death about 1792. Such churches as Bertie (Sandy Run), Lower Fishing Creek, Swift Creek, and Little Contentnea came from his ministry.[18]

Thus, by 1740, the close of this period, Southern Baptists had established 11 churches: 5 in South Carolina, 3 in Virginia, and 3 in North Carolina. However, the Euhaw church in South Carolina was not actually separated from Charleston in 1740; the church in Surrey County, Virginia, may have gone out of existence; and the church in Chowan County, North Carolina, had died before the end of this period. This makes it likely that there were but 8 Baptist churches of record functioning in the South by 1740. Their total membership could not have been more than 300 or 400 persons. Probably most of them were General Baptists (in Virginia and North Carolina), while all but one of the churches in South Carolina (Stono) were Particular Baptists.

It appeared that it would take an unusual outpouring of blessings from God to permit the survival of these several feeble Baptist churches, and such an outpouring occurred in what is known as the First Great Awakening in America. This inaugurated a new phase in the life of Southern Baptists.

Notes

1. Original of the letter in Backus Collection, Newton, Massachusetts. Reprinted in the *Journal of Southern History,* November, 1963, Vol. 29, No. 4, pp. 495-97.
2. See Leah Townsend, *South Carolina Baptists 1670-1805* (Florence: Florence Printing Co., 1935), p. 11.
3. Baker, *The First Southern Baptists,* p. 55.
4. *Ibid.,* pp. 62 ff.
5. *Ibid.,* p. 48.
6. *Ibid.,* for this story in some detail.
7. *Ibid.,* pp. 36 ff.
8. Morgan Edwards, *Materials Towards a History of the Baptists in the Province of South Carolina* (1772), Crozer mss, p. 18 n.
9. Townsend, *op. cit.,* p. 61.
10. *Ibid.,* pp. 76-77.
11. Baker, *Source Book,* p. 7.
12. Paschal, *op. cit.,* I, p. 172.
13. Baker, *Source Book* for documents, p. 7.
14. Alvah Hovey, *A Memoir of the Life and Times of the Reverend Isaac Backus* (Boston: Gould and Lincoln, 1859), p. 273.
15. For all known information on Palmer, see Paschal, *op. cit.,* I, pp. 131-64 *passim.*
16. Baker, *Source Book,* p. 8.
17. Paschal, *op. cit.,* I, pp. 140-41.
18. *Ibid.,* pp. 168 ff.

RAPID EXPANSION IN THE SOUTH
1740-1814

From the First Great Awakening to the First Baptist General Body

3 Fire Falls

The second general period of Southern Baptist history in America (1740-1814) brought numerous and radical changes. At the opening of this period the colonies north and south experienced the widespread religious revival known as the First Great Awakening. Following this and not unrelated to it was the struggle for political and religious liberty. After the War of Independence, the South was greatly influenced religiously by what has been called the Second Great Awakening (west of the Alleghenies). At the close of the period, the principal story concerned the developing missionary thrust engendered both by the receding frontier in America and the English foreign mission enthusiasm sparked by William Carey.

These several developments between 1740 and 1814 will be sketched in three chapters. This chapter will deal specifically with the First Great Awakening and its effect upon Southern Baptists. Chapter 4 will describe the participation of Southern Baptists in the Revolutionary War and the struggle to include the principle of religious liberty in the new federal Constitution. Chapter 5 will note the expansion of Southern Baptists into the newly-developing western areas and their participation in the revival and missionary movements that developed with the turn of the century.

Progress by the Older Baptists

Between 1740 and the American Revolution, despite the developing political crisis in the American colonies, the older Baptist groups in South Carolina, Virginia, and North Carolina, which were discussed in the previous chapter, made good progress.

South Carolina. The Charleston church, which had been greatly weakened by controversy in the 1730's and 1740's, was revived when George Whitefield visited that city in 1745. The coming of Oliver Hart, a minister from the Philadelphia Association, to be pastor of the Charleston church in 1749 gave new impetus to the work. He remained as a successful pastor until driven north by the Revolutionary War in 1780.

In 1740 the General Baptists meeting at Stono, bolstered by a new pastor from England, Henry Heywood, entered suit to secure the property of the old undivided church and were successful in securing this property on Lot No. 62, while the Particular Baptists were awarded the parsonage. The General Baptist congregation dwindled away until the time of the Revolution, and subsequently the Particular Baptists were able to secure the old meetinghouse on Lot No. 62 again.

Important low-country churches organized before the Revolution included Coosawhatchie in 1759 and Pipe Creek in 1775. Other churches were establishing branches which would ultimately become separate churches. In the Peedee section of South Carolina, the Welsh Neck church expanded into the Catfish area, where a church was organized in 1752. The Beauty Spot church was organized from Catfish in 1768, and a number of smaller churches developed in the Catfish area thereafter. Another branch of the Welsh Neck church formed a separate congregation at Cashaway in 1756, and from this area thereafter a number of branches and private-home churches were established before the Revolution. These included Muddy Creek, Black Creek, two churches on Lynches Creek, Flat Creek, and others. Important ministers during the period were Philip James, Nicholas Bedgegood, Evan Pugh, and others.

The first Baptist association in the South was organized at Charleston, South Carolina, on October 21, 1751, and took the name Charleston Baptist Association.[1] Its minutes before 1775 have been lost or destroyed, but they were used by Wood Furman in his history of the association published in 1811. These minutes declared that the object of the association was

> the promotion of the Redeemer's kingdom, by the maintenance of love and fellowship, and by mutual consultations for the peace and welfare of the churches. The independency of the churches was asserted, and the powers of the Association restricted to those of a Council of Advice.[2]

This association was formed primarily from the initiative of Oliver Hart, who had become pastor of the Charleston church in 1749. He had been an active member of the Philadelphia Association prior to his southern ministry and was familiar with "the happy consequences of union and stated intercourse among Churches maintaining the same faith and order." The original organization was approved by "delegates" from the Charleston, Ashley River, and Welsh Neck churches. In the early years the association met annually, usually at Charleston. This association contributed greatly to the unity and edification of Baptists in South Carolina. It kept the churches current with respect to contemporary religious issues, not only in South Carolina but with happenings in all Baptist life in the colonies. Among other things, in 1775 it secured John Gano, a distinguished minister of the Philadelphia Association, to preach the gospel in the back country, which he did for a year very effectively.[3]

Virginia. The older Baptists in Virginia made good progress during the period between 1740 and the Revolution. A General Baptist church was organized at Opekon on Mill Creek, now Berkeley County, West Virginia, by immigrants from Maryland in 1743. After their minister had been excluded for licentiousness, they applied to the Philadelphia Association for assistance. Benjamin Miller, Isaac Sutton, John Thomas, and John Gano (all Particular Baptists) met at the Opekon church in 1752, and finding that the church had General Baptist doctrines, proceeded to sift out the chaff, "retaining the supposed good grain." John Gano reported to the Association:

> We examined them, and found that they were not a regular church. We then examined those who offered themselves for the purpose, and those who gave us satisfaction we received, and constituted a new church. Out of the whole who offered themselves, there were only three received. Some openly declared they knew they could not give an account of experiencing a work of grace, and therefore need not offer themselves. Others stood ready to offer if the church was formed. The three before mentioned were constituted, and six more were baptized and joined with them. After the meeting ended, a number of old members went aside and sent for me. They expressed their deplorable state, and asked me if I would meet with them that evening, and try to instruct them. They were afraid the ministers blamed them. They had been misled, but it was not their fault, and they hoped I would pity them. I told them I would with all my heart, and endeavored to remove their suspicion of the ministers. They met, and I spoke to them from these words: *"They being ignorant of God's righteousness, and going about to establish their own righteousness, have not submitted themselves unto the righteousness of God."* I hope I was assisted to speak to them in an impressive manner, and they to hear, at least some of them, so as to live. They afterwards professed and became zealous members, and remained so, I believe, until their death.[4]

The church was received into the Philadelphia Association in 1754. It was to this church that Daniel Marshall, the outstanding Separate Baptist, came in 1754 where he was baptized and licensed. That story will be told in connection with the Separate Baptist movement.

In 1751 John Thomas organized a church of eleven members at Ketocton, Virginia, and in the following year the church appealed to the Philadelphia Association for assistance in administering the ordinances. John Gano was sent by the Association, and both on this occasion and intermittently during the next several years assisted them in their services. In 1754 this church was received into the fellowship of the Philadelphia Association.[5]

Probably as early as 1745 a group of Pennsylvania Baptists settled on Smith's Creek in Frederick County, Virginia, and in 1756, John Alderson organized the Smith's Creek Baptist Church there and remained as its pastor until the Revolutionary War.[6] After 1756, the three churches at Opekon (Mill Creek), Ketocton, and Smith's Creek arranged to have a fellowship and communion meeting together each year, and this was done when circumstances permitted. In 1762, Smith's Creek church was admitted to the Philadelphia Association, reporting thirty members at that time. Two significant names in this church were Silas Hart and Nicholas Fain.

One of the outstanding early leaders of Virginia Baptists was David Thomas, who came to Opekon from Pennsylvania in 1760. His zeal resulted in the organization of the Broad Run church in 1762 with twelve members. Thomas was an educated and talented preacher, and Broad Run, through his leadership and the assistance of half a dozen young ministers whom he had influenced, took the gospel throughout the entire area. These ministers included Nathaniel Saunders, who became pastor of the Mountain Run church in 1768; Richard Major, who became pastor of the Little River church in 1768 and subsequently served at Bull Run church; Daniel Fristoe, who became co-pastor with David Thomas at Chappawamsic in 1771; William Fristoe, ordained in 1769 and served extensively in the churches among which was Broad Run after 1787; John Creel, who became pastor of the Birch Creek church in 1771; and Jeremiah Moore, who was ordained about 1771 and served many churches, the one in Alexandria in particular being significant. The sweep of the work of David Thomas and these men included the organization of the church at Chappawamsic (1776) with several arms, Mountain Run in 1768, Little River in 1768, Birch Creek in 1769, and Thumb Run in 1771.

Other Baptist preachers helped found several other churches of this period, including Joseph Thomas, who helped constitute New Valley in 1767; Isaac Sutton, who organized Great Bethel in 1770;

and John Marks and John Garrard, who planted the church at Buck Marsh in 1771.[7]

On August 19, 1766, messengers from the three churches that belonged to the Philadelphia Association (Opekon, Ketocton, and Smith's Creek), along with David Thomas and Joseph Metcalf from Broad Run, met at Ketocton and organized the Ketocton Baptist Association, the first in Virginia, comprised of four churches with 142 members. By 1772 the minutes of the association showed 13 churches with approximately 1150 members. Although the association adopted no confession of faith for many years, its leaders were of the Particular Baptist persuasion.

North Carolina. Before the Revolution the General Baptists in North Carolina had advanced under the leadership of Joseph Parker, William Sojourner, and Josiah Hart, assisted by many faithful General Baptist preachers associated with them. Parker continued his service to the Meherrin church, and doubtless had a large part in the founding of churches at Bertie (Sandy Run), Lower Fishing Creek, and the Swift Creek church in the 1740's. William Sojourner evidently left Burleigh, Virginia, in 1742 with a number of the members of that church, due to an epidemic of some sort which had taken the lives of many of the people in that area. Sojourner and his flock promptly organized the Kehukee church near the present town of Scotland Neck. This became one of the influential centers of Baptist life in the area. Josiah Hart, evidently a long-time resident of the province, probably founded the Pungo church in Beaufort County and the Fishing Creek church in Warren County. Hart is best known for the large number of preachers whom he had either baptized or ordained, including such influential pastors as William Walker, Henry Ledbetter, James Smart, John Thomas and his two sons Jonathan and John, Charles Daniel, John Moore, Sam Davis, and probably others.

Through the efforts of these men there were sixteen General Baptist churches in North Carolina by 1755.[8] These churches were located as far west as Granville and as far south as the Great Cohara, and the records intimate that their influence far outweighed any other religious group in eastern North Carolina during this period.

To a greater extent than either South Carolina or Virginia, Baptists in North Carolina underwent a radical doctrinal revolution between 1750 and 1760 in the transformation of practically all of the General Baptist churches into Particular Baptist churches.[9] George W. Paschal followed Morgan Edwards in crediting the initiation of this Calvinizing process to a Welsh Neck pastor, Robert Williams.[10] A native North Carolinian, Williams had gone to the Welsh Neck church in South Carolina in 1745, and upon his return in 1750, he exercised remarkable influence in turning the minds of the preachers from the General

Baptist doctrines to those of the Particular Baptists. Some of the stalwarts whom Williams won to these views were James Smart, Henry Ledbetter, William Walker, John Moore, Thomas Pope, Edward Brown, and, later on, Charles Daniel. It is difficult to understand how such fundamental theological shifts could take place with such seeming ease, but doubtless the movement was accelerated because most of these General Baptist preachers were untrained theologically, were aware of the lack of discipline in their churches, and were conscious of the absence of assurance on the part of their parishioners.

Williams was not satisfied to make individual conquests but notified the Philadelphia Association of the situation and urged that preachers be sent from that Calvinistic center to help the North Carolina General Baptists to find the true faith. John Gano came in response to this plea and in May, 1755, visited Fishing Creek in Warren County and preached with great power. After his report to the Association, they voted to send further assistance to North Carolina, and on October 28, 1755, Peter Van Horn and Benjamin Miller left Philadelphia for this purpose.[11] They visited the Kehukee church first where Thomas Pope, the pastor, had already accepted Calvinistic views. The church was reorganized on December 11, 1755, although only ten members formed the new church. Within six years, all of the North Carolina General Baptist churches except Meherrin, Pungo, and Grassy Creek were reorganized on a Calvinistic basis. It is significant, however, that in the reorganization of these churches, an average of less than ten members began each of the reorganized churches. Paschal estimated that only about 5 percent of the older General Baptist members were in the new churches.

This Calvinizing movement was significant in that it brought new emphasis upon regeneration, church discipline, and a church covenant, all of which had been minimized under the old order.[12] W. L. Lumpkin is doubtless correct in suggesting that many of the General Baptists became a part of the Separate Baptist movement which was beginning about this time.

Maryland. Just after the opening of this new period in 1740, Baptist work was begun in the Roman Catholic colony of Maryland. In the interest of securing settlers, the proprietors of this colony granted religious toleration to most trinitarian Christians. However, there is no record of Baptists in the colony until a General Baptist from England, Henry Sater, invited visiting Baptist ministers to preach in his house on Chestnut Ridge, not far from Baltimore. As a result, in 1742, a church was organized in Sater's home, known at first as Chestnut Ridge church, then as Sater's Baptist Church. The first pastor was Henry Loveall. A second church was organized in 1754 by Benjamin Griffith and P. P. Van Horn at Winter Run, which was later called the Harford church, but was admitted to the Philadelphia Association in 1755 as the Baltimore church. These were the only Baptist churches in Maryland before the Revolution.

Without minimizing the importance of these events in the story of the older Baptists in the South between 1740 and the American Revolution, it should be reiterated that the most significant and far-reaching event of this period in the Baptist story was the Separate Baptist movement that developed from the First Great Awakening.

Whitefield's Chickens Become Ducks

The First Great Awakening in America, probably begun through the work of Jacob Frelinghuysen, Gilbert Tennant, and Jonathan Edwards in the second and third decades of the eighteenth century, affected Baptists in the South secondhand. George Whitefield, the Calvinistic associate of the Arminians John and Charles Wesley, brought to a climax in New England the earlier controversy stirred up by Jonathan Edwards concerning the need for a personal experience of grace through the power of the Holy Spirit. The New England Congregationalists had been at odds over this question since the Cambridge Platform of 1648 and the Half-Way Covenant of 1662. New England Congregationalism divided between the "New Lights," who affirmed that God brought new light into the hearts of men by a conversion experience, and the "Old Lights," who said that baptized babies, as children of the covenant, needed no such new light. The intensification of this conflict by 1744 closed the open doors that Whitefield had found when he first came to New England in 1740. In spite of this he toured New England and preached to large crowds. Some of the New Lights, unable to form new churches without the permission of the older ones and being unable to get that permission, separated themselves from the established Congregational church and were known as Separates. Two of these Congregational Separatists who became Baptists were used of God to transmit the fire of the revival to Baptists in the South.

The first of these was Shubal Stearns, a member of the Congregational church in Tolland, Connecticut, who became a New Light under the preaching of Whitefield in 1745.[13] Stearns led a small group of the New Lights to meet apart, and shortly they became a Separate church. After studying the Scriptures, Stearns declared that he had become a Baptist by conviction, and in 1751 he was immersed by Wait Palmer, the New Light pastor of a Baptist church nearby. Stearns became pastor of a new Baptist church in Tolland on May 20, 1751, where he remained as pastor for about three years.

His companion, Daniel Marshall, also born in 1706, was a prosperous farmer in Windsor, Connecticut, not far from Tolland. He had been a deacon in the First Congregational Church there for about twenty years. Marshall, however, had questions about the Old Lights as early as 1744. When George Whitefield toured Connecticut in 1745, Marshall listened avidly and the fires of revival were kindled within his heart. By 1747, when he married Stearns' sister, Martha, he was a confirmed Separatist and after 1750 became a Baptist.[14]

Of the two, Stearns was the natural leader. He was small in stature, possessed a musical and strong voice that he used very effectively in reaching the convictions and emotions of his hearers, and had a very penetrating eye, which seemed to impress his hearers. Although not formally well educated, he was an avid reader of books and was a man of sound judgment, according to Morgan Edwards.[15] Daniel Marshall, while not as gifted as Stearns, was a man of overpowering earnestness and zeal, which made his plain exhortations most effective in presenting the gospel.

These two mature men, each almost fifty years of age when they came to North Carolina, were used of God to make fundamental changes in the character and development of Southern Baptists. No wonder George Whitefield, a Church of England Methodist who disdained the use of much water in baptizing infants or adults, as he pondered how he had helped produce many Baptists who immersed their candidates fully into the baptismal pool, ruefully said, "All my chickens have become ducks."

Onnaquaggy, Opekon, and Sandy Creek

Although Stearns became the leader, it was Daniel Marshall that acted first upon his inner convictions of a special Christian mission. In 1751 or 1752, with his wife and three children, Marshall traveled northeastward in a wagon to witness to the Mohawk Indians in east-central New York. The friendly Indians permitted them to settle at Onnaquaggy, where the Marshalls and perhaps one other couple witnessed for eighteen months. The English-French rivalry among the Indians disrupted the work, and after a brief stop in Pennsylvania, the Marshalls drove southward to Virginia, arriving at Opekon in 1754. Here Marshall became acquainted with the Baptist church and its pastor, Samuel Heaton. He and his wife were baptized by Heaton in that year, and Joseph Breed and his wife, who may have been at Onnaquaggy with the Marshalls, were also baptized. Marshall was soon licensed by this church to exercise his gifts. He must have exercised them zealously, for some of the church complained to the Philadelphia Association about this display of enthusiasm. However, Benjamin Miller from that body was delighted with the warmhearted Christians that he found when he visited the church there.[16]

Meanwhile, Shubal Stearns in Tolland, Connecticut, felt God's call to a missionary service. In August, 1754, he and five or six couples from his church, most of them related to him, loaded their possessions into a wagon and before the close of the year joined the company of Daniel Marshall in Opekon, Virginia. Together the party moved to Cacapon Creek and constructed homes for a new settlement. The response to their witnessing in this neighborhood, however, was not good. For the first time, the differences between the new Separate Baptists, as they were called, and the older Baptists, brought a strained relationship between the Stearns group and the older Baptists of the community. The zeal and emotional preaching of the Separates, the use of uneducated ministers, the "noisy" meetings, and even the extensive ministry of women in the services alienated the more formal older Baptists, who became known as Regular Baptists. This confrontation, along with the impending Indian hostility, caused Stearns and his party to consider another location. The decisive factor probably was a letter which Stearns received from North Carolina describing the needs of the people there. In the summer of 1755, unnoticed by contemporary historians, Stearns and company traveled to Sandy Creek in what is now Randolph County in central North Carolina, arriving, according to Morgan Edwards, in the late fall, to begin a revolution in Southern Baptist life. Here the eight men and their wives promptly formed themselves into a church of sixteen members and built a meetinghouse.

An Alarmed Neighborhood

Sandy Creek, North Carolina, indeed the South, were never the same after this group settled at Sandy Creek. The immediate impact was obvious. Morgan Edwards remarked that "the neighborhood was alarmed," and so it was. In an area of the back country where the population was growing rapidly, particularly with settlers uncommitted to Christianity, the impact of these sixteen people was remarkable. Three of the busiest roads of the entire South converged at Sandy Creek: the Settlers Road running from north to south along the edge of the Alleghenies, the Boone Trail from Wilmington west to the Yadkin settlements, and the Trading Path from southeastern Virginia to the Waxhaw country.[17]

This little church promptly sounded the alarm in the immediate neighborhood. Not only the preachers, but the entire congregation were conscious of standing under the judgment of God. All of the church looked to the leadership of the Holy Spirit. No less than 125 ministers were called into service during the next seventeen years from this church and her daughters. Preaching tours promptly began to characterize the ministry of the ministers. A strong organizational structure was developed as each church was planted, perhaps a result of the Congregational background of Stearns and Marshall. Every sermon was preached with compassion and zeal in an effort to win the hearts of those not yet committed to the service of Christ. The preachers themselves in the early years steadfastly refused to receive any remuneration for their services, which helped to win the confidence of the masses about them, but at the same time perpetuated an untrained, part-time ministry of zealous men who earned their own livings as they preached.

It is difficult to describe in a few words what Paschal devoted almost a hundred pages to outlining—the expansion of this Sandy Creek church in every direction. Stearns and Marshall made repeated tours into almost every part of the province. Large throngs gathered, and many conversions resulted wherever they went. Many years later in describing some of these results, Morgan Edwards said:

> Sandy Creek church is the mother of all the Separate Baptists. From this Zion went forth the word, and great was the company of them who published it: it, in 17 years, has spread branches westward as far as the great river Mississippi; southward as far as Georgia; eastward to the sea and Chesapeake Bay; and northward to the waters of the Potomac; it, in 17 years, is become the mother, grandmother, and great-grandmother to 42 churches, from which sprang 125 ministers. . . . I believe a preternatural and invisible hand works in the assemblies of the Separate Baptists bearing down the human mind, as was the case in the primitive churches, I cor. xiv:25.[18]

Before 1760, a large band of stalwarts had been called out of God to become preachers in the Separate movement. Among these were James Younger, John Newton, Ezekiel Hunter, James Reed, John Dillahunty, Philip Mulkey, Joseph and William Murphy, Dutton Lane, Charles Markland, Nathanel Powell, James Turner, Jeremiah Walker, Elnathan Davis, and perhaps the most influential of all the converts, Samuel Harris, who became the "Apostle of Virginia."

William L. Lumpkin summarized the early rapid progress of the Separates in North Carolina:

> Within three years of the Separates' settlement at Sandy Creek there were three fully constituted churches with a combined membership of over nine hundred. Vigorous branches thrived in the region of Sandy Creek at Little River in Montgomery County and Grassy Creek in Granville County, and other branches were located well to the eastward at Southwest in Lenoir County, Black River in Duplin, New River in Onslow, and as far away as Lockwood's Folly in Brunswick. Preaching had been carried on from the Moravian settlements to the Cape Fear and northward into Virginia.[19]

The Separate Baptist movement was also set forward by the organization of the first Separate association in 1758.[20] Shubal Stearns felt that an association would "impart stability, regularity and uniformity to the whole." So he visited each Separate congregation and urged them to meet at Sandy Creek for the purpose of organizing such a general body. As many as nine or ten congregations may have been represented in the meeting, probably held on the second Monday of June, 1758. The utmost democracy prevailed at this meeting, even the election of a moderator not being attempted lest the free work of the Holy Spirit might be counteracted. This was the second association to be organized in the South, the first being Charleston seven years earlier. The inspiration from these annual meetings of the association gave great impetus to the zeal of the preachers. Lumpkin judged that a definite missionary strategy was planned by the leadership. Shubal Stearns worked primarily in eastern North Carolina and to the west of Sandy Creek; Daniel Marshall itinerated to the north; Philip Mulkey preached primarily in the east and southeast.

However, in 1770 a new direction was taken at the meeting of the Sandy Creek Association. Usually no action was taken at the meeting of this association without unanimous approval, but such was the division among the representatives in 1770 that they could not agree even on a moderator. The only unanimity came when it was agreed to divide into three bodies, one for North Carolina (the Sandy Creek Association), one for Virginia (the General Association of Separate Baptists in Virginia), and one for South Carolina (the Congaree Association). Morgan Edwards described the cause for this division in the following words:

> The cause was partly convenience, but chiefly a mistake which this association fell into relative to their power and jurisdiction; they had carried matters so high as to leave hardly any power in particular churches, unfellowshipping ordinations, ministers and churches that acted independent of them; and pleading "That though complete power be in every church yet every church can transfer it to an Association"; which is as much as to say that a man may take out his eyes, ears, etc., and give them to another to see, hear etc. for him; for if power be fixed by Christ in a particular church they can not transfer it; nay, should they formally give it away yet it is not gone away.[21]

In addition, David Benedict noted that a part of the reason for this division was the somewhat autocratic attitude of Shubal Stearns himself.

> The good old Mr. Stearns, who was not wholly divested of those maxims which he had imbibed from the traditions of his fathers, is said to have been the principal promoter of this improper stretch of associational power, which, however, was soon abandoned by those, who, for a time, tampered with it, to their embarrassment and injury.[22]

Through the withdrawal of churches in Virginia and South Carolina and the heavy migration of Separate Baptists to Kentucky and Tennessee, as will be described in the following chapter, the strength of Separate Baptists in North Carolina greatly diminished. In 1771 only nine churches were represented in the Sandy Creek Association, and some of these were quite small in membership, including the parent church itself. The story, then, must turn toward Virginia, South Carolina, and Georgia, if the trail and influence of the Separate Baptists is to be followed.

Growth of Separate Baptists

Virginia. The story of Separate Baptists in Virginia has political, economic, social, and religious antecedents. The early center of the Virginia commonwealth was the tidewater section of the state, where the older settlements had stopped some sixty or seventy miles from the coast line. Wesley M. Gewehr drew the line separating the Old Dominion from the Piedmont area as running south through Fredericksburg, Richmond, and Petersburg. West of this line the political, social, economic, and religious atmosphere was completely different from that of the tidewater. In the older section, life centered around large estates operated by tobacco planters who constituted the aristocracy. Williamsburg was the capital and center of their activities, and most of them were engaged in political scuffles that influenced the entire state. Democracy and equality were not popular words with this group, and religion was generally not taken seriously.

West of the tidewater, however, the land had been settled by numerous marginal farmers, some from the tidewater and some newcomers, for attractive terms had been offered to the poorer class who would move to the frontier in the Piedmont and the Valley of Virginia and defend the frontiers against the Indians. After 1732 a steady stream of immigrants moved down the Valley, mainly Scotch-Irish and Germans. These counties in central and western Virginia west of the Blue Ridge were settled by sturdy men who opposed almost everything the planters in the tidewater section espoused. Equality in the state, absolute liberty in religion, and freedom of choice in all matters social or political characterized these new settlers. The non-English background of many of them helped intensify the tension with England.

Between 1742 and 1758 the Presbyterians under William Robinson and Samuel Davies worked strenuously with considerable success among these settlers, not without ecclesiastical opposition. As mentioned earlier in this chapter, the Regular Baptists also began work in this area as early as 1743 and gathered several churches.

The Separate Baptists initiated their work in Virginia in 1760 and by the time of the Revolution had spread phenomenally. Their expansion into Virginia can be glimpsed in four rather distinct phases.

The first phase began in August, 1760, when Daniel Marshall and Philip Mulkey from the Sandy Creek Association in North Carolina established the Dan River church in Pittsylvania County, just across the line from North Carolina. The church consisted of sixty-three white and eleven Negro members originally. The most distinguished of them was Samuel Harris, a leading citizen of the area who had been honored with almost every public office in the county. He had experienced a remarkable conversion under the preaching of Joseph Murphy and had been baptized by Marshall in 1758. Other Separate churches were at Staunton River and Black Water, both organized in 1761, and both just across the line from North Carolina.

The second phase of their expansion occurred in 1765. In January of that year a convert of David Thomas in Culpeper County, about a hundred miles north of the border, came to Harris and urged him to come far up into central Virginia and preach at Culpeper. Harris promptly responded to this call. This was the beginning of a new center of Separate Baptist work. Although driven from Culpeper by armed men, Harris preached extensively in Orange County and later, with James Read, evangelized the entire surrounding area. On November 20, 1767, with Dutton Lane, Harris and Read organized the first Separate Baptist church north of the James. It was called Upper Spotsylvania, and became the mother of churches in the entire section. Continued preaching by Harris and Read led to the organization on December 2, 1769, of the Lower Spotsylvania church and, two days later, the Blue Run church. Lewis Craig, Elijah his brother, and John Waller were ordained in the following year. Lewis became pastor of the Upper Spotsylvania church; Elijah became pastor of the Blue Run church; and Waller became pastor of the Lower Spotsylvania church.

A third distinct period of advance by Separate Baptists in Virginia took place in 1769, when the movement began to spread quite rapidly there. Samuel Harris was ordained in that year, and with Jeremiah Walker established the Amelia church in southern Virginia, where Walker remained as pastor. In November, 1769, James Ireland and Harris established Carter's Run church in Fauquier County, the first Separate church in northern Virginia, and it grew rapidly. A number of other churches were established in the next two years. One rather interesting situation developed at Ebenezer in what is now Amherst County where a church was constituted in 1771. Ordinarily the Separate Baptist pastors received no salary at all, which pleased the churches, of course. However, this church bound itself to pay its minister fifty shillings a year. Perhaps this was one reason for its rapid growth.

It will be recalled that the Sandy Creek Association decided to divide into 3 bodies in 1770.[23] In May, 1771, 12 of the Separate churches in Virginia met in Orange to organize the General Associa-

0

tion of the Separate Baptists in Virginia. Representatives to this organizational meeting came from 12 churches located in 11 counties with a total of 1,335 members. No representatives attended this meeting from 3 other Separate Baptist churches in Virginia. Some of the ministers who formed this body and were quite influential in this period of Virginia Baptist life were Allen Wyley, William Marshall, Thomas Hargate, Christopher Clarke, Rane Chastain, John Williams, John Burrus, William Webber, John Young, Reuben Pickett, William Lovell, James Shelburne, Elijah Baker, John King, Reuben Ford, and John Koontz.

The Virginia Association had grown so large by 1773 that it was divided into the Southern and Northern Districts, the James River being the dividing line. At the general meetings in 1774, the Northern District had grown to include at least 24 churches with a total membership of 1,921, while the Southern District included 30 churches with 2,083 members.[24]

The fourth phase of the Separate work in Virginia began about 1775. In that year both districts met at the Dover meetinghouse near Richmond, where letters from 60 churches were received: 29 from the Northern District and 31 from the Southern. It was reported that only abouut 300 had been baptized altogether since the last meeting of the association, and Semple remarked that this proved "that cold times were now not only appearing but actually arrived." This decline was probably caused by the outbreak of the Revolutionary War, the Arminian incursion as seen in the defection of strong leaders like John Waller and Jeremiah Walker, and the beginning of the Methodist revival about this time. Although the growth of the Separates was slowed and several problems appeared, they were an important influence during the American Revolution and in the struggle thereafter for liberty of conscience. Gewehr said that the Separate Baptists "were the greatest factor in destroying the Establishment and securing religious liberty."[25]

South Carolina. The Separate Baptist movement flowed into South Carolina like a vast refreshing stream pointed toward the center of the state, approaching within a hundred miles of the first Regular Baptist church at Charleston, then swerving to the west to fill up the Carolina back country and crossing into Georgia. Regular Baptists had been growing slowly in the low-country and the Peedee sections, but had done little in the back country of the state. It was in this area that the Separates made rapid growth, and in less than two decades, they had surpassed the number of Regular Baptists in the entire state.

The Separate Baptists thrust into South Carolina were led by Philip Mulkey and Daniel Marshall. Mulkey was a North Carolinian, reared as an Anglican, experienced a remarkable conversion, was baptized by Shubal Stearns at Sandy Creek in 1756 at the age of twenty-four, and was ordained in the following year. After several years as pastor of the Deep River church in North Carolina, he led twelve other members of the church in 1759 or 1760 to South Carolina and established a church at Broad River. Two years later, the church prospering meanwhile, the same thirteen members who had come from Deep River moved south about a hundred miles to constitute a Separate Baptist church at Fairforest, the oldest Baptist church in the back country. As was usually the case in connection with Separate Baptist churches, this church became a center from which a large area was evangelized. Growing out of the ministry of the church, additional congregations were gathered at Lawsons Fork, Thickety, and Enoree. Also probably related to the Fairforest ministry were churches constituted at Tyger River, Little River of Broad, Little River of Saluda, and Buffalo. Mulkey's preaching in the Congaree section, followed by Daniel Marshall and Joseph Murphy, led to the constitution in 1766 of the Congaree church. Other churches developing from the influence of this center probably were Wateree Creek, Mine Creek, Red Bank, Twenty-Five Mile Creek, Amelia, Four Holes, and, perhaps most important of these, High Hills of Santee. Joseph Reese was instrumental in constituting the High Hills church, and among his principal converts was Richard Furman. Furman became pastor of this church in 1774 at the age of twenty, and distinguished himself for the next half century in South Carolina Baptist life. The High Hills church in turn became a center for additional Baptist churches of the Separate type, and within a few years the churches at Bethel, Swift Creek, Ebenezer, Second Lynches Creek, and Upper Fork of Lynches were constituted.

Another whole set of Separate Baptist centers developed from the preaching of Daniel Marshall, who had been pastor of Abbotts Creek in North Carolina. In 1760 Marshall moved to South Carolina and organized a church at Beaver Creek near Broad River. Two years later he and his family traveled south to Stevens Creek, about ten miles from Augusta, Georgia, where a church was constituted in 1766. The leadership of Marshall is seen in the organization of the churches at Horns Creek, Bush River, and Raeburns Creek.

It will be recalled that the Sandy Creek Association divided in 1770 to permit the organization of bodies for Virginia and South Carolina. Separate Baptists in South Carolina formed the Congaree Association on December 26, 1771, with seven or eight constituent churches. Benedict described how this association began correspondence with the Philadelphia Association after Morgan Edwards from that body visited the churches in 1772. Probably the statement in the 1774 minutes of the Philadelphia Association referred to this correspondence. It said:

> A letter from the Association at Little River and Broad River, South Carolina, was read, by which it appears that sixty-six joined them by baptism the year past; their number of members six hundred and ninety-two. Good news from a far country.[26]

Although the name *Congaree* does not appear in this reference, later on in the minutes for the same year the Association approved letters of fellowship to be written to a number of associations including the Congaree in South Carolina.[27] The Congaree Association dissolved about the time of the Revolution, partly because of internal dissension and partly because of the war.

Georgia. It will be recalled that beginnings in Georgia Baptist life probably sprang from the older Regular Baptists, but that no church of that type was organized before 1773. It is probable that the Separate Baptists from South Carolina established the first organized church in Georgia. Daniel Marshall had been preaching extensively in the southwestern section of South Carolina and moved to Georgia in January, 1771. In the spring of the following year he led in the organization of the Baptist church at Kiokee, a few miles from the South Carolina border. From this Separate Baptist center a number of outstanding Georgia Baptist leaders developed, including Silas Mercer, father of Jesse Mercer.

Union of Separate and Regular Baptists

The early distrust between the Separate and Regular Baptists was quite marked. Instances of open antagonism are found in the histories of North Carolina, Virginia, and South Carolina. As Lumpkin points out, the principal story of the uniting of these two groups took place in Virginia, where all Baptists joined together to fight for liberty and a common revival was sweeping both groups. As a result, a formal union of Separates and Regulars took place in Virginia in 1787.[28] A formal union in North Carolina took place in 1788, when two Separate churches were received into the reformed Kehukee Baptist Association.[29] In South Carolina and Georgia there came the gradual elimination of distinctions between the two types of Baptists without formal action.

Importance of the Separate Baptist Movement

William L. Lumpkin evaluated the significance of the Separate Baptist movement at the close of his study of this group. After describing some of their weaknesses, including their strong appeal to the emotions, their neglect of ministerial education, their tendency to

alarm the people more than to feed them, their nonsupport of ministers, and their anti-confessionalism, he outlined some of their major
contributions, as follows: (1) They revived the Great Awakening in
the South in a unique way. (2) They helped establish the character
of American evangelical Christianity. (3) They provided religious
leadership for the American frontier. (4) They made moral and spiritual preparation for American political liberty. (5) They played a large
part in the triumph of free church principles in America. (6) They
contributed largely to the evangelization of the Negro in the South.
(7) They greatly advanced the cause of religion in America and shaped
the character of Protestantism in the South. (8) They brought great
numerical gains to Baptists in the South. (9) They provided the antecedents for the Southern Baptist Convention in such things as their
aggressiveness and evangelical outlook, their centralized ecclesiology
that was influential in 1845 when Southern Baptists chose their type
of organizational structure, and many other aspects, such as their
self-conscious attitudes, their hymnody, their lay leadership, many
ecclesiastical practices, and their strong biblicism.[30]

There seems to be a providential element in the mingling of the
Separate Baptist distinctives with those of the older General and
Particular Baptists in the South. Taken alone, any one of these three
large Baptist movements possessed many weaknesses. In the uniting
of the three movements, Southern Baptists were prepared fundamentally for the remarkable development that came in the next two
centuries. The General Baptists provided emphasis on the necessity
for human agency in reaching men with the gospel; the Regular
Baptists added doctrinal stability and a consciousness of the divine
initiative; while the Separates united some of the best features of
both and in addition to magnifying structural responsibility, emphasized the necessity of the presence and power of the Holy Spirit. Thus,
Baptists in the South were fundamentally equipped to begin the surge
in numbers and influence during the following centuries.

This summary has not included an account of the struggle for
political and religious liberty that developed during this period. That
story will be told in the following chapter.

Notes

1. Baker, *Source Book*, p. 16.
2. Wood Furman, *A History of the Charleston Association of Baptist Churches in
the State of South Carolina* (Charleston: Press of J. Hoff, 1811), pp. 8-9.
3. Baker, *Source Book*, pp. 26-27.
4. *Ibid.*, p. 12.
5. *Ibid.*, p. 12.
6. *Ibid.*, p. 13.
7. *Ibid.*, pp. 12-13.
8. Paschal, *op. cit.*, p. 176.

9. Baker, *Source Book,* pp. 13-14.
10. *Ibid.,* pp. 13-14.
11. *Ibid.,* pp. 13-14.
12. *Ibid.,* pp. 14-16.
13. *Ibid.,* pp. 17-18.
14. *Ibid.,* p. 19.
15. *Ibid.,* pp. 17-18.
16. *Ibid.,* p. 19.
17. William L. Lumpkin, *Baptist Foundations in the South* (Nashville: Broadman Press, 1961), p. 38.
18. Baker, *Source Book,* p. 20.
19. Lumpkin, *op. cit.,* p. 44.
20. Baker, *Source Book,* pp. 20-21.
21. *Ibid.,* p. 21.
22. *Ibid.,* p. 21.
23. *Ibid.,* p. 21.
24. Robert B. Semple, *A History of the Rise and Progress of the Baptists in Virginia* (rev. by G. W. Beale, Philadelphia: American Baptist Publication Society, 1894), pp. 79-80.
25. Wesley Gewehr, *The Great Awakening in Virginia, 1740-1790* (Durham: Duke University Press, 1930), p. 109.
26. A. D. Gillette, ed., *Century Minutes of the Philadelphia Baptist Association: 1707-1807* (Philadelphia: American Baptist Historical Society, 1851), p. 135.
27. *Ibid.,* p. 143.
28. Baker, *Source Book,* p. 22.
29. *Ibid.,* p. 23.
30. Lumpkin, *op. cit.,* pp. 147 ff.

4 Liberty: Political and Religious

The participation of Southern Baptists in the Revolutionary War and the victory of efforts to include the principle of religious liberty in the new American Constitution of 1789 will be discussed in this chapter. Both political independence from England and religious liberty had their roots in the First Great Awakening. The spiritual unifying of colonies that in many other respects were isolated from one another was an important factor in the preparation for American independence, and the extensive strengthening of minority denominational groups laid the foundations for achieving religious liberty in the new nation.

Baptists shared in the events leading to the Revolution and in the war itself. The whole drama of war and independence had such radical effects in every area of American life that anyone living in the colonies was involved. The many economic policies, for example, that bound the colonies tightly to English interests—mercantilism, the several Navigation Acts, the Sugar Act, the paper money regulations, the Stamp Act, etc.—were precisely those elements that made up the world for the colonists, giving direction to their day-by-day activities. The disruption of the economic structure alone, apart from the many other substantial factors that made up the complex story of the American colonial revolt against England, was bound to have radical effects upon every colonial.

The sequence of events conspired to lead the American colonies more fully toward revolutionary action after 1750. In the three earlier wars between France and England (King William's War, 1689-97; Queen Anne's War, 1701-13; and King George's War, 1744-48), the American colonies actually were on the periphery, and none of these wars determined which European nation should control the American continent. But the French and Indian War (1756-63) was significant. Its complex effects, both immediate and remote, were decisive: it gave England the controlling hand in America; it agitated the opening of the western American areas for colonization; it involved a closer cooperation among the American colonies than they had heretofore known; and, most immediately, it caused England to determine to **59** make radical reforms in colonial administration. British officials now saw firsthand the inept customs service in the colonies; they recognized the need to revise the obsolete Navigation Acts in the interest of mercantilism and the balance of trade; they reported numerous loopholes in the laws and widespread efforts to evade British trade restrictions; and they expressed their dismay at the refusal of the colonies to submerge individual interests in order to defend the interests of England. It was the effort of the British government to correct these deficiencies, brought to their attention by the French and Indian War, that led directly to repressive taxation and rigid enforcement; and, finally, to revolt.

Southern Baptists and the American Revolution

Baptists in each of the four southern states (Virginia, North Carolina, South Carolina, and Georgia) faced a somewhat different situation before and during the Revolutionary War, although their basic interest was liberty, political and religious. As was true with Baptists in the North, Southern Baptists did not hesitate to identify political liberty with religious liberty. For this reason, most Southern Baptists took the patriot side during the war. This can be glimpsed more clearly by reviewing developments in the four southern states named.

Virginia. The direct link between the French and Indian War and the American Revolution can be taken back one more step. The French and Indian War was probably triggered by the efforts of Virginia to colonize the western areas which she claimed by virtue of her original charter. One can imagine the bitterness of Virginia in 1763, after the war was won, when the crown issued a proclamation forbidding settlements west of the Allegheny watershed. This, along with "taxation without consent," brought Virginia into conflict with England.

While Baptists in Virginia were more or less remotely related to these political developments, their principal issue with England was at the point of religious liberty. The vigorous prosecution and persecution of dissenters from 1767 on, sometimes by legal authorities and sometimes by an aroused Tory populace, led Baptists almost to a man to believe that the only possibility of securing religious liberty was bound up with the achievement of political liberty. The climax for them came in August, 1775, when, after deliberate reflection and discussion, the combined northern and southern district associations of Separate Baptists, representing the great majority of Baptists in Virginia, submitted to the Virginia Convention (assembled to chart Virginia's course for freedom) a memorial proposing complete political independence of Virginia from England and the inauguration of total religious liberty in the colony, and pledging Baptist support.[1] This memorial produced a profound effect on the Virginia Convention and identified Virginia Baptists as strong patriots in the forthcoming struggle with England. They were active both on the field of battle and through political agitation in behalf of civil and religious liberty.[2] England recognized this, and Baptist churches were regularly burned by their troops during the war as "nests of rebellion."

North Carolina. What has been called the first battle of the American Revolution took place on May 11, 1771, at Great Alamance Creek between the state militia sent by Governor William Tryon and about 2,000 unorganized farmers from the back country, who had become known as Regulators. The causes of this conflict between the common people and the state authority included

> unlawful exaction of taxes under color of legislative authority, unlawful exaction of fees by clerks and county registers of deeds, unequal distribution of the burdens and benefits of government, unequal incidence of taxation, the land policy of Lord Granville's district, and the scarcity of money.[3]

There had been protests against official corruption and taxation without representation before Tryon became governor in May, 1765, but his spirited defense of those in authority, corrupt or not, and his active efforts to strengthen the hold of the Church of England in the province exasperated the victims of the system in the central and western sections. As early as 1758 a spontaneous meeting of about 700 farmers took place near Salisbury in a protest against political and religious injustices. The flames of the movement were fanned in 1767 and 1768 when Edmund Fanning in Orange County began to heap up unjust demands upon the people. Fanning was convicted of extortion in 1768, but retained his office through gerrymandering by Governor Tryon. The people began to react violently against Fanning by 1768. Despite continued efforts to petition the government to settle the matter peaceably, things went from bad to worse. Tryon launched a vendetta against the Baptists, whom he considered to be ringleaders in the Regulator movement. After Alamance, Tryon terrorized the countryside in the very areas where Baptists had their strength. He camped for a week at Sandy Creek after laying waste to plantations, burning homes, and arresting many men. Tryon then moved against the Baptist settlements near the Jersey church, followed by the intimidation of another principal Baptist area in the neighborhood of Shallow Fords.

Although Shubal Stearns had counseled his followers against violence, and the Sandy Creek church was divided over the issue, it is likely that many Baptists took part in the exciting events of this period. It cannot be determined whether it was Baptist involvement or despair in the failure of their efforts to secure justice that caused wholesale Baptist emigration from North Carolina after Alamance.

> Morgan Edwards reported in 1772 that fifteen hundred families departed straightway and that "a great many more are only waiting to dispose of their plantations in order to follow them." The Alamance region was almost emptied of Baptists and did not recover a considerable Baptist population for a hundred years. Sandy Creek Church in a few years was reduced from six hundred and six members to fourteen by 1772. Little River Church dropped from five hundred members to scarcely a dozen. Tidence Lane and some others from Abbott's Creek went northward into Virginia, but most went south and west. It was as though the Battle of Alamance and the death of Shubal Stearns six months later had been twin signals for most of the Baptist people of central North Carolina to disperse.[4]

When the Revolutionary War broke out, North Carolina Baptists supported it wholeheartedly with only a few exceptions.

South Carolina. As was true in both North Carolina and Georgia, South Carolina had experienced little religious persecution at the hands of the royal governor and council, but had been engaged actively for many years prior to the Revolution in the struggle to enlarge the prerogatives of the local government against royal control. Similar to the activities of the other colonies, South Carolina resisted the economic and political legislation following the French and Indian War, set up a provincial government in 1774, and drove out the royal governor in 1776. There were many Tories in South Carolina. Baptists were numbered among the colonial supporters, although in the back country many Separate Baptists were strongly pacifistic and refused to join in any type of military conflict. Leaders like Oliver Hart and Richard Furman strongly supported the Revolution and, in addition, were used extensively in persuading their fellow countrymen to become engaged in the struggle. So effective was Furman in this task that the British put a price on his head, and he was forced to flee from his church. In May, 1780, General Cornwallis captured Charleston, and for the next year British armies dominated South Carolina.

American leaders never forgot the part that Furman had in the struggle. Harvey T. Cook described how Furman happened to be passing through Washington some years later and met an acquaintance in company with Colonel James Monroe (later President) who introduced him to Monroe.

> Col. Monroe, in taking his hand, remarked thoughtfully, as if trying to recall something, Furman, Furman, of Charleston! The name and the countenance seemed familiar. "May I inquire if you were once of the High Hills of Santee?" said Col. Monroe. He was answered affirmatively. "And were you the young preacher who fled for protection to the American camp, on account of the reward which Lord Cornwallis had offered for his head?" "I am the same," said Mr. Furman. Their meeting was now deeply affecting and Col. M. could

hardly let him go, and did not until he related to the distinguished by-stander the circumstances to which he alluded. "It seems young Furman was not only an enthusiastic Baptist preacher, but an ardent advocate of rebellion, and everywhere, on stumps, in barns, as well as in the pulpit, prayed and preached resistance to Britain and alarm to the Tories. Urged by the latter, Lord Cornwallis who had been made aware of his influence and daring, offered a thousand pounds for his head. Ascertaining that the Tories were on his track, young Furman fled to the American camp, which, by his prayers and eloquent appeals he reassured, insomuch that it was reported Cornwallis made the remark that he feared the prayers of that godly youth more than the armies of Sumter and Marion." Col. Monroe related these particulars with much feeling and enthusiasm. Dr. Furman was now so much a lion in the national capitol that he prepared to leave immediately, but Monroe would not let him go—but made an appointment for him to preach in the Congressional Hall. In vain did the quiet minister disclaim his ability as a court preacher. All the elite, the honorable, the notable of the metropolis were there, including the president, Cabinet, Ministers, Foreign Ambassadors, etc., for his early adventures and eloquence had been noised abroad.[5]

Baptists as a group emerged from the war with the reputation of being strong supporters of the colonial cause, and many Baptists served with distinction in the colonial armies.

Georgia. This colony was late in joining the revolutionary movement, but did send delegates to the Second Continental Congress in 1775. There were few Baptists in Georgia at this time. Evidently most of them took the colonial side.

Struggle for Religious Liberty

Without question the battle for political liberty was a large factor in the South, as it was in New England, in advancing the struggle of Baptists to attain religious liberty. There had been little religious persecution in South Carolina during this period. One isolated instance of this kind was so frowned on by the community that there is no record of another such occurrence. In Georgia the only case of record was the arrest of Daniel Marshall in 1771, and the stout words of Martha Marshall and faithful testimony of Daniel brought the conversion of most of those involved in his trial. In North Carolina Morgan Edwards mentioned a persecution occurring about 1767, in which Baptists were charged with blasphemy, riots, and heresy, but he gave no particulars, and George W. Paschal, the North Carolina historian, could find no further record of this. It is true that in 1740 at New Berne, when several Baptists petitioned to register a house for Baptist preaching they were harrassed and put under bond to keep the peace. There is a tradition that even though charges against them were later dismissed, James Brinson, Nicholas Purefoy, and William Fulsher were publicly whipped or imprisoned.[6] Paschal also described similar harrassment in Beaufort and Pamlico counties in 1742.

However, the story was different in Virginia. Persecution there was of two kinds, popular and legal. Popular violence against the Baptists was aroused partly by their fidelity to their own convictions and partly by "frivolous" charges that "ignorance or malice" mustered against them. They were unpopular for dissenting from the Church of England, for refusing to commune with those of other denominations, for refusing to baptize infants, for immersion in baptism, and for making divisions. There were also reports that they condemned others in their preaching continually, that they had little human learning, and that they held noisy meetings; and it was even whispered that when they became strong enough they would massacre the inhabitants and take possession of the country. The earlier Regular Baptists were no more exempt from persecution than were the Separate Baptists. Of the former, David Thomas in 1763 was driven from Culpeper County by a mob, and in Stafford, a gang armed with firearms attacked the people at worship and a violent battle ensued. A similar scene took place at Bull Run against Richard Major. Even legal harrassment took place. In December, 1762, Thomas and seventeen of his members were indicted for absenting themselves from the parish church. Ministers had difficulty obtaining licenses to preach. Many other legal methods of intimidation were attempted.

A similar story can be told of the Separate Baptists. When Samuel Harris preached at Culpeper in 1765, he was driven out by a mob of armed men. Similar savage action was taken in Pittsylvania, Amherst, Louisa, Fauquier, Chesterfield, Middlesex, Orange, Caroline, and elsewhere.

Garnett Ryland, the Virginia Baptist historian, judged that the first legal attempts to suppress Separate Baptist preachers came before 1767 when Lewis Craig was fined in Spotsylvania County for preaching. The occasion proved to be dramatic and fruitful. Craig said to the grand jury that indicted him:

> I thank you, gentlemen, for the honour you did me. While I was wicked and injurious, you took no note of me, but now having altered my course of life and endeavoring to reform my neighbors, you concern yourself much about me.[7]

One of the jury, John Waller, known for his gambling and profanity as "Swearing Jack" Waller and the "Devil's Adjutant," was brought to Christian conviction by this testimony, was baptized and began preaching, and was himself presented to a grand jury the next year for his preaching.

The principal period of persecution of Virginia Baptists occurred between 1768 and 1774 with the exception of one isolated instance occurring in 1778. This legal persecution probably ended when it did because of the new phase of Baptist activity in 1775, which will be described hereafter.

Two instances of legal persecution occurred in 1768. The first was on June 4, 1768, when John Waller, Lewis Craig, James Chiles, James Read, and William Marsh were arrested in Spotsylvania. After forty-three days in jail, Chiles, Craig, and Waller were released, and promptly returned to their vigorous preaching. In July, 1768, in the adjoining county of Orange, Allen Wyley, John Corbley, Elijah Craig, and Thomas Chambers were arrested and committed to jail. It is known that Craig and Wyley spent a considerable time in prison in 1768 under very difficult circumstances.

In November, 1769, James Ireland, then a youth of twenty-two, was arrested in Culpeper County for his "vile, pernicious, abhorrible, detestable, abominable, diabolical doctrines." From November until April, Ireland lay in the Culpeper one-room jail. Ryland described the conditions of imprisonment as being shocking, his keeper the most avaricious and heartless, and his persecutors, most outrageous. Attempts were made to suffocate him through burning sulphur and pepper, to kill him by exploding gun powder under the jail, and a plot was hatched to poison him. He was released without trial when a competent attorney threatened the magistrates with prosecution for illegal action. Promptly Ireland began a missionary journey as far west as Ohio, preaching day and night despite opposition.

Two examples of persecution occurred in 1770. In Fauquier County in February, John Pickett was jailed for three months. In Chesterfield County in December, William Webber and Joseph Anthony were arrested for "itinerate preaching" and lodged in jail, where they remained for several months.

Between June and August, 1771, in Caroline County, John Young, Bartholomew Choning, James Goolrich, Edward Herndon, John Burrus, and Lewis Craig were arrested for preaching the gospel. It is not certain how long they remained in custody. In Middlesex County in the same year the authorities indicted several members of a new congregation for absenting themselves from the parish church. A petition for a place of public worship was denied. On August 10, John Waller, William Webber, and Thomas Wafford came to the community and promptly felt the hand of the law. John Waller described the experience in a letter from Urbanna Prison on August 12, as follows:

> At a meeting which was held at brother McCain's, in this county, last Saturday, whilst brother William Webber was addressing the congregation from James II; 18, there came running towards him, in a furious rage, Captain James Montague, a magistrate of the county, followed by the parson of the parish, and several others, who seemed

greatly exasperated. The magistrate, and another, took hold of brother Webber, and dragging him from the stage, delivered him, with brethren Wafford, Robert Ware, Richard Falkner, James Greenwood and myself, into custody, and commanded that we should be brought before him for trial. Brother Wafford was severely scourged, and brother Henry Street received one lash, from one of the persecutors, who was prevented from proceeding to farther violence by his companions; to be short, I may inform you that we were carried before the above magistrate, who, with the parson and some others, carried us, one by one, into a room, and examined our pockets and wallets for fire-arms, &c., charging us with carrying on a mutiny against the authority of the land. Finding none, we were asked if we had license to preach in that county; and learning we had not, it was required of us to give bond and security not to preach any more in the county, which we modestly refused to do, whereupon, after dismissing brother Wafford, with a charge to make his escape out of the county by twelve o'clock the next day on pain of imprisonment, and dismissing brother Falkner, the rest of us were delivered to the sheriff, and sent to close jail, with a charge not to allow us to walk in the air until court day.[8]

Waller, Ware, Greenwood, and Webber preached from the windows and carried on a fruitful ministry. They were released on September 26 of that year. It is possible that Patrick Henry, the great advocate of liberty, assisted in their release.

In 1772 three cases of imprisonment were recorded. In May in Chesterfield County, Augustine Eastin was arrested for preaching without a license. In August in King and Queen County, James Greenwood and William Lovell were imprisoned for sixteen days. In August in Caroline County, two laymen, James Ware and James Pitman, were imprisoned for sixteen days for preaching in their homes, and a month later John Waller was placed in jail for preaching. How long Waller remained there is not known.

The officers were busy in 1773. In Chesterfield County John Tanner, John Weatherford, and Jeremiah Walker were imprisoned. Patrick Henry paid the jail fees for Weatherford, but did not reveal this for many years. Jeremiah Moore was arrested in the same year in Fairfax County. In Culpeper County on August 21 of this year Nathaniel Saunders and William McClannahan were arrested and placed in jail. It is not known how long they remained there. In Orange County on October 23, 1773, Joseph Spencer was imprisoned for "teaching and preaching the Gospel as a Baptist, not having license." It is perhaps this case that led James Madison who lived nearby to write a friend in Philadelphia and remark:

> I have nothing to brag of as to the state and liberty of my country. Poverty and luxury prevail among all sorts; pride, ignorance and knavery among the priesthood, and vice and wickedness among the laity. This is bad enough; but it is not the worst I have to tell you. That diabolical, hell-conceived principle of persecution rages among

some, and, to their eternal infamy, the clergy can furnish their quota
of imps for such business. There are at this time in the adjacent country
not less than five or six well-meaning men in close jail for publishing
their religious sentiments, which, in the main, are very orthodox. I
have neither patience to hear, talk, or think of anything relative to
this matter; for I have squabbled and scolded, abused and ridiculed,
so long about it, to little purpose, that I am without common patience.
So I must beg you to pity me, and pray for liberty of conscience to
all.[9]

The year 1774 marked almost the end of this kind of legal harassment. In Chesterfield County David Tinsley was imprisoned for over
four months and suffered many indignities. In Essex, John Waller,
John Shackelford, Robert Ware, and Ivison Lewis were arrested for
preaching the gospel. They were released on bond after a few weeks.

In addition to these specific instances, Semple recorded arrests in
Culpeper County and imprisonment without dates of John Corbley,
Thomas Ammon, Elijah Craig, Thomas Maxfield, Adam Banks, and
John Delaney. Ryland added the name of Anderson Moffett as being
a prisoner in Culpeper, according to oral tradition.

With the exception of the imprisonment of Elijah Baker in Ac-
comack in 1778, these are the definite records of imprisonment. Ryland
remarked in summary:

> These imprisonments of more than thirty individuals in the jails
> of nine counties so far from arresting the Baptist movement had accel-
> erated it by arousing sympathy for the prisoners, by kindling interest
> in their message and by awakening understanding and appreciation
> of their insistence on unrestrained exercise of freedom of belief in
> religion and liberty to preach the Gospel to every creature.[10]

The Battle of Petitions

The story of the achievement of religious liberty in Virginia has
three phases. From 1770 to 1775, Baptists and other groups petitioned
the House of Burgesses (the legislature of the colony) to give relief
from the harassment and various restrictions placed upon them in
the colony. The second phase involved no less than demands for
complete religious liberty in the state and continued from 1775 to
1788. The third phase had to do with religious liberty in the new
national Constitution.

It should be observed that Virginia Baptists quite early in the story
of American Christianity engaged in active political lobbying to
achieve a spiritual end, utilizing their denominational strength and
political petitions for effective results. If some had qualms about this
kind of relationship between church and state, they said very little
publicly about it.

The first petition by Baptists to the House of Burgesses related to bearing arms, attending musters, and restriction on the preaching of ministers. It was presented in 1770 and was unsuccessful. In 1772 the House received petitions from Lunenburg, Mecklenburg, Sussex, and Caroline counties, in which the Baptists asked that they be treated with the same indulgence in religious matters as Quakers, Presbyterians, and other Protestant dissenters. Another petition from Amelia Baptists declared that Baptists were being discriminated against in matters of conscience.

In 1773 a petition from the Ketocton Association requested "liberty to preach in all proper places and in all Seasons without restraint." Both in 1774 and 1775 petitions were presented from Baptists and other Protestant dissenters complaining of a proposed bill which would prohibit public worship except in the daytime.

In August, 1775, at a joint meeting of the northern and southern district associations of Separate Baptists meeting in what is now Powhatan County, "was taken the first organized action in Virginia for religious freedom and the separation of church and state." [11] (This was referred to previously in this chapter.) Because of the exciting developments that led to the Revolutionary War, the House of Burgesses had replaced the colonial government with a Virginia Convention. This Convention was sent a petition asserting the support of Baptists in the struggle against Great Britain and asked that Elijah Craig, Lewis Craig, Jeremiah Walker, and John Williams be permitted liberty to preach to the troops without molestation. This Baptist meeting also determined to circulate petitions to be submitted to the Virginia Convention asking for the abolishing of church establishment, allowing each religious society protection in the peaceable enjoyment of its own principles and methods of worship. In reply to their petition, the Convention granted dissenting clergymen the right to conduct worship for those who may not choose to attend the services by the chaplain.

On May 19, 1776, the Baptist church at Occaquon in Prince William County addressed a petition to the Virginia Convention, urging that in the struggle for civil rights and liberties of mankind, religious privileges should be given to all men to allow them to worship God in their own way, to permit them to maintain their own ministers and no other, and to allow their ministers to marry, bury, and carry on similar ministerial duties.

When the Virginia Assembly met in October, 1776, a petition containing about ten thousand signatures was presented asking that the ecclesiastical establishment be eliminated and that every other yoke of religious oppression be removed. Many Presbyterians were numbered among the signers of this petition, and in addition, many Presbyteries sent petitions urging that the establishment of the Anglican Church be discontinued. Thomas Jefferson later remarked that

> after desperate contests almost daily from the 11th of Octob. to the
> 5th of December we prevailed so far only as to repeal the laws which
> rendered criminal the maintenance of any religious opinions, the for-
> bearance of repairing to church or the exercise of any mode of worship:
> and further, to exempt dissenters from contributions to the support
> of the established church; and to suspend, only until the next session,
> levies on the members of that church for the salaries of their own
> encumbents. For although the majority of our citizens were dissenters,
> as has been observed, a majority of the legislature were churchmen.
> Among these, however, were some reasonable and liberal men, who
> enabled us, on some points, to obtain feeble majorities.[12]

This still left, however, many distressing restrictions on dissenters.
Only the Anglican Church could perform legal marriage ceremonies,
and although they could not levy tithes to support that church, they
still conducted a systematic program of relief for the poor, and assessed
taxes for this project. Baptists determined to petition for complete
freedom. Sometimes they were supported by other denominations and
sometimes they were not. In October, 1778, a petition from the General
Association was received by the General Assembly urging that all
ordained ministers of every denomination be authorized to celebrate
marriages. A similar petition was presented in May, 1780, and in
October the General Association and the Ketocton Association of
Regular Baptists united to send a memorial to the Legislature further
protesting the marriage inequities. Finally, in December, 1780, the
Legislature authorized the granting of licenses to four ministers of
each denomination in a county to perform marriage ceremonies in
that county alone; at the same time, marriages already celebrated
by dissenting ministers were declared valid. The General Association
sent memorials in 1782 and 1783 noting that Baptists had joined their
brethren in the cause of liberty, and that it was only equitable that
there be religious liberty for all denominations. The Vestry Act and
those concerning marriages were specifically mentioned. Another
memorial was sent in 1783, noting, "We have patiently waited, while
the great matter of the war was the subject of deliberation, but as
the struggle is now happily over, we hope that our former petitions
and memorials may be attended to in the depending session." Nothing
was done by the Assembly, however.

The Formation of the General Committee

A determinative phase of the movement toward religious liberty
in Virginia came in 1784 with the formation of a General Committee,
which was to consist of not more than four delegates from each Baptist
association in Virginia. Their main task was to articulate the grievances
of the dissenters in an effort to eliminate the religious discrimination

that still existed. In October of that year delegates from four associations, including the Separates and the Ketocton Regular Baptist Association, constituted the new body. William Webber was named moderator and Reuben Ford, clerk, and these two men retained these two offices during most of the existence of this body. During the following ten years this Committee worked vigorously in four areas of religious discrimination: the right to perform marriages anywhere by all dissenting clergymen, the elimination of a general assessment, the protest against the Act of Incorporation, and the recovery of the glebe lands. One of the strong pillars of this Committee was John Leland, who had come from Massachusetts to Virginia as pastor in 1777. For fifteen years, this zealous and gifted man was prominent in the struggle for religious liberty in Virginia, after which he returned to Massachusetts.[13]

The Marriage Act. At the first meeting of this Committee in October, 1784, a petition was prepared and subsequently presented to the General Assembly, specifically mentioning the unjust provisions of the Marriage Act and the Vestry Law, and praying that all distinctions before the law be done away with, so that no denomination of Christians have special privileges allowed them. The General Assembly received this petition favorably, and as a result of this (and other petitions), the Marriage Act was so amended that all discrimination against dissenters was removed.

General Assessment. When the General Committee met in August, 1785, it learned that the General Assembly was about to pass a law which would levy a tax for the support of ministers or teachers of the Christian religion and for providing places of worship, with the understanding that each person could designate the denomination which should receive his tax. Most of the denominations in Virginia favored this kind of public support of the various churches. The Baptists were the only organized group that opposed it. The principal opposition in the Assembly was led by James Madison, who prepared his famous Memorial and Remonstrance.[14] The General Committee promptly recommended that petitions be prepared for the General Assembly protesting "that should the legislature assume the right of taxing the people for the support of the gospel it will be destructive to religious liberty." Madison later wrote Thomas Jefferson and said that the table was loaded with petitions and remonstrances from all parts against this uniting of church and state. However, the petition against assessment became superfluous, for the Assembly passed an Act for Establishing Religious Freedom, prepared by Thomas Jefferson.

> *Be it enacted by the General Assembly,* That no man shall be compelled to frequent or support any religious worship, place or ministry whatsoever, nor shall he be enforced, restrained, molested, or burthened

in his body or goods, nor shall he otherwise suffer on account of his religious opinions or belief; but that all men shall be free to profess, and by argument to maintain, their opinion in matters of religion, and that the same shall in no wise diminish, enlarge or affect their civil capacities.

And though we well know that this assembly elected by the people for the ordinary purposes of legislation only, have no power to restrain the acts of succeeding assemblies, constituted with powers equal to our own, and that therefore to declare this act to be irrevocable would be of no effect in law; yet we are free to declare, and do declare, that the rights hereby asserted are of the natural rights of mankind, and that if any act shall be hereafter passed to repeal the present, or to narrow its operation such act will be an infringement of natural right.[15]

The praise of this action by James Madison reflected the judgment of later historians who said that when this became a law in January, 1786, Virginia became "the first government in the world to establish by statute the complete divorce of Church and State,—the greatest contribution of America to the sum of Western civilization." [16]

The Act of Incorporation. The sweeping principle set out in the establishment of religious freedom did not automatically eliminate specific action of previous years which had been discriminatory. In June, 1784, the clergy of the Anglican Church that was in the process of forming a new body separate from England requested the Legislature to give the property to them that had formerly been used for the advantage of the Anglican Church. This was done in December, 1784. At their meeting in 1786 the General Committee of Baptists urged that petitions be circulated in different counties protesting the possession of this land by one denomination and suggesting that the land be sold and the money applied to public use. A memorial to that effect was sent to the Assembly on August 5, 1786. In response, the Assembly repealed most of the obnoxious Act, but that section dealing with possession of the glebe lands (which had provided homes and farms for the benefit of ministers of the old established church) was retained.

The Glebe Lands. In March, 1788, the General Committee discussed at length the possession of glebe lands by the new Episcopal Church. The property had been purchased in each parish by taxing the citizens, and the Committee felt that the retention of the property by the Episcopal Church was discriminatory.

We were left to fear it would be made use of in a future day and the established church have it to say, there was a reserve of property to them in preference to all other sects, and that establishment was only in part abolished, and this cockatrice egg produce in time a fiery, flying serpent.[17]

In 1790 the Committee prepared a memorial to the next General Assembly and urged that petitions be presented from all counties in Virginia. Letters were written to the Methodists and Presbyterians asking their assistance at this point, but neither group was willing to engage in this affair. Undeterred, the Baptists sent memorials year by year to the Assembly. In January, 1794, the General Assembly repealed every prior act that related to religion except the Act for Establishing Religious Freedom of 1786.

> This action, by which the ownership of the glebes reverted to the State, established so completely the freedom of religion from support, control, restriction or discrimination by the government, for which the Baptists had contended that the General Committee, "conceiving that the object that required its existence" had been obtained, did "not therefore think it expedient to exist any longer," and in 1799 dissolved. The principle having been won, the Baptists through their organizations, showed no interest in the ultimate disposition of the glebes.[18]

It should be said that this last struggle by the Baptists relative to the glebes aroused great unpopularity against them. Official and unofficial attacks were made against their motives and their understanding. Subsequently, leaders and historians of the Episcopal Church in Virginia have acknowledged that the possession of the glebes would have been quite injurious to their church had that situation continued.

Virginia Baptists and the Federal Constitution

This Virginia struggle for religious liberty occurred at a very auspicious time in the formative years of the American Republic. The Continental Congress had anticipated the need for some type of confederation after the close of the war for independence. On November 15, 1777, that body sent the Articles of Confederation to the states for approval. They were not ratified until March 1, 1781, and were not satisfactory thereafter. On May 25, 1787, a Constitutional Convention was assembled, purportedly for amending the Articles to correct some of their principal deficiencies. However, this Convention prepared an entirely new instrument of government produced in secret sessions. On September 17, 1787, the new Constitution was adopted by most of the Convention and submitted to the Continental Congress, who in turn sent it to the states for ratification. In Virginia, the General Committee of Baptists studied the proposed Constitution and unanimously agreed that it did not make proper provision for religious liberty, although it was recognized that any powers not specifically granted to the central government were reserved to the states. As a result, John Leland, popular Baptist pastor in Orange County, entered the campaign as a candidate for the Virginia Convention that would vote on ratification of the Constitution. His opponent was James Madison, who favored ratifying the document. After consultation with Madison relative to providing additional safeguards to religious liberty, Leland announced his support of Madison, who was elected. The Constitution was ratified, and Baptists supported Madison to the first Congress of the United States. In June, 1789, Madison introduced the amendments he had promised to make to the Constitution, the first of which said, "Congress shall make no law respecting an establishment of religion, or prohibiting the free exercise thereof."

An interesting exchange of correspondence took place between the Committee and the new President of the United States. The General Committee wrote a letter to George Washington in August, 1789, voicing their concern for liberty of conscience in the new Constitution, and expressing the confidence that "if religious liberty is rather insecure in the Constitution 'the administration will certainly prevent all oppression, for a *Washington* will preside.'" Washington replied in a letter of appreciation and assured them that "no one would be more zealous than myself to establish effectual barriers against the horrors of spiritual tyranny, and every species of religious persecution." [19]

While the principal struggle for religious liberty necessarily took place in the area of most persecution (that is, in Virginia), it is clear from various sources that Baptists in Virginia took counsel with Baptists in other states, both North and South, in this struggle. As early as 1776, North Carolina specifically granted all ministers of every denomination the right to celebrate matrimony and in a Bill of Rights asserted that all men have a natural and inalienable right to worship God according to the dictates of their own consciences. The North Carolina Constitution, adopted in 1776, contained the following religious liberty clause adopted partly as the result of Baptist influence:

> There shall be no establishment of any one religious church or Denomination in this State in Preference to any other, neither shall any person, on any pretence whatsoever, be compelled to attend any place of worship contrary to his own Faith or Judgment, or be obliged to pay for the purchase of any Glebe, or the building of any House of Worship, or for the maintenance of any Minister or Ministry, contrary to what he believes right, or has voluntarily and personally engaged to perform, but all persons shall be at liberty to exercise their own mode of worship. [20]

At the very time this struggle for religious liberty was taking place, Southern Baptists were multiplying in numbers, expanding into new areas, and finding new ways to share the gospel. These events will be considered in the following chapter.

Notes

1. Lumpkin, *op. cit.,* pp. 113-15, and Garnett Ryland, *The Baptists of Virginia 1699-1926* (Richmond: The Virginia Baptist Board of Missions and Education, 1955), p. 95.

2. See summary in Gewehr, *op. cit.,* pp. 188-218.

3. Lumpkin, *op. cit.,* p. 73.

4. *Ibid.,* p. 85.

5. Harvey T. Cook, ed., *A Biography of Richard Furman* (Greenville: Baptist Courier, 1913), pp. 72-73.

6. Paschal, *op. cit.,* pp. 186 ff.

7. Ryland, *op. cit.,* p. 60.

8. Baker, *Source Book,* pp. 33 f.

9. Ryland, *op. cit.,* pp. 81-82, quoting from Hunt, *Writings of James Madison,* I, p. 21.

10. Ryland, *op. cit.,* p. 84.

11. *Ibid.,* p. 95.

12. *Ibid.,* p. 103.

13. See Baker, *Source Book,* pp. 40-42, for an example of Leland's vigorous style.

14. *Ibid.,* pp. 36-38.

15. *Ibid.,* pp. 38-39.

16. William T. Thom, *The Struggle for Religious Freedom in Virginia: the Baptists* (Baltimore: The Johns Hopkins University Press, 1900), p. 78.

17. Ryland, *op. cit.,* p. 94.

18. *Ibid.,* p. 132.

19. Baker, *Source Book,* pp. 43-45.

20. *Ibid.,* p. 42.

5 Post-War Advance

At the same time the political and religious struggles described in the previous chapter were taking place, Southern Baptists experienced solid growth in the older southern states; expanded rapidly westward; participated in a widespread revival that began west of the Alleghenies in the opening years of the nineteenth century; and shared the missionary impulse generated by William Carey, which was implemented by the Second Great Awakening in New England and emphasized by the spiritual needs of the immigrants on the receding frontier.

Baptist Growth in the Older Southern States

During the years between the Revolutionary War and the close of this period in 1814, the older states of Maryland, District of Columbia, Virginia, North Carolina, South Carolina, and Georgia were experiencing radical readjustments. Independence brought massive problems politically, economically, socially, and religiously. Old colonial sectional jealousies made it difficult to form a political union. Questions concerning the nature of the federal union, liberty of conscience in the new Constitution, ultimate political sovereignty, ultimate legal authority, federal financing, land ownership, relations with other governments, the powers of each branch of the government in relations to other branches, and many other fundamental issues were faced head-on in the tumultuous events of the period, which included war with England in 1812.

The principal story economically in the southern states was in the area of agriculture. Usually the War of 1812 with England is counted the turning point between the old colonial economic dependence upon Europe and England and the development of American manufacturing, mining, weaving, and so forth to provide a self-sufficient nation. This was not entirely true of the South. The invention of the cotton gin by Eli Whitney in 1793 not only made it possible to separate the seed from the cotton more rapidly and economically, but it actually made it profitable to grow short-staple cotton in the uplands, thus enlarging greatly the land area that could be given to the raising **75** of cotton. The impact of this was immediate. The southern states had produced 2,000,000 pounds of cotton in 1791; by 1801 the output had grown to 40,000,000 pounds and by 1811, to 80,000,000 pounds, The results of this development were many: the institution of Negro slavery, which most Americans had thought was dying in the eighteenth century because it was economically unprofitable, began instead to enlarge, as can be seen by the statistics which will be given in the discussion of each of the southern states; the western area of the South began to gain rapidly in the number of Negro slaves in their population; a one-crop system (that of cotton) began to develop in many of the southern states; and the whole question of slavery or antislavery began to assume political proportions.

In this exciting milieu Baptists in the older southern states made good progress. Generally speaking, Baptists had grown very little during the Revolution itself, some of them had postwar revivals in the 1780's and 1790's, and practically all of them felt the impact of the revival after the turn of the century.

The United States Census Bureau has developed a regional demarcation that is both accurate and germane to this study. With slight modifications, that classification will be utilized in describing the geographical development of Southern Baptists. In this chapter only the South Atlantic, South Central, and North Central regions are involved; the first consisting here of Maryland, District of Columbia,[1] Virginia, North Carolina, South Carolina, and Georgia; the second, Kentucky, Tennessee, Mississippi, Louisiana, and Alabama; and the last, Missouri alone.

South Atlantic Region. In the period between 1790 and 1814 Baptists in the five South Atlantic states of Maryland, Virginia, North Carolina, South Carolina, and Georgia made excellent numerical advances.[2] In 1790, there were 422 churches, 838 ministers, and 36,100 Baptists in these five states. In about 1814, there were 39 associations, 618 ministers, 837 churches, and 75,666 members. This represented an annual average membership growth of 4.77%. At the very close of the period Baptists in District of Columbia were just emerging. As pointed out in the footnote appended to District of Columbia in the previous paragraph, there are several problems related to statistics there.

Both as a yardstick for measuring the growth of Southern Baptists and as significant data for estimating growth potential, a comparison will regularly be made of the population increases in each region and state. The total population in these five South Atlantic states in 1790 was 1,736,837; by 1810 it had grown to 2,496,748 (including 23,336 in District of Columbia, a sixth area). This represented an average annual increase of 2.08%. Thus, Baptists grew more than twice as fast as the population in the South Atlantic region during this period.

Another yardstick of economic and social relevance was the growth of Negro slavery. In 1790 the five South Atlantic states of Maryland, Virginia, North Carolina, South Carolina, and Georgia contained 633,373 slaves, many of whom were Baptists. In 1810, these five states (plus District of Columbia, which was first shown in 1800) contained 983,671 slaves. This represented an average annual increase of 2.63%, just a little larger increase than the total population and about one half of the rate of increase of Baptists. This relatively small increase in Negro slaves will be compared soon to the rapid increase in the South Central region during this period.

1. Maryland. It will be recalled that two Baptist churches had been organized in Maryland prior to the Revolution—Sater's Baptist Church (known earlier as Chestnut Ridge) and Winter Run (afterwards called both Harford and Baltimore). In 1756 John Davis, a Virginian, became pastor of the Winter Run church, and in 1785, Abraham Butler helped Davis found the First Baptist Church, Baltimore, as well as the churches at Taneytown, Gunpowder, and perhaps Frederick Town. A second Baptist church was founded in Baltimore through the work of John Healey, an Englishman, in 1797. The first association in Maryland dates from 1782, when a joint body for churches in Maryland and Virginia, known as the Salisbury Association, was formed on the eastern shore. This body was developed from the evangelistic preaching of Elijah Baker and Phillip Hughes. In 1808 the Virginia churches were dismissed to form the Accomac Association of Virginia. The Baltimore Baptist Association was formed on August 10-12, 1793, with messengers present from six churches (including Huntington, Pennsylvania).

The population of Maryland in 1790 was shown as 319,728, including 103,036 slaves. By 1810 it had grown to 380,546, including 111,502 slaves, or an average annual increase of .91%. Maryland had 12 Baptist churches, 11 ministers, and 776 members in 1790. At the close of the period there were 2 associations, 15 ministers, 32 churches, and 1,326 members. This represented an average annual growth of 3.08%. It far outdistanced the population growth. The number of slaves in Maryland increased from 103,036 in 1790 to 111,502 in 1810, for an annual average increase of .44%.

2. District of Columbia. The new capital city of the United States received its land by small cessions from Virginia and Maryland. Although the city was being planned and developed under both Presidents Washington and Adams, the first President to take the oath of office there was James Madison on March 4, 1801.

District of Columbia churches were for many years included in the Maryland associational bodies, but they will be described briefly as a prelude to later separation from Maryland. 'Actually, District of Columbia Baptists have been related to both Northern and Southern Baptists; their story will be summarized here for completeness. The small number involved will not affect the reliability of overall statistical percentages of Southern Baptists.

Baptists met in a worship service in Washington on July 5, 1801, soon after the new capital city was occupied by the federal government. On March 7, 1802, the First Baptist Church, Washington, D. C., was organized with six charter members. Four ministers were present: Lewis Richards, pastor of First Baptist Church, Baltimore, who had preached at the first worship service eight months before; Adam Freeman; Jeremiah Moore; who preached the sermon at the organizational service; and William Parkinson, recently named as chaplain of the House of Representatives. On May 31, 1807, Obadiah B. Brown was elected pastor and served for the next forty-three years. Brown had a finger in every important Baptist program in this city during these years. The second Baptist church was organized on June 3, 1810, (as the Navy Yard Baptist Church), and S. E. Moore served as pastor until his death in 1814.

At the close of this period these 2 churches were members of the Baltimore Association of Maryland, and reported 78 members. The population in the District of Columbia was shown as 14,093, including 3,244 slaves, in 1800 (the first time it is shown in the United States census). It increased to 24,023 (including 5,395 slaves) in 1810.

3. Virginia. Virginia was the most populous state in the nation by far at the first census in 1790, although New York and Pennsylvania showed a larger white population at that time. Virginia had 748,308 people (including 293,427 slaves). The invention of the cotton gin in 1793 was, of course, a great boon to this state in the growing of cotton and the use of Negro slaves, but ultimately this worked against a healthy economy by encouraging a one-crop system. The population increased to 974,622 (including 398,518 slaves) in 1810, which represented an average annual growth of 1.44%. Negro slaves increased at an average annual rate of 1.70%, somewhat faster than the population in general. In 1810, Virginia had more slaves than any other state. Several factors slowed the increase of slaves in the South Atlantic states, as will be noted in the discussion of the South Central region.

The rapid growth of Virginia Baptists subsided during the Revolutionary War. The war itself, western migration, economic stringency, and the inroads of Methodism took their toll. Not only did Methodism slow Baptist growth by winning many of the unreached people to their denomination and organizing them into churches, but as well the Arminian doctrine of that denomination attracted such Baptist leaders as John Waller and Jeremiah Walker. Waller pursued an independent course, disdaining cooperative relationship, from 1776 until 1787.

The effect of the Revolutionary War may be glimpsed in the fact that in 1776, 74 churches sent letters to the General Association of Separate Baptists in Virginia; in the following year "the associations were but thinly attended and little business done," and in 1778 only 32 churches sent letters. This gave occasion for sharp questioning as to whether associations were useful and worthy of continuation. The answer was finally given that "a society of churches combined to seek mutual good of the whole is desirable"; however, the same statement contained a warning that "associations are not to interfere with the internal concerns of churches, except where their advice is requested by any church." Only 29 letters were presented at the association in 1780, and the body appointed a day of fasting and prayer "in consequence of the alarming and distressing times." Only 16 churches sent messengers in 1781, probably fearful of General Cornwallis who was marching nearby.[3]

However, Ryland pointed out, despite the problems of war and the internal troubles due to the Methodist incursion, the Separate Baptists organized 37 new churches in 28 different Virginia counties during the Revolution. In 13 of these counties, there had been no Baptist churches before. A part of this increase came from the work of Elijah Baker on the peninsula and the Eastern Shore, Lewis Lunsford in the Northern Neck, and the work of John Leland, who came to Virginia from Massachusetts in 1777. It is interesting to note that Baker was a Separate Baptist, having been baptized by Samuel Harris, while Lunsford was a Regular Baptist. Concerning Lunsford, Semple said that it was hardly probable "that any man ever was more beloved by a people, when living, or more lamented when dead." He was a most effective witness.

From 1785 to 1791 the "Great Revival" swept through Virginia. Ryland judged that nothing like it had ever been heard of before in the state. There were thousands of conversions, particularly among the Baptists, who were its chief promoters and beneficiaries.

> The revival was attended by the emotional outbursts characteristic of the period. Many of the preachers did not at first approve of them. Others fanned them as "fire from heaven." Singing had a large part in the revival. Bands went singing to meetings, sang after the preaching, went singing home and from fields, shops and houses "made the heavens ring" with "spiritual songs." These were generally the compositions of Isaac Watts but a number originated in Virginia. Young Andrew Broaddus I, forbidden by his father to attend the Baptist night meetings in neighboring homes, would go out doors and listen to the

singing, softened by the distance and made more impressive by the stillness of the night. In his latter years it still seemed to him "more like the music of heaven" than any to which he had ever listened.[4]

The revival greatly strengthened the Baptist churches by reaching people of education and leadership. Baptists became leaders in religious influence in much of the state. Gone were the peculiar mannerisms in tones and gestures, partly received from Shubal Stearns and partly the result of preaching to large crowds in the open air. Semple judged that their zeal was less mixed with enthusiasm and their piety became more rational.

In addition, as Baptists assumed religious leadership in Virginia, they developed more of that cooperative attitude that additional responsibility usually brings. The General Committee of Correspondence that operated from 1784 to 1799 exchanged letters with Baptists everywhere in the United States, and there was discussion concerning the need for a general body composed of messengers from all states in Baptist life. In fact, almost a score of years before the organization of the first state body by South Carolina Baptists in 1821, Virginia Baptists rather extensively discussed the need for such a state body. The General Committee also discussed an official history of Virginia Baptists, general and ministerial education, and even agitated the question of the wrongfulness of slavery. Negroes had always been admitted to Baptist churches in Virginia, and many "exercised their gifts" with great effectiveness. In 1792 the Roanoke Association purchased a Negro called Simon and set him free to preach the gospel. Several Negro Baptist ministers were outstanding during the two decades before the close of this period, including Jacob Bishop, William Lemon, Gowen Pastor, and Gowan Pamphlet.

Virginia Baptists were slowly becoming united. Separate and Regular Baptists had joined in the organization of the General Committee of Correspondence in 1784. By 1787 an official union in Virginia was effected, and the parties expressed the "desire hereafter that the names Regular and Separate, be buried in oblivion."[5] Even John Waller was officially restored to full fellowship in 1787 in the spirit of union that was present. In addition, when the General Committee of Correspondence was dissolved in 1799, efforts were made in the following year to establish a meeting of all associations within the state under the title General Meeting of Correspondence of the United Baptist Associations in Virginia. Although in 1802 a majority of the delegates from seven associations rejected the effective organization of what amounted to a state body, efforts continued to develop some sort of inter-association correspondence. By 1808 the Albemarle, Appomattox, Dover, Gochen, Meherrin, and Roanoke delegates met to elect Robert B. Semple as moderator to replace the lamented William

Webber, and Reuben Ford was named clerk. This body, probably dating from 1803, became the forerunner of the General Association of 1823. At the very end of this period, revival began in Upper Essex and Upper King and Queen counties in the churches of Theodorick Noel and spread through adjoining counties and associations for several years.

The statistics show that Virginia Baptists had excellent growth between 1790 and 1814. In the former year they had 204 churches with 20,443 members, served by 150 ordained and 112 licensed preachers. By the close of the period they had 16 associations, 283 churches, 283 ministers, and 35,164 members. This represented an average annual growth of 3.13%, much more than double the rate of population growth. The number of slaves grew more slowly in Virginia, as has been noted, than either the general population or the Baptist increase.

4. North Carolina. Historians among the Baptists in North Carolina generally divide the development of the Baptist work in the state into three geographical sections—the eastern, which included at first some of the north central area; the central; and the area west of the Yadkin.

In the eastern section, the old Kehukee Association was "reformed" and reorganized in August, 1777. The new membership was made up of 10 churches, which included 6 Regular Baptist churches in North Carolina and 4 Separate churches located in Virginia. Despite the presence of Separate Baptist messengers (some historians say, because of them) a confession of faith was adopted which was rather rigidly Calvinistic. After some growth, a condition of "apathy and coldness" prevailed from about 1785 until the turn of the century. Leaders in this period were Lemuel Burkitt, Henry Ledbetter, John Tanner, John Meglamre, Jeremiah Walker, Jeremiah Dargan, Martin Ross, and Henry Abbot.

By 1793 there were 49 churches in the Kehukee Association. As a result, Tar River became the dividing line between the Kehukee and the new association, the Neuse, which was formed in 1794. The Neuse Association consisted of 28 churches dismissed from the Kehukee Association along the Neuse River and south of it to the South Carolina line. The Kehukee Association still retained churches north of the Neuse River to the Virginia line and westward through Franklin and Warren counties. In the same year (1794) the Roanoke Association, which had included 36 churches from both Virginia and North Carolina, divided along the state line, and the Flat River Association in North Carolina was formed with 9 member churches. One of the most interesting and able Separate Baptists who labored in this area was John Dillahunty, whose church subsequently joined the Kehukee

Association. Another excision from the Kehukee Association came in 1805 when the churches north of the Roanoke withdrew to form the Chowan Association, which was organized in 1806. Like Virginia Baptists, North Carolina Baptists were looking toward a state body as early as 1809. Martin Ross introduced a resolution calling for a General Meeting of Correspondence. This was created, and at the close of this period in 1814 preliminary steps were being taken that ultimately led to a state convention.

In the central area of North Carolina, in 1805 both the Raleigh Association and the Cape Fear Association were organized out of the Neuse Association, primarily because of the long distance required for attending meetings of the Neuse Association.

Despite the proximity of Sandy Creek, there were few churches in Anson, Rowan, and Mecklenburg west of the Yadkin in 1781. Through treaties with the Indians, western North Carolina was thrown open to the whites by 1800. The work of Joseph Murphy, David Allen, William Cook, William Petty, and Lazarus Whitehead was outstanding. The Yadkin Association was formed in 1790 when 13 North Carolina churches sent messengers. Because of its large size, the Yadkin Association divided in 1799 with the organization of the Mountain Association.

West of the Blue Ridge a Baptist church had been organized as early as 1789, known as the French Broad church. By 1807 the French Broad Association was organized with 6 churches sending messengers.

From the tables given in the appendix of M. A. Huggins, *A History of North Carolina Baptists,* it appears that between 1776 and 1783, there were 25 new churches organized; between 1783 and 1790, there were 37 new churches organized; and between 1790 and 1814, there were 85 new churches organized. These figures probably are not scrupulously accurate because there were questions about the dates of the founding of some of the churches shown, but they do show the type of growth that took place. These figures also suggest the impact of the sweeping revival that took place after 1800. Part of the reason for this revival in North Carolina was the visit of Lemuel Burkitt to Kentucky and Tennessee.

> The desirable news seemed to take such an uncommon effect on the people, that numbers were crying out for mercy, and many praising and glorifying God. Such a Kehukee Association we had never before seen. . . . In some churches where they had not received a member by baptism for a year or two, would now frequently receive, at almost every conference meeting, several members. Sometimes twelve, fourteen, eighteen, twenty, and twenty-four at several times in one day. Twenty-two and twenty-four were baptized several times at Flat Swamp, Cashie, Parker's meeting-house, Fishing Creek, Falls of Tar River, &c. Some of the churches in the revival received nearly two

hundred members each. In four churches lying between Roanoke and Meherrin Rivers, in Bertie, Northampton, and Hertford counties, were baptized in two years about six hundred members; and blessed be God the work seems yet progressing. The work has engaged the attention of all sorts of people—rich and poor, and all ranks. Many very respectable persons in character and office have been called in this revival. There are a few churches within the bounds of the Association that have not as yet experienced a revival, but we hope for them. According to the accounts returned to the two last Associations fifteen hundred have been added to the churches by baptism in the Kehukee Association.[6]

In 1790 there were 94 Baptist churches, 154 ministers, and 7,503 members in North Carolina. At the end of the period, there were 11 associations, 194 churches, 110 ministers, and 12,083 members. This represented an average annual increase of 2.65%. The population of the state grew from 393,751 (including 100,783 slaves) in 1790, to 555,500 (including 168,824 slaves) in 1810. This represented an average increase of 1.96% annually, much less than the Baptist growth. The increase of slaves averaged 3.21% annually.

5. South Carolina. Just as the Revolution erupted, South Carolina Baptists were beginning to feel the strong spiritual influence of the Separate Baptist movement in the back country. By 1777 this movement had reached the coast. Two years later Elhanan Winchester reported 240 members added to the Welsh Neck church. The coming of the Revolution, however, dampened the revival fires, but by 1789 another revival movement had reached its climax in the state. A sweeping revival occurred about 1800. Growing out of the Second Great Awakening west of the Alleghenies, South Carolina entered into the camp meeting movement that had been established in Kentucky. Richard Furman, the distinguished pastor at Charleston, attended a meeting at the Waxhaws on May 21, 1802, and being a regular correspondent with David Benedict, the historian, wrote him on August 11 concerning the joint meeting which took place about 170 miles from Charleston. Furman estimated the number present as between 3,000 and 4,000, and 21 ministers preached intermittently to the great crowds—5 Methodists, 5 Baptists, and 11 Presbyterians. The Presbyterians had taken the lead in this meeting, but both Baptists and Methodists cooperated wholeheartedly in it. Two public services were appointed at each of two stands each day and three for the sabbath, accompanied by the administration of the Lord's Supper. Furman noted:

> The communion service was performed with much apparent devotion, while I attended, which was at the serving of the first table. The Presbyterians and Methodists sat down together; but the Baptists, on the principle which has generally governed them on this subject, ab-

stained. Several persons suffered at this meeting those bodily affections, which have been before experienced at Kentucky, North-Carolina, and at other places, where the extraordinary revivals in religion within this year or two have taken place.[7]

Interest in education of the ministry among South Carolina Baptists can be traced to Oliver Hart, pastor in Charleston from 1749 to 1780. When several young men surrendered to preach under his ministry, this gifted and alert pastor promptly became concerned about their education. In 1755 a fund was begun in the Charleston Association to aid young ministers in securing their education. Following the Revolutionary War, Richard Furman, who had succeeded Hart at Charleston, took the lead in this enterprise. In 1791 a General Committee was named by the association to raise money for this purpose and to determine the form and the amount to be provided. Between 1791 and 1810, at least thirteen young preachers were aided by this fund. Generally during this time a young minister was placed in some capable minister's home where he received instruction, was given the use of the minister's library, and carried on a practical internship.

Before the close of the period, Roberts' Academy was established to train young ministers, and continued from about 1800 to 1810. It provided the equivalent of the first two years of college.

The general picture of Baptist life in South Carolina can be summarized through statistics. In 1772 Morgan Edwards counted 24 organized churches with approximately 50 ministers, licensed preachers, and exhorters. In 1790, out of a population of 249,073, there were 67 churches, 91 ministers, ordained preachers, and itinerants, and 3,878 white and Negro members. By 1800, there were 96 organized churches, 63 ministers, and 5,583 white and Negro communicants. Joe M. King pointed out that in 1772, about half of the 1,100 members reported by Edwards were in the low country and the Peedee section, with half in the back country. By 1790, of the total of 44 churches, 27 were in the back country, 12 in the Peedee, and only 5 classed as low-country churches. Of the 2,763 members, 1,505 were members of back-country churches, 751 of Peedee churches, and 507 of low-country churches. By 1800 the membership of 54 back-country churches was 2,978, of 14 Peedee churches was 714, and of 6 low-country churches, 515. At the close of the period, there were 5 associations, 96 ministers, 157 churches, with 10,794 members in all of South Carolina.[8]

The average annual rate of increase among South Carolina Baptists during the period was 7.43%. The population in 1790 was 249,073, of whom 107,094 were slaves. By 1810 it had grown to 415,115, of whom 196,355 were slaves. This represented a population increase of 3.17% average annual growth, well below half of the Baptist growth.

The increase in slave population showed an average annual growth of 3.97%, more than the population growth but below the Baptist rate of growth.

6. *Georgia.* It will be recalled that the first Baptist church in Georgia at Kiokee was established just before the Revolutionary War. The churches grew from 1 in 1772 to 42 in 1790, and in the latter year, there were 33 ordained ministers, 39 licensed ministers, and 3,211 church members. At the close of the period, there were 5 associations, 171 churches, 115 ministers, and 16,299 members. This represented an average annual increase of 17.72%, the largest increase shown in any South Atlantic state. Meanwhile, the population increased from 82,548 (including 29,264 slaves) in 1790, to 252,433 (including 105,218 slaves) in 1810. This was an average annual increase of 9.80%, barely over half of the Baptist growth. The slave population, meanwhile, had an average annual growth of 12.36%, much larger than the general population but well below the Baptist rate.

The rather large rate of increase among Georgia Baptists stemmed partly from the large number of licensed and ordained ministers working in the state, as well as the sharing of Georgia in the revival of about 1800. Most of the associations had been organized before the beginning of the revival. Georgia Association was formed in 1784, and from this body came the Hepzibah Association in 1794 to the south, the Sarepta Association in 1799 to the north, and the Ocmulgee Association in 1810 to the west. In 1802 the Savannah Association was formed on the coast. All of these reflected the growing revival after the turn of the century. Jesse Mercer, an outstanding leader in the Georgia Association, baptized about 300 persons in two years. In 1809 the revival became active in the Georgia and Sarepta associations. By 1812, the revival had spread all across Georgia. In the course of that year alone, the four associations (Ocmulgee, Sarepta, Georgia, and Savannah) added 3,800 members. Savannah alone added about 1,500, while Sarepta added over 1,250.[9]

A strong missionary spirit was evident in Georgia, as well as a sense of unity among the Baptist people. Three conferences were held in 1801 through 1803 at Powelton in an effort to unite Baptists in the state. At the last one on April 29, 1803, a permanent committee was formed which was influential in developing the state body later on. Among the Negroes, the first Baptist church was organized in 1788 by George Leile and Andrew Bryan. As well, the first Baptist missionary magazine in the nation and the earliest religious magazine in the South was founded in 1802 when Henry Holcombe, pastor of the Savannah church, began the publication of *The Georgia Analytical Repository.* The paper ran through six issues from May, 1802, to April, 1803.[10]

Expansion Westward

The expansion of the original thirteen colonies toward the west after the Revolutionary War is a complex story, punctuated by conflicting claims to vast stretches of land, political bargaining, swapping of areas larger in size than all of the thirteen colonies put together, and surprisingly amicable settlements of what seemed to constitute insoluble problems. The claims of the seaboard colonies based upon their original grants were abruptly silenced by England through her Proclamation of 1763 and the Quebec Act of 1774. But after independence from England was secured, renewed efforts were made by several of the colonies to gain control of the territory as far west as the Mississippi River. Virginia had the largest claims, although six of the other thirteen colonies also had their eyes turned toward the west. Finally, Kentucky was carved out of a portion of Virginia's claims, and was admitted to the Union in 1792. Tennessee was admitted to the Union in 1796 composed of land ceded by North Carolina. Mississippi and Alabama were formed out of western lands won from the British in the war. Mississippi (including the territory later separated to form Alabama) was given territorial status in 1798 and statehood in 1817, while Alabama became a separate state in 1819. Louisiana was a part of the Louisiana Purchase of 1803. Missouri also was a part of the Louisiana Purchase of 1803, although Spain had encouraged the coming of American settlers after securing possession of this territory in 1762. Following territorial government from 1804 to 1821, Missouri was admitted to the Union.

Before the Revolution, the westward immigration was but a trickle. The immigrants represented what W. W. Sweet called "woodchoppers, game hunters, and Indian fighters" whose contributions generally were short-lived. Some Baptists accompanied these early explorers, i.e., those fleeing from North Carolina across the rugged mountains into what became Tennessee after the Battle of Alamance in 1768, and some who accompanied Daniel Boone, for example, into what became Kentucky.

Economic and social factors, however, turned this trickle of immigrants into a flood after the Revolution. The winning of political independence meant that new economic lines would have to be established. What good were bumper crops without markets to absorb them? The British West Indies closed their ports to American trade, an immediate blow to the southern states in particular. England abruptly substituted an antagonistic policy of trade for her former paternalistic attitude. Even France and Spain were initially cool at the emergence of a new economic factor in trade among the nations, and their policies did not assist the stringent economic situation. The new governmental structure inaugurated by the colonies was not effective in establishing any sort of trade policies to alleviate the crisis. Bankrupt and dispossessed farmers looked to the western country for the opportunity to start over, and the migration began.

As Theodore Roosevelt pointed out, this post-Revolutionary immigration was of different character than the earlier groups. Sweet remarked:

> It was this population which transformed Kentucky and Tennessee from backwoods communities into states. This immigration was made up not only of small farmers and people of the lower middle class, which included many Baptists, but also there were young planters, lawyers and some men of means, impoverished by the long civil war which had accompanied the Revolution in Virginia, among them. This was the class of people which laid the foundations for the cultural life of the new communities, and in whose path schools and churches soon appeared.[11]

Nor was the economic pinch the only factor that caused people like the Baptists to move westward. The social stratification in Virginia turned many toward the democratic back country.

> Most of the Virginia Baptists who left the East were motivated in part by dislike of the snobbery of aristocrats and large landowners. They were tired of being looked down upon as inferior. On the frontier a man could be a man, and hard work and integrity received their just reward.[12]

Baptist ecclesiology and doctrine were particularly suited to the democratic atmosphere of the developing western frontier. The Baptist gospel was simple, minimizing complex theological formulations, and emphasizing a life-changing confrontation with Jesus Christ. Like Paul, most of the frontier Baptist preachers were tentmakers in the sense that they provided for their own livelihood. The distinction between "laity" and "clergy" existed only in the fact that the latter had fire in their bones to preach the gospel in response to a divine summons.

> The Baptist preachers lived and worked exactly as did their flocks; their dwellings were little cabins with dirt floor and, instead of bedsteads, skin-covered pole-bunks: they cleared the ground, split rails, planted corn, and raised hogs on equal terms with their parishioners.[13]

The fact that each Baptist church was completely independent appealed to frontier democracy and eliminated problems of ministerial appointment and ecclesiastical authority. It is no wonder, then, that the Baptists played a large part in the significant frontier movement and made great gains from their ministry among the people on the growing edge of American life.

South Central Region. The census of 1790 showed returns on only two states in what is called the South Central region—Kentucky and Tennessee. The former had a population of 73,677, while the latter had 35,691, or a total of 109,368. By 1810, however, the reports list Alabama with 9,046, Mississippi with 31,306, Louisiana with 76,556, and the growth of Kentucky to 406,511 and Tennessee to 261,727. This brought the total in 1810 in these five "western" states to 785,146, representing an average annual increase in population in this region of 29.44%. This should be contrasted with the South Atlantic annual average of 2.08% population increase as an illustration of the rapid migration to the western areas. Along with this, it should be noted that in 1790 only Kentucky and Tennessee reported slaves, a total of 15,247. By 1810 the number of slaves in these two states had grown to 125,096 and, in addition, Mississippi and Louisiana were shown as having slaves, to bring the total slaves in the South Central region in 1810 to 176,844, an average annual increase of 50.42%. This means that the movement of slavery from the eastern areas was so rapid that the number of slaves in the South Central states more than doubled the original number every two years during this period. This should be compared with the annual rate of increase in the number of slaves in the South Atlantic area during the same period of 2.64%, showing the very rapid move of the center of slavery from the old South Atlantic states to the South Central area.

Baptists, meanwhile, increased from 60 churches, 82 ministers, and 3,994 members in 1790 in the two states of Kentucky and Tennessee, to 21 associations, 304 ministers, 457 churches, and 34,848 members in Kentucky, Tennessee, and Mississippi at the close of the period. This represented an average annual increase in this region of 33.59%. This was a far greater increase than the population, but not as large as the increase in the number of slaves. This rate far outstripped the South Atlantic Baptist increase of 4.77% during the same period.

1. Kentucky. The area that became Kentucky was considered the western part of Virginia during the early years, and many from that state and from North Carolina moved into this new region. The population in 1790 was 73,677, including 11,830 slaves. Ten years later it had risen to 220,955, including 40,343 slaves, and by 1810, the number of inhabitants reached 406,511, including 80,561 slaves. This represented an average annual population increase of 21.73%.

Baptists came to Kentucky quite early. In 1772 Squire Boone, a Baptist preacher, accompanied his renowned brother, Daniel Boone, in exploring eastern Kentucky. Whether Squire preached during this time is not certain. It is known that in the spring of 1776, William Hickman and Thomas Tinsley from Virginia pushed as far west as the fort at Harrodsburg and preached there. John Taylor and William Marshall also made preaching tours from Virginia to eastern Kentucky in 1779 and 1780. The first Baptist church in Kentucky was organized June 18, 1781, called Severn's Valley Baptist Church at Elizabethtown.

Less than a month later the Cedar Creek church in Nelson County was organized. The third church organized in this area was the Gilbert's Creek church, famous because of its colorful history. On November 20, 1767, twenty-five persons constituted a church at Upper Spotsylvania, Virginia, and in the fall of 1781, under the leadership of its pastor, Lewis Craig, this "traveling church" emigrated to Kentucky. Four other preachers accompanied this church—Joseph Craig, Elijah Craig, Ambrose Dudley, and William E. Waller. After exciting adventures along the way, the church camped on Gilbert's Creek, twenty-five miles southeast of Harrodsburg, from which it got its name, and on the second Sunday of December, 1781, worshiped at its permanent home. This was the third Baptist church in Kentucky.

By 1785, eighteen Baptist churches had been organized in Kentucky, partly through the enthusiastic preaching of men like John Taylor and William Hickman, who cast their lot with the new state about 1784. Large numbers of both Regular and Separate Baptists poured in from Virginia, many of them products of the great revival in that state in 1785.

On September 30, 1785, the first association in Kentucky was organized, known as the Elkhorn Association. A month later the Salem Association was constituted.

After a decade of decline, in 1800 a remarkable revival occurred in Kentucky, beginning among the Presbyterians but vitally affecting Baptists also. For several years thereafter the growth was phenomenal. After another dry season, an additional revival between 1810 and 1813 brought great growth.

In 1790 Baptists in Kentucky had 42 churches, 61 preachers (of whom 21 were licensed and the remainder ordained), and 3,105 members. At the close of the period, there were 13 associations, 263 churches, 148 preachers, and 21,660 church members. This represented an average annual increase of 25.98%, a remarkable record of growth. Slaves increased between 1790 and 1810 at an average annual rate of 26.10%, slightly larger than the Baptist increase and much larger than the population increase.

2. Tennessee. The flow of immigrants into what became the state of Tennessee was very rapid between 1790 and 1814, particularly from Virginia and North Carolina. In 1790 there were 35,701 inhabitants in Tennessee, including 3,417 slaves. By 1810 the population had reached 261,727, including 44,535 slaves. This population increase averaged 30.15% annually. The slave population increase averaged 57.30% annually, the largest average percentage of growth ever experienced by any state in slave population.

Among the pioneers in Tennessee were many Baptists. The early Regulator troubles in North Carolina had caused many Separate

Baptists to flee from the reprisals of Governor Tryon after 1768. After the Battle of Alamance in 1771, a small group of members from the Sandy Creek church settled on Boone's Creek in what is now Washington County, Tennessee, and soon received accessions to their party from·Sandy Creek. Although no records have been preserved, it is likely that these Separate Baptists organized three churches. The Indian wars of 1774 evidently destroyed the records and dispersed the people.

David Benedict provided the information generally used to describe the first Baptist life of Tennessee, as follows:

> But the beginning of the first churches which have had a permanent standing was in the following manner: About the year 1780, William Murphy, James Keel, Thomas Murrell, Tidence Lane, Isaac Barton, Matthew Talbot, Joshua Kelly, and John Chastain, moved into what was called the Holston country, when it was in a wilderness state, and much exposed to the ravages and depredations of the Indians. These ministers were all Virginians, except Mr. Lane, who was from North-Carolina. They were accompanied by a considerable number of their brethren from the churches which they left, and were followed shortly after by Jonathan Mulky, William Reno, and some other ministers and brethren, and amongst the other emigrants there was a small body which went out in something like a church capacity. They removed from the old church at Sandy-Creek, in North-Carolina, which was planted by Shubael Stearns; and as a branch of the mother church, they emigrated to the wilderness, and settled on Boon's Creek. The church is now called Buffaloe Ridge.[14]

Benedict then related how in 1781, the five or six churches this group had established were organized into a temporary association which was under the supervision of the Sandy Creek Association in North Carolina. On August 31, 1786, this body was organized into a separate group known as the Holston Association consisting of seven churches, and including both Regular and Separate Baptists. On December 5, 1802, this association was divided to form a second body known as the Tennessee Association. These were the only two associations in East Tennessee by 1814, the close of this period.

General James Robertson led about forty families from Virginia and North Carolina to the luxurious banks of the Cumberland River in 1780. Benedict noted that "a church of a temporary existence" was formed in 1786 called Sulphur Fork, but that after a short time its pastor, John Grammer, removed elsewhere and the church was dissolved. In 1791 the Tennessee church was constituted by Ambrose Dudley and John Taylor from the Elkhorn Association in Kentucky, who had traveled at the request of the Tennessee brethren through about two hundred miles of wilderness, with menacing Indians everywhere, to organize this church. Three years later the White's Creek church near Nashville became the second Baptist church in this wilderness. Another church, organized in North Carolina and moved as a body to the head of Sulphur Fork about 1794 or 1795, was the third church in this western area. In 1793 several of these churches and two new ones organized the first Baptist association in Middle Tennessee called Mero District Association. This body was dissolved in 1803 over internal strife, and in its place the Cumberland Association was formed, becoming the mother of all Baptist associations in Middle Tennessee. Stockton's Valley Association was formed in 1805, and a daughter, Caney Fork Association, was constituted in 1813. Seven churches formed the Elk River Association in 1808, and in the following year, the Concord Association, the oldest association in Middle Tennessee to remain missionary, was organized.

In 1790 Tennessee had 1 association, 18 churches, 21 preachers, and 889 members. By the end of the period, there were 7 associations, 174 churches, 133 ministers, and 12,294 members. This represented an average annual increase of 55.78%. This Baptist increase was greater than the large population increase, and almost as large as the increase of slaves.

3. Mississippi. Before the American Revolution ended, small parties had moved into the area now known as Mississippi. The territory was first included in the census of 1800, when it had 8,850 population, including 3,489 slaves. In 1810, the total population was 40,352, including 17,088 slaves. The growth of the population represented an average annual increase of 32.36%. The slave population increased at an average annual rate of 35.43% during the ten years, which was almost the same as the growth of the total population.

A group of Baptists from the Peedee section of South Carolina made their way to Natchez County, Mississippi, in 1780, traveling overland due west, then floating down the Holston, Tennessee, Ohio, and Mississippi rivers. Richard Curtis was leader of the group, and his son, Richard, Jr., a licensed preacher, led in worship services until October, 1791, when the Salem or Cole's Creek Baptist Church was organized with eleven members and young Curtis as pastor. The Catholic clergy was aroused, and after violent harassment from them, Curtis and his companions returned to South Carolina in 1795. In his absence, the Salem church continued to meet and even built a log church house. Curtis returned to this church in 1798. By 1806, six churches had been constituted in Mississippi and together organized the Mississippi Baptist Association. Some of their prominent leaders were Bailey Chaney, William Thompson, Thomas Mercer, David Cooper, David Snodgrass, Ezra Courtney, Moses Hadley, and John Stampley. From this association went leaders to nearby Louisiana to assist in the beginning of work in that state. There are no Baptist statistics for Mississippi in 1790 but at the end of this period, Mississippi Territory had 1 association, 20 churches, 13 ministers, and 894 members.

4. Louisiana. Some Americans had entered what is now the state of Louisiana shortly after the close of the American Revolution, although the Spanish owners tried to restrict this immigration in every way. The settling of Louisiana was quite rapid after the Louisiana Purchase of 1803. The 1810 census showed the population as 76,556, including 34,660 slaves.

The Baptist story began before the purchase of the area by the United States. Bailey Chaney, referred to as a leader in Mississippi, entered Louisiana in 1798 with his family and attempted to establish a church, but the Catholics resisted him. The organization of the first church was delayed until October 12, 1812, when the Half Moon Bluff Baptist Church, not far from the present town of Clifton, was constituted. It is uncertain as to exactly who organized this church, although the messengers from the Mississippi Baptist Association sent Joseph Lewis, Joseph Irwin, and later David Cooper and Thomas Mercer to assist the Louisiana brethren in the organization. The Louisiana story mentions Ezra Courtney, the only preacher in east Louisiana at that time. This church dissolved about 1870, but Hay's Creek church was later organized from it. Leaders from the Mississippi Association also sent Cooper and Lawrence Scarborough to ordain Joseph Willis and help organize the second Baptist church in Louisiana, the first west of the Mississippi River, on November 13, 1812. At the close of this period there were only about half a dozen small churches with a membership probably of less than a hundred.

5. Alabama. Baptist work in Alabama parallels the story of the settlement of the area by all groups. In 1807 the United States quashed the Indian title to the land and authorized a survey of the public lands in 1807 for settlements, although statistics on population were first included in the 1820 census. It was at first a part of Mississippi Territory. Several thousand pioneers traveled to Alabama, primarily from Virginia, North Carolina, and Georgia. Among the early group were John Nicholson, John Cantebury, and Zadock Baker, three Baptist ministers. On October 2, 1808, Nicholson assisted in the organization of the first church in Madison County, when about a dozen members constituted the Flint River Baptist Church a few miles northeast of Huntsville. On September 26, 1814, the Flint River Association was organized, consisting of 17 churches with 1,021 members, some of whom were located in Tennessee. The transient nature of the settlers undermined these churches during the next few years.

North Central Region. During this period only one state was included in the North Central region. Missouri had a central place in the political controversies during the first decades of the nineteenth century, which partly accounts for its late entry into the Union. It was acquired as a part of the Louisiana Purchase in 1803 and, was successively ruled by a military government, became a part of the District of Louisiana (which became the Territory of Louisiana), and in 1812 was constituted as the Territory of Missouri. It first appeared in the census of 1810 with a population of 20,845, including 3,011 slaves.

Some Baptist settlers appeared in southeast Missouri as early as 1796, including Thomas Bull, his wife, and her mother. Others settled near St. Louis. Thomas Johnson, an aged Baptist missionary from Georgia, moved to Missouri and performed the first Baptist immersion in the state in 1799.

The Bethel church, near what is now Jackson, has been called the first church permanently organized in Missouri. It was dated July 19, 1806. It later became antimissionary and died. The oldest continuous church in Missouri was organized near St. Louis, known as the Fee Fee church, in 1807 by Thomas R. Musick from Kentucky. By the close of this period in 1814 the number of Baptists in Missouri probably did not exceed two or three hundred.

Second Great Awakening in the South

During the American Revolution and immediately thereafter, the vitality of Christianity in America fell to a low ebb. Part of the reason was the bitterness and cynicism that war always brings. In addition, English deism and French infidelity greatly influenced the colonies. The anti-Christian writings of Voltaire (1694-1778) in France and Thomas Paine (1737-1809) in America were widely circulated. The 1790 census reported only about 275,000 out of 3,929,214 inhabitants in the new nation to be Christians. Remarkable religious awakenings, however, took place both in New England and in the South. There was considerable difference between the Second Great Awakening in New England around the turn of the eighteenth century and the earlier First Awakening stirred up by Whitefield. The Second Awakening in New England had less emotional excitement, little immediate controversy over methods of revival, and fewer outstanding leaders. Most of the power of the Second Awakening consisted not simply in large numbers of additions to the churches, but as well in the initiation of extensive benevolent Christian ministries, such as home and foreign missions, Bible distribution, Sunday School extension, the printing and circulation of Christian tracts, and the organization of many societies for carrying on these Christian benevolences.

Although occurring about the same time that the second New England revival took place, a revival of a different sort was begun west of the Alleghenies in Tennessee and Kentucky. Many descriptions have been written of the rough and violent society that had gathered on this southwestern frontier in the closing years of the eighteenth century. Revival for these multitudes began through the agency of James McGready, a Presbyterian minister, who assumed charge of Presbyterian churches in Logan County, Kentucky, in 1796. As he traveled from one church to another under his supervision, he found responsive hearts and evidences of revival. In 1799 two brothers, William and John Magee, one a Presbyterian and one a Methodist, stirred the fires of revival in both Kentucky and Tennessee as they preached. In July, 1800, the first American camp meeting occurred in Logan County, Kentucky, and great crowds of people from miles around drove to the preaching services. The climax to these meetings came at Cane Ridge, Tennessee, in August, 1801, when between twenty and thirty thousand persons assembled on the camp ground. These meetings in general were characterized by excessive emotional display, including the jerks, the barks, dancing, rolling, shouting, fainting, and similar exercises.

Baptists, while engaging in many of these services, for the most part refused to be involved in the emotional manifestations taking place. As has been mentioned already, this revival spread into the older states among the Baptists and spurred revivals there. Benedict described the effect of this Awakening upon Kentucky Baptists as follows:

> This great revival in Kentucky began in Boone county on the Ohio River, and in its progress extended up the Ohio, Licking, and Kentucky Rivers, branching out into the settlements adjoining them. It spread fast in different directions, and in a short time almost every part of the State was affected by its influence. It was computed that about ten thousand were baptized and added to the Baptist churches in the course of two or three years. This great work progressed among the Baptists in a much more regular manner than people abroad have generally supposed. They were indeed zealously affected, and much engaged. Many of their ministers baptized in a number of neighbouring churches from two to four hundred each. And two of them baptized about five hundred a-piece in the course of the work. But throughout the whole, they preserved a good degree of decorum and order. Those camp-meetings, those great parades, and sacramental seasons, those extraordinary exercises of falling down, rolling, shouting, jerking, dancing, barking, &c. were but little known among the Baptists in Kentucky, nor encouraged by them.[15]

Part of the increase in Baptist statistics in Kentucky and Tennessee, mentioned heretofore, came from the Baptist participation in the revivals in these states.

The Missionary Impulse

Baptists in America had no organizational structure beyond the local churches from 1639 to 1707 when the Philadelphia Association was formed. The second association (Charleston, South Carolina) was not formed until 1751 and was a direct offshoot from the Philadelphia body. It was promoted by one of her ministers who had accepted the pastorate in South Carolina. It took more than a full century after the first association was organized to develop a general denominational body for missionary purposes, and the first state convention was not formed until 1821.

This rather long period of time before bodies beyond the local congregation were formed suggests that American Baptists were true followers of the principle of congregational authority. Other denominational bodies beyond the local congregation were important for the *bene esse* (well being) but not the *esse* (being) of Baptist life. This point of view reflected explicit statements by English Baptists of the seventeenth century. John Smyth, for example, in an answer to Henry Ainsworth in his *Paralleles* said that "Christ's ruling power is originally and fundamentally in the body of the Church, the multitude." He voiced the belief that "the last definitive determining sentence is in the body of the Church." Both the General and Particular Baptists in England followed this view. In the Confession of Faith of 1611, Thomas Helwys reflected the language of Smyth as in Article XI he defined the church as consisting of particular congregations, with each congregation a whole church and authoritative. The Particular Baptist confession of 1644 said in Article XXXVI that every individual church has power given them from Christ for their better well-being

> to choose to themselves meet persons into the office of Pastors, Teachers, Elders, Deacons, being qualified according to the Word, as those which Christ has appointed in his Testament, for the feeding, governing, serving, and building up of his Church, and that none other have power to impose them, either these or any other.[16]

It was the departure of General Baptists from this earlier principle of the autonomy of the local body that caused the downfall of the General Assembly of General Baptists. Conversely, the extreme efforts of the Particular Baptists to maintain the total autonomy of the local congregations left their general body without effective powers.

American Baptists maintained this view of the authority of local bodies. The first association in the colonies was organized in 1707 at Philadelphia. In 1749 this body adopted an essay on the power of an association and specifically said that

> each particular church hath a complete power and authority from Jesus Christ, to administer all gospel ordinances, provided they have a sufficiency of officers duly qualified, or that they be supplied by the officers of another sister church or churches, as baptism, and the

Lord's supper, &c.; and to receive in and cast out, and also to try and ordain their own officers, and to exercise every part of gospel discipline and church government, independent of any other church or assembly whatever.[17]

In the correspondence of the Philadelphia Association during the eighteenth century, it is clear that the Association was quite sensitive to the authority of the churches at every point. In 1768, for example, it was reiterated that "the Association claims no jurisdiction, nor a power to repeal any thing settled by any church; but if, before settlement, parties agree to refer matters to the Association, then to give their advice." [18]

In the South, it will be recalled that one reason for the division of the Sandy Creek Association in 1770 was the "improper stretch of associational power." It will also be recalled that in Virginia as late as 1778 there was a serious debate as to whether any extra-church body like the association was necessary. It was finally agreed that so long as an association did not threaten the authority of the churches, it was helpful for advice and counsel.

However, American Baptists in the South as in the North saw the necessity of organization beyond the local level for inspiration, fellowship, and the achievement of tasks too large for a single church. Committees of correspondence were established in Virginia, the Carolinas, and Georgia, and were influential in assisting Baptists in the struggle for religious liberty. In the case of Virginia, their General Committee of Correspondence had fraternal relations with Baptist bodies in the North, as well.

Baptists in the North, perhaps as a reflection from the political developments in that area, were quite sensitive to the need for more cooperation on the part of Baptists. As early as 1767, when the Warren Association was formed, the Philadelphia Association wrote to the leaders of the new body and said:

> For, as particular members are collected together and united in one body, which we call a particular Church, to answer those ends and purposes which could not be accomplished by any single member, so a collection and union of churches into one associational body may easily be conceived capable of answering those still greater purposes which any particular Church could not be equal to. And, by the same reason, a union of associations will still increase the body in weight and strength, and make it good that a three-fold cord is not easily broken.[19]

Four years later Morgan Edwards suggested a plan by which the Philadelphia Association might be incorporated and delegates from other associations be admitted to the corporation to form a type of national body. In 1775 the Warren Association (Rhode Island) urged that a meeting be called of delegates from Baptist bodies in every colony to forward religious liberty. A "Continental Association" was called to meet in 1776, perhaps a reflection of the Continental Congress which was then in session, but the religious meeting was not held. In 1799 the Philadelphia Association called for a national meeting of all Baptist bodies to form a General Conference "composed of one member, or more, from each Association, to be held every *one, two,* or *three* years, as might seem most subservient to the general interests of Christ's kingdom." [20] At the turn of the century Richard Furman of Charleston was in correspondence with northern leaders concerning a possible national union of all Baptists.

Despite all of this agitation for a general body, Baptists were not willing to organize such a structure unless they saw a real necessity for it. That real necessity occurred in the great missionary impulse. The desire to win others beyond the local church field can be called either evangelism or missions. At any rate, warmhearted pastors quite early in American Baptist history began itinerating for the purpose of winning others to Christ. An example was John Clarke, pastor at Newport, who traveled to various sections of New England for gospel preaching. The next step, as Albert L. Vail pointed out, was the missionary church. The outstanding example of this was the Sandy Creek church in North Carolina with Shubal Stearns and Daniel Marshall as its leaders. Other examples were the church at Middletown, New Jersey, under the leadership of Abel Morgan; Cazenovia, New York, under John Mason Peck; and Brentwood, New Hampshire, under Samuel Shepherd.

Not unexpectedly, the Philadelphia Association, the first in America, became a missionary body, although tardy in this movement. Vail remarked:

> The year 1755 is the fountain-head year of Baptist mission work in America beyond the individual and the church. In this year the Philadelphia Association first reached the realization of itself as a missionary organization.[21]

In that year two ministers were appointed to visit North Carolina, their expenses to be borne by the several churches making up the associational structure. In 1766 another large step was taken by the Philadelphia Association, when a permanent missionary fund was provided "the interest whereof to be by them laid out every year in support of ministers traveling on the errand of the churches, or otherwise, as the necessities of said churches shall require." This fund was developed through quarterly collections by the churches to be handled by trustees of the Association. By 1773 the fund had grown to over five hundred dollars. Other associations, as they were formed, followed the example of the Philadelphia. In 1751 the Charleston, in 1758, the Sandy Creek, and in 1767, the Warren Association of

Rhode Island became involved in associational missionary programs. The climax to the associational method of missionary work came in 1802 when the Shaftsbury Association of Vermont adopted a plan that resembled on a small scale the type of structure subsequently adopted by the Southern Baptist Convention; namely, a committee of the association was appointed to handle mission contributions, examine the candidates, recommend the time and place of appointments, and pay salaries of missionaries.[22] Two years later, a plan was developed to make pledges in advance for missionary contributions. Other associations followed suit, and it appeared that missions, both domestic and foreign (as some associations sent missionaries into Canada) were firmly entrenched in the hands of associational bodies.

However, this kind of organizational mission structure was challenged by another method. William Carey in England had made impassioned appeals to the association of which he was a part to support a missionary program in their official capacity. When they refused to do so, the famous Baptist Missionary Society at Kettering was organized apart from the association in 1792. In America, this missionary society method was eagerly adopted, at first including members of various denominations who were endeavoring to minister to the Indians and others in their immediate vicinity. Vail listed five of these societies, beginning in 1796, with which Baptists were connected. The very simplicity of the pattern made it appealing, for weak and unorganized denominations who could not afford to carry on extensive missionary operations even if they had been organized to do so, could have members in this type of society based strictly upon what each person felt that he could do. In addition, without authorization from any denomination, without previous experience, without a complex pattern, a small group of individuals could meet in a home, take a small offering, and use the funds as seemed best to them.

The climax to the society type of structure came on May 26, 1802, when the Massachusetts Baptist Missionary Society was organized. Three missionaries were appointed, not for full-time service but for taking certain missionary tours. One of these, Joseph Cornell, traveled northward through New York beginning on December 2 and in a sixteen-week tour preached in many areas of Canada.[23]

Thus, by 1802 there were two types of missionary structure among American Baptists. As fully developed, the two methods presented different philosophies, one of which (the society) was used by Baptists in the North until 1907, while the other (the associational) was used by Southern Baptists from the beginning to the present.

Some of the differences between these two methods are quite evident. The associational method was *geographically* based, while the society method was *financially* based. That is, as associations became more completely geographically oriented, the support of the missionary projects of an association included those who were geographically a part of the area covered by a particular association. The society method, on the other hand, could never be limited by geography. Those individuals interested in giving to missions, regardless of geography or structural form, were related immediately to the enterprise by the giving of their money to the society.

Another difference between the two methods of operation was that the associational method usually involved a denominational structure fostering many benevolences, while the society became involved with only one benevolence. In the former, a denominational body (the association) already in existence simply took up another aspect of denominational life, which was added to other benevolent activities such as the education of the ministry, the publication of circular letters on doctrine and program, etc. The missionary society, on the other hand, had no other interest than missions. In its full development after 1826, the society method disclaimed all but one specific interest, whether it be home missions, foreign missions, or publication and tract work. If additional benevolences were to be undertaken, a new society for each one would be organized.

A third difference between the two methods was the relationship sustained to the churches. Under the associational plan, as developed, no one could engage in the missionary program unless he were a member of a church related to the association. That is to say, relationship to the program was channeled through the agency of the churches as they in turn were a part of the associational ministry. On the other hand, although it was expected that a member of a missionary society would be a member of a Baptist church, the relationship of the individual to the society was in no way connected with the relationship of the church to the society. The churches were entirely bypassed in this type of mission program, as pointed out by President Francis Wayland of Brown University during the abolitionist controversy.[24]

A fourth difference between the two methods was the fact that the associational method was denominationally centered, while the society plan was benevolence centered. Under the associational plan all of the interests of the denomination were fostered through the association, and the missionary program, as one part of the entire denominational thrust, had its place. The interests of the entire denominational program were always considered in setting up the mission program of an association. On the other hand, a missionary society was totally autonomous and utilized its entire efforts in one direction only; viz., for the promotion of the particular benevolence represented by that society. Thus, the focus of the individual in the missionary society was not primarily on the balanced objectives of the whole denomination, but rather upon the immediate work and finances of the particular society to which he belonged. Ultimately, this was the principle that brought the change from the missionary society plan in the North in 1907 and the development of the Northern Baptist Convention.

Finally, there was an interdependent and connectional relationship in all the benevolent work through the association that was not evident in the independent and voluntary societies organized for a particular benevolence.

Before 1814, then, American Baptists had developed two rather distinct methods of carrying on benevolent work. One looked toward a denominational body with churches as its base; the other emphasized a society entirely separate from the churches and consisting solely of individuals interested in missions. Vail remarked that it was the "collision of these two currents" of thought that produced a "revolution" in Baptist organizational life.[25] The victory was quickly, although temporarily, won by the society method. Although the associations had been conducting missionary work for over half a century, within a decade the society plan was almost universally adopted in American Baptist life. In the opening decade of the nineteenth century, Vail estimated that at least sixty-five societies were organized north of Philadelphia alone to raise money for missions. He felt that the principal reason for this revolutionary change to the society method took place because of the extreme sensitiveness of the Baptist churches and leaders toward the development of ecclesiastical bodies that might usurp the autonomy of the local congregations. He wrote:

> The excessive sensitiveness in behalf of church independency then characteristic of Baptists probably had influence. In those times even the Association must protest its innocency on this score very distinctly. The churches were exceedingly jealous for their authority. We have seen how long the Philadelphia Association fumbled over this point, and when the Warren came into being it was under keen suspicion, so that at first some of the best pastors stood aloof. This state of mind prevailed more or less everywhere, and although necessity had pushed the Associations into mission work, it had been done gingerly and from hand to mouth in the main. In this situation the society opened the way out of some of the perplexity. The Associations were based in the churches, having some organic or semi-organic relation with them, therefore they were specially and inevitably watched with reference to centralization. But start a society without any direct connection with the churches, and thus free from the suspicion of usurpation in that measure of authority essential to effectiveness, and there would be plainer sailing. Mission-minded brethren might tolerate in the society what they would not in the Association, and omission-minded brethren would keep out of the way by keeping out of the society. This might have constituted to judicious and irenic leaders a reason

for the society, and probably it was the chief reason with those who thought thoroughly.[26]

Summary

Between 1740 and 1814, Southern Baptists made substantial advances in many areas. At the opening of the period they had only one organizational structure—the local congregation (although some of the churches of the South were affiliated with the Philadelphia Association, the only one in America until 1751). In the seventy-five years of this period, their churches increased from fewer than 10 to more than 1,282. (The figures from Benedict do not include churches in Louisiana and Missouri, but his Mississippi statistics perhaps include what became the early Alabama churches). The first association in the South was organized in 1751 in South Carolina, and by 1814, there were at least 60 in the South. The total number of Baptists in the South increased from several hundred in 1740 to over 110,514 in 1814.

This growth took place both in the South Atlantic states and the South Central states. The South Atlantic states had 68.47% of all Southern Baptists in 1814. Virginia alone had more Baptists than all of the South Central states combined. In 1814, 31.82% of all Southern Baptists were in Virginia. The other South Atlantic states had substantial percentages of the total Southern Baptist population: Maryland, 1.20%; North Carolina, 10.93%; South Carolina, 9.77%; and Georgia, 14.75% (second largest number in the South Atlantic states and third in the South).

The South Central states had 31.53% of all Southern Baptists in 1814. Kentucky, with 19.60% of them, was second only to Virginia in the number of Baptists. Tennessee had 11.12% of all Southern Baptists, while Mississippi had .8%. The South Central states had 21 of the 60 associations in the South.

Revival and migration accounted for growth in the several areas. The First Great Awakening sparked the rise of the Separate Baptists, whose remarkable expansion was responsible for much of the growth. The westward trek accelerated after the Revolution, and by 1810 the South Central states had 708,590 inhabitants, including 166,256 slaves. It is hard to overestimate the effect of this migration on Baptists. Large numbers were transported to the very areas where a democratic people's church movement like that of the Baptists was very popular. In the next period (1814-45) this rapid westward flow will multiply geometrically, as will the movement of slaves into the South Central section. The invention of the cotton gin in 1793 rescued and proliferated the institution of slavery.

The Baptist image was almost totally reversed during this period.

They had been vilified and scorned in the pre-Revolutionary period, particularly in Virginia, but their rapid growth, support of the patriot cause, and successful leadership in securing religious liberty enhanced their status. Gewehr judged that the social status of Baptists, even in Virginia, was equal to any other religious group by 1790. Life on the frontier maintained primitive social and economic patterns, and church and revival meetings became a social as well as religious exercise, as neighbors would make long trips from isolated farms to meet for fellowship and worship.

As many historians have noted, church life provided moral discipline and order on the frontier. Both Negro and white Baptist members were subjected to rigid surveillance by the corporate religious judicature at the church business session. There are many extant church minutes which paint this picture clearly.[27] The early Baptist associational structure provided a responsible body which gave answers to knotty social and doctrinal queries from the churches; and although careful to observe the independence of the local congregation, associations often settled controversies which had gone beyond the control of the churches.[28] They also engendered a wider fellowship by the exchange of correspondence and by swapping ministerial assistance of various sorts.

Southern Baptists were groping toward a wider unity. The committees of correspondence in the principal southern states presaged the development of the state bodies in the next period. It is likely that the struggle for religious liberty accelerated greatly the uniting of the newer Separate Baptists and the old Regulars. The General Baptists, with their Arminian doctrines, were greatly reduced by the "Calvinizing" activities of the Philadelphia Association and the work of strong individual ministers. Paschal pointed out that only a small percentage of the older General Baptists joined the reconstituted Calvinistic churches. It is likely that the remainder were either swallowed up in the Separate Baptist movement or continued in a local fellowship as a separate group. The integration of the General Baptists, the Regulars, and the Separates laid the doctrinal foundation for the religious activism of Baptists in the South: a mild Calvinism that involved active human agency in spreading the gospel. This stance brought rejection of antimission and anti-effort groups.

The achievement of religious liberty released the Baptists to new opportunities. Their thrust in this period was primarily missionary or evangelistic, but other benevolences were beginning to develop. Before the South had a denominational college, many of the states supported Rhode Island College, later named Brown University.[29] Ministerial education was promoted by societies and associations in several of the southern states. Southern Baptists were ready for the larger challenges of the nineteenth century.

Notes

1. The proper statistics for Southern Baptists in the District of Columbia constituted a problem. Some in the District were Northern Baptists and some Southern. Many of the constituency affiliated with adjacent state bodies, whose statistics would include them. However, the small number of Baptists in the District had practically no effect on the percentages of comparative growth in the South Atlantic region over a period of the years included in each chronological division, so no effort was made to cull Southern Baptist figures in the earlier years.

2. See Appendix #A for the source and evaluation of the Baptist statistics used in this study. The preface described how the several percentages have been figured. The population statistics are always from the reports of the United States Census Bureau. Most of the summaries of state Baptist histories were compiled from Norman W. Cox, ed., *Encyclopedia of Southern Baptists* (Nashville: Broadman Press, 1958), Vols. I and II, and Davis C. Woolley, ed., *Encyclopedia of Southern Baptists* (Nashville: Broadman Press, 1971) Vol. III. Hereafter, these will be referred to as Cox-Woolley, eds., *Encyclopedia.*

3. This summary is taken from Ryland, *op. cit.,* pp. 112 ff.

4. *Ibid.,* p. 142.

5. Baker, *Source Book,* p. 22.

6. *Ibid.,* pp. 47-48.

7. *Ibid.,* pp. 50-51.

8. *Ibid.,* p. 51; and see King, *op. cit.,* p. 136.

9. David Benedict, *A General History of the Baptist Denomination in America and Other Parts of the World* (Boston: Lincoln and Edwards, 1813), II, p. 188.

10. See Baker, *Source Book,* p. 52, for a sample of the style of this publication.

11. William W. Sweet, ed., *Religion on the American Frontier—*Vol. I, *The Baptists 1783-1830* (New York: Henry Holt & Co., 1931), p. 20.

12. Lumpkin, *op. cit.,* p. 124.

13. Theodore Roosevelt, *The Winning of the West* (New York, 1890), III, p. 101.

14. Benedict, *op. cit.,* II, pp. 214-15.

15. *Ibid.,* II, pp. 251-52.

16. McGlothlin, *op. cit.,* p. 184.

17. Baker, *Source Book,* p. 17.

18. *Ibid.,* p. 18.

19. Quoted by W. W. Barnes, *The Southern Baptist Convention* (Nashville: Broadman Press, 1954), p. 2, from R. A. Guild, "The Denominational Work of President Manning," *Baptist Review,* 11 (1880), p. 559.

20. John Rippon, ed., *The Baptist Annual Register* (London, 1790-1802), II, p. 262.

21. Albert L. Vail, *The Morning Hour of American Baptist Missions* (Philadelphia: American Baptist Publication Society, 1907), p. 67.

22. Baker, *Source Book,* pp. 24-26.

23. *Ibid.,* p. 26, has the constitution of the new society.

24. See also Vail, *op. cit.,* pp. 150-55; and Robert A. Baker, *Relations Between Northern and Southern Baptists,* 2nd ed., (Fort Worth: 1954), p. 15. Hereafter this will be referred to as Baker, *Relations.* Note also Wayland's earlier essays that set forth this view, which can be found in Baker, *Source Book,* pp. 70-71.

25. Albert L. Vail, *Baptists Mobilized for Missions* (Philadelphia: American Baptist Publication Society, 1911), p. 309.

26. Vail, *The Morning Hour of American Baptist Missions,* pp. 150-51.

27. See, for example, John Taylor, *A History of Ten Baptist Churches* (Frankfort, Ky.: J. H. Holeman, 1823), pp. 75 f.

28. See Lemuel Burkitt and Jesse Read, *A Concise History of the Kehukee Baptist Association* (Halifax, N. C.: A. Hodge, 1803), pp. 40 ff.

29. See Reuben A. Guild, *Chaplain Smith and the Baptists* (Philadelphia: American Baptist Publication Society, 1885), pp. 133-34.

6 Baptists United for Benevolences

The first half of the nineteenth century was one of the most significant periods in American Baptist history. Most important, chronologically, was the organization of the first Baptist general bodies in America for benevolent purposes. Baptists North and South cooperated in these enterprises. The story will be told in this chapter. Contemporaneously, Baptists in the southern states advanced rapidly in many ways, as will be described in the next chapter. The final chapter in this period will discuss the several controversies of these years, coming to a climax with the sectional division between northern and southern Baptists in 1845.

The thirty-one years between 1814 and 1845 marked an era of organized benevolent activity by northern and southern Baptists on a national scale. Structural and methodological patterns were developed that still influence Baptist thinking. In the midst of an exciting and revolutionary era (which will be described briefly in the next chapter). American Baptists united to meet the challenge of missions abroad and at home.

Three principal benevolent societies were formed jointly by northern and southern Baptists: one for foreign missions (the General Missionary Convention of the Baptist Denomination in the United States for Foreign Missions) in 1814; one for the publication and distribution of religious tracts (the Baptist General Tract Society) in 1824; and one for home missions (the American Baptist Home Mission Society) in 1832. The organization of these three societies and the work that they did during the united period will be the burden of this chapter.

The General Missionary Convention

The initial factor that led to the organization of a foreign mission society among American Baptists was the beginning of the modern foreign missionary movement in England by William Carey in 1792. American societies were formed to support Carey, and the several denominations in England and America were challenged to become active in this new and blessed ministry. In the midst of this milieu, and perhaps encouraged by it, the Second Great Awakening in New England occurred with the coming of the nineteenth century. This Awakening was different in character from the First Great Awakening of about 1740. There was less emotional excitement and mass evangelism, and much of the power of the revival was channeled into benevolent activity for advancing the Christian cause, similar to the work of Carey. Increased efforts were made to evangelize the American Indians, and the Christianizing of the American frontier was vigorously attempted. American Congregationalists formed their American Board of Commissioners in 1810 to begin foreign mission work. Baptists developed their foreign mission body in 1814. An interdenominational society for Bible printing and distribution was begun in 1816, along with the American Sunday School Union in 1824 and the American Home Mission Society in 1826. Baptists formed their Tract Society in 1824, just one year before the interdenominational American Tract Society. Baptists organized their Home Mission Society in 1832.

In addition to bringing into existence these various benevolent organizations for Christian activity, the Second Great Awakening undoubtedly played a substantial role through Charles G. Finney and Theodore D. Weld in laying the foundations for the abolitionist movement of the fourth decade.

Two men were involved in this flurry of missionary organization and activity after the turn of the century. Both of them were initially related to the American Board of Commissioners of the Congregationalists, and both of them played large roles in the organization of the first foreign mission general body by American Baptists in 1814. These two men were Adoniram Judson and Luther Rice.

Judson was born at Malden, Massachusetts, on August 9, 1788. His father was a Congregational minister. Graduating from Brown University in 1808, young Judson entered Andover Seminary, and, caught up in the desire to take the gospel around the world to every creature, he along with other Andover students petitioned the Congregational Association of Massachusetts for advice and assistance. In 1810, the Congregationalists organized the American Board of Commissioners for Foreign Missions. On February 5, 1812, Judson married Ann Hasseltine, and two weeks later the couple sailed for India as missionaries of the Congregational Board. On February 14, 1813, Ann Hasseltine Judson wrote her parents and sisters to say that enroute to India, "Knowing he [Judson] should meet the Baptists at Serampore, he felt it important to attend to it [the Baptist position] more closely, to be able to defend his sentiments." [1] That is to say, he knew that William Carey, Joshua Marshman, and William Ward had been on the field for about two decades and that he would be expected to be able to give an accounting for the faith that was in him. Thus, simply the presence of Carey and others in India turned Judson toward a serious consideration of his denominational views. After several weeks of intensive study in Serampore, Judson addressed a letter to Carey, Marshman, and Ward, in Calcutta on August 27, 1812, advising them of his entire conviction "that the immersion of a professing believer is the only Christian baptism." He then asked for Mrs. Judson and himself the opportunity to "profess our faith in Christ by being baptized in obedience to his sacred commands." On September 1, 1812, Judson sent his letter of resignation to the Congregational Board, and on the same day wrote Lucius Bolles, a prominent American Baptist, appealing to Baptists in America for support in his mission work.[2]

At the very time these things were taking place, one of Judson's companions was undergoing a similar experience. Luther Rice was born at Northborough, Massachusetts, on March 25, 1783. When almost nineteen, he joined a Congregationalist church. Two years later he entered Leicester Academy and in October, 1807, enrolled at Williams College as a sophomore. He was a member of the famous Haystack Prayer Meeting group, and in 1810 was one of several, including Judson, who urged the Congregationalists to form a foreign mission body. Rice was appointed to go to India on the condition that he should raise the necessary money for expenses to reach the field. On a ship separate from that of Judson, Rice sailed on February 18, 1812, for Calcutta. He also became convinced by independent study of the correctness of the Baptist position. On November 1, 1812, he was baptized by William Ward, who had also baptized Judson and Ann Hasseltine. On October 23, 1812, he wrote Thomas Baldwin, prominent Boston pastor, concerning his change of views and soliciting Baptist support.[3]

Baptists in America received several letters from the English missionaries in India urging them to form a missionary society to support these new missionaries. When some influential American Baptist leaders suggested that English Baptists assume the care of the Judsons and Rice, the English missionaries in India urgently replied that this was the time for American Baptists to begin this important enterprise. The gracious nature of William Carey is suggested in one of his letters, probably about December 20, 1812. Despite the fact that at this very time America was at war with England, Carey, after urging American Baptists to "take these two brethren under their protection," ended up by saying, "We shall not desert them, nor their companions, should they be in want." [4]

In an earlier letter William Carey said to Thomas Baldwin, "Do stir in this business; this is a providence which gives a new turn to American relations to Oriental Missions." [5] There is evidence of a peculiar providence that shaped the events of these days. For one thing, there had been an extensive amount of missionary correspondence between Carey and his companions in India and American Baptist leaders, particularly William Rogers and William Staughton of Philadelphia, and Thomas Baldwin of Boston.

Not only so, but what was considered a harsh blow turned out to be the forwarding of the gospel. In the opening years of the nineteenth century the British East India Company resented the English Baptist missionaries working in India, feeling that it would hurt their business if the masses were Christianized. After many threats, the blow finally fell: no more missionaries would be allowed to sail from England to India. Through their control of shipping between England and India, the British East India Company felt that they could stop any missionaries from making the journey. However, providentially the missionaries were routed by way of America. In America these dedicated men would sometimes have to wait many weeks before a ship could be found to take them from America to India. While they waited, they stayed in the homes of American Baptist leaders, sharing their zeal for foreign missions with American Baptists. For about ten years American Baptists were conditioned in this way to begin their own foreign mission program.

Furthermore, Baptist leaders knew that it would be possible to raise funds for foreign missions among the Baptist people in America. Out of the contributions made to send Rice and the Judsons to India, more than $3,000 was given by American Baptists. Not only so, but American Baptists contributed over $20,000 for foreign missions during the years 1806 through 1814.

It is no wonder, then, that in October, 1812, upon learning about the Judsons and Rice, Boston Baptists promptly organized a society by the name of "The Baptist Society for Propagating the Gospel in India and Other Foreign Parts." [6] Other societies were organized elsewhere, including one at Savannah, Georgia.

Meanwhile, it was agreed by the three missionaries in India that one must return to raise funds to support the others, and the logical one was Luther Rice. He returned to Boston in September, 1813, and at the suggestion of the New England leaders, made an extensive tour through the seaboard states as far south as Georgia.

In the December, 1813, edition of *The Massachusetts Baptist Missionary Magazine,* the editor reported that Luther Rice had been received in every part of the country with utmost cordiality, and had suggested that delegates promptly be appointed to meet in Philadelphia to organize a national body for missionary work.

Organization of the Foreign Mission Body. On May 18, 1814, at the First Baptist Church in Philadelphia, thirty-three representatives (of whom more than half were from the Philadelphia Association) organized the General Missionary Convention of the Baptist Denomination in the United States of America for Foreign Missions. Difficulty in preparing an agreeable constitution was experienced, and the convention was in session, forenoon and afternoon of each day except Sunday, from Wednesday, May 18, until Tuesday, May 24. Albert L. Vail paid tribute to these pioneers and the work of their hands in eloquent words.

> The modifying of this constitution will soon begin, indeed; the responses of the denomination will be comparatively sluggish, fluctuating, and inadequate; sources then unsuspected of disruption will arise, waves of protest and assault will surge against the craft there launched, the ambitions of men, the defections of friends, the deficiencies of missionaries and administrators, will follow each other and combine with each other to wreck the enterprise almost; but that was begun there on which God will lay his hand to steady it when men stumble, and crown it when human laurels fail! For that was in some appreciable sense the inauguration of one of the great forces for the salvation of the world. And it may be deliberately questioned whether any Baptist vote ever meant more for the denomination or for mankind.[7]

Struggle for Direction. It will be recalled that at the very time this convention met in 1814, there had been two points of view concerning the proper type of denominational structure for a general body carrying on missionary work among Baptists. The associational method of organization stressed denominationalism, while the society type magnified church independency and benevolences. These two divergent types of thought unquestionably met in the Philadelphia meeting, and part of the extended length of the meeting probably stemmed from warm discussion at this point. A compromise resulted. The new organization had elements of both views. Two things suggested the influence of the associational stream of thought. (1) The organization was given a denominational name—the General Missionary Convention of the Baptist Denomination in the United States of America for Foreign Missions. Because the constitution arranged that the body should meet every three years, this organization was popularly known as the Triennial Convention. (2) Its constituency, according to Vail, included only Baptist organizations—societies, churches, and other groups, but no individuals. It should be said, however, that Francis Wayland interpreted the constitution to mean that individuals formed the base.[8] On the other hand, there were elements suggesting the society idea in the constitution, for it specifically named one benevolence only (foreign missions) as its object. Furthermore, membership was fixed upon a modified money basis, thus reproducing to some extent the *modus operandi* of the society plan of operation, rather than the associational idea which permitted *all* churches to associate themselves together regardless of financial contributions.

The body had hardly been organized before evidences of the struggle for direction were apparent. Luther Rice himself favored a strong denominational body. In his diary he noted:

> While passing from Richmond to Petersburg in the stage, an enlarged view of the business opened upon my contemplations. The plan which suggested itself to my mind, that of forming one principal society in each state, bearing the name of the state, and others in the same state, auxiliary to that; and by these large, or state societies, delegates be appointed to form one general society.[9]

It is hardly coincidental that Rice received this impression while traveling in the South, for Southern Baptists in general held more centralized views organizationally than did Baptists in the North. In fact, Rice probably received a suggestion from W. B. Johnson at this point.[10]

It appeared that the denominational proponents would achieve a quick victory. At the first triennial meeting in 1817, in a carefully worded statement the convention voted "That the powers of this Convention be extended so as to embrace home missions and plans for the encouragement of education."[11] Perhaps the influence of Richard Furman of South Carolina was involved in this move. In his presidential address in 1817, Furman had said, "The same gracious direction which it becomes all Missionary Societies earnestly to solicit, and conscientiously to obey, is opening other spheres on our own continent." Furman continued by observing the need for home missions in New Orleans and in the West, as well as the great opportunities in the field of education. Relative to the latter, he mentioned that a scheme for carrying out this benevolence had been suggested to the board, and added, "It is hoped that something on this point will be speedily and vigorously attempted."

As a result, the General Missionary Convention modified its original plan to promote only foreign missions, and, as mentioned, voted to include home missions and the sponsorship of a Baptist college. John M. Peck and James E. Welch were appointed as missionaries in Missouri Territory. They were set apart in a moving service of dedication for home mission work.[12] Columbian College was chartered in 1821, and opened in Washington, D. C., in that year under the auspices of the General Convention.

The adoption of these additional benevolences was a definite move toward the associational emphasis, for if this body were to assume control of all benevolent interests of all of its constituent members, it would become a general denominational body according to the associational pattern. The flow of favorable public opinion evidently continued in this direction in the second triennial meeting in 1820, when the additional functions of the convention were recognized, and perhaps the avenues were opened for additional enlargement in various directions by the adoption of an addenda to the title showing the object of the body, which said, "for foreign missions and other important objects relating to the Redeemer's kingdom."

Still another factor moving American Baptists toward the organization of a denominational-type structure was the development of the first Baptist state convention in America in 1821 by South Carolina Baptists. Its original constitution described the state convention as a "coalition of Associations," and its membership consisted of delegates from the associations in the state, along with representatives from other religious bodies of the Baptist faith. Richard Furman was the first president of this state body, which had another characteristic of the associational or denominational type of structure; namely, it looked toward the promotion of many benevolences, not just one. Interestingly enough, the editors of the *American Baptist Magazine* in Boston, Massachusetts, taking note with favor of the action of the South Carolina group, urged that a state body be established in Massachusetts, remarking, "Our Associations united our churches; why should not a Convention unite our associations?" [13] Other signs hinted that at the 1826 meeting there would surely come a strong movement to develop a national body for Baptists based upon delegates from various state bodies that were rapidly organizing.

One important factor that looked in this direction was a series of articles written by Francis Wayland, at that time the associate editor to Thomas Baldwin of the *American Baptist Magazine* in Boston. Baldwin's centralizing ideas were well known, and doubtless he influenced his associate at this point. Under the pseudonym "Backus," Wayland wrote six letters between November, 1823, and May, 1824, in which he made observations about contemporary Baptist organizational forms and suggested ways of improvement. The first four letters described the defects of the contemporary system: the most striking defect was that the plan was unfinished, in that there was no national body that represented Baptists in the various parts of the nation; the associations should send delegates to a general convention, thus bringing the whole denomination into concentrated and unified action; the General Missionary Convention

> at present is composed of delegates from missionary societies, and of course must, in its very nature, be mostly composed of persons elected from the vicinity of its place of meeting. And besides, were the meeting ever so universally attended, its foundation is radically defective. A missionary society is not a representative body, nor can any number of them speak the language of a whole denomination. . . . Every one sees at a glance the difference between the representative of a state convention, which comprised two or three hundred churches within its limits, and thus the bearer of their opinions, and him who is only the delegate from a missionary society which contributes fifty or one hundred dollars to the treasury.[14]

In fact, Wayland went so far as to suggest a Baptist world alliance whereby "Baptists on both sides of the Atlantic, would be united together in a solid phalanx."[15]

Just prior to the 1826 meeting, Luther Rice reflected these statements of Wayland in his suggestion that the missionary body be changed into a structured denominational body through state convention representation.

However, as Winthrop Hudson has pointed out, the very man who had spoken so clearly in the *American Baptist Magazine* (Francis Wayland) became the leader of the movement which reversed all centralizing trends that looked toward a more rigid denominational structure. With the aid of the Massachusetts and New York delegates, who constituted almost two thirds of the entire General Convention of 1826, three major goals were accomplished—Columbian College was separated from the convention, Boston was able to retain control of the foreign mission program, and the proposal to centralize the convention by causing it to be composed of delegates from state conventions was defeated.[16] The *American Baptist Magazine* for June, 1826, and July, 1826, reported the removal of the seat of foreign missions from Washington to Boston and the elimination of the educational program, and gave reasons for this action.[17] Later on Francis Wayland, without describing his own radical reversal in thinking, made reference to the struggle in these words:

> An attempt was made, pretty early in the history of this organization, to give it the control over all our benevolent efforts. It was proposed to merge in it our Education Societies, Tract Societies, Home Mission Societies, and our Foreign Mission Societies, so that one central Board

should have the management of all our churches, so far as their efforts to extend the kingdom of Christ were concerned. After a protracted debate, this measure was negatived by so decided a majority that the attempt was never repeated, and this danger was averted. We look back, at the present day, with astonishment that such an idea was ever entertained.[18]

As the result of this internal struggle, American Baptists in 1826 chose to decentralize their denominational operations and utilize only the society plan, previously described, for all general benevolent work. As will be seen shortly, new societies, each autonomous in itself, were organized for additional benevolences. This remained the principal denominational structure, with some variations in representation in the societies, until 1907 in Northern Baptist life.

Work of General Missionary Convention. The activity of the convention during the thirty-one years between 1814 and 1845 falls naturally into two sections, separated by the year 1832. From 1814 to 1832 the principal fields were Burma and Africa, although between 1820 and 1822 India was briefly entered, and in 1832 a beginning was made in Siam.

From the early center at Rangoon, the work was expanded into other sections of Burma. Particularly in 1826, when George Dana Boardman began a new mission in eastern Burma, this expansion accelerated. Although Boardman died in 1831, he had enlarged the vision and work in India, including extension into Tavoy and, after his death, the opening of a center in Siam. The work of Judson in Burma struck a responsive chord in the hearts of American Baptists. The imprisonment of Judson during the first Burman war between 1823 and 1826 brought to him great suffering, followed shortly by the death of his beloved Ann Hasseltine. It is likely that these sacrifices inspired the expansion of Baptist work after the war. By 1832 there were 14 missionaries in Burma, 5 more under appointment, and another 5 awaiting appointment.

Missionary work in Africa was begun at the initiative of the African Baptist Mission Society formed in Richmond by Negroes in 1814. In 1819 the General Convention assisted financially in the sending of Lott Cary and Collin Teague to what became Liberia. Calvin Holton was the first white missionary to be sent to Africa by Baptists in 1824. However, due to the diseases and fevers that attacked white missionaries in Liberia, it became necessary to withdraw the white missionaries from the field for a season.

The second period of activity brought a considerable enlargement of the program of this body. France was entered in 1833; the incomparable John G. Oncken began work in Germany in 1834, which soon spread under his influence to Denmark to the north and Switzerland to the south; J. Lewis Shuck and his wife were sent to China in 1835; and in 1836, South India and Assam were entered.

By 1845 the reports of the General Missionary Convention revealed an impressive achievement in foreign mission work. Curiously enough, until 1865 work among Indians in North America was included in the foreign mission program. By 1845 the convention had work among the Ojibwas, Ottawas, Tonamondas, Tuscaroras, Shawanos, Chero- kees, Creeks, and Choctaws. In the European field, which included France, Germany, Denmark, and Greece, the report in 1844 showed 3 missions, 21 stations and 34 outstations, 4 preachers and 5 female assistants, 28 native preachers and assistants, 28 churches with 900 members and 123 baptized the previous year, and 1 school with 50 pupils. In the African field, the report showed 1 missionary, 2 stations and 1 outstation, 2 preachers with 1 assistant and 2 female assistants, 2 native assistants, 1 church with 24 members, and 2 schools. In the Asiatic field, which included Burma, Siam, China, Assam, and India, the report showed 7 missions with 51 stations and outstations, 66 missionaries and assistants and 84 native assistants, 34 churches re- porting 2,360 baptisms in 1844 along with 2,257 members, and 42 schools with about 1,000 students.

In a recapitulation of this significant work, the 1845 report named 17 distinct missions, 130 stations and outstations, 109 missionaries and assistant missionaries of whom 42 were preachers, 123 native preachers and assistants, 79 churches, 2,593 baptisms, more than 5,000 church members, and 1,350 students in 56 schools.

The Baptist General Tract Society

The second of the important societies organized by American Bap- tists in the united period between 1814 and 1845 was a body to publish Baptist tracts and distribute them. Impetus was given to this movement by the beginning of the foreign mission program in 1814. As early as 1819 or 1820 such leaders as Luther Rice, William Staughton, and Irah Chase, among others, were discussing the need for establish- ing a Baptist tract society.

A dramatic scene may have provided the inspiration for the organi- zation of the body. At Washington, particularly among the leaders who had moved the seminary from Philadelphia to the nation's capital in 1820, repeated calls came to establish a tract society for Baptists. Luther Rice, George Wood, James D. Knowles (editor of the *Colum- bian Star*), along with preachers like O. B. Brown and William Staughton, often met to discuss this project. At one of these meetings a newly-ordained young minister, Noah Davis, was listening to the discussion, when Samuel Cornelius came into the room. He wore a bell-crowned hat, and as he removed it upon coming into the room, out of the tall top of it fell a number of tracts. Cornelius was a walking depository, and this scene so fired the emotions of Davis that he wrote to Editor Knowles proposing a tract society be organized immediately.

As a result, on February 25, 1824, the Baptist General Tract Society was organized and a constitution was adopted.[19] George Wood was named the first General Secretary and served two years. Within ten months 86,500 copies of nineteen tracts were printed. It was soon obvious that a printing center like Philadelphia was needed for this work, and despite the opposition of Luther Rice, who wanted to make Washington a Baptist center of influence, on November 14, 1826, the society moved to Philadelphia. Before 1845 the society had moved five times to different locations in rented quarters in Philadelphia. Financial problems beset them severely during these early years. Between 1824 and 1840 the society issued over 3,500,000 copies of 162 different titles of tracts. Its ministry reached to Burma to help Adoniram Judson, and to Germany to assist J. G. Oncken; and by 1838, had provided tracts for Africa, Nova Scotia, Canada, Texas, Mexico, and South America.

A radical reorganization took place in 1840. The constitution of the society was amended to enable it "to publish such books as are needed by the Baptist denomination, and to promote Sunday schools by such measures as experience may prove expedient." The term "books" included tracts, Sunday School books, and biographical, doctrinal, historical, and other religious works, chiefly of a denominational character. A new name was adopted which in 1845 became its permanent title: the American Baptist Publication Society. In the years between 1840 and 1844, the society published 34,750 bound volumes, 5,000 pamphlets, and 266,573 copies of tracts. In addition it circulated over 100,000 bound volumes, of which about one fourth were its own publications.

It should be said that Baptists in the South enthusiastically supported this society. At the close of its second year of history, it had 26 persons enrolled as life-members, of whom 21 were living in the South. Of the $1,010.33 received during the first two years, all but $133.73 came from the South. Noah Davis succeeded Wood as General Secretary and remained until 1830; Ira M. Allen served until 1838; J. Rhees Morgan, from 1840 to 1842; and John M. Peck, from 1843 to 1845.

American Baptist Home Mission Society

American Baptists recognized the need for home mission work from their earliest years. Antedating Eliot, Brainerd, and Jonathan Edwards in their ministry with the Indians was Roger Williams, who began preaching to them as early as 1631. Before there was any organized work, warmhearted pastors like John Clarke, at considerable risks to themselves, preached the gospel in a wide area surrounding what is now Rhode Island. As previously pointed out, the Philadelphia Association began a home mission program as early as 1754, which was quickly imitated by other associations as they were organized thereafter. Before 1832 when the American Baptist Home Mission Society was formed, there were Baptist bodies in fourteen states carrying on home mission work. In the story of the General Missionary Convention it was mentioned that in 1817 this foreign mission body decided to enlarge its task to include home missions and Christian education. Two home missionaries, James Welch and John Mason Peck, were appointed in 1817. Peck was then a young man of twenty-eight years, with a wife and three small children. Peck had met Luther Rice in 1815, and a fire was kindled in his heart to work on the western frontier. Promptly after his appointment, Peck and his family braved the wilderness in a small one-horse wagon for 128 days. He united and inspired the small group of Baptists in the area of St. Louis, and in the following year the Missouri Association was formed. In 1819 his plan for a society to spread the gospel was approved by this association and one in Illinois, and its achievements in missionary work, education, and Indian work were remarkable.

However, in 1820, as has been noted, the General Missionary Convention voted to eliminate home missions from its support, due primarily to the lack of funds and internal opposition. For two years Peck supported himself, then he was accepted as a missionary by the Massachusetts Baptist Missionary Society. His labors were prodigious. In 1826, while on a visit to the East, Peck met Jonathan Going, pastor of the church at Worcester, Massachusetts. So impressed was the board of the Massachusetts Baptist Missionary Society by the message of Peck that the board requested Going to study the conditions of the western mission fields and report his findings. He arrived at Peck's home on June 20, 1831, five years after their first meeting in Worcester. For three months Going and Peck traveled in Missouri, Illinois, Indiana, and Kentucky, and when they separated in September, 1831, at Shelbyville, Kentucky, Peck wrote in his journal: "Here we agreed on the plan of The American Baptist Home Mission Society." When Going returned to Massachusetts and reported what he had seen and felt in his journey to the Massachusetts Baptist Missionary Society in November,

> the Board without a dissenting vote solemnly declared its conviction that a general home mission society should be formed, and in a resolution recorded their belief that Jonathan Going himself should give his full time and strength to the promotion of its work.[20]

A committee consisting of Daniel Sharp, Lucius Bolles, and Going went from state to state discussing the need for the general home mission society. As a result a Provisional Committee was formed and a circular issued to meet on April 27, 1832. This date coincided with the meeting of the General Missionary Convention, and consequently the representation was gratifying. Fourteen out of the twenty-three states and one of the five territories were represented. Careful consideration was given to the kind of organization to be formed. Two distinct plans were debated.

> The first contemplated "an independent society" with officers separate from the General Convention (for foreign missions) and with headquarters at New York City. The second plan proposed that the General Convention be changed from a foreign mission society into a general denominational body with power to appoint a board for foreign missions and one for home missions, "each with their Treasurers and Secretaries, the first to be located at Boston, and the last in this city." The first plan (the *society* method) prevailed, and the constitution provided for the organization of a separate society for domestic missions. The idea of converting the General Convention into a general denominational body was rejected.[21]

On April 27, 1832, the American Baptist Home Mission Society was formed.[22] Its first secretary was Jonathan Going (1832-37), followed by Luther Crawford (1837-39), and Benjamin M. Hill (1839-62) during this united period. Between 1832 and 1845 its contributions and legacies totaled $165,586.71; its missionaries, 1,116; baptisms reported, 14,426; churches organized, 531; and missionary years of labor, 829.[23]

The interest shown in this aspect of mission work is emphasized by the fact that during the first year 50 missionaries served the society in 10 states, 2 territories, and Lower Canada. The western states included Ohio, Indiana, Michigan, Illinois, Missouri, and Arkansas. In the following year, 80 missionaries were appointed, and work was begun in Louisiana and Upper Canada. By 1835-36 there were 150 missionaries and agents at work in 14 states, 2 territories, and 2 provinces. They supplied 300 churches or congregations, to which 1,040 were admitted by baptism and 736 by letter. These missionaries reached 1,676 people for Christ, helped ordain 33 ministers, constituted 96 churches, and organized 7 associations. Wisconsin and Iowa were entered in 1837, Texas in 1840, and Oregon in 1845.

The work was most difficult. White described some of the problems that constantly faced the missionary in these words:

> Fancy to yourself a man obliged, through a rough country and over miserable roads, to travel from thirty to fifty miles a day, without where to lay his head; to preach, perhaps, to ten or a dozen members in open houses, and be exposed to all kinds of weather, dangers and

difficulties; to be opposed and maligned by those calling themselves the children of God, and accused of preaching for lucre's sake—and you have some idea of a missionary.[24]

Some idea as to the rapid development of the ministry of this society can be glimpsed from the reports of the first decade which show that 804 missionaries had been appointed for 31 states and territories, and that a total of $99,368.00 had been expended in this task. In the states of Kentucky, Missouri, Indiana, and Michigan in 1832 there were but 955 Baptist churches, with 484 ministers, only 10 of whom were regular pastors; in contrast in 1842 in the same states there were 1,689 churches with 772 ministers.

This brief resume of the cooperative work carried on by both Northern and Southern Baptists in the three great benevolent societies does not describe the growth and expansion of Baptists in the southern states during this period, nor does it recount the several controversies of the period, one of which caused Northern and Southern Baptists to adopt separate bodies for home and foreign missions in 1845. These events will be discussed in the following chapters.

Notes

1. Baker, *Source Book,* p. 53.
2. *Ibid.,* pp. 53 ff.
3. *Ibid.,* pp. 55-56.
4. *Ibid.,* p. 59.
5. *Ibid.,* p. 58.
6. *Ibid.,* p. 56
7. Vail, *The Morning Hour of American Baptist Missions,* pp. 384-85.
8. Francis Wayland, *Notes on the Principles and Practices of Baptist Churches* (Boston: Gould and Lincoln, 1856), p. 184.
9. Baker, *Source Book,* p. 61.
10. See *The Christian Index* (Georgia), January 27, 1835.
11. Baker, *Source Book,* p. 67.
12. *Ibid.*
13. *Ibid.,* pp. 76-77.
14. *Ibid.,* pp. 68-71.
15. *Ibid.,* p. 71.
16. See Winthrop Hudson, "Stumbling Into Disorder," in *Foundations,* April, 1958, pp. 55-71.
17. Baker, *Source Book,* pp. 71-73.
18. Wayland, *op. cit.,* p. 185.
19. Baker, *Source Book,* pp. 73-74.
20. Charles L. White, *A Century of Faith* (Philadelphia: American Baptist Publication Society, 1932), p. 36.
21. Baker, *Relations,* p. 28.
22. See Baker, *Source Book,* p. 74, for its constitution.
23. Henry L. Morehouse, *Baptist Home Missions in North America* (New York: American Baptist Home Mission Society, 1883), p. 551.
24. White, *op. cit.,* p. 51.

7 Across the South

The period between 1814 and 1845 was one of considerable turmoil and rapid change across the South. It is difficult to separate the history into economic, social, political, or religious compartments, for most of the factors impinging upon the history of the South during this period overlapped into all of these areas.

The invention of the cotton gin by Eli Whitney in 1793 greatly influenced the history of this period, as has been pointed out. It started a chain reaction that led to the profitable cultivation of the short-staple variety of cotton, contributing to the resuscitation of the institution of slavery which now could be profitably utilized. In turn, this led to the extension of the cotton area from the tidewater region of the coastline to the states of the interior, and, of course, immigration was accelerated to the interior states in such fashion as to increase their political strength and prosperity. Meanwhile, the textile industry had greatly benefited by the invention of the spinning jenny and the power loom, and the development of the factory system. The older seaboard states of Virginia and North Carolina began to lose their people and prosperity to the growing areas of South Carolina and Georgia and the interior states. As an illustration of this, the cotton crop in 1791 totaled 2,000,000 pounds and was produced entirely by South Carolina and Georgia. By 1811, South Carolina produced 40,000,000 pounds, Georgia produced 20,000,000 pounds, Virginia produced 8,000,000 pounds, and North Carolina produced 7,000,000 pounds, while Tennessee showed a crop of 3,000,000 pounds and Louisiana a crop of 2,000,000 pounds. By 1834, however, the interior states of Tennessee, Louisiana, Mississippi, Alabama, Florida, and Arkansas produced over 297,000,000 pounds, as compared with only 160,000,000 pounds produced in Virginia, North Carolina, South Carolina, and Georgia.

The rapid migration to the West was accelerated by the extinguishing of the Indian titles to the lands between 1812 and 1830, principally the result of the victory of Andrew Jackson in the Gulf region. In the nine-year period between 1812 and 1821, Kentucky grew in population 22%, Louisiana 41%, Tennessee 61%, Mississippi

81%, and Alabama 142%.

Closely related to these developments was the nagging problem of slavery. The South had at first rejected slavery, then protested against it, and, after 1793, began to embrace it because of its economic importance. Slave insurrections in San Domingo in 1792, the Vesey conspiracy of 1822, and the Nat Turner rebellion of 1831, accentuated by harsh abolitionist attacks of the 1830's, may explain the extreme bitterness of the slavery controversy both in religious life and in politics during this period. The slavery issue was raised in 1818 with the question of the admission of Missouri to the Union, as well as in the annexation of Texas that was proposed in 1836 and accomplished in 1845.

The political pot boiled considerably during this period. In addition to the slavery issue, politicians quarreled extensively in 1824 and 1827 over the question of the tariff, many raising the constitutional question of whether a protective tariff was permitted by the Constitution. This almost brought civil war in 1832 apart from the question of slavery. Intermingled with this political agitation was the rise of Jacksonian democracy, marking a radical turn from the existing political norm.

All of this radical change was interspersed with economic depressions. A panic in 1819 was induced by the speculator reaction following the War of 1812. Cotton prices had risen as high as thirty cents a pound, and $78.00 an acre was bid for government land in the Southwest. The credit system of selling land by the government brought reckless purchase of public lands. Pioneers, planters, and speculators purchased large quantities of land on credit, expecting bank loans to finance their purchases and, in the case of the speculators, hoping to sell the land before payments became due. The United States Bank contributed to this movement, but in 1818, facing ruin, it demanded that the state banks redeem their notes or close their doors. The country was in a panic by the spring of 1819. Interestingly enough, one of the results of this panic was the change of policy in disposing of public lands. In 1820, Congress reduced the land from $2.00 to $1.25 per acre, abolished the system of credit, and allowed purchasers to secure as little as eighty acres. This meant that a pioneer would need to pay cash for his lands. As a result, not anticipated by the congressional leaders, a great number of Americans crossed the Sabine River into the Mexican province of Texas where land could be secured without cash.

Between 1825 and 1829, another depression occurred, but it was of a rather mild character. A very severe depression occurred in the middle and late 1830's and early 1840's. Excessive bank expansion, land speculation, large loans for state internal improvements, European bank failures, and crop failures in 1835 and 1837, compounded by the Deposit Act and the Specie Circular of 1837, brought the Panic of 1837. Despite active steps by President Van Buren, this depression lasted until 1843, greatly affecting public confidence and causing much loss and suffering.

New important religious movements were begun in this changing world. Campbellism, Mormonism, Universalism, and Unitarianism moved into the religious picture and materially altered the work of established denominations.

In the midst of these turbulent events and directly affected by them, Southern Baptists made substantial progress during the period from 1814 to 1845. An effort will be made in this chapter to tell the story of their numerical and geographical expansion, as well as the development of organizational structures in the several states.

South Atlantic Region

Between 1814 and 1845, Baptists in the South Atlantic states containing Baptists before the end of the period (the older six states of Maryland, District of Columbia, Virginia, North Carolina, South Carolina, and Georgia, plus a newcomer, Florida) increased in number from 39 associations, 618 ministers, 837 churches, and 75,666 members in 1814 to 87 associations, 1,294 ministers, 2,019 churches, and 202,703 members in 1845. This represented an average annual gain in membership of 5.25% in this region, and may be compared with the 4.77% average annual growth between 1790 and 1814. The population increased in this region from 2,602,239 in 1810 to 3,782,770 in 1840, an average annual increase of 1.48%, less than one third of the Baptist growth rate. The rapid movement of the slave population into the western areas is evident in the slow rate of growth in the South Atlantic region compared to the rate of growth in the South Central region during the same years. In the seven South Atlantic states there were 983,671 slaves in 1810; by 1840, there were 1,422,934, or an average annual growth of 1.46%. In the previous period (1790-1814), the annual average rate of growth of slaves in the South Atlantic region had been 2.63%.

Maryland. Maryland Baptists grew slowly during this period. From 2 associations, 15 ministers, 32 churches, and 1,326 members in about 1813, they increased to 2 associations, 15 ministers, 32 churches, and 1,960 members in 1845. The membership growth was at the average rate of 1.49% each year. This annual growth may be compared with the 3.08% rate of growth between 1790 and 1814.

Meanwhile, the population grew from 380,546 in 1810 to 470,019 in 1840, an average annual growth of .76%, just slightly more than half of the Southern Baptist growth. The slave population decreased from 111,592 in 1810 to 89,737 in 1840. Evidently many of the slaves had been manumitted by 1840, for the free blacks increased from 33,927 in 1810 to 62,078 in 1840.

The antimission schism in the Baltimore Association in 1836, described in the following chapter, seriously hindered Baptist work in Maryland for many years to come. S. P. Hill, pastor of the first Baptist Church in Baltimore, and G. F. Adams led in the formation of the Maryland Baptist Union Association in 1836, not, the leaders said, to wage war on any existing body, nor to engender strife, but to spread the gospel in Maryland and the northern part of the District of Columbia.

> We wanted something to answer the purpose of State Conventions in other States. And as there were no Associations that would be likely to combine their influence in such an object, we thought it best to combine what few churches we could find of the proper stamp.[2]

The principal leaders of Maryland Baptists during this period were John Davis, founder of most of the churches in the Baltimore Association, S. P. Hill, G. F. Adams, and a layman, William Crane. At the very close of the period the distinguished Richard Fuller came as pastor in Baltimore.

Maryland Baptists claim that theirs was the first Sunday School and the first Sunday School using volunteer teachers in America during this period.

District of Columbia. Baptists in the city of Washington also grew slowly in the period between 1814 and 1845. Only one permanent church was added, the E Street Baptist Church, which later became Temple. It is true that black members of the First Baptist Church moved to a separate building in 1833, but they were counted as a part of the membership of First Baptist Church long after this time. At the close of the period, the venerable O. B. Brown was still pastor of First Baptist Church. It is likely that in 1845 there were about 4 churches, affiliating with associations either in Maryland or Virginia, with 5 pastors, and a total membership of 706.

Meanwhile, the population of the District increased from 24,023 in 1810 to 43,712 in 1840, an average annual increase of 2.55%. The slave population was numbered at 5,395 in 1810 and 4,694 in 1840.

It will be recalled that Luther Rice, who had been converted to Baptist views while en route to India as a missionary of another denomination, returned to America on September 7, 1813. He made Washington his headquarters until his death in 1836. He helped in the establishment in Washington of the first nationwide Baptist journal, *The Columbian Star,* a religious weekly begun in 1818; the first Baptist missions magazine, *The Latter Day Luminary;* the first Sunday School in the city, begun in the First Baptist Church in 1819; the establishment of the first Baptist college in the South, Columbian

College, chartered in 1821; and the first Baptist publication society, the General Tract Society. Through Rice, District of Columbia Baptists were at the center of Baptist denominational life until 1826, when the General Missionary Convention for Foreign Missions severed its connection with Columbian College, and Rice began spending most of his time traveling about the country in a buggy raising money for the school and other Baptist benevolences. *The Columbian Star* was later moved to Georgia and became *The Christian Index,* the state paper; the theological department of Columbian College left the school in 1825 to establish the Newton Theological Institution in Massachusetts; and in 1826 the foreign mission headquarters were moved to Boston, and the Baptist Tract Society moved to Philadelphia.

The principal leaders in District of Columbia among Baptists were Rice, Obadiah B. Brown, and Spencer H. Cone, who later moved to New York City and became quite active in the national benevolent societies.

Virginia. The rate of growth by Baptists in this state far outdistanced the population gains during this period. Baptists increased from 16 associations, 283 ministers, 283 churches, and 35,164 members to 23 associations, 303 ministers, 498 churches, and 78,645 members. This was an annual average growth of 3.86%, compared with 3.13% between 1790 and 1814.

Meanwhile, the population increased from 974,622 to 1,239,797 between 1810 and 1840, an average gain of .88% annually, less than one fourth the Baptist rate. The slave population grew from 392,518 in 1810 to 449,087 in 1840, or an average annual increase of .46%, showing the rapid excision of slave labor to the western areas. Free blacks increased during the period from 30,571 to 49,852, or 2.03% growth, much larger than the increase of the slave population.

Although Virginia Baptist gains were slowed by the diminishing of their revivals and the incursions of other denominations, especially the Methodists, their rate of growth outstripped the population and represented substantial progress. The reasons for this growth lay in the missionary activity centering around the work of Luther Rice and the organization of the General Missionary Convention in 1814, the development of organizational bodies for various kinds of benevolence, and the continuance of strong leadership among Baptists in this state.

The missionary spirit of Virginia Baptists did not begin with the foreign mission emphasis of this period, of course. Local evangelism or missions had characterized them from the very beginning of their history, and early in the nineteenth century they had cooperated with North Carolina Baptists in a missionary society to reach the Indians.

However, missionary interest was greatly stimulated by the return of Luther Rice from India after his conversion to Baptist views. With the assistance of Rice, the Baptist Missionary Society of Richmond was organized on October 28, 1813. The Richmond Female Baptist Missionary Society was organized in 1813 also. Rice was very active in Virginia. Generally speaking, the district associations were in favor of the missionary enterprise, and Rice helped organize many mission and educational societies and raised large sums of money for benevolent purposes in Virginia. In the year preceding April, 1820, for example, Rice spent six months in Virginia forwarding the missionary and educational (Columbian College) enterprises. At the third triennial meeting of the General Missionary convention in 1820, Virginia was entitled to more representatives than any other state, having exceeded $100 per year in gifts from four male mission societies, four female mission societies, four education societies, one African mission society, and one association. Rice listed more than 780 individual subscriptions from Virginia for Columbian College. Robert B. Semple of Virginia was named president of the General Missionary Convention in 1820 and held that office for four terms thereafter.

Of particular interest was the organization in April, 1815, of the Richmond African Baptist Missionary Society, whose contributions were earmarked for an African mission. The black members of the Richmond churches had been inspired through the work of Lott Cary who, with another black preacher, Collin Teague, in January, 1821, went to Liberia under the American Colonization Society. A description of Teague and Cary was contained in a letter from William Crane of Richmond, which illustrates the zeal and ability of these Negro missionaries. Crane wrote on March 28, 1819, to the board of the General Missionary Convention, as follows:

> You will probably recollect, that I introduced you to two of our coloured brethren in this place, who are accustomed to speak in public; one named Collin Teague, the other Lott Cary. Ever since the missionary subject has been so much agitated in this country, these two brethren, associated with many others, have been wishing they could, in some way, aid their unhappy kindred in Africa; and I suppose you have heard of their having formed a missionary society for this sole purpose. . . . They are now determined to go themselves to Africa; . . . They both possess industry and abilities, such as, with the blessing of Providence, would soon make them rich. It is but two or three years since either of them enjoyed their freedom; and both have paid large sums for their families. They now possess little, except a zealous wish to go and do what they can. Brother Lott has a wife and several little children. . . . Brother Collin has a wife, a son 14 years of age and a daughter of 11, for whom he had paid $1300, and has scarcely anything left. Both of their wives are Baptists; their children, amiable and docile, have been to school considerably; and I hope, if they go, will likewise be of service. Collin is a saddler and harness maker. He had no early education. The little that he has gained, has been by chance and piece-meal. He has judgment, and as much keenness of

penetration as almost any man. He can read, though he is not a good reader, and can write so as to make out a letter. The little knowledge he has of figures, has been gained by common calculation in business. Lott was brought up on a farm; and for a number of years has been chief manager among the laborers in the largest tobacco warehouse in this city. He has charge of receiving, marking and shipping tobacco; and the circumstance that he receives $700 a-year wages may help you to form an estimate of the man. He reads better than Collin, and is, in every respect, a better scholar.

They have been trying to preach about ten or eleven years, and are both about forty years old. . . . Their object is to carry the tidings of salvation to the benighted Africans.[3]

A church composed of Cary and his wife, Collin Teague and his wife and son Hillary, and Joseph Langford and his wife was organized before they left Richmond and was transported to Liberia. Their contributions there were impressive.

A word should be said concerning the religious instruction of the Negroes in Virginia. Virginia followed the usual pattern of other states and other denominations in dealing with the Negroes. They were members of the white churches, baptized on a personal confession of faith, and subject to the same discipline that obtained for white members. Black deacons were chosen to look after the black members, and generally discipline was meted out at their recommendation. Negro preachers were licensed and set apart to the ministry. It was not unusual for the Negro minister to preach to a church in the absence of the white pastor. Sometimes the church preferred the preaching of the substitute.

Separate statistics for white and Negro members are first shown in 1838, when the Dover Association reported 9,112 black and 5,755 white members in the affiliated churches. A few years later, nine Virginia associations gave separate figures.

The reports from the various associations during all of this period show a kindly and concerned attitude on the part of the white leadership for the spiritual condition of the Negroes. At the same time, however, the introduction of slavery into national politics, the bloody insurrection by Nat Turner in Southampton County in 1831, and the increasingly radical incendiary propaganda blanketing the South from northern abolitionists brought increasing tension between the races. Legislatures in the various southern states restricted the assembling of Negroes to guard against additional insurrections. Propaganda from northern abolitionists urging violence was countered in the various southern states by laws making it illegal to teach Negroes to read. Frederick J. Turner estimated that two thirds of the population of Virginia was white and one third Negro in 1830. The white majority was lessened by 1850, due to the westward migrations to the virgin lands that had not been exhausted by constant crops of tobacco and cotton. As a rule, Baptists were in the lower economic class, and very few of them were a part of that small society which owned a large number of slaves.

Virginia also provided three young couples for the foreign fields in William Mylne, who went to Liberia in 1835 for a brief three-year stay, when ill health required his return to Virginia; Robert D. Davenport and his wife Frances, who went to Bangkok, Siam, in 1835; and J. Lewis Shuck and his wife Henrietta Hall, who went to China in 1835. Shuck later became one of the first missionaries appointed by the Southern Baptist Convention, at which time he was already in China.

It will be recalled that Virginia Baptists had organized a General Meeting of Correspondence, made up of associations, as a unifying body, but not all associations cooperated in this movement during the opening decades of the nineteenth century. In an effort to find an effective organization to relieve the spiritual destitution in Virginia, messengers (from five of the twenty associations in Virginia) at the June, 1822, meeting recommended the formation of a new body called the General Association of Baptists of Virginia. The first meeting of this new organization on June 7, 1823, was encouraging, but there was a gradual lessening of interest and support during the next several years. In 1829 a revised constitution was adopted to provide a financial basis of representation, and the fortunes of this body improved from that time. The General Association slowly became the center of state benevolent activities. In 1836 the Virginia Baptist Education Society and the Virginia Foreign Mission Society began holding their annual meetings at the same time and place as the General Association. So did the Virginia and Foreign Baptist Bible Society, organized in 1836 to aid in the translation of Judson's Bible into Burmese. In 1838, the Virginia Baptist Sunday School Association was organized, which, in 1840, became the Virginia Baptist Sunday School and Publication Society, auxiliary to the American Baptist Publication and Sunday School Society. The slow unification of these several benevolent societies continued until 1855, after the close of this period, when a change in the constitution developed an organic relationship among them.

Virginia Baptists also cooperated in support for the Baptist General Tract Society and organized a temperance society and a ministers' meeting in 1826 and 1829, respectively.

In 1826, under the editorship of Henry Keeling, a monthly paper was begun which, in 1828, became a weekly paper called the *Religious Herald*. The principal editor and publisher became William Sands.

Virginia Baptists made progress in the area of education. As early as 1819, efforts were made to make provision for ministerial education, but these efforts were not successful. Columbian College was a beneficiary both of liberal financial support and of students. However, during the General Association in 1830, a meeting was held to wrestle with the need for the education of young ministers. The Virginia Baptist Education Society was organized in that year, and in October, 1830, a school was opened in Powhatan County with six students. In 1832 the society purchased a farm four miles north of Richmond, and on July 4, the Virginia Baptist Seminary was opened with ten students under the tutelage of Robert Ryland. Two years later this farm was sold and seven and three-quarters acres were purchased in the suburbs of Richmond. In December, 1834, the seminary moved to this new location, with sixty students, and W. F. Nelson as principal. On March 4, 1840, the Education Society secured a charter for a college from the Virginia Legislature. The state would not incorporate an institution of a religious nature, so that it was necessary to eliminate the year of theological instruction that had been earlier provided. Manual labor also was discontinued. This was the beginning of the University of Richmond with Robert Ryland as president and a faculty of five.

At the very time Virginia Baptists were active in missionary and benevolent enterprises and organizing societies for more effectively carrying these out, their ranks were split by the anti-effort controversy of the 1820's and 1830's. William Gilmore, a Virginia pastor, was elected moderator of the "Particular Baptists of the Old School" meeting at Black Rock Meeting House in Baltimore, Maryland, in September, 1832. The Address of this body asserted violent opposition to tract societies, Sunday Schools, Bible societies, missionary societies, colleges and educational societies, theological schools, and protracted meetings. Along with the Kehukee antimissionary effort in North Carolina, this Maryland group vigorously assailed all benevolent societies. Men like William F. Broaddus in Virginia, who fought for these missionary agencies, were reviled and refused a seat as messengers in many associations. The controversy of the 1830's and thereafter affected practically every association in the state. Many of them divided over the missionary enterprise, and new associations were organized by either the missionary or the antimissionary groups which had split. The progress of Virginia Baptists was considerably retarded by this extensive controversy during the remainder of the period under study. They were also affected quite early by the Campbell movement.

Some of the principal leaders of Virginia Baptists during this period were R. B. Semple, John Bryce, William Crane, Edward Baptist, Spencer H. Cone (who later moved to New York), J. B. Jeter, Henry Keeling, Noah Davis, William Sands, James B. Taylor, William F. and Andrew Broaddus, and Robert Ryland.

North Carolina. Baptists in this state grew rapidly in the period from 1814 to 1845. From 11 associations, 110 ministers, 194 churches, and 12,083 members, they increased to 22 associations, 311 ministers, 454 churches, and 32,671 members, an average annual growth of 5.32%. This 5.32% growth may be compared to the 2.65% growth they experienced between 1790 and 1814.

The population of the state increased from 555,500 in 1810 to 753,419 in 1840, an average annual increase of 1.05%, less than one fifth the rate of North Carolina Baptists. The slave population increased from 168,824 to 245,817, an average annual increase of 1.47%, larger than the general population increase. Free blacks increased from 19,266 to 22,732.

North Carolina Baptists moved gradually toward a state body. As early as 1805, Martin Ross led the Kehukee Association to form the Baptist Philanthropic Missionary Society, but this "was essentially an interassociational committee of correspondence and did not have a general plan for the support of missions." Consequently, at the suggestion of Ross, the North Carolina General Meeting of Correspondence was formed in 1812 "to extend religious acquaintance; to encourage the preaching of the Gospel, and to diffuse useful knowledge." The address of 1812 to the associations urged them to extend their correspondence to embrace the entire state. The idea of a statewide body was beginning to develop. For the next seven years the various associations of the state named delegates who met in annual sessions, which were primarily involved with preaching and the reading of letters to and from similar bodies in other states. In 1821, however, this General Meeting ended, probably because the sponsoring association (Chowan) had decided not to continue its cooperation. However, these meetings were valuable in preparing the way for further statewide activity.

The body that supplanted this General Meeting of Correspondence had been formed on March 19, 1814, with the name the North Carolina Baptist Society for Foreign Missions, whose object was "to aid in sending forth and supporting Missionaries for the purpose of translating the Scripture, preaching the Gospel, and gathering Churches in Heathen and Idolatrous parts of the world." Membership was on a financial basis, and this proved to be a great advantage over associational delegates since anyone interested in foreign missions could join. In 1819 the name was changed to include domestic missions. This society became very active in the first decade of its existence. Again, however, it became evident that a better structure was needed for the enlistment of all North Carolina Baptists. In 1826, Martin Ross introduced into Chowan Association a resolution calling for the formation of a Baptist state convention, but he died before much could be done.

Meanwhile, the antimissionary movement led by Joshua Lawrence in the Kehukee Association in 1826-27, described in the following chapter, brought the demise of the North Carolina Baptist Society for Foreign and Domestic Missions.

The friends of missions met in early 1829 to form the North Carolina Baptist Benevolent Society looking to mission work within North Carolina. However, the leadership recognized that a larger vision was needed. Consequently, on March 26, 1830, at the meeting of this benevolent society, a resolution was unanimously adopted to the effect that this society be transformed into a state convention. Thomas Meredith brought to this meeting a written draft of a constitution, and this was read and adopted, article by article. Its objects included ministerial education, domestic missions, and cooperation with the General Convention in promoting missions in general. Membership was financially based in that any association, church, society, or individual, could send one Baptist delegate for every $10 paid into the treasury.

Within two years this new state convention had commanded considerable support of the missionary followers in North Carolina. In the 1832 meeting, the convention learned with approval that Thomas Meredith was planning to publish a periodical. The first edition was issued in January, 1833, under the name the *North Carolina Baptist Interpreter,* but on January 7, 1835, this monthly was replaced by a weekly newspaper called the *Biblical Recorder* with Meredith as its editor.

Also in 1832 the convention adopted a report urging the founding of a school for ministerial education. A committee was appointed and purchased a farm in the forest of Wake County, where on February 3, 1834, the Wake Forest Manual Labour Institute was opened.

The antimission movement provided powerful opposition to the work of the convention. In three of the existing associations, Kehukee, Country Line, and Abbott's Creek, the Old School or Primitive Baptist forces, as they called themselves, were able to secure control. All of the other associations felt the impact of antimission minorities.

At the session of the convention in 1836 a Bible society was suggested and organized with Meredith as its president. Soon it was promoting both Bible circulation and Sunday Schools as well. The 1838 report said that there had been Sunday Schools in North Carolina since about 1805, and that they presently totaled 200 schools with 10,000 pupils.

Some of the outstanding leaders in North Carolina Baptist life during this period were Martin Ross, Patrick Dowd, Thomas Meredith, A. J. Battle, Robert T. Daniel, and Samuel Wait.

South Carolina. Baptists here made excellent progress during this period. From 5 associations, 96 ministers, 157 churches, and 10,794 members in about 1814, they increased to 13 associations, 232 ministers, 389 churches, and 40,237 members, representing an average annual growth of 8.52% by 1845. This 8.52% average increase may be compared to the 7.43% increase shown in the previous period from 1790 to 1814.

The population increased from 415,115 to 594,398, an average annual growth of 1.39%, which was about one sixth of the Baptist growth rate. The slave population increased from 196,365 in 1810 to 327,038 in 1840, a growth of 2.15% annually.

Reference has been made in a previous chapter to the leadership of the Charleston Association in missions and education before 1814. In fact, Joe M. King in his story of South Carolina Baptists noted that before 1810 no association in South Carolina, except the Charleston, had shown any interest in education, evangelism, or missions, and only a few of the churches in that body had assisted in this work.[4]

Two great stimuli took place in this period, however, that strengthened and unified South Carolina Baptists and doubtless assisted in the considerable progress made by the Baptists in this state by 1845.

The first of these was the conversion of the Judsons and Luther Rice to Baptist views, and the return of Rice to secure support for the new foreign mission enterprise of American Baptists. Rice appeared at the meeting of the Charleston Association in November, 1813, and was cordially received. The General Committee, which had been utilized for both missions and education during the previous twenty-three years, became the coordinating center of their efforts to rally around the cause of missions. The following May (1814), thirty-three men convened at Philadelphia to form the first general body among Baptists in America. South Carolina was represented by Richard Furman, pastor at Charleston, called by Albert L. Vail "perhaps the foremost Baptist in America." There were five other delegates at Philadelphia who were related strongly to South Carolina. William Staughton, an eloquent Englishman, had begun his American ministry at Georgetown, South Carolina, after the Revolution, in response to an appeal from Furman. Henry Holcombe, pastor of the First Baptist Church, Philadelphia, was a Virginian who had become a Baptist in South Carolina, was ordained there, and served as pastor of several churches for over a decade before moving to Georgia, thence to Pennsylvania. William Bullein Johnson was a protege of Furman, but was serving as pastor in Savannah, Georgia, in 1814. Lewis Richards, another delegate, came to South Carolina from South Wales, was baptized and ordained by Furman. He became pastor of the first church in Baltimore in 1784, and was serving there in 1814.

Matthis B. Tallmadge, "by far the most distinguished 'layman' in the Convention," was an outstanding lawyer in New York. He regularly spent his winters in Charleston, South Carolina, and was a very close friend to Furman.

Furman was elected president of this new general body, both in 1814 when it was organized and 1817 at its second meeting. In his presidential address in 1817, Furman moved the assembly with a powerful address on the need for an educated ministry. The General Convention approved of this addition to their foreign enterprise, and South Carolina Baptists generously supported both the first theological institution in Philadelphia opened in 1818 and Columbian College in Washington, D. C., when it opened in 1822. Meanwhile, South Carolina Baptists were continuing their significant program of providing financial assistance to needy young ministers. Not only so, but South Carolina also supported the home mission program of the General Convention which was carried on between 1817 and 1820. As well, when the Baptist General Tract Society was organized in 1824 and the American Baptist Home Mission Society in 1832, these benevolences also were generously supported by South Carolina Baptists.

The second great thrust during the period from 1814 to 1845 by South Carolina Baptists was the organization of a state convention, the first in the South and indeed, the first in the nation. A. H. Newman is mistaken in suggesting that the Massachusetts body was a state convention. It was transformed into one later on, but the true picture may be seen in the editorial in 1821 by a Boston editor, who suggested that Massachusetts ought to follow the example of South Carolina.[5]

The movement for a state body began in November, 1819, in the Charleston Association, but many of the associations would not support the proposed organization. Despite this, however, at the call of the Charleston Association, seven ministers and two laymen from three associations met December 4, 1821, to organize a state convention. Richard Furman was elected president, and a constitution was adopted emphasizing the spread of the gospel and the education of the ministry.

After some hesitation because of the possibility of a joint venture with Georgia Baptists, and further delay caused by the death of Richard Furman and a severe struggle with inertia, the Furman Academy and Theological Institution was opened at Edgefield, on January 15, 1827. The principal was Joseph A. Warne. Two years later both the site and the plan of Furman were abandoned, but the ministerial beneficiaries were placed under the care of Jesse Hartwell at High Hills, who carried on under difficult circumstances. Before the close of the period, the institution was moved to Fairfield and modified as to its character. Theological education took precedence after 1837. A new day began in December, 1844, when James C. Furman, son of Richard, came to head the school.

Efforts were made during this period to establish a Baptist paper in South Carolina, without success.

It is difficult to list the principal leaders of South Carolina Baptists during this period, but doubtless the names of Richard Furman, James C. Furman, Richard Fuller, William Bullein Johnson, Basil Manly, Sr., and Jesse Hartwell were among the foremost.

Georgia. Baptists in this state also showed a large numerical growth in this period. From 5 associations, 115 ministers, 171 churches, and 16,299 members in 1814, they increased to 26 associations, 401 ministers, 620 churches, and 47,151 members in 1845, an average annual increase of 5.91%. This 5.91% growth rate may be compared with their growth rate of 17.72% between 1790 and 1814.

The population increased from 252,433 in 1810 to 691,392 in 1840, or an annual rate of 5.62%, not as rapid as the Baptist increase, but a large population growth. The slave population increased from 105,218 in 1810 to 280,944 in 1840, or at an average annual rate of 5.39%, not as fast as the general population increase.

As was true in South Carolina, Georgia Baptists were given great impetus by two parallel movements during the period between 1814 and 1845. The first of these was the development of the national missionary body in 1814 growing out of the conversion of the Judsons and Rice. Rice visited the state in 1813 and was received enthusiastically. Under the influence of William Bullein Johnson, who had come from South Carolina in 1811 for a four-year pastorate at Savannah, a foreign mission society was formed on December 17, 1813. Rice later wrote that it was a conversation with Johnson that encouraged him to suggest the formation of the General Missionary Convention of 1814.[6] When Johnson as president of the Savannah Baptist Society for Foreign Missions prepared the address, he used, apparently for the first time, the expressions so characteristic of him, as he urged that the "energies of the whole Baptist denomination throughout America may be elicited, combined, and directed." Although Johnson was only thirty-two years of age at the time, his address "of extraordinary elegance and power" was termed by Daniel Sharp "the most able appeal in behalf of Baptist missions which was written by anyone at that period." Johnson represented Georgia at the 1814 meeting.

Promptly, additional local missionary societies sprang up in Georgia, including female societies as early as 1817. In July, 1819, the first Sunday School in Georgia was organized, and the movement grew rapidly during this period, probably accounting for some of the large gains made. It is likely that the missionary work among the Creeks and Cherokees beginning about 1819 was the outgrowth of this missionary spirit.

As was to be expected, the rapid thrust of the missionary movement alienated some. Several associations adopted antimissionary resolutions and turned away from cooperation in the several benevolent enterprises engaging Georgia Baptists during this time.

The second factor that marked the forward progress of Georgia Baptists was the development of a state body in 1822. Adiel Sherwood offered a resolution in the Sarepta Association in October, 1820, urging the organization of the associations into a "general meeting of correspondence." After some preliminaries, on June 29, 1822, at Powelton, representatives from the Georgia and Ocmulgee Associations organized The General Baptist Association of the State of Georgia. Each association, according to the constitution that was adopted, could send not less than three and not more than five delegates to represent them. The objects of the body were to unite the influence and pious intelligence of Georgia Baptists, form and encourage plans for the revival of experimental and practical religion in the state and elsewhere, promote uniformity of sentiment and discipline, aid in giving effect to useful plans of the association, assist in the education of pious young men for the Christian ministry, promote plans for pious and useful education in the Baptist denomination, and correspond with other bodies on topics of general interest to the Redeemer's kingdom. The name of the body was changed in 1827 to the Baptist Convention for the State of Georgia.

Although during the following decade the state body was disturbed by differences of opinion concerning missions, educational institutions to train the ministry, and several types of doctrinal questions, in all the body made marked progress. In 1831, upon motion of Adiel Sherwood, the convention approved a resolution to establish a classical and theological school for those preparing for the ministry as soon as funds justified it. The following year it was agreed to admit other students than those in divinity. Through the bequest of $2,500 by Josiah Penfield, Mercer Institute (later Mercer University) was opened at Penfield in 1833. It was the beginning of a number of educational enterprises by Georgia Baptists.

The state periodical of Georgia had begun as *The Columbian Star* in 1821 in Washington, D. C., under the leadership of Luther Rice for promoting the work of the General Convention. Its name was changed to *The Christian Index,* and in 1833, Jesse Mercer purchased the paper and moved it to Washington, Georgia, serving as editor for some time. The paper was transferred to the convention in 1840. It provided an important medium of communication during all of the period under study.

Some of the outstanding leaders of Georgia Baptists during this period were Adiel Sherwood, Jesse Mercer, William T. Brantly, James Armstrong, J. P. Marshall, and B. M. Sanders.

Florida. This area became a part of the United States in 1821 under terms of the Adams-Onis Treaty, by which Spain relinquished her claims. Baptists had already moved across the border from Georgia and Alabama to farm the land, then to reside. As early as January 7, 1821, Fleming Bates, assisted by Isom Peacock, organized the Pigeon Creek Baptist Church, the first one in Florida. This church was received into the Piedmont Association in Georgia. Farther west another church was organized on March 12, 1835, under the leadership of E. H. Calloway and Jeremiah Kembrill, known now as the Campbellton Baptist Church. This church was received into the Chattahoochee Association of Alabama.

By 1835 there were eight Baptist churches in Florida, and on September 26, 1835, the Suwannee Association was formed. The antimissionary party in the state, however, agitated vigorously against the benevolent activities of the missionary majority. By a political parliamentary trick, the antimissionary minority secured control of the association and voted to become antimissionary. Already, however, on October 22, 1842, the missionary Baptists in middle Florida had organized the Florida Association, under the leadership of William B. Cooper.

Growth in this state was remarkable under the circumstances. Before 1840 it was necessary to carry guns to church for protection against the Indians. In 1845 the state had 1 association, 32 churches, 26 ministers, and 1,333 members. Florida is first shown in the census of 1830, when it had 34,730 population, including 15,501 slaves. By 1840, it had grown to 54,477, with 25,717 slaves.

South Central Region

The remarkable migration from the South Atlantic to the South Central region is reflected in the statistics for this era. Between 1810 and 1840 the population of the South Central states of Kentucky, Tennessee, Alabama, Mississippi, Arkansas, and Louisiana increased from 785,146 to 3,025,430, an average annual growth of 9.20%. This may be compared with the population growth of the South Atlantic region of 1.48%. The slave population increased during the same period from 176,844 to 1,002,447, or an average increase annually of 15.06%, compared with the slave population growth in the South Atlantic region during the same period of 1.46% average annual increase.

This great increase in population (including slaves) was very significant for Baptists, both in their growth and their development. In 1814 only three states in this region had a Baptist population (Kentucky, Tennessee, and Mississippi). By 1845, however, Baptists in these three states had increased substantially and there were four additional states in which Baptists were found: Alabama, Arkansas, and Louisiana, and, in addition, the new state of Texas, admitted to the Union in 1845. They increased from 21 associations, 304 ministers, 457 churches, and 34,848 members in 1814 to 105 associations, 1,253 ministers, 2,042 churches, and 146,277 members in 1845, or an average annual membership growth of 9.99%, quite as impressive as the population growth, and larger than the Baptist increase in the South Atlantic states of 5.25%.

These figures confirm that the South Atlantic states, for a variety of reasons, were losing their people to the inland areas. Also indicative of this is the fact that in 1811, only two South Central states (Tennessee and Louisiana) were producing cotton, and these two states showed a crop of 5,000,000 pounds. By 1834, twenty-three years later, Mississippi and Alabama had joined with them in producing cotton, and their product had ballooned to 277,000,000 pounds, which far surpassed the cotton crop of all of the South Atlantic states in 1834. Frederick Jackson Turner remarked that between 1830 and 1850, the South Central states became the repository of over half the slaveholders of the entire Union.[7] Indicative of this also is the fact that in the 1830's, the population of North and South Carolina remained almost stationary, while Virginia showed an increase of but 7% in whites and 3.5% in slaves. Alabama in the same period showed an increase of 76% in whites and 115% in slaves, and Mississippi showed an increase of 154% in whites and 197% in slaves.[8]

Economically and politically, the South Central section was affected to a large extent in the same way as the South Atlantic states relative to the periods of financial crisis and sectional political loyalty because of the "peculiar institution" which had become a part of the new lands.

Kentucky. It will be recalled that this state was admitted to the Union on June 1, 1792, and grew rapidly thereafter. Her population increased from 406,511 in 1810 to 779,828 in 1840, an average annual increase of 2.95%. The slave population during this period increased from 80,561 to 182,258, an average annual increase of 4.07%. The growth of Baptists outstripped both the population and the slave increase, as substantial as these were. When the period began, Kentucky had 13 associations, 142 ministers, 263 churches, and 21,660 members. By 1845 there were 42 associations, 449 ministers, 685 churches, and 60,371 members, or an average annual increase of 5.58%. Kentucky was second only to Virginia in the number of Baptists within her borders in 1845.

The postwar revival had ceased by 1803 in Kentucky, but another revival occurred between 1810 and 1813, following a period of schism and quarrel over slavery and other issues. Although Kentucky had no representation at the meeting of the General Missionary Convention in 1814 at Philadelphia, the arrival of Rice in 1815-16 brought great missionary enthusiasm, and six missionary societies were promptly organized. As usual, the rise of the missionary fervor brought anti-effort forces into activity after 1816, and the adoption of home missions as a part of the General Convention's program in 1817 brought additional opposition from the anti-effort forces. As will be mentioned in the following chapter, John Taylor, Daniel Parker, and Alexander Campbell were principal leaders in the anti-effort movement. Taylor was from Kentucky, but the writings and influence of Daniel Parker of Tennessee were a strong deterrent to progress in Kentucky. After 1823 Campbell was busy in Kentucky, and by 1827 many associations in Kentucky were splitting over the Campbell movement. The effect of the work of these three and many lesser lights was devastating. In 1829, Kentucky Baptists numbered 45,442, but by 1832 they numbered only 35,862, and despite a sweeping revival between 1837 and 1840, the membership of 1839 was numbered at only 39,806.

In the face of the anti-effort opposition, Kentucky Baptists made remarkable progress during this period. In 1832 Uriel B. Chambers began a weekly Baptist paper, which subsequently became the *Western Recorder,* and under the able editorship of John L. Waller and W. C. Buck, this paper became the leading Baptist journal in the West. In 1829, Georgetown College was begun.

As early as 1813 there had been a proposal for the forming of a general body, but nothing came of it. After a preliminary appeal by the Frankfort Association, the Kentucky Baptist Convention was organized on March 29, 1832, with thirty-four delegates representing three associations and nine churches. However, it was recognized that a more effective body was needed, and on October 20, 1837, the General Association of Baptists in Kentucky was organized by fifty-seven Kentucky Baptist leaders, including twenty ordained ministers, one licensed preacher, and thirty-six laymen. This body was composed of representation from Baptist churches and associations which contributed annually to the causes sponsored by the body or cooperated through auxiliary associations.

For several years some of the antimission Baptists, who had remained in the several associations auxiliary to the new body, did their best to destroy the new organization, but by 1842 the antimissioners had withdrawn.

Tennessee. This state also grew rapidly after being admitted to the

Union on June 1, 1796. From 261,727 in 1810, the population increased to 829,210 in 1840, an average annual increase of 6.99%. Baptists during this same period increased from 7 associations, 141 ministers, 162 churches, and 12,294 members to 18 associations, 292 ministers, 440 churches, and 32,159 members in 1845, an average annual increase of 5.05%, somewhat less than the population growth. As did Kentucky, Tennessee showed a large increase in the number of slaves during this period, increasing from 44,535 slaves in 1810 to 183,059 in 1840, an average annual increase of 10.03%. The social, economic, and religious influence of this institution was beyond computation.

Other denominations were active in Tennessee. The Presbyterians and Methodists far outstripped the Baptists during the post-Revolutionary revivals, but Baptists assumed an important place by the opening of this period, many of them holding high offices in the new state. They were influential in the preparation of the constitution of 1834, as well as the earlier one of 1796, where full religious liberty was specifically granted.

As the Baptists spread westward, there came a threefold division of the state because of geographical barriers and the size of the state. Work in East Tennessee naturally was begun first and during this period the original Holston and Tennessee Associations multiplied westward as far as Jefferson County. Middle Tennessee Baptists centered around Nashville and slowly increased through this period to include churches between the mountains on the east and the Tennessee River on the west. West Tennessee Baptists began organizing associations in 1822, and included everything west of the Tennessee River.

Although Tennessee had no representation at the General Missionary Convention of 1814, the organization of that body precipitated both support and opposition, as was true in other states. Luther Rice visited Tennessee several times after 1815, but almost singlehandedly, Daniel Parker, pastor at New Hopewell church in Concord Association in Middle Tennessee, provided vigorous opposition to the new mission movement. In 1821 he moved to Illinois, but the anti-effort cudgel was taken up again by 1827, when the teachings of Alexander Campbell infected many Baptists in the area. As an example of the influence of Campbell, the Concord Association was reduced in a few years from 49 churches and 3,399 members to 11 churches and 805 members. In 1834, however, R. B. C. Howell of Virginia became pastor of the remnants of the Nashville church (which had followed Campbell), and missionary Baptists took heart. In 1833, under the leadership of James Whitsitt, a state body known as the Tennessee Baptist Convention was organized near Nashville,

> but the individual and combined attacks of Primitive Baptists, Gospel Mission Baptists, and the Disciples of Christ were too much for it.

> The dissenting Baptists looked upon the new convention with dire misgivings and regarded with suspicion anything which tended toward the centralization of authority or threatened the autonomy of their churches.[9]

It changed its name in 1842, but this did not placate its enemies. During the remainder of this period and for many years thereafter, there was no state convention in fact. Instead there were three sectional conventions: the East Tennessee General Association of Baptists, the Middle Tennessee Association of Baptists, and the West Tennessee Convention of Baptists.

Alabama. Geographical and political factors delayed large immigration into Alabama. When the tide began, it soon reached flood proportions. Until 1813 Spain held a large southern strip of this area, but by 1817 Alabama Territory was organized. It was admitted as a state on December 14, 1819. A great deal of Indian warfare continued until 1832, when the Creeks by treaty ceded their lands to the United States.

The population of the state was first shown in the 1820 census, when it numbered 127,901, including 41,879 slaves. In twenty years the number of slaves had risen to 253,532, and before the outbreak of war in 1860 Alabama ranked second as a cotton-producing state. There is little wonder that the Confederate government was set up at Montgomery. By 1840 the population was 590,756.

There were perhaps 1,500 or 2,000 Baptists in this area in 1814, but so great was the growth, primarily through immigration, that the statistics in 1845 showed 17 associations, 242 ministers, 427 churches, and 28,210 members.

The early Baptists in this state faced many problems. For one thing, the constituency was formed from Baptists who had come from many different states and who held varying doctrinal emphases. An untrained ministry and leadership often found itself bewildered by the multiplicity of doctrinal and ecclesiastical views. In the earlier years many of the churches were "house churches," very mobile and easy to move. This did not tend toward stability, although it provided great opportunity for witnessing among the common people and subsequently did enlist many people. In the primitive frontier settlements, there was often local opposition to any kind of preaching, and threats against Baptist ministers in the Tombigbee settlements, for example, were not unknown. Although not directly involved in the organization of the General Missionary Convention in 1814, the settlers from the older states were familiar with the missionary thrust of that movement, as well as the anti-effort response, which also appeared in early Alabama life. Early Baptists had some difficulty in securing land titles because they "squatted" on the territory before titles were issued, and subsequently had to move farther west, which slowed down the growth in some sections. The terrain itself gave difficulty. This was canebrake country, when sometimes the cane was so thick and so high that it was difficult to move freely through the countryside.

Despite these factors, Alabama Baptists grew phenomenally during this period. One great reason for this was the grass roots nature of the ministry, who came from the people, served with little formal education or salary, and with zeal and sincerity overcame every obstacle. Alexander Travis, for example, who came to Alabama from South Carolina, frequently would walk forty miles to preach, swimming streams and rivers and ignoring the clutching overgrown canebrake. What the people lacked in education and training, they made up in zeal and conviction.

Probably the principal factor that brought such amazing growth in this period to Alabama Baptists was the rapid immigration into distinct geographical areas, each of which became a center of Baptist activity. The earliest center was the Tennessee River Valley, where immigrants from Virginia, North Carolina, and Georgia settled rather early. A pioneer like John Davis (known by choice as "Flat-footed" John Davis because of his plain and forcible style of preaching) was very effective here. The Tombigbee settlements, north of the West Florida boundary line, was a second principal area. After the War of 1812 and the mollifying of the Creek Indians, "the flood-gates of Virginia, the two Carolinas, Tennessee, Kentucky, and Georgia were hoisted, and mighty streams of emigration poured through them. . . . Never before or since has a country been so rapidly peopled." Early leaders were James Courtney, Alexander Travis, Joseph McGee, and Jacob Parker. The third region of settlement was found in the Coosa and Alabama River valleys, with early leaders like James McLemore, Electius Thompson, Lee Compere, and R. S. Daniel. One colorful leader was L. C. Davis, who called himself "The Club-Ax," an eccentric and forceful pioneer. The fourth general area of infiltration was the Black Warrier and Cahaba River valleys, which boasted such stalwart pioneers as Hosea Holcombe and Joseph Ryan.

Through the leadership of J. A. Ranaldson, on October 28, 1823, the Baptist State Convention of Alabama was organized. Fifteen delegates from missionary societies constituted the body, and elected Charles Crow as president and Ranaldson as secretary. During the early years of this body, there was considerable opposition to missions in many parts of the state. An effort was made to hold together Baptists both of mission and antimission views, but near the close of the period the antimissionary forces withdrew and formed their own churches and associations under the name Primitive Baptists.

Along with the antimissionary schism, Alabama Baptists also found their relationship with the General Missionary Convention and the Home Mission Society jeopardized by the activities of the abolitionists. In 1843 the convention revised the constitution to eliminate reference to the General Missionary Convention as an agency of cooperation and magnified the various benevolences as the principal purpose of their body. In the agitation over this matter, in 1844 the Tuscaloosa church inquired of the state body if it were proper to continue supporting financially the northern movements when there was so much misunderstanding and disagreement among them. The convention replied that constitutionally all members of the northern societies were entitled "to receive any agency, mission or other appointment, which may fall within the scope of their operations or duties." It was the Alabama Resolutions along this line to the General Missionary Convention of 1844 that precipitated the organization of the Southern Baptist Convention in 1845.

The state body vigorously supported significant activities. Offerings were made at first to Columbian College, and then efforts were made to establish an institute near Greensboro, which was killed by the financial panic of 1837. Aid was provided to ministerial students and preachers. Howard College was opened in 1842 at Marion, and in that year the convention accepted a four-year-old school, Judson Female Institute, also at Marion. Also in 1842 the convention approved *The Alabama Baptist* as the state paper, and S. S. Sherman, president of Howard College, became its editor.

In 1836 the Alabama Baptist Bible Society was organized as an auxiliary to the convention to distribute Bibles and secure gifts for Bible publication and translation. Baptist leaders also were active in 1838 in the organization of a temperance convention.

Mississippi. Mississippi also experienced remarkable growth in every way during this period. In 1810 the population was 40,352, and by 1840 it numbered 375,651, or an average annual increase of 26.78%. The census of 1810 showed 17,088 slaves, but the number had risen by 1840 to 195,211, an average increase of 33.61% annually.

At the opening of the period, Baptists had 1 association, 13 ministers, 20 churches, and 894 members. By 1845 they had grown to 15 associations, 182 ministers, 326 churches, and 19,539 members. This was an average annual membership increase of 65.10%.

The dynamic in the early growth of Mississippi Baptists was the Mississippi Baptist Association, which had been organized in 1806. It took the initiative to foster missions both in Mississippi Territory and in southern Louisiana. In 1817, following the organization of the General Missionary Convention in 1814, Mississippi Baptists organized the Mississippi Society for Baptist Missions, Foreign and

Domestic, with Benjamin Davis as president and William Snodgrass as secretary. A Mississippi Baptist Education Society was organized in 1818 by the Mississippi Association, and reorganized in 1835, in an effort to provide ministerial education.

By 1824, with the rapid multiplication of churches and associations, a state body was organized, but due to the anti-effort opposition it was dissolved in 1829. For the next five years Baptists were engaged in internal dissension, a part of the problem being the Campbell controversy.

A new day dawned with the coming of Ashley Vaughn in 1833 as missionary from the American Baptist Home Mission Society. He was active in every forward-looking movement of Mississippi Baptists. In September, 1836, he began the publication of *The South-Western Religious Luminary* at Natchez. In 1836, Vaughn traveled horseback across the Baptist area of the state, then issued a call for the formation of a state convention. On December 23, 1836, from the efforts of Vaughn, the Convention of the Baptist Denomination in the State of Mississippi was formed. Vaughn was named president of the new body. As usual, the anti-effort element in the state opposed the formation of this convention.

In an effort to meet the mission needs of the area, the convention began cooperation with the Southern Baptist Home Mission Society, formed in 1839 by R. T. Daniel at Columbus. However, when Daniel died three years later, this society also died. As early as 1838 special attention was given to the Sunday School movement as a part of organizational life in the churches.

In addition to those named in areas of leadership, other outstanding men were L. B. Holloway, T. S. N. King, and Norvell Robertson, Jr.

Arkansas. George Gill, who migrated into northeastern Arkansas and probably preached the first sermon in the state by a Baptist, was the early pioneer in this state. The formation of the first Baptist church probably was the work of James P. Edwards, missionary from the Bethel Association of Missouri, who, with Benjamin Clark and Jesse James, organized in 1818 a church, later called Salem, in what became the Columbia settlement. One of the members of this church, John Y. Lindsey, was an outstanding leader among Arkansas Baptists for almost half a century.

Arkansas Baptists faced many difficulties. The wild country, danger from the Indians, a shortage of preachers, the incursions of Campbellism, and a strong antimissionary party hampered their growth. The oldest church in the state with a continuous existence was not organized until 1832 and was known as the Kentucky church.

Other pioneers included Silas Toncray and his brother-in-law, Isaac Watkins, who came from Kentucky in 1824. Probably the outstanding early preacher was David Orr, who came from Missouri in 1827 and promptly began organizing Baptist churches and at least two associations. When the American Baptist Home Mission Society was organized in 1832, Orr was appointed a missionary of that society, as well as W. B. Karr, Benjamin Clark, and Thomas Mercer. The southern part of the state had only three of seventeen active churches in 1832.

Statehood was attained on June 13, 1836, and marked a forward thrust in the organization of churches and associations in all parts of the state. Missionaries like George Gill, William Nutt, Sherrod Winningham, and T. S. G. Watson organized new churches and associations in the early 1840's.

However, two movements greatly slowed the progress of Arkansas Baptists. The followers of Alexander Campbell were able to win some of the churches from Baptist ranks. The Calvinistic antimission party confronted the missionary Baptists in the 1830's and began a long struggle between the two opposing views.

Arkansas grew rapidly from immigration. The population was first shown in the 1820 census and consisted of 14,273 inhabitants, including 1,617 slaves. The 1840 census showed 97,574, including 19,935 slaves, an average annual increase of 53.94%. By 1845, Baptists had 6 associations, 67 churches, 24 ministers, and 2,015 members.

Louisiana. This state was admitted to the Union in 1812, the first state to be formed from the Louisiana Purchase of 1803. The population in the first census in which it was shown in 1810 was 75,556, of which 34,660 were slaves. By 1840, it had increased to 352,441, with 168,452 slaves. This represented an annual average population increase of 11.62%, and an average increase annually in slaves of 12.29%, slightly larger than the population gain. It is likely that there were fewer than 100 Baptists in Louisiana in 1814. By 1845 there were 5 associations, 50 ministers, 73 churches, and 3,311 members.

In the opening years of this period, Joseph Willis, organizer of the Calvary Baptist Church near Bayou Chicot, the oldest Baptist church in the state with a continuous history, took the lead in evangelizing southwestern and central Louisiana. With Ezekiel O'Quin, he spent almost a half-century in faithful witnessing. All five of the churches which formed the Louisiana Baptist Association in 1818, the first in the state, had been organized by Willis. In New Orleans proper, efforts were made as early as 1818 to form a Baptist church, but not until 1843 was a permanent body, now the First Baptist Church, planted.

In north Louisiana James Brinson from Tennessee and Henry Humble from Mississippi were active after 1820. A group of Baptists who had come in a party from the Edgefield district of South Carolina organized the Mount Lebanon Baptist Church on July 8, 1837, with

Henry Adams, a freeborn mulatto, as the first pastor. This church and the surrounding community became the center of Louisiana Baptist work about the middle of the century.

There was no state body in Louisiana during this period. The strong Roman Catholic hostility, the poorly educated Baptist leadership, the widely scattered population in north Louisiana, the lack of a denominational organ, the anti-effort opposition that was common in all of these early Baptist communities, and the divisive effect of the movement of Alexander Campbell contributed to the disunited condition of Louisiana Baptists at the close of this period in 1845.

Texas. Texans declared their independence from Mexico on March 2, 1836, but Baptists had been active in the area long before this. Freeman Smalley, Joseph Bays, Thomas Hanks, Isaac Reed, Abner Smith, Daniel Parker, Thomas J. Pilgrim, and many others of the Baptist persuasion were active in Texas in the 1820's and 1830's. Some of these were missionary Baptist preachers, some were antimissionary, and Pilgrim was a young schoolteacher who contributed mightily through Baptist Sunday Schools.

Migration into Texas was very rapid, especially after the financial panic in the 1820's made it difficult to secure land without cash in the United States. Texas was admitted to the Union on December 29, 1845. The first census including this area took place in 1850, when 212,592 people were listed, including 58,161 slaves.

Antimissionary Baptists formed the earliest churches in Texas. Daniel Parker moved a church he had organized in Illinois into Texas in 1834, while Abner Smith probably brought a church from Alabama in the same year.

The first missionary Baptist church in Texas was organized by Z. N. Morrell, an outstanding pioneer from Tennessee, in November, 1837. This church appealed to the Baptist mission societies, and James Huckins and William Tryon came in 1840 and 1841. These two men, along with Morrell and R. E. B. Baylor, greatly set forward the Baptist witness before the close of this period.[10]

In 1840 the Union Association was organized, and in the following year, the messengers to this body formed an education society and the Texas Home Mission Society. Both of these were active. The education society led in the founding of Baylor University in 1845 at Independence, while the mission society promptly appointed several ministers to serve as state missionaries (principally without pay).

As was true in many states in this period, both Campbellism and antimissionism brought problems. Churches were lost through pastors who held the views of Campbell, but the early purging of Texas Baptists of this movement evidently prevented more difficulties later. Most of the antimission Baptists in Texas either had their own churches or very early withdrew from the missionary churches, although some of this element remained within Texas Baptist life.

In 1845 Texas Baptists had 2 associations, 24 churches, 14 ministers, and 672 members.

North Central Region

Missouri. Although Missouri did not become a Territory until 1812 and a state until 1821, it grew rapidly during this period. First shown in the census of 1810, it had 20,845 inhabitants, 3,011 of them slaves. In 1840 the population was 383,702, an average annual increase of 56.15%. The slave population in 1840 was 58,240, an average annual increase since 1810 of 59.17%. Baptists increased from several hundred in 1814 to 21 associations, 212 ministers, 334 churches, and 16,366 members in 1845.

In the 1820's and early 1830's, Missouri Baptists, composed of pioneers from many different parts of the country with various types of theology and ecclesiology, endeavored to unify their people. Most of them were known as United Baptists, but at first they were quite disunited.

> (But) many factors combined during the early statehood days of Missouri to impede their progress and hinder their co-operation, such as the antimission controversy, the bitter agitation of the slavery question, the troublesome presence of wandering Indian tribes, the Mormon migration, war, and the terrible cholera epidemic in St. Louis, which created alarm throughout the state.[11]

A large step toward unity was taken when messengers gathered in June, 1835, and formed what became the Missouri Baptist General Association. Leaders in this movement were Thomas Fristoe, Fielding Wilhite, and Ebenezer Rodgers, as well as the first moderator of the association, the veteran Jeremiah Vardeman. This state body was handicapped because of the antimission party within the association. Through the influence of the pioneer missionary in the area, John Mason Peck, the body became allied as an auxiliary with the American Baptist Home Mission Society in 1841.

Peck first arrived in St. Louis in 1817 and served effectively until 1822, when he moved across the line to Illinois. With James E. Welch he helped organize churches, missionary societies, and Sunday Schools around St. Louis. In 1818 Peck helped organize the first missionary society in the West, the United Society for the Spread of the Gospel. Other early Missouri leaders were William Mansfield, Anderson Woods, and James Suggett.

Summary of the Period

During this period Southern Baptists added to their two functional ecclesiastical bodies (the churches and the associations) the remaining structures of their organized life—the general bodies beginning in 1814 and the state bodies beginning in 1821. The Baptist World Alliance would be added in the next century, but this basically was not a part of their functioning structure. It is rather curious that American Baptists as a whole developed churches and associations in their logical order, but that structured state bodies were not adopted until after the general bodies (the three principal benevolent societies) had been formed. This may be accounted for by the fact that the society method, popularized because of its adoption by William Carey in England in 1792, represented an organizational option for benevolent work that had more appeal to the ecclesiology-conscious Baptists of the early nineteenth century than strictly denominational structures did. Rice proposed the formation of a logical denominational structure that began with the churches and built organizational forms through associations, state bodies, and finally a national denominational convention in a sort of ascending judicature. This plan was not adopted initially in 1814 nor was the extensive effort to introduce it successful in the 1820's. Instead, the society-type of general structure was chosen, which magnified benevolences more than denomination and was refined to magnify each benevolence separately to the weakening of denominational unity.

In the thirty-one years from 1814 to 1845, Southern Baptists increased from no state bodies to 9, from 60 associations to 213, from 1,282 churches to 4,395, and from a membership of 110,514 to 365,346. This represented an average annual increase in membership of 7.20%, compared with the average annual population growth in the same area of 3.63%, about half the Baptist rate.

Good growth was experienced by Baptists in the South Atlantic region, averaging 5.25% annually, but the effect of western migration can be glimpsed in the comparison of this rate of growth with the 9.99% average annual increase in the South Central region. Slavery moved rapidly to the West: in 1850 this area was the repository of over half the slaveholders of the entire Union.[12] Slaves in the South Atlantic region increased from 979,820 in 1810 to 1,422,934 in 1840, an average annual rate of increase of 1.46%; while slaves in the South Central region increased from 176,844 in 1810 to 1,002,447 in 1840, an average annual rate of increase of 15.06%. Meanwhile, the population in the South Atlantic region increased from 2,602,239 in 1810 to 3,837,247 in 1840, an average annual growth of 1.53%; while the population in the West (the South Central region plus Missouri) increased from 785,146 in 1810 to 3,025,430 in 1840, an average annual rate of 9.20%.

Baptists in the South Atlantic region represented 55.48% of all

Southern Baptists in 1845, a drop from their relative strength in 1814 of 68.47%. Baptists in the South Central region represented 40.04% of all Southern Baptists in 1845, compared with their 31.53% figure of 1814. This lower percentage of Baptist population in the South Atlantic states did not represent a lessening of growth in that region but reflected the remarkable increases shown in the West. Virginia still led in the percentage of Southern Baptists in a state with 21.53% in 1845. She was followed in the South Atlantic region by Georgia with 12.90%, South Carolina with 11.01%, North Carolina with 8.94%, Maryland with .54%, Florida with .36%, and District of Columbia with .19%. In the South Central region, Kentucky was still the leader and next to Virginia the state with most Southern Baptists in its borders, with 16.52%; Tennessee followed with 8.80%, then Alabama with 7.72%, Mississippi with 5.35%, Louisiana with .91%, Arkansas with .55%, and Texas with .18%. The Baptist growth in the South Central region during this period averaged 9.99% annually, slightly more than the substantial population increase of 9.20%. Missouri, in the North Central region, increased in population from 20,845 in 1810 to 383,702 in 1840, an average annual increase of 56.12%. Baptists in that state, meanwhile, increased to 16,366 by 1845 from a few at the opening of the period. These Missouri Baptists in 1845 constituted 4.48% of all Southern Baptists.

The substantial growth of Baptists during this period did not result so much from sweeping revivals, involving some dominant central figure (like George Whitefield in the previous period) or some single event (like the First Great Awakening). Rather, growth came from active evangelism by warmhearted ministers; more structured missionary work by associations, state bodies, and missionary societies; more zeal accelerated by increasing unity in state bodies and the challenge of great benevolent societies on a national scale; the popularity and appeal of the "grass roots" denominations (like Baptists and Methodists) on the western frontier; the improved communication and enlightenment afforded by the publication of Baptist papers in many of the southern states; and the contributions of missionaries appointed by the American Baptist Home Mission Society after 1832. Still an important factor was the nature of Baptist ecclesiology. Where some other denominations had great difficulties relative to securing and supporting proper ministers, Baptist views provided accessible avenues for zealous, self-supporting men to be ordained on the basis of a divine call to preach. Such a situation neglected ministerial education and ecclesiastical support, but under the circumstances it solved knotty problems of ministerial personnel and support and blended well with the democratic ideas of the frontier.

Yet Southern Baptists were already busy during this period in providing educational opportunities for their ministry. The state bodies sprang forth partly as an answer to educational and missionary needs. Four of the seven principal schools founded during this period were advocated fervently in corporate meetings and initiated by the action of the state bodies. This included Furman (South Carolina), whose founding in 1827 followed the action of their convention two years before; Mercer (Georgia), which opened its doors in 1833 as the result of a resolution at the Georgia Baptist Convention two years before; Wake Forest (North Carolina), begun in 1834 from the initiative of their convention; and Howard (Alabama), whose founding in 1842 followed the action of the state body. Georgetown (Kentucky) in 1829 developed from community action; University of Richmond (Virginia) in 1832 was sponsored by the Virginia Baptist Education Society organized two years before; and Judson (Alabama), opened in 1839 as a school for girls, was initiated by private gifts (including the sponsorship of E. D. King), but was accepted by the state body in 1843. King also had a part in the founding of Howard, now known as Samford University.

E. C. Dargan remarked that the "hireling" ministry under the Virginia establishment and the difficulty of securing an education, particularly for a dissenting clergyman, had initially caused Southern Baptist ministers to pass up "book learning" as not being a significant part of their preparation for ministry; but that during this period the denomination gave more emphasis to "scholarly and accomplished men." The pattern of leaders like Richard Furman, Henry Holcombe, Jesse Mercer, and Richard Fuller, to name a few, commended the use of educational preparation for an effective service. In addition, in one of those curious turns that history occasionally takes, the Campbell controversy distinctly forwarded theological education by showing the need for training to serve apologetic and polemical purposes. Furthermore, Baptist newspapers began to spring up rapidly in this period, providing both stimulation to education and opportunity for its use by Baptist writers. In a little more than a decade, six of the principal Southern Baptist state papers were born: *The Christian Index* (Georgia), 1822; the *Western Recorder* (Kentucky), 1826; the *Religious Herald* (Virginia), 1828; the *Biblical Recorder* (North Carolina), 1833; the *Alabama Baptist* (Alabama), 1835; and the *Baptist and Reflector* (Tennessee), 1835. Other states published less permanent periodicals of various sorts.

Without question, many important contributions to Southern Baptist life flowed from their relationship with the national benevolent societies organized in 1814, 1824, and 1832. Every southern state cooperated with these benevolent societies, inculcating a larger sense of unity than Baptists had ever known. The Bible translation controversy, begun in this period, flowered in Southern Baptist life in the next period. The Campbell and anti-effort excisions from Southern Baptist life were not unmixed evils: by the end of this period most of the dissidents had been expelled or had withdrawn from the large missionary-minded majority of Southern Baptists, and the improved fellowship and cooperative spirit in the ranks of the missionary churches and associations gave impetus to their advance. It should be said, however, that Baptists in some southern states were still involved in the struggle with these alien groups at the end of this period.

Southern Baptists were bound up with the culture of their region. This does not mean that they were substantially involved in slavery, but the one-crop system, predicated upon the use of slave labor, brought almost total collateral economic dependence upon King Cotton. All of society, religion, and economics were affected by this system, and when sectional prejudices and political rivalry over a relatively long period were added to the mixture, an explosion occurred. For American Baptists, this explosion included a rupture of cooperative relations between Baptists North and South.

Notes

1. For this general resume, see Frederick Jackson Turner, *Rise of the New West 1819-1829* (New York: Harper and Brothers, 1906), p. 70.
2. From a letter of G. F. Adams in 1843, found in Benedict, *op. cit.,* 1848 edition, p. 634.
3. Ryland, *op. cit.,* pp. 202-3.
4. King, *op. cit.,* p. 167.
5. Baker, Source Book, pp. 76-77.
6. *The Christian Index* (Georgia), January 27, 1835.
7. For this resume, see Turner, *The Rise of the New West,* p. 47, and Turner, *The United States 1830-1850* (New York: P. Smith, 1950), p. 214.
8. *Ibid., The United States 1830-1850,* p. 214.
9. Cox-Woolley, eds., *Encyclopedia,* II, p. 1363.
10. For a detailed story, see Baker, *The Blossoming Desert* (Waco: Word Books, 1970).
11. Cox-Woolley, eds., *Encyclopedia,* II, P. 910.
12. Turner, *The United States 1830-1850,* p. 215.

8 Divisive Controversies

At the very time Baptists in Philadelphia formed a foreign mission society to support the Judsons and Rice in 1814 and endeavored to find the proper method of structuring their national benevolent bodies, three divisive movements were developing that would either wrench large numbers from Southern Baptist ranks, or, as in the case of the last one, bring a structural separation between Baptists in the North and those in the South in home and foreign missions. These were Campbellism, antimissionism, and sectionalism deepened by the slavery-abolitionist controversy.

Another less significant conflict began during this period, but it had more impact among Southern Baptists during the following one. In 1835 many American Baptists belonged to the American Bible Society, founded in 1816 on an interdenominational basis. Some of them requested that the society aid in printing a Bengali version of the Bible in which Baptist missionaries had translated *baptizein* by the native word for *immerse*. The society refused to aid in a translation of this sort because it would not be used by denominations that did not immerse for baptism. Whereupon, a relatively large number of Baptists organized the American and Foreign Bible Society in 1837 at Philadelphia. When this body in 1850 also declined to print a version of the Bible with the Baptist interpretation of *baptizein*, another Baptist society was formed for this express purpose, called the American Baptist Union. Southern Baptists were in somewhat of a dilemma as to which society to support, as will be noted in the events of the next period.

Campbellism

Thomas Campbell and his son Alexander were Scotch-Irish Presbyterians, greatly influenced in their biblicism by men like Greville Ewing, John Glas, and Robert Sandeman in the Glasgow community. In America, after a careful study of the Scriptures, both Campbells and their families were immersed by a Baptist preacher in 1812, and remained loosely affiliated with American Baptist life from then until the 1820's.

148

However, the theological and practical orientation of Alexander Campbell made him uncomfortable in Baptist life. Even his view of baptism, which had originally turned him toward the Baptists, differed from the Baptist position. Campbell looked upon baptism as the formal washing away of the sins of penitent believers, while Baptists viewed it simply as a symbol of cleansing from sins already forgiven. In 1823 Campbell began publishing *The Christian Baptist* (replaced by *The Millennial Harbinger* in 1829), and this soon became an organ for attacking practically all Baptist beliefs. He opposed missionary societies, Bible societies, Sunday School and tract societies, ministerial education, salaries to ministers, and similar practices of Baptists.

In 1825 Campbell preached at the Baptist church in Virginia where Robert Semple was pastor, and in December, 1825, Semple wrote to Campbell as follows:

> Your opinions on some other points are, I think, dangerous, unless you are misunderstood, such as casting off the Old Testament, exploding experimental religion in its common acceptation, denying the existence of gifts in the present day commonly believed to exist among all spiritual christians, such as preaching, &c. Some other of your opinions, though true, are pushed to extremes, such as those upon the use of creeds, confessions, &c., &c. Your views of ministerial support, directed against abuses on that head, would be useful, but leveled against all support to ministers (unless by way of alms) is so palpably contrary to scripture and common justice, that I persuade myself that there must be some misunderstanding. In short your views are generally so contrary to those of the Baptists in general, that if a party was to go fully into the practice of your principles I should say a new sect had sprung up, radically different from the Baptists, as they now are.[1]

By 1830 the Appomattox Association of Virginia, following the lead of several western associations, condemned the teachings of Campbell and officially advocated disfellowshipping him. The Virginia association specifically condemned Campbell's assertions that there was no promise of salvation without baptism; that baptism should be administered to all who say they believe that Jesus Christ is the Son of God without examination on any other point; that there was no direct operation of the Holy Spirit on the mind prior to baptism; that baptism brought the remission of sins and the gifts of the Holy Spirit; that the Scriptures were the only evidence of interest in Christ; that obedience placed it in God's power to elect to salvation; that no creed was necessary for the church, but simply the Scriptures literally interpreted; and that all baptized persons had a right to administer the ordinance of baptism.[2] About 1832, with Barton W. Stone and others, Alexander Campbell founded the Disciples of Christ.

The movement of Campbell did not make a great impact on the Atlantic seaboard Baptist churches from Pennsylvania and Jersey southward, partly because his Arminian theology could not counter the vigorous Calvinism of that section. West of the Alleghenies, however, the strict biblicism which he asserted, along with a latent Arminianism that had moved westward after the American Revolution, attracted large numbers of Baptists. Many Baptist ministers were won to his views and brought their entire churches into his movement. As far west as Texas in 1841, Campbell's followers split Baptist churches.[3] No definite figures are available, but there can be little doubt that hundreds of Baptist churches left the denomination to follow Campbell. State bodies felt the influence of the movement long after the beginning of the next period in 1845.[4]

Antimissionism

The antimission movement among Southern Baptists has complex roots. Robert G. Torbet is correct in assigning many contributing factors, including theological differences, the development of organizations for carrying on the work, hostility toward the Indians when missions were directed toward them, the fear that eastern leaders might get financial and political control of Baptist church polity through administering the missionary funds, misunderstanding and misinterpretation of the work being done, jealousy toward the better trained clergy of the East who came as missionaries, the low state of vitality in many churches that opposed anything demanding effort or finances, and the opposition of charismatic leaders. In addition to these, one can glimpse the appeal made by antimission leaders to a rigid unenlightened biblicism, the Old Testament flavor of the denunciatory tones of the antimission leaders (some of whom tried to leave the impression that they were of the prophetic order), and various other sectional and local factors.[5]

It cannot be determined exactly who began the southern phase of the antimission movement. Daniel Parker claimed to be the first one "to draw the sword against the error," but B. H. Carroll, Jr., doubted the truth of this. Carroll felt that John Taylor of Kentucky, a pioneer in the settlement of Kentucky and Tennessee, antedated Parker in advocating antimissionism. In many ways Taylor was the most admirable of all the antimission leaders, although even his language sometimes was unkind and incorrect. His principal polemic was a pamphlet entitled *Thoughts on Missions,* written on October 27, 1819, when Taylor was sixty-seven years old. In this document Taylor charged that missionaries were simply involved in the movement because of their love for money, and that the missionary system was hierarchical in its tendencies and contrary to Baptist church government.[6]

Daniel Parker first wrote on antimissionism a year after Taylor had published his pamphlet. Parker was born in Culpeper County, Virginia, in 1781, reared in Georgia, and was described by John Mason Peck, who apparently was not impressed by him, as "without education, uncouth in manner, slovenly in dress, diminutive in person, unprepossessing in appearance, with shrivelled features and a small, piercing eye." [7]

Parker's doctrine of the *Two Seeds in the Spirit* divided the human race into the predestined children of God and the predestined children of the devil. God will save his own; the devil will claim his own. There was no place for missions in his theology. Most of his ministry was carried on in Tennessee and Illinois. In 1833 he led a church from Illinois into the Mexican province of Texas, probably the first Baptist church there. He died in 1844 after organizing a number of churches in east Texas.[8] He greatly influenced Wilson Thompson, another well-known antimissionist.

As has been mentioned previously, Alexander Campbell was also a strong opposer of missions. Most of the other antimission leaders were strong Calvinists or hyper-Calvinists, claiming that it was blasphemy for men to attempt to win people to salvation whom God had not elected, or to try to win people whom God had elected, because these efforts amounted to taking the work of God out of God's hands. Campbell, on the other hand, was an Arminian. He claimed that his opposition was primarily to methods rather than the principle of missions, but as one reads his vitriolic and sarcastic arguments against missions and missionaries, many of which were manifestly untrue as well as unfair, it seems likely that his views concerning the church and the ministry were more dominant than his view of the atonement.[9]

Another influential antimission leader in the South was Joshua Lawrence, veteran pastor in Edgecomb County, North Carolina, who had many followers in Georgia, Alabama, and Mississippi. The Kehukee Association, to which he belonged, had been missionary from almost the time it was founded in 1769. About the year 1820 Lawrence published a pamphlet opposing missions. By 1826 the antimission party in this association became organized and vocal. In 1827 the association adopted a resolution to "discard all Missionary Societies, Bible Societies and Theological Seminaries, . . ." The exact action that was taken at this time was disputed from the beginning.[10] At any rate, the year 1827 marked the beginning of the antimission schism in North Carolina. The Kehukee Association became the rallying point for antimissionism in a large area surrounding it. "Kehukeeism" became synonymous with "Hardshellism," "Primitivism," and the anti-effort movement.

Still another center of antimissionism developed in the old Baltimore Association. This association was formed in 1793 and was an active missionary body in its early years. After the adjournment of the 1832 meeting at the Warren church, however, the anti-effort party called for a meeting to "oppose all these inventions of men"—missionary, Bible, and tract societies; Sunday Schools; etc.—declaring they were the "progeny of Arminianism." A call was then made for "all Old School Baptist Churches" to send delegates to a convention. On September 28-30, 1832, this convention met at the Black Rock church, Baltimore County, Maryland. The nonlocal leadership of this meeting was shown by the fact that William Gilmore of Virginia was elected moderator, while Gabriel Conkling of New Jersey became clerk. The principal voice in the meeting was that of Gilbert Beebe, pastor in New York, who edited *The Signs of the Times* for forty-nine years proclaiming the anti-effort position. His language may be glimpsed in the address published by this group.

upholding the principles of genuine Christianity, and denouncing the Arminian men-made societies that had so rapidly increased in number and influence within a few years, and which seemed designed to supplant the church of God itself, and scatter to the winds the faith and practice and all the ancient landmarks of God's chosen people.[11]

This address, prepared by a committee of seven (including Beebe), was totally anti-effort. Missions, Christian tract distributions, Sunday Schools, theological education, and Bible societies were pungently anathematized.[12]

Four years later, on May 12, 1836, the Baltimore Association's regular meeting was held at the Black Rock church, "attended by only 28 persons, seven of whom were not properly authorized messengers, and the one elected as moderator was not a member of the body." [13] By a vote of sixteen to nine, a resolution expelling all "uniting with and encouraging others to unite in worldly societies" was passed. The missionary-minded churches formed another association with the same name as the old one, but this body was greatly weakened when several of the stronger churches affiliated with the Maryland Baptist Union Association, organized in 1836.

The effect of the antimission movements (including Campbell) on Southern Baptists was devastating. Many churches and sometimes whole associations declared themselves antimissionary. The western frontier, in particular, felt their blighting effect.[14]

From 1820 to 1840, they wrecked the missionary cause on the frontier and created confusion in the older states, throughout the South and beyond. They reached their zenith about 1840. From that time they began to decline, but not before causing untold harm to the cause of missions in the South.

Baptists lost a large percentage of their total strength to the antimission movement. A large number left the denomination with Campbell, though the exact figure cannot be accurately estimated, as no sources on this point are available. Others refused to join the Baptists because of the controversy. Schools and colleges were not founded in the West during this time, further delaying the growth and progress of Baptists for lack of trained leadership.[15]

Sectionalism

Nowhere can the overwhelming effects of social, economic, and political factors upon religious life be glimpsed more clearly than in the story of the separation between Northern and Southern Baptists in 1845. The settlement of the West, for example, was likely the principal factor that brought the formation of the American Baptist Home Mission Society in 1832; it was this settled West that within a few years became the greatest political threat to eastern suzerainty, particularly in the Senate, and fanned the flames of sectionalism to the consuming point.[16] As Marcus Lee Hansen pointed out, the problem of slaveholding was not in itself divisive, but translated into political control through the support of a common institution of this sort, it multiplied sectionalism to its highest component.

Simply stated, sectionalism is the advocacy of any particular interest by a community, whether local or widespread, that shares in that interest. Sectionalism has played a large part in American history. Perhaps the classic treatment is that of Frederick Jackson Turner, *The Significance of Sections in American History*. Sectionalism may be glimpsed in the Constitutional Convention, for example, when Gouverneur Morris of Pennsylvania, asserting the sectional interests of the Atlantic states, wanted to arrange the ratio of representation in the national government so that the number of representatives from the Atlantic states would always be larger than the number from the western states. As A. L. Burt pointed out, the early West was strongly conscious of its peculiar needs and struggled vigorously for its sectional interests. New England displayed sectionalism in the Hartford Convention; so did Georgia in the litigation with the Creek and Cherokee Indians. The Nullification Ordinance of 1832 by South Carolina almost brought civil war over sectionalism without reference to slaveholding or abolitionism.[17]

The literature has many instances of sectional differences between Northern and Southern Baptists during this period. The Annuals of the Home Mission Society printed complaints from different parts of the West (the South Central region) and the South to the effect that their sections were being neglected in the appointment of missionaries and asserting that a mission society in the remote northeast could not understand the needs of other sections. The Kentucky Baptist paper, for example, in 1837 alleged that the southern states were being neglected in the appointment of missionaries, and urged the formation of a southern home mission society.[18] The Georgia Baptist paper in 1840 advocated the formation of a "Southern society" to transmit funds for the "Texian mission" in the event the Home Mission Society did not heed the call.[19] Both papers alleged that the southern states were sending more money to the society than was being expended on sending missionaries to the South.[20]

Relative to the claims that the South was furnishing more money to the society than was being expended for missionaries to work in the South, it is difficult to untangle the true facts. C. B. Goodykoontz insisted that Kentucky, Tennessee, and Missouri were *western*, not *southern* states at this time; if this be so, southern states gave $28,149 for missions between 1832 and 1841 through the society, while the society expended only $13,646.50 in the South during that time. However, if these are counted southern states during that period, the society expended about the same amount as was contributed by the South. It is true that the Southwest (Kentucky, Tennessee, Louisiana, Mississippi, Arkansas, and Missouri) was greatly neglected in comparison with the amount of missionary work done by the society in the Northwest (Illinois, Indiana, Michigan, and Ohio).[21] The greatest problem faced by the society at this point was to find missionaries willing to work in the South because, according to Goodykoontz, the missionaries were principally northern people who preferred not to live in the midst of Negro slavery, they felt that they would not be welcomed by the people in the South, and many feared the enervating climate. Another element was the fact that the northern valley of the Mississippi River was filled with people from the North, especially from New England, and northern missionaries preferred to work among their own people in that area.[22]

It was likely this sectional wrangle over home missions that caused Robert T. Daniel to organize a Southern Baptist society for home missions, with headquarters in Columbus, Mississippi, asserting that the mission needs of the region were the only motivation for forming the body.[23] Similarly, the attempt to form "a general organization for home missionary operations throughout the western valley" in 1839 at Louisville, Kentucky, was motivated only by home mission needs in the Mississippi Valley, and not by abolition-slavery considerations.[24]

However, the greatest sectional issue ever to confront the American nation was Negro slavery. It had been introduced into Virginia in 1619, and at first was vigorously resisted by the southern colonies. Against the wishes of the colonists and nullifying repeated acts by some of the colonial legislatures, Great Britain forced a profitable slave trade to be continued.[25] In the Declaration of Independence, as originally drawn by Thomas Jefferson, it was stated that among the grievances which produced the Revolution was that the King of England had steadfastly resisted the efforts of the colonies to prevent the introduction of slaves.

W. W. Barnes pointed out that slavery was not a divisive issue until the 1830's.

> The principle and practice of slavery were not divisive issues when the national government was established on the basis of the federal Constitution. There was opposition to slavery in the South and in the North. It had not become a sectional issue. In the 1787 convention that framed the constitution, it was proposed to give Congress the authority to limit the trade in slaves. A committee, the majority of which were from the free states, reported adversely, denying Congress the power at any period to prohibit the African slave trade. Later, another committee, the majority of which were from the slave states, reported a new section giving Congress the authority to prohibit the trade after 1800. The commercial interests of New England especially hindered leaders in the Southern and Middle states from including provisions in the federal Constitution that would curtail the traffic both in time and extent. A manumission society was formed in Tennessee in the second decade of the century, and in 1817 it presented a memorial on slavery to the legislature. The leader of the society, Elihu Embree, published in Jonesborough, Tennessee, in 1820, *The Emancipator,* the first antislavery paper in the United States.
>
> Baptists in the Southern states contributed their part of the opposition to slavery. They gained their first supporters among the population within the lower economic brackets. Hence, most of their members were found among the nonslaveholding majority of the population of the South. In the upper South, where plantation life was not on a scale so extensive, this was especially true. In Virginia, Kentucky, and other states, associations passed resolutions against slavery. In 1828, the Cherokee church sent a remonstrance to the Holston Association, Tennessee, against the traffic in slaves. The association unanimously approved the remonstrance. In Kentucky, Baptist churches and associations, known as the "Friends of Humanity," passed resolutions of nonfellowship with slaveowners. Many of these Baptists left Kentucky for Missouri, thus strengthening the antislavery sentiment in that state. Many Baptist families, among them that of Thomas Lincoln, father of Abraham Lincoln, left Kentucky for Indiana and Illinois, because of opposition to slavery south of the Ohio.
>
> Of all the divisive issues in American life in the second quarter of the nineteenth century, slavery cut the deepest because it was at once a political, economic, social, moral, and religious issue. But not until the opposition took the form of abolitionism in the 1830's did the issue begin to portend those divisions in the religious and political spheres realized in the following decades.[26]

As late as 1832, when the American Baptist Home Mission Society was formed, the issue was not yet divisive. Two men who later became active leaders of Baptist abolitionism (Elon Galusha and Duncan Dunbar) were on the Board of Directors for the society; and in a resolution offered by Galusha, he made it plain that at that time he saw no objection to cooperating with the South in home missions.

The documents reveal almost exactly the time the issue became divisive among American Baptists. Baptists in England had been in the forefront of the agitation in that country to eliminate slavery in the West Indies. In 1833 the English Parliament passed legislation designed to eliminate all slavery in the Empire by 1838. Rejoicing in this victory, English Baptists on December 31, 1833, addressed American Baptists in a lengthy treatise and described the victory of the English emancipation movement. The letter concluded by asking:

> Is it [slavery] not an awful breach of the Divine law, a manifest infraction of that social compact which is always and everywhere binding? And if it be so, are you not, as Christians, and especially as Christian ministers, bound to protest against it, and to seek, by all legitimate means, its speedy and entire destruction? [27]

This letter promptly divided American Baptists, although the division was not yet clearly between the North and the South. On September 1, 1834, Corresponding Secretary Lucius Bolles replied for the General Missionary Convention, enclosing official resolutions by the Boston board. The gist of these resolutions was that the constitution of the General Convention precluded any discussion on this subject.

> We have the best evidence that our slaveholding brethren are Christians, sincere followers of the Lord Jesus. In every other part of their conduct, they adorn the doctrine of God our Savior. We cannot, therefore, feel that it is right to use language or adopt measures which might tend to break the ties that unite them to us in our General Convention, and in numerous other benevolent societies; and to array brother against brother, church against church, and association against association in a contest about slavery. [28]

However, as soon as this correspondence was published, about fifty Baptist ministers met at Boston on May 26-27, 1835, and voted their approval of another reply, which was subsequently signed by about 130 Baptist ministers before it was mailed. This letter acknowledged the guilt of slaveholding and pledged all efforts "to labor in the use of weapons not carnal but mighty through God to the overthrow of this as well as every other work of wickedness." [29]

The supporters of abolitionism increased rapidly in numbers in American Baptist ranks. Agitation from abroad continued. During 1835 two distinguished Baptist abolitionists from England toured America in behalf of their views, although they said very little about the slavery issue. [30] In 1836 a flood of strong abolitionist resolutions were published from English Baptist associations. Meanwhile, the slave uprisings in the South, which endangered the lives of the whites there, and the increasing political emphasis in abolitionism tended to polarize the antagonists North and South. Baron Stow, one of the leaders in the General Convention, is an example of the shift toward dominant abolitionist sympathies. In 1837, answering for the General Convention another letter from the English abolitionists, Stow said that since "the constitution of the Board limits them to the business of Foreign Missions, they will not, under existing circumstances, intermeddle in any way the question of slavery." However, in the following year Stow replied to still another letter from the English Baptists, and this time he urged the English brethren to be patient "and not think us tardy in accomplishing an object which we, as well as they, are anxious to see immediately effected." By this time he had become an avowed abolitionist proponent.[31]

Baptist abolitionism was accelerated by the organization of the American Baptist Anti-Slavery Convention. The initial meeting took place in New York on April 28-30, 1840, with about 100 in attendance. At this meeting two addresses were prepared, one to Northern and one to Southern Baptists. The address to the South was vigorously written and widely circulated throughout the South. Recognizing that most of the states had passed laws, because of slave uprisings, which legally forbade southerners to free their slaves, the address urged the Baptists to "forsake, like Abraham, your father-land, and carry your children and your households to the vast asylum of our prairies and our wilderness."[32] Partly as a result of this agitation and the bitterness it engendered among Baptists in the South, the several societies felt it necessary to issue circulars affirming their neutrality. Both the General Convention for Foreign Missions and the Home Mission Society based their neutrality upon their constitutions. The foreign mission body took this action in December, 1840, while the Home Mission Society published their disclaimer on February 16, 1841.[33] The editor of the *Christian Watchman* of New York frowned upon the agitation taking place in 1840, remarking that the fellowship of the churches should not be "a matter of convenience, a matter of retaliation, nor a tool of political philanthropy."

When the General Convention met in Baltimore in 1841 for its triennial session, a determined effort was made by northern and southern leaders to maintain the unity of the body. At a caucus in mid-April just before the opening of the convention, a group of northern and southern leaders prepared a Compromise Article which in effect condemned abolitionists as introducing new tests for Christian fellowship in benevolent work. This was signed by seventy-four of the principal northern and southern leaders.[34] It probably delayed the separation of the two sections for a few years.

The newspaper controversies over slavery-abolitionism, however, intensified during 1842 and 1843. A literary battle of particular vehemence and bitterness erupted just before the meeting of the three societies in 1844. This set the stage for the critical anniversaries of 1844. Controversy began on December 27, 1843, when an anonymous inquiry in the Baptist paper of New Hampshire asked whether or not it was true that James Huckins and William Tryon, missionaries of the Home Mission Society in Texas, were slaveholders. Baptist papers in North Carolina, Boston, Maine, Georgia, and other areas quickly joined a lively discussion. It developed that James Huckins of Vermont had purchased a slave after beginning his work in Texas, while William Tryon had married a Georgia woman who owned slaves. This confrontation continued to the very week of the benevolent anniversaries. The minutes of the societies made explicit reference to this last extensive newspaper fuss. The Home Mission Society in 1844 appointed a committee to work out plans for the amicable dissolution of the society,[35] while the General Convention revealed that it was overwhelmingly abolitionist in its spirit.

An exception to the abusive language of the time was provided by the literary debate in Baptist papers between President Francis Wayland of Brown University and Richard Fuller, pastor in South Carolina at this time. Although they advocated opposite sides of the issue, the two men were courteous, logical, and explicit, qualities which most of the literature of this period did not exhibit.[36]

Meanwhile, on May 4, 1843, Baptist abolitionists met in separate convention and organized a mission society which subsequently supported both foreign and home missions.[37] Some of the prominent abolitionists preferred not to join this society but to remain within the constituted bodies and make strong efforts to separate Southern Baptists from these bodies.[38]

The crisis came in 1844. Georgia Baptists were not satisfied with the neutrality assurances of the Home Mission Society, since many of the leaders of the society were busy in abolitionist activities. On August 2, 1844, the Georgia Baptist Executive Committee submitted to the Home Mission Society the name of James E. Reeve for appointment, openly volunteering the information to the society that Reeve was a slaveholder.[39] After many discussions about Reeve, the Executive Board refused to consider the application for the appointment of Reeve because this application constituted a test, and as such, violated the purposes and letter of the constitution, compromised the principles of the neutrality circular issued by the society in 1841, ignored a resolution introduced in 1841 by Richard Fuller which denied the right of anyone to introduce the subject of slavery or anti-slavery into the society, and, because of all of this, threatened to destroy the harmony of the society. Georgia Baptists were wroth.[40]

The final event that led to separation was initiated in Alabama. The Baptist state convention met in November, 1844, and on November 25, addressed a resolution to the General Convention demanding the distinct avowal that slaveholders were equally eligible to all the privileges enjoyed by nonslaveholders, especially with reference to the appointment of agents and missionaries. Under date of December 17, 1844, although not released for publication until much later, the Acting Board replied to the Alabama Resolutions to the effect that if anyone having slaves should offer himself as a missionary "and should insist on retaining them as his property, we could not appoint him. One thing is certain; we can never be a party to any arrangement which would imply approbation of slavery."[41]

When this correspondence came to the attention of the Virginia Baptist Foreign Mission Society, they issued an official call for a consultative meeting of Baptists of the South "to confer on the best means of promoting the Foreign Mission cause, and other interests of the Baptist denomination in the South." Augusta, Georgia, was suggested as a meeting place, and the first part of May was named as a possible date.[42]

In 1845, when the anniversaries of the three principal societies were held at Providence, Rhode Island, there were few Baptists from the South in attendance. They had turned their eyes toward Augusta.

Notes

1. Baker, *Source Book*, pp. 77-78.
2. *Ibid.*, p. 78.
3. Baker, *The Blossoming Desert*, pp. 78-81.
4. See Errett Gates, *The Early Relation and Separation of Baptists and Disciples* (Chicago: R. R. Donnelly & Sons, 1904), pp. 67 ff.
5. Robert G. Torbet, *A History of the Baptists* (Valley Forge: The Judson Press, Fifth Printing, 1953), pp. 268-69.
6. See Baker, *Source Book*, pp. 79-81, for copious extracts from this pamphlet.
7. B. H. Carroll, Jr., *The Genesis of American Anti-Missionism* (Louisville: The Baptist Book Concern, 1902), p. 91.
8. J. M. Carroll, *A History of Texas Baptists* (Dallas: Baptist Standard Publishing Co., 1923), pp. 45 ff.
9. B. H. Carroll, Jr., *op. cit.*, pp. 124-55.
10. C. B. Hassell, *History of the Church of God From the Creation to A. D. 1885,* revised and completed by Sylvester Hassell (Middletown, New York: Gilbert Beebe's Sons, 1886), pp. 763 ff. See also Henry Sheets, *Who Are Primitive Baptists?* (Raleigh, N. C.: Edwards and Broughton Printing Co., c1908).
11. Hassell, *op. cit.*, p. 900.
12. See Baker, *Source Book* for excerpts from the *Address*, pp. 82-84.
13. Cox and Woolley, eds., *Encyclopedia*, II, p. 830.
14. Sweet, op. cit., p. 62, pp. 67-68.
15. Cox and Woolley, eds., *Encyclopedia*, I, p. 54.
16. Baker, *Relations*, pp. 16-26.
17. *Ibid.*, pp. 16-19.
18. Baker, *Source Book*, p. 84.

19. Baker, *Relations,* pp. 33, 36 ff.

20. Baker, *Source Book,* pp. 84-85.

21. Baker, *Relations,* pp. 34-37.

22. *Ibid.,* pp. 38-39, and note the documentation.

23. Baker, *Source Book,* pp. 84 ff.

24. *Ibid.,* pp. 86-87.

25. *Ibid.,* pp. 88-89.

26. Barnes, *op. cit.,* pp. 18-19. See also Baker, *Relations,* pp. 18-21.

27. Baker, *Source Book,* pp. 87-88.

28. *Ibid.,* pp. 89-90.

29. *Ibid.,* p. 90.

30. Baker, *Relations,* p. 42.

31. Baker, *Source Book,* pp. 90-91.

32. *Ibid.,* pp. 92-94.

33. *Ibid.,* pp. 55 ff.

34. *Ibid.,* p. 100.

35. See Baker, *Relations,* pp. 67-68 for the detailed story.

36. Richard Fuller and Francis Wayland, *Domestic Slavery Considered As a Scriptural Institution* (New York: Lewis Colby, 1845), pp. 101-4.

37. Baker, *Source Book,* pp. 94-95.

38. See J. A. Smith, *Memoir of Nathaniel Colver* (Boston: George A. Foxcroft, Jr., 1875), p. 199; also *The Emancipator* (New York), May 25, 1843.

39. Baker, *Source Book,* pp. 105-6.

40. Baker, *Relations,* pp. 74-75.

41. Baker, *Source Book,* pp. 106-8 has the Alabama Resolutions and the reply.

42. *Ibid.,* pp. 109-13.

PERIOD FOUR
A NEW DIRECTION
1845-1860

From the Formation of the Southern Baptist Convention to Civil War

9 The Southern Baptist Convention

When Baptists from various parts of the South met at Augusta, Georgia, on May 8, 1845, in response to the call issued by the Virginia Baptist Foreign Mission Society, some of them had been giving considerable thought to the kind of denominational body or bodies that Baptists in the South should organize. The kind of structure finally adopted was, in fact, somewhat of a departure from the former practice of carrying on benevolent work through separate, autonomous societies. The ancient dilemma that they faced, the kind of organization that they formed, and their new relationship to the older societies in the North will be considered briefly in this chapter.

An Old Dilemma

Southern Baptists in 1845 faced the same basic problem that has confronted all Baptist groups who have attempted to establish denominational bodies; namely, how to unite independent churches into an effective denominational structure without overwhelming the autonomy of the local congregations. It should be noted that this was a relatively new problem in the history of Christianity. This does not mean that the principle of congregational autonomy was new. In intensive linguistic and theological research, non-Baptists like **161**

F. J. A. Hort, as well as non-Landmark Baptists like John L. Dagg, John A. Broadus, John R. Sampey, and H. E. Dana have described the autonomous nature of the primitive churches. *Clement of Rome,* one of the earliest noncanonical writings, provides evidence that at the close of the first century this autonomy still existed among the churches. This letter, addressed by the church at Rome to the church at Corinth about A.D. 96, was written because the latter church had dismissed some of their elders who had been put into office by the apostles themselves. The Corinthian church had taken this action without asking the permission of anyone, and the letter from Rome was an appeal for reconsideration. The Roman letter gives no indication that any other church or individual could require the Corinthian church to reinstate these leaders.

However, even though congregational autonomy was practiced in primitive Christianity, the problem of the best way to structure independent churches for benevolent work was not faced because no such general bodies were organized during the period of congregational autonomy. There were no associations, state conventions, missionary societies, or national bodies for benevolent work in the first century. One could hardly confuse Paul's concept of the church as the Body of Christ with a geographic and organizational structure.

The assumption of church government by the bishops interrupted further development in this area. There were probably monarchical bishops in Asia Minor by A.D. 165 and in Rome not long thereafter. The Council of Nicaea in A.D. 325 made reference to large areas of control by strong bishops, and a papal structure was evident by the time of Chalcedon in A.D. 451. The independence of the local congregations was swept away with the rise of territorial bishops, so there was no particular problem in structuring a strong hierarchical body under an authoritative judicature which ultimately was headed by the pope at Rome. After Constantine, the Roman Empire provided both the pattern and the assistance for developing a Catholic church which held sway almost universally until the Reformation. In sixteenth-century England the *imperium* and *sacerdotium* were united in the person of the sovereign, bringing to its ultimate form in this country the concept of Constantine that the sovereign was the bishop of the bishops. In this same country and in the same century, the rise of congregationalism, in which the authority of the local body was enunciated, set the stage for a new type of polity.

Thus, all groups in the sixteenth century holding to congregational autonomy were forced to pioneer in the development of denominational structures beyond the local level. English independency developed on theological and historical grounds, and serious consideration was not given initially to the question of how that type of ecclesiology could be utilized in forming effective denominational structures. As a matter of fact, both English and American Congregationalists have wavered at the point of denominational structure. A "semi-Presbyterian conception of the internal government of the church," says Williston Walker, "instead of a democracy of Browne, dominated all early English and American Congregationalism." [1]

English Baptists, emphasizing extensively and precisely the authority of the congregation, were faced with the problem of devising denominational structures beyond the local church in such fashion that congregational autonomy would be maintained. In the 1650's English Baptists developed associations, and General Baptists structured their General Assembly of General Baptist Churches. However, in their struggle to prevent heresy and maintain unity through their General Assembly, General Baptists compromised the autonomy of the congregations related to this general body, as mentioned in an earlier chapter. They gave so much authority to general bodies that the local congregations lost their autonomy. It is no wonder that the historian of General Baptists in Suffolk remarked that their church order was more Presbyterian than Baptist.

English Particular Baptists, on the other hand, were reluctant to organize beyond the associational level. A loose type of union was created in 1689 called the General Assembly of Particular Baptists. Their point of view with reference to polity was seen in a Confession of 1677, reprinted by order of the new body in 1689, which said:

> These messengers assembled are not intrusted with any church-power properly so-called; or with any jurisdiction over the churches, themselves, to exercise any censures either over any churches or persons; or to impose their determination on the churches or officers. [2]

General Baptists in England, therefore, dealt with the problem of local church autonomy versus denominationalism by making the denominational structure inhibitive, while Particular Baptists attacked the same problem by limiting the effectiveness of the general body as a means of safeguarding the autonomy of the churches.

American Baptists also faced the question of church independency as they began to organize beyond the local level. The first association in America organized in Philadelphia in 1707 carefully refrained from usurping the autonomy of the churches. In 1749 it adopted an Essay which plainly said that an association

> is not a superior judicature, having such superior power over the churches concerned; but that each particular church hath a complete power and authority from Jesus Christ, to administer all gospel ordinances, provided they have a sufficiency of officers duly qualified, or that they be supplied by the officers of another sister church or churches, as baptism, and the Lord's supper, &c.; and to receive in

and cast out, and also to try and ordain their own officers, and to exercise every part of gospel discipline and church government, independent of any other church or assembly whatever.[3]

As pointed out previously, it is likely that the rapid swing from the associational program for carrying on missions to the society plan for carrying on these activities was caused by the extreme sensitiveness toward developing ecclesiastical bodies that might usurp the autonomy of the local churches.

The struggle of the founding fathers of the General Missionary Convention in 1814 to find the proper direction between 1814 and 1832 has already been described. Through the influence of Francis Wayland, the autonomy of the churches was safeguarded by the organization of independent societies for carrying on the several benevolences of American Baptists between 1814 and 1845. Wayland, in fact, was so opposed to denominational structures that might inhibit the local congregations that he even urged the elimination of state conventions and their replacement with missionary societies in each state.[4]

Thus, in 1845 when Southern Baptists met at Augusta, Georgia, the old dilemma of how to unite independent churches for effective denominational functions without violating their autonomy was one of their basic problems and a very live issue.

A Proposed Structure

One of the ablest minds among Southern Baptists in 1845 was that of William B. Johnson, president of the South Carolina Baptist Convention. He was the only person at the meeting in 1845 who had been in the organizational sessions of the General Missionary Convention in 1814 and had served as president of that body. He also had been a member of the committee to prepare the constitution of the General Convention. His genius had been displayed on many occasions in his defense of missionary societies and the organization of state bodies when they were very much opposed by some of his brethren.

Johnson, as president of the state body, called a special meeting of the South Carolina Baptist Convention on May 3, 1845, one week before the meeting to take place at Augusta, Georgia. In a lengthy address he confessed that despite his personal involvement in the organization of the General Missionary Convention, he had now reluctantly come to the conclusion that there must be separation. He compared the situation to that when Paul and Barnabas had sharp contention and separated one from the other on the second missionary journey, and as a result, "two lines of service were opened for the benefit of the churches."

Such, I trust, will be the result of the separation between the Baptists of these United States in their general benevolent Institutions. When we embarked in the cause of Foreign Missions, the union of the whole denomination was necessary, for it was then comparatively small. But now, such state of things, that we may part asunder and open two lines of service to the heathen and the destitute, instead of one only, and the vast increase in our numbers, and the wide extent of territory, over which we are spread, seem to indicate the hope, that our separation will be attended with no sharpness of contention, with no bitterness of spirit. We are all the servants of the same Master, "desirous of doing the will of God from the heart." Let us, then, in generous rivalry, "provoke each other to love and good works." [5]

Johnson went on to say in this message that in view of the need for a new organization, he wished to offer a suggestion. He called their attention to the fact that they had been functioning for years past through the use of a separate and autonomous society for each benevolence. He then proposed the formation of

one Convention, embodying the whole Denomination, together with separate and distinct Boards, for each object of benevolent enterprise, located at different places, and all amenable to the Convention. [6]

This kind of organization, Johnson said, would provide judicious concentration, which he termed "of the first moment in all combinations of men for important enterprises."

In its successful operation, the whole Denomination will be united in one body for the purpose of well-doing, with perfect liberty secured to each contributor of specifying the object or objects, to which his amount shall be applied, as he please, whilst he or his Delegation may share in the deliberations and control of all the objects, promoted by the Convention. [7]

It is evident from this that Johnson was suggesting a different kind of denominational organization than the one utilizing the three autonomous benevolent societies as had been done heretofore. Disdaining the possibility of overwhelming the authority of local congregations, Johnson was suggesting a more centralized body that would have control over all the benevolent objects projected by Southern Baptists.

The Consultative Convention

In his study of the enrollment of the messengers at the meeting in Augusta, Georgia, on May 8, 1845, W. W. Barnes concluded that there were 293 separate accredited messengers attending the meeting. All but twenty of these were from Georgia, South Carolina, and Virginia. The others were from Alabama, District of Columbia, Kentucky, Louisiana, Maryland, and North Carolina. In addition, one corresponding messenger from Pennsylvania and the American Baptist

Publications Society attended. The messenger from Kentucky was Isaac McCoy, the renowned Indian missionary.

Most of the leaders in Kentucky, as well as Tennessee and Mississippi, questioned the wisdom of separation at this time. Editor W. C. Buck of Kentucky pointed out that the Acting Board (which served for the full Board between its annual meetings and for the full General Missionary Convention between its triennial meetings and had made the reply to the Alabama Resolutions) could not finally speak for the full Board nor for the General Convention, and that Southern Baptists should wait until the next full meeting of the convention in 1847 before taking precipitate action. The editor of the *Biblical Recorder* of North Carolina, Thomas Meredith, agreed with this, as did the Board of the Tennessee Baptist Foreign Mission Society. R.B.C. Howell of Nashville sent a letter to Augusta asking for a delay in the meeting, remarking that Tennessee, Mississippi, Arkansas, Missouri, and Kentucky did not have time to appoint representatives, and also suggested that the General Convention probably would not sustain the Board at its meeting in 1847. The call issued by the Virginia Baptist Foreign Mission Society was not published until April 10, and there was hardly time for many of the southern societies and state bodies to meet, elect messengers, and discuss the issues, even if there had been good communication and transportation. That almost three hundred messengers appeared at Augusta was remarkable. At the first meeting it was announced that Mississippi, Tennessee, Arkansas, and Florida had sent letters, due to the fact that the short notice of the meeting prevented further representation.

On the opening day, William B. Johnson of South Carolina was named president; Wilson Lumpkin of Georgia and J. B. Taylor of Virginia were vice-presidents; and Jesse Hartwell of Alabama and J. C. Crane of Virginia were secretaries. A committee of one from each state represented, along with seven others, was appointed to prepare a preamble and resolution. In the afternoon Richard Fuller, the chairman, submitted the report, which was discussed during the remainder of the day.

The entire second day (Friday, May 9) was spent reviewing and making verbal amendments to the preamble and resolution presented by the committee on the previous day. The preamble specifically named the action of the Boston board, in their answers to the Alabama Resolutions, as evidence that the board "most clearly and unnecessarily exceeded their power and violated their trust." The preamble continued:

> It is a question admitting no debate, that the Triennial Convention was formed on the principle of a perfect equality of members, from the South and North. And what is all important, the very qualifications

of missionaries are prescribed by the original constitution of that Convention,—the fifth article providing that "such persons as are in full communion with some regular church of our denomination, and who furnish satisfactory evidence of genuine piety, good talents and fervent zeal for the Redeemer's cause, are to be employed as missionaries."

Besides this, too, the declaration of the Board, that if "any one should offer himself as a missionary, having slaves, and should insist on retaining them as his property, we could not appoint him," is an innovation and a departure from the course hitherto pursued by the Triennial Convention, (such persons having been appointed). And lastly, the decision of the Board is an infraction of the resolution passed the last spring, in Philadelphia; and the General Board at their late meeting in Providence, have failed to reverse this decision.[8]

The resolution that accompanied this preamble read:

Resolved, That for peace and harmony, and in order to accomplish the greatest amount of good, and for the maintainance of those scriptural principles on which the General Missionary Convention of the Baptist denomination of the United States, was originally formed, it is proper that this Convention at once proceed to organize a Society for the propagation of the Gospel.[9]

The preamble and the resolution were adopted separately after extensive discussion. Then, upon motion, eight additional names were added to this same committee, including William B. Johnson to act as its chairman, "who should prepare and report a Constitution for a Southern Association."

On the third day (Saturday, May 10) the body met at 8:00 A.M., and the day was spent receiving and approving a preamble and constitution for the new body. In the preamble the purpose of the new body was named as "carrying into effect the benevolent intentions of our constituents, by organizing a plan for eliciting, combining and directing the energies of the whole denomination in one sacred effort, for the propagation of the Gospel." The constitution finally adopted was almost precisely, in many instances word for word, the one suggested by William B. Johnson during the previous week at the meeting of the South Carolina convention. The critical section of the new constitution was Article V, by which the body departed radically from the society principle that each organization should deal with only one benevolence. The new article provided:

The Convention shall elect at each triennial meeting as many Boards of Managers, as in its judgment will be necessary for carrying out the benevolent objects it may determine to promote, all which Boards shall continue in office until a new election. . . . To each Board shall be committed, during the recess of the Convention, the entire management of all the affairs relating to the object with whose interest it shall be charged.[10]

This constitution was discussed seriatim and adopted unanimously. One change was discussed carefully. The committee had suggested that the body should be called the Southern and Southwestern Baptist Convention. When the motion came to strike out "Southwestern," many expressed their fears that "Southern" was such a sectional name that their constituents might take exception to it.

This completed, the convention upon motion appointed William B. Johnson, Thomas Curtis, Richard Fuller, and C. D. Mallary as a committee to prepare an Address to the Public setting forth the reasons which led to the formation of this body.

J. B. Jeter of Virginia then submitted a resolution raising a question that had been in the minds of all during the first two days of the meeting. His resolution proposed:

> That the individuals, churches and other bodies, approving the constitution of the Southern Baptist Convention, adopted by this body, be recommended to meet, according to its provisions, for organization, by members or delegates, on the Wednesday after the first Lord's day in June, 1846, in Richmond, Va.: And that this Convention now proceed to the election of its Officers and Boards of Managers, to continue in office until said meeting.[11]

This resolution brought an extended discussion about whether this consultative convention had the power to take this action. Some messengers said that they had come without instructions from their constituency and for that reason were loath to take part in initiating any organizational action. The presiding officer, W. B. Johnson, expressed a doubt that this body had the power to organize even a provisional government. However, after a long break for lunch the resolution was adopted in the afternoon session, and a provisional structure was organized. W. B. Johnson of South Carolina was elected president, while Wilson Lumpkin of Georgia, James B. Taylor of Virginia, A. Dockery of North Carolina, and R. B. C. Howell of Tennessee were named vice-presidents. M. T. Mendenhall, a medical doctor from South Carolina, was elected treasurer, while Jesse Hartwell of Alabama and James C. Crane of Virginia were named secretaries. A Board of Managers for Foreign Missions, to be located at Richmond, Virginia, was named, with J. B. Jeter of Virginia as president and C. D. Mallary as corresponding secretary. A Board of Managers for Domestic Missions was located at Marion, Alabama, and Basil Manly of Alabama was named president. J. L. Reynolds was elected corresponding secretary of this body.

On Monday the convention met for its closing session, only about a hundred members being present. Several resolutions were passed, as follows: (1) an invitation for auxiliary societies to affiliate with this new body; (2) a request that state conventions and other bodies who might have funds for foreign or domestic missions to forward such funds to the treasurer of the proper board; (3) an appeal for the support of the Indian Mission Association; (4) an instruction to the Board of Domestic Missions to take all prudent measures for the religious instruction of the Negro population; (5) an instruction to the Foreign Mission Board to communicate with the proper board of the General Missionary Convention relative to any claims each may have upon the other; (6) an authorization to the Foreign Mission Board to enter into an arrangement with the General Missionary Convention "to take a portion of its Missions under the patronage of this Convention"; (7) a committee to apply for a charter of incorporation from the state of Georgia; and (8) a recommendation to the Board of Domestic Missions to give attention to the needs of the city of New Orleans. The convention then adjourned to meet the following year in Richmond to perfect a permanent organization.

Meanwhile, however, a charter was secured on December 27, 1845, from the state of Georgia, incorporating the convention "for the purpose of eliciting, combining, and directing the energies of the Baptist Denomination of Christians, for the propagation of the gospel." The two boards also began to function. However, the numbering of the sessions of the Southern Baptist Convention was reckoned from 1846 from the very beginning.

The Address to the Public

There is no evidence that the convention in 1845 saw or approved the Address to the Public which was prepared by its authorization. The document is dated May 12, 1845, and perhaps the committee named to prepare the address simply remained at Augusta after the adjournment of the body.

The address began with a statement that a painful division had taken place in the missionary operations of American Baptists, but remarked that the extent of this disunion should not be exaggerated.

> At the present time it involves only the Foreign and Domestic Missions of the denomination. Northern and Southern Baptists are still brethren. They differ in no article of the faith. They are guided by the same principles of gospel order.[12]

Three main emphases were made by this address. In the first division, it endeavored to show that the cause of the separation was constitutional. It noted that in the early years of the history of the General Missionary Convention "there was no breath of discord between them." It affirmed the resolution passed in the 1841 convention that "in co-operating together, as members of this Convention, in the work of foreign missions, we disclaim all sanction, either expressed or implied, whether of slavery or anti-slavery." The reply to the Alabama Resolutions was described as "a new qualification for missionaries" and a "usurpation of ecclesiastical power." By this decision, continued the address, the Boston board had placed itself in direct opposition to the constitution of the convention. It was noted that at the full meeting of the Board of Managers at Providence in April, 1845, they were entreated to revise and reverse the obnoxious interdict, but instead a resolution expressed sympathy with the Acting Board and sustained them.

The address asserted secondly that the new Southern Baptist Convention would carry on under the principles of the General Missionary Convention.

> The Constitution we adopt is precisely that of the original union; that in connection with which, through his missionary life, Adoniram Judson has lived, and under which Ann Judson and Boardman have died. We recede from it no single step. We have constructed for our basis no new creed; acting in this matter upon a Baptist aversion for all creeds but the Bible. We use the very terms, as we uphold the true spirit and great object of the late "General Convention of the Baptist denomination of the United States." It is they who wrong us that have receded. We have receded neither from the Constitution nor from any part of the original ground on which we met them in this work.[13]

The third emphasis of the address affirmed that the object of the new body was to extend the Messiah's kingdom and the glory of God.

The reason given for separation was basically constitutional. This had been asserted in the call for the consultative convention by Virginia Baptists, had been the burden of the address by William B. Johnson at the called meeting of the South Carolina Baptist Convention just one week before the meeting of the consultative body, and, of course, was the principal thrust of the Address to the Public. It is likely that Francis Wayland had this aspect in mind when he wrote William B. Johnson at the time of the consultative convention and said:

> You will separate of course. I could not ask otherwise. Your rights have been infringed. I will take the liberty of offering one or two suggestions. We have shown how Christians ought not to act, it remains for you to show us how they ought to act. Put away all violence, act with dignity and firmness and the world will approve your course.[14]

It is likely also that it was this constitutional aspect that caused a northern Baptist historian like H. C. Vedder to speak favorably of the southern withdrawal.

Another of the reasons alleged by the South for withdrawal could be called the missionary imperative. Southern leaders were saying, in essence, that the General Missionary Convention and the Home

Mission Society will not appoint slaveholders to serve as missionaries; therefore, under the present situation we are cut off from carrying out the Great Commission. This is what Johnson meant in the address when he asserted that the northern brethren were "forbidding us to speak unto the Gentiles." The argument was that if the South wanted to have any part in sending missionaries, it must form its own organization to do so.

A third argument for separation was based upon ecclesiology. The abolitionists, said the southerners, claim that the missionary societies have the right to judge the moral character and Christian integrity of the slaveholders when, as a matter of fact, it was argued, these prerogatives belong only to a local church. Discipline, it was asserted, is the privilege and responsibility only of the local body of which the person in question is a member. Thus, as Johnson said in his message to the South Carolina convention on May 3, 1845, the prerogatives of the autonomous local body were being taken over by some portions of the missionary societies, which was a breach of Baptist ecclesiology.

Underlying all three of these arguments for separation, of course, was the involvement of the South with the "peculiar institution," and the ordinary prejudices of sectionalism fanned into flames by the political consequences of the spread of this institution into the West.

Another southern argument for separation, however, had nothing to do with slavery. Before this matter ever became seriously controversial, there had been cries from all parts of the South to the effect that a separate body was needed for this section because their missionary needs were not being met by the Home Mission Society. As early as 1837 the editor of the Kentucky Baptist paper wrote:

> It appears from the "last report of the Executive Committee of the American Baptist Home Mission Society" that they have not a single missionary in all Kentucky, Alabama, Louisiana and Florida, and that they partially or entirely sustain one missionary in Mississippi, three in Tennessee and three in Arkansas, making in all seven missionaries for these six states and one Territory . . . only one missionary to every 428,581 souls, while in the state of Michigan, . . . they have sixteen missionaries . . . one missionary to every 4,000 souls. . . . Why are these states (Illinois and Indiana) so liberally supplied? Are they more needy? Are they more destitute? They are more liberally supplied because of Northern contributions, and because Northern preachers refuse to come to the south. . . It is, therefore, apparent, that the only way to produce effort in the south must be brought about by the formation of a Southern Baptist Home Mission Society.[15]

Similar editorials came from other southern states.

Almost simultaneously in 1839, as has been mentioned already, there had been two efforts to establish missionary bodies in the South.

On May 11, 1839, William C. Buck of Kentucky was chairman of a meeting to organize a separate body to have "the general supervision of home missions in this field." It was planned that the organization would be formed

> by delegates from State conventions and associations, and other Baptist bodies, in each State where such general organizations have been formed, and by delegates from Baptist associations, churches, and missionary societies under Baptist management, where such State organizations do not exist.[16]

The skillful maneuvering of John Mason Peck prevented the organization of this body.

However, on May 16, 1839, Robert T. Daniel led in the organization of the Southern Baptist Home Mission Society, with headquarters at Columbus, Mississippi.[17] In the circular calling for this organization, published on March 21, 1839, there is no mention at all made of abolitionism or slavery, which had not yet become critical issues. The mission needs of the Southwest were the only motivation for the formation of this body. When Daniel died in 1842, the society died with him.

These two movements, however, show clearly that in addition to slavery-abolitionism, there were other strong considerations for a separate southern body.

Why This Kind of Structure Was Chosen

The adoption by Southern Baptists of this kind of denominational structure poses some questions. Manifestly, the organization of one convention to oversee multiple benevolences differed from the former method of utilizing three separate and autonomous societies for benevolent work.[18] What was there in the background of W. B. Johnson, who proposed this shift, and the consultative convention of representative Southern Baptists who adopted the new plan with remarkable unanimity, that would provide antecedents for such action?

W. W. Barnes has suggested that Southern Baptists were generally more centralized in their thinking than were Baptists in the North because of three rather basic factors: first, the widespread popularity in the South of the Philadelphia Confession of Faith with its general, invisible church view; second, the predominance of centralizing English General Baptists among the original settlers in the South; and third, the influence of the Separate Baptist movement, which was just one step removed from New England Presbyterian ecclesiological thinking.[19] Also, the centralizing patterns of the southern culture, as seen in the system of large plantations and in the top-heavy state political structures, provided their influence upon Southern Baptists.[20]

Other factors were involved. One was the development of state conventions in the South after 1821. The South Carolina Baptist Convention organized the first state body in America in 1821; it was built on associations, looked toward sponsoring multiple benevolences, and had other centralizing features. Many southern states had adopted similar state structures in the succeeding years. The experience of Southern Baptists with these bodies led them to feel that there was little to fear that any of them might ever become oppressive.

Another influence in the direction of centralization in the South was what could be called the Furman-Johnson tradition. Richard Furman, pastor of the First Baptist Church, Charleston, from 1787 until his death in 1825, was well-known for his centralized ecclesiological views. Johnson had been trained by Furman and shared his ecclesiological ideas. In fact, the local church ideas of Francis Wayland in the North and, later on, of J. R. Graves in the South, did not represent the ecclesiological views of Southern Baptists in 1845. Rather, Furman and Johnson were in the tradition of the centralizing ideas of the Separate Baptists, as were their contemporaries such as A. M. Poindexter of Virginia and J. L. Dagg of Georgia. Dagg's work, *A Treatise on Church Order,* published in 1858 at Charleston, South Carolina, was actually an anti-Landmark polemic, particularly with respect to the High Church ecclesiology of J. R. Graves.[21]

That this centralizing tendency in 1845 in favor of a single denominational structure overseeing all benevolences was not a novel concept to Southern Baptist ecclesiology, finds support in the events of almost half a century earlier. The new convention of 1845 favored the old associational pattern of the days before 1802 when all benevolences in a given geographical area were fostered by a single denominational body, the association. It will be recalled that the structure of the General Missionary Convention of 1814 limited it to foreign missions alone, but that in 1817, undoubtedly through the influence of Richard Furman, its president, the convention widened its scope to include other benevolences than foreign missions. The Southern Baptist Convention of 1845 resembled most closely this 1817-20 General Missionary Convention which in those years concerned itself with foreign missions, home missions, and Christian education. Whether W. B. Johnson, who was present and active in the organization of the 1814 body and subsequently served as its president, deliberately fashioned his proposal to the South Carolina convention in 1845 along the lines of the 1817-20 General Missionary Convention's structure can only be conjectured; but the parallel is there and the Address to the Public by the 1845 body asserted that the new convention was fashioned after the structure of the General Missionary Convention.

It is quite evident from the literature and the choice of denominational structure in 1845 that Southern Baptists were not uneasy that the new convention might threaten the autonomy of the churches. It has been mentioned already that there had developed considerable concentration on the state level without any diminution of the independence of the churches related to these bodies. Another protective factor was the nature of the constituency. The members who made up the new convention were also members of the local churches. The abolitionist controversy with the two missionary societies had been widely interpreted as an infringement upon the authority of the churches, and church authority was viewed as primary.

Another strong control for keeping such a new body from usurping the authority of the churches was the democratic nature of the convention. The vote of the floor at the annual meeting was the final authority in the body, and this inhibited usurpation. The constituents of 1845 felt that should there be any evidence of misplaced authority, the matter could be firmly and quickly settled through free discussion and decisive vote. It is true that the boards had authority to act in behalf of their own benevolence on matters arising between the meetings of the convention, but review by committees and discussion from the floor were the regular pattern in each case. This public review of decisions made and activity carried on opened the way for public discussion of any item in the work of the boards or of the convention itself. The relatively small numbers attending the conventions before the opening of the twentieth century made it possible for the convention to act almost as a committee of the whole in the supervision of its work.

The location of the headquarters of the two benevolent boards (for foreign and home missions) in different cities may have had some protective overtones to inhibit over-centralization, but this feature may simply have copied the former practice of the united period.

Undoubtedly, however, the principal reason that Southern Baptists were not unduly sensitive about church independence as they organized in 1845 was that a fundamental safeguard, authenticated by many years of experience, was retained in the structure which they adopted. The fact is that with all of the centralization implicit in the adoption of one organization for all benevolences, the continued use of the society plan of financial representation totally isolated the centralized convention from any interference whatsoever with the autonomy of the churches. Article III of the constitution asserted that the convention would "consist of members who contribute funds, or are delegated by religious bodies contributing funds," exactly after the pattern of the society method. In his preconvention address, William B. Johnson specifically mentioned that the interests of the constituency would be safeguarded by the power of financial designation. If the constituency were to see tendencies toward usurping the authority of the congregations, it would be a simple matter for finances to be withheld, quickly undermining the general body. Indeed, this was the weapon that the South had used during the abolitionist controversy in the decade preceding separation. Doubtless one of the reasons that almost three hundred Southern Baptists were willing to change from the society type of organization to the more centralized associational plan in the concentration of benevolences was the fact that the financial basis of representation provided an effective method of control.

It is also quite possible that the radical structural potentialities of the new body were not generally recognized. For several decades the body was referred to as the "missionary organization," not conceding that every type of denominational activity was contemplated in the structure. At any rate, by subjecting the activity of the new body to popular support financially by designated gifts, the founding fathers built in the safeguards of the society method as well as the centralization of the associational method of fostering many benevolences through a single denominational body. This was not a convention of churches, but a gathering of money-giving Baptists organized to do their benevolent work through a centralized structure.

In the new structure, however, there were two tensions that would surface repeatedly during the next eighty years. Both of them stemmed from the attempt to put new wine into old wineskins: the new type of convention structure could not be contained in the old society type of financing and representation. The founding fathers of the Southern Baptist Convention recognized no ambivalence in retaining the financial basis of representation, which both provided funds for operations and determined the voting constituency in a society. They sensed no limitation in the potential thrust of the new body through the retention of the older financial basis. This had been the accepted and effective method followed by the several societies during the lifetime of most of those present in 1845. The minutes of the new body, the denominational newspaper accounts, and the several reminiscences by actors in the drama give no hint that any of the messengers to the consultative meeting in 1845 desired to change this basis of representation. As a matter of fact, except for relatively minor adjustments designed to improve the choice of constituency, the constitutional pattern set in 1845 for financing the work of the convention remained rather constant until 1925. Actually, there was nothing inherently wrong in the financial basis of representation, for it followed the equitable principle that those who give the money should be allowed to spend it.

However, the adoption of this financial base provided a limitation that was not intended. The potential thrust of the convention was limited by the popular support accorded to any benevolence, since all finances were provided by designated giving. The convention as such had no funds of its own; even money to print the minutes had to be taken from designated home and foreign mission gifts. Since there were no convention headquarters, who should keep the minute book of the convention? The body voted that it should be kept at the foreign mission office in Richmond. For many decades the convention was looked upon simply as a missionary body, not a structure for implementing all of the varied benevolences of Baptist people in the South as the constitution originally envisioned. This is the reason that additional benevolences during this period like the Southern Baptist Publication Society in 1847 and Southern Baptist Theological Seminary in 1859, unable to share financial support within the framework of the convention, were developed outside of the body and given individual support under the old society plan.

The second point of tension within the structure of 1845 was the method of determining the constituency. For almost a century this strictly financial plan of representation was severely criticized as not being representative and equitable. Many alternatives were offered, but this basis of representation survived chronic tampering until the coming of a new century.

Thus came the separation of 1845 between Northern and Southern Baptists. At the time it took place, there was almost complete agreement North and South that this was the best course. J. B. Jeter was assured by northern leaders that this action prevented division within churches and associations throughout the North.[22] John Mason Peck felt that separation would bring more zeal by each group. Many expressed the feeling that with the separate organization and immediate responsibility for the task, Southern Baptists would become more involved in the whole enterprise—management, agencies, appointments, finances, etc.—and would correspondingly enlist more of their people to take part in these tasks.

Notes

1. Williston Walker, *A History of the Congregational Churches in the United States* (New York: The Christian Literature Co., 1894), p. 46.
2. McGlothlin, *op. cit.,* p. 268.
3. Baker, *Source Book,* p. 10.
4. Wayland, *op. cit.,* pp. 181 ff.
5. See the *Edgefield Advertiser* (Edgefield, South Carolina), May, 7, 1845.
6. Baker, *Source Book,* p. 114.
7. *Ibid.,* p. 114.
8. *Annual,* Southern Baptist Convention, 1845, pp. 12-13. The title *Proceedings* is sometimes used, but this reference hereafter will show *Annual.*
9. *Ibid.*
10. Baker, *Source Book,* p. 117.
11. *Annual,* Southern Baptist Convention, 1845, p. 14.

12. Baker, *Source Book,* p. 118.

13. *Ibid.,* p. 120.

14. *Ibid.,* p. 116.

15. *Ibid.,* pp. 84-85.

16. *Ibid.,* pp. 86-87.

17. *Ibid.,* pp. 85-86.

18. It should be observed, however, that even as recently as 1843, the Free Mission Society (first called the American and Foreign Baptist Missionary Society), organized by Baptist abolitionists when they withdrew from the General Convention and the Home Mission Society, contemplated both home and foreign missions through the single body. See Baker, *Relations,* pp. 62-64.

19. Barnes, *op. cit.,* pp. 6-8.

20. Baker, *Relations,* pp. 147-49.

21. J. L. Dagg, *A Treatise on Church Order* (Charleston: Southern Baptist Publication Society, 1858), p. 292, and *passim.*

22. J. B. Jeter, *The Recollections of a Long Life* (Richmond: The Religious Herald Co., 1891), p. 233.

10 The Antebellum Years

Southern Baptists, of course, were a part of the economic, social, and political patterns of the 1840's and 1850's. Economically, cotton had become the king of the crops. Because of the rapid expansion into the south central and southwest portions of the country, the growing of cotton increased geometrically. In 1830 over 500,000 bales were exported; in 1850, this had increased to nearly 2,000,000 bales; while in 1860, exports had reached the amazing total of about 4,000,000 bales. Despite this huge increase in production, the demand was such that the price of cotton itself even began to increase slowly. The price reached an all-time low of below six cents a pound in 1845, but slowly increased until the average in 1857 was nearly fourteen cents a pound. By 1860 the cotton crop reached the enormous total of 5,300,000 bales, seven-eighths of the world's supply. Meanwhile, particularly in Virginia and Kentucky, the tobacco crop was also bringing prosperity. In 1849 this crop had amounted to less than 200,000,000 pounds, but by 1860 it exceeded 430,000,000 pounds.

It should not be overlooked that Baptists in the South were mainly of the lower economic class. Very few, if any of them, were among the 8,000 planters who owned over 50 slaves each and used them on huge plantations in a commercial enterprise. Two thirds of the white families of Virginia in 1850 owned no slaves; three fourths of the white families in North Carolina owned no slaves; half of the white families in South Carolina owned no slaves; about two thirds of the white families in Georgia held no slaves. Frederick Jackson Turner noted that in about 1845 two thirds of the white families in all the South Central states (which included Kentucky, Tennessee, Alabama, Mississippi, and Louisiana, the repository of most of the slaves in America) were not slaveholders. This meant that while there was general prosperity in the raising of cotton, in particular, Baptists as a group rarely participated directly in such profits. However, the entire culture was built upon King Cotton, and the general prosperity engendered in the whole society by the raising of cotton also affected the Baptists. Even the panic of 1857 did not greatly affect the South, where cotton crops were good, prices were high, and banks were sound.

However, there were three factors that combined to destroy the antebellum culture. These were the deepened sectionalism in the 1840's and 1850's, the rapid development of slavery into a political issue, and the humanitarian reforms of the same decades which centered their attacks on slavery.

The three areas, Northeast, South, and West, it will be recalled, had given evidence before the 1840's of their sectional loyalties. The severe struggles of the 1830's over a protective tariff, the Bank of the United States, and the nature of the constitution had brought wounds that never quite healed. With the rapid economic prosperity based upon cotton which, in turn, used Negro slavery, the South united as a section. The Northeast with her new manufacturing interests, and the West with her agrarian interests vied with the South for political and economic control.

It was to be expected that such sectionalism would fall into the political realm. The war with Mexico over the annexation of Texas' brought strong antislavery repercussions because of the fear that this would open the door to further introduction of slavery to the West. The antislavery Wilmot Proviso of 1846 was the reply of the abolitionists. This argument brought a congeries of sectional antislavery legislation and struggle. The North was rapidly drawing away from the South in population and in senatorial voting. New political parties favoring abolitionism, such as the Free Soil Party, arose. In 1849-50, tension deepened when California, New Mexico, and Utah applied for admission as free states. The Compromise of 1850, supported by President Millard Fillmore, doubtless delayed actual military conflict between the sections. However, the Kansas-Nebraska Bill debate in 1854, and the Dred Scott decision in 1857 led to the organization of the new Republican Party and the election of Abraham Lincoln.

Along with this sectional and political antagonism, the 1840's and 1850's were decades of strong humanitarian reforms. Almost every type of reform agitation occurred in these years over labor, education, women's rights, temperance, prisons, peace, and so on. It was unthinkable that the vulnerable slavery system in the South should not be involved in these humanitarian reforms.

In the midst of these critical and exciting events Southern Baptists moved in new directions during the years between the provisional formation of their convention in 1845 and the close of the period in 1860.

Increasing Activity Through State Bodies

The formation of Baptist state bodies in the southern states, accentuated by the organization of the new southwide body in 1845, brought an increased unity among Baptists in the South during this period. This does not mean that all Baptists in each state promptly joined with the new state body in a common cause. There were still large pockets of antimission Baptists of various sorts, such as the Primitives, Hardshells, followers of Campbell, and Daniel Parker's Two-Seeders. Some of these remained within the missionary churches. In addition, some missionary Baptists were not yet ready for an additional organizational structure like a state body. But large impetus was given in the several states to a new Baptist unity in both structure and function through the formation of these state organizations.

New State Organizations. Nine Baptist state bodies were in operation in southern states before the organization of the Southern Baptist Convention in 1845. These were formed in South Carolina, 1821; Georgia, 1822; Alabama and Virginia, 1823; North Carolina, 1830; Missouri, 1834; Maryland and Mississippi, 1836; and Kentucky, 1837.

Between 1845 and 1860, four additional states organized new general bodies. The first chronologically was Texas. On September 8, 1848, the Texas Baptist State Convention was organized by fifty-five messenge , from twenty-one churches gathered at Anderson. The financial basis of representation was initially adopted, but in 1860 the constitution was altered to provide numerical representation from churches and associations. Reflecting the increasing areas of activity of state bodies, from the first this organization manifested its interest in education, publication of a Baptist newspaper, foreign missions, home missions, distribution of the Bible, and the religious condition of the black population. A second state body was organized on May 24, 1855, and in 1868 its name was changed to the Baptist General Association of Texas.

On September 21, 1848, the Arkansas Baptist State Convention was organized by seventy-two messengers at Tulip, Arkansas. Membership was composed of "delegates from Baptist Associations, Churches, and individual contributors who are members of Baptist Churches in good standing. Associations shall be entitled to five and Churches to three delegates to the Convention." Because this body was located in the southern part of the state, Baptists in the north organized the White River Baptist Convention on September 14, 1850, with messengers from about twenty churches. After 1850, Baptists in eastern Arkansas organized the General Association of Eastern Arkansas.

After several futile efforts to form a state body, Louisiana Baptists on December 2, 1848, at Mount Lebanon, organized the Baptist State Convention of North Louisiana. The word "North" was dropped in 1853. Representation was on a financial basis until well after the close of this period.

Florida Baptists organized their state body on November 20, 1854, near the Concord Baptist Church, Madison County. During the remainder of this period the great distances to travel and the financial condition of the people greatly hindered the work of the convention.

Thus, by the close of this period in 1860, Baptists in thirteen of the fifteen states cooperating in the work of the Southern Baptist Convention had developed state bodies. Tennessee remained divided into three sectional conventions despite efforts at unification, while the District of Columbia was still charting its direction. There is considerable evidence that the states organizing new bodies took counsel with the leaders in the states already so structured in an effort to provide the very best kind of organization. In fact, it is quite characteristic of the minutes of the several state bodies to name distinguished visitors from many other states at each of their annual sessions. These visitors were both teachers and pupils in states not their own, which helped to create a new atmosphere of unity and cooperation that had heretofore been limited to associational or church meetings. Common patterns of state activity clearly began to emerge under these new conditions. State structures were often quite similar; independent state benevolent societies soon began to merge with the state body to bring more unity of action; and the functions of the state bodies began to polarize around common objectives—growth, missions (state, southwide, and foreign), education, state papers, and specialized benevolences (hospitals, orphanages, widows' relief, old ministers' assistance, etc.).

There is also evidence of a new unity among Baptists in the South because of the organization of the Southern Baptist Convention in 1845. This would be expected, of course, as an immediate sectional reaction to withdrawal from cooperation with the General Missionary Convention and the American Baptist Home Mission Society, but signs occasionally appear in the literature that reveal distinct efforts to forward this unity. For example, it is likely that the appearance of W. B. Johnson at the North Carolina state meeting in 1845 and of J. B. Jeter at the Kentucky meeting in the same year marked a planned purpose by leaders of the new Southern Baptist Convention to strengthen the ties of the general body with the several states.

The rapidly increasing activity of state bodies can be glimpsed in the following brief summary.

South Atlantic Region. Baptists in the states comprising this region (Maryland, District of Columbia, Virginia, North Carolina, South Carolina, Georgia, and Florida) showed a substantial growth between 1845 and 1860. They increased from 87 associations, 2,019 churches, and 202,703 members in 1845 to 116 associations, 3,107 churches, and 328,666 members in 1860, an average annual growth of 3.88%.

This should be compared with their growth from 1790 to 1814 of 4.77%, and from 1814 to 1845 of 5.25%. Meanwhile, the general population in these seven states grew from 3,837,247 in 1840 to 5,252,487 in 1860, an average annual increase of 1.74%, much less than half of the 3.88% figure of Southern Baptist growth. The slave population between 1840 and 1860 increased in these seven states from 1,422,934 to 1,838,647, an average annual growth of 1.39%. This growth was below the rate of the general population and, as will be noted, was far below the average annual gain of 4.73% during the same years in the states of the South Central region.

The identification of leadership in the South Atlantic region during this period must necessarily be arbitrary, but has been based primarily upon the names nominated for the *Encyclopedia of Southern Baptists* by the states themselves and by professional historians. In Maryland were George F. Adams (1802-77), pastor and educator, and "the unmatched preacher of the time," Richard Fuller (1804-76). The District of Columbia provided O. B. Brown (1779-1852), pioneer pastor and leader. In Virginia were pastors Edward Baptist (1790-1863) and Andrew Broaddus (1801-76); J. B. Jeter (1802-80), pastor and editor; Robert Ryland (1805-99), educator; and William Sands (1793-1868), layman editor. In North Carolina, Thomas Meredith (1795-1850) was best known as editor of the Baptist paper, and Samuel Wait (1789-1867) was the principal educator. In South Carolina, J. C. Furman (1809-91) was the principal educator; J. B. O'Neall (1793-1863) was an active layman and denominational leader; and William Walker (1809-75) was recognized for his musical leadership. The seminary cluster at Greenville in 1859 included James P. Boyce (1827-88), John A. Broadus (1827-95), Basil Manly, Jr. (1825-92), and William Williams (1821-77). Leaders in Georgia were Joseph S. Baker (1798-1877), editor of *The Christian Index;* Enoch Callaway (1792-1859), whose family produced forty Baptist preachers for Georgia and the South; J. H. Campbell (1807-88), historian; N. M. Crawford (1811-71), who became president of Mercer University; J. E. Dawson (1805-60), pastor; J. H. DeVotie (1813-91), first executive secretary of Georgia Baptists; J. H. T. Kilpatrick (1788-1869), pastor; C. D. Mallary (1801-68), author and denominational leader; J. G. McCurry (1821-66), a lay musician and composer; Humphrey Posey (1780-1846), pastor; B. M. Sanders (1789-1852), editor and denominational leader; Adiel Sherwood (1791-1879), denominational and educational leader; Alfred Shorter (1803-82), lay philanthropist; and Thomas Stocks (1789-1876), lay denominational leader.

1. Maryland. Although almost a decade had passed since the Black Rock antimissionary defection, the remaining missionminded Baptists of Maryland, now in the Maryland Baptist Union Association, still felt the influence of their presence in Maryland and District of Columbia. The work was slow and discouraging. The associational letter of 1847, in particular, was pessimistic. Part of the problem was the frequency with which pastors would leave the churches of the association because of the difficulty of making progress, while the lack of financial support for all the Baptist churches was regularly noted. In 1847 Franklin Wilson was elected corresponding secretary of the Executive Board and served well during the period. A general missionary was employed in 1851, but served for only about a year. In that year the report said that of the twenty-seven churches in correspondence with the association, only four were self-supporting. In 1856 the funds were so low that missionaries of the board had not been paid for many months.

Maryland Baptists displayed cordial interest toward Negro Baptists. William Crane, in particular, who had moved earlier from Richmond to Baltimore for the express purpose of forwarding mission work, gave substantial financial support to the Negro churches. Noah Davis, a black Baptist preacher from Fredericksburg, Virginia, secured his freedom through donations of Baltimore Baptists, and became a missionary of the board among his own people.

Maryland Baptists supported Columbian College with scholarship pledges, although a proposed Board of Education for more substantial help was not structured. At the close of the period the association voted its support for the new Southern Baptist Seminary at Greenville, South Carolina. The Sunday School movement was pressed during the entire period, and the benefits of the Widow's Fund were extended to superannuated ministers in 1848.[1]

Despite many difficulties, Maryland Baptists grew from 1,960 in 1845 to 4,143 in 1860, an average annual increase of 6.96%. This was the largest percentage increase of any South Atlantic state. Meanwhile, the population of Maryland increased from 470,019 in 1840 to 687,049 in 1860, an average annual increase of 2.20%, less than one third the increase of Baptists. The slave population decreased from 89,737 in 1840 to 87,189 in 1860.

2. District of Columbia. Baptists in the District, who affiliated with various state bodies, increased from 706 to 1,069 during the period, an average annual growth of 3.21%. Meanwhile, the population increased from 33,745 in 1840 to 75,080 in 1860, an average annual increase of 5.83%, far exceeding Baptist growth. The slave population dropped from 4,694 in 1840 to 3,185 in 1860.

3. Virginia. Baptists in Virginia had taken the lead in calling for a consultative convention to consider a separate organizational structure for Southern Baptists, and at the meeting in Augusta, Georgia, in 1845 they had thirty-one delegates from twenty-six churches and two associations present. The new foreign mission body was located at Richmond, and many important posts in the new body were filled by Virginians.

The state mission program during this period grew slowly. However, the state structure was strongly unified. Before 1855 the education society, the Bible society, and the foreign mission society were separate bodies, but in that year these societies were made boards of the state body.[2]

Virginia Baptists had chartered the University of Richmond in 1840; in 1845 the curriculum was enlarged to add the final two years of college and their first B.A. degree was conferred in 1849. Virginia Baptists played an active part in the founding and support of Southern Baptist Theological Seminary in 1859. They also had a number of private female institutions, as well as a school for boys.

The principal periodical was the *Religious Herald,* published by its owner, William Sands, although Henry Keeling published the *Virginia Baptist Preacher,* a monthly sermonic-type paper, from 1842 to 1858.

Baptists in this state grew from 78,645 in 1845 to 108,888 in 1860. The average annual rate of growth was 2.40%. Meanwhile, the population of Virginia grew from 1,239,797 in 1840 (this figure includes both Virginia and what later became West Virginia, since they had not been divided at this time) to 1,596,318 in 1860, an average annual increase of 1.32%, far below the Baptist rate of growth. The slave population in Virginia increased from 448,987 in 1840 to 490,865 in 1860, an average annual growth of .44%.

4. North Carolina. Baptist activity was quite evident in North Carolina. The 1845 minutes of the state convention mentioned that W. B. Johnson of South Carolina (now president of the new Southern Baptist Convention) was visiting, and the body approved the organization of the Southern Convention and its boards. The 1846 session of the state convention reorganized the structure of the body to form three boards: foreign missions, state missions, and education. In 1854 an executive committee was appointed. A Western Convention was organized as an auxiliary to the State Convention in 1845, but in 1857 it became a separate body for the area west of the Blue Ridge.

The mission work was actively stressed in cooperation with the several associations. A general agent was appointed in 1853 to create more support for the mission cause.

Both the State Convention and the Western Convention were active in educational interests. Regular reports were made on Wake Forest; female schools and academies were founded; the planting of Southern Baptist Seminary at Greenville, South Carolina, was supported vigorously between 1856 and 1860. Chowan College in 1848 and Mars

Hill in 1856 were opened. A Sunday School and Publication Society was developed in 1844 and made its first report in 1845.[3]

Overall, Baptists in North Carolina grew from 32,671 in 1845 to 60,532 in 1860, an excellent annual average of 5.33%. They had 9.38% of all Southern Baptists in 1860. The population increased from 753,419 in 1840 to 992,622 in 1860, an average annual increase of 1.51%. Baptists grew more than three and one-half times faster than the population in this state. The slave population grew from 245,817 in 1840 to 331,059 in 1860, an average annual increase of 1.65%, almost the same rate as the total population growth.

5. *South Carolina.* Baptists in this state played a large part in the development of the new Southern Baptist Convention in 1845. Their state convention as late as 1844 had deprecated disunion between Baptists North and South, even in the face of the Alabama Resolutions; but in their called convention at Edgefield on May 3, 1845, just one week before the consultative meeting at Augusta to form the southwide body, their presiding officer, W. B. Johnson, proposed the more centralized structure that Southern Baptists approved at Augusta. Johnson became president of the new southwide body. The state body named twenty delegates to represent them at Augusta. One of the first actions of the state body in its regular meeting in 1845 was to approve the formation of the Southern Baptist Convention, and urge additional benevolences to be sponsored by the new body.[4]

In 1851 the South Carolina body restructured its organization to emphasize its missionary character and to absorb education and Bible societies, the whole to be embodied into three boards—home missions, Bible, and education. The result of this move brought more missionary support and educational interest. Furman University was relocated in 1850 at Greenville, and made good progress during the remainder of this period. A female school was also begun in Greenville in 1855 and flourished.

The increasing influence of the state body continued until the end of this period. An average of three associations had become affiliated with the body during each of the first three decades of its life (1821-50), but in the 1850's, six new associations related to the body.[5] In numbers, Baptists increased from 40,237 to 62,984 in this state during this period, or an average annual growth of 3.53%. The population, meanwhile, grew from 594,398 in 1840 to 703,708 in 1860, an average annual increase of .87%, less than one-fourth the rate of Baptist growth. The slave population increased from 327,038 to 402,406, or an average annual growth of 1.10%.

6. *Georgia.* At the very beginning of this period, Georgia Baptists had a strong state structure, including an executive committee that

provided excellent efficiency. Their close relationship to the new Southern Baptist Convention was emphasized through their participation in a strong program of Indian missions (which subsequently was taken over by the Convention) and their nomination of James Huckins and William Tryon as missionaries under the Marion board to the state of Texas. Their constitution was amended in 1854 to provide more of a numerical representation to parallel the financial basis.

The state mission program was actively developed in all parts of the state. Reference was made several times to "many seminaries for the education of males and females" sustained under Baptist influence in the state. Mercer University was the object of much attention, including a typical Baptist hassle in the 1850's, but it emerged with added strength. Every year at the convention (except from 1852 to 1855) an education sermon was preached, and in 1850 it was noted that twelve young ministers were receiving aid from the education fund "and there was still room for more." The Hearn Manual Labor School, opened in 1839, continued during this period.[6] An abstract of the minutes spoke often of the large amount of Sunday School activity, the excellent financial support of the Bible Board, the merging of the state publication society with the new Southern Baptist Publication Society in 1856, and the prosperous condition of the state paper, *The Christian index.* Typical of the many visitors who seemed to be going from one state to another during this time was the report of distinguished men in the 1855 state convention: J. M. Chiles of South Carolina; G. L. Sandidge, J. H. Eaton, and J. R. Graves of Tennessee; A. M. Poindexter of Virginia; S. Henderson and I. T. Tichenor of Alabama; J. P. Tustin of Charleston, South Carolina; A. C. Dayton of Nashville; H. F. Buckner, missionary to the Indians in Indian Territory; A. D. Phillips, soon to sail for Africa; and A. E. Stevens from Burma.

This substantial activity was reflected in the statistics of growth of Baptists in Georgia. Baptists in this state surged from 47,151 in 1845 to 84,567 in 1860, an average annual increase of 4.96%. The population grew from 691,392 to 1,057,286, or an average annual increase of 2.52%, barely more than half the rate of Southern Baptist growth. The slave population increased from 280,944 in 1840 to 462,198 in 1860, an average annual growth of 3.07%.

7. Florida. Before the formation of a state body in 1854, Florida Baptists were led by outstanding pioneer missionaries (several from the Southern Baptist Convention after 1845) like John Tucker, William B. Cooper, Richard J. Mays, Joshua Mercer (brother of Georgia's Jesse Mercer), James MacDonald, and J. M. Hayman, in particular. The antimission struggle affected Baptists here, but when Suwanee

Association became antimissionary in 1845, it began an excision of those who opposed missions from Florida churches and associations. This was a healthy development for the inner structure of early Florida Baptists.[7]

Even before a state body was formed, Florida Baptists seriously discussed the founding of a college. Several academies were formed after 1851. E. E. Joiner judged that problems of sectionalism and race played little part in early Florida Baptist history. There was no state paper during this period, but good books were distributed by colporteurs, and active interest was expressed in increasing Sunday School work.

The state body was organized in 1854, and their constitution was probably modeled after that of Georgia Baptists.[8] It is rather interesting to note that the ubiquitous J. R. Graves of Tennessee showed up at this organizational meeting.[9]

The statistics show that Florida Baptists grew substantially during this period. They increased from 1,333 in 1845 to 6,483 in 1860, an average annual increase of 2.41%. The population grew from 54,477 in 1840 to 140,424 in 1860, an average annual increase of 7.51%, the largest rate of population growth in the South Atlantic region. The slave population also showed a large increase, growing from 25,717 in 1840 to 61,745 in 1860, an average annual increase of 6.67%.

South Central Region. The westward migration from the South Atlantic states into Kentucky, Tennessee, Alabama, Mississippi, Arkansas, Louisiana, and Texas, which comprised this region, continued at a rapid pace during this period. It is startling to notice that of all the natives of South Carolina alive in 1850, over 40 percent were residents of other states. About one third of the natives of North Carolina had left the state of their birth, and about one fourth of those of Georgia. Nearly one half of the people of Alabama, Mississippi, and Louisiana were born outside the state in which they resided. Kentucky was principally settled by Virginians; Tennessee, by North Carolinians. Georgia natives were the majority in Alabama, followed by South Carolina. Noting the sources of Georgia's population, the two Carolinas furnished the bulk of Alabama's people. Alabama was the chief contributor to Mississippi, while Louisiana's population came principally from Mississippi. In Mississippi and Louisiana the Negroes were more numerous than the whites in 1850.[10] Kentucky and Tennessee also were recipients of many inhabitants from the seaboard during this period.

In the seven South Central states, Baptists increased from 105 associations, 2,042 churches, and 146,277 members in 1845 to 163 associations, 3,904 churches, and 271,675 members in 1860, an average annual increase of 5.36%. This rate of growth should be compared with the 33.59% rate from 1790 to 1814, and the 9.99% rate from 1814 to 1845. It is also instructive to compare it with the 3.88% growth experienced in the South Atlantic states during this period.

Meanwhile, the population of these South Central states grew from 3,025,430 in 1840 to 5,768,658 in 1860, or an average annual increase of 4.32%; a large increase but still not equaling the 5.36% Baptist increase for this period. The slave population jumped from 1,002,447 in 1840 to 1,998,320 in 1860, or an average annual increase of 4.73%, over three times as fast as the slave population increase in the South Atlantic states. The percentage of westward migration of slave population had slowed considerably from the 1790-1810 increase of 48.38% annually and the 1810-1840 increase of 15.06% annually, although the *number* of slaves increased more between 1840 and 1860 than at any other earlier period. (An increase of almost a million slaves in the South Central region was shown in the 1840-1860 period, compared to 825,603 in the 1810-1840 period and about 161,000 in the 1790-1810 period). Texas and Arkansas, in particular, showed very large increases, due, likely, to the efforts of the eastern states to find a sanctuary for their slaves in the face of mounting tension that led to civil war.

The principal leaders in the South Central region, as determined from the *Encyclopedia of Southern Baptists,* were as follows: In Kentucky, noteworthy for their service, were W. C. Buck (1790-1872), editor and author; Warren Cash (1760-1849), the pioneer preacher; R. T. Dillard (1797-1878), editor and pastor; T. F. Fisher (1812-66), the evangelist; Alfred Taylor (1808-65), pastor; William Vaughn (1785-1877), pastor; George Walker (1777-1860), pastor; and J. L. Waller (1809-54), pastor, editor, and author. Tennessee provided J. H. Borum (1816-?), pioneer West Tennessee pastor; A. C. Dayton (1813-65), author, editor, and a part of the Landmark triumvirate; Obadiah Dodson (1792-1854), pastor; P. S. Gayle (1802-53), pastor; J. R. Graves (1820-93), pastor, editor, and founder of Landmarkism; and R. B. C. Howell (1801-68), pastor, editor, and author. Leaders in Alabama included D. P. Bestor, Sr. (1797-1869), educator; Lee Compere (1790-1871), pastor, translator, and missionary; J. L. Dagg (1794-1884), theologian, author, and college president; E. D. King (1796-1862), lay educator and benefactor; Basil Manly, Sr. (1798-1868), educator and pastor; and I. T. Tichenor (1825-1902), pastor, educator, and denominational executive. Norvell Robertson, Jr. (1796-1878), pastor and author, was outstanding in Mississippi during this period.

Farther west in Louisiana, two men stand out: Bartholomew Egan (1795-1879), physician and lay educator, and Joseph Willis (1758-1854), pioneer preacher known affectionately as "Father Willis."

Joseph Islands (?-1848) was called the "Apostle to the Indians" in Indian Territory. Texas was developing a strong band of pioneer leaders; G. W. Baines (1809-82), pastor, educator, and editor; R. E. B. Baylor (1793-1873), preacher and educator; Joseph L. Bays (1786-1854) preacher; Gail Borden, Jr. (1801-74), deacon and benefactor; Richard Ellis (1781-1846), lay leader and outstanding patriot; H. L. Graves (1813-81), pastor and educator; Sam Houston (1793-1863), president and governor of Texas and lay leader; James Huckins (1808-63), pastor, missionary, and educator; Z. N. Morrell (1803-83), pioneer pastor and denominational leader; T. J. Pilgrim (1805-77), Sunday School leader; and William Tryon (1809-47), pastor, missionary, and educator.

1. Kentucky. This period was characterized "by increased organization of the friends of missions for the spread of the gospel in all the world." [11] This statement was alluding particularly to the elimination of antimissions from Kentucky churches and associations, and the consequent new unity provided among the mission-minded Baptists.

At the 1845 meeting in Georgetown, the new Southern Baptist Convention was the chief topic of discussion. Kentucky Baptists heartily endorsed the organization of the new body, and welcomed J. B. Jeter of Virginia, the president of the new Foreign Mission Board of the southwide body. Plans were made to forward the "union among the various societies and associations of Baptists in the south." The China Missionary Society of Kentucky was placed under the operation of the southwide convention.

A unifying reorganization took place beginning in 1850 in which all separate benevolent societies were united under one board with one agent, and by 1852 it was reported that this movement was already bearing fruit. Refinements in structure were continued, almost annually, until 1857. At the 1857 meeting, many Southern Baptist Convention leaders arrived early for the southwide gathering which met the day following the adjournment of the Kentucky convention, and a long list of distinguished Baptists from the South were present at the Kentucky meeting, including, of course, J. R. Graves of Tennessee.

Year by year the mission program in the state advanced. In 1853, for example, the Board of Managers reported: "Perhaps in no year since the organization of the General Association has more missionary labor been performed than the present." [12] In 1857, unusual because it antedated a general movement of the kind, the body adopted a resolution urging all pastors to endeavor to form "Female Missionary Societies" in their respective churches.

Educational activity among Kentucky Baptists continued during this period. Georgetown College was regularly promoted by the state body;

in 1855, in particular, reports showed that Bethel College at Russell-ville had been developed; eight "Female Schools" of various grades were flourishing; and some Baptist high schools for both male and female were being well patronized.[13] The Ministerial Education Society was active. The new Western Baptist Theological Institute at Covington, Kentucky, which will be discussed later, "ought not, under present circumstances, to receive support of the Baptists of Kentucky," said the General Association in 1845. A committee of the state body was appointed to confer with trustees of the Institute in 1847, and in 1851, the school was commended for young ministers. The minutes of 1853 report the dissolution of the school.[14]

The name of the Baptist paper in Kentucky was changed to the *Western Recorder* in 1851 when John L. Waller again became editor, and the people were urged to patronize the paper. The state body also recommended the *Western Baptist Review*, which was published from 1845 through 1851, principally by Waller; it was renamed the *Christian Repository* and continued during the remainder of the period under the same editorship.

The minutes of the General Association reflect that the Mexican war (1846-48) took many of their young men into service, while occasional epidemics in 1848-49 retarded the work. The Sunday School was urged after 1854 as an aid to evangelism and religious education, and a Kentucky Baptist Ministers' body was promoted during the 1850's.

Two rather divisive matters during this period in Kentucky involved abolitionism and Landmarkism. Baptists were divided on the question of slavery in this state, some being fervent on each side. A strong anti-slavery paper was established in Lexington in 1845, and the constitutional convention of 1849 showed the divided opinion of the people. J. M. Pendleton, who wrote the Landmark tract, "An Old Landmark Re-Set," in 1854, was pastor at Bowling Green, Kentucky, but in 1857 moved to Tennessee, thence, when war came, to Pennsylvania. Pendleton's Landmark views brought a literary controversy in 1854-55.[15]

Despite hindrances, Baptists in Kentucky showed good growth during this period. They increased from 60,371 in 1845 to 81,588 in 1860, an average annual growth of 2.20%. This percentage of increase may be compared with the state's gain of 25.98% between 1790 and 1814 and 5.58% between 1814 and 1845.

The population of Kentucky increased from 779,828 in 1840 to 1,155,684 in 1860, an average annual increase of 2.29%, just about the same rate as the Baptist increase. The slave population grew from 182,258 in 1840 to 225,483 in 1860, an average annual increase of 1.13%. Kentucky was not now far enough to the west and to the south to show a large increase in the slave population. The average increase had slowed considerably from the 26.10% from 1790 to 1810 and the 4.07% increase from 1810 to 1840.

2. *Tennessee.*   There was no single state body in Tennessee during this period. Instead, after the disintegration of the Tennessee Baptist Convention in 1842, three sectional bodies developed: the General Association of Baptists of East Tennessee; the Baptist General Association of Tennessee, which in 1849 took the name Baptist General Association of Middle Tennessee and North Alabama; and the West Tennessee Baptist Convention. Unification into a single body was delayed because of differences involved in geographical location, lack of communication, localized historical background, and diverse reactions to the various controversies sweeping Tennessee during this and the previous period.

The East Tennessee body organized Carson College in 1850 and carried on missionary work in its section during the period. It split in 1859 over the Graves-Howell controversy.

The Middle Tennessee body established Union University at Murfreesboro in 1848 under the aegis of the Tennessee Baptist Education Society. The school closed with the outbreak of civil war. R. B. C. Howell dominated this Middle Tennessee body until he accepted a pastorate in Virginia in 1850, after which J. R. Graves assumed this function. The controversy between these two men after Howell returned to Nashville in 1857 almost wrecked this Baptist General Association, but Graves retained control of it.

The West Tennessee Baptist Convention carried on an active missionary program in its section during this period. It established a male institute in Madison County which took the name Madison College in 1859.

The denominational paper, *The Baptist,* owned and published by R. B. C. Howell at the opening of the period, was given by him to the Middle Tennessee body in 1846, after which it came under the control of J. R. Graves and had a wide circulation, even beyond the borders of Tennessee.

During these exciting days Baptists in Tennessee increased from 32,159 in 1845 to 46,564 in 1860, an average annual growth of 2.80%. This may be compared with an increase of 55.78% in 1790-1814 and 5.05% between 1814 and 1845.

The total population of the state increased from 829,210 in 1840 to 1,109,801 in 1860, an average annual growth of 1.61%, far below the Baptist growth. The increase in the slave population also slowed considerably. From 183,059 in 1840, they grew to 275,719 in 1860, an average annual increase of 2.41%, compared to 10.03% in the 1810-40 period and 57.30% in the 1790-1810 period.

3. Alabama. Baptists in this state body played a large part in the confrontation of 1845 that brought the organization of the Southern Baptist Convention. Fourteen messengers were appointed to attend the Augusta meeting, and during the summer and fall of 1845, churches, associations, and the state convention approved the new southwide convention structure. The Domestic Mission Board was located at Marion, Alabama, a strategic and significant choice.

During this period the state body "became well established and was accepted as the unifying agency among Alabama Baptists as a whole." The antimissionary forces had withdrawn to form a separate body, although there continued to be antimission and anti-convention sentiment in northern Alabama. The agitation over slavery distracted Baptists. Despite this, as will be noted, Alabama Baptists had phenomenal growth. State missions were aggressively promoted; after 1850 (when a southwide emphasis was placed upon Sunday Schools) the strength of the Sunday School movement grew rapidly; and the state body was moving toward assistance for aged or disabled ministers and their widows. J. R. Graves visited Alabama often, and many Baptists there read his paper with its strong Landmark views after about 1850. He sowed distrust of the denominational boards and the Southern Baptist Convention itself.

Judson Female Institute, at Marion, which had been chartered in 1841, was given to the state body in 1843, and flourished during this period. Howard College (for men), which had been chartered in 1841, was razed by fire in 1844 and again in 1854. It had barely been rebuilt and occupied before war came. In addition to Judson and Howard, almost a dozen Baptist local schools were scattered across the state.

A state paper, *The Alabama Baptist,* began publication in 1843. Evidently the scholarly M. P. Jewett was the chief editor and manager of the paper in the beginning. In 1850 the paper changed its title to *The South Western Baptist,* which it retained until the close of civil war. Another short-lived paper was edited by W. C. Buck in 1859.

As suggested previously, Alabama Baptists experienced excellent growth during this period. They increased from 28,210 in 1845 to 61,219 in 1860, an average annual increase of 7.31%. The population grew during this period from 590,756 in 1840 to 964,201 in 1860, an average annual increase of 3.01%, a substantial growth, but not half of the Baptist increase. The slave population grew from 253,532 in 1840 to 435,080 in 1860, or an average annual increase of 3.41%.

4. Mississippi. Baptists here wholeheartedly approved of the new southwide body and cooperated in its work.[16] Despite transportation and communication difficulties, missionary activity by both the state body and through the associations was effective. Sunday Schools were promoted and a Bible and colportage society was organized in 1859. Several papers were begun during this period. The *Tennessee Baptist,* published by J. R. Graves, was often recommended to the people (and Graves was often in the state during the 1850's). At the very close of the period, Mississippi Baptists experienced a serious controversy over Graves and his Landmark views. The 1860 convention appointed a committee to help mediate between Graves and the First Baptist Church, Nashville, Tennessee, which allayed some of the pro-Graves feelings in the state.[17] Intermittently the *Mississippi Baptist* was published between 1846 and 1862. Many private Baptist schools flourished, but in 1850 Mississippi College at Clinton was accepted by the Mississippi Baptist Convention, and it quickly became the largest such institution in the state. Mississippi Baptist Female College was established in 1851 under the leadership of William Carey Crane. A state education society promoted the raising of funds during this period.

The number of Baptists increased from 19,539 in 1845 to 41,610 in 1860, an average annual growth of 7.06%, compared with their increase in the 1814-45 period of 65.10% annually. The general population in Mississippi increased from 375,651 in 1840 to 791,305 in 1860, an average annual growth of 5.27%, quite sizeable but not close to the Baptist 7.06% increase. The slave population of Mississippi increased from 195,211 in 1840 to 436,631 in 1860, an average annual growth of 5.89%, compared to the 1810-40 growth of 33.61%.

5. Arkansas. In 1848, thirty years after the organization of the first church in the state, Arkansas Baptists formed a state body. J. S. Rogers, their historian, remarked that in 1848 the "80 to 100 Baptist fathers . . . found they had no State-wide organization, no newspaper, no schools of college grade, in fact no State-wide institution of any kind." There was still the opposition of antimission groups, preachers needed training, and a Baptist paper was needed.[18] The new state body brought zeal and growth. Before the close of the period the number of associations had doubled, a state paper had been established, and two Baptist academies had opened.[19]

In 1858 the convention authorized the publication of the *Arkansas Baptist* under the editorship of P. S. G. Watson. The promising beginning in January, 1859, was soon destroyed by civil war.

The Landmark movement, which would become severely divisive in a later generation, was introduced into Arkansas as early as 1851 when J. R. Graves held a sweeping revival meeting at Helena and organized a strong church there. The church was a liberal and loyal supporter of the state body, but Graves "had a commanding and enthusiastic following among Arkansas Baptists from about 1850 to

1870 or later." [20]

Despite many difficulties, Arkansas Baptists made remarkable numerical gains. They increased from 2,015 in 1845 to 11,341 in 1860, an average annual growth of 28.93%. The general population increased from 97,574 in 1840 to 435,450 in 1860, an average annual increase of 16.49%, the largest percentage increase in this period in all the South. As indicated, however, even this remarkable increase lagged far behind the Baptist growth of 28.93% annually. The slave population of Arkansas also grew rapidly during this period. From 19,935 in 1840, it grew to 111,115 in 1860, an average annual increase of 21.78%, which was a growth faster than the population but still far behind the Baptist gains.

6. *Louisiana.* In his story of Louisiana Baptists, John T. Christian judged that in the period between about 1835 and 1850, Louisiana Baptists had no common rallying point. They were few in number, new in the land, opposed and despised by many enemies, and had not one minister of commanding influence. [21] During these years the antimission forces of Hardshellism or Primitivism and of Campbellism brought dissension and lethargy. [22] The turning point in Louisiana Baptist history was the organization in 1848 of the Baptist State Convention of Louisiana. At first some associations withheld cooperation, but within a relatively few years the new state body provided the nucleus for the unity needed by Louisiana Baptists.

New Orleans was one of the first recipients of assistance from the new Domestic Mission Board of the Southern Baptist Convention. Russell Holman and I. T. Hinton of New Orleans had assisted in the organization of the southwide body in 1845 at Augusta. The most severe yellow fever epidemic New Orleans had yet known occurred in 1847 and took the life of Hinton along with many others. The discovery of gold in California in 1849 caused many New Orleans Baptists to emigrate to the West. The organization of the new state body came at a very critical time in these early years.

In 1852 the state body founded Mt. Lebanon University, which had a promising beginning that was interrupted by civil war. A female college was also organized at Mt. Lebanon but also died with the war. Keachie Female College was chartered in 1857 and flourished, but its operations were suspended during the war.

Baptists in the state increased from 3,311 in 1845 to 10,264 in 1860, an average annual increase of 13.12%. The population of Louisiana increased from 352,411 to 708,002 between 1840 and 1860, for an average annual increase of 4.80%, slightly more than one third the increase shown by Baptists. The slave population increased from 168,452 in 1840 to 331,726 in 1860, an average annual growth of 4.61%.

7. Texas. This newest Baptist frontier state began the period in 1845 with 672 Baptists recorded, but the number increased to 19,089 by 1860, an annual average increase of 171.29% (due to the small numbers involved). The population in the 1860 census numbered 604,215 with 182,566 slaves.

Much of the rapid progress of Texas Baptists in this early period was due to strong leaders like Z. N. Morrell and R. E. B. Baylor, and the two great missionaries, James Huckins and William M. Tryon, both of whom were first sent by the Home Mission Society of New York before 1845 and by the Domestic Mission Board of the South thereafter.

In 1840 the first association (Union) was formed, and in 1848 the Texas Baptist State Convention came into being. Unfortunately, in a sectional disagreement, a second state body was organized in 1853, which was re-formed two years later under the name Eastern Texas Baptist Convention. Both bodies prosecuted missionary and Sunday School work actively during the remainder of the period. Sunday School interest was kindled quite early with the coming of Thomas J. Pilgrim in 1828, who spent a long life promoting this movement. Negroes, Germans, and Mexicans were the targets of missionary activity.

A newspaper, *The Texas Baptist,* was published from 1855 to 1860, when it became an early casualty of the war. J. R. Graves was quite influential in Texas, his Tennessee paper being widely circulated and his Landmark publications finding numerous sympathetic readers.

At the second meeting of the Union Association in 1841, two important bodies were organized: the Texas Baptist Home Mission Society and the Texas Baptist Education Society. Working through the latter body, William M. Tryon fathered Baylor University, chartered in 1845 by the Republic of Texas. At the end of the period this school was involved in a serious internal controversy. Meanwhile, over a dozen institutes and female colleges were organized during this period, including Waco Classical School in 1855 and two colleges at Tyler in east Texas.[23]

North Central Region. Only one state in this region was involved in Southern Baptist life during this period—Missouri. The general body, organized in 1835, became auxiliary to the Southern Baptist Convention in 1845. State missions were vigorously promoted, including the organization of a German Mission Society in 1853 to carry the gospel to the large numbers of Germans entering Missouri.[24] There was considerable strife after 1847 over the question of employing paid agents in missionary promotion.

After disappointing delays, William Jewell College was chartered in 1849 and, except for a two-year closure between 1855-57, flourished until it was closed by the war in 1861.

Despite several vigorous efforts to establish a state denominational paper, a satisfactory publication was not developed during this period. *The Western Watchman* was published intermittently after 1848, but its disfavor was indicated by the beginning of a rival paper in 1860, *The Missouri Baptist*. Both died with the coming of war.

Missouri was constantly agitated during this period over the question of slavery, but despite this its population increased from 383,702 in 1840 to 1,182,012 in 1860, an average annual increase of 9.91%. The number of slaves increased from 59,814 in 1840 to 118,503 in 1860, an average annual increase of 4.67%. Baptists in the state grew at an average annual rate even more rapid than either of these groups. They increased from 21 associations, 334 churches, and 16,366 members in 1845 to 37 associations, 749 churches, and 44,877 members in 1860, an average annual increase of 10.89%.

In this region, William Jewell (1789-1852) was an outstanding physician and lay benefactor to education, while A. P. Williams (1813-68) was a pastor and author. Identified with the boards of the Convention during this period were T. F. Curtis (1815-72), Russell Holman (1812-79), and Joseph Walker (1804-95) in the home mission movement, and A. M. Poindexter (1809-72) and James B. Taylor (1804-71) with the foreign mission effort.

Benevolences Outside the Convention

Although the official minutes and the newspaper accounts at the time of the 1845 meeting of Southern Baptists at Augusta make no reference to it, it is evident that there was some ambivalence relative to the nature of the convention to be organized by Southern Baptists. The plan adopted at Augusta provided that the new body could carry on as many benevolences as it desired, and contemplated an all-inclusive denominational structure through which Southern Baptists might carry on every type of work. This was reflected in the call issued by the Virginia Baptist Foreign Mission Society, the address of William B. Johnson to the South Carolina Baptist State Convention on May 3, 1845, and in the constitution that was adopted.

However, although many additional benevolences were being discussed by Southern Baptists in 1845, such as a new Bible society or board, a new publication society, and an education society to provide a school for theological training, none of these was included in the 1845 structure of the Southern Baptist Convention. Instead, during this period Southern Baptists developed a publication society, a Sunday School union, and a seminary outside the structure of the Convention.

Southern Baptist Publication Society. Although there is no explanation of the fact in the records, it is evident that the principal target of protest at the consultative meeting in 1845 and in the Address to the Public was the foreign mission society. The Home Mission Society of New York and the American Baptist Publication Society of Philadelphia received little attention, if any, although the action of the consultative body brought separation from the home mission body but not from the publication body. The silence of the records on the latter is noticeable, since the call of Virginia Baptists for a consultative convention specifically suggested that Southern Baptists might organize a separate publication society. At the 1844 meeting of the Georgia Baptist Convention, James Davis had introduced a motion calling for the formation of a southern publication society, but it was defeated. At the 1845 consultative meeting in Augusta, J. S. Baker, the aggressive editor of *The Christian Index* of Georgia, introduced a resolution concerning a publication society, although not recorded at the time, which was also voted down.[25] Perhaps one of the reasons for the silence concerning the American Baptist Publication Society was that J. L. Burrows came as a corresponding delegate from the publication body of Philadelphia and was invited to participate in the discussions. In fact, on the second afternoon of the meeting Burrows addressed the body in behalf of the American Baptist Publication Society. The Address to the Public emphasized that the extent of the disunion between North and South should not be exaggerated, since it involved "only the Foreign and Domestic Missions of the denomination." When it is recalled that there were only three principal Baptist benevolent societies, the General Missionary Convention for foreign missions organized in 1814, the American Baptist Publication Society organized in 1824, and the American Baptist Home Mission Society organized in 1832, the southern separation from the two missionary societies but not the publication body in 1845 is noteworthy. The abolitionist literature said that the publication body had not given any cause to the southerners for separating from them.

At any rate, after the 1845 consultative meeting, there came continued appeals for the organization of a publication society for Southern Baptists from almost every part of the South. Editor J. S. Baker published many of these in *The Christian Index* of Georgia. However, the various newspapers of the South were divided on this matter. When Secretary J. M. Peck of the American Baptist Publication Society suggested to Georgia Baptists in the summer of 1845 that an agent be permitted to collect funds in Georgia for the society, the Executive Committee of the Georgia Baptist Convention replied that it was their hope that a southern board for publication and Bible distribution would be organized. After this reply was published, Editor John L. Waller of the *Western Baptist Review* of Kentucky promptly protested that.there should be no more divisions.

> We wish to see no further alienation of feeling between the North
> and South. Discord has already done enough. . . . Being wholly unap-
> prized of the existence of any necessity for further division, we solemnly
> enter our protest against withdrawing from the Bible and Publication
> societies, merely because their Boards are located north of Mason and
> Dixon's line.[26]

There was another important factor that caused .many Southern
Baptist leaders to refuse or delay the publication enterprise. This was
the financial stringency of the period. The Panic of 1837 had brought
a depression that lasted until the consultative convention of 1845 at
Augusta. Even the American Baptist Publication Society, with
twenty-five years of financial rootage and expertise, was severely
shaken by this financial crisis, and southern members of that society,
acquainted with the details of that fierce financial struggle, shrank
from venturing into a competitive enterprise with such related perils.

The division of opinion manifested in the discussions between the
Georgia and Kentucky editors in 1845 came to the floor of the Southern Baptist Convention when it met at Richmond, Virginia, in 1846.
Thomas Stocks of Georgia introduced a resolution calling for the
appointment of a committee of two from each state to consider organizing a Board of Managers for Bible and publication work. An
extensive discussion followed the report of the committee, and there
were numerous amendments. Finally, however, relative to the question
of organizing a Southern Publication Board within the Convention
structure, the Convention approved the statement that it "does not
deem it advisable to embarrass itself with any enterprise for the,
publication and sale of books." This victory for the Kentucky position
provided an attitude toward the publication of books by the Convention that was often repeated during the remainder of the century.

The issue was not settled, however. The Central Baptist Association
of Georgia in its 1846 session issued a call to all Southern Baptists
for a convention to meet at Savannah on May 13, 1847, just prior
to the gathering of the state body, to consider the organization of
a separate society for carrying on publication work in the South.
Approximately 100 well-known leaders of Southern Baptists gathered
at that time and formed the Southern Baptist Publication Society.[27]
A constitution was adopted providing membership on a financial basis
for individuals, Baptist churches, and Baptist societies. The object
of the body was "to publish and distribute such books as are needed
by the Baptist denomination in the South." An appeal was made
to all Baptists in the southern states to affiliate with this society.[28]

This action, of course, was not novel in the sense that Southern
Baptists had never organized independent societies of this kind. They

had done so both on the state level and on an interstate level, as seen, for example, in the home mission society of R. T. Daniel in 1839. However, this was significant in that it magnified an optional way for benevolent work after the Convention as such had refused to carry on the particular benevolence. It simply meant that a minority of Southern Baptists could organize for benevolences without reference to the action of the Southern Baptist Convention. It provided another safeguard, if one were needed, against the centralization of the Convention, and still constitutes a live option that has been repeated in various spheres of activity, as will be noted.

Many southern organizations which had been auxiliary to the American Baptist Publication Society of Philadelphia changed their affiliation to this new Southern Baptist body. As a matter of fact, the American Baptist Publication Society refrained voluntarily from working in the South from this time until after the Civil War. The question of bringing this southern publication body into the structure of the Convention was agitated regularly after 1858, but nothing came of it. Sometime during the Civil War, perhaps in late 1863, this southern publication society ceased operations, a casualty of the war. During the 16 years of its existence it printed more than 80 different books and booklets, totaling almost 250,000 copies. Southern Baptists gave more than $100,000 for the work during these years, showing the interest in this type of ministry by many.[29]

Southern Baptist Sunday School Union. In all denominations the Sunday School was becoming recognized as an excellent teaching and enlistment opportunity. In 1840 the Baptist Tract Society changed its name to the American Baptist Publication and Sunday School Society to emphasize its entrance into the area of Sunday School work.

In 1857, R. B. C. Howell, president of the Southern Baptist Convention, introduced a resolution at the Concord Association of Tennessee urging the formation of a Sunday School union. Delegates from eight states met at Nashville on October 23, 1857, and organized the Southern Baptist Sunday School Union. The body became suspect, however, when the Landmark leader, A. C. Dayton, was elected its president. Despite some opposition, the union continued until it was killed by the Civil War.

Southern Baptist Theological Seminary. Practically all of the southern states recognized quite early the need for ministerial education and endeavored to meet these needs. At least ten southern states provided Baptist colleges which were founded for the specific purpose of providing literary and theological training for ministers. However, in 1835 Basil Manly, pastor of the First Baptist Church, Charleston, South Carolina, wrote that these efforts in various states were not enough.

He suggested a coalition of several states to cooperate in founding a southwide theological school. Nothing came of this suggestion. In 1841 North and South Carolina Baptists pondered a plan for all collegiate students from each state to go to Wake Forest in North Carolina, while all theological students from both states would go to Furman in South Carolina. This also fell through. J. L. Dagg of Mercer in Georgia wrote Robert Ryland of Virginia agitating the question, and in response the Virginia Baptist Education Society appointed a committee in 1844, which reported in the following year that despite the importance of this enterprise, nothing could be done for the present.

> The difficulty lies in selecting a site for such a School. Our Brethren, in South Carolina, Georgia, and Alabama, have, in each of those States, an Institution, partly endowed, which they would gladly have adopted as the common Theological School of the Southern and South-western Baptists.[30]

At the consultative meeting of Southern Baptists in 1845 at Augusta, leaders from the seaboard states discussed the need for such an institution, but all recognized that the Baptist colleges in the South which had theological departments felt they did not need such a southwide body and provided formidable opposition.

Baptists in the West made the first beginning of a cooperative enterprise for theological education. Agitation had begun as early as 1833, and a Western Baptist Education Society was formed. Under their auspices the Western Baptist Theological Institute opened in Covington, Kentucky, in 1845, but unfortunately for the enterprise, at the very height of northern-southern tension over slavery, the faculty were all northern men of antislavery sentiments in a school located in a slave state. After legal controversy, the school was closed and its property divided.[31]

For almost a decade the pros and cons of a southwide theological institution were discussed in editorials from various states in the South, some opposing and some supporting it. Significant action came in 1855 when an Education Conference, meeting between sessions of the Southern Baptist Convention at Montgomery, called an Education Convention to meet in Augusta, Georgia, in April, 1856. At that meeting there were sixty-eight delegates from Maryland, District of Columbia, Virginia, North Carolina, South Carolina, Georgia, Alabama, Florida, Mississippi, Tennessee, and Louisiana. All but twenty of these were from South Carolina and Georgia. The group recognized that the location of the school and funds for its founding and operation were basic in considering the establishment of a southwide school, and named a special committee to study these matters and report at a meeting in the following year. Two months later, the South

Carolina Baptist Convention proposed that the theological funds of Furman University would be turned over to the trustees of a general theological school, and that South Carolina would increase these funds to $100,000 on the conditions that the proposed seminary would be located in Greenville and that the other states would raise an equal amount. When the Education Convention met in 1857 at Louisville between sessions of the Southern Baptist Convention, there were eighty-eight delegates from twelve states. After earnest discussion, the South Carolina offer was unanimously accepted, despite sharp disagreement on the part of advocates of other schools.

The Education Convention met in Greenville, South Carolina, May 1, 1858, but plans to organize the new institution were delayed because a faculty had not been completed. An Abstract of Principles was prepared and adopted by the Education Convention.[32]

The seminary opened in Greenville, South Carolina, in the fall of 1859 with James P. Boyce as chairman of the faculty, along with John A. Broadus, Basil Manly, Jr., and William Williams as professors. There were twenty-six students in the first session, representing six southern states. The work of the seminary was soon suspended by civil war.

The First Years of the Southern Baptist Convention

Although the Convention was structured as a triennial body (after the pattern of the General Missionary Convention), it actually convened eight times from the 1845 consultative meeting at Augusta to the May, 1861, meeting at Savannah, Georgia, after civil war had begun. The more frequent gatherings were inaugurated by an unfortunate experience in 1849. The Convention was scheduled to meet at Nashville, but a cholera epidemic in that city caused a sparsely attended meeting that was convened there by Vice-president R. B. C. Howell to be shifted to Charleston, South Carolina, for the completion of the session. By a vote of forty-two to seventeen, the Convention adopted a resolution to amend the constitution to arrange for biennial rather than triennial meetings. An effort was made at this time to establish annual meetings, but this suggestion was not supported by the body. The presiding officers during these eight meetings, William B. Johnson (1845-49), R. B. C. Howell (1851-57), and Richard Fuller (1859-61), were gifted and wise leaders.

The general attendance at these meetings of the Convention was somewhat discouraging. Except for the session at Richmond in 1859 (where Virginia alone reported 241 delegates), the average attendance was around 160. The finances, although shaky at first, were bolstered by the use of agents in the various states to appeal for funds. In a review by the *Religious Herald* of Virginia, it was pointed out that during the thirty-three years previous to separation, while all American Baptists were united in missionary work, the South had contributed $250,656 to home and foreign missions; while by 1859, during the thirteen years the Southern Baptist Convention had been in existence, the southern states had contributed $266,359 for domestic and Indian missions and $384,339.07 for foreign missions, or a total of $650,698.07. This amounted to an average annual contribution seven times greater than that given by the South before the organization of the new body.[33]

During these first fifteen years of its existence, the new Southern Baptist Convention was confronted with several severe threats to its life.

One of these was the problem of communication and transportation. Long distances, mountain ranges, and wide rivers were formidable enemies of unity, understanding, and fellowship. To send a package of books from Richmond, Virginia, to Charleston, South Carolina, for example, it was necessary to send them to Baltimore, Maryland, first; and to send a bookcase from Tuscaloosa, Alabama, to Penfield, Georgia, it must be sent to Mobile, Alabama, to New York City, back to Savannah, Georgia, thence to Penfield by way of Augusta or Atlanta, Georgia.[34] Small attendance at conventions, expensive and slow gathering of funds, and provincial prejudices were faced.

Another virulent foe was the antimission movement. As pointed out in the resumé of the state activities, most antimission followers had withdrawn or been expelled from missionary churches, associations, and state bodies by 1845, but enough of them remained to provide vigorous opposition to the new southwide body.

Still another threat to the Convention may be called localism. A vital factor in assuring the continuance of the Convention was the ability to secure funds from the constituents to promote the benevolent work. Most Southern Baptists recognized the need for giving funds for foreign missions, but missionary work on the home field was another matter. There was widespread spiritual destitution in every state of the South, and there was reluctance to give funds for home mission work somewhere else when the needs were so great within a local area. The Convention's first corresponding secretary for home missions resigned after less than six months of service and said that he was convinced that the people preferred to work through their associations and state bodies rather than provide funds for the Domestic Mission Board of the southwide body.

> Throughout the period from 1845 to 1894, there was friction between the Home Mission Board of the Convention and those states which desired to keep their funds and do their own work. Some of the Southern leaders gently chided these states by reminding them that they had clamored for aid from a general organization before 1845,

but now that an agency had been organized to render such aid they were unwilling to give it their support. For many years the funds collected and expended by the various Southern states for domestic missions greatly exceeded the amount provided for the Southern Convention's Domestic or Home Board.[35]

Gathering up this localism, J. R. Graves and his Landmark movement, which will be described later in this chapter, provided a severe test for the new southwide body.

Some structural changes were made in the body during this period. The Indian Mission Association had been organized as an independent society in 1842, and its work was principally supported by Southern Baptists. In 1855 the association proposed union with the Convention, who instructed its Domestic Mission Board to take over the work of the association.[36] For a short time the name of the board was the Domestic and Indian Mission Board.

Also, a new board was created. From 1846 to 1851 the Convention authorized its mission boards to act as agents for the distribution of the Bible. Year by year, however, there was agitation to create a separate board for this work, and in 1851 a Bible Board, to be located at Nashville, was authorized.[37] The controversy between the American Bible Society and Baptists desiring a literal translation of the Scriptures had brought a schism in 1850 with the formation of the American Bible Union. It was evident that Southern Baptists, rather than choosing officially one way or another, preferred to organize their own Bible Board. From that time until the close of the period, the board made reports to the Convention concerning funds raised for Bible distribution and the work that was done.

Functionally, the Southern Baptist Convention had not as yet departed substantially from the old society plan followed before separation in 1845. Representation in the body still depended upon designated gifts, and agents for each benevolence in the field continued the sense of rivalry that had existed under the old society plan. The potential thrust of the Convention that was implicit in providing Boards of Managers for multiple benevolences, as set out in Article V of the constitution, was limited by the method of financing under which designated giving provided support for only two benevolences, foreign and home missions.

In addition, there was no authoritative *ad interim* body or committee to represent the Convention between the regular meetings of the body. This made it necessary to continue allowing boards to be totally autonomous between sessions of the Convention. The designated giving to two benevolences (foreign and home missions) and then three (the Bible Board) eliminated any financing for the Convention body itself.

However, there were signs that the new character of the body was beginning to emerge. This was not yet recognized by those involved in it, but from a later point of vantage it can be seen. At the 1846 meeting, out of the total of 135 who were present, 91 of them were from missionary societies, churches, and individuals making gifts to the Convention, while state bodies and local associations had 42 representatives. By 1861, however, missionary societies, churches, and individuals sent only 8 representatives, while state bodies and local associations accounted for 169 of the 177 delegates. This is exactly the reverse of the development between 1802 and 1814 when the missionary program was rapidly taken from the hands of the associations and put into autonomous missionary societies. Now, in Southern Baptist life, missionary societies were giving way to structured bodies like the associations and the state bodies as agencies to raise money for missions. Perhaps Southern Baptists were beginning to recognize the truth of what Francis Wayland had said in 1823 when criticizing the make-up of the General Missionary Convention that "missionary societies are not representative bodies," so that many were advocating that representation for a body such as the Southern Baptist Convention must be sought in structured organizations like associations and state conventions, rather than in missionary societies.

Although rather minor, another straw in the wind in the developing multi-benevolence function of the Convention may be glimpsed in the fact that at first the Convention sermon was concerned only with foreign missions. Belatedly, it was recognized that the Domestic Mission Board also had an interest in the matter, so a second sermon was arranged for the purpose of forwarding domestic missions. Then, after a brief period, the Convention sermon was separated from the functions of the boards, and the subject of it was left to the initiative of the preacher.

The Foreign Mission Board. At the 1846 session in Richmond, it was reported that C. D. Mallary, who had been elected Corresponding Secretary for the Board of Foreign Missions, had been unable to take the post because of failing health. James B. Taylor, pastor at Richmond, had temporarily assumed leadership, and the Convention enthusiastically named him as permanent corresponding secretary. He served with distinction until his death in 1871.[38] Taylor reported that by agreement with the General Missionary Convention, the northern body would retain the property that had been accumulated but would also assume responsibility for the substantial debts involved therewith. Relative to the transfer of any fields to the new body, the Boston board notified the Foreign Mission Board late in 1846 that if any of the missionaries should prefer to change their relations from the Boston board to the southern board, they should "in the spirit of fraternal regard" be allowed every facility for doing so.

The board at Richmond corresponded with J. Lewis Shuck and I. J. Roberts, southerners in China, who indicated their desire to serve under the southern board. The first appointee, however, was Samuel C. Clopton, named on September 1, 1845, while George Pearcy was appointed in November. Shuck became a missionary of the board in March, 1846, and Roberts was accepted at the same meeting.[39] Other able missionaries were sent to the East Asia field, including two giants—R. H. Graves to Canton and Matthew T. Yates.

The other field of service of the southern Foreign Mission Board during this period was Africa. John Day, an American Negro missionary in Liberia, decided to leave the service of the northern board and work under the new Convention, and he was appointed in 1846. The first missionary sent from this country by the new board was B. J. Drayton, a member of the First African Baptist Church in Richmond, who sailed in January, 1848. Thomas J. Bowen was appointed for Central Africa in 1849. Many other missionary couples and individuals were appointed to Africa but were felled there by death or broken health. Bowen himself had to return to America, and although he worked briefly in 1859 among the Yoruba slaves in Rio de Janeiro, his health prevented further service. In 1856 the northern Baptist board transferred its Liberian work to the southern board.

The board began the publication of the *Southern Baptist Missionary Journal* during the first year as a means of communicating with the constituency through the reports of the missionaries.

Gifts to foreign missions increased steadily in these antebellum years. The following chart gleaned from Convention *Annuals* does not include offerings at Convention meetings and some other receipts, so it is not completely accurate, but it will illustrate the general increase in gifts year by year:

1846	$11,735.22
1849	30,000.00 (estimated)
1851	44,805.65
1853	57,797.10
1855	52,246.87
1857	58,436.13
1859	79,964.12
1861	75,000.00 (estimated)

The Domestic and Indian Mission Board. The first year brought many dismal hours to the new Domestic Mission Board, located at Marion, Alabama. Both the president and the corresponding secretary of the board resigned shortly after their appointment at Augusta. Still another corresponding secretary reluctantly accepted the post, then resigned with the comment that "our brethren prefer carrying on their domestic missionary operations, through their Associations and State Conventions." Russell Holman then served from 1846 to 1851. T. F. Curtis retained the office for two years, and was succeeded by Joseph Walker from 1853 to 1856. Holman again took the post in 1856 and served throughout the remainder of this period.

The board outlined its field as the fourteen states of the South, covering nearly 1,000,000 square miles and a population of about 8,000,000.[40] During this period work was begun among the white population, the Negroes, the Indians, the Chinese in California, and the Germans in Missouri and Maryland. It will be recalled that in 1855 the board took over the work of the American Indian Mission Association.

Meanwhile, the Home Mission Society was withdrawing its missionaries from the South in implicit recognition of the territorial field of the southern convention. In 1846 they supported two in Arkansas, one in Florida, three in Kentucky, five in Missouri, one in North Carolina, one in Texas, and one in Virginia; in 1847, there were two in Arkansas, one in Florida, two in Kentucky, four in Missouri, one in Texas, and one in Virginia; in 1848, there were two in Arkansas, two in Kentucky, one in Missouri, and one in Texas; in 1849, there were one in Texas and one in New Mexico; in 1850, there were one in Missouri and one in New Mexico. Thereafter, only Missouri generally had a missionary until the outbreak of the war.[41]

In 1847, when the Home Mission Society appointed a missionary to Texas, having previously withdrawn from this field, Secretary Russell Holman of the southern board wrote:

> Texas was abandoned by them previous to the division; after the Southern organization it was occupied by this Board. This, together with its geographical position, will furnish an apology for calling it "our field." Yet, if the Northern Board have sufficient funds to "preach the gospel to every creature" in the Northern and Western States, and Territories, and can occasionally send a Missionary to Texas, we will find no fault.[42]

The northern society left the field after a few months.

That the society might reenter the South did not seem to occur to either the society or the southern convention during this period. Since the appointment of missionaries was so closely linked to the area of receipts, and since it was not contemplated that the southern states would voluntarily leave their own Convention to provide receipts for the northern Home Mission Society, the possibility of rivalry on the home field seemed rather remote. Yet, this remote possibility became a reality during the next period as a result of a reappraisal of its mission by the Home Mission Society of New York. That story will be told in succeeding chapters.

The following chart shows the increase of receipts and missionaries during this period.[43]

Year	Number of Missionaries	Cash Receipts
1846	7	$ 1,824
1847	30	9,594
1848	50	11,239
1849	57	12,176
1850	50	10,692
1851	50	12,176
1852	66	10,939
1853	77	13,074
1854	88	19,019
1855	99	21,153
1856	125	23,088
1857	136	39,002
1858	138	32,072
1859	139	41,710
1860	159	48,966
1861	111	35,273

The Bible Board. The third board added to the structure of the Convention in 1851, as mentioned previously, was the Bible Board, located at Nashville, Tennessee, which had several secretaries during its brief life. Southern Baptists were beginning to glimpse the potentialities of Article V of their constitution, which allowed additional benevolences to be promoted by the body. They were somewhat divided over the proper Bible society to support because of the conflict over the translation of the word *baptizein.* Since both the American and Foreign Bible Society and even the older American Bible Society were receiving rather generous gifts from Southern Baptist contributors, the leaders of the Convention thought that the formation of a Bible Board within the Convention structure would promptly guarantee that funds would be diverted from the older societies to the new board. They were mistaken. The Bible Board's report at each biennial meeting mentioned the large sums still being sent to the other Bible societies by Southern Baptists. Its receipts were shown as follows during this period:

1851-53	$ 8,073.86
1853-55	8,972.99
1855-57	32,182.24
1857-59	4,376.74
1859-61	6,505.97

The unusual increase in 1855-57 receipts was caused by a different plan of operation. The reported receipts of state auxiliaries were counted and promptly assigned on paper to the state where the money was raised, resulting in a misleading statistic for that biennium.

The Convention's Greatest Internal Crisis

Campbellism and Primitivism, which had been so divisive in the previous period, had now been identified and for the most part had separated from the ranks of missionary Baptists. Daniel Parker, the outstanding leader of the hyper-Calvinists, died in Texas in 1844, and there was no one of his stature to replace him. This does not mean that the antimission movement had disappeared, but its strength within Southern Baptist life had dissipated. A new and potentially divisive movement was articulated during this period, however, the effects of which are still evident in Southern Baptist life.

The Beginning of the Landmark Movement.[44] The principal figure in this developing conflict was J. R. Graves, who was born in Vermont in 1820. At fifteen he left Congregationalism and united with the North Springfield Baptist Church in Vermont. His family moved to Ohio in 1839, where young Graves taught school. During his two years here he was ordained as a Baptist minister, and along with his pastor entered fiercely into the struggle with Campbellism. Moving in 1841 to Kentucky, he spent four years teaching school, at the same time carrying on an intensive program of self-study to compensate for his meager formal education.

In 1845 he went to Nashville, Tennessee, to take a teaching position, and for a brief season was pastor of the Second Baptist Church. In 1846, however, he returned to membership in the First Baptist Church where R. B. C. Howell was pastor and editor of *The Baptist* (*The Tennessee Baptist* after 1847). In November, 1846, he became assistant editor to Howell, and in June, 1848, succeeded Howell as editor. Howell moved to Virginia in 1850 to accept a pastorate there, but returned to Nashville in 1857 to serve his old church. While he was away, Graves launched the Landmark movement, and as soon as Howell returned, conflict began between the two former associates. Before describing the tumultuous events of the next several years, it would be well to describe the nature of the Landmark movement which Graves constructed piecemeal. The background of Landmarkism includes a great deal of Graves's Vermont ecclesiology, his unusual skill in integrating various elements into a single theological system, his personal aggressive nature and love for conflict, and his ability to attract strong and able lieutenants for his cause. These personal factors were matched by the immediate context of his ministry. He had learned in earlier years the art of confronting Campbellism and had breathed the heady air of victory in debate. Now in Nashville Graves found himself in a stronghold of Methodist and Disciples leadership that had the temerity to challenge the truth of the Baptist position. As editor of the Baptist paper in Nashville he had the opportunity to strike a blow as a champion for Baptist principles.

Literary controversies between Baptists and pedobaptists were quite common both in England and in America. The foreign mission enthusiasm at the turn of the nineteenth century slowed somewhat the doctrinal assaults by Baptists against pedobaptists and the reverse, but the Bible controversy beginning in 1835 and continuing for many decades thereafter renewed the warfare. As described previously, in that year the American Bible Society declined to print a revised edition of Carey's Bengali Bible because pedobaptists did not want the word *baptizein* translated by a word in the language for *immerse*. The society insisted that the translation of this work must "comport with the known views of other Christian denominations." Many Baptists withdrew in 1836 from this society and formed the American and Foreign Bible Society. They were incensed when the American Bible Society used political influence to prevent the issuance of a charter to the new body by the New York legislature. After six years of struggle, the charter was finally secured in 1848, but not before the whole bitter conflict had been widely publicized in Baptist papers everywhere. The Bible translation controversy proved to be a springboard into discussions of other doctrinal differences that separated Baptists and other denominations.

In the very year the Bible translation controversy was touched off, Graves left Congregationalism to become a Baptist in Vermont. Evidently he followed the course of the controversy avidly during the next several years. In his debates later with the pedobaptists, Graves showed an intimate knowledge of this baptismal controversy that marked the days when he chose the Baptist way.

Graves seemed to thrive on controversy. As soon as he became assistant to Howell in 1846, the paper immediately took a more aggressive stance. In an editorial in 1849 he admitted that he deliberately gave attention to controversial topics, asserting that as long as there was conviction about the truth, there must be conflict. Confrontations with pedobaptists, he remarked, had won many of them to Baptist views, and such conflict was the best way to make progress. Before Landmarkism had taken form, Graves already had the temperament, the means for propagation, and the basic views that entered into the movement.

The Principal Emphases of Landmarkism. When matured, the system of Graves had three principal emphases, each of which was spun out into various applications in doctrine and polity. The first was the authoritative nature of the local and visible New Testament congregation. Of course he identified a New Testament congregation as a Baptist church only, since Baptists alone were admittedly reproducing the total primitive pattern described in the Scriptures. From this emphasis Graves adopted an antagonistic attitude toward any doctrine or organization that would wrest the primacy from the local churches. General bodies were suspect. Their basis of membership must not be financial, associational, or denominational: they should draw their authority from the local body. They must not exercise authority over the local body, directly or indirectly. Their programs should not usurp the work of the local churches. Although Graves had formerly been of another mind, he came to the position that only members of a local church could participate in the Supper in that church. No persons "of like faith and order" could be allowed, since these persons were not amenable to the discipline of the church observing the Supper unless they were members of it.

The second principal emphasis of Graves asserted that the kingdom of Christ was made up of the aggregate of local congregations that were true churches of Christ. Since he recognized only Baptist churches as true churches, this sounded suspiciously as though he meant that only Baptists could be saved, and he was forced many times to protest that he did not mean this. The kingdom of Christ (that is, the true churches) has had an unbroken continuity from the days of the New Testament to the present, since Christ said that the gates of death would not prevail against it. Graves wrote:

> Landmark Baptists very generally believe that for the Word of the Living God to stand, and for the veracity of Jesus Christ to vindicate itself, the kingdom which he set up "in the days of John the Baptist," has had an unbroken continuity until now. I say kingdom, instead of succession of churches, for the sake of perspicacity. Those who oppose "church succession" confuse the unthinking, by representing our position to be, that the identical organization which Christ established—the First Church of Judea—has had a continued existence until to-day; or, that the identical churches, planted by the apostles, or, at least, *some one* of them, has continued until now, and that Baptist ministers are successors of the apostles; in a word, that our position is the old Romish and Episcopal doctrine of apostolic succession. I have, for full a quarter of a century, by pen and voice, vehemently protested against *these* misrepresentations, as Baptists have, for twice as many more, against the charge of teaching that no one can be saved without immersion, and quite as vainly; for those who oppose us seem determined to misrepresent, and will not be corrected. We repudiate the doctrine of apostolic succession; we do not believe *they* ever had a successor, and therefore, no one to-day is preaching under the apostolic commission any more than under that which Christ first gave to John the Baptist. They are our opposers who, in fact, hold to apostolic succession; for the majority do believe that, if ministers, they are preaching by the authority contained in that commission! So much for this charge.
>
> Nor have I, or any Landmarker known to me, ever advocated the succession of any particular church or churches; but my position is

that Christ, in the very "days of John the Baptist," did establish a visible kingdom on earth, and that this *kingdom* has never yet been "broken in pieces," or given to another class of subjects—has never for a day "been moved," or ceased from the earth, and never will until Christ returns personally to reign over it; that the organization he first set up, which John called "the Bride," and which Christ called his church, constituted that visible kingdom, and to-day all his *true* churches on earth constitute it; and, therefore, if his *kingdom* has stood unchanged, and will to the end, he must always have had true and uncorrupted churches, since his kingdom can not exist without true churches.[45]

Graves denied that it was necessary for him to prove by incontestable historical facts that this Kingdom had stood from the day it was set up by Christ, for to question this continuous succession would be to doubt Christ's promise when he said that the gates of death would not prevail against it.

We believe that his kingdom has stood unchanged, as firmly as we believe in the divinity of the Son of God, and, when we are forced to surrender the one faith, we can easily give up the other. If Christ has not kept his promise concerning his *church* to keep it, how can I trust him concerning *my salvation?* If he has not the power to save his *church,* he certainly has not the power to save me. For Christians to admit that Christ has not preserved his kingdom unbroken, unmoved, unchanged, and uncorrupted, is to surrender the whole ground to infidelity. I deny that a man is a believer in the Bible who denies this.[46]

Despite his claim that he did not need to prove historical succession, Graves early (about 1855) republished in America a book by C. H. Orchard of England, which attempted to trace Baptists from the New Testament days to the present.

The third corollary of Graves's system was the assertion that true churches must possess all the doctrinal and ecclesiastical characteristics of the primitive churches in order to be a part of this unbroken and unmoved Kingdom. This meant that all pedobaptist bodies were unscriptural. Methodists, Presbyterians, Roman Catholics, and other pedobaptist groups, said Graves, were not *churches* at all because they did not follow the scriptural pattern of the New Testament. He called them *societies.* They, therefore, could not authorize or practice scriptural baptism, and could not conduct the Supper. Their ministers were not New Testament ministers and should not be invited into Baptist pulpits, even to pray. Their ordinations were not valid and their activities were without scriptural authority. This is the rationale of "close communion." This aspect of Graves's system, it should be said, was the initial thrust of the movement.[47]

It is no wonder, in view of these strong assertions, that Graves was difficult to interpret. As distinguished a Baptist historian as

W. H. Whitsitt accused Graves of saying that salvation was impossible outside of a Baptist church. But in reply, Graves said explicitly that "Old Landmarkism" did not deny the spiritual regeneration of those with whom they declined to associate ministerially or ecclesiastically; that Landmarkism was not the denial of the honesty and conscientiousness of pedobaptists and Campbellites; that Landmarkism was not a proof of the uncharitableness of Baptists, since they were simply following the Scriptures; that Landmarkism was not a denial of the right of others to exist as professed churches or their ministers to preach their views.[48]

The Sources of Graves's Views. A number of complex factors unquestionably provided materials for the system of Graves. He was self-educated, choosing his own reading and areas of study, and as a consequence his theology showed the lack of a complete and systematic understanding of Christian doctrine. James E. Tull has demonstrated that Graves was quite at loss in trying to handle some of the basic Christian doctrines.[49] His early training in Vermont shaped his ecclesiology, particularly the several historical factors that called for the New Hampshire Confession of Faith, which was developed during his formative years, to magnify only the local congregation. His immediate associates furnished some of the grist for his system. The strong article on pulpit affiliation by J. M. Pendleton implemented his own ideas. The integrative ability of Graves is evident as one notes how he took ideas from these associates and wove them into his thinking. For example, he published an excerpt from *Theodosia Ernest,* a novel by A. C. Dayton, in a periodical he was publishing in 1856, in which Dayton asserted that the word *church* was never used in an "invisible, universal" sense in the New Testament. Graves put a footnote to the article and said: "The view is original and against the 'received authorities,' but is it not correct?" [50] Thereafter Graves incorporated this idea more completely into his writing. He could have noted the idea of historical succession in John L. Waller, R. B. C. Howell, or Jesse Mercer and others. His church-kingdom emphasis he could have found in Howell or J. Newton Brown. Long before the aggressive assertion of the view by Graves in 1851, there were many references in Baptist papers to the Baptist belief that pedobaptists were unscriptural. In fact, there was a startling letter in *The Christian Index* (Georgia) for April 21, 1843, in which a writer asked Editor Joseph S. Baker almost precisely the questions raised by Graves at Cotton Grove in 1851. In his reply Baker remarked that there were many who viewed pedobaptist churches merely as religious societies. Jesse Mercer of Georgia held many views that were reflected in the Landmark movement; Graves called him an "Old Landmarker." [51] When Graves tried to call James P. Boyce a Landmarker, however, Boyce protested.[52] Other portions of Graves' system can be glimpsed in various parts of Southern Baptist life before he appeared.[53] The system of Graves, when it matured, took these and many generally received Baptist doctrines and projected them to the extreme at every point.

The Rapid Spread of Landmarkism. The synthesis of Graves became popular in many sections of the South, particularly in the Southwest, in a remarkably short time. He was an eloquent and persuasive platform speaker and was widely sought for general meetings. He and his lieutenants were vigorous and skilled writers, Dayton, in particular, entering many homes through his novel, *Theodosia Ernest*. Graves controlled many media for propagation of his views. His newspaper, *The Tennessee Baptist*, was the most influential Baptist paper in all the Southwest, reaching about 12,000 subscribers by 1860. He also edited several regular periodicals, such as *The Southern Baptist Review and Eclectic*. He was a frequent visitor to many southern states and usually "swept the deck" when called upon to speak.

Graves had a reputation of being a champion of Baptist views in the struggle against Campbellism. Even J. B. Jeter, later to become his principal antagonist, admired Graves in the earlier years for their mutual efforts against Campbell. Not only so, Graves was widely known for his active participation in denominational affairs. He had a significant role in forming societies for education and for Indian missions, assisted in raising funds for Union University, organized a woman's college in Kentucky, and through his newspaper and publishing firm wielded vast influence in supporting many Baptist causes. He had a finger in forming the Bible Board and the Southern Baptist Sunday School Union, and by his opposition, sowed distrust for the Southern Baptist Publication Society, Charleston, South Carolina, probably in the hope that he would become the "orthodox" publisher for Southern Baptists.

One not inconsiderable factor was the plain fact that his tenets pleased many Baptists as they were identified with true New Testament doctrines and practices to the discredit of other denominations. In a day when doctrinal debates were common, Graves provided much new grist for the mill, and in the midst of some very trying and disheartening experiences, gave Southern Baptists a sense of "divine right" in their work.

It is no wonder, then, that Graves' system evoked a mixed response. Some viewed him as the champion of orthodoxy against the forces that would dilute the pure Baptist position; others, like John L. Waller, Kentucky editor, denied that Graves and his group held views that were Baptist at all.[54] Apart from the dubious authority and logic in his doctrines, Graves alienated many by his lack of Christian charity, his belligerent attitude, his pejorative stance, his spiritual arrogance, and his personal ambition.

The Development of Controversy. Just how long Graves had been formulating his system in his mind is not clear, but evidently his interest in asserting a radically sectarian and integrated system of Baptist beliefs was sparked by a letter from a Baptist association in Alabama to the *Western Baptist Review,* Louisville, Kentucky, on February 25, 1848, asking if immersion on profession of faith by a pedobaptist minister was a valid baptism. John L. Waller, editor of the paper, discussed the question at some length. He noted that it was impossible to trace a succession of "valid" baptisms back to New Testament times, so that no one could be certain whether even a Baptist administrator had an unbroken line of "valid" baptisms leading up to his own. He closed by saying:

> Let all those who can furnish clear and indubitable evidence of the validity of their baptism, according to the terms of the affirmative of this question, vote non-fellowship for those churches and ministers who believe it right to receive a member who has been immersed on profession of faith by a Pedo-Baptist minister, and let all the rest keep silence. . . . What can be more fair? Surely no brother in all Alabama would wish to condemn in another what he allows in himself.[55]

In direct response to Waller's letter, Graves under a pseudonym in his paper denounced the reply, saying that "the unbroken practice of the Baptist Church, from deep antiquity till now or within a few years, is higher authority than scores of Reviews."

W. W. Barnes felt that it was this discussion that "precipitated the several elements of succession that had been held in solution in Baptist life." He identified four aspects of this succession: church succession (each congregation must be formed by the authority of another true New Testament congregation in historical succession back to the New Testament days); apostolic succession (each ordination must be conducted by an orthodox [Baptist] and properly constituted presbytery which had historical succession from the New Testament); baptismal succession (each baptism must be performed by a "validly" baptized and authorized minister); and spiritual succession (through the centuries "there are traces of our principles and of adherents to our principles").[56] Graves, said Barnes, conjoined the first three views (church, apostolic, and baptismal succession) into a "logical rigid system" after about 1850. James E. Tull felt that the view of Graves was basically church succession.

The first evidences of the developing synthesis appeared when Graves issued a call for interested Baptists to meet at Cotton Grove, Tennessee, on June 24, 1851, and he submitted the following questions for discussion:

> 1st. Can Baptists consistently, with their principles or the scriptures,

recognize those societies, not organized according to the pattern of the Jerusalem Church, but possessing a *government,* different *officers,* a different *class of membership,* different *ordinances, doctrines* and *practices,* as the Church of Christ?

2d. Ought they to be called Gospel Churches or Churches in a religious sense?

3d. Can we consistently recognize the ministers of such irregular and unscriptural bodies, as gospel ministers in their official capacity?

4th. Is it not virtually recognizing them as official ministers to invite them into our pulpits, or by any other act that would or could be construed into such a recognition?

5th. Can we consistently address as brethren, those *professing* christianity, who not only have not the doctrines of Christ, and walk not according to his commandments, but are arrayed in direct and bitter opposition to them? [57]

In the following month at the annual meeting of the Big Hatchie Association at Bolivar, Tennessee, these questions were discussed. Question 4 was unanimously answered yes while the others were unanimously answered no as expressing Baptist views.

In the following year (1852), Graves was joined by J. M. Pendleton, at that time pastor of the First Baptist Church, Bowling Green, Kentucky. Pendleton had invited Graves to come to the church for a revival, and in addition to holding an evangelistic meeting, Graves enlisted Pendleton in support of his views. He asked Pendleton to write a tract on the question of whether Baptists ought to recognize pedobaptist preachers as gospel ministers. Graves published this tract in 1854 under the title, "An Old Landmark Re-set," referring to Proverbs 22:28, which said, "Remove not the ancient landmark, which thy fathers have set." From this the movement got its name. The publication of this tract brought immediate controversy. [58]

About this time Graves met A. C. Dayton, who had recently left the Presbyterians to join the Baptists. Graves was impressed with Dayton's writing ability, and soon made him associate editor of the Tennessee Baptist paper. One of Dayton's principal contributions to the movement was his novel, *Theodosia Ernest* (in two volumes), published in 1857, which told the story, complete with romance, of a lovely girl who became a Landmark Baptist by conviction. As James E. Tull has demonstrated, however, these three, acknowledged as the "triumvirate" of the Landmark movement, never completely agreed on the doctrines and emphases of the movement.

The Southern Baptist Convention felt the impact of Graves' views in their 1855 meeting, the year after Pendleton's tract on nonpulpit affiliation and about the time Graves republished Orchard's history of Baptists (tracing Baptist succession from the days of the New Testament to the nineteenth century). After the Convention had completed its initial organization, the usual resolution was offered inviting ministers of other denominations to join the deliberations of the body. This resolution was sharply challenged, and the debate that followed lasted the whole day. Writing almost forty years later, John A. Broadus described the surprise of many at the views and strength of the Landmark followers. He closed by saying:

> After the day's discussion, it was proposed to end the matter by letting the resolution be withdrawn, upon the understanding that those who saw no objection to its passage would concede thus much to the views of their brethren who objected so strongly. Some present thought already that there was no such extreme difference of opinion among us as appeared to exist. The controversy in the next few years rose high, and in some quarters threatened division. But it has now long been felt by most brethren that we could agree to disagree upon the matters involved, and that the great bulk of us were really not very far apart.[39]

When R. B. C. Howell returned to become pastor again of the First Baptist Church, Nashville, in 1857, he found a minority of his church to be avid followers of Graves. Graves was unawed by the return of his mentor, and when Howell refused to cooperate in Landmark objectives, Graves unleashed a scurrilous attack against him. The church brought charges against Graves on September 8, 1858. He was found guilty on five counts and excluded on October 18, 1858. Meanwhile, Graves and a minority had withdrawn from the First Baptist Church and claimed that their schismatic group was the true church.[60] Landmarkers were in control of the General Association of Tennessee and North Alabama and the Concord Association of Tennessee, and each of these bodies recognized Graves and a handful of followers as the true First Baptist Church of Nashville and unseated the pastor, R.B.C. Howell, and the majority of the members, although Howell had been president of the Southern Baptist Convention since 1851. Graves had some difficulty in his ecclesiology explaining how an autonomous New Testament church (such as the First Baptist Church, Nashville) could be rejected in favor of a small, schismatic minority.[61]

At the same time he was jousting with Howell, Graves launched severe attacks against the boards of the Convention, particularly the Foreign Mission Board. When a colleague, President N. M. Crawford of Mercer University, Georgia, published an article in 1858 in *The Tennessee Baptist,* in which he denied that the Foreign Mission Board had authority over autonomous Baptist churches on the mission field, Graves volunteered his agreement in a footnote:

> No man has lower views of the authority of a Missionary Board to dictate to missionaries or churches than we have. . . . We, no more than Brother C., believe that our missionary machinery is scriptural or expedient. The scriptural plan is clearly exemplified in the New

Testament, and it is simple and effectual, and the sooner we return to it as a denomination, the better for us and for the world. . . .

We do not believe that the Foreign Board has any right to call upon the missionaries that the churches send to China or Africa, to take a journey to Richmond to be examined touching their experience, call to the ministry, and soundness in the faith. It is a high-handed act, and degrades both the judgment and authority of the Church and presbytery that ordained him, thus practically declaring itself above both.[62]

What better method, a correspondent wrote him, could be followed than the present system of entrusting foreign mission matters to a board to administer? Graves said that the scriptural method would be to follow the example of Paul: let local churches unite informally to send a missionary to a foreign field and remit funds by a commercial house, thus eliminating the present nonscriptural plan of allowing a board or convention to override autonomous Baptist churches on the foreign field.

An ominous note was sounded in February, 1859, just a few months before the biennial meeting of the Convention at Richmond. Graves reflected his animosity toward the president· of the Convention, R. B. C. Howell, and his dissatisfaction with the Foreign Mission Board. He wrote in his paper:

There are elements at work that threaten the disruption of the relation of the Convention and the Foreign Board to the body of the Southern Baptists. There are schemes of consolidation and centralization now urged by certain brethren who exercise a controlling influence in the Biennial Convention which, if they succeed in consummating, will as certainly destroy the present union of Southern Baptists in Foreign Missions as the Convention meets in May next. And there is a determination on the part of some, moved more by partizan than missionary zeal, to make the next Biennial Convention an ecclesiastical Court and to force its decision into antagonism with Churches and Associations.[63]

Graves came to the Convention at Richmond in May, 1859, determined to have his Nashville minority seated as the true First Baptist Church, to prevent the reelection of R. B. C. Howell as Convention president, to kill the Bible Board from which A. C. Dayton had been forced out as president, and to confront the Foreign Mission Board. It was indeed unfortunate for the Landmark faction that the Convention was meeting in Virginia, the center of anti-Landmark leadership. Because of the location, there were 241 "delegates" from Virginia alone, more than from all of the Landmark states put together. When the 97 from North and South Carolina were added, these three anti-Landmark states always had a majority of the 574 "delegates" attending the 1859 session. It is no wonder that Graves failed in most of his objectives. Howell's group was seated at the Convention, and

Howell was reelected president on the first ballot. Recognizing, however, that Graves had enough popular support to embarrass if not to split the Convention (as Graves had openly threatened if Howell were elected), Howell promptly declined the office, and after three ballots Richard Fuller, universally beloved and not actively engaged in the controversy, was named to the presidency. The strength of the Landmark faction may be glimpsed when motions to invite ministers of other denominations to seats or even to invite them "to witness our proceedings" could not be passed.

Although Graves also failed in his efforts to abolish the Bible Board, he had more success in his confrontation with the Foreign Mission Board. He was given ample opportunity to present every objection and did so eloquently and with fervor. After a full day of debate, Graves met with the two secretaries of the board, J. B. Taylor and A. M. Poindexter, and discussed the issues until the "east was glowing and the roosters crowing." [64] As a result, a committee was appointed to inquire about improving the system of missions and missionary operations. In their report, this committee recommended that no change be made in the existing plans of missionary operation, but that if

> any churches, associations, or other bodies entitled to representation in this Convention, should prefer to appoint their own missionaries, and to assume the responsibility of defraying their salaries and entire expenses, that the respective Boards are authorized, under our present organization and fundamental rules, to become disbursing agents of the bodies so appointing missionaries and appropriating funds, . . .; provided such expenses of forwarding the money, as have to be specially incurred, be borne by the contributors.[65]

Such were the evidences of personal and ideological antagonism that the final action of this 1859 Convention urged that "personal controversies among pastors, editors, and brethren, should, from this time forth, be more than ever avoided." On motion of I. T. Tichenor, it was agreed that all Baptist papers be instructed to publish this resolution.

About two weeks after the close of this Convention, Graves' paper contained an editorial which said:

> There is no reason why our denomination may not co-operate harmoniously in missionary matters. All those who prefer that the Board at Richmond shall have the appointing power and be held responsible for its exercise, can throw their funds unconditionally into its treasury. Those Associations and Churches that prefer appointing their own missionaries can do so, and the Board will transmit their funds, while the missionaries will be amenable to the Associations and Churches sending them forth. Here are two plans of operation submitted to the brethren. Let them make their election. Let them remember that they

have no good excuse for doing nothing. The missionary spirit enters essentially into a Church organized according to the gospel.[66]

However, still embroiled in the controversy with Howell and the First Baptist Church of Nashville, Graves spent the fall and winter of 1859 touring Alabama, Arkansas, Georgia, Louisiana, Mississippi, Texas, Virginia, and perhaps other states, pressing his cause and seeking vindication. It appeared that he was trying to bring about a schism in the denomination. He won many followers in these states. In May, 1860, as an example, the Mississippi state Baptist convention appointed a committee to attempt to mediate between Graves and the First Baptist Church, Nashville. A light note was injected into the deliberations of the Mississippi body over Landmarkism when T. C. Teasdale, one of their eminent leaders,

> prayed for the peace of Zion with a bias to one side of the mooted question manifested in his prayer; and when he had completed his prayer, some one moved that one be appointed by the chair to answer Dr. Teasdale's prayer.[67]

At the very close of this period in 1860, Graves and his lieutenants were powerful and popular. Their fortunes were radically affected by the outbreak of war, as will be described in the next period under study.

Summary of the Period

Southern Baptists grew in this period from 365,346 to 645,218, an average annual increase in membership of 4.79%, well below the 7.20% growth during the period from 1814 to 1845. The number of churches increased from 4,395 in 1845 to 7,760 in 1860, the associations increased from 213 in 1845 to 316 in 1860, and the state bodies from 9 to 13. This decrease in the rate of membership growth was not confined to a particular section, for the South Atlantic region grew only 3.88% during this period compared to 5.25% during the previous period; the South Central region grew only 5.36% during this period compared to 9.99% during the previous period; and the rate of growth in the single North Central state of Missouri, while impressive, could not compare with the large percentage previously attained when they had begun with few and increased to 16,366. It is true that the South Atlantic region decreased in the percentage of Southern Baptists found in that region from 55.48% in the previous period to 50.94% in this period; while the South Central region increased in this respect from 40.04% to 42.10%, and the North Central state increased from 4.48% to 6.95%; but here again, the larger percentages in the latter two regions do not mean that the South Atlantic region did not make good progress in Baptist work. This can be seen in the fact that the average annual population growth in the South Atlantic region was but 1.74%, while Baptists in that region increased by 3.88%, more than double the population rate. The South Central region increased in population at the rate of 4.32% during this period, while Baptists in that region increased by 9.99% annually, a little more than double the population rate. Missouri, the only North Central state, had a population increase during this period of 9.91%, compared to the Baptist increase of 10.89%. Thus, in every instance, Baptist growth exceeded the population rate, more than doubling it in the South Atlantic and South Central regions. Overall, the population increase in all southern states involved in this study was 3.25%, compared to the Baptist average annual growth of 4.79%. In 1860 Southern Baptists comprised 5.29% of the population, compared with 5.03% in 1845.

The South Atlantic region states, as pointed out, had 50.94% of all Southern Baptists in 1860, compared with 55.48% in 1845, and 68.47% in 1814. Virginia still had more Baptists than any other southern state in 1860 with 16.86%. Georgia showed a very large growth in this period and had 13.11% of Southern Baptists. South Carolina with 9.76% was barely ahead of North Carolina with 9.38%. Florida had 1.00%; Maryland, .64%; and District of Columbia, .16%.

The South Central region had 42.10% of all Southern Baptists, compared with 40.04% in 1845 and 31.53% in 1814. Kentucky still led the South Central region with 12.64% of all Southern Baptists, but had dropped behind Georgia to third among all southern states. Alabama had moved to second in this region with 9.49% by reason of a whopping 7.30% increase in this period. Tennessee had 7.21% of all Southern Baptists; Mississippi, 6.45%; Texas, 2.96%; Arkansas, 1.76%; and Louisiana, 1.59%.

The North Central state of Missouri had 6.95% of all Southern Baptists, compared with 4.48% in 1845 as a result of a 10.89% average annual increase during this period.

The states of the South were active during this period in prosecuting what is known as state missions. As a matter of fact, southern leaders noted a vigorous rivalry for funds between the state work and the work of the Domestic Mission Board of the Convention. The receipts of the southwide body, however, increased from $1,824 in 1846, with which 7 missionaries were employed, to $29,878 for the regular work and $19,088 for Indian missions in 1860, with 110 missionaries employed for the former and 49 for the latter work.

The foreign mission enterprise also advanced. In the first year, two missionaries had been sustained in China and the gifts were shown as $11,735.22, while by 1860, work was being supported on three fields (China, Liberia, and Nigeria) and receipts were approximately $75,000.

The new Bible Board was not receiving adequate support and would be abolished soon after the close of this period.

Scores of local academies and preparatory schools sprang up throughout the South during this period. Sometimes the founder was the principal, teacher, and sole proprietor. This was particularly true on the frontier where schools of this type for girls were very popular. It kept dangerous travel to a minimum and provided local interest in education. Some of these local schools persevered through wars and depressions of various sorts. Typical of these was the Harrison-Chilhowee Baptist Academy (Tennessee), which was founded about 1840 under the sponsorship of interested citizens.

It is rather significant in illustrating this "grass roots" educational interest to note that of the nine permanent advanced schools developed between 1845 and 1860, not a single one was initiated by the action of a structured state body, although in some cases there was collateral action. Baylor University (Texas) opened in 1845 under the auspices of the Texas Baptist Education Society. Bessie Tift (Georgia) began in 1847 under local auspices. Chowan (North Carolina) was opened in the following year by the Chowan Association. William Jewell College (Missouri) began classes in 1849 through private gifts to the state body, but the school has retained a self-perpetuating Board of Trustees. Carson-Newman (Tennessee) was sponsored in 1851 by the Baptist Education Society of East Tennessee. Bethel College (Kentucky) was opened in 1854 as a community project. Mars Hill (North Carolina) was sponsored by local Baptists in 1856. Hannibal LaGrange (Missouri) opened in 1858 under the sponsorship of a local association. Averett (Virginia) was begun in 1859 by the citizens of Danville.

Although originally the state bodies were organized to promote missions and education, additional functions began to be added as the people developed more confidence in the new structure and achieved a new unity through state cooperative enterprises. One of these added functions was the publication of a state paper. T. T. Eaton counted about thirty-six Baptist papers or periodicals begun before 1860 in the South.[68] Most of these were owned and edited by private individuals. Increasingly, the state bodies recognized the need for such a periodical both to provide religious news and the promotion of benevolent programs in the state.

Southern Baptists were becoming more articulate during this period. A few outstanding histories and biographies had been produced during the previous period, like Burkitt and Read's story of the Kehukee Association (1803), William Fristoe's history of the Ketocton Association (1808), Wood Furman's history of the Charleston Association (1811), Jesse Mercer's history of the Georgia Association (1838), Hosea Holcombe's history of Alabama Baptists (1840), and Charles D. Mallary's biography of Jesse Mercer (1844). In addition, the beginning of Baptist state papers before 1845 had offered an opportunity for extensive writing of various sorts—editorials, news writing, doctrinal monographs, sermonic literature, and the like.

Between 1845 and 1860, the amount and diversity of the literature increased. Much sermonic, doctrinal, and controversial material was published in the Baptist state papers and periodicals. In addition, several categories of books made their appearance. Doctrine and polity accounted for many: William B. Johnson on church polity (1846), R. B. C. Howell on communion (1847), J. L. Reynolds on church polity (1849), T. F. Curtis on communion (1850), P. H. Mell on baptism (1853) and a treaties on church discipline (1860), James B. Taylor on communion (1856), J. L. Dagg's two-volume work on theology (1857-58) and a single volume on moral science (1860), and Richard Fuller on baptism (1859). There were several historical and biographical books published, including James B. Taylor's *Memoir of Rice* just before the opening of this period (1840), J. B. Jeter on Andrew Broaddus (1852), George W. Purefoy's history of the Sandy Creek Association (1859), and R. B. C. Howell's story of Virginia Baptists (n.d.). J. R. Graves published a volume on sufferings in behalf of religious liberty in New England (1857), which may belong to this category. Polemical literature (particularly after the Landmark controversy began) was plentiful. Graves wrote four books; A. C. Dayton, one on pedobaptist and Campbellite immersions (1858); Pendleton published his Old Landmark Re-set article twice. In a miscellaneous category, two very popular books were novels: Sallie R. Ford published *Grace Truman* (1856) and A. C. Dayton, *Theodosia Ernest,* in two volumes (1857), the latter strongly Landmark. T. J. Bowen, missionary to Africa, published some descriptive material in 1857, and in the following year brought out a grammar and dictionary of the Yóruba tongue. Richard Furman (grandson of the distinguished preacher) published a book of poetry in 1859, while in 1860 H. F. Buckner, missionary to the Indians, published his grammar of the Creek language.

This list is not intended to be exhaustive but to illustrate the increasing amount of published materials by Southern Baptists during this period.

This period witnessed a growth in the number of outstanding leaders in the South, both among laymen and ministers. New categories of denominational service began to appear with the addition of new functions in the state and Southwide bodies. These categories will be expanded considerably during the next two periods of history.

Distinguished Negro Baptist preachers also served in the South during this period. There were some churches of wholly Negro membership, especially in the larger cities. Typical of this class was the church in Savannah, Georgia, organized in 1788, founded under the preaching of Andrew Bryan, who served as its pastor for twenty-four years until his death in 1812. Sometimes these independent Negro churches were under the pastoral care of a white minister. Robert Ryland, first president of Richmond College, was pastor of the Negro church in Richmond for twenty-five years beginning in 1841, and baptized over 3,800 persons into its membership. Sometimes the whites and blacks in a single church had separate organizations, each with its own pastor, deacons, business sessions, preaching, and so forth. The First Baptist Church, Montgomery, Alabama, was an example of this. Two thirds of its 900 members about 1860 were Negroes.

Most Negro Baptists before 1860 were members of white churches and occupied separate sections reserved for them. It was not uncommon to find a church with three rather distinct sections: the white men in one area, white women in another, and the Negroes in still another. Sometimes the rigorous state laws, which set specific rules for allowing manumission, were by-passed in a rather interesting fashion. The Alabama Association, for example, recognized the great ability of Caesar McLemore as a preacher and desired to employ him to win the Negroes to Christ in the area of the association. State laws, however, would not permit this; so the association purchased him and appointed a committee to direct his work as a missionary of the association. He was very effective, despite the fact that a Baptist association had to become a slaveholder to secure his services.[69]

Accurate statistics as to the number of Negro Baptists in 1860 are almost impossible to secure. A scholarly guess of 400,000 has been made, and this may be as accurate as can be secured.[70]

Thus, between 1845 and 1860, Southern Baptists made good progress, both in their Convention and across the Southland. They had begun their task in a difficult time. At the end of the period they were just beginning to recognize the potential involved in the new type of organization; namely, a denominational body structured to engage in every type of benevolence, with separate boards located in various cities. The financial basis of representation, however, limiting both the representative nature of the constituency, and through designated giving, narrowing the number of benevolences, served to hold in check the larger ministry of which the Convention was capable.

The culture with which Southern Baptists were inextricably bound up was rapidly deteriorating and would soon die. The sectional conflict and the reconstruction that would follow provided a stern test of their ability to persevere. Furthermore, there was a hint during this period of other conflicts to come. The Home Mission Society of New York had played an important part in the establishing of churches in Texas through the appointment of able missionaries like James Huckins and William Tryon. The field had been abandoned by the society and the Southern Baptist Convention promptly appointed missionaries there in 1845. When the Home Mission Society reentered Texas in 1847, Secretary Russell Holman of the Domestic Mission Board protested mildly.[71] This brief skirmish was the prelude to a major confrontation later in the century to determine fields of service of the two sectional bodies.

Notes

1. See Joseph T. Watts, *The Rise and Progress of Maryland Baptists* (Baltimore: State Mission Board, c1951), *passim* for this resumé.

2. Ryland, *op. cit.,* pp. 294-95.

3. This summary taken from M. A. Huggins, *A History of North Carolina Baptists 1727-1932* (Raleigh: General Board, Baptist State Convention, 1967), *passim.*

4. King, *op. cit.,* pp. 218 ff.

5. *Ibid.,* pp. 230-31.

6. Cox-Woolley, eds., *Encyclopedia,* I, p. 604.

7. See E. E. Joiner, *A History of Florida Baptists* (Jacksonville: Florida Baptist Convention, 1972), p. 30.

8. *Ibid.,* p. 38.

9. *Ibid.,* p. 39 n.

10. For this summary, see Turner, *The United States 1830-1850,* pp. 214 ff.

11. Frank M. Masters, *A History of Baptists in Kentucky,* (Louisville: Kentucky Baptist Historical Society, 1953), p. 283.

12. *Ibid.,* p. 301.

13. *Ibid.,* p. 304.

14. *Ibid.,* pp. 290, 291, 299, 300.

15. See *ibid.,* pp. 308-311 for a good review.

16. See R. A. McLemore, *A History of Mississippi Baptists, 1780-1970* (Jackson, Miss.: Mississippi Baptist Convention Board, 1971), pp. 142 ff.

17. *Ibid.,* pp. 150 ff; and see also Lynn E. May, Jr., *The First Baptist Church of Nashville, Tennessee, 1820-1970* (Nashville: First Baptist Church, 1970), p. 90.

18. J. S. Rogers, *History of Arkansas Baptists* (Little Rock: Executive Board of Arkansas Baptist State Convention, 1948), p. 445.

19. *Ibid.,* p. 451.

20. *Ibid.,* p. 588.

21. John T. Christian, *A History of the Baptists of Louisiana* (Shreveport: The Executive Board of the Louisiana Baptist Convention, 1923), p. 98.

22. *Ibid.,* pp. 102-107.

23. See Baker, *The Blossoming Desert,* for this story.

24. W. Pope Yeaman, *A History of the Missouri Baptist General Association* (Columbia E. W. Stephens Press, 1899), p. 90.

25. See the *Southern Baptist* (Charleston, S. C.,), August 29, 1855, p. 3.

26. John L. Waller, ed., *Western Baptist Review* (Frankfort, Kentucky: 1845), I, pp. 57 ff.

27. Jesse H. Campbell of Georgia claimed credit for its initiation. See Jesse H. Campbell, *Georgia Baptists: Historical and Biographical* (Macon: J. W. Burke & Co., rev. ed., 1874), p. 81.

28. See Baker, *Source Book,* pp. 126-28 for the constitution.

29. For a summary of this story in larger perspective, see Baker, *The Story of the Sunday School Board* (Nashville: Convention Press, 1966), pp. 6-11.

30. See *Proceedings of the Baptist General Association of Virginia* (Richmond, 1845), p. 21.

31. W. C. James, *A History of the Western Baptist Theological Institute* (Louisville: Baptist World Publishing Co., 1910), Kentucky Baptist Historical Society Papers, No. 1, pp. 31-100. See also Cox-Woolley, eds., *Encyclopedia*, II, p. 1486.

32. See Baker, *Source Book*, pp. 137 ff for this document and the discussion of it by James P. Boyce.

33. *Religious Herald* (Virginia), May 11, 1876, p. 2, col. 2.

34. *Ibid.*, August 13, 1847.

35. Baker, *Relations*, p. 151.

36. Baker, *Source Book*, p. 129, has the document.

37. *Ibid.*, pp. 128-29.

38. Baker J. Cauthen, ed., *Advance: A History of Southern Baptist Foreign Missions* (Nashville: Broadman Press, 1970), p. 28.

39. *Ibid.*, pp. 78-79.

40. *Annual,* Southern Baptist Convention, 1846, pp. 17, 34. See also W. W. Barnes, "The Dimensions of the Home Mission Task," in *Southwestern Journal of Theology* (Fort Worth), II, 2, pp. 49 ff.

41. Baker, *Relations*, pp. 86 ff.

42. *The Christian Index* (Georgia), April 8, 1847, p. 4, col. 2.

43. Arthur B. Rutledge, *Mission to America* (Nashville: Broadman Press, 1969), p. 245.

44. The best account of the Landmark movement is James E. Tull, *A Study of Southern Baptist Landmarkism in the Light of Historical Baptist Ecclesiology* (privately circulated Ph.D. dissertation at Columbia University, 1960), 790 pages.

45. Baker, *Source Book*, pp. 142-43.

46. *Ibid.*

47. See J. M. Pendleton's statement in the *Western Recorder* (Kentucky), February 22, 1877, p. 1.

48. Baker, *Source Book*, p. 144.

49. Tull, *op. cit.*, pp. 519 ff.

50. J. R. Graves, A. C. Dayton, and N. M. Crawford, eds., *The Southern Baptist Review and Eclectic* (Nashville: Southwestern Publishing House, 1855), Vol. II, September-October, 1856, p. 544.

51. See J. R. Graves, *Old Landmarkism—What Is It?* (Memphis: Baptist Book House, Graves, Mahaffy and Co., 1880), p. 262.

52. See letter of Boyce in *Religious Herald* (Virginia), May 11, 1899.

53. See, for example, J. H. Grime, *History of Middle Tennessee Baptists* (Nashville: Baptist and Reflector, 1902), pp. 22 ff.

54. See *Western Recorder* (Kentucky), September 20, 1854.

55. *Western Baptist Review* (Kentucky), III, March, 1848, pp. 276 ff.

56. W. W. Barnes, *The Southern Baptist Convention*, pp. 100-101.

57. Baker, *Source Book*, p. 142.

58. See, among other accounts, Masters, *op. cit.*, pp. 308-311.

59. John A. Broadus, *Memoir of James P. Boyce* (New York: A. C. Armstrong and Son, 1893), pp. 98-99.

60. See May, *op. cit.*, pp. 87-88.

61. See Robert A. Baker, "The North Rocky Mount Baptist Church Decision," *Review and Expositor* (Louisville, Ky.), January, 1955, pp. 59-60.

62. *The Tennessee Baptist* (Nashville), September 4, 1858.

63. *Ibid.*, February 5, 1859, p. 2, col. 4.

64. For this story, see W. W. Barnes, *The Southern Baptist Convention*, pp. 110-12.

65. Baker, *Source Book*, pp. 145-46.

66. *The Tennessee Baptist*, May 21 and May 28, 1859, p. 2, col. 1.

67. Cox-Woolley, eds., *Encyclopedia*, I, pp. 583-84.

68. A. H. Newman, ed., *A Century of Baptist Achievement* (Philadelphia: American Baptist Publication Society, 1901), pp. 262-70.

69. *Ibid.*, pp. 163 ff.

70. *Ibid.*, p. 165.

71. See *The Christian Index* (Georgia), April 8, 1847.

WAR AND RECONSTRUCTION
1860-1877

From Civil War to the End of Reconstruction

11 Resort to Arms

In retrospect, one feels a sense of unreality as he watches the rapid outbreak in 1861 of the bloodiest war yet fought, sometimes involving brother against brother. Differing constitutional interpretations, constantly irritated by every sectional issue that arose, caused men to abandon reason and turn to violence. On April 9, 1861, the troops of South Carolina fired on Fort Sumter, and less than a week later war had begun. It continued almost exactly four years, ending with the surrender of Lee at Appomattox on April 9, 1865. Reconstruction was the name given to the painful military, economic, social, and political control of the South during the following twelve years, ending with the final withdrawal of troops from the South in 1877.

Little needs to be said about the war itself, which the South had hoped to win with her cotton. The antebellum culture was totally destroyed, and Lincoln's plan of restoring the seceding states was scrapped after his assassination. President Andrew Johnson was bludgeoned at every point. By one vote a bill of impeachment against him failed. The South was divided into five military districts, with commissioners appointed to determine who could vote. The financial position of many southern states was temporarily ruined by reckless bonding programs which provided northern control at a fraction of

226

the actual value of posted securities. The sharecropper system became an extension of the control of northern capital. Abolitionist idealism was replaced by economics and politics. Intelligent Negroes noticed that not one of their number had been appointed to a federal office in the North and none had a place in a northern state legislature. When Reconstruction became politically ineffective, it was brought to a close.

The economic situation of the South improved slowly during the period. Five years after the close of the war the yield of cotton and tobacco, the "money crops" of the South, was still barely over half of what it was in 1860. Cotton production was 5,387,052 bales in 1860 and 3,011,996 bales in 1870; tobacco had dropped from 434,209,461 pounds in 1860 to 262,735,341 pounds in 1870. "You have no idea of the total prostration of everything in Virginia. Our people are the subjects of great suffering." wrote James B. Taylor in 1866 to President William Carey Crane of Baylor University in Texas. Such was true in most southern states.

Civil War (1861-65)

Practically every Baptist state convention in the South passed resolutions favoring the Confederate cause after the outbreak of hostilities.[1] The Southern Baptist Convention meeting in Savannah in 1861 issued a strong declaration justifying the formation of the Confederate States of America, and altered its name to recognize the political change. When the Convention met at Augusta in 1863, it heard a very gloomy report on the disruption of its work because of the war.

> Colleges have suspended, some of them indefinitely. Doctor Talbird, President of Howard College, has raised a company and gone to the wars, and the students of most of our colleges have enlisted in the Confederate army. The Revision Association is prostrate, and we pre sume the whole work of Revision is indefinitely suspended. Our female schools, in several localities, show signs of distress. Some six or seven Baptist papers have gone down in the past six months, while the Mississippi Baptists and the Texas Baptists issue half sheets, and the Tennessee Baptist is cut down in size to one-third less than the Western Recorder. Added to this gloomy picture, our Foreign Missions are paralyzed, our Home Missions almost suspended, and our State organizations unable to carry on their work. Ministers have been forced through stern necessity to leave their fields of usefulness in order to provide bread for their families.[2]

It will be recalled that when the war began, Southern Baptists had three benevolent boards in the structure of their Convention: one at Richmond, Virginia, for foreign missions; one at Marion, Alabama, for domestic and Indian missions; and the Bible Board at Nashville, Tennessee. Loosely related to the Convention were the seminary at

Greenville, South Carolina, which closed temporarily in 1862, the Southern Baptist Publication Society, Charleston, South Carolina, and the Southern Baptist Sunday School Union, Nashville, Tennessee. The last two-named bodies were permanent casualties of the war, although the records of their demise are incomplete. The Bible Board was abolished by the Convention in 1863 after Nashville was captured by the Union armies.[3]

Foreign Mission Board. Mission work in China and Africa limped along during the American war. The Brazilian mission, briefly conducted by Thomas J. Bowen, was abandoned early in 1861 because of Bowen's ill health. The board faced many problems during the war. In 1863 it reported to the Convention that it had not been able to meet during the previous year; that the two periodicals, the *Home and Foreign Journal* and *The Commission,* had been suspended; that there were no agents in the field to help raise mission funds; and that civil war in China and the outbreak of Asiatic cholera there had brought much suffering and death on that field. Receipts in 1863 were $51,000 for the previous two years; at the next meeting in 1866 the board reported $68,000 had been raised during that period.

The board experienced difficulty both in raising money for the foreign mission cause and in getting money to the fields. Quite early in the war, Richmond was cut off from land contact with northern ports, and the Union fleet blockaded the southern coast to keep ships from carrying cotton to other nations. The board devised several means of raising and sending funds. (1) Under a flag of truce the board in Richmond forwarded the money that it had collected to Baltimore, where it was then shipped to the missionaries. This means of communication failed as the war progressed. (2) Isaac T. Smith, the financial agent of the Foreign Mission Board in New York, anticipating the very difficulty which they faced, had already made advances to the missionaries. (3) In the fall of 1862, a Provisional Board was constituted at Baltimore, and foreign mission contributions were received from Maryland, District of Columbia, Kentucky, and Missouri, as well as from friends in northern cities. (4) A rather unique means of financing missions in China and Africa involved the running of the Union blockade. The board invested about $1,500 in bales of sea-island cotton. After the ship on which it was loaded had successfully run the blockade, the cotton netted nearly $5,000 in England, and this sum was credited there to the account of the missionaries in China and Africa. (5) Some of the missionaries, particularly in China, were able to secure secular work on their fields. Matthew T. Yates, for example, became an interpreter for the United States government and also made wise investments in land near Shanghai. (6) Some foreign residents in China, noting the need of the missionaries that were cut off from the States, made contributions to them to assist in the work. Even missionary societies of other denominations assisted the Baptist missionaries in China. All indebtedness incurred during the war in the foreign mission program was paid shortly after the close of hostilities.

Courageous men and women served well in China during this period. Roswell P. Graves, M.D., had come to South China through the appeals of J. Lewis Shuck and was for a considerable time alone in the important work at Canton. In Central China, the eminent Matthew T. Yates and his wife continued throughout all of this period. In North China, J. L. Holmes and his wife arrived in 1860 to open mission work in Chefoo. In the following year Holmes was murdered by bandits. Mr. and Mrs. J. B. Hartwell and Mr. and Mrs. T. P. Crawford performed important service in this field during the period. An attempt was made to open the mission field in Japan in 1860, but two missionaries were lost at sea and others were not appointed because of the war and lack of finances.

Throughout all of the critical war period, James B. Taylor served as corresponding secretary of the board. His arduous labors took their toll on his health.

Domestic and Indian Mission Board. The home field was devastated by the war. Work with the Negroes, Chinese, Germans, English-speaking whites, and city population promptly ceased with the outbreak of war. There had been over 150 missionaries serving in the home field before the war, but their work was promptly suspended. The Indian work, in particular, suffered severely. Southern Baptist schools in Indian Territory, for which the United States government had appropriated $75.00 per year per pupil, were closed. Many Southern Baptist missionaries and ministers became chaplains or colporteurs in the Confederate army. The several states, as well as the board, were zealous in supplying tracts and Bibles for the soldiers. In 1863, for example, Virginia alone provided 5,000,000 pages of tracts for distribution in the Confederate army through the colporteurs. W. W. Barnes felt that "there was never an army in which a greater religious work was done than in the Army of Northern Virginia," where revival occurred on several occasions. When federal troops gained control of the Mississippi River, the board sent J. B. Link, one of their agents in Mississippi, to Texas to serve as an arm of the board in raising and distributing home mission funds. The executive committee of Louisiana was similarly empowered.

In the fall of 1863, the Home Mission Society of New York, through its president, United States Senator Ira Harris, applied to the War Department for authority to seize abandoned Southern Baptist meetinghouses in the areas overrun by the troops of the Union army.

The War Department granted them more than they asked, and ordered its commanding officers to seize and deliver to the society "all houses of worship belonging to the Baptist Churches South, in which a loyal minister of said church does not now officiate." [4] The society explained that this was an effort to protect Baptist property in the South from marauders and, in some cases, from "others than Baptists" who had denied the society's right to use them. The society went on to say that the whole object of this move was to occupy the property and save it from being destroyed or passing into other than Baptist hands, reserving it as an inheritance for future Baptists to own and occupy. J. W. Parker of Boston was appointed to head this program, and during the first four months of 1864 about thirty Southern Baptist edifices were seized. Some of them, as in the case of the Coliseum Place Baptist Church of New Orleans, had not been abandoned, but were seized from Southern Baptists by force. While their motives were good, the society embittered many Southern Baptists in carrying out this program.

As the armies of the North captured southern areas, the Home Mission Society sent its missionaries into those areas to labor. In 1862, there were three such missionaries in South Carolina and one in Missouri; in 1863, one each in Kentucky, Louisiana, and Tennessee, two in Virginia, three in Missouri, and four in South Carolina; in 1864, one each in District of Columbia, Kentucky, Louisiana, and North Carolina, two in Mississippi, three in South Carolina, four in Virginia, six in Missouri, and seven in Tennessee; while in 1865, there were one each in Alabama, Arkansas, and Kentucky, two each in Louisiana and Mississippi, four each in Georgia and South Carolina, five in North Carolina, seven each in Tennessee and Virginia, and twenty-three in Missouri. Most of these were working among the Negroes in those states.[5]

The receipts of the southern board during the war were greatly affected by the inflation of the Confederate currency. In 1860 gifts amounted to $37,659.34; in 1861, $35,274.50. From 1862 to 1865 receipts were in Confederate currency and dropped to $14,996.73 in 1862, but inflation began to appear in 1863 when $29,072.12 was secured. In 1864 receipts totaled $118,937.91, while in 1865, they were shown as $156,491.76, most of it in almost worthless Confederate currency.

Russell Holman returned for his second stint as corresponding secretary in 1857 and served until 1862. He was succeeded by M. T. Sumner.

Bible Board. The third of the existing boards when the war began was the Bible Board, which had been established in 1851. The Convention appointed a special committee in 1861 to look into the condition of this board. When the Convention met again in 1863, the headquarters of the board at Nashville were in the hands of the northern army, and the Convention promptly abolished it. Its death prepared the way for the organization of the first Sunday School Board.

First Sunday School Board. In the very midst of the dark days of the war, a new board was organized which, both in its own ministry and in the long shadow it cast toward the future, rendered a significant service. After the vote of the Southern Baptist Convention in 1863 abolishing the Bible Board, Basil Manly, Jr., introduced a resolution calling for a committee to look into the need for a board to promote Sunday Schools. As chairman of that committee, Manly wrote in most eloquent language the first apologetic for the Sunday School movement ever adopted by the Southern Baptist Convention.

> All of us have felt that the Sunday School is the nursery of the Church, the camp of instruction for her young soldiers, the great missionary to the future. While our other benevolent agencies relate primarily to the present, this goes to meet and bless the generation that is coming, to win them from ignorance and sin, to train future laborers, when our places shall know us no more.[6]

Despite many strong objections, Manly and his supporters were able to secure the organization of the first Sunday School Board in 1863. He was named president of the new board, with headquarters at Greenville, South Carolina, and inaugurated an ambitious program for providing books and for enlisting volunteer agents for each state. In that fall a second great name was attached to the history of the board, that of John A. Broadus. Like Manly, he had been professor in the first Southwide seminary at Greenville, South Carolina, which had closed its doors in 1862 because of the war. The amount of work done by these two men was remarkable. Broadus said in his report to the Convention in 1866 that the work they had accomplished was "sadly little," but he was mistaken. Hymnbooks, children's question books and catechisms, teacher's and pupil's class books, and other printed helps of various sorts were provided in large numbers for the Sunday Schools in the South. Outstanding men in many southern states served voluntarily to promote the work of the board.[7]

In his report in 1866 Broadus described the beginning of a small monthly paper entitled, *Kind Words for the Sunday School Children.*

> The plan adopted was to issue quite a small sheet and at a very low price. Children are rather pleased than otherwise that theirs should be a *little* paper, strikingly different from the papers for grown people.

This little paper for children became "the golden thread" that linked this first Sunday School Board with the second board that was organized in 1891. In his closing word Broadus appealed for "the lively sympathy and the liberal support of all that love Him who loves little children."

The Reconstruction Period (1865-77)

Progress in the Several States. Before describing numerical gains made across the Southland during these tumultuous days, mention should be made of two events which brought large excisions from the ranks of Southern Baptists. The adoption of the Virginia Secession Ordinance constituted the breaking point between eastern and western Virginia as the culmination of a number of economic, social, and political tensions, and on June 20, 1863, the new state of West Virginia was formed. In 1868 nearly 15,000 members in 249 churches left the General Association of Virginia to form the West Virginia General Association. The other event was the withdrawal from the white Baptist churches by most of the Negro Baptists in the South in order to form their own church bodies. Perhaps around 400,000 Baptists were in this way removed from the rolls of the white churches. This excision was encouraged by the northern Home Mission Society and the military forces stationed in the South, and of course was very appealing to the Negroes themselves as an evidence of their total freedom.

The reaction of white Southern Baptists to this withdrawal was fairly uniform. As a rule, this withdrawal was expected and accepted along the seaboard, but farther west the feeling seemed to exist that Negroes were not yet sufficiently trained and grounded in the basic Baptist doctrines to the point that they could carry on Baptist church life without some supervision and assistance from the whites. As early as September, 1865, the Dover Association of Virginia discussed the separation of the African churches to form an independent Negro association, and that action took place by seven African churches in Richmond, Manchester, and Petersburg. Several white associations in Virginia published the view that separate organizations "should neither be required nor encouraged," but this did not slow down the pace of the withdrawal. By 1868 there were 3 Negro associations with 129 churches and almost 39,000 members. A Negro state body was organized in May, 1868.

The Tar River Association of North Carolina mentioned that during the first few years after the war, such excisions were numerous.[8] In 1866 the South Carolina State Convention noted the formation of separate organizations by the Negroes and urged that the whites be helpful and sympathetic in dealing with them.[9] Between 1872 and 1876, the Negro membership in the white churches of South Carolina diminished rapidly.[10]

In Georgia the statistics show the beginning of rather rapid excision from the churches after 1867. A new Negro association was shown in 1868 with 2,335 members, which had been organized in 1866.[11] Two additional Negro associations, both organized in 1866, were shown in the minutes of 1870. By 1875, there were only 3,295 Negroes remaining in the 34 white associations in Georgia out of a total membership of 74,545.

In Alabama, reference was made quite early in the war to the possibility of separate churches by the Negroes, which the whites felt should be discouraged. In 1865, while recognizing the right of the Negroes to withdraw from the white churches, it was urged that their highest good would be subserved by maintaining their relationship in the churches with those that know and love them. However, evidently after 1868 the Negroes were withdrawing rapidly, and reference was made to their churches which were separate from the white churches. In 1868 the state body urged that wherever possible that white assistance be given to any organization of black churches.[12]

In Mississippi the state body made reference in 1867 to aiding the Negroes in organizing their churches.[13] The parting of the Negroes in Kentucky occurred shortly after the war; while in Texas, between 1865 and 1870, there was a drop in Negro church membership in the white churches from 35% to 7.7% in ten associations selected for study.[14]

On the whole, the division was an amicable one. In some cases the white churches gave their buildings to the Negroes and moved elsewhere to build their own; often the white churches provided financial aid to Negro Baptists as they attempted to construct their church edifices.

Even during Reconstruction and while experiencing the losses just described, Southern Baptists made substantial numerical progress.

1. South Atlantic Region. The war was disastrous in its effect upon Baptists in the southern seaboard states in particular. Virginia, for example, was almost prostrate at the close of hostilities. The land was devastated. Garnett Ryland, the Virginia Baptist historian, named over two dozen Baptist meetinghouses damaged or destroyed by Union troops; he mourned the execution of Albert C. Willis, a young preacher in the Shiloh Association, and noted the imprisonment of eight other ministers. Men and boys from sixteen to sixty had been called into the Confederate army, and ministering by colporteurs to soldiers became the principal organized activity of Virginia Baptists. Richmond College had been stripped of its library, scientific apparatus, and everything else portable by marauding troops. The endowment of the school was worthless. The entire plant of the *Religious Herald* had been destroyed. President Ryland of Richmond College milked his own cow and sold the milk to sustain his family, making personal deliveries morning and evening.

After the war closed, Baptists in this region resolutely set about to repair the extensive physical damage. A constructive attitude was reflected in the renewed meetings of the state bodies. In Virginia, for example, promptly after the war ended, the General Association adopted a resolution earnestly recommending to brethren throughout the state "to prove themselves to be loyal citizens of the United States; and enter with zeal and activity upon the discharge of the responsibilities devolved on them by their new social and civic relations."

The minutes of each state body reflected a desire to begin immediately the significant benevolent ministries interrupted by war. State missions, Sunday School promotion and leadership, ministerial relief, rehabilitation of the schools, and cooperation with the Southwide Baptist body were topics which were discussed in every state. Hardly an annual session of a state body during all of this period went beyond the first day without someone earnestly presenting the needs of the Negroes and appealing for an active witness to them. Every state in this region took steps to restructure its convention or general association during this period to unify the several programs in the state or to make the body more efficient.

The several state minutes provide inspiring examples of perseverance amidst difficulties. The postwar convention meetings in Florida, for example, were poorly attended and the financial picture was bleak. Kinsey Chambers began work as a part-time state evangelist in 1873 in an effort to turn the tide. His report for five months showed that he traveled 1,688 miles, spoke 105 times, made 54 family visits, helped constitute 1 church, baptized 7, and collected $68.95. His expenses for these five months were shown as $10.75.

A new permanent educational institution was begun by Georgia Baptists in 1873, although it did not come under the control of the state body until 1902. Alfred Shorter, a Baptist in Rome, Georgia, organized a private stock company to sustain a liberal arts college for girls in his community, stipulating that its trustees should always be members in good standing of some Baptist church.

Old Mercer University was moved in 1871 from Penfield to Macon, Georgia, in an effort to improve its financial condition and enlarge its enrollment.

Under these difficult circumstances Baptists in the seven South Atlantic states increased from 116 associations, 3,107 churches, and 328,666 members in 1860 to 185 associations, 4,458 churches, and 361,575 members in 1877, representing an average annual growth of .56%. Between 1860 and 1880, the population of this region increased from 5,252,487 to 6,832,132, an average annual growth of 1.43%. The largest Baptist percentage of growth in this region occurred in District of Columbia, where Baptists increased from no associations,

5 churches, and 1,069 members to 1 association, 31 churches, and 10,061 members, or an average annual membership increase of 46.73%. The small numbers involved in this growth account for the large percentage of increase. Maryland Baptists increased from 1 association, 34 churches, and 4,143 members to 1 association, 48 churches, and 7,607 members, an average annual membership growth of 4.64%. Georgia Baptists increased from 38 associations, 994 churches, and 84,567 members to 86 associations, 1,855 churches, and 119,470 members, an average annual membership growth of 2.29%. Florida Baptists increased from 5 associations, 134 churches, and 6,483 members to 12 associations, 221 churches, and 9,020 members, an average annual membership growth of 2.17%. North Carolina Baptists increased from 27 associations, 696 churches, and 60,532 members to 40 associations, 986 churches, and 83,904 members, an average annual membership increase of 2.14%. Both South Carolina and Virginia Baptists showed losses in the number of Baptists during this period. South Carolina had 18 associations, 473 churches, and 62,984 members in 1860 and 23 associations, 625 churches, and 60,239 members in 1877, an average annual decrease in membership of .24%. Virginia decreased from 27 associations, 771 churches, and 108,888 members to 22 associations, 692 churches, and 71,274 members, an average annual membership loss of 1.92%.

 2. *South Central Region.* Despite the many problems that they faced, the Baptists in the South Central region made an excellent record of growth during this period. Baptists increased from 163 associations, 3,904 churches, and 271,675 members in 1860 to 308 associations, 7,007 churches, and 464,953 members in 1877, representing an average annual growth of 3.95%. The population, meanwhile, increased from 5,768,658 to 8,919,371, an average annual growth of 2.60%, which means that Southern Baptists in these states outstripped the population substantially.

 The largest Baptist percentage of growth took place in Texas, which increased from 22 associations, 456 churches, and 19,089 members to 55 associations, 1,176 churches, and 65,453 members, an average annual membership growth of 13.49%. Arkansas Baptists increased from 16 associations, 321 churches, and 11,341 members to 32 associations, 708 churches, and 31,602 members, an average annual membership growth of 9.92%. Mississippi Baptists increased from 22 associations, 598 churches, and 41,610 members to 42 associations, 1,183 churches, and 89,426 members, an average annual membership growth of 6.38%. Louisiana Baptists increased from 10 associations, 209 churches and 10,264 members to 20 associations, 376 churches, and 19,179 members, an average annual membership growth of 4.82%. Tennessee Baptists grew from 24 associations, 663 churches, and 46,564 members to 42 associations, 1,074 churches, and 85,001 members, an average annual membership increase of 4.59%. Kentucky Baptists grew from 39 associations, 849 churches, and 81,588 members to 64 associations, 1,367 churches, and 109,510 members, an average annual membership increase of 1.90%. Alabama Baptists grew from 29 associations, 808 churches, and 61,219 members to 53 associations, 1,193 churches, and 64,782 members, an average annual membership increase of .32%.

These seven states were also eyeing their state bodies. There were varying attitudes toward such structures. In Kentucky and Arkansas, for example, undoubtedly through the influence of Landmarkism, fierce struggles took place between those who rejected the concept of state structures and those who favored such organizations. In Kentucky the fear of centralization was very strong all during this era, and the district associations looked upon the general body as a competitor rather than a channel of work. In 1869 the General Association reaffirmed its aims, which included better understanding and cooperation, assistance for feeble churches, the use of experienced evangelists in the state, and an effort to reach neglected areas, especially in the mountains of eastern Kentucky. The functioning agency of the General Association was a General Executive Board, later named the State Board of Missions. In 1866 the title of the General Agent, as he had been called, was changed to Corresponding Secretary, which was filled at this time by annual election.

Arkansas Baptists, likewise, had an active controversy over the centralized authority involved in the use of a state structure and an authoritative board whose functions appeared to jeopardize the autonomy of the churches, some thought.

It will be recalled that Tennessee had not been successful in establishing a permanent state body during the previous period. On April 10, 1874, through the cooperation of leaders in the three sectional bodies in the state, a unified state structure was organized at Murfreesboro, but the de facto unification of the state was a process requiring many years beyond this period.

Mississippi Baptists began refining their state body shortly after the close of the war. In 1871, not satisfied with the structure, a complete reorganization took place; this was repeated in 1873. At the close of the period these Baptists were still struggling with the proper structure of the state body.

Texas Baptists still had two rival state bodies at the opening of the period, and additional sectional organizations soon began to organize in various areas of this vast state. Alabama Baptists modified their convention to emphasize the growing Sunday School movement.

In addition, as was true in the South Atlantic region, the seven states in the South Central region turned to the antebellum benevolences of state missions, Sunday Schools, and so forth in an effort to restore and advance these programs during the dark days of Reconstruction.

Several educational advances were reported during this period. In 1873 the distinguished Confederate officer, Mark P. Lowrey, with the aid of his two daughters, opened Blue Mountain Female Institute, later to become Blue Mountain College. It was operated as a private school until 1919, when the Mississippi Baptist Convention assumed control of it. Foundations were laid for what became Belmont College in Nashville, Tennessee, when a female school called Ward Seminary was established in 1865.

Texas Baptists during the period of war and Reconstruction faced serious problems in their educational work. In 1861, in open hostility, Rufus C. Burleson, president of Baylor University at Independence, resigned and took his entire senior class to Waco University. Throughout the remainder of the Reconstruction period both Baylor at Independence and Waco University kept open their doors. In 1866 the Female Department of Baylor became a separate institution and moved its campus to Belton, Texas. The rivalry between the school at Independence and the one at Waco was lively during the remainder of the Reconstruction era.

3. North Central Region. Missouri in the North Central region underwent serious internal convulsions during this period. This state had been almost evenly divided during the war between those loyal to the North and those favoring the South. As a result, in 1865 a separate Baptist body was formed by those desiring to work with the North. However, through the efforts of A. H. Burlingham, members of this new body returned to the older general association three years later. In order to promote harmony, the general association eliminated from its constitution the statement that the body would be auxiliary to the Southern Baptist Convention. As a result, Missouri Baptists, while in the same state body, divided in their support of a general body. In 1878 the executive board was consolidated with the board of the Sunday School convention. This constituted the Missouri structure during all of this period. The number of Baptists increased from 37 associations, 749 churches, and 44,877 members to 66 associations, 1,328 churches, and 79,546 members, or an average annual membership increase of 4.29%. Meanwhile, the population of Missouri grew from 1,182,012 to 2,168,380 between 1860 and 1880, an average annual increase of 3.97%, a rate somewhat slower than the growth of Baptists.

The Southern Baptist Convention. The period of Reconstruction was one of continuing struggle for the Convention and its boards. The crop failures of the late 1860's, the financial panic of 1873, and the political agitation that led to the withdrawal of the troops from the South in 1877 affected all of the activities of the several agencies of the Convention. Presidents of the body in these critical years were Richard Fuller (1861-63), P. H. Mell (1863-72), and James P. Boyce (1872-79).

1. The Question of Reunion. Since the societies in the North had so enthusiastically supported the Union cause and the Southern Baptist Convention had vigorously defended the Confederacy, it was unlikely that either side would be interested in the question of reunion during the war period from 1861 to 1865. However, even before the close of the war, the American Baptist Home Mission Society of New York was sending its workers into the occupied areas of the South to do missionary work, primarily among the Negroes. This story will be given in some detail a little later. After Appomattox and the elimination of the "peculiar institution" that had played such a large part in the sectional quarrels between the North and the South, the whole question of reunion was broached. The initiative came from the Home Mission Society, but Southern Baptist state bodies that met in 1865 were practically unanimous in voting nonaffiliation with this society and the foreign mission body in the North. The South was still embittered because of the seizing of church property in the South by the society, calling this action unbaptistic and illegal. Angry words were published, adding to the sectional alienation. The Virginia Baptist General Association, for example, urged its churches "to decline any co-operation or fellowship with any of the missionaries, ministers, or agents of the American Baptist Home Mission Society." Completely impatient with this attitude, Secretary J. S. Backus of the Home Mission Society wrote a vigorous article, a part of which said:

> And now if it is politically and morally wrong to support "the Southern Confederacy," how can it be religiously right to support "the Southern Baptist Convention?" If the Government is to be one, why should not the Baptist denomination be one, and, as a united people, give their influence and example in support of a united Government? Is not the spirit which would have it otherwise, disloyal? Would not the spirit which seeks now to perpetuate the Southern Baptist Convention, were it in its power, reproduce and sustain the Southern Confederacy? [15]

The Southern Baptist Convention did not meet in 1865, but in 1866 it went about its work on the assumption that it would continue its operations as before. In 1868, 1870, 1871, 1875, and implicitly in other years, the Southern Baptist Convention vigorously took the position that "separate action in general denominational enterprises is the policy of true peace and surest progress." [16] Although this issue was to come up again in the next period, there never was the slightest suggestion that Southern Baptists seriously favored scrapping their denominational body, different in kind from the several independent and autonomous societies of the North as it was, and returning to the old arrangement. Basically, apart from differences in ecclesiology and sectional temper, there were four reasons given by Southern Baptists for remaining apart organically, even though fellowship was resumed: (1) the combined body would be too large (note that this conceived of a single convention rather than a series of societies); (2) at convention time, few cities in the North and none in the South would be able to accommodate a meeting of the size required; (3) distances were so great that few from the South would be able to attend the meetings in other sections of the country; and (4) a separate body in the South would allow southern leadership to develop and bring familiarity by the members of the southern churches with their leaders, thus deepening their interest.

2. *The Domestic and Indian Mission Board.* The Domestic and Indian Mission Board labored arduously on its field "from Maryland to Texas" during the Reconstruction era. Under the leadership of M. T. Sumner (1862-75), the program reflected the oscillation of mission gifts. When the funds were provided, the board eagerly commissioned missionaries to the Negroes, to the Indians, and to destitute fields across the South. With dismal regularity, however, a year of good offerings was followed by one with decreased funds, necessitating a cutback in the program and the discouragement of indebtedness. When Sumner resigned in 1875, he was succeeded by W. H. McIntosh, who served during the remainder of this period.

A growing financial crisis may be seen by the following table of its receipts:

1866	$23,058.28
1867	34,257.58
1868	27,071.58
1869	18,205.53
1870	21,549.73
1871	31,223.17
1872	38,014.83
1873	27,199.20
1874	32,465.00
1875	23,260.54
1876	19,359.81
1877	16,816.64

This board (called the Home Mission Board after 1874) was caught up in the agitation about the use of agents for raising funds. Stoutly supporting this practice, the board emphasized that as expensive as this method of collecting was, much more money was received for missions by the use of agents than without them. Nearly half of all the offerings until almost the very close of this period ·was used for collection and administration. In 1876, for example, the board collected $19,359.81. Of this amount, 44% or $8,518.32 was needed for administration, leaving $10,841.49 for the principal task. Another cause of agitation was the assertion by some of the state bodies that a home mission board was not really needed, since the various states could take care of their own needs with their own state mission boards. In 1873, for example, the receipts of the Convention's board were $27,199.20; in this same year, seven states reported having expended $18,367.68 on their own fields. By the close of this era in 1877, the states were spending more money on their own fields than the receipts of the Home Mission Board. The reports of the board constantly called for the cooperation of the various states. With respect to the use of agents, in 1876 when it was reported that more than 53% of the collections was used for paying the agents, the board was ordered to dispense with the use of agents for collecting funds. The drop in receipts shown for 1877 was caused, said the board, by the continuing economic depression that had begun four years before and the adoption of the policy of not using agents on a percentage basis to collect funds.

This critical financial dilemma of the board was greatly compounded by developments in the Baptist Home Mission Society of New York. In 1862, after the society had surveyed the missionary needs in the Virginia peninsula around Fortress Monroe, then occupied by Union armies, the question of providing missionaries there was discussed at the meeting of the full society. The first response of the society was that its financial resources were "inadequate to the necessities of any new territory," and asserted that no justification could be found for "attempting such extension of operations." [17] This attitude was replaced, however, by an enthusiasm that swept the society "to the occupancy of a field broader, more important, more promising than has ever yet invited our toils." A resolution was passed providing that steps should be taken immediately to send missionaries and teachers both to the free and to the slaves throughout the whole southern section. In justifying this extension of operations into the South, the society later asserted that the withdrawal from the older states of the South after 1845 was simply an expediency, while the return to the South was the assertion of the society's "original birthright to the cultivation of this entire continent." [18]

The society was reorganized to include a Southern District, which comprised all of the territory south of New York. A special Freedman's Fund was provided to secure collections for this work in the South. The society sent Edward Lathrop on a tour of the churches, both white and black, along the southern Atlantic coast with a resolution urging Southern Baptists to cooperate with the society in spreading the gospel. Most of the white churches did not welcome him, but the society said that their mission remained unchanged. "The work must not be stopped by State lines, nor sectional hatreds, nor complexion of man." [19] Missionaries rapidly began following the advancing Union armies, so that by 1865 the society reported sixty missionaries in twelve southern states. This included one each in Alabama, Arkansas, and Kentucky; two each in Louisiana and Mississippi; three in New Mexico; four each in Georgia and South Carolina; five in North Carolina; seven each in Tennessee and Virginia; and twenty-three in Missouri. [20]

Thereafter, the society engaged in considerable activity in three areas of work in the South—evangelism, education, and assistance in building church edifices. By 1867, the society had almost a hundred missionaries in twelve states of the South, of whom perhaps fifty-nine were teachers, although the records are not explicit. In addition, loans for building church edifices had been made in Missouri to both white and Negro churches, as well as in South Carolina to churches of both races, and doubtless elsewhere, although the records are not complete.

The Southern Baptist Convention took note of the society's activity in 1867 and defined what it considered to be a basis of rapprochement with the society by resolving:

> That this Convention having learned, though informally and unofficially, that the American Baptist Home Mission Society is desirous of aiding the religious instruction of this class of our population (the Negroes), the Domestic Mission Board be directed to make known to that Society our willingness to receive aid in this work, by appropriations made to the Boards of this Convention. [21]

In the following year (1868), a committee from the society visited the Southern Baptist Convention and offered a resolution of amity and fellowship. The Convention welcomed "the brethren from abroad—brethren laboring in their own field" and said:

> Could the Home Mission Board (the Society), while conforming to its constitutional obligations, render us assistance here, we are sure that much good might be effected so far as this class is concerned. . . . Conscious of the risk of being misunderstood, and restricted in utterance by a sense of the proper and the becoming, we yet feel constrained by the great interests at stake to renew the suggestion made in the concluding report of the Minutes of 1867. The Domestic Mission Board have peculiar advantages for prosecuting this work—experience, proximity to the field, interest in the people, and they are willing to receive aid in its conduct. [22]

The Southern Baptist Convention appointed representatives to meet with the society in 1868. The chairman of the group was J. B. Jeter and with him were John A. Broadus, Richard Fuller, Basil Manly, Jr., J. R. Graves, and H. A. Tupper, some of the ablest veterans of the Convention. During the exercises, Broadus (who was known in the North for his catholic attitudes and conciliatory views) addressed the society relative to the freedman task and suggested that only missionaries selected by the southern board be sent among the southern people; or, if such missionaries were selected by the society, they should be approved by the southern board. The society officially replied that they were unwilling to operate in this fashion; that they had a right and an obligation to Christ to send their missionaries to any point without endorsement by the South; and that if they restricted themselves according to the desires of the South, the sources of their benevolence would dry up, for their supporters would be unwilling to make contributions for a program of this kind. Thirty years later, Secretary H. L. Morehouse of the society approvingly pointed to this assertion by leaders of the society during this period as being the immediate response to the requests of the South for the society to make appropriations to the boards in the South or to secure the Convention's approval of missionaries sent to the South.[23]

The issue, then, was joined. The society refused to recognize the Southern Baptist Convention as a territorial general body which had supervision of Baptist work south of the Mason-Dixon line. The Southern Baptist Convention, on the other hand, demanded that it should be considered the only general organization for missions within the territorial limits of the South, and insisted that any work done by "brethren from abroad" should be channeled through its Domestic Mission Board. Its attitude was expressed by Basil Manly, Jr., who said in an address before the society: "We ask for help and co-operation, but if you repel our confidence, our heart of love which we proffer, we will at least not oppose whatever you may choose to do." [24]

A twofold conflict, which had been implicit from the very organization of the Southern Baptist Convention in 1845, was revealed in the contrasting views. The first conflict was ideological. It will be recalled that the three principal societies in the North were organized in such fashion as to minimize denominationalism while emphasizing the appeal of a particular benevolence. The society method stressed independency; the convention method stressed connectionalism or denominationalism. The latter related those supporting its program to all of the interests promoted by the denomination. The associational or convention type of structure chosen by Southern Baptists in 1845 was actually a new *kind* of general organization, in that it was a throwback to the associational missionary philosophy used by associational bodies before 1803 and partly utilized by the General Missionary Convention between 1817 and 1820. The organization by Southern Baptists of a convention with separate boards for benevolent work, rather than of societies for each type of benevolent activity, sowed seeds for this ideological conflict. Had the South simply formed separate benevolent societies for each type of activity, it would have been possible for the various societies, conceived as they were, to relate to one another on the basis of their common task, whether located in the North or the South. It is doubtful that a denominational rigidity would have developed. Any church might have had individuals contributing to two or more societies doing the same type of work, depending entirely upon the sympathy of the individual for the general aims and attitudes of the societies involved. The organization of a territorial convention, on the other hand, brought a geographical consciousness and a total denominational loyalty, still intensified by sectional passions, into structured form in the South.

The second conflict was geographical. The constitution of the Home Mission Society, adopted in 1832, provided that its field was all of North America. The constitution of the Southern Baptist Convention, endeavoring to reproduce the General Missionary Convention's constitution of 1814, named the United States as the area of its constituency. This meant that there was a complete geographical overlapping of the territory to be cultivated by the two bodies. This geographical tension did not develop immediately after separation in 1845 for several reasons. For one thing, the cohesive force resident in the institution of slavery, binding together a distinctive geographical area in a cultural, social, and economic unity (combined with the preference of northern missionaries not to work in the South), brought a territorial consciousness to the new convention. The Home Mission Board of the Convention constantly reiterated that its field was the South during all of the period from 1845 throughout the remainder of the Reconstruction era. Furthermore, the voluntary withdrawal of the Home Mission Society from the older states of the South between 1845 and 1862 gave impetus to the conception of a distinct geographical division. When the Home Mission Society briefly sent a missionary to Texas after having withdrawn from the field when separation came, the South's Domestic Mission Board secretary referred to Texas as "our territory," as over against the northwestern area which was looked upon as the society's territory. In addition, the normal development of the southern body was abruptly interrupted by the war in 1861 before it could be determined how far the organization would go toward carrying out the constitutional definition of its field. Reconstruction projected this situation for more than a decade after the war. Finally, the different organizational character of the new southern body tended to magnify territorial ideas more than a society type would have. The convention type of organization encouraged denominational unity involving all benevolences, rather than a benevolent unity that divided the constituency into groups loyal to one or more particular phases of activity. The new kind of organization encouraged *intensive* or multibenevolent development in a given geographical area rather than an *extensive* promotion of a single benevolence in any geographical area.

For these, and perhaps other reasons, the geographical tension did not display itself until the renewed activity of the society led it to send missionaries to the South during and after the Civil War.

During all of this period from 1860 to 1877, the Home Mission Society endeavored to secure organic union of Northern and Southern Baptists, but the Convention consistently refused to take this step. As a result, the American Baptist Home Mission Society simply bypassed the Convention and worked in and with the various states of the South. Between 1867 and 1877, when Reconstruction closed, the society made 686 annual appointments in the South covering 22,402 weeks of missionary labor in an average of 14 states of the South each year. Much of this work was among whites. In addition, in educational work, between 1872 (when specific figures are first available) and 1877, the society conducted 7 schools for Negroes and Indians in that many states of the South, employing 20 teachers in 1872 whose number increased to 41 in 1877. Pupils in these schools averaged about 800 each year, with 871 enrolling in 1877.[25]

Thus, in the closing decade of this period, an open rivalry developed between the older Home Mission Society of New York and the Home Mission Board of the Convention. The society's work in the South grew rapidly and prospered; its leaders announced that it was ministering to all races in the South in every type of missions, and that they saw no need for Southern Baptists even to have a board for home missions. At the same time, the Home Mission Board was in dire straits. Its finances were less than half as much in 1877 as in 1867. Even some Southern Baptists were calling for the elimination of this board from the work of the Convention. In addition, the death of the first Sunday School Board in 1873 in the early stages of a severe financial depression caused the Convention to assign the debts and work of that agency to the Home Mission Board. This was well-nigh a last straw for the struggling home mission body.[26]

3. The Death of the First Sunday School Board. After the close of the war, the Sunday School Board secured C. C. Bitting as its corresponding secretary. He worked strenuously to improve the financial condition of the board, but came to the 1868 Convention with an $1,800 indebtedness for that year. He was conscious of the antago-

nism that such a debt aroused in the Convention, and in justifying
the situation he presented a melancholy picture:

> This Board has existed only five years. Part of this time, a desolating
> war raged over all our territory, and the remaining time has witnessed
> the great poverty and oppression of our people. The postal facilities
> were almost the only means of communication in our business, and
> these were greatly diminished, while those existing were deranged and
> irresponsible. In the State where we are located there were, even this
> year, only about 141 in all, where in 1862, there were 478 offices.
> During this brief and disastrous period; without experience; without
> one dollar of permanent capital; dependent only on uncertain and
> small receipts; without the general and active interest among our
> brethren which is so beneficial and important, this Board has issued
> *fourteen publications,* and of these, over 200,000 copies, besides the
> establishment and improvement of a monthly Sunday-school paper
> of large circulation and at a cheaper rate than any other such paper
> known to us. It has aided and established many Sunday-schools. It
> has circulated many copies of the Word of God. Through its officers,
> missionaries, publications and appeals, it has contributed, not a little,
> to the awakening of that increased and general interest in the Sunday-
> school work which now prevails among our brethren.[27]

The Convention voted to move the board to Memphis, thinking
perhaps its financial state might be improved in the West. However,
the removal was disastrous for Secretary Bitting, for he was totally
unknown in the West. He resigned in 1869. Later in the year Thomas
C. Teasdale replaced him and for three years struggled with the
financial crisis. During Teasdale's secretaryship, some of the tension
that had lingered below the surface in the relations between the
southern Sunday School Board and the northern American Baptist
Publication Society's work in the same area began to appear. In his
first report to the Convention, Teasdale noted with considerable impa-
tience that some Southern Baptists were purchasing their literature
from the northern publication society, and acidly remarked:

> If we can command the general patronage of our own Southern
> people, we will give them a Sunday School paper, at once most excellent
> and attractive, which shall be alike free from offensive sectionalism
> and unsound theology; and which shall be in every respect adapted
> to the peculiar civilization of the South, and the scriptural piety of
> our people.

In the following year, after the Publication Society answered his
request for free books by suggesting that if the churches asked for
them, such requests should be referred to the Publication Society,
Teasdale angrily wrote:

> It was thus made apparent that the American Baptist Publication
> Society of Philadelphia is not disposed to render aid to the South
> through the medium of the Sunday School Board of this convention.

If it shall do anything to aid our people, it would seem that it must be done independently of any of our Southern organizations. Until this policy of that society in this regard shall have been modified, we must abandon all hope of co-operation with it on such terms as will not compromise the self-respect of our people, nor interfere with the integrity of the Boards of this Convention.[28]

In the fall of 1872 he resigned and the board could not find a replacement. Samuel Boykin was elected secretary pro tem, but when the Convention met in 1873, the board was abolished and its work and debts were transferred to the Domestic and Indian Mission Board, whose name was changed in the following year to the Home Mission Board. This competition for selling Sunday School and other publications smouldered during the period of Reconstruction, but in the next period it broke into flame.

4. The Foreign Mission Board. The Foreign Mission Board promptly resumed its work in Africa and China after the war. A new field was opened in Rome, Italy, in 1870. William N. Cote was the pioneer there, but in the following year he was replaced by George B. Taylor, son of the executive secretary of the board. An appeal for missionary cooperation came from São Paulo, Brazil, in 1873, where some of the Confederate leaders had migrated after the war, but there was a delay of almost a decade before the challenge was answered.

The corresponding secretary of the board, as pointed out, was James B. Taylor, whose distinguished service safely guided the foreign mission venture through the difficult days of beginning and of civil war. He resigned in December, 1871, shortly before his death, and was replaced by Henry Allen Tupper, who continued in that office during the remainder of this period.

The following table shows the receipts of the Foreign Mission Board year by year, reflecting in part the effect of the economic conditions of the period:

1867	$21,678.85
1868	14,832.44
1869	19,192.41
1870	21,938.53
1871	25,750.00
1872	28,500.00
1873	50,000.00
1874	32,770.13
1875	---
1876	45,000.00
1877	37,276.98

The *Home and Foreign Journal* was begun again as the promotional periodical of the boards. During this period there was considerable discussion at the meetings of the Convention concerning the use of agents to raise money for the several boards. In 1871, for example, even though the agent could keep 20% of what he collected for foreign missions, the board felt that his services were indispensable. In 1874 the Foreign Mission Board reported that agents were costing about 25% of what they collected. During the Reconstruction period women began their local and state organizations in a movement that was destined to bless the foreign mission program during the years to come. Lottie Moon had gone to China to be there a brief period with her sister, Edmonia, who had to return to the States in 1877 because of her health.

In the closing year of the period, a glimpse of a struggle to come was seen in a message delivered by T. P. Crawford, one of the missionaries in China, in May, 1877, at a mission conference. Crawford spoke on the advantages and disadvantages of the employment of native agents. He was so impressed by the disadvantages of such employment that he was thrown into controversy with the Foreign Mission Board itself, and during the following decades he was the principal figure in the Gospel Mission controversy.

5. Theological Education. The Southern Baptist Theological Seminary at Greenville, South Carolina, found it necessary to close in June, 1862, after its third session. Most of the faculty and student body became chaplains or soldiers in the Confederate army. After the war, the four stalwarts constituting the faculty (Boyce, Broadus, Williams, and Manly) vowed that they would die before letting the seminary die, despite almost hopeless conditions. The seminary reopened on November 1, 1865, with seven students. It soon became evident that South Carolina, so severely mauled by the war, could not support the school. Plans were set in motion early in the 1870's to move to a more favorable location and secure endowment, but the Panic of 1873 inhibited this. In 1877 the seminary was moved to new quarters in Louisville, Kentucky. Baptists in that state made herculean efforts to provide cash and pledges to insure its survival. At the close of this period the issue was still in doubt.

The Women's Work. Baptist women in the South, of course, had been active in missionary societies since before the forming of the General Missionary Convention in 1814. In fact, many female societies sent funds for foreign missions to the General Convention between 1814 and 1844, and were permitted on the basis of these contributions to appoint men to represent them at the triennial meetings.

A large step toward organizational articulation came when Mrs. Ann J. Graves of Baltimore, whose son, R. H. Graves, had been appointed by the Foreign Mission Board of the southern body in 1855 to China, began 'to call informal meetings of Baptist women of Baltimore together to hear letters from her son who was working in Canton. Perhaps the initial convention-related meeting of record occurred in 1868 when the Southern Baptist Convention convened in Baltimore. Promptly the women of several states began to organize to forward the missionary enterprise. Baltimore Baptists sent a circular throughout the South appealing to the women of Baptist churches to become active in the missionary enterprise. In this circular the women of Baltimore said that they had adopted a plan of having mission boxes in their homes, each member pledging to put at least two cents a week into this box, preferably on Sunday. The circular also suggested the organization of societies in each state to attend to business, and regular meetings in each church or neighboring churches for prayer and dissemination of missionary intelligence. By 1874, the Foreign Mission Board recommended that an executive or central committee for women's work be appointed for each state. At first the board made these appointments in consultation with brethren in the state concerned, but within ten years the women's committees became self-perpetuating. In 1875 the Southern Baptist Convention commended the significant work of "these gentle and loving servants of Jesus." By the close of the Reconstruction era, the Convention was urging that a female missionary society be organized in every church. The exhortation in 1877 was prophetic of things to come.

> Let the Christian women of our Churches generally, adopt some such plan, and press it with zeal and energy, and like the rock smitten by the Prophet's rod, the dry places shall become fountains of blessing to the needy.[29]

The Fortunes of Landmarkism

Civil war and Reconstruction were quite hurtful to the Landmark movement. Homer L. Grice remarked: "The war brought at least one great blessing to Southern Baptists: It ended the greatest controversy that ever afflicted them." It is true that Landmarkism never again had strength enough to confront the Southern Baptist Convention as it did in 1859 at Richmond, but the movement was far from terminated at the close of the war. The fall of Nashville to Union forces in February, 1862, in which J. R. Graves lost everything—book stock, press, and equipment—was only the first of many blows that wasted him. The postwar yellow fever epidemic claimed his mother and his wife. He accepted the pastorate of the First Baptist Church, Memphis, in 1867, leaving the familiar and beloved environs of Nashville. He was able to begin the publication of *The Baptist* at Memphis, but he was defeated again and again in his struggle to establish a publication agency. His paper was quite popular in what James E. Tull termed "the Landmark belt"—Tennessee, Arkansas, Mississippi, Texas, Louisiana, and North Alabama. With the close of the war,

Graves began a strenuous decade of preaching, lecturing, and writing. "All was energy, toil, and frequent physical breakdowns." Perhaps his own trials brought a kindlier spirit to Graves. Late in this period he wrote in his paper:

> It has been a long time since anything of a personal character appeared in this paper. . . . The older we grow the more we are convinced that it were better to let the most bitter things pass unnoticed.[30]

Homer L. Grice wrote that many of Graves' followers

> were not willing to help split associations, state conventions, and the Southern Baptist Convention on the personal and denominational issues he had stressed, for they knew what the Campbellite and antimission splits had done to Southern Baptist life. Increasingly, they tired of warfare and yearned for peace.[31]

In addition, Grice felt that Southern Baptists, "suffering sorely from the ravages of the Civil War and grappling with the many difficult problems of the Reconstruction era, had other things to think about than the Graves-Howell controversy." [32]

However, despite this improved spirit by Graves and the quiescence of his followers, the ecclesiological views of such an influential man as J. R. Graves (and he never relinquished them) continued to develop polarities in churches, state bodies, and the Convention itself. Strong Landmark leadership was a significant factor in several spin-offs just before and after Graves's death in 1893. At the same time, as James E. Tull pointed out, Landmark doctrines were entering the bloodstream of Southern Baptists. As will be described in the next period, second-generation Landmarkers adopted those aspects of Graves' system that they preferred, and overlooked others. Consequently, Landmarkism, apart from Graves himself, exhibited no monolithic character, even among the original triumvirate. This will be glimpsed more clearly in the next period when various controversies developed, several of them clearly based on Landmark ideas; but because of varying emphases, none of these controversies commanded the general support of all types of Landmark followers; and despite the fact that at least two of them, embodying basically the thrust of Graves, appeared at precisely the same time, there was little coalescence in the controversies because of their varying emphases.

Summary of the Period

Baptists in the fifteen southern states increased from 316 associations, 7,760 churches, and 645,218 members in 1860 to approximately 559 associations, 12,864 churches, and 906,074 members in 1877. This represented an average annual membership growth of 2.25%. It was the smallest average annual increase Southern Baptists had yet experienced, dropping from the average increase annually between 1814 and 1845 of 7.20% and from the average annual increase between 1845 and 1860 of 4.79%. There were several reasons for this. The withdrawal of the West Virginia churches diminished Virginia Baptists by approximately 15,000. Furthermore, before 1877 most of the Negro Baptists had withdrawn from the white churches to form their own churches, associations, and state bodies. This diminished the number of Baptist church members by perhaps 400,000. In addition, the fatalities of the war and diminution of efforts because of the dislocation of all areas of life by war and Reconstruction provided further reductions in the number of Baptists in the South. It is likely, also, that the relatively large size of Southern Baptists militated against a high percentage of increase in succeeding periods.

Despite such adverse factors, the rate of Baptist growth exceeded the population increase. In these fifteen southern states the population grew from 12,203,157 in 1860 to 17,919,883 in 1880, or an average annual increase of 2.23%. The population of the entire United States during this same period averaged 2.50% annually, so the population of the southern states grew less rapidly than the national average. The census reports show that the population growth in the South slowed down radically during the war, then gradually began to accelerate. The national average increase between 1860 and 1870 was 22.6%, but of the fifteen southern states, only Texas with 35.5%, Missouri with 45.6%, and Florida with 33.7% increases in their population during this decade were able to exceed the national average. Virginia sustained a loss of 23.3% or 371,155 in population during this decade. South Carolina had a gain of only .3% (1,898 people in ten years), while Alabama and Mississippi had gains of 3.4% and 4.6%, respectively. Louisiana gained only 2.7% during this decade. Between 1870 and 1880, however, most of the southern states again began to grow substantially.

The Baptist slow-up in growth during this period took place in all three of the geographical regions, but it was most radical in the South Atlantic region. The total average annual increase for the seven states in that region was .56%, compared with the average annual increase of 3.95% in the South Central region and 4.29% in the single state of Missouri in the North Central region. Meanwhile, the population increase in the seven South Atlantic states averaged 1.43% annually, almost three times the rate of Southern Baptist growth. Virginia and South Carolina Baptists were hard hit in the South Atlantic region, the former showing an average annual loss of 1.92% and the latter, of .24%. The excision of the Negroes from the white churches, the carving of a new state from Virginia, and the vicissitudes of war and

Reconstruction were particularly hurtful to the growth of Baptists in the South Atlantic states.

The South Atlantic region contained 39.90% of all Southern Baptists in 1877, compared with 50.91% in 1860, 55.48% in 1845, and 68.47% in 1814. This rapid shift of Baptist strength in the South in sixty-three years suggests several factors: that Southern Baptists played a large part in populating the receding frontier to the west; that the center of Baptist influence was rapidly moving westward; and that doctrinal conservatism, which was so characteristic of frontier and western Baptists, would become increasingly influential as the percentages of Southern Baptists in the western areas began to mount. In 1871 the Convention met at St. Louis, Missouri; in 1874 a Convention session was held at far-off Jefferson, Texas; and in 1877, at New Orleans, Louisiana. Virginia dropped out of first place as the state containing the most Baptists. Georgia with 13.19% had replaced Virginia, which fell to 7.87%. North Carolina had 9.26%; South Carolina, 6.65%; District of Columbia, 1.11%; Florida, .99%; and Maryland, .84%.

The South Central states also experienced some losses from the excision of the Negroes and the rigors of war and Reconstruction. Baptists in Alabama, the capital of the Confederacy, had an average annual gain of only .32%, compared with a population gain in the same period of 1.47%. Texas Baptists increased at a whopping 13.49% annual average, compared with the population gain of 7.78%. Arkansas Baptists gained 9.92% annual average, while their population showed a 4.01% gain. Mississippi Baptists gained 6.38%, compared with the population gain of 2.05%. Louisiana gained 4.82%, compared with the population gain of 2.05%. Tennessee Baptists gained 4.59%, compared with the population gain of 1.86%. Kentucky Baptists gained 1.90%, compared with the average annual population gain of 2.03%, the second South Central state in which Baptists grew less rapidly than the population. In the entire South Central region Baptists showed an increase of 3.95% annually during this period, compared with the population increase of 2.60%. This larger Baptist growth, as can be glimpsed above, developed from larger relative increases in Texas, Arkansas, Mississippi, and Tennessee.

Kentucky was now second only to Georgia in the number of Southern Baptists in the state (12.09%). Excellent growth had brought the percentage of all Southern Baptists in Mississippi to 9.87%. Tennessee had 9.38%; Texas (with a 13.49% increase annually) had 7.22%; Alabama, greatly hurt by war and Reconstruction, had 7.15%; Arkansas had 3.49%; and Louisiana, 2.12%. The percentage of all Southern Baptists in the South Central region increased to 51.32% in 1877, as compared with 42.06% in 1860, 39.92% in 1845, and 30.62% in 1814.

Missouri Baptists, in the North Central region, increased from 37 associations, 749 churches, and 44,877 members in 1860 to 66 associations, 1,328 churches, and 79,546 members in 1877, an average annual increase in membership of 4.29%, while the population had an annual average increase of 3.97%. This may be compared with their growth between 1845 and 1860 at the rate of 10.89% annually. The percentage of all Southern Baptists in Missouri increased to 8.78% in 1877, compared with 6.95% in 1860, 4.4% in 1845, and none in 1814.

Thus, by 1877 the South Central region had the majority of Southern Baptists within its area, and the two western regions contained over 60% of all Southern Baptists.

The educational level of the Baptist ministry was much higher than before. New schools were founded and old ones reopened even during the difficult postwar years. Of the 131 ministers named by the *Encyclopedia of Southern Baptists* as outstanding during this period, 70 or 53% of them were shown as having at least a college or university education. Approximately 42 of these 131 ministers were described as "educators," which included the administration of many colleges, universities, and seminaries, as well as professors in these schools. In the period between 1860 and 1877, 4 permanent academies, colleges, and universities, and 1 permanent seminary were founded in 4 states, making a total of approximately 24 permanent schools in 10 southern states by the close of Reconstruction.

In addition, Southern Baptists had permanent state papers, either privately or denominationally owned, in 9 of the 15 states of the South by 1877. Some of the most distinguished leaders in the South were denominational editors, and a considerable amount of denominational and doctrinal writing was published from the pens of scores of writers. Of the 152 leaders listed in the *Encyclopedia of Southern Baptists* for this period (of whom 21 were laymen and 6 were lay-benefactors of denominational objects), 33 men were listed as editors of papers. The stress of the times prevented a great deal of book publishing, but Kerr Boyce Tupper summarized a surprisingly large amount of literature of this period.[33] Outstanding in this list are the two books by John A. Broadus, *On the Preparation and Delivery of Sermons* (1870) and *Lectures on the History of Preaching* (1876). Of the 152 leaders listed in the *Encyclopedia* for this period, 32 were authors of one or more books.

Although the explosive Landmark movement had been temporarily crippled by the war, J. R. Graves himself was very active during this period and continued to popularize his distinctive views. The other two members of the old Landmark triumvirate were out of the movement. A. C. Dayton died in 1865, while J. M. Pendleton, after spending the war period and some of the Reconstruction era in the North, returned to the South with little sympathy for Landmark doctrines. Graves did develop a better spirit and did not again challenge the right of the Convention to live during the remainder of this period, but he tried regularly to curtail its program and rework its constituency as a safeguard to the rights of the local congregations.

Organizational structures across the South were strengthened during this period. Preparation was being made in the various states for a new unity through strong state structures that would emerge in the next period. The Southern Baptist Convention itself eliminated the Bible Board and the first Sunday School Board, primarily because the system of designated giving, which was implicit in the old society method of financing benevolent work, had not provided support for these two benevolences.

There is evidence during this period that Southern Baptists were becoming accustomed to the larger liberties involved in the new kind of structural body they had adopted. More and more one can see the denominational emphasis simply in a cursory reading of the minutes. For example, by 1861, out of 177 messengers attending the Convention, 169 of them were from associations or state bodies; in 1863, all but 9 of 185 messengers were from associations and state bodies. This tendency seems to prevail in the following years, suggesting that auxiliary societies in the various states were giving way to the structured associations and state bodies.

Efforts were made to keep this liberty from getting out of hand. For a brief season, individual churches facing crises were permitted to make appeals for financial help during the meetings of the Convention, but in the closing years of this era, there were several instances where such appeals were not permitted. An exception, of course, was the Coliseum Place Baptist Church of New Orleans, which had been seized by the American Baptist Home Mission Society under the order that they secured from the War Department during the Civil War. The Convention assumed a continuing helpful stance toward this particular church throughout the remainder of this period, even taking a second mortgage on it in order to acquire legal domain. The whole question of the use of agents to collect funds for the boards, under an arrangement by which the agent received a certain percentage of what he collected, came under serious criticism during the latter years of this period. It is also notable in the Convention meetings of this period that the gatherings were small enough for vigorous individual dissent. The inclination for this was not lacking, and on many occasions it was necessary to limit the time of a speaker to five or ten minutes. The procedures were very democratic because of this and on account of the extensive use of committees appointed to study the various aspects of the operations of the several boards.

Most of the Negroes had withdrawn from Southern Baptist churches before 1877. The attitude of Southern Baptists officially toward the Negro was one of concern for his welfare and the need to win him to Christ. However, in the periodical literature it is plain that the whites still retained the antebellum paternalistic attitude toward the Negro.[34] Like all other Christian groups, North and South, Southern Baptists in this period failed to grasp the principle of total equality. As had been prophesied by some northern leaders during the abolitionist controversy, the laissez-faire economic system was unwilling to allow unprepared and unassisted Negroes, suddenly catapulted into the full responsibilities of citizenship and self-survival, to reap the fruits of freedom, and like many marginal people of all races in this period of industrialization, they became second-class citizens socially and economically despite their political emancipation.[35]

The Southern Baptist Convention, refusing to enter into organic union with northern societies, was confronted during this period by the American Baptist Home Mission Society of New York as a rival for its home field, and a severe controversy was in the offing over the choice of a publication body to provide literature for the Sunday Schools and the churches in the South. The failure during this era of two boards established by the southern body; the diminishing strength exhibited in both home missions and publications, compared to rival bodies in the North; the increasing recognition of the ideological struggle between the society principle of promoting extensive geographical support for a particular benevolence, and the convention principle of promoting all benevolences for Baptists in a limited geographical area; and the manifest sympathy of many Southern Baptists for a return to the old days of unified operations by all American Baptists—all of these factors dampened any feeling of optimism by southern leaders concerning the future of the Convention.

Notes

1. See, for example, *Minutes of Georgia Baptist Convention,* 1861, pp. 5-6.
2. *Annual,* Southern Baptist Convention, 1863, pp. 34-35.
3. Baker, *Source Book,* pp. 128-29 has the documents.
4. *Ibid.,* p. 126.
5. Baker, *Relations,* p. 90.
6. *Annual,* Southern Baptist Convention, 1863, p. 45.
7. For the detailed story, see Baker, *The Story of the Sunday School Board,* pp. 16-20.
8. Cox-Woolley, eds., *Encyclopedia,* III, p. 1953.
9. *Minutes of the 45th and 46th Anniversaries of the State Convention of the Baptist Denomination in South Carolina,* held in July, 1865, and July, 1866 (Greenville: C. E. Elford's Job Press, 1866), pp. 238-41.
10. See, for example, *Minutes of the Edgefield Baptist Association,* 1871, pp. 3-4.
11. See *Minutes of the Forty-Sixth Anniversary of the Georgia Baptist State Convention,* 1868, p. 27.

12. *Minutes of the Forty-Sixth Annual Session of the Alabama Baptist State Convention*, 1868, pp. 11-12.

13. *Proceedings of the Twenty-Eighth Session of the Mississippi Baptist State Convention*, 1867, pp. 20-21.

14. Paul W. Stripling, *The Negro Excision from Baptist Churches in Texas (1861-1870)*, unpublished Th.D. dissertation, Southwestern Baptist Theological Seminary, Ft. Worth, Texas, May, 1967, pp. 218 ff.

15. See Baker, *Relations,* pp. 95-96.

16. *Annual,* Southern Baptist Convention, 1870, pp. 35-36.

17. *Annual Report,* American Baptist Home Mission Society, 1862, p. 21.

18. See *Home Mission Monthly* (of American Baptist Home Mission Society, New York), VI, pp. 225 f.

19. *Annual Report,* American Baptist Home Mission Society, 1864, pp. 20 f.

20. Baker, *Relations,* p. 90.

21. *Annual,* Southern Baptist Convention, 1867, p. 79.

22. *Ibid.,* 1868, pp. 20 f.

23. *Home Mission Monthly,* XVI, p. 406.

24. Morehouse, *op. cit.,* pp. 427 f.

25. Baker, *Relations,* p. 119.

26. *Ibid.,* pp. 153-165.

27. Baker, *The Story of the Sunday School Board,* p. 22.

28. *Annual,* Southern Baptist Convention, 1871, p. 16 of Appendix.

29. *Ibid.,* 1877, p. 59.

30. On April 24, 1875. Quoted in Tull, *op. cit.,* p. 499.

31. Cox-Woolley, eds., *Encyclopedia,* I, p. 684.

32. *Ibid.,* pp. 584-585.

33. Newman, *op. cit.,* pp. 355 ff.

34. See Rufus B. Spain, *At Ease in Zion* (Nashville: Vanderbilt University Press, 1961 and 1967), pp. 68 ff; and David M. Reimers, *White Protestantism and the Negro* (New York: Oxford University Press, 1965), pp. 18 ff.

35. For earlier warnings of this, see Baker, *Relations,* pp. 20-22.

RECOVERY AND ADVANCE
1877–1917

From the End of Reconstruction to
the First Executive Committee of
the Convention

12 The Struggle to Live

The post-Reconstruction decades were crucial for Southern Baptists. Some of their difficulties developed from internal and inter-Baptist rivalries growing out of doctrinal or sectional ideologies. On the other hand, many of their problems were thrust upon them by the kind of world in which they lived in the forty years between 1877 and 1917. In many respects these years were most remarkable, defying any attempt to unravel their complex components. The aspects of the world that were most influential on the growth and life of the Southern Baptist Convention may be described in general terms. The rapid growth of the population in the United States (from 47,141,000 in 1877 to 103,414,000 in 1917) challenged Southern Baptists with potential converts. Immigration reached new heights, totaling more than 23,000,000 people during these years. In fact, between 1905 and 1914, six of the ten years showed immigration exceeding 1,000,000 each year, while the lowest number of immigrants in the other years was 751,786. The frontier to the west ceased to exist by about 1890, due partly to extensive purchase of western land by speculators, and partly by achieving control of the Indians in the West by eliminating their basic meat supply through destroying the huge buffalo herds and by establishing reservations for them. At the same time the development of the railroads provided more rapid and convenient transportation. In 1860 total trackage was 30,625 miles. This figure grew steadily until 1920, when total track mileage approximated 260,000. Southern Baptists spread rapidly to the southwestern and western areas, affecting the sectional nature of their general body and bringing additional missionary activity to the new settlements along the railroads. Better communication was secured by the invention of the telephone to supplement the telegraph, while the automobile and even the flying machine had their beginnings in this period.

Technological improvements helped the United States become the world leader in many areas. The typewriter, the linotype (accelerating effective journalism), the phonograph, and the electric light were only a few of the significant inventions. The refinement of agricultural implements had revolutionized the operation of farms. Industry kept pace. Before the turn of the century the United States had surpassed England and Germany in the production of iron and steel and was the leading industrial nation. Mass production that inhibited individual craftsmanship and creativity in work already was well under way. The number of wage earners engaged in manufacturing more than trebled between 1869 and 1914. The gross value of manufactured products rose at the same time from about $3,400,000,000 to $24,200,000,000. The American labor movement became effectively organized for the first time in this period. This was the age of giant corporations, huge personal fortunes, and unbelievable corruption in financial and political life. Monopolies brought government intervention in industry. The only interruption in the spiraling prosperity of this period was the panic of 1893. Reflecting instability in the British market in 1890, foreign capital movement to America was stopped, bringing a market collapse in New York and substantial exports of gold. The inflexible banking system was helpless to stop the completion of the cycle, and a severe financial panic gripped the nation from about 1893 to 1897. The effects of this depression were reflected in every Baptist institution or activity during that important decade.

One problem that was not met in this period was racial. After the withdrawal of troops from the last of the southern states in 1877, a new era was begun in southern history. The elimination of the slavery system had revolutionized nearly every aspect of southern life—social, economic, political, and religious. Unfortunately, due to a variety of causes emanating from both the North and the South, first-class citizenship was not accorded the freedmen or even seriously advocated by any section of the nation during this entire period.[1]

As southerners returned to the national political arena, they found that northern financial and industrial leaders, without the opposition in Congress by southern planters, had utilized the Federal Government to forward and protect their sectional interests; but by the close of this period, the South was involved in the new nationalism that had developed rapidly after the Spanish-American War and the new enthusiastic idealism that accompanied the First World War. The Spanish-American War in 1898 catapulted the United States into the position of a world power. After its close the United States annexed Hawaii on July 7, 1898, and on December 10, 1898, received the Philippines, Puerto Rico, and Guam from Spain. At the very close of the period, World War I was fought to make the world safe for democracy. War was declared on April 6, 1917, and peace was signed on November 11, 1918.

The greatest influence on Southern Baptists, of course, came from the religious climate during this period. In both European and American religious life the baneful carry-over of rationalism and scepticism from an earlier period formed a foundation for religious confrontations in all denominations. The nineteenth century was characterized both in Europe and the United States by a strong anti-supernaturalistic thrust. The French Revolution inaugurated forms of free thought and liberalism that radically affected politics, culture, and religion in the following century. Successive blows were aimed, in particular, at the basic supernaturalism that undergirded the Christian movement. Scientific thought was used to erode the theological assertions of a creative and providential God, and indeed, the necessity of his existence. In 1859 Charles Darwin published his *Origin of the Species,* which developed the theme that human life evolved from lower forms through the survival of the fittest: this was projected into religious and metaphysical structures to undermine many of the most evident arguments for the existence and providence of God. Historical and radical literary critics attempted to reconstruct the Scriptures in such fashion as to eliminate the meaning of biblical inspiration. Loisy and Tyrrell in the Roman Catholic Church and Wellhausen and Strauss of the Protestant community published radical works in this vein. An increased sociological emphasis, interpreting Christianity in humanitarian terms rather than individualistic regeneration, resulted in extensive application of the "this-worldly" social gospel in the place of an "other-worldly" individual-redeeming gospel. A part of the move toward church unity and ecumenism stemmed from not only the needs of the mission fields but from the attempt by Christian liberals to unify all Christian denominations in the struggle against hostile critics. Philosophy, taking its cue from the upward direction of the evolutionary process in the hypothesis of Darwin, began to reflect an optimistic attitude toward the future and potentiality of man, who indeed might evolve into deity.[2]

These scientific, literary, sociological, ecumenical, and philosophical trends formed the religious community in the world of Southern Baptists from 1877 to 1917. All of them appear in some aspect of Southern Baptist life. This chapter will describe the fierce internal ideological struggles within Baptist ranks that threatened the destruction of the Southern Baptist Convention. Chapter 13 will examine the development of the Convention's program in the midst of its revolutionary world during this period; while chapter 14 will survey the concurrent advances made by the constituency of the Convention.

The critical internal and inter-Baptist attacks against the Convention during this period occurred precisely at those points where this body broke with the old society-type ideology in 1845 when organizing on the associational or convention concept: (1) opposition to the effort to establish a specific geographical base; (2) opposition to the effort to sustain a multibenevolent ministry; and (3) opposition to the effort to "elicit, combine, and direct" the energies of all Southern Baptists in a united denominational thrust. The first two attacks stemmed from the desire of the older societies (for home missions and for publication) in the North to retain the geographical field and the publication ministry in the South that had been theirs before the organization of the southern Baptist body. The third attack was launched by the Landmark movement within the Southern Baptist Convention as a protest against the centralization of denominational life in general bodies to the detriment of the authority of the local churches. Had the Convention failed to survive any of these confrontations, it would have been badly mutilated or utterly destroyed.

Establishing a Geographical Base

As mentioned heretofore, the convention ideology differed radically from the society plan in that the former desired a geographically-based denominational body that would assume leadership in all of the benevolences the constituency might desire to cultivate. Each society, on the other hand, was benevolence-centered. It functioned for one benevolence only, minimized geography and denominational unity in favor of widespread financial support, and ignored all other denominational emphases as being the province of other societies. Consequently, from the very time that the Southern Baptist Convention was organized in 1845 there was a potential confrontation between the Domestic Mission Board of the new body and the older Home Mission Society of New York relative to the geographical base each would cultivate. Not only so, but the increasing home mission programs of the several associations and state bodies in the South presented rivals for funds to the Home Mission Board (so called after 1874) of the Convention.[3]

Rivalry by Southern States. The rivalry with the state bodies in the South not only radically diminished the receipts of the southern board but also closed many areas of work to it. It was reported at the meeting of the Convention in 1881 that because of this rivalry the only areas of mission service left in the hands of the Home Mission Board were Florida, Arkansas, Louisiana, Texas, Indian Territory, and California. W. H. McIntosh, secretary of the board, remarked at the Convention's session in the following year that the geographical area which constituted the largest resources of the board and in which the greatest results had been accomplished—the older southern states—had been taken over by the state boards, thereby diminishing the contributions to the southwide board "whose labors are bestowed upon regions that need assistance and can give but little." As a matter of fact, the board was denied the right of collecting funds and prosecuting missions in some of these states by official action of the state conventions.[4]

Confrontation by the Home Mission Society. But the paucity of receipts from its constituency was not the severest trial of the Home Mission Board. At this very time, the Baptist Home Mission Society of New York, under the able leadership of Henry L. Morehouse, disregarding protests by Convention leaders, was aggressively striving to supplant the Convention's Home Mission Board entirely. The society was not only pressing a mission program in the older states of the South, but was rapidly enlarging its work in the few states and territories left in the hands of the southern board because of southern state convention rivalry.[5]

When the receipts of the board plunged to a new low of $12,960.43 in 1878 and the Home Mission Society of New York continued its domination of the southern home field, Southern Baptists began to debate seriously both in the Convention sessions and elsewhere whether a southern Home Mission Board was really needed, since the associations and state bodies in the South and the northern society were so active in the work. The year 1882 was critical. This marked the fiftieth anniversary of the northern society, and it used its great resources and history to call for additional cooperation by the South. In that year, for example, the society had 67 missionaries in 13 states of the South in their evangelistic program, 13 schools with 78 teachers and 2,329 pupils (principally Negro) in the South, and had provided extensive assistance to churches of all races in the constructing of church buildings. Baptist state bodies in Texas, Arkansas, Georgia, and Mississippi were in more or less formal alliance with the society in its southern work, and financial support was given the society by Baptists in other southern states without formal alignment.[6] The society's receipts during the previous ten years had amounted to almost

$2,000,000. In contrast with this, the Convention's home mission receipts during the same period were less than $225,000 (of which perhaps 40% was probably used for collecting agents and administration).

A New Location and Secretary. On the second day of the 1882 session of the Convention, Joshua Levering of Maryland offered a resolution that a committee consisting of one from each state be appointed to study the Home Mission Board and make such recommendations as might "promote its usefulness to the enlargement of the work committed to its trust." Two days later the committee appointed made the following report:

> Your Committee to whom was referred the consideration of the present condition, prospects and enlargement of the Home Mission work of this Convention, beg leave to report that we find a want of enthusiasm on the part of the denomination in the work of this Board, and since from the experience of a series of years, it seems impossible to arouse this enthusiasm without making material changes, your Committee feel constrained, as on the whole promising the best results, to recommend the following resolutions, viz;
>
> 1st. That the Home Mission Board be removed from Marion, Alabama, to Atlanta, Georgia, as soon after the adjournment of this Convention as such transfer can be made.
>
> 2nd. That the Board be instructed to employ a Corresponding Secretary, and in addition thereto, one or more district Secretaries, if found best for the efficient prosecution of its work.
>
> 3d. That the Committee on Nomination of new Boards be instructed to render their report in accordance with the foregoing resolutions.
>
> Your Committee desire, in presenting the above recommendations, to state distinctly and emphatically, that in all their inquiries, they have heard no word of complaint against any of the brethren composing the present Board, but, on the contrary, only words of commendation and praise for their faithful attention to the work committed to their trust, and they cannot close this report without recommending the adoption of the following resolution, viz:
>
> "That the earnest and sincere thanks of this Convention be and are hereby tendered to the Home Mission Board, at Marion, Alabama, and to its Corresponding Secretary, and to each member thereof, for long and faithful services rendered so willingly and gratuitously." [7]

Pursuant to these instructions, the Home Mission Board elected I. T. Tichenor as the successor to McIntosh, and moved the headquarters of the board to Atlanta, Georgia. Tichenor faced what he called later "a great defeat and a lost cause."

> He surveyed the area west of the Mississippi, and judged that the entire territory had passed out of the hands of the Southern Board. East of the river the outlook was not much brighter. Mississippi was allied with the Publication Society of the North, Georgia was co-operating with the Home Mission Society in freedman missions, while Florida was seriously considering an official alignment with the Home

Mission Society. Tennessee Baptists also were studying the possibility of Northern alignment. Indian Territory and Louisiana were the only areas that offered the possibility of alignment with the Southern Convention, and in the former the Home Mission Society was pressing an aggressive campaign.[8]

Tichenor promptly began to challenge the Home Mission Society. During the next five years he made an intensive effort to attend, meetings of all state bodies in the South and as many of the associational gatherings as time and strength permitted. In August, 1882, President E. T. Winkler of the Home Mission Board wrote an article that was widely publicized in many periodicals, in which he openly questioned the propriety of the aggressive program of the Home Mission Society in the South. Probably for the first time this article alerted many Southern Baptists to the issues involved in the extensive program of the northern society in the South. Winkler noted the several plans of cooperation between the Home Mission Society and various southern states, and pointed to the announced new program of the society which would greatly affect the work of the Home Mission Board if it succeeded. He concluded his article by saying:

Every one of the border States of the South is occupied by the Home Mission Society; and most of our older States are in co-operative alliance with the American Baptist Publication Society in colportage and Sunday School work. . . . The missionaries employed in the South by the Home Mission Society is 120—just three times the number of those under commission of our own Home Mission Board. The total expenditures of the Northern Society at the South, for regular missionary and educational work and school buildings, during the past year, was over $84,000, while, on the other hand, the entire contribution of Southern Baptists to their Home Mission Board did not amount to $29,000.[9]

This article by Winkler was the beginning of a widespread newspaper controversy over the right of the society to work in the South, which the Southern Baptist Convention called its territory. Corresponding Secretary H. L. Morehouse of the Home Mission Society affirmed that the society was in the South to stay, and said vigorously that in its constitution the society named North America as its field, which, of course, included the South. The *Religious Herald* of Virginia and the *Foreign Mission Journal* of the Convention openly debated this question with the *Home Mission Monthly* of the society. In 1887 the Home Mission Society published an article in its journal which remarked:

We observe that some influential Southern Baptists are openly asserting that the Home Mission Board of the Southern Baptist Convention is a superfluity and ought to be dispensed with entirely. Its field is covered by old and efficient State conventions, the only new mission fields to which it devotes attention being portions of Florida and Texas. It is felt that a special organization for such limited work is not now called for, whatever may have been the demands for it in the past.[10]

Tichenor worked strenuously to overcome the lassitude of Southern Baptists in their home mission program. His vision was large. Year after year he challenged the Convention with significant programs couched in appealing terms. In 1885, for example, he said to the Convention:

> For once let us try what the united energies of this Convention can accomplish when it determines to do a deed of noble daring for our kindred, and for our Saviour's cause. Long enough we have been creeping timidly along the shore. Let us launch out into the great deep of human necessity, and let down the gospel net where the thousands are perishing. For forty years we have been pursuing a policy which has distrusted our God and been hurtful to ourselves. We are weary of following every other Christian host into the battle for the world's deliverance. We want to move up to the front, and as good soldiers bear our full part in the conflict.[11]

His vision encompassed many new facets of work, including schools, hospitals, homes for orphans and for the aged and infirm, and "indeed all those means which lift up our humanity from the degradation of the fall, and prepare it for the work of God in this life, and to dwell with Him in the life to come." His eloquence was stirring.

> The breath of the Divine Spirit can dissipate the mists of worldliness that bedim the vision of His people, and show us even now that both duty and happiness require such consecration. A new Pentecost, with its disparted tongues of fire, may impart new life, even in our day, to His children. . . . A mighty revolution, shaking as with the might of an earthquake, the sleeping Christians of our time, may break upon us as a meteor breaks through the midnight sky. The voice of the Almighty may call to this valley of dry bones, "O, ye dry bones, hear the word of the Lord," and starting from their long slumbers, they may stand up an exceeding great army, prepared for the conquest of the world.[12]

He found it difficult to stir his comrades. In 1891, for example, he expressed disappointment at the meager funds received for carrying on the work, describing extensively the economic and material development of the South that should cause Southern Baptists to advance. He closed by exclaiming,

> Brethren of this Convention, you have laid this work upon us. Its vastness has awed our souls. Its sore pressing needs have touched our spirits. Its crying wants have moved our hearts to pity, and sometimes to tears. Its boundless opportunities have excited our enthusiasm. We want to do the work you have assigned us, but how can we when we are trammelled by the slowness of our churches and the scantiness of our resources. Take from hands that are eager to do what we see

so plainly needs to be done these shackles that restrain our efforts and limit our action.[13]

Despite such expressions of disappointment, Tichenor accomplished much. Perhaps he more than any other single person should be credited with saving the home field. As a result of his energetic policy,

in five years (after he took office in 1882) there was not a missionary to the white people of the South who did not bear a commission from either the Home Mission Board of the Southern Baptist Convention, or one of our State Boards in alliance with it.[14]

Even in the troublesome border states of Missouri and Indian Territory, where the controversy between the Home Mission Society and the Home Mission Board was so vigorously waged, Tichenor was able to negotiate a *modus vivendi.* In Missouri, committees from the two general bodies worked out a compromise by which they shared this important field of service, but in 1890, so unsatisfactory was the arrangement that the state body asked both of the home mission bodies to withdraw and permit the state forces to collect and divide home mission funds.[15] This arrangement seemed to please all participants. In Indian Territory, J. W. Murrow, the venerable missionary of the southern board, disagreed with Tichenor's aggressive pro-southern policies and in 1891 was forced to resign. He was promptly appointed by the society as their missionary and continued his work.[16] Thenceforth, Tichenor worked actively in Indian Territory for southern interests.

During Tichenor's last year as secretary in 1899, 671 missionaries were supported jointly with the state boards. Alabama, Arkansas, Florida, Georgia, Indian Territory, Kentucky, Louisiana, Maryland, Missouri, Mississippi, North Carolina, Oklahoma Territory, Tennessee, Texas, and Virginia were cooperating with the board in part or all of their work. The receipts of 1899 were $79,366.68.

Joe W. Burton has suggested ten significant contributions made by Tichenor, as follows: (1) he saved the Southern Baptist Convention through saving the Home Mission Board; (2) he laid the foundations for the Cooperative Program through his plea for systematic giving; (3) he established a church building department; (4) he fostered and built up the Sunday School work; (5) he inaugurated the board's work in Cuba; (6) he actively promoted city missions; (7) he assisted Negroes through conducting institutes and training them for efficient service; (8) he inaugurated the chain of mountain mission schools; (9) he promoted direct missions on the frontier, among the Indians and among the foreigners; and (10) he led Baptists to see the South as a base for world missions.[17]

The Beginning of Comity Agreements. At the 1894 meeting of the

Convention, T. T. Eaton, Kentucky Baptist editor, submitted the following resolution, which was approved.

> *Resolved,* That a committee of five be appointed to confer with a similar committee to be appointed by the American Baptist Home Mission Society with reference—
> 1. To coöperation between our Home Board and the Society in work among the colored people of the South; and
> 2. With reference to a more definite understanding in regard to the territorial limits of the work of the Board and the Society among the native white people, the Indians and the foreign populations of the country.[18]

1. The Fortress Monroe Conference. The Convention appointed a committee consisting of T. T. Eaton, H. H. Harris, I. T. Tichenor, J. B. Gambrell, T. P. Bell, Noah K. Davis, and O. F. Gregory. The society named James L. Howard, T. J. Morgan, H. L. Morehouse, J. B. Thomas, E. H. Johnson, A. S. Hobart, Nathan E. Wood, and, by invitation, M. MacVicar. The combined committee met at Fortress Monroe, Virginia, on September 12, 1894, where Howard was elected chairman and Gregory and Wood were named secretaries. Despite the fact that on each of these committees were those who had been strenuously opposed to the work of the other body, an excellent spirit prevailed. After two days of deliberation, the group unanimously adopted two items, and a third one, which was proposed by the South, was reported favorably, although the northern committee had no instructions about approving it. The first item concerned schools among the Negro people. It was unanimously agreed that the Home Mission Board should appoint a local advisory committee at each point where a school was controlled by the society; that control of the schools shall remain in the hands of the society, but these local advisory committees shall make recommendations to the society concerning any changes needed for the school; that the board and the Southern Baptist Convention shall appeal to Baptists of the South for moral and financial support of these schools and encourage promising young black people as students. The second item concerned mission work among the Negroes. It was unanimously recommended that the two bodies cooperate in the mission work among the Negro people of the South in connection with the Baptist state bodies, white and black, in the joint appointment of general missionaries, in holding Ministers' and Deacons' Institutes, and in the better organization of the missionary work of Negro Baptists. The third item concerned territorial limits. The committee of the society referred to their board (which subsequently approved it) the proposition of the committee of the Southern Baptist Convention, which read as follows:

We believe that, for the promotion of fraternal feeling and of the

> best interests of the Redeemer's kingdom, it is inexpedient for two
> different organizations of Baptists to solicit contributions, or to establish
> missions in the same localities, and for this reason we recommend
> to the Home Mission Board of the Southern Baptist Convention and
> to the American Baptist Home Mission Society, that in the prosecution
> of their work already begun on contiguous fields, or on the same field,
> that all antagonisms be avoided, and that their officers and employees
> be instructed to co-operate in all practical ways in the spirit of Christ.
> That we further recommend to these bodies and their agents, in opening
> new work, to direct their efforts to localities not already occupied by
> the other.[19]

Despite the fine words and good spirit of the Fortress Monroe
Conference, however, the agreement was not effective. Some white
Baptist state conventions refused to enter into it, while Negro Baptists
generally either showed little interest or in many cases were so separated by factions within the states that they could not agree on any
program. The Home Mission Board seriously and energetically endeavored to make the program a success. It refused to aid black
Baptists who would not cooperate with the society, and turned away
from educational activities among the Negro race since the society
was majoring in that field. However, the program increasingly became
less effective, and within a decade many felt that it was no longer
operative.

2. *The Washington Conference.* Another comity agreement was
attempted after the opening of the twentieth century. The Home
Mission Board had been receiving frequent requests for aid from
churches composed of Southern Baptists in New Mexico. At the
Southern Baptist Convention in 1894 a Texan offered a resolution
that New Mexico should be entered as a mission field, and the Convention approved. However, after the resolution that led to the Fortress
Monroe Conference was approved later in the same session, the Home
Mission Board was directed not to enter New Mexico until after the
conference with the society had been held. The requests for aid from
churches composed of Southern Baptists in New Mexico were especially numerous and urgent in 1907 and 1908. When the Convention
began looking favorably toward assisting these churches, Secretary
H. L. Morehouse of the society protested and cited the Fortress
Monroe agreement. The southern board again requested a conference
with the society to settle this question. A conference was held in
Washington, D. C., on April 15, 1909, and before beginning their
new discussions, all parties agreed that the Fortress Monroe agreement
had expired and that its stipulations were not now in force or binding.

The combined committee recommended that the southern board,
with the consent of the New Mexico Convention, take over all the
work of the society in New Mexico, and that any question of territorial

adjustment on the part of both boards be considered settled for a period of at least five years.[20] When this recommendation came to the Southern Baptist Convention, however, J. B. Gambrell of Texas added a statement declaring that nothing in the agreement should be construed to limit any church, association, or other Baptist body in the free exercise of the inalienable right to make such alignments for cooperation as will, in its judgment, be for its own good and for the furtherance of its work.[21] The society was unwilling to accept this qualification and refused to approve the recommendations of the Washington Conference.

3. Old Point Comfort-Hot Springs Conference. Agitation in New Mexico, which had initiated the Washington Conference, continued, and their state body split in two, one portion affiliating with the society and one with the board of the southern convention. At the request of the northern brethren, on September 27-28, 1911, a meeting of committees appointed by the Northern and Southern Baptist Conventions took place at Old Point Comfort, Virginia, and later at Hot Springs, Arkansas. With reference to New Mexico, this committee recommended that a new state body be organized, composed of the two existing rival conventions, and that the new convention should affiliate solely with the southern board and convention. This plan was subsequently adopted by the society, the Home Mission Board, the two New Mexico conventions, and the Northern and Southern Baptist Conventions. The Northern Baptist Convention had been organized in 1907, but the Home Mission Society still retained its former functions.

In addition to settling the New Mexico problem, the joint committee in 1911-12 also set forth some principles of comity that have continued to be recognized to the present time. The committee asserted its belief in the independence of local Baptist churches, in the moral inter-dependence and cooperation of Baptist churches, and in the advisory nature of all denominational bodies. Based upon these fundamental principles, the joint committee formulated three comity statements that were subsequently unanimously approved, as follows: (1) the giving of financial aid by a denominational body should not impair the autonomy of any church; (2) denominational organizations should carefully regard the rights of sister organizations and of the churches, to the end that unity and harmony and respect for the liberties of others should be promoted; and (3) Baptist bodies should never in any way injure the work of any other Baptist group.[22]

4. The Oklahoma Decision. Growing directly out of the New Mexico decision by the joint committee from Northern and Southern Baptists came another territorial adjustment during this period, as referred to previously. Both Northern and Southern Baptists had worked in Indian and Oklahoma Territory for many years. At times there were four or five sectional bodies organized, each affiliating with either the North or the South in carrying on their programs, and in general ignoring the other bodies. However, beginning in March, 1901, there came a series of harmonious conferences among the several bodies in Indian and Oklahoma Territory. These conferences resulted in the formation of the Baptist General Convention of Oklahoma in 1906. In the following year, Oklahoma became the forty-sixth state of the Union. The new Baptist General Convention of Oklahoma adopted dual alignment, sending funds both to the society and to the board.

The question of alignment had plagued Oklahoma Baptists for years. The predominantly southern population of Oklahoma was constantly being augmented by new southern immigrants. The settlement by the joint committee from both Northern and Southern Baptists in New Mexico was the decisive factor in causing Oklahoma Baptists to change their affiliation. The chief consideration for asking New Mexico Baptists to cooperate with the Southern Baptist Convention, the joint committee had said, "was the fact that the tide of immigration into New Mexico from Texas and other Southern States in recent years had been so great. The result has been that the population of New Mexico has become largely Southern in tradition and sympathy and preference." [23] A committee of Oklahoma Baptists, facing the same problem in that state, said that every reason given for New Mexico being turned to the Southern Baptist Convention applied with more weight to them. Consequently, in November, 1914, the Oklahoma body voted to adopt single alignment with the Southern Baptist Convention. No question of doctrine was involved.

> The reasons assigned for the action were that it was best in Oklahoma, as it was in New Mexico, for a State Convention to be affiliated with only one general society and that the preponderating sectional element in the denomination in the State should determine which one it should be.[24]

Thus, by the close of this period in 1917, the Convention had established its geographical base and in its struggle to accomplish this, had begun the development of a denominational consciousness that substantially deepened the loyalty of its constituents.[25] This loyalty would soon result in the reassessment of the geographical base when southern people, accustomed to their affiliation with the Southern Baptist Convention, moved into every section of the nation and preferred their old affiliation.

Sustaining a Multibenevolent Ministry

The second crucial struggle of the Southern Baptist Convention in this period developed from its ideology that conceived of all denom-inational and benevolent activity in the geographical area of its work as being properly a part of its mission. At this point there was a growing rivalry between the American Baptist Publication Society of Philadelphia, which had been faithful in providing Sunday School publications for Southern Baptists since 1840, and Southern Baptist leaders who desired to incorporate this ministry in the structured work of their Convention. It will be recalled that the first Sunday School Board of the southern body survived only from 1863 to 1873, after which, because of financial difficulties, its duties were assigned to the Domestic or Home Mission Board, along with a debt of $6,565. This was the situation in 1877.

The Home Mission Board Period. The financial panic of 1873, which brought the demise of the first Sunday School Board, caused the Convention to instruct its Home Mission Board to incur no additional debts whatsoever on the Sunday School publications. Consequently, the Home Mission Board let a contract with J. W. Burke and Company to publish *Kind Words* and lessons leaflets, with the understanding that there would be no expense of any kind to the board and any profits would accrue to the publisher. Later, because of the profit made by this contract, J. W. Burke and Company allowed a royalty of $800 a year under a new contract, which was increased on June 1, 1881, to $1,000 a year. Burke had been publishing over 100,000 copies of *Kind Words* each month, together with lesson leaflets in the number of about 40,000 a month. The old Sunday School debt had been pared down to about $3,000. By January, 1884, all of the old debt of the first Sunday School Board was paid off through these royalties.

The financial profit shown in the publication of the Sunday School material did not go unnoticed. In 1885 a committee of the Convention complimented the board for the paper, but went on to say the follow-ing:

> Neither brother Boykin nor any other man can supply all the de-mands of the literature essential to efficient Sunday-school work. The very best writers of our denomination are needed to supply, in adequate measure, what is now needed. If, therefore, we expect to meet these varied demands, we must very materially increase the facilities for producing this literature. Multitudes of our churches are already order-ing their publications from Northern and Western publishing houses, not only on account of their cheapness, but because of the ability with which they are prepared, as many of their ablest men are editing these publications. Whether we can, under present circumstances, compete with these houses in these respects, is a question to be determined. On some accounts it may be well to make the experiment. We only speak what we all feel when we say that no one man can supply the demands of this service. We must have something adapted to all stages

> of mental and moral development—a graded series reaching from our infant classes to mature age.
>
> In view of the early expiration of the contract for the publication of *Kind Words*, we suggest to the Home Board to mature some plan by which these growing demands may be met. With Rev. Smauel Boykin as chief, supported by such talent as can be found in our midst, this paper would meet all the demands of the case, and none of our people would look either North or West for any Sabbath-school literature.[26]

The "Northern publishing house" referred to in this report was, of course, the American Baptist Publication Society, the principal publisher of Sunday School materials in both northern and southern Baptist life. In that same year Secretary I. T. Tichenor of the Home Mission Board bluntly urged the Convention to consider enlarging the area of Sunday School literature to provide all Baptist churches in the South with needed materials. When the committee report suggested that the board "mature some plan by which these growing demands may be met," Tichenor promptly responded. In the following year he reported to the Convention that the board was "fully convinced that it was the duty of the Board and Convention, if possible, to supply the Sunday-school needs of its constituents." He said that he had awarded a five-year contract to publish several editions of *Kind Words,* and in addition to publish a full grade of *Quarterlies* in the number of three, and a *Magazine for Teachers.* The board would receive an annual royalty of $1,000 without assuming any risk under the contract. The Convention approved this without a word of opposition or dissenting voice. With this approval of a series of Sunday School publications, there developed what Tichenor called "the heaviest denominational conflict of the century." The northern publication society enjoyed a large and profitable business among the Baptist churches in the South, and was not willing to give up this business without a struggle. For the next several years the rivalry rocked along quietly, but there were evidences of it. For example, in 1887 Tichenor reported that outstanding Southern Baptist writers like Basil Manly, Jr., F. H. Kerfoot, J. M. Frost, H. H. Harris, and Samuel Boykin had contributed material, and that the patronage was so gratifying that the publisher had been forced to enlarge his facilities materially. On the back of the Convention *Annual* in 1887 was an advertisement for the series, including weekly *Kind Words,* the semimonthly *Kind Words,* the monthly *Kind Words,* lesson leaflets, the *Child's Gem, Kind Words* quarterlies for three age groups (primary, intermediate, and advanced), and the *Kind Words Teacher.* The board reported in 1888 that the total issues of the series promised to reach 5,000,000 during that year.

The tension was apparent at the 1889 Convention meeting in Memphis. A committee appointed to confer with the American Baptist Publication Society during the previous year reported that they could not reach an agreement on points of difference in the prosecution of their work.[27] The board's report on *Kind Words* was rather brief and seemingly harmless, but the subject was so sensitive that a motion was passed referring the whole publication question to a special committee, with the understanding that any question or comment about publications would be referred without debate to that committee. When the committee reported, it simply pointed out that the contract with the publisher of the series would not expire until June, 1891, so that nothing could be done by the Convention until that time.

All of this agitation greatly aroused James M. Frost, a mature and experienced pastor in Richmond, Virginia.

> Frost was deeply stirred by the issues involved. He had the insight to perceive that this was no mere squabble over finances. The future of the Southern Baptist Convention and all its work were involved in the right answer. His conviction was deepened by a chance visit with Dr. Tichenor. Frost described later how he and Tichenor had met at Selma, Alabama (perhaps in 1889 when the Alabama State Convention met there). Tichenor had attended the deliberations of the State Mission Board; he and Frost stood at the front gate of the house where Tichenor was staying and for two hours they talked. "Rather he talked and I listened. I was sympathetic, but unable to follow his sweep of thought in outlining the future,.showing what the Baptists of the South might accomplish, and the imperative need that a people make their own literature." [28]

What else Tichenor said to Frost on this occasion has not been revealed, but it is significant that among the first to commend Frost for moving toward providing a board for Sunday School work was I. T. Tichenor. On February 27, 1890, Frost published in the *Religious Herald* of Virginia an announcement that when the Convention next met he planned to offer resolutions to the effect that a new board should be organized for publication work. Strangely enough, Frost at this time did not know that there had formerly been such a board. However, he soon learned of this fact and pored over the story of the earlier movement. He later remarked:

> I saw at once that without knowing it I had in my proposition only gathered up the broken threads of history as if knitting them together again. Manifestly the unseen hand that touched the heart and mind in the night time was weaving the life plan for Southern Baptists.[29]

Frost presented his resolutions, which were referred to a committee of one from each state and Frost as chairman. The committee could not agree, but the majority report by Frost was adopted. It provided that a standing committee of nine be appointed to take over all the interests of the Sunday School promotion and publications from the Home Mission Board. Frost later remarked that with only two exceptions, every denominational paper in the South opposed his proposition.

The Sunday School Committee. The attitude of I. T. Tichenor was significant. He reported to the Convention that these publications had attained a success most gratifying to the Home Mission Board. He praised their writers, their teachings, and their rapidly enlarging circulation. Their value, he said, had increased sixfold in the previous three years. However, he concluded, if the Convention should commit this

> great and growing interest to a separate Board, we will rejoice that the success it has attained in our hands has made such a separation an act of wisdom, and we will heartily co-operate with the new Board in the work of the Convention. Should the Convention continue these publications in our hands we will, as heretofore, comply with its instructions and use our best endeavors to increase their circulation and their usefulness.[30]

Such a spirit on the part of Tichenor revealed the greatness of the man, for this growing, prosperous, and influential ministry of the Convention was one which any board would have been glad to retain under its control.

The Sunday School Committee authorized by the Convention in 1890 carried on the publication work for one year, and then reported that the needs of the denomination required either a considerable enlargement of the powers of this committee or, preferably, the appointment of a board to whom these great interests could be entrusted. This report was referred to a committee composed of one representative from each state. They soon learned that the members could not agree, so with considerable acumen, they chose one representative from each party to act as a sub-committee to recommend to them a report for the Convention. J. B. Gambrell of Mississippi, who did not favor the separate board at this time, and J. M. Frost of Virginia were appointed to work out some kind of report. They spent the day in the hotel room discussing what kind of report to make to the full committee. Twenty years later Frost wrote that Gambrell proposed to let Frost write the report and even name the location of a proposed board, provided Gambrell could write the closing paragraph. Frost agreed, with the proposal that he be allowed to add one sentence. The report was written under these circumstances. It recommended that a new board be created to be called the Sunday School Board of the Southern Baptist Convention and be located at Nashville, Tennessee. At the close of this report, Gambrell wrote his paragraph mentioning that "there are widely divergent views held among us by brethren equally earnest, consecrated, and devoted to the best interest of the Master's Kingdom." It was recommended, therefore, that the fullest freedom of choice be accorded to everyone as to which literature he would use or support without any disparagement "on account of what he may do in the exercise of his right as Christ's freeman." Frost added his final sentence urging all brethren to give the board a fair consideration and not to obstruct it in the great work assigned to it by the Convention.[31]

When the report was read to the Convention, men in every part of the congregation were ready to speak for or against it. John A. Broadus, however, the patriarch at Southern Baptist Theological Seminary, quickly moved to the rostrum and with deep emotion requested there be no debate, but that immediately the Convention take its vote on the report. With only thirteen dissenting votes, the board was approved. A. T. Robertson wrote later on:

> And even as I write, the tears come unbidden, as I think of the old veteran sitting there, his head buried in his hands and his whole frame heaving with emotion, which, if I mistake not, found relief in sobs.[32]

Thus, the Home Mission Board, which had conserved this significant ministry from 1873 until 1890, was relieved of the privilege and task of publication work as the new board was founded.

The Rebirth of the Sunday School Board. The problems facing the new Sunday School Board authorized by the Convention at Birmingham in 1891 were many and large. There was still a great deal of opposition within the Southern Baptist Convention to a separate board; the headquarters must be moved from Atlanta, Georgia, to Nashville, Tennessee; the trustees of the new board were totally inexperienced in this kind of operation; a new secretary would have to be secured; and, although there were many signs of its coming, few people recognized the scope and extent of the financial panic that had its birth in the same year as the Sunday School Board. To face this situation, the new board had practically no resources; indeed, until the sale of periodicals provided funds in December, 1891, the only finances available to the board came from two short-term loans amounting to about $1,200 from a Nashville bank on endorsements by members of the board.

Only ten trustees were in attendance out of the forty making up the board when the first meeting took place on May 26, 1891. When their first choice for corresponding secretary declined, the board met two weeks later to elect James M. Frost who, after severe personal struggles, accepted the post on July 1, 1891.

The committee report adopted by the Birmingham Convention spelled out the work of the new board. Its task was to publish the

Sunday School series, doing its best to improve them and increase the circulation, but to assume no other publication work except the proposed catechisms of John A. Broadus; to assume the Sunday School interests in the territory of the Convention, including statistical information, keeping the Convention informed in matters of Sunday School work; to enter into a printing contract rather than follow the leasing system in the publication of the Sunday School series; to prepare a list of books for recommendation to the various Sunday Schools; to aid mission Sunday Schools by contributions of literature and money through state organizations, with the understanding that no system of state or subagencies should be organized; and to take over the work of the Sunday School Committee after the issuance of the third quarter's series of literature. With his own private desk, money secured from his wife, and a small office borrowed from the Tennessee state paper, Frost began his work.

The first year was a critical one. Frost knew, as did everyone else, that if the new board failed to show a profit during this first year, it would likely be dissolved. Frost arranged for the transfer of Samuel Boykin, who had been editing the Sunday School literature for the Home Mission Board in Atlanta, and Boykin arrived in Nashville on January 1, 1892. Frost negotiated a printing contract for the following year, which brought comfortable quarters for the board without charge, and then busied himself as editor, writer, promoter, and business manager during the remainder of the first year.

As he reported to the Convention in May, 1892, Frost eloquently related the new board to the golden days when Basil Manly, Jr., and John A. Broadus produced the *Kind Words* series from Greenville, South Carolina. He then announced that the new board had a balance of over $1,000 after paying all operating expenses for the previous year, and capitalizing on this achievement, he called for the increased use of the periodicals of the board. He closed with a challenging word: "We stand in the present, but we speak for the future; we work in the present, but shall gather and garner our harvest in the centuries and the ages and the eternities." [33]

In a surprising move, Frost resigned on January 1, 1893, to become pastor of the First Baptist Church, Nashville. His successor was Theodore P. Bell, a staunch southerner in his thinking, who accepted the post on March 16, 1893. During this three-year secretaryship Bell rendered outstanding service. In the midst of a deepening financial panic the receipts of the board increased year by year, climbing to $63,141.12 in 1896, with a reserve fund of $2,500.

One of the most important of Bell's contributions was the nurturing of the new movement for the training of young people in Baptist life. The Christian Endeavor movement had been begun in 1881 among the Congregationalists and quickly began to cut across denominational lines to claim young people. The various American denominations recognized the danger of losing their young people and glimpsed at the same time the opportunity of enlisting this group in active service. In 1891 the Baptist Young People's Union of America was organized in Chicago and began to attract many Southern Baptist young people. In 1893 the Southern Baptist Convention adopted a resolution which marked the beginning of this program in its structure. The resolution recommended that young people form societies that were "strictly Baptistic and denominational and be under the sole authority of the local church without interdenominational affiliation." It also suggested that the Sunday School Board provide literature for the churches to forward this work. Isaac J. Van Ness was secured to lead this movement in the board, and promptly showed great ability.

After considerable Convention-wide discussion, the Baptist Young People's Union, Auxiliary to the Southern Baptist Convention, was formed at Atlanta, Georgia, on November 21-22, 1895. This was at first an independent body, not organically related to the Convention, but year by year its relationship became closer.

It is likely that T. P. Bell was influenced to move to another area of denominational life by the continuous friction between himself and the American Baptist Publication Society of Philadelphia. His correspondence was filled with emotional resentment against the Philadelphia body. More than once he wrote that the purpose of the Publication Society was to destroy the Sunday School Board. Just a few weeks before his resignation Bell remarked in a letter to a friend that perhaps he (Bell) was "too strongly *Southern* Baptist" in his sentiment, and that the time had come when he had better let others of a broader spirit take the lead in some things. On January 22, 1896, Bell purchased *The Christian Index,* the Georgia Baptist paper. He resigned from the board the following week to become editor of the paper.[34]

After Bell resigned the board enthusiastically elected J. M. Frost as corresponding secretary again. Frost made it clear that he was now burning his bridges behind him so far as leaving the secretaryship was concerned; that he was setting his face and heart to the future of the board. It was well that he dedicated himself to the task, for the twenty years left to him were filled with strenuous labors.

Rivalry with the American Baptist Publication Society. The immediate struggle in which Frost became engaged involved the very existence of the board itself. The American Baptist Publication Society had befriended the first Sunday School Board in the 1860's and 1870's, but increasingly in the 1880's and 1890's it had become aware of the large amount of its business that was being secured by the Sunday

School Board of the South. Under a new secretary the society determined to challenge the board, knowing that many in the South would for various motives support the society against the board. Secretary A. J. Rowland of the society wrote Frost early in February, 1896, suggesting that there be a closer relationship between the two bodies. On February 11, 1896, Frost replied to Rowland that if the suggestions of Rowland were carried out, it would be a serious threat to the very life of the board. Despite this, on March 18, Rowland sent a series of propositions which, in essence, simply meant the swallowing up of the southern Sunday School Board by' the society. On April 1, Frost replied that the board was unwilling to accept this proposition because it involved "not only the integrity and efficiency of the Board but its very existence, and contemplates the destruction of our own Sunday school periodicals." Rowland then threatened to take the matter to the floor of the Southern Baptist Convention. Frost later on recorded the dramatic scene that took place at the Convention meeting in 1897 in these words:

> Prior to Chattanooga the Society had first proposed to the Sunday School Board to absorb its life and business, and when this was declined, it then circularized the Baptists of the South to make the offer effective through the approaching session of the Convention. I had just returned to the secretaryship to encounter this new phase of the opposition, but it failed to get any public consideration, though the situation was painful in private circles.
>
> At Wilmington, however, a year later the opposition got into the open and produced a scene well-nigh dramatic. It was commonly reported that the Society had seventeen officials and employees in attendance. One of them made an open attack from the platform on the Sunday School Board, especially on its Bible work in a lengthy and elaborate speech. . . . It created a stir of resentment in the audience as could be easily seen. At its close many men made an effort to get to the floor. I never saw so many heavy guns unlimber so quickly and get ready for action. Dr. William E. Hatcher, of Virginia, got the floor, and in twenty-five minutes made a speech that was a marvel even for him. All of his powers with an audience came into play in that short time. He told how he had not favored making the Board at first; how it had won its place in the denomination; how the Baptists of the South had set it out as their policy; . . . Can anyone who was present ever forget how he stirred and swept the people as he turned with a mighty sweep in the declaration: "I have been a life-long friend of the Publication Society, but it must not come here to interfere with our work." [35]

This was the climax of the struggle. Increasingly the leadership and the constituency of the Southern Baptist Convention turned their support to the Sunday School Board, and by the close of the period its manifold ministry was writing new chapters in Southern Baptist history.

Eliciting, Combining, and Directing the Denomination

The third crisis involving the life of the Convention stemmed basically from the Landmark movement of J. R. Graves. It will be recalled that Graves's attacks on the functions of the Convention when it met in 1859 reflected his view that general bodies among Baptists must not assume spiritual or denominational authority which was granted only to local Baptist churches by the New Testament. He was partially mollified in 1859 when the Convention said that churches or groups of churches may send their own home or foreign missionaries independently of the Convention's boards, and the Convention even agreed to assist in forwarding funds to foreign missionaries so independently engaged.[36] It has been mentioned that Landmarkism was relatively quiet during the period between civil war and the end of Reconstruction. James E. Tull felt that this happened because the movement had become "engulfed in the general impoverishment and paralysis of Southern life and culture" during Reconstruction and so had little vitality to incite controversy during that period. In fact, the personal losses of Graves himself in the war and thereafter would complement this suggestion. Homer L. Grice attributed the noncombative spirit of the movement to another significant factor—the mellowing of Graves himself.

> A reading of his writings in *The Baptist* after 1877, the year his publication society failed, reveals that the man of thunder and conflict had subsided and a man of gentler and sweeter spirit was developing. He gave much less attention to controversial matters and dealt much more gently with those who did not agree with him. He magnified the doctrines of grace and preached with tenderness and love, becoming a revered and widely loved man. It is this Graves his friends and admirers, and their descendants, largely remember.[37]

It is also undoubtedly true that Landmarkism had no monolithic pattern that was widely accepted. Even the original Landmark triumvirate of Graves, J. M. Pendleton, and A. C. Dayton never really agreed on a unified system of Landmark doctrine. Indeed, Tull makes it plain that Graves himself had critical doctrinal tensions which, if generally known, would have alienated many Baptists from him.[38] Thus, the tendency of Landmarkism was to create small islands of "mild," "moderate," "radical," or "schismatic" Landmarkers, and this was the pattern that developed between 1877 and 1917. It is significant that when the Landmark resurgence came in this period, each appearance was triggered in a historical situation that did not involve the entire Landmark syndrome as such. In each case, however, the controversy led unerringly back to the taproot of Landmarkism: the sacrosanct nature of the authoritative local congregation.

Why was there a resurgence of Landmarkism in the 1880's and

1890's after the quiescence of the 1860's and 1870's? Tull interpreted it in terms of four factors: (1) the shift of regional dominance to the Southwest in the Southern Baptist Convention precipitated the most strongly Landmark area of the Convention into a position of ascendancy and brought newly located Convention agencies under intensive Landmark cultivation; (2) the continuing influence of Graves radiating out from Memphis provided a vital infusion of strength; (3) denominational newspapers, the majority of whom were sympathetic to Landmarkism, spread the Landmark doctrines among the people; and (4) the intellectual currents of the denomination showed that Landmarkism was still a "virile, grass-roots, people's movement."[39] Another considerable element was the immediate historical context of the four aspects of the Landmark resurgence. The four began completely independently, and although without question they interacted on one another, the initial thrust of each had its own peculiar characteristics and emphases. The contextual coloration gave each movement a somewhat individualistic character, and caused its focus to shift perceptibly. They related to one another because of their Landmark base, despite differences in historical milieu.

The four out-croppings of various aspects of Landmarkism in the 1880's and 1890's were the Gospel Mission movement, the Whitsitt controversy, Haydenism, and Bogardism.

The Gospel Mission Movement. The founder of this movement was T. P. Crawford (1821-1902), a missionary to China for fifty years, forty of which were under the Foreign Mission Board of the Southern Baptist Convention. He arrived at Shanghai in March, 1852, to begin his long service, but in 1863 he and his wife were transferred to North China and made Tengchow their center for thirty years. His first impression of the missionary methods in China was unfavorable. When he and his wife arrived at Hong Kong, a scandalous situation involving a Presbyterian missionary in China was brought to his attention. This missionary employed a hundred native assistants whom he sent to different cities not accessible to foreigners and provided them with Scriptures and tracts, purchased from a Chinese printer, to be distributed free. Instead, however, most of these assistants were selling the Bibles to the Chinese printer at a reduced price, who resold them again and again to the missionary. This had gone on for years, and the native assistants provided excellent statistics on Bible distribution. From this time until 1886, Crawford recorded his distaste for the employment of native workers with foreign funds on the grounds that it contributed to making them insincere, dishonest, cheats, and parasitic. Undoubtedly his visit to the United States in 1859 greatly influenced Crawford to sharpen his weapons and perhaps forge new ones. He attended the Convention at Richmond in that year when

J. R. Graves spoke at length against the authority of the Foreign Mission Board to examine, choose, support, and direct the missionaries on the foreign field. These prerogatives, said Graves, belonged only to churches or groups of churches, and not to boards.[40] W. W. Barnes noted:

> The Gospel Missioners made the same attack on the Convention and its boards that the antimissionaries and J. R. Graves, . . . had previously made; they proposed the same methods in the homeland and on the foreign field.[41]

This similarity is not surprising. Crawford's exposure in 1859 to Graves provided him with considerable grist for the mill, although he may have come into contact with Graves in Tennessee before he left for the mission field. His Quaker inheritance from his mother's side doubtless demanded that his inner light on mission methodology be revealed; his judicious investments in China provided him with financial stability apart from the board's salary; and his independent nature chafed at every hindrance to carrying out his long-standing ideas. In 1878 he visited the United States and on a leisurely tour of about five months, propagated his views North and South, climaxing it with an address at the 1879 Convention. After he returned to China, Crawford increasingly demanded that foreign fields be self-supporting and that indigenous churches be autonomous. In 1881 he disbanded the mission boarding schools because he felt that the young men educated in them were unfit to make their way among their countrymen and could not subsist without foreign employment. Curiously enough, the Foreign Mission Board was partly responsible for the stepped-up activity of Crawford. In 1885 the board had mailed to their missionaries a copy of the book of C. H. Carpenter, *Self-Support, Illustrated in the History of the Bassein Karen Mission from 1840 to 1880,* thinking it would be of interest and encouragement. Crawford evidently thought that the board might be weakening in its opposition to his views on self-support. He devoured this book and writings by J. L. Nevius, a Presbyterian missionary in China who advocated "self-supporting and self-propagating" indigenous churches.

In March, 1885, Crawford again returned to the United States, this time without informing the board of what he was about to do. He finally visited the board on October 12 and demanded that a committee be appointed to hear him express his views. Missionaries from Africa and Rome were present, and other missionaries expressed their views in letters. On November 6, 1885, this committee agreed that self-support was the end toward which the missionary should work, but recognized that it might not be possible to adopt it quickly on every mission field. Three reasons were given for this position: first, that the original agreement with the missionaries now in the field involved using native workers, and their program would be radically upset to make a change; second, the circumstances and conditions were not the same on every mission field, and a general law against native employees would be very hurtful in some areas; and third, to adopt this principle would be to affirm that the gospel cannot lift the Chinese or Africans above the corrupting influences of money.

After this committee had reported, the board suggested to Crawford that he return to his field, but he would not go. He spent several months traveling and making speeches derogatory to the interests of the board. He attended the Convention in May, 1886, and addressed that body on the work in China, but was not supported in his appeal to change the decision of the board. At the 1887 meeting of the Convention, resolutions were adopted providing for a review of mission methods of the board, but the committee that reported in 1888 recommended that existing methods not be changed.

From 1886 to 1889, Crawford had no communication with the board although he continued to draw a salary. In 1890, with three other missionaries and four Chinese Christians, Crawford organized the first Gospel Mission Association in North China. There is no record that this association met after it was organized until 1893.

The climax came in 1892 when Crawford published a small four-teen-page tract entitled *Churches to the Front!* In this his Landmark views were clearly expressed. He attacked the centralization involved in the board system which would overthrow the independence and self-respect of the churches and reduce them to mere "tributary appendages." All ecclesiastical bodies except churches are encroaching upon the prerogatives of the "only religious organizations recognized in the New Testament." Baptists are different from other denominations.

> Centralization and ring-government may suit the policy of other denominations. They do not suit ours, but are deadly hostile to it. Yet, strange to say, this dangerous element was first introduced among us with the first session of the Old Triennial Convention in 1814; and, stranger, still, the Northern Baptist Union and the Southern Baptist Convention have continued it down to the present day. Their Boards are . . . self-perpetuating, irresponsible central bodies with unlimited permission to grow in power by absorbing the prerogatives and resources of our Churches, as the old Roman hierarchy grew by absorbing those in the early ages of Christianity.[42]

As a result of this frontal attack on the Convention and its boards, Crawford was removed from the list of missionaries. A few other missionaries followed him, but the movement never gained the support one would have supposed Crawford's direct appeal to solid Landmark doctrines would have created.

The Whitsitt Controversy. The second of the four movements involving Landmarkism was occasioned by the views of W. H. Whitsitt (1841-1911), who was professor of church history and president of Southern Baptist Theological Seminary when the agitation arose in the 1890's. Based principally upon information from the so-called "Kiffin" manuscript and the minutes of the Jessey church in England, Whitsitt had come to the conclusion that Baptists both in England and in America had not baptized by immersion before the year 1641. He published two anonymous editorials in a Congregationalist weekly of New York *(The Independent)* on September 2 and September 9, 1880, advocating this position. In 1895 he wrote the article on Baptists in *Johnson's Universal Cyclopaedia* over his own name and asserted these same views. Led by T. T. Eaton, who was one of the trustees of the seminary, pastor in Louisville, and editor of the *Western Recorder,* a storm of protests took place. It is curious that Eaton had antecedents that were anti-Landmark: his gifted father was strongly anti-Landmark, and the son himself had been pastor in Petersburg, Virginia, a strongly anti-Landmark atmosphere, for over a decade before coming to Louisville. In the following year (1896) Whitsitt published *A Question in Baptist History,* which reviewed his research and conclusions about the use of immersion by Baptists. In his article on Whitsitt, W. O. Carver remarked that the fight was carried on all across Convention territory—in associations, state bodies, and at the Southern Baptist Convention.[43] In addition to Eaton, John T. Christian and S. H. Ford vigorously opposed Whitsitt's views. This controversy, aimed as it was at a central tenet of Landmarkism (Baptist church succession), infuriated the disciples of Graves (who had died in 1893). The climax took place in May, 1898, when Whitsitt submitted his resignation as president and professor to the trustees of the seminary and retired to Virginia.

The Hayden Controversy. The third Landmark spin-off was not directed toward the Southern Baptist Convention, but it brought virulent controversy and schism in Texas Baptist life that resulted in the withdrawal of some of their churches from affiliation with the Convention. The agitation was rooted in the intense rivalry between S. A. Hayden, who purchased *The Texas Baptist* (later the name *and Herald* was added) and became its editor in June, 1883, and J. B. Cranfill, who founded *The Texas Baptist Standard* in 1892. In April, 1894, Hayden began accusing the executive board of the Texas convention of paying excessive salaries to its leadership and of being ineffective in its administration of the mission enterprise in Texas.[44] When an investigation revealed no basis for these charges and the state body supported its executive board, Hayden unleashed an extensive and scurrilous barrage through his paper against his opponents.

The emotional depth reached in this controversy may be judged through language used in public denunciation of Hayden by the usually composed George W. Truett, who said:

> For several years an agent has been at work in our state Capitol undermining the mission work, drying up the mission spirit, and sowing down our once fertile fields with salt. That agent has persistently, ruthlessly, and openly in public print attacked this board, its methods and work, charging it directly and indirectly, and by various methods of innuendo and insinuation, with misappropriation, wanton extravagance, and reckless waste of public funds. . . . With this agent nothing pertaining to this work is sacred or ever settled. He evinces open disrespect of the decisions of this body, going back each year behind its approval and finished work to dig up and galvanize such issues or events as by his unrighteous use of them may best contribute to add to the general distrust, discord and divisions he himself has gendered. . . . Who, then, is this agent? His name is S. A. Hayden, of Dallas.[45]

Hayden was finally denied a seat in the Texas state body in 1897. He sought relief in the secular courts. His followers seceded from the Baptist General Convention of Texas by organizing a separate body on July 6, 1900, at Troup, Texas, which subsequently adopted the name Baptist Missionary Association. Hayden himself vigorously opposed the organization of a schismatic body, but later identified with it. This association joined with Arkansas Landmarkers and others in 1905 to form a general body.

The significance of the Hayden controversy in this context was the exposure of his Landmark views at two points. First, his initial attacks on particular activities of the executive board constantly revealed Landmark antagonism against the board method of missionary work. Second, when the Texas convention refused to seat him in 1897, Hayden appealed to Landmark ecclesiology by contending that conventions are made up of churches and derive their authority from them: therefore, a convention could not refuse to seat delegates accredited from the sovereign churches else the sovereignty of such churches would be overwhelmed.[46] He did not seem to notice that if conventions were made up of churches, every vote that was not unanimous would mean the reversal of the will of sovereign churches. The Texas convention and its leaders rejected both of these Landmark tenets.[47]

The Bogard Schism. The immediate impact of J. R. Graves is more evident in the Arkansas background of Landmarkism than in any other of these controversies. As early as the 1872 session of the Arkansas Baptist State Convention, Graves preached a magnificent three-hour sermon and captivated the audience. His views among Arkansas Baptists appeared openly in the 1888 session of the state body when objections were raised to the "unscriptural" methods being followed in the employment of a paid Corresponding Secretary of Missions, and in the ensuing controversy many of the typical Landmark views were displayed. The arrival of a rabid Landmarker, Ben M. Bogard, in 1899 to become pastor of the Searcy church provided a strong and aggressive leader for the Landmark forces. During the following two years he was the rallying point for a Landmark effort to incorporate their principles into all cooperative work in the state. When they were not successful, the Landmark group organized the General Association of Baptist Churches on April 10-11, 1902, at Little Rock. This separation became final in 1903 when committees from the Arkansas Baptist Convention and this General Association failed to reach a compromise. As a matter of fact, the Landmarkers were unwilling to budge from their radical basic demands, which included the right of individual churches to commission and send out missionaries, the church basis of representation in association and state body with each church entitled to the same number, the abolition of the office of corresponding secretary for the state body, the right of churches to instruct their messengers on matters to be raised, and the elimination of the current plan of cooperation with the mission boards of the Southern Baptist Convention.[48]

The next logical step was taken after a short delay. With the aid of Texas Landmarkers and other dissidents, Bogard and his group, numbering about 150 from 52 churches, met at Texarkana, Arkansas, on March 22, 1905, and prepared a memorial to the Southern Baptist Convention demanding that the money and associational basis of representation be eliminated in favor of a church basis, that the boards of the Convention be shorn of their power to appoint and remove missionaries at pleasure, and that the boards should eliminate any influence "by what is known as denominational comity." These were described as the minimal demands, and unless they were met "we have done our duty and shall trouble you no more." A strong committee of the Convention assigned to study and reply to this memorial declined in gracious but firm words to accede to these demands.[49] On November 24-26, 1905, representatives from 107 churches in 12 states and territories met at Texarkana and organized a Landmark general body, which changed its name in 1924 to the American Baptist Association and suffered a major schism in 1950.

The failure of these four movements to cause a widespread schism among Southern Baptists is surprising. Each one had dedicated and gifted leadership. Their zeal is reflected in the hardhitting and radical literature that they produced. One can hardly glance through J. A. Scarboro's book, *The Bible, The Baptists, and The Board System*, published in 1904 at Fulton, Kentucky, for example, without finding the strongest antagonism for the Southern Baptist Convention and its boards on almost every page. Various Baptist papers in many states regularly publicized articles on the several controversies. Yet all of this agitation in a single decade failed to ignite a widespread Landmark conflagration. Some of the reasons for this may be as follows. The Landmarkers felt that they had won the Whitsitt controversy. The four controversies occurred almost simultaneously and involved different aspects of the Landmark viewpoint, thus dissipating a possible concentrated attack by all Landmarkers. Landmarkers themselves were divided in the nature and intensity of their views. For example, in Texas some of the leaders James E. Tull identified as Landmarkers were on the Convention side of the several controversies. J. B. Gambrell is an illustration of this. Gambrell took the Convention side of the Crawford controversy; he defended Whitsitt's right to historical research by strongly asserting that no man could be called non-Baptistic or heretical because of his views on history; [50] he was the leader of the fight against Hayden in Texas; and he was an opponent of the Bogard movement in Arkansas. The conservative position of men like this and the opposition they displayed to Landmark agitation doubtless influenced their many admirers to turn away from schismatic ideas. There were other factors: the severe financial depression of the 1890's demanded that principal attention be turned to keeping alive; the formation of the second Sunday School Board in 1891 and its victory at Wilmington over the American Baptist Publication Society were strong blows to true Landmarkers; a generation of experience with the convention-type pattern had convinced many that Graves was wrong in 1859 in prophesying that the churches would be overwhelmed by this kind of general body; a new nationalism was everywhere apparent even in religious circles after the Spanish-American War in 1898 and the turn of the century; the victory of the Convention in its severe struggles with the northern benevolent societies had imbued a new loyalty to the general body; and perhaps even the mellowing of J. R. Graves and his death in 1893 as a faithful member of the Southern Baptist fellowship had some influence in strengthening the place of the Convention. James E. Tull is probably correct in suggesting that Landmark ideas had filtered into the bloodstream of Southern Baptists, for some of them are still evident; but the radical denominational enlargement and concentration beyond the local church level that took place in the early decades of the twentieth century in the structure and functions of the Southern Baptist Convention point unerringly to the disintegration and overbalancing of Landmark views. A strong Landmark undercurrent would have rendered impossible what took place in Southern Baptist organizational life between 1917 and 1972.

Notes

1. Reimers, *op. cit.,* p. 82.
2. For a summary of these developments, see Clyde L. Manschreck, *A History of Christianity—Reformation to the Present* (Englewood Cliffs, New Jersey: Prentice-Hall, Inc., 1964), pp. 315 ff, and 411 ff.
3. For this story, see Baker, *Relations,* pp. 158-59.
4. *Annual,* Southern Baptist Convention, 1892, p. xi of Appendix A.
5. For this story in some detail, see Baker, *Relations,* pp. 154 ff.
6. *Ibid.,* pp. 134 ff.
7. *Annual,* Southern Baptist Convention, 1882, p. 29.
8. Baker, *Relations,* p. 160.
9. *Ibid.,* p. 161.
10. *Ibid.,* p. 164.
11. *Annual,* Southern Baptist Convention, 1885, pp. xv-xvi.
12. *Ibid.,* p. xvii.
13. *Ibid.,* p. xliv.
14. *Ibid.,* 1892, p. xl of Appendix A.
15. *Annual Report,* American Baptist Home Mission Society, 1890, p. 23.
16. See William A. Carleton, "Not Yours But You"—The Life of Joseph Samuel Murrow (unpublished dissertation, Southwestern Baptist Theological Seminary, Ft. Worth, Texas, 1945), p. 98.
17. Joe W. Burton, *Epochs of Home Missions* (Atlanta: Home Mission Board, 1945), pp. 77-84.
18. *Annual,* Southern Baptist Convention, 1894, p. 16.
19. Baker, *Source Book,* pp. 161-62.
20. *Ibid.,* pp. 162-63 for this agreement.
21. *Annual,* Southern Baptist Convention, 1909, pp. 31-32.
22. Baker, *Source Book,* pp. 163 ff has this document.
23. *Annual,* Southern Baptist Convention, 1912, pp. 46 ff.
24. Baker, *Relations,* p. 198.
25. *Ibid.,* pp. 168-69.
26. *Annual,* Southern Baptist Convention, 1885, pp. 24-25.
27. *Ibid.,* 1888, p. 28.
28. Baker, *The Story of the Sunday School Board,* p. 38.
29. J. M. Frost, *Sunday School Board History and Work* (Nashville: Sunday School Board, 1914), p. 11.
30. *Annual,* Southern Baptist Convention, 1890, pp. vii-viii.
31. Baker, *Source Book,* pp. 149-51.
32. A. T. Robertson, *Life and Letters of John A. Broadus* (Philadelphia: American Baptist Publication Society, 1901), p. 394.
33. *Annual,* Southern Baptist Convention, 1892, p. lxiv.
34. Baker, *The Story of the Sunday School Board,* p. 70.
35. Frost, *op. cit.,* pp. 81-82.
36. Baker, *Source Book,* pp. 145-46.
37. Cox-Woolley, eds., *Encyclopedia,* I, p. 577.
38. Tull, *op. cit.,* pp. 519 ff.
39. *Ibid.,* pp. 486 f.
40. See Graves's assertions in Chapter X.
41. Barnes, *The Southern Baptist Convention,* p. 115.
42. See Baker, *Source Book,* pp. 177-80 for excerpts from this work.
43. See W. O. Carver, "William Heth Whitsitt: The Seminary's Martyr," *Review and Expositor* (Louisville), October, 1954, p. 450.
44. For this story in great detail, see J. M. Carroll, *A History of Texas Baptists,* pp. 705 ff. For a brief summary, see Baker, *The Blossoming Desert,* pp. 157 ff.
45. *Proceedings,* Forty-Eighth Annual Session of the Baptist General Convention of Texas, 1896, p. 23.

46. See Baker, *Source Book,* p. 180.
47. See J. M. Carroll, *op. cit.,* pp. 752 ff.
48. *Minutes,* Arkansas Baptist State Convention, 1903, pp. 15 ff.
49. *Annual,* Southern Baptist Convention, 1905, pp. 42 ff.
50. See the *Baptist Standard* (Texas), June 11, 1896.

13 The Convention Claiming Its Birthright

While the struggle for existence described in the previous chapter was the most dramatic episode in the history of the Convention during this period, of parallel importance were the week-by-week ministries of the three boards, the enlarging areas of service within the Convention, and the continuous efforts to modify the structure of the general body to provide a better instrument for the work Southern Baptists were trying to do.

The Ministry of the Three Boards

During all of this period the Foreign and Home Mission Boards, in addition to their struggles to preserve their existence, steadfastly pursued their main tasks, and before the period closed in 1917 showed excellent advances in their work. The Sunday School Board, founded in 1891, also made large strides in achieving the goals set for it by its founders.

Foreign Mission Board. The period of Reconstruction had thoroughly tested the dedication of the missionaries on the foreign field as well as the foreign mission leadership at home, for both had faced trying circumstances.

1. The Field in 1877. The stresses experienced at home were clearly reflected in the skeletal staff on the mission fields at the close of Reconstruction. These have been termed the "lonely days" on the foreign field, due to the fact that missionaries were few and for the most part isolated. Three fields were sustained during the rigorous days through which the South had gone. In Africa the missionaries were W. J. David at Abeokuta and W. W. Colley, a Negro missionary, at Lagos. This mission was facing very knotty problems and would experience dark days during the next decade. The second field was China, the oldest mission effort by Southern Baptists. In North China at Tengchow, Mr. and Mrs. T. P. Crawford, Mrs. S. H. Holmes, and Miss Lottie Moon were the mission staff. In Central China at Shanghai, Mr. and Mrs. Matthew T. Yates were the only missionaries. In South China at Canton, R. H. Graves, his wife, Miss Lulu Whilden, along with E. Z. and Maggie Simmons, were the mission staff. In Italy **287** at Rome, George B. Taylor, assisted by native pastors, carried on the work. Despite the extension of the panic of 1873, the offerings from the states for foreign missions in 1877 amounted to $31,789.42.

2. *Progress by Three Secretaries.* It will be recalled that the great patriarch of the Foreign Mission Board, James B. Taylor, died at the close of 1871, and Henry A. Tupper was elected his successor in 1872. Tupper served effectively until 1893, and many advances were made in the work of the board during his secretaryship. In 1887, Lottie Moon wrote from China to suggest that Southern Baptist women set apart a week just before Christmas as a time of prayer and offering for world missions. In 1888 Tupper presented the challenge of Lottie Moon to Woman's Missionary Union, which had just been organized in Richmond, Virginia. They set their goal for $2,000, but typical of many later goals, it was exceeded by the women, and $3,315.26 was given. During the administration of Tupper, 147 missionaries were appointed, new stations were established in China and Nigeria, and new fields were opened in Mexico, Brazil, and Japan. In these years a total of $1,330,747.27 was given by Southern Baptists for foreign missions.

An intimate glimpse of the relationship between the executive secretary and the missionaries around the world was given in Tupper's parting word in 1893 when he wrote:

> I feel as if I were saying good-bye to a great family, loved as life itself. We have had many joys together and many sorrows. My soul is knit to them as to my own flesh and blood. I love and honor every one of them. A braver band never fought the Lord's battles. I rejoice in the crowns awaiting them, as a father rejoices in the glory of his children! [1]

R. J. Willingham was elected corresponding secretary to succeed Tupper, and promptly began an aggressive program of outreach. This was made possible partly by the rapid improvement of the financial situation of the board. Its annual income increased from $110,000 in 1893 to $600,000 in 1914. The number of missionaries grew from 92 to 298 during the same period. Three new countries—Argentina (1903), Macao (1910), and Uruguay (1911)—were entered, and many new mission stations were begun on old mission fields. Willingham was an avid builder of schools and other institutions. During his tenure, six hospitals were built in China; the first building was secured for the seminary in Canton, China; theological schools (in some instances, both a college and a seminary) were established in Nigeria, Italy, Mexico, Brazil, China, Japan, and Argentina; and Baptist publishing houses were established in China, Brazil, Japan, and Mexico. Willingham became ill in 1913, and died in December, 1914.

J. F. Love succeeded Willingham as corresponding secretary in 1915.

By 1917, when this period closed, Love had already given evidence of his outstanding ability. Work was opened in Chile in 1917. Cash receipts for current support in 1917 were $852,923.73, and Love remarked that "Southern Baptists have put more money into the regular work during the past twelve months than they have contributed to current support in any previous year of the seventy-three of the Board's history." For the first time in ten years the board reported that they were totally out of debt. Typical of the increasing magnitude of the work on the field, Love reported that during 1917 there had been 6,290 baptisms, 6 churches constituted, contributions of $152,874.16 by the native Christians, 26 churches becoming self-supporting, and treatment of patients numbering 102,271 by medical missionaries. During the year of 1917, Woman's Missionary Union contributed over $250,000 in cash to foreign missions, while the new Laymen's Movement involving men had raised $6,000 for a project missionaries. In 1917 the board reported 172 missionaries in China, 16 in Africa, 19 in Japan, 4 in Italy, 29 in Mexico, 58 in Brazil, 16 in Argentina, and 2 in Chile. This made a grand total of 316 missionaries in 8 countries.

Home Mission Board. During the period between 1877 and 1917 the Home Mission Board carried on eight distinct ministries. Most of these had been originally outlined in 1845 as the task of the board when it was constituted by the Convention, but additional areas of service were entrusted to it during this period.

One of the principal ministries of the board was the founding of new churches and missions. Even in the older states, a committee reported in 1889 that there were many important towns without a Baptist ministry in them. A careful study of the *Annuals* of the Convention indicates that year by year a strong emphasis was made during this period upon constituting new churches and missions. In many reports the exact number is not shown, but typically there were 244 churches constituted in 1891, 133 in 1894, 195 in 1900, and 213 during 1917. As a part of this movement, strenuous efforts were made during the 1880's to establish an active church building department, but this did not receive the support of the people, and the effort was abandoned for the time. Under the leadership of Woman's Missionary Union, in 1903 a campaign was launched to raise a building and loan fund honoring I. T. Tichenor, and in 1908 the $20,000 goal was reached. In reporting this to the Convention in 1910, the amazing statement was made by the board that one or more of what were then the strongest churches in the capital city of every southern state had been helped by the Home Mission Board.[2] At the very close of this period, with a new Department of Church Extension, Louis B. Warren led in what would be a very successful drive for funds to lend to churches who needed to build.

A second major area of ministry looked to the winning of the cities. The board had always used some of its meager resources in this ministry. New Orleans, for example, repeatedly appears as an area of service during the first fifty years of Convention life. A new thrust was made in 1905 to increase this assistance to cities with their peculiar problems. Typical of the need for this ministry, in 1907 it was pointed out that there were thirty-six white Baptist churches in the three cities of Baltimore, St. Louis, and New Orleans. Of these churches, twenty were able to make their own way, but sixteen of them were being assisted by the state mission boards or the Home Mission Board, and could not continue to exist without this assistance. The population of these cities was increasing 177 times as fast as the membership of the Baptist churches.

During this period the board began an active program of reaching the mountain people of the Southeast. In cooperation with Baptists of western North Carolina the board carried on a joint mission program in the mountainous areas in the 1880's, and in addition, began the development in 1905 of a system of mountain schools in cooperation with other Baptist groups.

The frontier mission program was a fourth area of the board's work during this period. As the western frontier slowly receded, the board sent many missionaries to the frontier. In the 1880's and 1890's, in particular, the interest of the Convention in frontier missions was high. In 1905 a field secretary was appointed for the western territory. By 1910, there were over 700 missionaries at work west of the Mississippi River in this frontier category.

The Negroes, both during and after their days of bondage, were the object of the ministry of the board. As pointed out before, most of the blacks withdrew from the white churches shortly after the Civil War. Negro Baptists began organizing their first conventions in 1880, and by 1895 three separate bodies became the National Baptist Convention of the United States of America. However, in 1915 this body divided into two organizations, one the National Baptist Convention, U.S.A., Incorporated, and the other the National Baptist Convention of America. In 1905 the Home Mission Board entered into a joint program with the National Baptist Convention, involving an outlay of a maximum of $15,000 per year by each board. When the division in this Negro body took place in 1915, after some confusion, the board primarily carried on its cooperation with the National Baptist Convention, U.S.A., Incorporated.

One extremely valuable ministry of the board to Negro Baptists during the period from 1877 to 1917 was what has been called Ministers' Institutes, although subsequently deacons and other leaders of the Negroes were involved in the program. These institutes aimed to gather a group of uneducated ministers for a short study, usually about ten days, of fundamental doctrines. Evidently it was begun by E. W. Warren, of Atlanta, Georgia, whose work along this line was enthusiastically described in northern Baptist newspapers as early as May, 1873.[3] The Southern Baptist Convention endorsed his program in 1875, and in the following year the Home Mission Board began conducting institutes of this sort across the South. Three years later the Home Mission Society of the North voted to cooperate with the Southern Baptist Convention in providing these institutes. In the first full year after this program was begun, it was reported that 1,119 ministers and deacons had participated in 33 institutes, and that every southern state had been reached with one institute or more of about three days' duration.[4] In a touching and significant move, W. H. McIntosh, formerly the executive secretary of the board, was first appointed in 1883 as missionary to the Negroes.

Directly as a result of the Fortress Monroe agreement of 1894, the board worked with the Home Mission Society of New York in what was called the New Era Plan. After nine years, this plan was modified and called the Enlarged Plan of Negro Work, in a closer cooperative arrangement between the Home Mission Board and the similar board in the National Baptist Convention. In implementing this plan, the Southern Baptist Convention named A. J. Barton as its first field secretary for Negro work in 1904. The board provided matching contributions from National Baptists to a maximum of $15,000 the first year. In 1906, there were thirty-three missionaries employed jointly by the cooperating boards. Two years later there were thirty-seven missionaries jointly employed. By 1914, there were forty-seven. The division in the following year in the National Baptist Convention interrupted the significant growth of this program.[5]

Although not departmentalized in earlier years, the next large division of the work of the Home Mission Board could be described as language missions. Reference to this work in the earlier periods has already been made. Between 1877 and 1917, however, the language mission program enlarged greatly. During this period some of the great names in Indian mission work in Indian Territory and Oklahoma Territory were H. F. Buckner, Joseph S. Murrow, and E. Lee Compere.

Work was begun among the Germans in earlier periods, but the need for this distinctive program disappeared after World War I. One outstanding name in German missions in Baltimore was Marie Buhlmaier, who served for about twenty-five years beginning in 1893. The opening wedge for Baptist work among the French in Louisiana was the conversion of Adolphe Stagg, who made an outstanding contribution. Work was begun among the Italians in Florida in 1908, one of the chief names in leadership being J. F. Plainfield.

Reference has already been made to the work of the board in California under J. Lewis Shuck and B. W. Whilden. During the period under study, J. B. Hartwell, veteran Chinese missionary, served in San Francisco and helped constitute the first Chinese Baptist church of that city in 1880.

An active ministry to the deaf began in 1906 when John W. Michaels, a deaf mute, was appointed to this field.

One of the significant challenges in language missions has been those speaking the Spanish tongue who immigrated to the United States from Spain, Mexico, Cuba, Puerto Rico, or some other South or Central American country. In 1881 a mission was begun in San Antonio as the first permanent Spanish Baptist work in Texas. In 1884, a beginning was made in Florida among this group, also. Charles D. Daniel, foreign missionary to Brazil and Cuba, was appointed general superintendent of the Spanish-language missions in Texas in 1906, and under his leadership, the Mexican Baptist Convention of Texas was constituted in 1910.

As early as 1879 appeals had come from Cuba for missionaries. In 1886 the Convention voted that the Home Mission Board should be the agency for Cuban work, rather than the Foreign Mission Board. Both Secretaries Tichenor and Gray became enthusiastically involved in Cuban missions. The outstanding name in this area was M. N. McCall, who began his work in 1905 in Havana. In 1906 a seminary was begun, and the churches were organized into the Western Cuba Convention.

Work was begun in the Panama Canal Zone in 1906. Under the leadership of J. L. Wise, advance was slow, partly because the construction of the canal, completed in 1914, encouraged a transient population.

The military chaplaincy had engaged the board, as described earlier, during civil war, but for over half a century thereafter the board had no need for these services. In 1916, with the involvement of the United States in World War I, the Convention called for men to serve as chaplains to the men in the armed forces. At the very close of the period the board inaugurated a program of camp ministries, with George Green as director.

The eighth thrust of the board was all-encompassing; that is, it was the basic principle involved in all the ministries of the board. In 1906, after a careful study by the Convention, the board was instructed to create a Department of Evangelism. This was not achieved before a tense and critical battle on the floor of the Southern Baptist Convention. In the midst of the struggle, B. H. Carroll of Texas turned the tide in an eloquent address.

If I were the secretary of this [Home Mission] board, I would come before this body in humility and tears and say: "Brethren, give me evangelists. Deny not fins to things that swim against the tide, nor wings to things that must fly against the wind." [6]

W. W. Hamilton was elected as the first general evangelist. Everywhere this work met with favor because it was so primary in the entire program of Southern Baptists. Throughout the remainder of this period, this department served well and was mainly self-supporting through the offerings given to the evangelists. In 1917, for example, there were 20 evangelists who reported over 9,000 baptisms and 11,000 additions, as well as almost 1,100 volunteers for special service, all of which was performed at a net cost of about $18,000.

Although not distinctly set out as one of the programs of the board, one of the most important supporting services was the use of publications to inform and inspire the people about the work of the board. It will be recalled that the two mission boards shared the *Southern Baptist Missionary Journal* under several names until about 1874. During most of the period under study the official organ, *Our Home Field,* was used with slight variations of title to publicize the work of the board. For the most part the corresponding secretaries carried the editorial load of publishing these magazines. In 1909 the board established a Publicity Department and employed Victor I. Masters as its first editorial secretary in charge of publicity. He continued this service throughout the remainder of this period.

As a means of glimpsing the increasing work of the board during this period, the following chart will show the number of missionaries and the receipts at five-year intervals during these years.[7]

Year	Number of Missionaries	Receipts
1877	22	$ 16,816
1882	40	28,370
1887	251	110,590
1892	365	214,144
1897	372	161,193
1902	674	100,615
1907	865	232,113
1912	1,309	377,684
1917	1,507	474,375

After the retirement of I. T. Tichenor in 1899, F. H. Kerfoot became secretary of the Home Mission Board until 1901; F. M. McConnell, from 1901 to 1903; and B. D. Gray, from 1903 to 1928. The report for 1917, under the last-named secretary, showed cash receipts of $474,375. Forty-five Baptist camp pastors were supported to work in the United States Army after the outbreak of war with Germany. Twenty evangelists, twenty workers encouraging enlistment of the home field, an active department for church extension, thirty-five workers in Cuba, and three workers in Panama Canal Zone were reported. An enrollment of 5,190 was shown in mountain schools in Virginia, Kentucky, Tennessee, North Carolina, South Carolina, Georgia, Alabama, Arkansas, and Missouri, which had 210 teachers. An active Publicity Department was spreading tracts and books on home missions. Much credit for the excellent progress during the closing years of this period should go to B. D. Gray, whose policy of expansion and cooperation was reaching its climax before the difficult days of the 1920's.

Sunday School Board. When J. M. Frost began his work in 1891, the Home Mission Board had operated eight types of programs of Sunday School work. The principal effort, of course, had been the publication of church literature. It had been the success of this program that prompted the organization of the new board in 1891. The seven related programs of Sunday School promotion, cooperative work with state boards, church music publishing, the production of church supplies, church library service, research and statistical analysis, and the distribution of religious books can be glimpsed in the work of the Home Mission Board before 1891. During the three-year service of T. P. Bell, two additional programs were developed: Training Union promotion and Convention support. These ten programs of work were enlarged and strengthened during the second secretaryship of Frost between 1896 and 1916. In addition, a very significant organizational advance took place at the turn of the century. Frost secured Bernard W. Spilman, a strong and experienced Sunday School leader in North Carolina, as the first field secretary of the board in order to provide a direct tie with the field. For two years Spilman served alone, making passenger trains his office. During the next decade eleven additional field workers were added. Between 1896 and 1916 a remarkable increase in the percentage of Southern Baptist church members enrolled in Sunday School took place, rising from 38 percent in the former year to 65 percent in the latter. Great advances were made in grading the Sunday School, providing standards for measuring the quality of work, the training of Sunday School teachers, the integration of the Sunday School program, the providing of assistance in methodology for busy lay workers, and the upgrading of the quality of Sunday School lessons.

In addition to these ten programs of work continued from previous years, when Frost began his second term as secretary, he introduced six additional activities; some of which, while not altogether new, were enlarged or restructured.

One of the most significant of these new programs concerned the publication of books. It will be recalled that for more than half a century Southern Baptists had plainly said they did not desire to go into the field of book publication. Frost understood the objections to this activity. The Landmarkers had opposed it on the grounds that a denominational board should not be in the book publishing business; the opening of a new area of competition with the Publication Society of Philadelphia distressed some; while a large body of Southern Baptists objected to book publishing because of the financial risks involved. Now, however, J. R. Graves, the leader of Landmarkism, was dead, and there had come a recession of Landmark influence. The confrontation at the Convention in 1897 between the Publication Society and the Sunday School Board had won many Southern Baptists to the support of the board's activities in every sphere. Frost planned to limit the financial risk by establishing a book fund. On December 31, 1897, the board authorized the setting aside of a $500 fund for publishing the life of Matthew T. Yates, the pioneer Chinese missionary, a manuscript for which had already been prepared by President Charles E. Taylor of Wake Forest College. Frost published this book on his own initiative after writing many of the important leaders of the Convention urging their support of this type of work. At the Convention in 1898 Frost reported publishing the book and "asked to be allowed liberty in this, using for its advancement such money as we can appropriate from the business, or such as may be given to the Board for this purpose." The committee of the Convention reporting this recommended that the board be allowed to publish books as a part of its work, noting the far-reaching significance of this advance, but expressing its confidence in the board for this enlargement of its work.[8] The climax came in 1910. T. P. Bell, editor of *The Christian Index* of Georgia, learned that the Publication Society of Philadelphia had closed its branch houses in the South. He presented a resolution authorizing the board to supply the churches with "books, tracts, hymn and song books, and indeed all supplies for churches, Sunday schools, missionary societies, Young People's unions, such as are suitable and desirable." The vote was unanimous by the Convention. Frost responded with deep emotion that he counted this the greatest hour of his life.[9]

In addition to this new enterprise, under the leadership of Frost the board enlarged its ministry in Bible and general tract distribution, organized a Home Department "to carry into the home all the influences of the Sunday-school in the way of religious training," provided assistance in church architecture, began a new thrust in student work, donated funds to Southern Baptist Theological Seminary to provide teaching in Sunday School work, and saw the Convention establish a Baptist assembly ground at Ridgecrest, North Carolina, which subsequently assumed a large place in the training program of Southern

Baptists for lay leaders and workers in the churches.

Frost died on October 30, 1916, ending the pioneer era in the life of this board. The impact of these first twenty-five years of the Sunday School Board was many-sided. In its initial thrust of promoting Sunday Schools it had fared remarkably well. In 1891 there were approximately 8,600 Sunday Schools in Southern Baptist churches; by 1917 this number had increased to 18,134 schools, enrolling 1,835,811. Training Unions numbered 4,827 by 1917. Receipts of the board were over $450,000 when Frost died and in the following year were reported as $537,695.14. Resources were fixed at over $700,000 in 1917. Perhaps even beyond this impressive growth in long-time influence were the new methodology and unifying thrust of the new board. As will be mentioned in the following chapter, standardized methods and uniform structural patterns were developed by talented men in leadership and exploited through financial assistance to seminaries and state bodies, magnified in the literature used by almost every Southern Baptist church, and promoted through field workers, study courses, state papers, and all other media of Southern Baptist information. The effect on the life of Southern Baptists can hardly be estimated. New direct leadership was provided at the Convention level and channeled through parallel structures developed in the states and associations for each benevolence (i.e., Sunday School, Training Union, Vacation Bible School, etc.) so that churches were provided patterns, motivation, and nearby assistance in the promotion of all of these areas of service. These were large factors in developing the denominational consciousness of Southern Baptists that tied them to the structures, methods, and doctrines of the Southern Baptist Convention.

Expanding Horizons

The larger economic, social, political, and religious world described at the opening of the previous chapter brought new challenges to the Southern Baptist Convention in the two-score years after Reconstruction closed. The true significance of the denominational-type organization adopted by Southern Baptists in 1845 began to be displayed. In addition to directing the activity of its three functional boards, the Convention expanded its ministry in several additional areas.

The Enlistment and Organization of Lay Constituency. Interacting with the developments in the religious community, the Convention found itself faced with a multitude of women who desired to serve their Lord in the best possible fashion; became conscious of the world of young people, both in the local churches and in university settings, who were competent and eager to play a larger part in Christian service; recognized the vast potential involved in the enlistment of laymen for a larger participation in the Kingdom enterprise; and gave consideration to Christian schools and an assembly for training of leadership.

1. Women. Reference has been made to the increasing interest of Southern Baptist women in the foreign mission enterprise before 1877. In 1875, at the close of the previous period, the Convention for the first time took official cognizance of the "enlarged zeal and practical wisdom" of Southern Baptist women in the cause of foreign missions, and commended their unusual qualifications for this ministry.[10] But the women did not need the urging of the Convention to meet, pray, and give. They were rapidly forming missionary societies in all of the territory of the Convention, fostering home as well as foreign missions.

In 1878 the Convention's committee on women's work urged the organization of central committees of women in each state, and this marked a large step toward a convention-wide structure for women. As early as 1883, women began holding meetings for their group at the annual sessions of the Convention. The men made it rather plain that women were not entitled to be seated officially as Convention messengers.[11] Not until 1918 were they so seated. The year 1887 brought crystalization of the desires of many of the women leaders to provide a convention-wide structure. Under the leadership of Miss Martha McIntosh of South Carolina and Miss Annie W. Armstrong of Maryland, resolutions were adopted which urged each central committee in the several states to appoint three lady delegates "to meet during the next session of the Southern Baptist Convention, to decide upon the advisability of organizing a general committee; and if advisable, to provide for the appointment, location, and duties thereof." [12]

On May 11, 1888, in the basement of the Broad Street Methodist Church, Richmond, Virginia, thirty-two delegates from twelve states and other women from three more states met to discuss a general organization. This meeting differed from any other one held heretofore in that it contained official representation from the several states and had come to discuss the possibility of general organization. When it appeared that most representatives would vote for such an organization, the formal program was set aside and a committee was named to prepare a proposed constitution. On May 14 this committee reported and the constitution was adopted, with Baltimore selected as the site of the executive committee.[13] Martha McIntosh was elected first president; ten vice-presidents (one from each of the original states) were named; Annie W. Armstrong became corresponding secretary; and nine residents of Baltimore composed the executive committee. The name originally adopted was changed two years later to Woman's

Missionary Union, Auxiliary to the Southern Baptist Convention, and this has remained unaltered since that time.

> Several factors distinguished the new organization from other denominational woman's organizations. It combined home, foreign, and state mission interests in one body. Through its auxiliary relation to the Southern Baptist Convention, it would not handle money and duplicate mission boards; its collected money would be disbursed by Convention boards; it would not independently appoint its own missionaries. The Convention was relieved.[14]

The organizational structure was enlarged during the remainder of this period. In 1896 the Union assumed responsibility for the Sunbeam Band (now called Mission Friends), which had been initiated by George B. Taylor in 1886 in Virginia, to provide missionary education for children under nine years of age. In 1907 the name "Young Woman's Auxiliary" (now called Baptist Young Women) was adopted for the specific program of the Union for young women. In 1908 the Union began the promotion of the Order of Royal Ambassadors as an organization for missionary education for boys. In 1913 a new department was created to provide training for girls between the ages of the Sunbeams and the Young Woman's Auxiliary and given the name Girls' Auxiliary (now called Girls in Action and Acteens). Miss Lottie Moon, missionary in China, suggested in 1887 that Southern Baptist women institute a week of prayer and offering for foreign missions in connection with Christmas. This plan was adopted and shortly after the close of this period the offering was named the Lottie Moon Christmas Offering for Foreign Missions. The goal set in 1888 was $2,000 and over $3,000 was raised; this overreaching of challenging goals has been the pattern year by year as the annual offerings have been counted in millions of dollars. In 1894 a Week of Self-Denial was structured to pray and give to home missions, and not long after the close of this period, that became the annual Annie W. Armstrong Offering for Home Missions. From almost the very beginning of Woman's Missionary Union, the four fundamentals of its program have been promotion of mission study, stewardship, community missions, and prayer; and these were formally adopted in 1913.

Recognizing the need for the training of women missionaries for the foreign field, some of the women of Louisville, Kentucky, rented a private house in 1904 where single young ladies could live while attending seminary classes. As the number of applicants grew, the local committee appealed to the Union for assistance. In 1907 the trustees of the seminary surrendered to the Union the management and control of the Woman's Training School and offered the young ladies the privilege of attending their classes. The Union adopted this project, and with the aid of a gift from the Sunday School Board, a building was purchased and occupied during the remainder of this period.

Another significant missionary ministry of the Woman's Missionary Union began in 1904 with the establishment of a fund to provide a home for children of missionaries. This became the Margaret Fund, named after the mother of the donor. For ten years this provided a home in Greenville, South Carolina, but in 1914 the home was sold and the funds invested for use in educating missionaries' children. The first scholarship was awarded just after the close of this period.

The executive secretaries of Woman's Missionary Union during this period were Annie W. Armstrong (1888-1906), Elizabeth Crane (1907-12), and Kathleen Mallory (1912-48). The presidents of the Union were Martha E. McIntosh (1888-92), Fannie Exile Scudder Heck (1892-94, 1895-99, and 1906-15), Mrs. Abby Manley Gwathmey (1894-95), Mrs. Charles Stakley (1899-1903), Mrs. J. A. Barker (1903-06), and Mrs. W. C. James (1915-25).

2. Youth. Another large part of the Southern Baptist constituency—the young people—were rarely seen or heard before the Civil War. The development of organized groups of young people for fellowship and religious training slowly took place after the war, particularly in the North, in several denominations. The founding of the Christian Endeavor societies among the Congregationalists in 1881 accelerated this movement, and by the 1890's practically all major denominations in the United States were involved in providing unions, leagues, or societies for their young people.

Baptists North and South had provided such organizations under various names by 1891. To pull these together into a single Baptist organization, the Baptist Young People's Union of America was formed in July, 1891, at Chicago, specifically noting that the local group could call itself by whatever name it chose. The society plan necessarily was involved in the organization of this national Baptist youth body, since none of the existing Baptist societies in the North fostered this type of work or even favored it. Young Baptists from the South were grouped as one department in the national body.

In 1893 the Southern Baptist Convention took note of the movement, urging that Baptist young people's societies of this sort in the South be "strictly Baptistic and denominational," and that they be under the authority of the local church without interdenominational affiliation. The Sunday School Board was asked to provide literature for their use.[15] After considerable wrangling during the next two years, a consultative meeting was held on November 21, 1895, at Atlanta, Georgia, consisting of 236 delegates from 10 states (Alabama, Georgia, Mississippi, and Tennessee provided 210 of these). This body organized the Baptist Young People's Union, Auxiliary to the Southern Baptist

Convention. This action was approved by the Southern Baptist Convention in the following year, although at that time it was simply an independent society of Southern Baptists. However, by 1901 the minutes of this union were printed with those of the southern convention; after 1909 the officers and executive committee were elected by the Southern Baptist Convention; and in 1918, just after the close of this period, this body was disbanded and the work assumed by the Sunday School Board of the Convention.[16] In that year the enrollment in the various unions in the South was shown as 230,540.

What became the Baptist Student Union in the next period had its beginnings during these years. Southern Baptist leaders recognized that there was a definite need for some program to cultivate the religious life of young people who had gone away to colleges and universities. As early as 1914 Baptist educators discussed the problem and possible solutions. Under the leadership of Charles T. Ball, professor of missions in Southwestern Seminary, the Baptist Student Missionary Movement of North America was formed on November 16, 1914. Ball was without doubt greatly influenced by the interdenominational Student Volunteer Movement and the Laymen's Missionary Movement. The aim of the body, as the name suggested, was specifically missionary, but it did desire to reach all Baptist students to pray, to give, and to promote at home and abroad the missionary enterprise. The movement was still developing at the close of the period, but within a few years it would be swallowed up into a new student organization with wider objectives.[17]

3. Laymen. As will be mentioned in the following chapter, this period found many strong Baptist laymen in the South. Indeed, in the forty years from 1877 to 1917, laymen served as presidents of the Southern Baptist Convention for no fewer than nineteen of these sessions. A new impetus was given to their enlistment in 1906-07 by interdenominational attention to the Student Volunteer Movement and a commemoration of the one hundredth anniversary of the Williams College haystack prayer meeting that triggered organized foreign mission work in the first decade of the nineteenth century. On November 13-14, 1906, a group of prominent laymen of several denominations met in New York to pray and face the challenge of missions. From this conference the Laymen's Missionary Movement was launched, which was defined as being an effort to enlist laymen to participate in and promote the foreign mission cause in their own denomination. In 1907 Joshua Levering and W. J. Northen led in a conference of "some two hundred" Baptist laymen meeting the day before the Richmond session of the Southern Baptist Convention. This conference recommended that the Convention express "its hearty approval of the spirit and purpose of the Laymen's Missionary Movement." [18] Such was done, together with the approval of a proposed executive committee for the Laymen's Missionary Movement of Southern Baptists.

In 1907 J. T. Henderson was elected general secretary for the movement and began his work the following year. Following the direction of the interdenominational movement, the thrust of this body in the early years was missions only, and the concept of a general denominational body for men was disavowed. The centripetal nature of the Southern Baptist Convention, however, slowly pulled this body toward the organizational structure and the ideals of the Convention, and in the next period this development can be discerned more distinctly. During the remainder of the present period the Laymen's Missionary Movement of the Convention provided Convention-wide leadership, inspiration, and guidance. Organization in the various states developed slowly, sparked by several annual "conventions of men" after 1912. Headquarters of the group was moved from Baltimore to Chattanooga, Tennessee, in 1914. There are no statistics available for the period closing in 1917.

4. Christian Education. At the meeting of the Southern Baptist Convention in 1913, a resolution was presented in behalf of forming a Board of Education, principally because Southern Baptist involvement in Christian education at many levels was increasing rapidly and needed to be correlated and because "practically all large Christian bodies have some general agency for promoting this work." [19] In 1915 the Convention authorized its president to appoint a committee of one from each state to be called the Education Commission of the Southern Baptist Convention. In 1916 this commission presented a survey of the involvement of Southern Baptists in educational programs and made four recommendations, which were adopted, as follows: (1) that an effort be made to arouse the people to the importance of Christian education; (2) that a literature be created for use by the various state education boards and commissions; (3) that with the cooperation of the Sunday School Board the Convention authorize an Education Day in Sunday Schools of the South; and (4) that adequate statistics of Southern Baptist educational institutions be gathered.[20] The implementing of these goals was still being attempted at the close of this period.

5. Ridgecrest. The Convention became mildly involved in another distinct movement during this period which would subsequently become a significant factor in lay organization and enlistment. When B. W. Spilman was Sunday School leader in North Carolina in 1895, he earnestly desired a Baptist assembly for promotion and inspiration. In 1907, at the suggestion of Spilman, the North Carolina Baptist Convention purchased almost 1,000 acres of land in the Swannanoa

Gap area, and the Southern Baptist Convention endorsed this type of ministry. In 1909 Spilman, who had been named the first general secretary of the Ridgecrest Baptist Assembly (although that name was not adopted until 1912), held the first conference on these grounds with emphasis on all types of denominational activity. Although sorely tried during the early years of its operation by financial difficulties, fires, hurricanes, and lawsuits, this assembly was making its place in Southern Baptist life at the close of the period.

Theological Education. A second area of enlargement in the ministries of the Southern Baptist Convention during this period was theological education.

1. Southern Baptist Theological Seminary. It will be recalled that the seminary moved from Greenville, South Carolina, to Louisville, Kentucky, in 1877 at the very close of the previous period. As John A. Broadus remarked humorously:

> It was physically no great task to remove the Seminary from Greenville to Louisville. There was nothing to move, except the library of a few thousand volumes, and three professors,—Broadus, Toy, and Whitsitt,—only one of whom had a family.[21]

James P. Boyce, the other faculty member and its chairman, lived in Louisville from 1872 to 1877 and endeavored to raise an endowment to enable the move from Greenville to take place. Only eighty-nine students were enrolled during the first session in Louisville, but the number almost doubled by the second year. Endowment, so diligently sought, reached $400,000 about 1891.

The first professor to be added to the original distinguished four faculty at the seminary had been Crawford H. Toy. In May, 1869, President Boyce memorialized the trustees to appoint another member for the faculty, and Toy was elected as professor of Old Testament. He had volunteered as missionary to Japan but was prevented from going by civil war, and instead had studied for two years in Berlin. During his first session as teacher at the seminary in 1869, however, he revealed that in his German training he had accepted Darwin's evolutionary hypothesis and favored the Kuenen-Wellhausen theory of Pentateuchal criticism.[22] When Toy refused to desist from these teachings, he was dismissed in May, 1879, by the trustees.[23]

The pioneer James P. Boyce died in 1888. Previously called chairman of the faculty, he had been elected the first president of the school seven months before his death. In May, 1889, John A. Broadus was elected president by the trustees and served until his death in 1895. Although there were but six faculty members when both Boyce and Broadus died, the catalogs from 1895 through the remainder of this period mentioned that the student body was larger than that of any other theological seminary in America.

Upon the death of Broadus, William H. Whitsitt became president and served for four years. The controversy that has already been described forced him to resign in 1899, when E. Y. Mullins succeeded him as president. At this time the faculty numbered seven. Several important achievements came during the remaining years of the period after Mullins became president. In 1901 the Sunday School Board founded a Sunday School lecture series, in 1906 the Home Mission Board began an evangelism lecture series, and in 1910 the George W. Norton lectures were endowed by Norton. *The Review and Expositor,* at that time the only Baptist theological quarterly published in the South, was begun in 1904. In 1907 the Woman's Missionary Union Training School opened near the seminary, and women were taught in seminary classes along with the men. At the close of this period in 1917, the enrollment consisted of 292 men and 91 women, and a faculty of 12.

2. *Southwestern Baptist Theological Seminary.* A new Southern Baptist seminary was formed in Texas during this period. It developed from the theological department of Baylor University. In 1901 B. H. Carroll became head of that department at Waco, Texas. In 1905 this department was enlarged into the Baylor Theological Seminary with Carroll as dean. By private appeal he had raised an emergency fund of $30,000 to support the new school for three years. At the end of these years Baylor University and the seminary were separated, and on March 14, 1908, the new institution was chartered. The trustees were to be appointed by the Baptist General Convention of Texas unless other states desired to assist in supporting the school. Ten state bodies indicated their desire to help and were permitted to name trustees. In the first year as a separate school, the seminary enrolled 188 men and 26 women and graduated 21 men. The faculty consisted of B. H. Carroll, A. H. Newman, C. B. Williams, Calvin Goodspeed, J. D. Ray, J. J. Reeve, and L. R. Scarborough. Carroll was president and Newman was dean.

The trustees appointed a committee on location of the new seminary. After examining several offers and visiting possible sites, this committee recommended on November 2, 1909, that the seminary be located in Fort Worth. The first session in Fort Worth began in a partially-completed building on October 3, 1910, with 201 enrolled throughout the year. Of these, 171 were ministers and 30 were women, and 15 were graduated. The faculty was the same as in 1908 with the addition of W. T. Conner and two special lecturers (Henry C. Mabie and J. B. Gambrell). Carroll continued to serve as president until his death on November 11, 1914, when he was succeeded by L. R. Scarborough, professor of evangelism.

Southwestern Seminary was coeducational from its founding. In

1914 ground was broken for a building to house the Woman's Missionary Training School, and in the following year it was occupied. The women of Texas contributed $110,000 toward its cost. From the beginning women were admitted to all degree programs, including the doctorate, on the same basis as men. In 1915 a full department of religious education was established, and John M. Price was secured to head it. In the same year I. E. Reynolds was named head of the department of gospel music. The beginning of these two departments resulted in the admission of more women and laymen to the student body. At the close of this period in 1917, the seminary enrolled 188 men, 135 women, and 14 laymen, and graduated 38 (26 ministers, 11 women, and 1 layman). The faculty in 1917 had changed considerably. Scarborough was president and teacher, and with him were C. B. Williams, Charles T. Ball, W. W. Barnes, J. B. Weatherspoon, W. T. Conner, J. M. Price, and I. E. Reynolds.

Relations with Other Christian Groups. New or enlarged relations with other Christian bodies began to develop during this period. The story of cooperation with Negro Baptist organizations is told in connection with the work of the Home Mission Board. Two other groups, one Baptist and the other interdenominational, became a part of Southern Baptist interest during this period.

1. Baptist World Alliance. Suggestions had been made on several occasions that Baptists around the world should have some common organization for fellowship and inspiration.[24] J. N. Prestridge, editor of *The Baptist Argus,* Louisville, Kentucky, evidently was responsible for the initial call by that paper in 1904 for a world conference of Baptists. At the Convention in that year he introduced a resolution calling for the appointment of a committee to study the best means of accomplishing this. In October, 1904, British Baptist leaders invited Baptists of the world to meet in London on July 11-18, 1905, and representatives from twenty-three nations responded. On July 17 a plan of organization and a proposed constitution were adopted. The preamble magnified fellowship "in the Lord Jesus Christ as their God and Saviour of the Churches of the Baptist order and faith" and disclaimed the exercise of functions of any existing organization. Article 2 limited the membership to any "general Union, Convention or Association of Baptist churches," so individuals and churches related to the body only through organized general structures with which they might affiliate. Meetings every five years were suggested. Principal direction of the alliance was entrusted to a general secretary. During the remainder of this period this office was held by John H. Shakespeare, who was the secretary of the British Baptist Union. The second session met at Philadelphia in 1911; the third, delayed by World War I, did not convene until 1923 at Stockholm, after the close of this period. The proceedings of each congress have been published in detail after each meeting. They reflect the great inspiration and international fellowship that always accompany such meetings.

2. The Ecumenical Movement. To some extent Baptists have been involved with the movement toward interdenominational cooperation since its modern beginning. The burst of enthusiasm that followed the inception of the modern mission movement by William Carey crossed denominational lines in the last decade of the eighteenth century. In the United States a number of local interdenominational societies for foreign missions were formed, and Baptists often were a part of them before 1814. Baptists helped send Congregationalist missionaries to the foreign field, as in the case of Luther Rice.[25] After the organization of the Southern Baptist Convention in 1845, the annual sessions of that body often joined other denominations in a joint attack on immorality and drunkenness.

The immediate historical antecedents of the modern movement can be found in the interdenominational missionary conferences. Foreign missionaries of many denominations, wrestling with mutual problems in their efforts to witness for the Christian gospel, met together in conferences, sometimes informally, sometimes officially. As early as 1854 a significant conference by this group was held in London, followed by intermittent meetings in England during the rest of the century. The actual involvement by Southern Baptists probably developed from the pronouncement of the decennial meeting by the bishops of the Anglican communion in 1888 in Lambeth Palace in London. Following the lead of American Episcopalians, this London conference named four items that it considered minimum for church union: acceptance of the Old and New Testaments as the rule and standard of faith; the Apostles' and Nicene creeds as the doctrinal statement of faith; the observance of baptism and the Lord's Supper as sacraments of the church; and the historic episcopate to preserve the continuing unity of the church. In response to this, the Southern Baptist Convention suggested in 1890 that the several denominations select representative scholars to "seek to determine just what is the teaching of the Bible on the leading points of difference of doctrine and polity between the denominations." The Disciples of Christ exchanged correspondence with the Convention's committee, but nothing came of it.

Meanwhile, the Federal Council of Churches of Christ in America was formed, tentatively in 1905 and formally in 1908. Northern Baptists joined this group, but Southern Baptists did not. The Foreign Missions Conference of North America, formed by representatives from many denominations in 1893 for consultation on common problems related to foreign missions, invited the Foreign Mission Board of the Southern Baptist Convention to join them and the Board did so. Its secretaries attended these meetings during the remainder of this period. However, when a comparable Home Missions Council was formed in 1909, the Home Mission Board declined to participate in its deliberations. Part of the reason for this probably was the strained relations between northern and southern Baptists at this time because of geographical claims by each.

In 1910 the climax of interdenominational missionary conferences took place. Meeting at Edinburgh, Scotland, on June 14-23, over 1,200 official delegates representing 159 mission boards and societies of England, Europe, and America voted unanimously to organize a continuing official body for the promotion of church unity. John R. Mott, outstanding leader of the Student Volunteer Movement, was named chairman of the new Continuation Committee. In the following year the Southern Baptist Convention was invited to participate in a world conference of all Christian bodies to consider questions relating to faith and order. The Convention promptly appointed a committee, headed by the president of the body, E. C. Dargan, to make fraternal response and attend the proposed conference as fraternal messengers. During the remainder of this period, this committee made annual reports to the Convention. These reports were quite open in their attitude. "We shall count ourselves happy on the basis proposed to confer with our brethren of other communions, on the great matters which have been referred to us by our various Christian bodies," said the 1911 report. W. W. Barnes felt that at the close of this period there was a favorable attitude by Southern Baptists toward the question of participating in conference with other evangelical denominations.[26]

Social Aspects of the Gospel. Southern Baptists were aware of the various currents that magnified the humanitarian thrust of the gospel. As a matter of fact, from their earliest history they had responded to social issues of various sorts. They were active patriots in the Revolutionary War; used political methods to gain guarantees of civil and religious liberty; stressed temperance, marital fidelity, and good citizenship quite early; debated slavery on both sides; were involved in secession and war in the 1860's; and with the decline of the rural South, discussed urbanization, immigration, and labor agitation. Other such expressions of "practical religion" as the founding and operation of orphanages, hospitals, and schools for mountain people and various types of assistance to needy people on a local level were regularly a part of their programs.

As Rufus B. Spain and John Lee Eighmy have asserted, however, before the opening of the twentieth century the general stance of

Southern Baptists on social issues resembled a cultural establishment "sanctifying a secular order devoted to states' rights, white supremacy, laissez faire economics, and property rights." [27] Eighmy felt that three major forces restricted Southern Baptists in their social thought and action: (1) an ecclesiastical system of independent churches discouraged denominational activities other than mission work; (2) revivalism kept the local churches preoccupied with the spiritual and moral welfare of individuals rather than the social problems of society; and (3) the pressure of the social environment usually produced the silence, if not the sanction, of the local churches relative to the basic attitudes of the secular world.[28] W. W. Barnes said that the Convention was so busy rethinking its own character and objectives and so engaged in controversies that it had neither time nor opportunity for consideration of social problems.

There were other factors of some moment that should not be overlooked. Although Eighmy felt that Southern Baptists had not embraced the social gospel movement when it moved south, the fact is that the social gospel movement practically ignored the principal social problem of the South—the race question. As David M. Reimers made plain, in the social gospel movement "the plight of the Negro was scarcely considered." [29] As far as the race problem was concerned, the northern white Protestant churches, as well as the general culture, differed little in their general attitude from the South by the turn of the century.[30] Even such social gospelers as Walter Rausenbusch, Lyman Abbott, and Josiah Strong dismissed this sore dilemma of North and South with silence or endorsement of the southern attitude.[31]

In addition, the whole social gospel thrust had liberal doctrinal overtones that did not appeal to Southern Baptist conservatives. Eighmy illustrated this point. A. J. Barton, the first chairman of the restructured Social Service Commission of the Southern Baptist Convention in 1914, accurately defined the doctrinal stance of Southern Baptists in relation to social service when he wrote,

> Southern Baptists have never preached and will never preach social service as a substitute for the work of grace in the individual heart. In our social service we take the individual work of grace for granted and on that basis we stress social and civic obligations.[32]

However, Eighmy severely criticized Barton by saying that in making social religion the product of personal religion,

> Barton missed one of the main contributions of the social gospel, the idea that the Christian message addressed only to individuals does not ensure justice in social relations.[33]

This antithesis which Eighmy felt between personal or individual regeneration and social Christianity cropped out here and there in his study. The fact is that some Southern Baptists feared such an antithesis and thus shied away from the social gospel movement for that reason. They were unwilling to supplant an individual gospel of personal regeneration with a sociological gospel that ignored the salvation of the individual, and had not learned to relate them as Barton had.

In any event, the first action of the Southern Baptist Convention toward identifying and dealing with the whole gamut of social justice came in 1907 when a resolution was passed instructing the president to appoint a committee to arrange for a mass meeting at the next session to consider social questions. In 1913 a Social Service Commission was formed, soon absorbing the long-standing Committee on Temperance, and calling for a wholehearted attack on social ills in a report characterized by insight and thoroughness.[34] Most of the state bodies of Baptists structured similar committees. This action did not mean that Southern Baptists were yet ready to do something about racial discrimination, for this was practiced and sanctioned by both northern and southern churches at this time. But under the leadership of men like A. J. Barton, E. C. Dargan, Charles S. Gardner, and W. L. Poteat, the way was being prepared for the revolutionary changes of mid-century as Southern Baptists struggled with their own culture and heritage. In social areas other than race, Southern Baptists were already involved in many of the states.[35]

Structural Tensions in the Convention

The language of the founding fathers of the Southern Baptist Convention shows that they deliberately chose to organize in a way different from the society pattern, preferring instead to copy the older associational-type of structure.[36] They wanted a "judicious concentration" of all benevolent activity into one convention

> embodying the whole Denomination together with separate and distinct Boards for each object of benevolent enterprise, located at different places, and all amenable to the Convention.[37]

They felt that this kind of structure would be more effective, more responsive and representative, and more denominationally unifying than the separate and independent benevolent societies with which they had been affiliated between 1814 and 1845.[38] They recognized that the old society method was fundamentally antidenominational at several points. First, the zealous regard by each of the completely autonomous societies for its own benevolence brought a rivalry with the other Baptist societies in the collection of funds and in the magnitude of each program. This was one of the basic factors that led to the abandonment of the society method by northern Baptists in

1907. Second, the society pattern brought a neglect of many areas of denominational concern which were not specifically related to the immediate program of any of the societies. Third, the autonomous nature of each of the triennial bodies allowed no holistic concept or true denominational representation. The denomination was pared into benevolent slices that overlapped but were not united. The possibility that such judicious concentration might threaten the autonomy of the churches did not trouble Southern Baptists, as has already been pointed out, and the history of the body during this period from 1877 to 1917 confirmed their view.

However, the grand denominational concept of W. B. Johnson was crippled radically at the initial meeting in 1845. The Preamble and Article V of the constitution provided for it—one body to direct all benevolent activities that Southern Baptists might wish to promote. Yet Johnson himself did not realize that when they retained some of the old society characteristics in the structure of the new body, they were introducing antidenominational elements to set in motion ideological and functional tensions that would ultimately need to be confronted. Some of these society characteristics that were structured into the new body by the founding fathers were the priority of the benevolence over denominational solidarity, the use of designated giving for support of the benevolences, financial gifts as the basis of representation in the Convention, the placing of the mission boards in separate cities, the extensive authority given the boards between meetings of the Convention, the long period of time between meetings of the Convention, and the widespread concept that the functional existence of the Convention ceased when the triennial meeting adjourned.

During the period between 1877 and 1917 Southern Baptists began to recognize that these society characteristics, imbedded into a convention-type structure, inhibited the development of those denominational goals which had initially moved the founders of the Convention to leave the old society method; namely, the desire to form an effectively functioning, responsive and representative, and denominationally unifying body. The efforts to achieve these goals through modifying the structure during this period will be described briefly.

Improving the Convention's Effectiveness. The potential effectiveness of the new Convention was markedly reduced in 1845 when the founding fathers retained at least three of the society's antidenominational characteristics in the structure of the new body. For one thing, the old society concept of the nature of general bodies was retained. They were viewed as aristocratic, inspirational gatherings somewhat aloof from the total life of the denomination, having no corporate or functional existence between sessions. The fact that each society fostered only one benevolence resulted in partitioning the denomination in such fashion as to exclude a holistic conception. The meetings of the societies occurred only once every three years, and each society took cognizance only of its own benevolence. Each benevolence took precedence over the denominational emphasis. In the second place, W. B. Johnson's scheme for structuring all benevolent activities under one convention was rejected, and some benevolences were organized outside the structure of the Convention. In the third place, support for the benevolences of the Convention came from designated giving to specific benevolences, and the method of securing these funds was quite haphazard.

These basically antidenominational society characteristics, which were placed in the structure of the new denominational Convention by Southern Baptists in 1845, resisted any major change for over half a century. There were four principal reasons for this. For one thing, many Southern Baptists, particularly in the border states, clung to the hope that reunion of all American Baptists might be achieved. They desired to hold the new body to a limited program of benevolences lest there should come further alienation with Baptists in the North. When Georgia Baptists suggested that the southern body immediately adopt all benevolences for the South, Editor John Waller of the *Western Baptist Review* of Kentucky wrote a sharp reply in which he vigorously opposed any more divisions between the northern and southern Baptist bodies "merely because their Boards are located north of Mason and Dixon's line." [39] A second deterrent to any rapid move toward the convention ideal of promoting all benevolences was introduced after 1851 by J. R. Graves and the Landmarkers, who opposed authorizing any nonlocal body to enlarge the area of its benevolent work. Third, many Southern Baptists doubted their financial ability to promote all benevolences desired by the southern constituency through one denominational body, as demonstrated by their lengthy refusal to enter into the book publishing enterprise. Finally, the heterogeneous nature of Baptist life in the South, heightened by difficulties in communication and transportation, blunted the efforts of leaders to elicit, combine, and direct the energies of the whole denomination in one sacred effort through the new Convention.

In this ambivalent context, then, it is no wonder that the grand design of the Southern Baptist Convention to become an effective, all-inclusive denominational body to promote all benevolent activity of Southern Baptists was almost obliterated, and the Convention was often called "the missionary convention," suggesting the old society emphasis, during this period. It had no funds of its own, even to print minutes of the sessions, so designated mission funds were conscripted for this purpose. There was even a debate about where to keep the Convention minute book and records, since the Convention had no de facto existence or headquarters.

However, the very nature of the new Convention challenged these society characteristics. Four steps illustrating the struggle of the convention thrust may be distinctly observed. First, there were demands for more frequent meetings of the Convention. The many denominational emphases that went beyond missions required sessions more often than every three years. In 1851 the meetings of the Convention were changed from triennial to biennial, and in 1866, they became annual. Second, there were repeated efforts to bring all benevolences into the structure of the Convention. Four benevolences were structured within the Convention during the first twenty years of its history: a foreign mission body, a domestic mission body, a Bible Board, and a Sunday School Board. Three additional major benevolences were developed outside of the Convention following the old society pattern: a publication society in 1847, a Sunday School Union in 1857, and a Southwide theological seminary in 1859. These external benevolences, however, were so formed as to recognize the Convention and relate rather loosely to it. Third, in 1891 a significant and spectacular development occurred, although most Southern Baptists did not recognize it as such. In that year the second Sunday School Board was formed, and this board represented a large step toward bridging the gap between the old program of supporting a few basic benevolences and the total denominational thrust of the new southern convention. The new agency was able to carry on a large number of additional denominational functions, moving perceptibly toward the ideal of Article V of the original constitution. At the same time, this new agency provided a source of finances for the denomination over and above the expenses required for its operation. Thus, the Convention was now able to give leadership in many benevolent undertakings that could not have been fostered before 1891 because of financial limitation and designation. In part because the new board possessed these funds, it was assigned leadership in Sunday School and Training Union work, architectural assistance to the churches, periodical and book publishing, production of church supplies for every type of use in the churches, training in church budgeting, cooperative work with state boards, and many similar denominational programs. In addition, this board provided financial assistance to about a dozen denominational agencies in connection with its own distinctive program, which would not have been possible without this revenue.

Yet, even with the enlarged scope of benevolent activity potentially available in the formation of the Sunday School Board, the Convention was still far from possessing the "judicious concentration" necessary to make it denominationally effective. Finally, in 1917 a major breakthrough occurred which brought priority to the Convention as a denominational body for eliciting, combining, and directing Southern Baptist benevolences. The formation of the first Executive Committee was so important in this respect that it marked the beginning of a new era in Southern Baptist history. It resulted from increasing disenchantment of southern leaders with their structural body as an effectively functioning vehicle.

Before the turn of the century, there was a clamor for an improved structure to bring more denominational efficiency and structural unity. In 1898 Georgia Baptists introduced a resolution urging that the new century be celebrated by improving Baptist organization to meet the new challenges they would face.[40] Committees and commissions were named year by year to study and recommend, but disagreement was widespread.[41] The old society pattern of conceiving of the Convention as simply a solitary and isolated annual gathering with no official functional existence between meetings, was not compatible with the increasing complexity of the Convention's functions and the total denominational thrust being developed by the southwide body. Various proposals for resolving the tension were made, including suggestions for federation, division, nationalization, and consolidation.[42] In 1913 the Convention bluntly instructed a commission to study the structure, plans, and methods of the Convention to determine whether or not they were best adapted for "eliciting, combining and directing the energies of Southern Baptists and for securing the highest efficiency of our forces and the fullest possible enlistment of our people for the work of the Kingdom." [43] This was denominational language. The climax came in 1916 when M. H. Wolfe of Texas proposed the creation of a strong Executive Board "which shall direct all of the work and enterprises fostered and promoted by this Convention." A committee was appointed to study this matter. A minority report, interestingly enough, proposed a plan of consolidation calling for all the boards and agencies to be merged into a corporation, the Southern Baptist Convention, which should have a Board of Directors composed of the secretaries of the state conventions. This board would hold all of the property and direct all of the work of the Convention.[44]

The majority recommendation carried and a small Executive Committee of seven was named. One can detect a note of caution in the initial allocation of a few duties to this body. It was to have oversight of arrangements for the meetings of the Convention; to act ad interim on general business not otherwise provided for; to serve as an advisory group when requested to do so by one or more of the boards; and "this committee shall have no further duties except as other things may be specifically committed to it by the Convention itself at its annual meeting." [45] Yet even in the 1917 session, several additional matters for study and recommendation were referred to this committee. [46]

Thus, at the close of this period in 1917, Southern Baptists had begun a plan to exploit the genius of the convention-type structure which they had conceived in 1845. The strengthening and enlarging of this Executive Committee will be described in the next period.

Making the Convention More Responsive and Representative. The adoption of the society financial plan for determining the basis of representation in the Southern Baptist Convention in 1845 brought to this body one of the basic weaknesses of the society plan; namely, a structure for benevolent work of the denomination that was neither representative of nor responsive to the denomination itself. As early as 1824 Francis Wayland, who was to become the most influential figure for a long generation among American Baptists, remarked concerning the society plan of carrying on benevolent work:

> The convention at present is composed of delegates from missionary societies, and of course must, in its very nature, be mostly composed of persons elected from the vicinity of its place of meeting. And besides, were the meeting ever so universally attended, its foundation is radically defective. A missionary society is not a representative body, nor can any number of them speak the language of a whole denomination. [47]

It was this society plan of operation with respect to constituency and support that was adopted by the Southern Baptist Convention in 1845. While this structure provided a committed constituency, in contrast with the earlier associational plan which in many cases did not, the adoption of this plan by the Convention in 1845 made it impossible to unite the whole denomination in the manner desired by W. B. Johnson, the principal architect.

The truth of Wayland's comment was demonstrated in the years between 1877 and 1917. Not only was the basic nature of the society opposed to true representation of the denomination, but a number of specific elements enhanced the problem. The increasing size of the constituency of the Convention soon lessened the ratio of the decision-making attendants to about 1 percent of the denomination. The annual meetings became so large that sober deliberation was completely impossible. The agenda was so crowded with reports of work done and recommendations for work to be done that the Convention did not have enough time to give even brief consideration to many of them in the four or five days of meeting. The location of the Convention meeting place became overwhelmingly important. Nearby people would attend in large numbers and vote for any sectional issue that was favorable to them or pleased them. Resolutions were introduced that reflected the interests of a small sectional group, so that by reason of the time and location of the meeting, the well-being of the whole body was adversely affected. New plans and programs were often introduced at the meetings, and because of the lack of prior time to study them and judge their effects, the messengers were forced to vote on illogically conceived or improperly developed schemes that were foredoomed to failure. These and many more weaknesses in the operation of the Convention during this period were stressed by various leaders across the South.[48]

Almost every year during this period between 1877 and 1917 someone raised the question from the floor of the Convention relative to changing the method of representation. Changes actually were made half-a-dozen times. Despite this chronic tampering with the basis of representation, however, there was little consensus among Southern Baptists as to the proper method of determining the constituency in order to make it both representative and responsive. Serious consideration was given to four types of representation: associational, state, numerical, and church. Association representation, even without financial contributions to the Convention, was permitted during most of this period. Several attempts were made to eliminate this kind of representation in order to reduce the size of the Convention, but its popularity was such that this provision was retained and became a principal area of representation.

Support for state representation in the Southern Baptist Convention was surprisingly strong. In 1878 specific states were authorized to send messengers on a financial basis, and the state as a basis for general representation was seriously discussed in later years.

The numerical basis of representation was suggested many times. In 1891 and again in 1893 proposals from the floor were made to follow this plan. In the latter year, a large committee composed of some of the most important members of the Convention recommended that the basis of representation be changed either to a numerical basis or to a combined numerical-financial basis. The numerical plan suggested ten representatives from each cooperating state, plus one representative for each four thousand white Baptist membership within these states, and one representative from each cooperating district association. This plan was not adopted. In 1894, 1902, and after the close of this period, the numerical basis was stoutly championed. The most persuasive argument for this kind of representation was the assertion that most of the state conventions and other Baptist bodies had a numerical basis of representation. However, the effort to secure this kind of representation failed during this period.

The church basis of representation was most widely urged. As might be expected, J. R. Graves of Tennessee was one of its early champions. He wanted to limit the representation to membership of the churches only, and suggested that each Baptist church contributing any sum to the boards of the Convention should be allowed one delegate (in his terminology), and an additional delegate for each hundred dollars given. His point of view was reflected in 1905 at the Kansas City meeting of the Convention when a communication from fifty-two churches in Arkansas and other states was presented to the Convention. The principal demand of this memorial said:

> We want the money and the associational basis of representation eliminated from the Constitution and a purely church basis substituted instead. . . . The numerical basis is objectionable because such a basis carries with it the idea that the commission was given to the individual as such and not to the churches as such. Nothing short of exclusive church representation will satisfy us. We ask that you eliminate all other bases and adopt the church basis of representation.[49]

When the Convention refused this request, the Landmark group under B. M. Bogard and others withdrew from Convention and state cooperation.

However, this call for the church basis of representation was not limited to aggressive Landmarkers alone. A few weeks after the 1901 session of the Convention, the *Word and Way* of Missouri published an article on "Representatives of What?" The writer said in part:

> So far as I could see from the minutes of the Convention there was not a single church on the roll as being represented. The representatives were from the local association and those appointed by the State boards. . . . Is it any wonder that there is a hue and cry about ten thousand churches that do not co-operate with the Convention and its work? The basis of membership in the Convention is $250 for each messenger. This puts the Convention where not one church in five hundred can reach it. . . . Any regular Baptist church should be allowed to be represented in our associations and conventions. . . . Baptists believe in co-operation but not in centralization.[50]

A clear distinction should be made between the Landmark position of *delegated* church representation and the position of many non-Landmarkers which might be termed a *designated* church representation. The Landmarkers viewed the Convention as a body composed of autonomous and scripturally authoritative local churches officially represented through their delegates. Their ecclesiological theory asserted that otherwise there would be no basis for the general body even to exist, since the local church was the only scriptural and authoritative body among Baptists. The other view, which was magnified in the Hayden controversy in Texas in the last decade of the nineteenth century, denied both the necessity and the advantage of projecting the authority of local churches into general bodies. Instead, an anti-Landmark concept was championed in the struggle against Hayden. It conceived of general bodies as mass meetings of representative Baptists composed of messengers *designated* by the churches, but who did not officially represent their churches, nor possess any delegated authority from the churches, nor corporately exercise any authority over the churches. According to this view, the authority of the Convention stemmed from fraternal and widespread denominational consensus, not from the authority of the churches. In essence, this meant that all general bodies—associational, state, and convention-wide—were mass meetings of Baptists, not officially delegated bodies with any power over the churches that sent the messengers.

After the Convention refused to change its society-type of financial representation in 1905 at the demand of the Landmark group, it continued to ponder and debate the best way to secure a more representative and responsive basis. However, at the end of this period in 1917, Article V on membership still provided that the Convention should consist of (1) messengers who contribute funds, or were elected by Baptist bodies contributing funds on the basis of one messenger for every $250 paid into the treasuries of the boards and (2) one representative elected from each of the district associations cooperating with the Convention.

Deepening a Denominational Consciousness. A cursory glance at the appeals of W. B. Johnson in 1845 makes it plain that he desired more than simply an effective and responsive general body when he urged the adoption of a plan to "elicit, combine, and direct" all Southern Baptists in a concerted effort. Underlying all of this was the desire to unify Southern Baptists in such fashion that the tenuous "ropes of straw" holding together autonomous and sometimes noncooperative Baptist churches would be strengthened by a strong denominational loyalty as a means of supporting the domestic and foreign programs consistently and conscientiously. The South had always had a distinctive sectional cohesiveness. Social, economic, political, and linguistic patterns were different from those in the North. The presence of slavery after 1619 accentuated this sectional uniqueness. The struggles for religious liberty and the union of Regular and Separate Baptists brought a sense of southern unity. The strong blows of Primitivism and Campbellism severely affected Southern Baptists before their organization in 1845 and instilled a battle-field type of solidarity. The events of 1861 to 1877 deepened the southern sectional feelings.

Yet, in the period between 1877 and 1917, the Convention experienced the fiercest struggles it had known at this precise point: loyalty to the Convention. Doubtless the organization of benevolent work outside of the Convention was not intended to disparage the

Convention's purpose of becoming the structural body for all southern benevolences, but the lack of consensus for structuring such benevolences as publications, theological education, and a Sunday School union within the Convention structure, for reasons already suggested, could have destroyed the effectiveness of the southwide body. The severity of the struggles with the Home Mission Society of New York over the home field and the American Baptist Publication Society of Philadelphia relative to the multipurpose nature of the Convention, along with the several Landmark attacks involving the right of the Convention to carry on its work, showed the depth of the lack of loyalty to the Convention in the 1880's and 1890's. But it was in these very struggles that a strong denominational consciousness was developed.[50] The vision of southern leaders like I. T. Tichenor challenged the Convention's constituency to rally to the cause. The second Sunday School Board, organized in 1891, had a strong unifying effect through its literature and promotional activity. The tensions between the southwide and state programs lessened perceptibly by the turn of the century. The remarkable growth in several directions accelerated this denominational consciousness. When Southern Baptists moved to other states, they longed for the old ties and familiar denominational structures. This was the basic reason for the geographical expansion into other states during this and the following period. In this period Southern Baptists in New Mexico, southern Illinois, and Oklahoma sought ties with the southern convention from their new localities. It is likely that the appeals of Oregon Baptists in 1894 were unheard because of the territorial consciousness of the Convention at that time; but when Southern Baptist people began to swarm into all areas of the nation, territorial limitations could not stand in the face of the denominational consciousness displayed by them wherever they might live. The inability of the strong resurgence of Landmarkism in the 1890's to bring extensive schism in the Convention (despite some very strong attacks at many points) and the relative aloofness of Southern Baptists to the ecumenical movement probably resulted from the sense of identity developed in the convention-type structure of the South.

Thus, by 1917 the Southern Baptist Convention had totally recovered from the trauma of war and Reconstruction. Its ministry had been enlarged to three effective boards; it had greatly expanded its areas of service; and its organizational structure was being tested at the point of denominational effectiveness and responsiveness. There were evidences that the loyalty to the denomination requisite to maintaining and continuing a stable program was developing rapidly. Constituents and other Baptist agencies related to the general body had increased from 15 states, 559 associations, 12,864 churches, and

906,074 members in 1877 to 18 states, 909 associations, 24,883 churches, and 2,844,301 members in 1917, an annual average increase in membership of 5.22%.

Notes

1. *The Foreign Mission Journal* (Richmond), XXIV (July, 1893), pp. 353-54.
2. *Annual,* Southern Baptist Convention, 1910, p. 251.
3. See Baker, *Relations,* pp. 115-16. Note reference to these in *The National Baptist* (Philadelphia, 1865-1894), May 27, 1873.
4. *Annual Report,* American Baptist Home Mission Society, 1880, p. 37.
5. Rutledge, *op. cit.,* p. 135.
6. *Baptist Standard* (Texas), May 31, 1906, p. 2.
7. Rutledge, *op. cit.,* pp. 245 ff.
8. *Annual,* Southern Baptist Convention, 1898, p. 24.
9. Baker, *The Story of the Sunday School Board,* p. 89.
10. *Annual,* Southern Baptist Convention, 1875, p. 71.
11. Barnes, *The Southern Baptist Convention,* pp. 148 ff.
12. Baker, *Source Book,* p. 151, for this document.
13. *Ibid.,* pp. 152-53.
14. Cox-Woolley, eds., *Encyclopedia,* II, p. 1513.
15. *Annual,* Southern Baptist Convention, 1893, pp. 44 f.
16. Barnes, *The Southern Baptist Convention,* pp. 181 ff gives the story.
17. *Ibid.,* pp. 192 ff.
18. *Annual,* Southern Baptist Convention, 1907, p. 46.
19. *Ibid.,* 1916, p. 51.
20. *Ibid.,* 1916, pp. 50-56.
21. Quoted in William A. Mueller, *A History of Southern Baptist Theological Seminary* (Nashville: Broadman Press, 1959), p. 42.
22. See Broadus, *op. cit.,* pp. 259 ff.
23. Baker, *Source Book,* pp. 168-72 has this document.
24. Cox-Woolley, eds., *Encyclopedia,* I, pp. 127 ff. See also Barnes, *The Southern Baptist Convention,* p. 268, for this background.
25. Vail, *The Morning Hour of American Baptist Missions,* pp. 440 ff.
26. Barnes, *The Southern Baptist Convention,* p. 280.
27. John Lee Eighmy, *Churches in Cultural Captivity* (Knoxville: University of Tennessee Press, 1972), p. x of Preface.
28. *Ibid.,* p. 19.
29. Reimers, *op. cit.,* p. 54.
30. *Ibid.,* pp. 51 ff.
31. *Ibid.,* pp. 53-54.
32. *Annual,* Southern Baptist Convention, 1923, p. 101.
33. Eighmy, *op. cit.,* p. 97.
34. *Annual,* Southern Baptist Convention, 1914, pp. 37-38.
35. See, for example, Kenneth K. Bailey, *Southern White Protestantism in the Twentieth Century* (New York: Harper and Row, 1964); John Lee Eighmy, "Religious Liberalism in the South During the Progressive Era," *Church History* (September, 1969), pp. 359-72; and Wayne Flynt, "Dissent in Zion: Alabama Baptists and Social Issues, 1900-1914," *The Journal of Southern History* (November, 1969), pp. 523-42.
36. Baker, *Source Book,* pp. 24 ff.
37. *Ibid.,* p. 114.
38. This "convention-type" organization was rejected by the leaders of Northern Baptists in the 1820's. See Baker, *Relations,* pp. 15-16, and Hudson, *op. cit.*
39. John Waller, ed., *Western Baptist Review, op. cit.,* I, p. 57 ff.
40. See *Annual,* Southern Baptist Convention, 1898, p. 35, and note Cox-Woolley, eds., *Encyclopedia,* I, p. 428.
41. See *Religious Herald* (Virginia), June 28, 1900, p. 8, cols. 1-2; also *Annuals,* Southern Baptist Convention, 1901, pp. 179-88, and 1903, p. 3.

42. Barnes, *The Southern Baptist Convention,* pp. 176 ff.
43. *Annual,* Southern Baptist Convention, 1913, pp. 69 f.
44. Barnes, *The Southern Baptist Convention,* p. 178.
45. *Annual,* Southern Baptist Convention, 1917, pp. 33 f.
46. *Ibid.,* p. 109.
47. Baker, *Source Book,* pp. 70-71.
48. See, for example, the critique of the committee of E. Y. Mullins, *Annual,* Southern Baptist Convention, 1926, pp. 31-32.
49. Baker, *Source Book,* p. 174, has this document.
50. Baker, *Relations,* p. 168.

14 The Constituency in the New South

At the same time the Convention was struggling for survival and attempting to claim its birthright through operating as a multi-benevolent Convention for all Southern Baptists, the people across the South who made up its constituency were rapidly rebounding from the rigors of war and Reconstruction. A general reading of the state convention minutes and denominational newspapers for this period, however, discloses a surprising number of factors that tended to inhibit growth and advance.

This was a period of heated controversy. It will be recalled that in the struggle with the two northern societies during the 1880's and 1890's many Southern Baptist leaders took the side of the northern societies rather than that of the Convention because they envisioned a larger unity for American Baptists, deprecated separation from the North when each section could be helpful to the other, and had developed through the years strong personal ties with northern leadership. In the end, however, these struggles strengthened the bonds of the Convention with its southern constituency, and whatever their earlier preferences, the southern people worked effectively through agencies of the Convention.

It is remarkable that the Landmark resurgence described heretofore did not result in more extensive schism than actually occurred. None of the four outbreaks resulted in particularly large numbers of people leaving Convention affiliation, and the new unity that prevailed after the several schisms provided additional impetus to the work.

There were numerous financial recessions during this period. The minutes of the various states speak of critical financial problems in the 1870's, while almost the entire decade after 1890 was a time of financial panic. Alabama and Texas, in particular, complained of financial crises in 1907-08. As one looks at the statistics for these periods of financial crisis, he is impressed by the fact that although without doubt they were influential in diminishing the gifts, many other aspects of the work seemed to be little affected.

The Spanish-American war of 1898 was too brief to have much
320 effect, and at the close of this period in 1917 the First World War

was not yet underway, although the preparations for it were reported in various state annuals.

Still another deterrent to the work during this period was the several epidemics of sickness. In 1879, for example, reference was made in many state minutes to the "fearful scourge" that was taking place. It was mentioned that there were 40,000 cases of yellow fever at that time. In 1905-06 another yellow fever epidemic gripped the lower Mississippi Valley, resulting in many deaths among Southern Baptists. At other times there were references to epidemics of various diseases in the state reports. As a whole, however, it is difficult to detect any severe adverse reactions to these epidemics, probably because they touched only parts of the geographical area where Southern Baptists served.

Mention should be made, too, of natural catastrophies. In Missouri, for example, in 1880 a severe tornado was reported. Drought and crop failures were reported in Texas and Mississippi at the turn of the century and shortly thereafter. In 1907-08 the reports mentioned that there were crop failures in several of the states. In 1911 some of the states reported long droughts and extreme heat which destroyed many of the crops. In 1912 a number of the states reported a general drought. Again, however, despite the loss of financial revenue caused by these natural calamities, the overall effect on Southern Baptist life during the period was inconsiderable.

One other factor unquestionably was involved. The congenital tensions unintentionally built into the structure of the Southern Baptist Convention in 1845 had their effect upon the constituency of the body. In their efforts to cooperate with the Convention in its benevolent activity, the people were conscious of the ambivalence in many respects. As they attended the Convention sessions they noticed that some benevolences were discussed and some were not, that the financial basis of representation was not really satisfactory for a denominational body, and that designated giving brought a multitude of problems.

However, despite these several difficulties during this period, Southern Baptists made many gains across the South. Some of these will be described briefly.

Substantial Growth

Between 1877 and 1917 Southern Baptists grew from 15 states, 559 associations, 12,864 churches, and 906,074 members to 18 states, 909 associations, 24,883 churches, and 2,844,301 members, representing an average annual membership growth rate of 5.22%. This meant that Southern Baptists were more than doubling their original number every two decades.

Two comparisons show the substantial nature of this growth by Southern Baptists. The general population in the states involved in these Baptist figures increased from 17,922,000 in 1880 to 41,688,784 in 1920. This represented an annual average growth rate of 3.23%, just more than half the Baptist rate. Furthermore, other denominations provide a tool for measurement. Presbyterians grew from 553,000 in 1877 to 1,579,000 in 1917, an increase of 1,026,000 or 185.53%. This comes to 4.53% annual average growth, below the Southern Baptist average of 5.22%. Methodists grew from 2,346,000 in 1877 to 5,970,000 in 1917, an increase of 3,624,000 or 154.47%. This is an annual average increase of 3.77%, also below Southern Baptists. The Roman Catholic Church grew from 8,277,000 in 1891 (the earliest figures available for this body) to 17,023,000 in 1917, an increase of 8,746,000 or 105.66%. This is an annual average of 3.91% increase.

Where and to what extent this growth took place may be glimpsed from the following summary.

South Atlantic Region. In this region (consisting of Maryland, District of Columbia, Virginia, North Carolina, South Carolina, Georgia, and Florida), Southern Baptists increased from 185 associations, 4,458 churches, and 361,575 members in 1877 to 258 associations, 7,732 churches, and 1,021,616 members in 1917. This represented an average annual membership growth of 4.45%. The general population in this region grew from 6,832,132 in 1880 to 12,303,568 in 1920, or an average annual rate of 1.95%, less than half the Baptist rate.

Percentage-wise, Florida Baptists showed the largest increase (due to the small number of Baptists there in 1877): from 12 associations, 221 churches, and 9,020 members in 1877 to 29 associations, 730 churches, and 60,894 members in 1917, an average annual membership growth of 14.03%. The largest numerical growth in this region was experienced by North Carolina Baptists: from 40 associations, 986 churches, and 83,904 members in 1877 to 64 associations, 2,172 churches, and 284,927 members in 1917, an average annual membership growth of 5.84%. The state of this region with the largest number of Baptists was Georgia, who grew from 86 associations, 1,855 churches, and 119,470 members in 1877 to 94 associations, 2,473 churches, and 315,801 members in 1917, an annual average membership increase of 4.01%. The statistics from District of Columbia showed a decline in the number of Baptists from 1 association, 31 churches, and 10,061 members in 1877 to 1 association, 9 churches, and 4,436 members in 1917. However, as mentioned previously, the organizational structures and the varying denominational affiliations in the District have made it next to impossible to identify proper southern statistics up to and including this period. The loss shown is probably a paper realignment rather than an actual diminution.

The remainder of the South Atlantic states more than doubled their Baptist population during this period. Maryland Baptists grew from 1 association, 48 churches, and 7,607 members in 1877 to 3 associations, 88 churches, and 15,464 members in 1917, an annual average membership increase of 2.52%. Virginia Baptists increased from 22 associations, 692 churches, and 71,274 members in 1877 to 29 associations, 1,127 churches, and 178,980 members in 1917, an average annual membership growth of 3.68%. South Carolina Baptists increased from 23 associations, 625 churches, and 60,239 members in 1877 to 38 associations, 1,133 churches, and 161,114 members in 1917, an average annual membership growth of 4.08%.

South Central Region. Baptists in this region—consisting of Kentucky, Tennessee, Alabama, Mississippi, Arkansas, Louisiana, Oklahoma (and Indian Territory), and Texas—increased from 308 associations, 7,007 churches, and 464,953 members in 1877 to 535 associations, 14,465 churches, and 1,540,072 members in 1917. This represented an annual membership growth rate of 5.64%. The population in this region grew from 8,919,371 in 1880 (Oklahoma and Indian Territory are first shown in the 1890 census) to 19,135,531 in 1920. This represented an average annual growth of 2.65%, not half the rate of growth by Baptists during the period.

The largest growth in this region both percentage-wise and numerically, occurred in Texas, which increased from 55 associations, 1,176 churches, and 65,453 members in 1877 to 149 associations, 3,709 churches, and 383,774 members in 1917. This was an average annual membership growth of 11.86%. Next to Texas in the rate of growth were Louisiana Baptists, who increased from 20 associations, 376 churches, and 19,179 members in 1877 to 32 associations, 746 churches, and 80,108 members in 1917, or an average annual membership increase of 7.75%. Arkansas Baptists increased from 32 associations, 708 churches, and 31,602 members in 1877 to 54 associations, 1,547 churches, and 122,635 members in 1917, an average annual membership growth of 7.03%. Next in percentage of growth were Alabama Baptists. They increased from 53 associations, 1,193 churches, and 64,782 members in 1877 to 64 associations, 2,070 churches, and 221,501 members in 1917, or an average annual membership increase of 5.90%. Tennessee Baptists increased from 42 associations, 1,074 churches, and 85,001 members in 1877 to 55 associations, 1,839 churches, and 208,636 members during this period, for an average annual membership growth of 3.55%. Kentucky Baptists during this period increased from 64 associations, 1,367 churches, and 109,510 members in 1877 to 76 associations, 1,897 churches, and 260,221 members in 1917, for an annual average membership growth of 3.36%. Mississippi Baptists increased from 42 associations, 1,183 churches, and 89,426 members in 1877 to 56 associations, 1,515 churches, and 172,480 members in 1917, for an average annual membership growth of 2.26%. For the first time Oklahoma and Indian Territory were included in the federal census reports. With the organization of the Baptist General Convention of Oklahoma in 1906 it became possible to secure accurate statistics about Baptists in the state. Single affiliation with the Southern Baptist Convention occurred in 1914, and by 1917 there were 49 associations, 1,142 churches, and 90,617 Southern Baptists in Oklahoma.

North Central Region. In previous periods, the only state in this region involved in Southern Baptist life was Missouri. The story of the Southern Baptist affiliation with Baptists in southern Illinois, which began in 1910, will be told elsewhere. The number of Baptists in this region increased from 66 associations, 1,328 churches, and 79,546 members (in Missouri only) in 1877 to 108 associations, 2,542 churches, and 275,906 members in both Missouri and Illinois by 1917. This represented an average annual membership increase of 6.02%. The population in Missouri and Illinois, meanwhile, grew from 5,246,251 in 1880 to 9,889,335 in 1920. This was an average annual growth of 2.16%, barely more than one third of the Baptist rate of increase.

Missouri Baptists grew from the statistics shown above for 1877 to 82 associations, 1,956 churches, and 212,544 members in 1917, or an average annual membership growth of 4.08%. Illinois Baptists affiliating with the Southern Baptist Convention had 26 associations, 586 churches, and 63,362 members in 1917.

Mountain Region. New Mexico was the only state related to the Southern Baptist Convention in 1917 in this region. The story of their initial affiliation is told elsewhere. By 1917 they had 8 associations, 144 churches, and 6,707 Southern Baptists. The population of New Mexico increased from 119,565 in 1880 to 360,350 in 1920, representing an average annual growth of 2.32%, but no comparison can be made with the rate of Baptist growth.

Common Patterns of Denominational Development

As previously mentioned, the size and purpose of this volume do not permit even a state-by-state resume of the constantly enlarging activities of the Baptist churches, associations, and state bodies related to the Southern Baptist Convention during this and succeeding periods, except in the case of newly-organized state bodies. Adequate source material for such a detailed study is readily available and is quite inspirational and instructive. The alternative method chosen for this story was to digest the extensive materials and identify patterns of development and activity common to most Baptists related to the Convention, thus keeping abreast of interacting factors between the constituency and the Southern Baptist Convention. These patterns include improved organizational structures and additional benevolent ministries by the various state bodies, significant population mobility as manifested in the transfer of church members from section to section, the importance of the evangelistic outreach, the increasing number and additional training of the ministry, and a growing denominational consciousness.

Improved Organizational Structures and Enlarged Ministries. Practically every state body affiliating with the Southern Baptist Convention improved its organizational structure during this period. In the South Atlantic region this pattern was quite prominent. A new district body was formed for District of Columbia in 1877. The Florida convention underwent several improvements in structure and constitution. Georgia elected its first mission secretary in 1877. In 1879 Maryland Baptists underwent a constitutional revision. North Carolina restructured several functions in her state body. Although South Carolina retained substantially the same organization it had approved in 1865, the headquarters were moved to Columbia in this period to provide a more central location. Virginia historians remarked that the 1880's constituted the most constructive decade in the history of the General Association up to that time.

More radical changes took place in the South Central region. Alabama reorganized its state body in 1914; a new constitution was adopted in Arkansas in 1902; Kentucky Baptists organized for more effective service during this period, but there was still opposition to associational and state bodies on the ground that they might overwhelm the autonomy of the churches. Louisiana reorganized its work in 1885, while Mississippi made several structural changes in the 1880's and in the last decade of this period. Tennessee Baptists modified their 1874 structure with a constitutional change in 1904 and thereafter. Texas Baptists united their several conventions in 1886, and in 1914 formed an executive board for more effective work.

Each of the eighteen states affiliated with the Southern Baptist Convention during this period showed a substantial increase in the kinds of ministries in which it was engaged. As pointed out, practically every state in the four regions of the South altered the structure of its state body in such fashion as to become more efficient in the task of spreading the gospel within the state. The general philosophy varied from state to state. For example, Tennessee in 1916 employed 68 field workers, while providing assistance to 66 missionary pastors. On the other hand, in that same year Texas employed but 2 field workers, while providing financial assistance to 332 missionary pastors. Year by year each state reported an increasing program of state missions. In 1916, for example, the 6 South Atlantic states (not including District of Columbia) employed 17 administrators for state mission work, 56 field workers, provided assistance for 680 pastors, and spent a total of $291,657 for state mission work during the year. In that year the South Central region employed 16 administrators for the 8 states, 102 field workers, and provided assistance for 955 mission pastors, with total expenditures reaching $353,823. The 2 North Central states of Illinois and Missouri employed 3 administrators, 56 field workers, and provided assistance for 121 mission pastors, raising $48,123 for this task. New Mexico in the Mountain region provided 1 administrator, 11 field workers, gave assistance to 56 mission pastors, and spent $19,047. The total state mission program of Southern Baptists in 1916, then, included 37 administrators, 225 field workers, assistance for 1,812 mission pastors, with a total of $713,270 raised for this task during the year. During that year, although Oklahoma and District of Columbia did not report, state missionaries in these areas reported having baptized a total of 31,059 persons.

Practically every state body by 1917 engaged in educational activity, operated orphanages, and many of them were involved in a hospital ministry. It was reported at the 1916 Convention, for example, that 5 of the 6 South Atlantic states (not including District of Columbia) were maintaining colleges, while 3 of them were operating 23 additional secondary schools. These same 5 out of the 6 states (with the exception of Maryland) were operating orphanages, while Georgia and South Carolina were operating hospitals. The 8 South Central states were operating 16 colleges, 17 secondary schools, 10 orphanages, and 5 hospitals. Each of the 2 North Central states was operating a college, while Missouri also had an orphanage and a hospital. This made a total of 23 colleges, 40 secondary schools, 16 orphanages, and 8 hospitals.

During this period from 1877 to 1917, several of the states purchased the denominational newspapers from private individuals and utilized them to promote the work of the state body.

Population Mobility. The size and mobility of the population have been important factors in the growth of all denominations. People provided grist for the mill. Baptists, of course, depended upon individual conversions for their membership. The rearing of children in a Baptist home might provide more favorable circumstances for winning those children to Christ and Baptist membership, but this did not guarantee that the children of Baptists would themselves choose the Baptist way. Prospects for Baptist life, then, included both children of the Baptist population and other unconverted and unenlisted persons in a given community. The net increase in population, which involved both births and immigrants, constituted a challenge for Southern Baptist people.

It has been noted that Southern Baptist growth far outstripped that of the population in all four of the regions. It is not always true that the state or region showing the largest population growth necessarily showed the largest Baptist growth. In the South Atlantic region, for example, North Carolina showed only an average population growth of 2.02% between 1880 and 1920, while in the comparable period the annual average Baptist growth was a whopping 5.84%. Similarly in the South Central section, for example, Alabama showed an average annual population increase during this period of 2.09%, while the Baptist growth showed an increase of 5.90%. It is noticeable, however, that usually a large population increase in any state or section resulted in a large increase in the number of Baptists in that section. As an example of this, Florida increased in general population at an annual average of 6.32% between 1880 and 1920, while the Baptist population during the comparable period increased annually 14.02%. In the South Central region, Arkansas increased an average of 2.89% in general population annually during the period, while the Baptist population increased 7.02%. Texas increased in general population at an average annual rate of 4.71%, while the Baptist increase was 11.86% annually. That is to say, population increases often were reflected in the rate of increase in Baptists in the state or region.

An important factor in determining where and why Baptists had their greatest increase involves the mobility of the population. Historians agree that the western frontier drew many people from the South Atlantic region until about 1890. Thereafter, the rapid industrialization of the seaboard states, providing railroads, mill towns, etc., served to stabilize the population, and the westward immigration declined substantially. An interesting reflection of this situation is seen in the transfer of letters from one Baptist church to another. In the South Atlantic region, most of the states showed an annual loss by letter during most of the period.[1] More Baptists were lettered out of these churches before 1900 than were received by letter during that same period. Florida was the general exception to this rule, since this area became a very popular place for settlers. The population increased at an average annual rate of 6.32% between 1880 and 1920. The opening of far southern Florida to railroad transportation before 1900 and the drainage of the Everglades begun about 1907 increasingly turned people toward the state. Except for the years 1877 through 1880, Florida Baptists received more persons by letter and statement than they lettered out. During the entire period from 1877 to 1917, they received 58,303 persons by letter and statement and lettered out 46,466. Adequate figures for District of Columbia cannot be secured, likely because of the dual nature of the relationship of many of the churches there. Georgia Baptists lettered out more persons than they received by letter and statement every year from 1877 to 1909 with the exception of 1878 and 1881. During this period they received by letter and statement 355,783, while losing 369,050. In this period before 1900, Maryland granted more letters during fourteen of the years and received more letters in nine of the years. Over the entire period, Maryland gained 10,869 persons by letter and statement, while losing 10,207. From 1877 to 1908, North Carolina Baptists lettered out more persons than they received by letter and statement. However, in six of the years between 1908 and 1917, they showed a few more letters received than letters granted. Over the entire period, North Carolina Baptists received by letter and statement a total of 204,488 persons, while lettering out 214,934. Approximately the same picture is seen in South Carolina. Between 1877 and 1904, South Carolina Baptists lettered out more persons every year than they received by letter and statement. However, beginning in 1904, South Carolina Baptists received more by letter every year through 1917 than they lost. With these substantial gains after 1904, South Carolina received during the entire period 136,381 Baptists, while losing only 134,641. Virginia Baptists reflect about the same picture. During the years between 1877 and 1890, they lost more Baptists by letter than they gained every year, with the exception of 1886. However, beginning in 1890, Virginia Baptists showed more received by letter and statement each year than they lost. Their totals for the entire period between 1877 and 1917 showed 132,615 gained by letter and statement, while they lost only 117,160.

This summary reveals that in the South Atlantic states during the period between 1877 and 1917, this region gained 898,439 members by letter and statement, while losing 892,458. Most of the losses came in the years before 1900, after which this region not only held as many of its own Baptist people as it lost by letter, but generally gained members in this fashion.

The eastern portions of the South Central region also showed the effects of western migration before the turn of the century. In only one year before 1901 did Alabama Baptists show more additions by letter and statement than losses. However, in fifteen out of the seventeen years thereafter during the remainder of this period, Alabama Baptists showed gains by letters over losses. Over the entire period they gained 237,384 by letter and statement, while losing 235,956. A similar picture is seen in Kentucky. Before 1909, only six of the thirty-two years showed more additions by letter and statement than losses. However, during the last nine years of the period there was not a single report of losing more by letter than gaining. Over the entire period, Kentucky Baptists received 191,332 by letter and statement, while losing 195,728 in this way. Between 1877 and 1905,

Mississippi Baptists lost more by letter every year than they gained. However, from 1905 to 1917, only four years showed losses at this point. Over the entire period, the state received by letter and statement a total of 159,951 persons, while losing 166,709. Tennessee had about the same experience. Before 1906, in only four of the twenty-seven years did Tennessee Baptists show more gains by letter and statement than they lost by letter. However, each year between 1906 and 1917 showed more gains than losses. Over the entire period Tennessee Baptists gained 152,486 by letter and statement, while losing 153,366.

Farther west in the South Central region, there was a different picture. In twenty-seven of the forty-one years of the period, Arkansas Baptists showed more letters received than lost. Their final totals for the period were 125,780 received by letter and statement and 116,563 lost by letter. Louisiana Baptists had rather small gains and losses before 1900. Between 1877 and 1900, this state showed only six years in which there were more members received by letter and statement than those lost. This may reflect the attraction of nearby burgeoning Texas. However, after 1900, Louisiana Baptists showed an increase every year. Their final totals between 1877 and 1917 showed 68,875 received by letter and statement, with losses totaling 59,333. Oklahoma (and Indian Territory, which were united in 1906) never had a year between 1877 and 1917 that did not show more gains than losses by letter. The total gains by letter and statement over the entire period were 94,833, while the losses were 63,269. Texas had the same experience. Every year during this entire period this state showed a remarkably large number of additions by letter and statement, far outdistancing the losses. The final figures showed 567,875 gained by letter and statement and 473,498 lost by letter during the entire period.

In the North Central region, Missouri showed the instability one would expect in a state that received many and sent many. Between 1877 and 1905, only nine years showed more additions by letter and statement than losses, but thereafter, eight of the fourteen years showed more gains than losses. Overall, Missouri Baptists gained 224,296 by letter, while losing 222,679. Southern Illinois Baptists, between 1911 and 1917, showed an increase during half of the years. Their total figures were 10,273 gained by letter and statement, with 10,342 lost in this way.

In New Mexico, from 1914 through 1917, Baptists showed a gain every year, the final figures showing 2,870 gained by letter and statement, with 1,471 lost.

This survey confirms for Southern Baptists what historians generally have noted concerning the entire population. Before the turn of the century the frontier drew many of the people from the East. Baptists were included in these, as evidenced by the fact that during this early period most of the South Atlantic states showed yearly losses by letter and statement. At the same time the Baptist migration continued to go West from the eastern South Central states, as seen in the losses in such states as Alabama, Tennessee, and Kentucky during the earlier years of this period. The largest gains by letter and statement were made by the southwestern states of Arkansas, Oklahoma, and Texas. After the turn of the century, the increased industrialization of the southeastern states, along with the extension of railroads, provided a more stable situation in these states.

Evangelistic Outreach. The most determinative single factor in Southern Baptist denominational advance in ·this period was the emphasis upon winning people to Christ. In the seven states of the South Atlantic region, 1,382,927 were baptized between 1877 and 1917; in the eight South Central states during this same period, 2,158,632 were baptized; in the two states comprising the North Central region, 393,771 were baptized; while in the brief period the single Mountain region state was a part of Southern Baptist life, 2,427 were baptized. The accelerated rate of baptisms after the first half of this period is shown by the fact that in the first twenty years of the period the number of baptisms in the South Atlantic section averaged 25,649 per year, while in the last twenty-one years of the period, baptisms averaged 65,854 each year. Similarly in the South Central section, during the first half of the period, baptisms averaged 36,572 each year, while in the latter half of the period, they averaged 67,961 yearly. In the North Central region, baptisms averaged 7,368 during the first half of the period, while each year during the second half of the period baptisms were 11,736. For all Southern Baptists, during the first half of the period baptisms totaled 1,391,777, while for the last half of the period they totaled 2,545,980. The grand total of all baptisms in this period was 3,937,757.[2]

Since the net Baptist gain between 1877 and 1917 was 1,938,227, only about half the number of baptisms, it might be well to scrutinize these statistics a little more closely to see what happened. At first glance it might appear that Southern Baptists were very lax in the matter of enlisting those who were baptized. However, the reverse seems to be true relative to laxness. The records between 1877 and 1917 indicate that 557,610 church members died, although this figure must be seen as a bare minimum, since in the early years the statistics from many of the states showed very few deaths in the white churches. The significant statistic was one showing that Southern Baptists excluded from their membership between 1877 and 1917 a total of 861,730 persons. This was an average of 20,018 per year for forty-one years. In addition, another 160,052 were erased from the roll during this period, making a total of 1,031,132 who were disciplined or dropped from the rolls. During this time the churches reported restorations numbering 336,348. This left 694,784 who were disciplined or removed from the rolls and not restored at any time.

These figures suggest, then, that the careful disciplining of church members was much more of a factor in diminishing the net gain between 1877 and 1917 than any failure to conserve the results of evangelism. This practice of sharp discipline was not limited to the earlier years of the period. In fact, this particular figure increased year by year through 1917. For example, in Texas alone there were 38,749 exclusions (including erasures, which were combined with this figure in the reports of 1915-17) during the last ten years of this period, indicating the continuance of the active practice of disciplining members in the churches. Had it not been for the extensive evangelistic outreach of Southern Baptists, the losses through discipline, deaths, and "trunk" Baptists would have eliminated any net gain.

A Growing and Better Equipped Leadership. One of the remarkable developments of Southern Baptist life, undoubtedly an important reason for the rapid growth, has been the enlistment and training of Baptist leadership. The theological stance of Baptists has included the conviction that preachers were called immediately of God without reference to educational, ecclesiastical, or intellectual prerequisites. Many a farmer plowing his furrow reproduced the experience of Isaiah by responding, "Here am I, send me." Soon he described his call to those in the tiny congregation where he worshiped, and if his character and life displayed evidences of Christian dedication, he was usually set apart by license or ordination to practice his gifts. The normal pattern found this man toiling during the week to support himself and his family, and using Saturday and Sunday to preach here and there, or to become pastor of a small congregation which would pay him no salary. Like Paul, most of the early Baptist preachers practiced some sort of "tentmaking" as a part of their regimen. This pattern almost eliminated the problems of ministerial recruitment, compensation, and ecclesiastical oversight that plagued some denominations, particularly on the frontier, but the other side of the coin was not so impressive: it provided little opportunity for an educated ministry. Indeed, for varying motives that were not always theological, some early Baptists felt that the experience of God's call was all that a person needed. God would provide the message and wisdom for his messenger's service. An unpaid preacher was exhibited as evidence that he was no "hireling" of man, and his lack of education showed his dependence upon God. The common people heard him gladly. It was to this large constituency that Alexander Campbell and Gilbert Beebe appealed so forcefully in the period just before the founding of the Southern Baptist Convention.

Had this attitude become general among Baptists and provided the norm for their ministry, the results would have been disastrous. But theological and cultural factors were an early corrective to this extreme position. The Scriptures needed interpretation and application, so the preacher found himself wrestling with theological and social problems in an effort to interpret God and his world to the congregation. Fierce controversies arose which demanded training in theology and logic if one wanted to reply. A Baptist historian remarked that Campbellism in Alabama was one of the important factors forwarding ministerial education for this very reason. The general educational level of the people began to challenge the minister's understanding. Many educated and eloquent men (particularly lawyers) received the call to preach, and their effectiveness was an object lesson to young ministers. Some ministers, like Richard Furman of South Carolina, who had struggled to secure an education and recognized its value, assumed the responsibility of providing opportunities for others.

As a consequence, even before the founding of the Southern Baptist Convention in 1845, Baptists in the South were rejecting the idea that human education was unnecessary for a man who had received a divine call. When the consultative meeting took place at Augusta in 1845, as pointed out previously, there were already at least seven permanent denominational senior colleges in six southern states, together with numerous smaller schools and academies that served for a relatively short time. In the period between 1845 and 1860, five junior colleges in four states, four senior colleges or universities in three states, and one theological seminary had been established. Between 1861 and 1877, one junior college and three senior colleges or universities were constituted. In the period now under study (1877-1917), permanent Baptist academies were begun in Louisiana and Texas and two in Virginia; permanent junior colleges were founded in Virginia, South Carolina, Georgia, Kentucky, Mississippi, Missouri, Texas, and two in North Carolina; and permanent senior colleges or universities were organized in North Carolina, Florida, Kentucky, Mississippi, Arkansas, Louisiana, Oklahoma, and four in Texas. A new theological seminary was formed also in the latter state.

The favorable attitude toward education and its importance became quite evident in this period. The ministers included in the *Encyclopedia of Southern Baptists* by the nomination of the states involved would certainly not represent the average Southern Baptist minister of the period from 1877 to 1917. The significance of their service, however, was recognized and constitutes a cross-section of the quality of leadership during the period. It should be noted here that in the South Atlantic region, 63 out of the 81 ministers named had a college education or beyond (almost 78%). In the South Central region, 97 out of the 151 ministers named had a college education or beyond (over 64%). In the North Central region, 4 out of the 10 ministers named had a college education or beyond (40%); while in New Mexico in the Mountain region, the single minister named was college educated. Total figures from this source, then, show that 165 of the 243 ministers named during this period in the *Encyclopedia* had a college education or beyond, or almost 68%.[3]

It should also be pointed out that Southern Baptist leadership was not confined to ministers or males alone, but that laymen and women in this period were increasingly holding important posts of denominational leadership. Furthermore, the significance of the educational enterprise becomes more apparent in the review of the large number of ministers and laymen engaged actively as teachers and administrators in higher educational institutions during this period. Evidence of expertise also is suggested by the number of authors and editors that were prominent during this period.

A biographical study of the 121 leaders named in the *Encyclopedia of Southern Baptists* for this period in the South Atlantic region is revealing. Of the 3 District of Columbia leaders named, all of them had a college education or beyond, 2 were educators, 2 were authors, and 2 were laymen. Of the 8 Maryland leaders, 3 had a college education or beyond, 1 was an educator, 1 an author, 1 a publisher, 3 were laymen, and 1 was a woman. Of the 24 Virginia leaders, 15 had a college education or beyond, 7 were educators, 7 were authors, 5 were editors, 4 were laymen, and 4 were women. Of the 32 leaders in North Carolina, 28 had a college education or beyond, 17 were educators, 9 were authors, 6 were editors, 10 were laymén (including 3 governors and 1 United States senator), and 2 were women. Of the 16 South Carolina leaders, 11 had a college education or beyond, 4 were educators, 2 were authors, 5 were editors, 3 were laymen, and 1 was a woman. Of the 34 Georgia leaders, 24 had a college education or beyond, 18 were educators, 7 were authors, 3 were editors, and 6 were laymen (including 2 governors and a United States senator). Of the 4 Florida leaders, 3 had a college education or beyond, 1 was an educator, 1 was an author, and 1 was an editor. In the entire region, of the 121 named, 87 had a college education or beyond, 50 were educators, 29 were authors, 1 was a publisher, 20 were editors, 28 were laymen (including 5 governors and 2 United States senators), and 8 were women.

In summary of the South Central region, a total of 207 leaders were included in the *Encyclopedia* for this period. Of the 32 leaders in Kentucky, 22 had a college education or beyond, 18 were teachers or educators, 20 were authors, 7 were editors, and 3 were laymen.

Of the 20 leaders named for Tennessee, 12 were college graduates or beyond, 7 were teachers or educators, 9 were authors, 1 was a publisher, 5 were editors, and 6 were laymen. Of the 29 leaders in Alabama, 18 were college graduates or beyond, 9 were teachers or educators, 8 were authors, 3 were editors, 7 were laymen (including a United States senator), and 2 were women. Of the 22 leaders named for Mississippi, 10 were college graduates or beyond, 8 were teachers or educators, 4 were authors, 4 were editors, 7 were laymen, and 2 were women. Of the 20 named Arkansas leaders, 12 were college graduates or beyond, 4 were teachers or educators, 3 were authors, 3 were editors, 4 were laymen (including a governor), and 1 was a woman. Of the 14 leaders in Louisiana, 10 were college graduates or beyond, 4 were teachers or educators, 3 were authors, 2 were editors, and 1 was a layman. Of the 28 leaders named in Oklahoma and Indian Territory, 9 were college graduates or beyond, 4 were teachers or educators, 2 were authors, 3 were editors, 1 was a layman, and 3 were women. Of the 42 leaders in Texas, 36 were college graduates or beyond, 26 were teachers or educators, 21 were authors, 16 were editors, 11 were laymen, and 3 were women. In the entire region, out of the 207 leaders named, 129 had received a college education or beyond, 80 were teachers or educators, 70 were authors, 1 was a publisher, 43 were editors, 40 were laymen (including a United States senator and a governor), and 11 were women.

In the North Central region, 7 leaders were named in Missouri and 5 in Illinois. In the former, 5 had college educations, 5 were educators, 3 were authors, 3 were editors, and 1 was a layman. In Illinois, 2 were editors and 1 was a layman.

In the Mountain region (New Mexico), of the 3 leaders named for this period, 2 evidently were college trained, 1 was an educator, 1 was an author, 1 was an editor, and 2 were laymen.

Although the choices made for inclusion in the *Encyclopedia* doubtless would not represent an average Southern Baptist group, it is true that this compilation suggests the emphasis on education being given by Southern Baptists during this period as seen in the college graduates, the educators (which included teachers and university presidents), authors, and editors. The large place of laymen and women in denominational leadership can also be glimpsed.

It is somewhat difficult to get exact figures on the number of ministers during this period. In 1877 it was reported that there were 6,903 ordained ministers, while the number of churches was 12,603; in 1917 the *Annual* reported 15,946 ordained ministers and 24,883 churches. This doubtless reflects the rural character and small size of many of the churches, who probably had "quarter-time" or "half-time" preaching; i.e., one person would be pastor of three or four small churches, alternating his preaching ministry among them. On the other hand, the rapid growth in the number of ministers after the close of this period suggests that perhaps the poor keeping of records provided a part of the disparity between the number of pastors and churches.

An interesting development during this period involved the image of an outstanding minister. During the earlier periods the principal leaders were those who could stand in the pulpit, take direct and eloquent aim with a sermon, and never miss the mark. A survey of the *Encyclopedia of Southern Baptists* indicates that the outstanding people of this period (chosen by the several states to appear in the volume from that state) were not primarily great pulpit leaders, but, on the contrary, were strong denominational figures. The mission secretary of a state, for example, was usually named in this and succeeding periods, while pulpit orators were sometimes overlooked. In addition, new categories of specialization in ministry were beginning to develop in this period—Sunday School, Training Union, music, Woman's Missionary Union, and laymen in both state and southwide structures. These church ministries grew rapidly after the turn of the century.

In the western regions, in particular, however, the number of ordained ministers listed in 1877 could be misleading. Even this late many simple farmers toiled throughout the week in various aspects of spiritual tentmaking, but when Saturday came, they were transformed into fiery messengers witnessing to the grace of God. In Texas, for example, during a part of this period there was an instance of the existence of only one paid minister in an entire huge county. The rest of the churches were served by self-supporting men or an occasional itinerant preacher who might appear. This situation is reflected somewhat by the fact that in the entire Southern Baptist Convention in 1877 there were almost twice as many churches as the number of ordained ministers recorded. At the close of the period in 1917 the number of churches and ministers reported had just about doubled.

A Heightened Denominational Consciousness. As mentioned previously in connection with the Convention's ministry, this period witnessed a substantial increase in the denominational consciousness of Southern Baptists. This was reflected by the state and associational bodies in a definite movement toward group promotion of benevolences common to all Southern Baptists. The denominational papers became agents of promotion, and the general spirit seemed to be that expressed by Basil Manly, Jr., in 1863 when he was attempting to show the value of group promotion in Sunday School work. He had then said:

There seems to be no imperative reason restricting this work to State limits. The same plan and means which are effectual in one region will apply, if extended, to another. The books which suit Virginia Baptist Sunday Schools, will be useful to Alabama, and the agencies for stimulating interest in the subject in Georgia, can be applied with little increase of expenditure, and great increase of efficiency to the Carolinas. In fact, while aggregate expense slightly enlarged, the expense to each is greatly diminished, since many thousands can be supplied at much smaller individual cost than few—and if it has been found in other operations, that a general union is desirable, all the arguments apply, and some of them with increased force, to show that Sunday Schools, too, may be more efficiently promoted by similar united efforts.[4]

In the period from 1877 to 1917, additional group promotional patterns were accelerated for the benevolences fostered by the state and Convention-wide structures. Uniform denominational emphases were developed by the various states in promoting the several church auxiliaries such as the Sunday School, Training Union, Woman's Missionary Union, and Brotherhood, as well as state missions, education, hospitals, etc. States copied from one another in improved structures and methodology. Statistical reports on progress were standardized, and Convention leaders crusaded for each church, association, and state convention to follow the patterns of structure and methodology that were found to be successful and were promoted in the denominational literature.

Consolidation of rival state structures was common during this period, as in the case of Texas, Tennessee, and Oklahoma, while other state bodies centralized more of their functions under a single authority. Executive secretaries became the principal statewide leaders in forwarding all state benevolences. Additional internal unity was provided as the Southern Baptist Convention's Sunday School Board assisted the states financially in employing leaders for promoting uniform methods in the various church-related auxiliaries.

Perhaps another distinctive practice among Southern Baptists during this period served to deepen their sense of denominational uniqueness. At a time when liberal winds were blowing, causing many denominations to magnify the social aspects of the gospel, sometimes even in opposition to the initial need for individual regeneration, Southern Baptists were placing great emphasis upon evangelism and mass revival meetings. A Department of Evangelism was added to the Home Mission Board in 1906, and state programs involving the holding of "protracted meetings" were the common pattern among Southern Baptists when other groups were abandoning it. L. R. Scarborough reflected the temper of Southern Baptists in 1911 when he asserted that the South was peculiarly suited to this method of winning souls. He pointed to the climate, the long summers and open winters; the general reverence for the sabbath; the strong evangelical influence in this section of the nation; the freedom from form and ritual that marked the simple life of the people in the South; the love for the spiritual in the South; and the conservative nature of the southern people and the southern gospel.

Another evidence of this growing denominational consciousness stemmed from the series of comity conferences with northern Baptists beginning in 1894. The story of the transfer of New Mexico affiliation from North to South has been told previously, one of the spin-offs from which was the decision of Oklahoma Baptists to turn to affiliation with the southern body only. The friction in Missouri, which has also been described, resulted in dual affiliation under rather strained circumstances until a joint committee, made up of representatives from both northern and southern bodies, recommended in 1911 that state bodies should affiliate with only one general body and that majority sentiment should determine which one. Two years after the close of this period the state voted overwhelmingly for single alignment with the Southern Baptist Convention.[5] More portentous was the change to southern affiliation by Baptists in Illinois. In 1907, in a move that did not initially involve the Southern Baptist Convention at all, a large body of Baptists in southern Illinois separated from the Illinois Baptist General Association and formed the Illinois Baptist State Association. There were several reasons for this. The southern section of the state had been settled over a century before by immigrants from Georgia, Kentucky, and Tennessee. The northern area, on the other hand, was settled principally from New England, and the Home Mission Society of New York centered in the northern section most of the institutional life that it engendered. Originally, separate sectional bodies had been formed, the southern section in 1807 and the northern in 1834.[6] The basic reason for separation in 1907 stemmed from the conservative doctrinal views of the southern section. Baptists in that area had looked uneasily at the liberal doctrinal influence of the University of Chicago for some years. In 1906 one of the professors there published a book which offended Baptists in the southern section by its views on inspiration and the deity of Christ. After a confrontation in the General Association led by Editor W. P. Throgmorton of *The Illinois Baptist*, the new body was formed on January 31, 1907, at Pinckneyville. It grew rapidly and at first determined to carry on its own mission work and other benevolences without affiliation with a general body. However, in 1910 it began cooperation with the Southern Baptist Convention.[7]

Reference has already been made to the unifying effect of the work of the Sunday School Board. Another significant factor was Woman's Missionary Union. Following the organization of their general body in 1888, they rapidly became a substantial cohesive force in their state and Convention-wide programs of devotion, missionary education, enlistment in missionary activity, and promotion.

The impact of these and other influences on the constituency of the Southern Baptist Convention, unifying all of their denominational loyalties in a single general body and interlacing their religious activities in common denominational patterns, can explain the reluctance of Southern Baptist people to affiliate with even other Baptist churches of the same general doctrinal stance in states outside of the South.

Summary

The constituency of the Southern Baptist Convention grew substantially between 1877 and 1917. For the purpose of comparison, in seventeen southern states (not counting New Mexico, for which earlier figures are not available), the general population increased from 17,922,000 in 1880 to 41,328,434 in 1920. This represented an average annual growth rate of 3.27%. Southern Baptists, meanwhile, between 1877 and 1917 increased from 15 state bodies, 559 associations, 12,864 churches, and 906,074 members to 18 state bodies, 909 associations, 24,883 churches, and 2,844,301 members, or an average annual membership growth rate of 5.22%. This meant that Southern Baptists were more than doubling their original number every two decades. This rate of growth compares favorably with the average annual Southern Baptist increase during the previous periods (2.25% between 1860-77; 4.79% between 1845-60; and 7.20% between 1814-45) since the larger number of constituents makes percentage of growth more difficult to maintain. Southern Baptists outdistanced most other major denominations in the rate of growth.

* Regionally, the western areas (the South and North Central regions) continued to increase in the number of Baptists slightly more rapidly than the eastern seaboard. The South Atlantic region averaged a membership growth annually of 4.45%; the South Central region averaged 5.64%; the North Central region (only two states) averaged 6.02%. The sudden addition of Baptists in southern Illinois accounted for almost 2.0% of the growth in the North Central region. It will be recalled that the South Central region was recipient of a large number of church letters from eastern sections, so that the actual number of new Baptists probably was added at about the same rate in all three of the regions.

The seven states constituting the South Atlantic region contained 35.91% of all Southern Baptists in 1917, compared with 39.92% in 1877. Whereas Georgia Baptists had the largest Southern Baptist population in 1877 (13.19%), they had dropped to 11.10% in 1917, despite a sizable increase, and were second to Texas in 1917 as the state having the largest number of Baptists. North Carolina with 10.02%, Virginia with 6.29%, South Carolina with 5.66%, Florida with 2.14%, Maryland with .54%, and District of Columbia with .16% made up the remainder of the South Atlantic region with respect to the percentage of total Southern Baptists in each state of this region.

By 1917, 54.14% of all Southern Baptists lived in the eight South Central states of Kentucky, Tennessee, Alabama, Mississippi, Arkansas, Louisiana, Oklahoma, and Texas. The remarkable growth in Texas enabled that state to lead all others in the number of Baptists in the states related to the Southern Baptist Convention, as well as the highest percentage of total Southern Baptists in the state. The 1917 statistics showed that 13.49% of all Southern Baptists lived in Texas. Not far behind was Kentucky where 9.15% of all Southern Baptists lived, followed by Alabama with 7.79% and Tennessee with 7.33%. Mississippi had 6.06% of Southern Baptists, followed by Arkansas with 4.31%, Oklahoma with 3.18%, and Louisiana with 2.82%.

In the two states of the North Central region (Missouri and Illinois), 9.70% of all Southern Baptists resided in 1917, the former containing 7.47% and the latter, 2.23%.

New Mexico, the new Mountain region state, contained .235% of all Southern Baptists in 1917.

As pointed out, Southern Baptists ended this period in 1917 with three more cooperating states than they had in 1877. District of Columbia statistics were first shown in the 1889 Southern Baptist Convention *Annual*, at which time they reported 1 association, 11 churches, and 2,865 members. By 1917 the figures were 1 association, 9 churches, and 4,436 members. However, as noted before, it is virtually impossible to secure accurate and consistent statistics for District of Columbia Southern Baptists. The first unified figures for Oklahoma and Indian Territory were shown in the 1907 *Annual* of the Convention. They reported for 1906 a total of 40 associations, 855 churches, and 44,971 members. By 1917 these had increased to 49 associations, 1,142 churches, and 90,617 members. The Illinois Baptist State Association began affiliation with the Southern Baptist Convention in 1910, in which year they reported 22 associations, 522 churches, and 49,398 members. By 1917, these statistics had increased to 26 associations, 586 churches, and 63,362 members. The Baptist General Convention of New Mexico began reporting in 1912 to the Southern Baptist Convention, in which year they showed 6 associations, 166 churches, and 6,323 members. Their figures in 1917 were 8 associations, 144 churches, and 6,707 members.

The significance of the addition of these new constituents by 1917 is more than the numbers involved, particularly in the cases of Oklahoma, southern Illinois, and New Mexico. These three states were burgeoning areas, and the addition of these churches and members provided a stepping-stone for additional geographical expansion.

As one surveys the story of Southern Baptists between 1877 and 1917, a clear picture emerges. The Baptist center was moving farther west, as the population generally was doing, and the southwestern states of Arkansas, Oklahoma, and Texas benefited with increased additions by letter and statement. The secret of Southern Baptist growth during the period, however, was in the winning of people to Christ and the emphasis on evangelism. A strong discipline was practiced in all of the states during this period, accounting for a smaller net gain than would be anticipated from the number of baptisms. The structure of the organizations in many states was refined and strengthened to permit enlarged ministries. Additional unity in objectives was developing across the South during all of the period, and especially after 1891. A significant item in growth was the geographical expansion into three new states during this period. The negative factors that could have severely stunted the growth of Southern Baptists were not sufficiently widespread to do this.

It was neither accidental nor incidental that Southern Baptists moved more rapidly toward a trained ministry as well as an educated constituency during this period. Very few Southern Baptists discounted the importance of education for both the ministry and the other constituency by 1917. The increasing number of schools, universities, and seminaries in this period reflect the two-fold foci of Baptist doctrine at the point of ministerial leadership. The unconditional and urgent ministerial call—disregarding age, education, or human circumstances—must unfailingly be matched with the Baptist doctrine of the priesthood of the believer, demanding intelligent interpretation of God's message and the individual application of divine principles to human conditions. The former doctrine drove men to their knees, while the latter sent them to their books. A call to preach became a call to study, and the next period will reveal a remarkable educational thrust by Southern Baptists.

Southern Baptists clearly developed a stronger denominational consciousness during this period because of the converging factors mentioned in the last three chapters. The structural tensions imbedded in the convention-type structure in 1845 through the retention of society-type characteristics were beginning to be debated in almost every session of the Convention. The founding of the first Executive Committee in 1917 was a large step toward minimizing one of these tensions by providing a de facto existence for the Convention between the annual sessions of the body. The fundamentalist-liberal and sociological-conversion confrontations being experienced by many denominations in this period were reserved to agitate Southern Baptists in later decades.

Notes

1. This material has been compiled by examining the year-by-year statistics in the *Annuals* of the Southern Baptist Convention.

2. *Ibid.*

3. These figures should be treated as not completely representative nor accurate, since many of the ministers constantly moved from one region to another, some could be included in more than one chronological period, and in some instances the information seemed to be incomplete. The persons included in the *Encyclopedia* were not average in their educational qualifications. The estimate that approximately 59% of Southern Baptist ministers in 1899 had no college training is probably rather accurate. See Rufus W. Weaver, "Life and Times of William Heth Whitsitt," *Review and Expositor* (Louisville), April, 1940, p. 121.

4. Baker, *Source Book*, p. 130.

5. Baker, *Relations*, pp. 198-99.

6. *Ibid.*, pp. 187-191.

7. *Ibid.*, p. 190.

THE MODERN ERA
1917–1972

From the First Executive Committee
of the Convention to the Present

15 Witnessing Across the Southland and Beyond

The war that opened the modern era of Southern Baptist life was symbolical of the revolutionary nature of the period that it ushered in. Revolutions of every sort have crowded the years that have followed. Many of the radical movements sprang from extreme personal tensions induced by the tumultuous events of the period. People have been ill-equipped to cope with events of fearful proportions when their faith has been undermined by massive scientific, philosophical, and even religious attacks. Frustration and cynicism often have had no outlet save dependence on alcohol and other drugs. Social injustices of many kinds have been confronted, often accompanied by physical violence. Some of the areas of confrontation have involved racial discrimination (blacks, Mexican-Americans, and Indians, in particular), war, atomic weapons, women's rights, population explosion, rampant inflation, distrust of big government and the established order, taxes, poverty, urban decay, abortion, traditional religious and moral patterns, school busing, the generation gap, loss of identity in the mass production and mass assembly syndrome, religious discrimination, prayers in public schools, environmental pollution, and communal living.

342   Politically, the period was marked by two world wars, not to speak of conflicts in Korea (1950-53) and southeast Asia (about 1964 to about 1973—a Vietnam peace treaty was signed on January 27, 1973, but the related war in nearby Cambodia went on with American support). In the Second World War (1941-45), the atomic age was inaugurated on August 6, 1945, adding a breathless fear to other stresses. A new kind of arms race was begun, involving the possibility of bombardment from satellites in orbit around the earth. A modified type of diplomacy has evolved in the recognition that any major power possessing atomic weapons could doubtless destroy the inhabitants of the world by explosion or radical pollution of the earth, water, and air.

The world waited anxiously when the two great powers—the United States and the Soviet Union—confronted one another in Berlin in 1948-49, which the United States may have won with the airlift of food and supplies when the Soviets had blockaded the roads to the city. Another sensitive spot has been Palestine, where the new state of Israel and the Arabs fought in 1956 and again in 1967, and remain hostile to the present time. The strategic location of this area and its vast oil resources could make it pivotal in world history. The successful structuring of an atomic bomb in 1964 by Communist China and her development of a satellite to deliver it to distant targets has brounght new dimensions to the strategic position of the United States. The Soviet-American confrontation over Cuban missles in 1962 brought widespread trepidation.

In this period the "sturdy individualism" of early America was eroded much more rapidly by governmental intervention. Gone was the old laisse faire principle which viewed as best the government that governed least. Under President Franklin D. Roosevelt (1933-45), all of the resources of government were tapped to bolster the economy during the great depression of the 1930's. Closely related to the federal involvement in the economic and social patterns of the nation has been the clout it has been able to muster in every area of private enterprise in insuring the constitutional rights of all of its citizens. The rapid growth of population (from 103,414,000 in 1920 to 203,184,000 in 1970) and the extreme mobility of the citizenry have had religious overtones. This mobility can be glimpsed, for example, in that in 1940 there were 31,000,000 people living on farms, 27,000,000 living in the suburbs, and 45,000,000 in the central city; but by 1970, there were but 10,000,000 on the farms, 74,000,000 had moved to the suburbs, and 63,000,000 lived in the central city.[1]

Economically, this has been an era of extreme fluctuations. The rural post-war recession of the 1920's was followed by the stock market collapse of 1929 and the worst depression in American history in the 1930's. After World War II ended in 1945, a prolonged and constantly worsening period of inflation developed, partly caused by governmental expenditures, foreign aid policies, and credit card over-spending by the people. Continuing battles between capital and labor have added to the inflationary process. Automation and the application of scientific technology to management and industry have mechanized white- and blue-collar workers and labor, almost eliminating creativity and a sense of personal achievement from the daily work of the majority of people. A restless, mobile population has developed from the exploitation of new resources in various parts of the nation, including the industrialization of the South.

In the religious sphere, the theological optimism and extreme liberalism of the early decades of the twentieth century were modified by the events of the 1920's and 1930's. The neoorthodoxy of Karl Barth and others, which took God, sin, and salvation seriously, attracted a large following. Confrontations between liberalism and fundamentalism or conservativism have occurred in many denominations. The ecumenical movement has been structured on a world basis, and a number of denominations have merged. Proponents of ecumenism were cheered by Vatican Council II, begun under Pope John XXIII (1958-63) in 1962. It is too soon to predict the results of this council. In the various social, political, and economic confrontations of the later decades of this period, religious activism has been prominent by leaders of many denominations. New "free" patterns of Christian sectarianism have appeared, some of which are radically different from traditional forms and beliefs. Religious revivals have been promoted through mass media of radio and television, as in the case of Billy Graham. Lay leadership has increased greatly, and social Christianity has been accelerated. Charismatic movements have sprung up in all old-line denominations. Such High Church advocates as the Roman Catholic Church and the Protestant Episcopal Church have developed large groups of such neopentecostals within their ranks.

In this context, Southern Baptists have made significant advances. The story of the constituency of the Southern Baptist Convention during this period falls naturally into two geographical sections: the older South where Southern Baptists had been prosecuting their work before the opening of the modern period, and the new geographical areas into which Southern Baptists have moved during this period. Such an outline will permit comparisons between the growth of Southern Baptists in the older regions with the growth experienced in the same regions during previous periods; at the same time, it will allow a unified description of the geographical expansion into the new areas, which has occurred in a distinctive pattern.

Substantial Progress in the Older Southern States

The annuals and histories of the various older states of the South reflect a common story during this period. In every state the general pattern has been similar: the loss of young men from the churches and the auxiliaries during World War I (1917-18); the great influenza epidemic of 1918 which caused baptisms to fall to a major low; the Seventy-five Million Campaign (1919-24); the agonizing struggles with debts during the two decades following the close of the campaign; the radical drop in baptisms between 1925 and 1929 and in gifts between 1930 and 1933; new problems of affluence and expansion after World War II (1941-45); cooperation in the evangelistic campaigns of 1950 and 1951, and the enthusiastic push for a Million More in '54 (in Sunday School); the Baptist Jubilee Advance (1959-64); and the numerous tensions occasioned by the political, economic, social, and religious upheavals that followed the Second World War.

There was also a rapid acceleration in the development of uniform patterns in structure and activity by churches, associations, and state bodies. Reference was made in the last period to the increasing growth of group planning, methodology, and promotion. In this period it becomes possible to identify "major items" common to all churches, associations, and states in their activity. Some of the reasons for this growth of uniformity may be briefly identified. (1) The centripetal nature of the Southern Baptist Convention. The kind of general body adopted by Southern Baptists in 1845 tended to pull all denominational activities into its structure. As a result, whenever a new benevolent movement developed in any part of the territory of the Convention and was operating successfully and fruitfully, the leadership in the Convention endeavored to incorporate that activity into its program on the theory that what was good in one locality would be good for the whole constituency. It should be remarked that this concept, with only occasional exceptions, is a sound one and undoubtedly has greatly forwarded the work of Christ. Examples of this pattern have been the Sunday School, Training Union, Baptist Student Union, men's work, and many other "major items" of Southern Baptist life which began outside of the Convention structure (either as an independent society or as an interdenominational movement) but were subsequently integrated into the organization and functions of the general body. This process utilized the gifts of the grass roots constituents who alone might know how to build a better mousetrap, and by maintaining openness toward the ideas of a widespread constituency, the Convention has tapped vast human resources. (2) The laisse faire nature of Southern Baptist ecclesiology. Baptist life centers in a local congregation. The leaders of each congregation (and especially the pastor) are eager for it to grow in all phases of Christian life. Individual initiative and creativity are encouraged as an aid to growth. It becomes the Convention in microcosm. As a local congregation discovered a fruitful methodology or new activity, it was copied by neighboring churches, associations, and states in an effort to reap the same type of harvest that could be observed in the original congregation. (3) The activity of the Convention's agency to which a new function or program was assigned. Customarily, those individuals who displayed the brightest gifts on the local level were asked to provide Convention-wide leadership. Then, through study and experience, an intern-type of expertise was developed which tested and refined the methodology involved in a particular activity, and an archetypal pattern was formed for promotion in all congregations. (4) The immediate utilization of the vast media of Southern Baptists for promotion. The literature of the Sunday School Board, for example, going into practically every Southern Baptist church, was available to advertise a new department or activity. News items in state Baptist papers were used to inform pastors and churches of the latest developments in the new activity or department of work. (5) The development of a whole new class of Christian vocational specialists. During the previous period, state Sunday School and Training Union secretaries, for example, were rare, as were a score of other vocational offices that have become common. Until almost the opening of this period, the seminaries of Southern Baptists paid little attention to Sunday School and Training Union methodology and training, but at present the religious education aspect of seminary life is a major one. The structuring of the music program, now one of the significant ministries of Southern Baptist churches, waited until late in the century. In all of these areas and many others, an entire curriculum has been developed and many types of new vocational areas have been provided. (6) The intrinsic excellence of the curriculum and methodology. Without being unduly immodest, Southern Baptists can claim credit for the development of a religious education program of high quality. Other denominations, for example, copied some of the advanced pedagogy and methodology of the outstanding layman, Arthur Flake, and others during the 1920's.[2] (7) The intensive promotional efforts by agencies of the Convention. Since the cultivation of most of the work of church auxiliaries was originally assigned to the Sunday School Board, that agency would naturally take the lead in promoting these areas of work. A series of gifted executives of that board provided strong leadership "to carry from the steps of the Sunday School Board building to the last church all that we have come to know about Sunday school and Training Union methods."[3] While this statement came from T. L. Holcomb in 1935, it manifests the spirit of all the secretaries with respect to all of the resources of the board. (8) The reinforcement of the Convention's programs and patterns by the promotion of state bodies and associations. As mentioned in the story of the Sunday School Board, that agency deliberately set out to promote religious educational activity in the churches across the Convention's territory by providing financial gifts to each state for use in employing workers in religious education. Year-by-year subsidies of this sort have assisted the states to organize their own departments of religious education, and to promote the activities and methodologies of the southwide board. In addition, pastors who have used the methods suggested by the Convention's leaders often have spoken at the Convention's annual program praising the results achieved and urging their fellow-pastors to try them.

As a result of these factors (and many more that form a part of the entire promotional and educational thrust of the Convention and its agencies), many "major items" have been standardized in the reports by churches to their associations, state bodies, and the Southern Baptist Convention: baptisms, additions by letter, resident membership, total membership, Sunday School enrollment, Vacation Bible School enrollment, Training Union enrollment, Woman's Missionary Union enrollment, Brotherhood enrollment, Church Music enrollment, church libraries, value of church property, total receipts, and total mission gifts. Other major items such as missions, hospitals, schools, children's homes, etc., are reported by associations and state bodies, making it possible to summarize the work of Southern Baptists in statistical form year by year.

In an effort to conserve space, these summarizing statistics will be utilized in describing the advances made by Southern Baptists in the older southern states between 1917 and 1972. Four of these summaries will be provided for each of the four regions of the South where Southern Baptists were active in 1917, as follows: (1) total growth of the region in number of states, associations, churches, and membership, along with comparisons with previous periods; (2) growth in each of the states of the region in associations, churches, and membership between 1917 and 1972; (3) growth in church auxiliaries in each state between 1917 and 1972; and (4) growth in benevolent work in each of the states between 1917 and 1972.

South Atlantic Region. The seven states comprising this region in 1917, using the modified categories of the Census Bureau, were Maryland, District of Columbia, Virginia, North Carolina, South Carolina, Georgia, and Florida.

1. Total Growth in the Region. In the modern period Baptists of this region increased from 258 associations, 7,732 churches, and 1,021,616 members in 1917 to 321 associations, 11,204 churches, and

4,041,430 members in 1972. This represented an average annual membership growth of 5.37%, which, in view of the large numerical base of 1917, compares quite favorably with the average annual growth in this region of 4.45% between 1877 and 1917, 2.25% between 1860 and 1877, and 4.79% between 1845 and 1860. The population, meanwhile, increased from 12,303,568 in 1920 to 28,378,996 in 1970 in these states, representing an average annual growth of 2.61%, less than half the Baptist growth. It should be mentioned that during this modern period the two states of Delaware and West Virginia were added to the South Atlantic region in Southern Baptist expansion, but that story and the statistics involved will be given later in this chapter.

2. Growth by States. The numerical growth of each state may be seen in the following comparative tables.

| | 1917 | | | 1972 | | | Annual % Mem. |
State	Assns.	Churches	Members	Assns.	Churches	Members	Increase
Md.	3	88	15,464	14	254	86,442	8.33
D.C.	1	9	4,436	1	62	39,766	14.48
Va.	29	1,127	178,980	43	1,411	540,705	3.67
N.C.	64	2,172	284,927	80	3,461	1,046,302	4.86
S.C.	38	1,133	161,114	43	1,605	603,515	4.99
Ga.	94	2,473	315,801	93	2,930	1,039,953	4.17
Fla.	29	730	60,894	47	1,481	684,747	18.63
Total	258	7,732	1,021,616	321	11,204	4,041,430	5.37

3. Growth in Church Auxiliaries. All of the statistics for the local auxiliaries (including Sunday School, Training Union, Woman's Missionary Union, Brotherhood, Vacation Bible School, and Music) are not available for 1917. The following table shows the extant statistics from the records of 1917.

State	Sunday School Enrollment	No. of Training Unions	No. of WMU Organizations
Md.	14,701	54	58
D.C.	6,607	–	18
Va.	137,875	328	1,677
N.C.	222,432	500	1,484
S.C.	113,453	150	1,531
Ga.	226,268	836	846
Fla.	39,558	182	350

The excellent growth shown in these three auxiliaries (the enrollment in Training Union and Woman's Missionary Union, not available in 1917, will be given in 1972 rather than the number of organizations) may be glimpsed in the following table supplying statistics for 1972.

State	Sunday School Enrollment	Church Training Enrollment	WMU Enrollment
Md.	62,467	11,650	9,582
D.C.	19,105	2,517	2,552
Va.	358,711	41,852	84,568
N.C.	693,176	119,230	136,768
S.C.	407,267	117,178	95,621
Ga.	586,954	171,301	105,365
Fla.	414,699	116,471	54,256

In addition, in 1972, the following new statistics speak of the enlargement of the ministries of the local churches.

State	VBS Enrollment	Music Ministry Enrollment	Church Libraries
Md.	38,513	8,566	168
D.C.	8,003	3,100	50
Va.	144,649	54,070	800
N.C.	284,350	125,676	1,585
S.C.	169,590	72,927	780
Ga.	266,743	108,228	1,075
Fla.	163,595	72,138	794

4. State Benevolent Patterns. Besides fostering the local auxiliary ministries through organized departments in the state structures, the several states developed a number of other ministries, which may be contrasted in 1917 with 1972. The picture in 1917 was as follows.

State	No. of Hospitals	No. of Schools	Mission Gifts	Total Gifts
Md.	—	—	$ 41,229.94	$ 223,349.75
D.C.	—	—	6,756.30	53,006.56
Va.	—	12	215,036.10	1,356,506.27
N.C.	—	6	158,698.28	1,287,780.95
S.C.	1	2	147,809.23	963,635.83
Ga.	1	4	161,686.52	1,418,587.78
Fla.	—	1	34,633.72	443,877.43

In these same categories in 1972, increases may be observed in the following chart.

State	No. of Hospitals	No. of Schools	Mission Gifts	Total Gifts
Md.	—	—	$ 1,618,219	$ 9,870,462
D.C.	—	—	650,104	5,741,728
Va.	1	7	8,419,135	49,718,892
N.C.	1	9	15,683,929	98,921,298
S.C.	2	4	10,531,961	64,845,866
Ga.	1	4	13,810,611	90,628,635
Fla.	—	3	10,016,081	67,589,889

Furthermore, new or increased ministries are reflected in 1972 in the following chart of state benevolent gifts.

State	Homes for Children	Homes for Aged	Ministerial Retirement	Baptist Hospitals	Gifts thru Exec. Com. to Cooperative Program [4]
Md.	$ 6,000	$ 22,000	–	–	$ 311,439
D.C.	35,777	30,072	$ 18,283	–	86,847
Va.	375,523	164,137	205,364	$123,567	1,873,004
N.C.	1,151,842	302,317	485,670	644,471	2,601,692
S.C.	773,780	326,677	352,500	438,166	1,886,669
Ga.	822,917	403,899	267,670	371,634	2,851,211
Fla.	285,053	209,417	316,216	29,984	2,130,661

South Central Region. The eight states in 1917 making up this region in the modified categories adopted from the Census Bureau were Kentucky, Tennessee, Alabama, Mississippi, Arkansas, Louisiana, Oklahoma, and Texas. For the purpose of continuing previous comparisons, this region will not be subdivided. .

1. Total Growth in the Region. Baptists grew in this region from 548 associations, 14,465 churches, and 1,540,072 members in 1917 to 553 associations, 17,490 churches, and 6,435,129 members in 1972, or an average annual percentage growth in membership of 5.78%. This may be compared with the percentages of growth in this region from 1877 to 1917 of 5.64%, from 1860 to 1877 of 3.95%, and from 1845 to 1860 of 5.36%. Meanwhile, in these eight states the population grew from 19,135,531 to 32,127,010, or an annual average percentage of 1.36%.

2. Growth by States. The following table will show the numerical growth by states.

State	1917 Assns.	Churches	Members	1972 Assns.	Churches	Members	Annual % Mem. Increase
Ky.	76	1,897	260,321	80	2,201	684,246	2.96
Tenn.	55	1,839	208,636	68	2,722	917,579	6.18
Ala.	77	2,070	221,501	75	2,950	876,237	5.37
Miss.	56	1,515	172,480	76	1,885	558,742	4.07
Ark.	54	1,547	122,635	44	1,192	367,020	3.62
La.	32	746	80,108	51	1,309	489,727	9.30
Okla.	49	1,142	90,617	41	1,386	575,747	10.71
Tex.	149	3,709	383,774	118	3,845	1,965,831	7.49
Total	548	14,465	1,540,072	553	17,490	6,435,129	5.78

3. Growth in Church Auxiliaries. The available statistics for 1917 are shown in the following table, along with the growth experienced by 1972 in the same categories. The enrollments of Training Union and the Woman's Missionary Union were not available in the records of 1917.

| State | 1917 | | | 1972 | | |
	S.S. Enrollment	No. of T.U.	No. of WMU	S.S. Enrollment	T.U. Enrollment	WMU Enrollment
Ky.	141,146	309	722	364,200	71,328	51,428
Tenn.	139,276	316	827	524,962	163,218	72,039
Ala.	134,936	144	479	516,821	221,991	85,073
Miss.	77,702	202	1,047	311,475	124,632	47,554
Ark.	61,359	200	334	212,555	84,772	27,184
La.	40,466	186	257	269,813	116,893	36,144
Okla.	47,211	268	541	312,505	99,021	36,830
Tex.	225,002	1,700	1,475	1,097,342	289,828	133,444

In addition, the following statistics of 1972 speak of other ministries developed during this period in the local congregations.

State	VBS Enrollment	Music Ministry Enrollment	Church Libraries
Ky.	170,870	50,376	804
Tenn.	222,953	81,945	1,082
Ala.	232,873	94,471	1,124
Miss.	134,041	65,182	792
Ark.	92,414	31,183	497
La.	124,927	48,145	564
Okla.	119,940	42,875	604
Tex.	476,338	173,580	2,237

4. State Benevolent Patterns. Besides fostering the local auxiliary ministries through organized departments in the state structure, the South Central states developed a number of additional ministries, and the tables that follow will emphasize the growth numerically or financially and suggest the variety of Christian ministries. The first table represents 1917.

State	No. of Hospitals	No. of Schools	Mission Gifts	Total Gifts
Ky.	—	6	$186,088.99	$1,239,700.45
Tenn.	1	4	104,882.54	850,224.72
Ala.	—	2	83,693.27	747,012.69
Miss.	1	4	88,937.77	691,178.62
Ark.	—	4	69,558.47	443,811.05
La.	1	3	41,405.70	390,292.52
Okla.	3	1	49,665.32	472,053.94
Tex.	2	9	418,393.72	3,019,041.06

In these same categories, substantial increases may be noted by 1972.

State	No. of Hospitals	No. of Schools	Mission Gifts	Total Gifts
Ky.	4	6	$ 7,833,021	$ 47,658,277
Tenn.	3	4	12,091,786	75,166,553
Ala.	4	3	11,516,723	74,537,554
Miss.	1	4	7,857,271	50,596,007
Ark.	—	2	6,048,726	31,672,637
La.	1	3	7,073,140	44,312,134
Okla.	9	1	7,339,317	42,919,893
Tex.	8	11	31,074,678	172,466,560

In addition, by 1972 a number of new or increased ministries were added, as seen in the following summary of state benevolent gifts.

State	Homes for Children	Homes for Aged	Ministerial Retirement	Baptist Hospitals	Gifts thru Exec. Com. to Cooperative Program [5]
Ky.	$ 240,350	—	$216,866	$ 76,528	$1,272,039
Tenn.	957,557	—	341,408	28,915	1,993,343
Ala.	595,743	—	295,165	—	1,915,694
Miss.	196,995	—	270,000	75,094	1,303,258
Ark.	174,294	—	108,496	—	911,129
La.	240,350	$14,014	216,866	4,927	1,194,701
Okla.	972,593	16,000	173,870	80,429	1,445,125
Tex.	1,166,322	—	533,044	1,381,584	4,914,964

North Central Region. The two states of this region containing Southern Baptists in 1917 were Missouri and Illinois.

1. Total Growth in the Region. Baptists grew in these states from 108 associations, 2,542 churches, and 275,906 members in 1917 to 114 associations, 2,715 churches, and 733,122 members in 1972. This represented an average annual membership growth rate of 3.01%. It is not possible to compare the rate of growth in Illinois with any previous period, since Baptists there became affiliated with the Southern Baptist Convention first in 1910; but the two states showed an average annual increase of 3.01% in the modern period (compared with Missouri's rate of 6.02% growth annually from 1877 to 1917, 4.29% from 1860 to 1877, and 10.89% from 1845 to 1860). The population in these two states during the period from 1920 to 1970 increased from 9,889,335 to 15,791,375, or an average annual increase of 1.19%, compared to the rate by Southern Baptists of 3.01%.

2. Growth by States. The following table will show the numerical growth by the two states.

| | 1917 | | | 1972 | | | Annual % Mem. |
State	Assns.	Churches	Members	Assns.	Churches	Members	Increase
Mo.	82	1,956	212,544	79	1,826	534,106	2.75
Ill.	26	586	63,362	35	889	199,016	3.89
Total	108	2,542	275,906	114	2,715	733,122	3.01

3. Growth in Church Auxiliaries. The available statistics for 1917 are shown in the following table, along with the growth experienced in this region by 1972 in the same categories as far as possible.

| | 1917 | | | 1972 | | |
State	S.S. Enrollment	No. of T.U.	No. of WMU	S.S. Enrollment	T.U. Enrollment	WMU Enrollment
Mo.	156,932	284	629	330,920	92,107	57,336
Ill.	44,780	—	—	135,661	34,890	17,310

In addition, the following statistics of 1972 speak of other ministries developed during this period in the local congregations.

State	VBS Enrollment	Music Ministry Enrollment	Church Libraries
Mo.	158,654	47,067	882
Ill.	74,833	15,577	404

4. State Benevolent Patterns. Besides fostering the local auxiliary ministries through organized departments in the state structures, the North Central states developed a number of additional ministries, and the tables that follow will demonstrate the growth numerically or financially and suggest the variety of Christian ministries. The first table represents 1917.

State	No. of Hospitals	No. of Schools	Mission Gifts	Total Gifts
Mo.	1	3	$128,173.39	$1,395,427.71
Ill.	—	—	26,842.56	294,121.07

The statistics in these categories in 1972 may be noted in the following table.

State	No. of Hospitals	No. of Schools	Mission Gifts	Total Gifts
Mo.	1	5	$8,362,447	$45,944,724
Ill.	—	—	2,603,141	17,481,691

In addition, by 1972 a number of new or increased ministries were developed, as may be seen in the following summary of state gifts to these causes.

State	Homes for Children	Homes for Aged	Ministerial Retirement	Baptist Hospitals	Gifts thru Exec. Com. to Cooperative Program [6]
Mo.	$154,127	$91,929	$197,437	$3,134	$1,505,436
Ill.	198,327	—	142,000	—	459,525

Mountain Region. The single state in this region containing Southern Baptists in 1917 was New Mexico. In 1917 this state had 8 associations, 144 churches, and a membership of 6,707. By 1972 these statistics had increased to 16 associations, 250 churches, and a membership of 94,089, for a huge average annual membership growth of 23.69%. Meanwhile, the population during this period increased from 360,350 in 1920 to 1,016,000 in 1970, or an average annual growth of 3.64%. The Sunday School enrollment in 1917 was 6,107, which increased to 49,702 in 1972. In 1917, New Mexico had 22 Training Unions and 45 Woman's Missionary Unions; by 1972 these figures (translated into enrollments) became 16,271 enrolled in Church Training and a total enrollment of 6,716 in Woman's Missionary Union. Other ministries developed in the local congregations by 1972 included 27,055 enrolled in Vacation Bible School, 7,150 enrolled in Music Ministry, and 131 church libraries reported. New Mexico Baptists had neither hospitals nor schools in 1917. Their mission gifts in that year were reported as $10,424.45, while total gifts for all purposes were $56,347.98. In contrast, by 1972 their mission gifts totaled $1,244,291, while their total gifts amounted to $7,832,330. Additional ministries included $106,483 for children's homes, $31,124 for ministerial retirement, and $143,813 given through the Executive Committee to the Cooperative Program of the Southern Baptist Convention.[7]

In a brief word anticipating the more extended summary at the close of this chapter, these impressive statistics reveal that the turbulence of the revolutionary twentieth century did not distract Southern Baptists from their main task of making and teaching disciples. The average annual membership increase of 4.75% meant that the large constituency of 2,844,301 in 1917 was almost doubling every two decades, an achievement unmatched by any other major denomination. The multiplying of auxiliaries for enlisting, teaching, and training in the local congregations from just a few in 1917 to many in 1972 provided agencies for large numbers of accessions to the churches and the presence of a reservoir of trained workers for the tasks of the churches and their auxiliaries. Vocational specialists have been developed for every age group and to utilize many types of talents through structures planned to complement one another in the growth of the congregations. Methodologies and effective structures have been refined through expertise gained by experience.

The benevolent programs of the state and regional bodies, usually with parallel structures in the associations, speak of the vitality and concern of the constituency for the children, the aged, the ill, the uneducated, and other needy groups, as reflected in financial gifts for these purposes. The strong state mission programs have been matched by participation in home and foreign missions through special offerings and in all the interests of the Southern Baptist Convention through the Cooperative Program. State papers have been a major factor in communicating with the constituency and promoting the various types of programs in the several states.

Geographical Expansion

The second section of this chapter relative to the constituency of the Southern Baptist Convention in the period from 1917 to 1972 will deal with the expansion of Southern Baptists into geographical areas of the United States (and obliquely into Canada) that had no Southern Baptist churches in 1917. Such a rapid denominational expansion has no parallel in American Christianity of this century. From a geographical base of eighteen states in 1917, the denomination in 1972 has enlarged its activity into all fifty states of the Union.

It will be seen from the state-by-state description later that this expansion followed no orderly or uniform pattern, precisely because it was not a "planned invasion." On the contrary, the basis for every occasion of expansion was the presence of Southern Baptist people living in the new areas. The strong denominational consciousness which they had absorbed from their earlier experience with Southern Baptists moved them to seek affiliation with the southern body from their new homes. Thus, the mobility of Southern Baptist people was the principal cause for the expansion of the geographical base of the Southern Baptist Convention. This haphazard pattern of expansion renders it almost impossible to tell the story chronologically. Instead, after a brief historical background and a description of the reformulation of the earlier principles of the Convention and its agencies in order to meet the developing situation, the principal thrust of this section will be to trace the story of this expansion in an orderly geographical fashion, using the regional categories developed by the United States Census Bureau.

Historical Background. It will be recalled that when Southern Baptists organized their Convention in 1845, the northern Home Mission Society slowly began to withdraw its missionaries from the southern states. However, in 1863, sparked by their concern for the freed Negroes in the South, the society enthusiastically entered into a program that provided extensive missionary personnel in the South carrying on evangelism and education, and assisting financially in church edifice building involving all races. The territorial rivalry before 1882 was rather one-sided, and territorial limitations were not disucssed. The northern society offered no serious objections when Southern Baptists stationed a worker in California to work principally among the Chinese, since no northern Baptist missionaries could speak the Cantonese dialect necessary for communication. Little was said when Southern Baptist missionaries followed the wandering Indian tribes from Oklahoma into Kansas to minister to them.

However, as described in previous chapters, Southern Baptists awakened to the issues involved in maintaining a geographical base, and principally through the work of I. T. Tichenor the home field was claimed. A new direction was foreshadowed in 1894 when Baptists in New Mexico and Oregon looked to the Southern Baptist Convention for affiliation. The pendulum, which had swung in one direction lustily for a generation, began to reverse its course. In practical effects, the only result of the three comity conferences (Fortress Monroe, Washington, and Old Point Comfort-Hot Springs) was to ask New Mexico Baptists to affiliate with the southern body, although Oklahoma was prompted to adopt single southern affiliation because of the principles enunciated by the joint northern-southern committee considering New Mexico. Perhaps Missouri also was influenced to adopt sole southern affiliation in 1919 because of the action of New Mexico and Oklahoma. The excision of southern Illinois in 1907 and her affiliation with the southern body in 1910 were evidently unrelated to these events.

Between 1917 and 1942, the foundations were laid for the expansion that would later come. Economic, social, and military factors combined to thrust millions of southern people into the West and North, large numbers of them being Southern Baptists. Porter Routh summarized the great mobility of the southern population during the period.

> With the coming of the dust bowl, the depression and World War II, there was a tremendous turnover in population. For example, Oklahoma lost 301,900 by interstate civilian migration in the period from 1930 to 1940, and more than 303,000 during the early days of World War II from April 1940 to November 1943. North Carolina lost nearly 63,000 in the depression decade and more than a quarter of a million from 1940 to 1943. Kentucky had a similar loss, and Arkansas lost more than a hundred thousand in the decade from 1930 to 1940 and a quarter of a million in the first three years of the decade of the forties. These four Southern states lost more during this thirteen-year period than any states in the United States. Mississippi, South Carolina, Georgia, Missouri and Alabama joined these four in substantial losses during the same period of time.
>
> The destination of many of these civilian migrants can be seen when you note that California led by a tremendous margin with more than

a million net gain in population during the decade from 1930 to 1940 and an additional 1,350,000 during the first three years of the forties. Michigan, Washington and Ohio were among the first five in net gain during the period from 1940 to 1943.[8]

As will be noted in the northern penetration by Southern Baptists, it was the thousands of Southern Baptists intermingled with these mobile multitudes that initiated Southern Baptist churches in every new area.

Why did not these Southern Baptist people unite with other Baptist churches in the localities to which they moved? It should be said that in some instances there were no Baptist churches in their area. Robert G. Torbet named four reasons given by Southern Baptists to justify their expansion beyond the traditional geographical bounds of the South.

> First, they feel that Southerners migrating to the North are not content with the religion which they find in the churches of the American Baptist Convention. Second, they charge that Baptist churches in the North differ theologically from Southern Baptist churches. By this they refer not to major issues, but to differences in the practice of open or closed communion, associate church membership, alien immersion and the wider contacts of American Baptists with ecumenical Christianity. Third, Southern Baptists are convinced that Southern Baptists migrating north will be lost to the Baptist cause if they are left to themselves. This deep conviction that Southern Baptists are responsible under God for an adequate evangelizing of America is a potent motivating force among them. Fourth, some Southern Baptists have interpreted as an aggressive act the Northern Baptists Convention's change of name to American Baptist Convention, with the accompanying invitation to all Baptists who desire fellowship within cooperative Christianity to unite under this name. The answer to this charge is that Southern Baptist expansion northward was well underway prior to 1950 when this change of name was effected in the North.[9]

Blake Smith, a Southern Baptist minister, added as another reason for this "invasion" that Southern Baptists have a "programatic" understanding of their existence, which he defined as the identification of the church with the institution. This, he said, affected the relationship of Southern Baptists with other Christians and other Christian bodies, determined their theological emphases, and involved their ethical behavior.[10]

Another question has also been sharply asked the Southern Baptist Convention: Why have you been so quick to give official recognition and provide assistance to churches popping up far beyond the traditional Southern Baptist geographical base? As a matter of fact, the southern body did refuse to affiliate with Southern Baptists in Oregon who petitioned in 1894 and 1897, primarily declining on geographical grounds. But between 1894 and 1942 (when affiliation with California

Southern Baptists was voted) significant events had taken place. Southern Baptists, after two decades of painful negotiations with northern Baptists, had affiliated with Southern Baptists in New Mexico. Voices began to be heard in the Convention calling for other westward mission thrusts.[11] Additional impetus was added to this movement by the affiliation with the southern body of Illinois (1910), Oklahoma (sole affiliation in 1914), and Missouri (sole affiliation in 1919). These excisions caused considerable resentment among northern Baptist leaders.

The determinative events in preparing the Southern Baptist Convention for additional expansion developed through local controversy, often bitter, in Arizona and California.

Expansion into Arizona. In March, 1917, at the very opening of this period, because of dissension between liberals and conservatives in the First Baptist Church of Phoenix, Arizona, seventy-two members withdrew and formed the Calvary Baptist Church in the following month. C. M. Rock, a Southern Baptist, was called as pastor. Four years later the Calvary church split over doctrine. On March 27, 1921, the conservative minority organized the First Southern Baptist Church and called Rock as pastor. This was the first of a number of churches formed principally of southerners which were organized in protest against doctrinal and ecclesiological views held by leaders of the Northern Baptist Convention. Beginning with the Phoenix church in August, 1921, nine other churches with similar views soon joined the Southwestern Baptist Association of New Mexico and through it affiliated with the Southern Baptist Convention.[12] The older Arizona Baptist Convention bitterly opposed this new relationship with New Mexico Baptists by these Arizona churches and protested vigorously.[13] The ten Arizona Southern Baptist churches organized the Gambrell Memorial Association of Arizona on October 29, 1925, and in the following month, this association was recognized by the New Mexico state body. On September 21, 1928, the Baptist General Convention of Arizona was organized under the leadership of C. M. Rock, and sent messengers to the Southern Baptist Convention the following year. They were not only seated, but some were appointed to the Executive Committee and the Home and Foreign Mission Boards.[14] In 1929 the Sunday School Board appropriated $15,000 to the Baptist General Convention of Arizona for assistance in Sunday School and mission work. A torrent of criticism followed, but the Convention approved this action and authorized continued help.[15] In 1932 the Northern Baptist Convention adopted a resolution protesting the Arizona situation,[16] as did the older Arizona Baptist Convention. The Executive Committee of the Southern Baptist Convention replied that the promotion and organization of the second state body in Arizona was not due to activity by any Southern Baptist Convention agency; that the request of the Baptist General Convention of Arizona for recognition was acted upon by the Convention on the same grounds they had considered similar requests in former years; that all differences of opinion between the two Arizona state bodies could be adjusted better by mutual conference between the two of them than by outside bodies.[17]

Growing directly out of this Arizona confrontation, the Southern Baptist Convention, in a constitutional revision of 1931, formally articulated some basic principles for affiliation and for the recognition of auxiliaries, which will be described more completely in the following chapter. Essentially, before 1931 the article on membership in the constitution of the southern body rested on the old financial plan which provided that the Convention would consist of messengers who contributed funds or were elected by Baptist bodies contributing funds, on the basis of one messenger for each $250 paid into the treasuries of the boards; and of one representative from each district association cooperating with the Convention. This meant that a church must give $250 to the work of the Convention before a messenger could be seated. It is likely that when the Convention adopted a substitute motion from the floor in 1931 to change this method of representation to allow a church to elect messengers for only a *bona fide* offering, rather than $250, they were reflecting their experience with the needy churches in Arizona several years before. It is more clearly evident that the Arizona application for membership on the boards of the Convention triggered the passing of Bylaw 17, which made provision for state representation on the boards and Executive Committee of the Convention. Later action provided for formal representation on boards and the Executive Committee when a state had 25,000 members in its churches,[18] and automatic representation on the other agencies of the Convention when membership in the churches of a state or area body reached 50,000 members. The importance of this state representation will be discussed in the following chapter.

This bitter controversy in Arizona did not disappear when the Southern Baptist Convention disavowed responsibility for it. At first it seemed that Southern Baptists in Arizona would have little success. By 1940 the state still had only 1 Southern Baptist association with 16 churches and 3,448 members. Twenty years later, however, there were 20 associations, 189 churches, and 40,789 members. Total gifts amounted to $2,402,023, of which $412,685 were for missions. Moreover, their relationship of baptisms to church memberships was one of the best in all of the Convention: one baptism for each 8.8 members.[19] By 1972 they reported 15 associations, 232 churches, and 78,187 members. Total receipts were $6,749,552, while mission gifts were $1,080,420. Under the leadership of Executive Secretary Willis J. Ray, the state body also extended assistance to Southern Baptist churches in Utah, Colorado, Idaho, Wyoming, North Dakota, South Dakota, Nevada, and Montana, in addition to initiating an extensive program of state benevolences, including Grand Canyon College.

Expansion into California. From almost the beginning of the state's history, Southern Baptists had expressed a desire to carry the gospel to California.[20] This state formed a part of the area ceded to the United States by Mexico after the war of 1848. Two years later, following the gold rush, California was admitted as a state. The northern Baptist society sent missionaries early in 1849. Southern Baptists in 1855 appointed J. Lewis Shuck, one of their missionaries returning from China, to serve in the area of San Francisco because of his proficiency in the Cantonese tongue. With other Southern Baptist missionaries and leaders he worked in San Francisco and Sacramento until the war of 1861 stopped this ministry.

> In these years all the California churches, whether they were organized by missionaries from the American Baptist Home Mission Society or the Southern Baptist Home Mission Board, were in the same associations and state convention. Very little friction existed between the Northern and Southern elements in the Baptist ranks.[21]

The agony of the Civil War was disastrous to southern activity, and most of the early churches organized by Southern Baptists affiliated with northern Baptist mission societies.

The modern era began about the turn of the century. Before 1940 the population had increased from about 2,000,000 to beyond 8,000,000. It has been estimated that one third of this increase came from southern states, especially Texas, Oklahoma, and Arkansas. One of these Oklahoma families, that of "Preacher" George Mouser, was the core of the First Southern Baptist Church, Shafter, which was organized with sixteen members on May 10, 1936. Every charter member had belonged to a Southern Baptist church elsewhere before moving to California.[22] Other independent Baptist churches were formed at Oildale and Lamont, which, with the Shafter church and an older church at Taft, organized the first association of Southern Baptists in California—San Joaquin Valley Missouri Baptist Association, on April 13, 1939.[23] R. W. Lackey, an early leader, wrote the constitution for this association and also for the Southern Baptist General Convention of California, which was organized on September 13, 1940, at Shafter, by fourteen churches at the associational meeting.[24] Because of the importance of motivation in this pivotal state, the words of the leaders at the first annual meeting were significant.

> It is not the purpose of the Southern Baptist General Convention of California to molest or disturb anyone in his religious life. If one

is already a member of some organization and is satisfied therein, we believe that he should be let alone. We are doing our best to enlist the unenlisted for Christ.[25]

Emphasizing their doctrinal disagreement with liberal ecclesiological practices of northern Baptist churches in California, the new state body petitioned the Southern Baptist Convention for recognition in May, 1941. The committee appointed to study the petition was conscious of the pivotal nature of the decision to be made and requested that the matter await resolution at the next session. At the 1942 session of the southern body, the chairman was absent and sent word asking for another year's delay. However, a member of the committee, J. B. Rounds of Oklahoma, moved "that the Southern Baptist General Convention of the state of California be admitted to membership in the Southern Baptist Convention." [26] Many of the leaders of the southern convention spoke against the motion, but the floor passed it almost unanimously. Perhaps the location of the meeting place (San Antonio, Texas) was part of the reason for such a resounding vote, since messengers from Texas, Oklahoma, Arkansas, and Louisiana provided the majority of messengers. On June 20, 1942, the General Council of the Northern Baptist Convention protested recognition of the California body by the southern convention, saying that

> these movements in California and elsewhere weaken our Baptist witness, cause unnecessary duplication of cost, seriously jeopardize our mutual confidence, and nullify much of our effort and purpose in the establishment of an enriching and mutually profitable fellowship.

The council also noted that recognition of the California group as a body violated the comity principles of 1912. In reply, the Executive Committee of the Southern Body reaffirmed its adherence to the comity principles and admitted that the recognition of the California churches as a body was an unfortunate wording of the motion. It proposed to correct this mistake by regarding the Southern Baptist churches in California as individual churches and agreed that Convention agencies' would not carry on promotional work in California except through the churches cooperating with the southern convention. Later the Convention approved this reply, but specifically stated that nothing in any agreement should prevent Southern Baptists from carrying on their work in California.[27]

Northern Baptists were wroth. William B. Lipphard, editor of the influential northern Baptist *Missions* said that the action at San Antonio should be declared void and invalid and in violation of an existing agreement; also, that this "divisive, disintegrating, competitive trend" seriously threatened comity, harmony, and unity.[28] Porter Routh judged that perhaps the contemporary conversations looking toward uniting northern Baptists and the Disciples of Christ were influential in the strong Southern Baptist reaction to California's petition.[29] At any rate, editorials in most Southern Baptist papers favored this new affiliation. One even suggested that all geographical boundaries for Southern Baptist work be immediately eliminated.[30]

On February 11, 1946, Fred A. McCaulley was appointed by the Home Mission Board as General Field Worker for the Western States, and was commissioned to assist in promoting mission work in New Mexico, Arizona, and California, and to aid the churches cooperating with the Southern Baptist Convention. Following the constitutional revision of 1946 by the southern convention which urged that existing state bodies become central in cooperative mission work in new adjacent states, California Baptists encouraged the organization of Baptists in Oregon-Washington from the South who had for many years carried on independent or loosely-affiliated relationships with various Baptist groups.[31] Honoring the agreement of 1942, McCaulley declined many invitations to work with churches in Oregon-Washington, but in late 1946 he accepted a speaking engagement at a church already affiliated with the Southern Baptist Convention through California and began a ministry in these northern areas.[32]

California Southern Baptists, meanwhile, sometimes under great difficulties, made an excellent record of advance. In 1960, for example, they reported 38 associations, 698 churches, and a total membership of 145,293. Mission gifts totaled $1,115,665, while total gifts were $8,791,587. It is significant that California Southern Baptists had one of the two best ratios of baptisms to church membership in the Southern Baptist Convention. They averaged one baptism for each 8.2 members, compared with the overall Southern Baptist ratio of one for each 23.1 members.[33] By 1972 they had 34 associations, 890 churches, and a total membership of 267,745. Mission gifts totaled $2,757,815, while total receipts were $23,133,920.

The Development of New Geographical Principles. Before 1894 there had been no geographical limitation specifically formulated because, as Henry L. Morehouse, corresponding secretary of the northern Home Mission Society, vigorously asserted, the society was in the South or anywhere else on the American continent

> by right of its original and unchanged constitution, which names *North America* as its field of operations; is there by the right which is derived from the law of love that requires the strong to respond to the calls of the needy . . .; is there by the right of and in keeping with the spirit of the new era of our nation when the old things have passed away, and all things have become new, when sectional lines and sectional feelings are being obliterated, and the spirit of fraternity is binding in its blessed bonds the Baptist brotherhood as well as the citizens of this land.[34]

This work was being carried on among all races in several aspects. The comity agreement between Northern and Southern Baptists at Fortress Monroe in 1894 was initiated by Southern Baptists because of a desire to establish territorial limits between the two bodies. But plain Baptist ecclesiology could not justify general bodies dividing geographical territory, which would clearly violate the autonomy of churches and other Baptist general bodies. This view was vigorously asserted when the Convention adopted a report in 1909 relative to their relationship to the interdenominational Home Missions Council. This pointed to the independent nature of the churches, which could not be committed by the Convention, and said that the Convention's "independence or liberty as to the fields which we are to occupy" must not be circumscribed.[35] The calls in the Baptist newspapers and the periodical literature for additional missionary expansion in the home field, the new affiliation with Illinois in 1910, the addition of New Mexico in 1912, sole affiliation by Oklahoma in 1914, and the sole affiliation by Missouri in 1919 caused the opening of the modern period to be one of readjustment in the older attitude of Southern Baptists relative to territorial limitations. The literature of the 1920's magnified a new view of unlimited home missions, and the 1928 resolution of the Convention defining its relationship with other Baptist bodies stressed the ecclesiology that would deny territorial limitations.[36] The Arizona confrontation was another step that required the development of principles by the Convention's Home Mission Board to deal with the realities facing them. The 1940's and 1950's brought rapid expansion. Increasing numbers of requests for assistance poured into the offices of the Home Mission Board from every part of the nation. The climax was reached in 1951 when the Southern Baptist Convention adopted a resolution which unequivocally asserted that in view of previous pronouncements on territorial limitations and of the change in name of the Northern Baptist Convention in 1950 to make it continental in scope (American Baptist Convention), "the Home Mission Board and all other Southern Baptist boards and agencies be free to serve as a source of blessing to any community or any people anywhere in the United States."[37] Clearly it was necessary for the Home Mission Board to establish principles of operation based upon the experience gained heretofore and the terms of the constitutional revisions of 1946. The gist of the board's new policies was approved officially by the Convention in 1955, as follows:

> 1. In the work directly committed to this Board by the Southern Baptist Convention, or historically a part of the home mission program, it is the responsibility of this Board to develop co-operatively various programs and act as a clearinghouse for the exchange of information as to methods of use and application of programs so developed.
> 2. State conventions which are financially able and administratively

prepared are encouraged to engage in a co-operative program of home missions within their own territory without financial aid from the Home Board so far as practical.

3. Where state conventions are not able financially to carry on a co-operative program of home missions, grants-in-aid of money should be made by this Board to the State convention for use in such programs under the administrative supervision of the state convention.

4. In western and new areas the work of this Board is co-operatively done through the state mission board nearest to the field or the convention with which the existing Southern Baptist churches are affiliated. (1) The Home Mission Board acts only upon request of the state board, and the work and workers are elected and directed by the state boards. The Home Mission Board aids only in providing funds and counsel for the work and approves the mission workers. The Home Board does not pay salaries directly to these missionaries or mission pastors but makes allocations to the state conventions for such salaries. (2) The Home and state mission boards do not solicit or invite Baptist churches already affiliated with some other convention to join our associations or conventions. In fact, we prefer that they not do so. (3) The Home Mission Board, in co-operation with the state boards, seeks to establish new churches in communities and in areas of larger communities where there is no other Baptist church. The Home Board requires a survey to be made of any community where a new church is to be located and this survey filed with the Home and state board offices. (4) The Home Board makes allocations through the state mission boards to aid mission pastors' salaries for new work. This is done only when satisfactory application has been received from prospective mission pastors and approved by both the Home and state boards. Allocations are made for periods of from three to six months, with the hope that the new work may become a self-supporting church within that period of time.

These policies have been followed carefully in the promotion of our work. Conferences have already been held with the secretaries of the American Baptist Convention in some of these states, and the plan is to hold such conferences with others during 1955. Southern Baptists in these fields will find many opportunities to plant new churches and to win the lost without going into the fields already occupied by any other Baptist group, and this is our policy.[38]

Since 1955 the board has refined its methodology regularly and has through cooperation with the states, seminaries, and other agencies played a large part in the remarkable expansion that will now be described. As has been noted, this expansion began with a westward thrust and leaped the mountains into California and Oregon-Washington, almost simultaneously pushed northward into the vast central plains of the nation, and finally engulfed the remainder of the United States from New England to Hawaii and Alaska. For the purpose of describing the expansion in an orderly fashion, this description will follow the geographical structure provided by the Census Bureau and adapted partly in previous periods of this study. It will begin with the New England region and work westward to the Pacific

Coast region in a description of the new areas of Southern Baptist expansion. It should be observed that the denominational consciousness and solidarity implicit in the convention-type organizational structure played an important part in this entire development. Neighboring Southern Baptist states have assisted the small churches in new areas; the older southern states have sponsored new work until a state body was formed; churches and associations in several states have united to form single regional bodies for strength; individual churches in the South have given financial support to particular areas; several agencies of the Convention have cooperated in the movement; and the Home Mission Board, in particular, has actively unified and aided in the support of this program in line with the principles set out in 1955. In this description it will not be possible to do more than sketch briefly Southern Baptist beginnings in the new areas, take for granted the prompt organization of typical Southern Baptist auxiliaries at local, associational, and state levels, and provide the latest principal statistics showing the progress of the work.[39]

New England Region. This region comprises the states of Maine, New Hampshire, Vermont, Massachusetts, Connecticut, and Rhode Island. The population in 1972 exceeded 11,000,000, Massachusetts having almost half the total. Three of the New England states are among the first four most densely populated states in the United States. In the early settlements of this region, Congregationalism was the preponderant denomination, but the rapid immigration of the nineteenth century has resulted in almost one half of the population being Roman Catholic in 1972.

Because of the closely-integrated character of Southern Baptist beginnings in this region, this section of the story will encompass all of the New England states together, rather than state by state. In a familiar pattern, the presence of Southern Baptists in this region provided the spark that began Southern Baptist expansion. In 1955, answering many requests from New England for information on how to start new Southern Baptist churches, the Home Mission Board of the southern convention sent A. B. Cash to make a survey of the needs of the area. Perhaps the organization of a Southern Baptist Church in western New York under the aegis of Ohio Baptists in that year spurred the interest of Southern Baptists living in New England. On August 18, 1958, near Portsmouth, New Hampshire, through the leadership of the Manhattan Baptist Church in New York City, a mission of forty-four persons was begun, the first in New England to affiliate with the Southern Baptist Convention. On February 22, 1960, this mission was constituted into the Screven Memorial Baptist Church. In April of that year this church, along with four other Southern Baptist churches in the New England region and beyond, formed the Northeastern Baptist Association. Paul S. James, pastor of the Manhattan Baptist Church and also director of Home Mission Board work in the Northeast, was the moderator of this new association. The development of Southern Baptist churches in the six New England states, as well as New York, Pennsylvania, New Jersey, and Delaware, brought the organization of a Northeastern Baptist Regional Fellowship on August 29-30, 1960, sponsored by the Maryland and Ohio Southern Baptist state bodies. On November 2, 1962, the New England Baptist Association was organized at Springfield, Massachusetts, composed of 8 churches, 13 missions, and 1,141 members. The first moderator was Owen Sherrill, and by 1966 this association reported 17 churches, 7 missions, and 2,609 members.

At a pivotal meeting on September 22-23, 1967, at Boston, following extensive discussion at several regional fellowship sessions, it was agreed that churches in the six New England states would form one organizational unit, while churches in other areas of the fellowship would form their own organizational units. As a result, at the October meeting of the New England Baptist Association in 1967, a new structure was adopted which divided the six states into three sections: Upper New England Baptist Association (Maine, New Hampshire, and Vermont) was constituted with 5 churches, 1 mission, and 699 members, with W. Edwin Jackson as the first moderator; Southern New England Baptist Association (Connecticut and Rhode Island) was organized with 11 churches, 6 missions, and 1,136 members, with Jim Schneider as moderator; and Massachusetts Baptist Association was formed with 8 churches, 1 chapel, 1,015 members, and Merwyn Borders as moderator. The New England Baptist Association and its three subsections continued cooperation with the Southern Baptist Convention through the Maryland convention. The executive secretary of the general body in New England was Elmer Sizemore.

The report for 1972 showed the following statistics for the six New England states.

States	Churches	Membership	Mission Expenditures	Total Receipts
Me.	5	565	$ 7,590	$ 77,034
N.H.	2	506	14,343	63,987
Vt.	1	144	51,640	53,919
Mass.	11	1,818	30,120	212,035
R.I.	3	1,006	20,709	173,785
Conn.	9	1,538	61,328	403,029

Middle Atlantic Region. Closely related to the developments in the New England states was the Southern Baptist expansion into the three states of New York, Pennsylvania, and New Jersey in this region.

1. New York. Southern Baptists in western New York developed independently from the New York City center. In 1954, R. Z. Boroughs from an Alabama Baptist church moved to Niagara Falls, New York, to minister to some of his nonresident members. On June 24, 1955, with the assistance of Southern Baptists in Ohio, this developed into the first Southern Baptist church in New York state—the LaSalle Baptist Church of Niagara Falls, constituted with fifty-four members and affiliating with the State Convention of Baptists in Ohio. From this church, with the aid of Paul Nevels from the Ohio convention, churches were planted at Syracuse and Buffalo. On May 1, 1958, with the assistance of Ohio Baptists, Arthur L. Walker was appointed area missionary for western New York and northwestern Pennsylvania by the Home Mission Board of the South. At that time there were four New York churches and one mission affiliated with the Cuyahoga Association of Ohio. After Walker's resignation in 1962, Charles E. Magruder succeeded him.

On September 23, 1958, the Frontier Baptist Association was formed in the LaSalle church and was constituted by representatives from five churches and two missions. Within three years this association included churches reaching from Erie, Pennsylvania, to Syracuse and Utica, New York, and from the upper Adirondacks to Endicott and Elmira in the southern tier. The Rochester Baptist Church was constituted in 1959 and became a mother of churches in the area. On October 24, 1969, the Greater Rochester Baptist Association was formed. In the older area of work, additional growth caused the formation of the Central Association out of the old Frontier Association on September 29, 1961, and in 1968, the Central Association divided into three: Adirondack, Central, and Southern Tier. In the following year a state body was formed, as will be described in succeeding paragraphs, through the cooperation of Southern Baptists in Ohio and Maryland.

Work in New York City, the significant watershed of Southern Baptist life in all the northeastern area, was initiated through the leadership of Ohio and Maryland Baptists. Ohio's executive secretary, Ray Roberts, and John Moore met with James Aaron and his family (who had come to New York City for graduate study) on February 3, 1957, to confer about the desires of Aaron to find a Southern Baptist church in which to worship. Growing out of this, a mission of twenty-seven persons was formed on May 5, 1957, in New York City, and two months later it was adopted by the College Avenue Baptist Church, Annapolis, Maryland, as sponsor. This represented the beginning of extensive Maryland Baptist participation in the northeastern expansion. Paul James became pastor of this New York mission on November 3, 1957, and at the same time he was appointed by the Home Mission Board as director of all Home Mission Board work in the Northeast. On January 10, 1958, this mission was constituted into the Manhattan Baptist Church with ninety-nine charter members. By the following year, sixteen missions sponsored by this church (two jointly with other churches) became churches, almost half of them being quite distant from New York City.

> The four oldest churches in the New England General Association were missions of the church, as was the first Southern Baptist work in the Philadelphia area, out of which grew the Delaware Valley Baptist Association and eventually part of the Pennsylvania state convention. Two of the first churches in the language ministry in New York were missions of the church along with two churches in upstate New York, and almost every church in the Metropolitan New York Baptist Association was either a mission of Manhattan Church or is directly descended from it.[40]

James resigned as pastor of this church in December, 1963, in order to devote full time to his duties as director of the work in the Metropolitan Baptist Association, whose story will next be sketched.

It will be recalled that in April, 1960, the Northeastern Baptist Association was formed by five churches in Pennsylvania, New Jersey, New York, and New Hampshire. After the final session of the Northeastern Association on October 20, 1962, it was dissolved, and three new associations were formed from its churches: the Delaware Valley, New England, and the Metropolitan Baptist Association of New York. On that October date, 40 messengers representing 8 churches (3 in New Jersey and 5 in New York and its environs) and 1,285 members, constituted the Metropolitan Baptist Association. Paul James was the first moderator. In 1963 he was appointed area director for the Metropolitan Association by the Home Mission Board, and remained in this office until the organization of the New York state body in 1969. This association was affiliated with the Baptist Convention of Maryland until the state body in New York was formed. The Nashville (Tenn.) Baptist Association adopted this association in 1963 and assisted it with "cash gifts to churches, arranging for loans and bond sales, and sending individuals and busloads of people for evangelistic work and Vacation Bible Schools." Other churches throughout the Southern Baptist Convention have provided similar help to churches and missions in the association.[41]

There were several antecedents to the formation of the first Southern Baptist state body in the Northeast. The old Northeastern Baptist Association (1960) and the Northeastern Regional Fellowship (1960) were found to be too large in geographical area to be effective, so in 1964 at a meeting of the last-named body, it was agreed that smaller fellowships units would be desirable. In September, 1965, the New York-Northern New Jersey Fellowship was formed. In 1967 the larger regional fellowship body suggested that the six New England states provide one organizational unit, while churches in New York state, northern New Jersey, and southwestern Connecticut should look toward forming their own convention. In the spring and fall of 1968, fellowship meetings of the churches in the last three states named above were held in New York.

On September 29, 1969, representatives from 70 churches, 27 chapels, and 10,494 members met at Syracuse, New York, where the Baptist Convention of New York was constituted. Kenneth Lyle was elected president of the body, while Paul S. James became executive secretary-treasurer and John M. Tubbs the director of the division of education.

In 1972 this convention reported affiliation by 6 associations, 85 churches, and 12,874 members. Total receipts were $2,650,181, of which $470,169 was provided for missions.

2. Pennsylvania and New Jersey. The Southern Baptist entrance into the two Middle Atlantic states of Pennsylvania and New Jersey has been related to the beginnings in New York City and was the outgrowth of assistance and leadership from the Maryland and Ohio conventions and the Home Mission Board.

Southern Baptist layman were instrumental in the beginning of churches in Pennsylvania almost simultaneously in the western, central, and eastern sections of the state. In western Pennsylvania, on May 3, 1958, representatives of the Home Mission Board and the Ohio convention met with Jack Edens at Pittsburgh to discuss plans for forming a church there, and on October 30, 1959, one was constituted with ninety-eight charter members as the culmination of many months of planning and preparation. In central Pennsylvania a Florida layman, Frank Brown, began a Southern Baptist mission in Middletown in May, 1958, which was formed into the Valley Baptist Church in the following May. In eastern Pennsylvania, after several interested Southern Baptist families met for fellowship and prayer in their homes, a mission was begun in October, 1958; and on March 20, 1960, the Delaware Valley Baptist Church of Levittown, Pennsylvania, was organized. Steady growth in the number of churches brought the organization of the Delaware Valley Baptist Association on October 27, 1962, with 3 churches, 3 chapels, and 460 members. Richard C. Bracken was the first moderator. The Keystone Baptist Association was formed in November, 1962, with 4 churches and 371 members. Kenneth A. Estep was the first moderator. The Greater Pittsburgh Baptist Association was organized on September 13, 1963, with four churches and five missions from the Upper Ohio Valley Baptist Association in Ohio. Prior to 1970, churches in the first two associations were affiliated with Maryland Baptists, while those in the third were related to Ohio Baptists.

In New Jersey, the organization of Southern Baptist churches began in two distinct areas. In the Jersey suburbs of New York, with the assistance of the Manhattan Baptist Church of New York City, the Madison Baptist Church, Madison, New Jersey, was formed on May, 1, 1960; and during the following decade, the Manhattan church assisted in the formation of sixteen other churches in northern New Jersey. All of them affiliated with the Metropolitan Baptist Association of New York. Churches formed in southern New Jersey developed in a different context. Located contiguous to eastern Pennsylvania, they were organized at Cherry Hill and Willingboro in the suburbs of Philadelphia, near Atlantic City and Cape May along the Atlantic coast, at the military installations at Fort Dix-McGuire and Lakehurst, and at Trenton. Prior to 1970, these affiliated with the Delaware Valley Baptist Association of Pennsylvania.

When the Northeastern Regional Fellowship voted to work toward establishing smaller fellowship groups, the churches in Pennsylvania and southern New Jersey formed the Pennsylvania-South Jersey Baptist Fellowship and held annual meetings until 1969. On October 3-4 of that year, plans were completed to organize a bi-state convention, and on October 2-3, 1970, the Baptist Convention of Pennsylvania-South Jersey was formed with approximately 50 churches and 9,000 members. By 1972 this convention reported 3 associations, 57 churches, and 9,819 members. Total receipts were $1,549,562, of which missions received $444,432.

South Atlantic Region. The story of Southern Baptist progress in the seven older states of Maryland, District of Columbia, Virginia, North Carolina, South Carolina, Georgia, and Florida, has already been sketched in the previous section. During this modern period Southern Baptists have entered or enlarged their work in the last two of the South Atlantic states—Delaware and West Virginia.

1. Delaware. Southern Baptist work in Delaware evidently began with the formation in 1951 of a mission in Wilmington which developed into the Bethany Baptist Church. Nick Salios was its pastor from the beginning.[42] In 1960, two missions of the church were constituted into churches on consecutive days.[43]

In October, 1967, the Delaware Baptist Association was organized at Dover, consisting of 6 churches and 2 chapels with 2,297 members. Prior to this time, the churches had affiliated with Maryland's Eastern or Susquehanna Associations. Charles W. Adams was the first moderator. The new association, covering the entire state, affiliated with the Baptist Convention of Maryland. Their report in 1972 showed 8 churches with 3,145 members. Total receipts were $326,324, of which $55,695 was provided for missions.

2. West Virginia. Not all of the early Southern Baptist churches in West Virginia withdrew from the Baptist General Association of Virginia when this state separated from Virginia in 1863.[44] The geographical location of the churches at Charleston, Martinsburg, and Princeton in the eastern panhandle, and in Mercer County in the southern section, made their relationship with Virginia Baptists·close and fraternal. As in the case of other border states, Southern Baptist work spilled over into West Virginia. In 1958 there were thirty-three Southern Baptist churches in West Virginia; nine of them affiliated with the state bodies in Kentucky and Ohio, and twenty-four with Virginia.

In 1958 the Home Mission Board employed John I. Snedden as area superintendent of missions in West Virginia, with additional support provided by Southern Baptists in Kentucky, Ohio, and Virginia. In 1959 a West Virginia Pastors' Fellowship was formed with Willard Jenkins as president. In 1966 the Baptist General Association of West Virginia was organized by representatives of fifty-four churches and four associations. Jenkins became its president. Meanwhile, in 1964, Francis R. Tallant was called to be religious education director for the state.

On October 29-30, 1970, the West Virginia Convention of Southern Baptists was constituted at Belle, West Virginia, with John I. Sneeden as executive secretary-treasurer. Its report for 1972 showed 6 associations, 54 churches, and 14,626 members. Total receipts were $1,228,468, of which $176,089 was provided for missions.

East North Central Region. It will be recalled that in the earlier story of Baptists in Missouri and Illinois, both states were included in the "North Central region." The extensive enlargement of Southern Baptist work in this period makes it necessary to use the Census Bureau's subdivisions of the East North Central region (Ohio, Indiana, Illinois, Michigan, and Wisconsin), and the West North Central region (Minnesota, Iowa, Missouri, North Dakota, South Dakota, Nebraska, and Kansas). In some cases, Southern Baptist regional bodies overlapped the geographical regions this structure marked off. Southern Baptist expansion in the East North Central region will be described first.

1. Ohio. As was true in many pioneer areas, Southern Baptist beginnings in Ohio resulted from the spilling over of southern people with Baptist views into this state.[45] Some of these who located just across the river from Kentucky desired to continue their old relationship with Southern Baptists, and several small congregations of Southern Baptists were organized before 1940.[46] On November 1, 1940, five such churches formed the White Water Association of Southern Baptists and affiliated with the state body in Kentucky.[47] V. B. Castleberry served this association as missionary for nine years, at the close of which there were 19 churches, 6 missions, and approximately 4,000 members.

In 1952, with the help of Kentucky Baptists and the Home Mission Board, Ray E. Roberts became missionary of this association, and under his leadership an aggressive home missionary program was launched that resulted in the formation of Southern Baptist churches as far to the north as the Great Lakes and to the east as New York and West Virginia.

On January 8, 1954, the State Convention of Baptists in Ohio was formed, representing thirty-nine churches in Ohio.[48] All but five of these had been affiliated with the White Water Association, which voluntarily dissolved and surrendered its name. The first moderator of the state body was John Kurtz, while Roberts was named first executive secretary-treasurer. Three new associations were planned: Southern, to include Cincinnati and the area surrounding it; Central, to include Dayton and the area surrounding it; and Northern, to include Akron and Cleveland and the areas surrounding them. Central Baptist Association was formed on February 25, 1954, with fourteen churches; Greater Cincinnati Association was formed on March 16, 1954, with twenty churches in the southern area; while Erie Association was formed on March 20, 1954, with eight cooperating churches and missions in the northern area. Three new associations were constituted in the following year, reflecting the aggressive evangelistic and missionary program of the new body. In addition, as has been indicated in the description of the beginning of churches in New York, Pennsylvania, West Virginia, and elsewhere, the activity of this new state body in aiding Southern Baptists in other pioneer areas was remarkable.

In 1972 this state convention reported 17 associations, 381 churches, and 91,540 members. Total receipts were $9,644,670, of which $1,671,177 was for missions.

2. Indiana.   Indiana Southern Baptists actually existed in the previous period. Southern Baptists from Illinois and Kentucky, in particular, had spilled over into Indiana. In 1914 the Second Baptist Church of Hymera, Indiana, was constituted and affiliated with the Palestine Association of the Illinois Baptist State Association.[49] In the intervening forty-four years before the formation of the state body in 1958, Southern Baptists churches were organized independently in four areas of Indiana. Beginning in the 1920's Southern Baptists in the Evansville section related themselves initially to Illinois associations, then to Kentucky associations. In 1931 a church was formed by Baptists from Kentucky near Brooksville, Indiana, and, with others in the area, for five years affiliated with a Kentucky association. These formed an independent association in 1951 and in 1954 related to the Illinois

Baptist State Association. In 1934 a church composed of Southern Baptists was organized in East Chicago, Indiana, but moved to Hammond and affiliated with the Illinois state body. With five other Southern Baptist churches in the Chicago area, the Hammond church formed the Great Lakes Baptist Association; but in 1955, with other churches in northern Indiana, it constituted the Lake Michigan Baptist Association and affiliated with the Illinois Baptist State Association. In 1948, just across the Ohio River from Louisville, Kentucky, the first Southern Baptist church of Clarksville was established, securing affiliation with a Kentucky association.

A significant forward thrust came in 1954 when the Illinois Baptist State Association took the initiative to employ a pioneer missionary in Indiana to correlate the work and look toward the formation of a state body. On September 29-30, 1955, a fellowship meeting of all Indiana Southern Baptists was held at Indianapolis under the leadership of E. M. Taylor, secretary of missions for Kentucky Baptists, and E. H. Moore, secretary of stewardship and missions of the Illinois state body. At a second such meeting in the following year, plans were laid for a new state body in Indiana. On October 3, 1958, the State Convention of Baptists in Indiana was organized, with 111 churches in affiliation.[50] S. H. Cobb was elected the first president of the body, and E. Harmon Moore was named executive secretary-treasurer. The report of the first year showed 6 associations, 124 cooperating churches, and 23,361 members. This state body was voted the status of a cooperative constituency by the Southern Baptist Convention in 1962. By 1972 this state reported 14 associations, 232 churches, and 59,234 members. Total receipts were $5,611,190, of which $785,266 was expended for missions.

3. Michigan. Independent churches composed of Southern Baptists sprang up quite early in this state, perhaps in 1914.[51] The church at Jackson was probably the first Southern Baptist church.[52] In the years of depression and war, large numbers of southerners moved to Michigan to work in the factories. Many of these were Baptists, who formed independent congregations without affiliation. Six of these "independent" churches, principally around Detroit, formed the Motor Cities Association of Southern Baptist Churches in Michigan in 1951. Olin Sisk was the interim missionary and Coy Sims, the first moderator. In the following year Fred D. Hubbs was elected as the first missionary.

In January, 1953, the Arkansas Baptist State Convention, along with the Home Mission Board of the Southern Baptist body, began actively supporting the Michigan association with prayers, finances, and personnel. On October 1, 1957, the representatives from the forty-nine churches in the Motor Cities Association met at Roseville and agreed to plan for a state body. In November, 1957, at Detroit, the Baptist State Convention of Michigan was constituted by representatives of fifty-two churches.[53] At the same time, the Motor Cities Baptist Association was dissolved, and five new associational bodies were constituted. H. T. Starkey was the first convention president, Fred D. Hubbs became the executive secretary, and Kenneth Day was named state director of missions. Truett Smith, who had come to Michigan in 1955 as missionary pastor and seminary extension director, became editor of the state paper.

By 1972 this state body represented 13 associations, 169 churches, and 37,384 members. Total receipts in 1972 were $3,733,774, of which $538,214 was for missions.

4. Wisconsin. Southern Baptist activity began in this state when four Southern Baptist couples in Madison, Wisconsin, explored the possibility of starting a Southern Baptist church. Their efforts resulted in the formation of the Midvale Baptist Church, Madison, on September 20, 1953.[54] Within three years there were six such churches, whose affiliation was with the Great Lakes Baptist Association and the Illinois Baptist State Association. In October, 1956, these six Wisconsin churches and the Southtown Baptist Church of Minneapolis, Minnesota, formed the Wisconsin-Minnesota Baptist Association, representing 411 members. In November of that year this association became affiliated with the Baptist General Convention of Texas, who also helped sponsor the work. By October, 1965, there were 21 churches and 3,000 members in this association, but the long distance between the places of meeting by the association demanded restructuring. In that month the Wisconsin-Minnesota Association disbanded. Minnesota Southern Baptists organized the Northland Baptist Association, while Wisconsin Southern Baptists organized the Lakeland Baptist Association and the Central Wisconsin Baptist Association. The Lakeland Association had eight churches, while the Central Association had nine churches and chapels. Frank B. Burress was named superintendent of missions for the state, and Texas Baptists continued to sponsor the Wisconsin work.

In 1972 the Southern Baptists of Wisconsin reported 19 churches and 3,452 members. Total receipts were $430,257, of which $57,373 was for missions.

West North Central Region. This section consists of the seven states of Minnesota, Iowa, Missouri, North Dakota, South Dakota, Nebraska, and Kansas. Southern Baptists in Missouri have already been described previously.

1. Minnesota. Transplanted Southern Baptists in the Minneapolis-St. Paul area began the process that led to the formation of the Southtown Baptist Church (at first called Tabernacle) on September 24, 1956, with twenty-eight charter members. Warren Littleford was its pastor.[55] The church became affiliated with a newly-organized Wisconsin-Minnesota Baptist Association. On November 6, 1956, this association became affiliated with the Baptist General Convention of Texas. In October, 1965, the Wisconsin-Minnesota Baptist Association was dissolved to form three new associations, two in Wisconsin (as mentioned in that story) and one in Minnesota. The Minnesota body was named the Northland Baptist Association, and Littleford resigned the Southtown church to become superintendent of missions. In 1972 Minnesota Southern Baptists reported 14 churches and 1,658 members. Total receipts of that year were $347,016, of which $47,794 was used for missions.

2. *Iowa.* The familiar pattern of beginning was followed in the case of Iowa Southern Baptists. Baptists from the South moved into the area near Anamosa, Iowa, and met in their homes for worship. On June 12, 1954, the Fairview Baptist Church, located in a village four miles southwest of Anamosa, was constituted with sixteen members, the first Southern Baptist church in Iowa. After the superintendent of missions for Missouri's North Grand River Association had assisted part-time in Iowa, the Home Mission Board and Missouri Baptists aided in the employment of a superintendent of missions in Iowa in April, 1960. On April 17, 1965, the first association was organized, composed of 24 churches and chapels and a total membership of 2,809.[56]

The principal population centers have been occupied since the first church was formed in 1954, and the report for 1972 showed 21 churches and 5,548 members. Mission gifts totaled $119,918, while total receipts were $772,815.

3. *North Dakota.* Oil-field workers from Southern Baptist life who moved to the area of Williston, North Dakota, initiated Southern Baptist churches in this state. Through the assistance of O. R. Delmar from Arizona Baptists, the First Southern Baptist Church of Williston was organized on March 15, 1953, with twelve charter members. On December 14, 1954, the North Dakota Southern Baptist Association was formed with five churches. This body affiliated with Arizona Southern Baptists, then changed to the newly-organized Colorado Baptist General Convention when it was formed in 1955. The Home Mission Board assisted with pastoral missionaries at Minot, Grand Forks, and Fargo in 1958, and in 1961 the Baptist State Convention of North Carolina became sponsor of the North Dakota work.

In eastern North Dakota, the activity of W. J. Hughes as pastoral missionary at Grand Forks led to the constituting of the Faith Southern Baptist Church (at first called the First Southern Baptist Church) on June 14, 1959. It became a fruitful center from which half-a-dozen other churches sprang. Primarily because of this growth, the original association was dissolved and two sectional associations were formed in September, 1962: the North Dakota Western Baptist Association and the North Dakota Eastern Baptist Association. As will be mentioned under the South Dakota story, North Dakota Baptists joined Baptists in South Dakota, Wyoming, and Montana to form the Northern Plains Baptist Convention on November 7-8, 1967.

4. South Dakota. A group of Southern Baptist military personnel stationed at Rapid City, South Dakota, in 1953 met in the home of Sergeant Clydal Donaho on March 25 and constituted the Calvary Baptist Church (at first called the First Southern Baptist Church) with twenty-two members. In July, L. H. Roseman became its pastor and served for ten years. "All the churches in South Dakota have been directly or indirectly influenced by the outreach of this first church." [57] Under Superintendent of Missions Robert L. Smith, who served both South Dakota and Wyoming (1955-57), Roy Owen (1957-61), and John Allen (1962-67), rapid progress was made.

Affiliated at first with the Arizona convention, South Dakota Southern Baptists became a part of the Colorado Baptist General Convention when that body was organized on November 21-23, 1955. On November 7-9, 1967, through the encouragement of Colorado Baptists, the Northern Plains Baptist Convention was formed with messengers from seventy-five Southern Baptist churches in North and South Dakota, Wyoming, and Montana.

5. Nebraska. United States Air Force personnel belonging to Southern Baptist churches and stationed at Lincoln, Nebraska, provided the initial leadership for Southern Baptists in eastern Nebraska. On Easter Sunday, 1955, a group met in the home of an Air Force sergeant for worship, and from this beginning the Southview Baptist Church (initially called the First Southern Baptist Church), Lincoln, was organized on September 11, 1955, with thirty-four charter members. The first churches in this area affiliated with a Kansas association, but in 1959 the Eastern Nebraska Baptist Association was formed, affiliating with the Kansas Convention of Southern Baptists.[58]

The western area of Nebraska has a different history. After an earlier attempt to provide a Southern Baptist church at Scottsbluff. was short-lived, a mission was organized in that town in 1955 sponsored by the Trinity Baptist Church of Longmont, Colorado. A Southern Baptist church at Greeley, Colorado, established a mission at Kimbell, Nebraska, and in February, 1956, the First Southern Baptist Church of Kimball was constituted. On September 6, 1960, messengers from five churches formed the Western Nebraska Southern Baptist Association which affiliated with the Colorado Baptist General Convention, but effective January 1, 1967, this affiliation was changed to the Kansas Convention of Southern Baptists so that all Nebraska

Southern Baptists churches could be united into one affiliation.[59] By 1972 Nebraska Southern Baptist churches numbered 23 with 5,418 members. Total receipts were $536,822, of which $89,166 was for missions.

6. Kansas. In the nineteenth century Southern Baptist missionaries had ministered among the Indian tribes who had wandered from Oklahoma into Kansas, but this ceased with the Civil War. Some Kansas Baptist churches composed of older Missouri Baptist members cooperated with a Missouri Baptist association about 1910, but accurate records are not available. The familiar pattern of Southern Baptists spilling over from adjoining states began in Kansas about 1910. In 1911 the Wirtonia Baptist Church near Crestline, Kansas, joined the Spring River Baptist Association of Missouri.[60] By 1945, churches at Baxter Springs, Lawton, Arma, and Macedonia had done likewise.

In 1943 Oklahoma Baptists listed ten Kansas Churches affiliating with them. When the Baptist General Convention of Oklahoma met in 1944 at Tulsa, plans were made to develop more unity among the Kansas churches which were affiliating with six Oklahoma associations.[61] In November, 1945, representatives from four Kansas Baptist churches cooperating with Oklahoma Baptists formed a Southern Baptist Fellowship, and on March 19, 1946, representatives from seven churches met at Chetopa and organized a state body, whose name became the Kansas Convention of Southern Baptists. N. J. Westmoreland became executive secretary-treasurer on October 14, 1946.[62] On May 11, 1955, sponsorship of work in Nebraska was authorized, and by 1967, all Southern Baptists churches and associations in Nebraska were affiliated with the Kansas body.[63] By 1972 Kansas Baptists reported 13 associations, 198 churches, and 57,666 members. Total receipts in 1972 were $47,658,277, of which $7,833,021 was for missions.

Mountain Region. The census structure for the Mountain region included the states of Montana, Idaho, Wyoming, Colorado, New Mexico, Arizona, Utah, and Nevada. The Southern Baptist regional structures, however, cut across these Census Bureau lines. The description of the beginnings will follow the census regional structure, but in Baptist organizational structure, North and South Dakota from the West North Central region joined with Wyoming and Montana from the Mountain region to form the Northern Plains Baptist Convention, as suggested previously. Utah and Idaho united to form a single regional convention, but both of them are in the Mountain region of the census structure.

1. Wyoming. On June 24, 1951, at Casper, Wyoming, a small group of Southern Baptist families principally related to the oil industry met for Bible study and discussion of plans to form a Southern Baptist church in the area. Two weeks later, at their invitation, O. R. Delmar of the Arizona convention conducted worship services. The following Sunday, July 15, the First Southern Baptist Church of Casper was formed with Delmar as pastor. By the end of 1952, as a result of missions conducted by this church, new Southern Baptist churches had been constituted at Wheatland, Cheyenne, and Cody. Three new churches were formed in 1953 and five more by 1954. The first association, Old Faithful Southern Baptist Association, organized on September 24, 1956, served all of the churches in the state initially, but on January 6, 1958, the Frontier Baptist Association was formed; on September 8, 1961, the Yellowstone Baptist Association was added; and on May 11, 1964, the Green River Baptist Association was organized. In the fall of 1952 Delmar was elected area missionary for Wyoming and Montana, and later North Dakota was added. Robert L. Smith came in May, 1955, to assume leadership in Wyoming as well as South Dakota.

From 1952 to 1956 all of the Wyoming Southern Baptist churches affiliated with Arizona Southern Baptists, but in 1956, after the organization of the Colorado convention, Wyoming churches affiliated with that body. In 1967 Wyoming representatives helped form the Northern Plains Baptist Convention, and statistics for 1972 will be shown for that body.

2. Montana. Southern Baptist churches in Montana stemmed from the Casper church in Wyoming. The W. C. King family from that church moved to Billings, Montana, and about that time the Alvie McCaslin family, whom the Casper pastor had known in Texas, moved to a ranch seventy-two miles west of Billings. With leadership from O. R. Delmar a mission was organized. Following a revival meeting held by Glen Braswell, a Texas minister, he was called as pastor of the mission, and on December 7, 1952, Emmanuel Baptist Church (initially called the First Southern Baptist Church) was constituted with thirty-two charter members. Through the efforts of this church, four new missions were begun and by the end of 1953 had become churches. Southern Baptists in this state, as mentioned, formed a part of the new Northern Plains Baptist Convention.

After careful plans had been laid in conference with the Colorado convention, a meeting was held in Rapid City, South Dakota, on November 7-9, 1967, composed of messengers from seventy-five Southern Baptist churches in Wyoming, Montana, North Dakota, and South Dakota, and the Northern Plains Baptist Convention was formed. John P. Baker was named executive secretary-treasurer of the body, and a typical structure of state leadership was provided.

By 1972 this convention (consisting of Southern Baptists in four states) reported 14 associations, 83 churches, and 14,247 members.

Total receipts were $1,542,412, of which $274,765 was given to missions.

3. Colorado. In 1930 a group of transplanted Arkansas Baptists organized a Baptist church known as Mt. Tabor, at Byers, Colorado, and in 1954, after an intermittent history of affiliation, this church affiliated with the Denver Association of Southern Baptists. The site of the first definite Southern Baptist church in Colorado was Alamosa, where a church was constituted in 1934 under the sponsorship of a New Mexico association.[64] Although this church disbanded later, the pastor, L. W. Rieschel organized a church in Cortez in 1938, "the oldest continuing Southern Baptist church in Colorado," [65] which affiliated with New Mexico Baptists. By 1950 half-a-dozen additional churches had been organized in Colorado, all affiliated with New Mexico Baptists. In 1951, after conference between the leaders of the several state bodies and the Home Mission Board, all Southern Baptist churches in Colorado came under the sponsorship of the Baptist General Convention of Arizona. On July 7, 1952, six churches formed the Southern Baptist Association of Colorado, affiliating with the Arizona body, and other associations followed shortly.[66]

Southern Baptist activity on the eastern slope expanded substantially with the organization of the Denver Temple Baptist Church on August 19, 1951, such growth coming partly from financial assistance given by individuals, churches, associations, and state bodies outside of the state.[67] Work on the western slope grew more slowly. A regional convention was formed at Denver on May 5, 1954, when 348 representatives from Southern Baptist churches in the five states of Colorado, Wyoming, Montana, North Dakota, and South Dakota combined their strength. This convention had no administrative or executive functions, but was organized for fellowship, promotion, and cooperation. It was dissolved at its third meeting in 1955 to prepare for the organization of a state convention in Colorado.

After carefully planning, a new state body was formed in Colorado on November 21, 1955, at Colorado Springs, involving 90 churches and 9,815 members.[68] Willis J. Ray was elected executive secretary-treasurer, and after his retirement in 1962, was succeeded by Glen E. Braswell. Colorado Southern Baptists worked very closely in the organization of the Northern Plains Baptist Convention, involving the states of Wyoming, Montana, North Dakota, and South Dakota, whom they had continued to assist until the organization of their own regional body in 1967. By 1972 Colorado Southern Baptists reported 10 associations, 129 churches, and 43,102 members. Total receipts were $4,323,470, of which $578,855 was for missions.

4. Utah and Idaho. Oil, uranium, and steel brought Baptists from the South into both Utah and Idaho. Under the sponsorship of a

Texas church, the first Southern Baptist church in Utah was organized at Roosevelt on July 2, 1944. It affiliated with Arizona Southern Baptists and with their assistance, churches were constituted at Clearfield and Vernal in 1946, Provo in 1948, and Gusher in 1951. Missions were also developed for the Indians.

In southern Idaho, the Calvary Baptist Church was organized in Idaho Falls in 1951; while in northern Idaho, the first church was the Orchards Baptist Church at Lewiston, constituted in May, 1953. These churches were composed of Southern Baptist migrants. Those in northern Idaho affiliated with the Oregon-Washington convention, while the churches in southern Idaho affiliated with the Arizona Southern Baptist Convention.

The first association in the two-state area was the Utah Association, formed in 1951 by four churches formerly affiliated with the Central Association of Phoenix, Arizona. In 1953 four churches in Idaho, formerly affiliated with the Utah Association, constituted the Twin Buttes Baptist Association, which in four years split into three associations.

After five years of regional cooperation, assisted principally by the Arizona Southern Baptist Convention, the Utah-Idaho Southern Baptist Convention was formed on January 1, 1965, by representatives from fifty churches which had formerly affiliated with the Arizona body. Charles H. Ashcraft was named executive secretary-treasurer, but was succeeded by Darwin E. Welsh in 1969. In 1972 this convention reported 8 associations, 62 churches, and 9,916 members. Total receipts were $835,437, of which $148,489 was given to missions.

5. Nevada.   The first Southern Baptist affiliated church in this state seems to have been the First Baptist Church, Boulder City, Nevada, just at the very southern tip of the state where it adjoins Arizona. The church was organized in 1951 with Maurice F. Wicker as its first pastor. Its report to the Arizona convention, with whom it affiliated in 1951 through the Mohave Association, showed fifty members. The Boulder City church, along with three churches in the northwestern edge of Arizona, formed the Mohave Association in 1951.[69] J. L. Eddings was assisted, along with Wicker, by the Arizona convention in the ministry of this early church.

The second principal thrust in Nevada came in the Las Vegas area. Charles Ashcraft, brotherhood secretary of New Mexico at the time, visited Las Vegas and became concerned about its spiritual needs. Without any sort of appointment or promise of support, he and his family moved to Las Vegas on January 14, 1955, and purchased a home there. On May 8, 1955, after visiting and witnessing, a mission was established, and on June 26, 1955, a church was established with thirty-three charter members. It became the nucleus for the organization of several churches in the Las Vegas area.[70]

In 1956 the Nevada churches formerly affiliated with the Mohave Association withdrew and formed the Lake Mead Baptist Association, and are hopeful that by 1980 a state body may be formed. In 1972 Nevada Southern Baptists reported 31 churches with 8,384 members. Total receipts were $759,362, while mission expenditures totaled $81,718.

Pacific Region. This region consists of five states: California, Washington, Oregon, Alaska, and Hawaii. The story of California Southern Baptists has already been sketched. Since the Oregon-Washington convention has also affiliated with Baptist churches in Canada and raised the question of Convention affiliation with Canadian churches, that decision will be discussed at this point.

1. Oregon-Washington. Baptists settled in Oregon and Washington as early as 1844, and on May 25 of that year organized the West Union Baptist Church, the first Baptist church west of the Rocky Mountains. From almost the very beginning of their history in these areas, Baptists emigrating from the North and those from the South disagreed sharply over many issues, some of them doctrinal.[71] In 1893 and 1897 one group applied to the Southern Baptist Convention for affiliation without success.[72] The confrontations between the Northern Baptist Convention and both Conservative Baptists and the General Association of Regular Baptists in the 1940's brought confusion and conflict in the area. However, many of the churches denied recognition in the 1890's had been Southern Baptist in constituency and leadership from their very beginnings.

The new policy of the Southern Baptist Convention, by which California began affiliation in 1942, brought encouragement to Southern Baptists of the churches in Oregon and Washington. Some of the churches affiliated with the California Southern Baptist body, the first being the First Baptist Church, Sweet Home, Oregon, in June, 1946.[73] On April 13, 1948, at the Antioch Baptist Church of Portland, Oregon, representatives from 15 churches with approximately 2,000 members organized the Baptist General Convention of Oregon-Washington. R. E. Milam was named executive secretary. In the following year this was granted recognition as a cooperating constituency of the southern convention.[74] At the time the regional convention was organized in 1948, two associations were formed: Oregon Baptist Association with eight churches, and the Washington Baptist Association with seven churches. In 1971 the Oregon-Washington body changed its name to the Northwest Baptist Convention. In 1972 it reported 22 associations, 234 churches, and 44,641 members. Total receipts were $4,498,421, of which $736,197 was given for missions.

The question of recognition for churches in Canada arose as early as 1951, when the Emmanuel Baptist Church, Vancouver, British Columbia, looked favorably toward affiliation with the Southern Baptist Convention.[75] In October, 1953, the church was received into affiliation with the Oregon-Washington convention, claiming doctrinal convictions different from those held by most Canadian groups.[76] The Convention emphasized that it was not entering Canada as a mission field, but simply responding to a request for affiliation, thus permitting state missionaries from the Oregon-Washington convention to work with the new affiliate in Canada. When other churches began to seek similar affiliation, the Oregon-Washington body petitioned the Southern Baptist Convention in 1954 asking that the agencies of the southern body be permitted to aid the regional convention in this work. The petition pointed out that the Home Mission Board was at work in Panama and Cuba, where there was a language barrier, and in Alaska, which was farther away than Canada. In presenting the petition, Secretary R. E. Milam said that many Southern Baptists had moved into Canada and were desirous of southern affiliation. He asked that any supporting agency of the southern convention be permitted to render aid to a Canadian church affiliating with the Oregon-Washington body. After much discussion, the motion was adopted.[77] When the Baptist Union of Western Canada protested in 1954, the Executive Committee appointed a committee from the Home Mission Board to meet with them. This committee's report was adopted by the board, agreeing (1) that the board shall recognize that Baptist brethren as individuals, local churches, associations, and state conventions are autonomous and may affiliate with whomever they will; (2) that the board may accept invitations from any Baptist church or groups of Baptist churches in Canada to help promote their programs for the development of their own members; (3) that no worker of the board whose salary is paid in part or in full by the board may establish residence in Canada or seek to align existing churches or new churches with Southern Baptists; and (4) that the board will render all assistance possible to help Baptists in Canada develop an indigenous denominational program to win Canada to Christ.[78] In 1957 the Convention voted to revise this statement to allow a salaried employee of the board to reside in Canada and work under the board. A joint committee was appointed to guide relations between Canadian Baptists and Southern Baptists. It was composed of representatives from the southern convention, the Baptist Federation of Canada, the Oregon-Washington convention, and perhaps from the Fellowship of Evangelical Baptist Churches of Canada.[79] In 1957 the Home Mission Board named Bertram King as liaison agent for Canada.[80]

The Oregon-Washington convention endeavored to secure the seat-ing of Canadian messengers at the Southern Baptist Convention in 1958 but failed. In 1963 the Oregon-Washington body had its annual session at Vancouver, British Columbia. In 1972 Canadian Baptists related to the Northwest Baptist Convention reported 21 churches, 1,627 members, total receipts of $351,965, and mission expenditures of $57,992.

2. *Alaska.*   Southern Baptist work in Alaska began with the organization of the First Baptist Church, Anchorage, with seventeen charter members on September 19, 1943.[81] There had been no Baptist church in Anchorage before this time, and only one Baptist church in all of Alaska. The initiative for this beginning came from Major Aubrey Halsell, a Southern Baptist chaplain who had been stationed at Anchorage, and after holding a revival there, took the lead in establishing the church.[82] Inspired by reports of this work, Felton II. Griffin, a Texas minister, moved to Anchorage in July, 1944, and in the following year became pastor of the Anchorage church. Additional Southern Baptist churches were organized in Juneau and Fairbanks. Messengers from these three Alaska churches met at Anchorage on March 27, 1946, and organized the Alaska Baptist Convention.[93] After some discussion between northern and southern Baptist bodies about the promotion of mission work in Alaska, the Home Mission Board of the South appointed B. I. Carpenter and his wife of Ketchican as their first missionaries to the territory in 1948. Until 1951 the only Northern Baptist church in Alaska (at Kodiak) sent messengers to the Alaska Baptist Convention, but after 1951, this action ceased. The first full-time executive secretary of the convention was L. A. Watson, who was named to that office in 1956. After statehood was secured by Alaska on January 2, 1959, the Southern Baptist work there was unified and strengthened. By 1972 this convention reported 4 associations, 37 churches, and 12,961 members. Total receipts were $1,397,110, of which $260,279 was given to missions.

3. *Hawaii.*   Southern Baptist activity in Hawaii sprang principally from the work of missionaries of the Foreign Mission Board when the war in the Orient closed mission fields in the late 1930's and early 1940's in that sector. There had been Baptist work prior to this time,[84] but after surveying the field, the foreign board led in the organization of the Hawaiian Baptist Mission on December 12, 1940, which was a trusteeship to hold deeds to church property. One of the trustees was Charles J. McDonald, a Baptist businessman and lay preacher, who evidently started Baptist work in Hawaii. By 1943 there were five Baptist churches in the Islands, and representatives from them met on July 16, 1943, to organize a Baptist association. Missionaries Edwin B. Dozier and Victor Koon served as moderator and treasurer, respectively. In 1945 the name of this body was changed

to the Hawaii Baptist Convention.[85] On March 2, 1959, Hawaii was granted statehood, at which time the assets of the mission were transferred to the Hawaii Baptist Convention.[86] Stanton Nash was elected first executive secretary of the new body on July 21, 1959, and he was succeeded on September 1, 1963, by Edmond Walker. In 1972 this convention reported 6 associations, 32 churches, and 9,572 members. Total receipts were $1,405,253, of which $208,377 was given to missions.

Summary

In order to permit comparison of growth with previous periods, this summary will first focus on the older states of the South; i.e., those who had Baptists at the opening of this period in 1917; then will describe the expansion areas where Southern Baptist activity has developed since 1917; and finally will note briefly the overall picture of the constituency of the Southern Baptist Convention in 1972.

Southern Baptists in the eighteen southern states where they were working in 1917 increased from 909 associations, 24,883 churches, and 2,844,301 members in 1917 to 1,004 associations, 31,659 churches, and 10,282,154 members in 1972, or an average annual membership growth of 4.75%. This compares quite favorably with the percentages of growth in previous periods (5.22% between 1877 and 1917; 2.25% between 1860 and 1877; 4.79% between 1845 and 1860; and 7.20% between 1814 and 1845) since the large number of constituents in 1917 made percentage of growth more difficult to maintain. The population in these same states increased from 41,688,784 in 1920 to 77,313,381 in 1970, or an average annual growth of 1.71%, far short of the Baptist growth.

Regionally, the southwestern areas of these older Baptist states continued to increase in the percentage of Baptist membership growth slightly more rapidly than the east. The South Atlantic region had an average annual membership growth during this period of 5.37%; the South Central region, 5.78%; the North Central region, 3.01%; and the Mountain region (only one state—New Mexico), 23.69%.

The seven states constituting the South Atlantic region (Maryland, District of Columbia, Virginia, North Carolina, South Carolina, Georgia, and Florida) contained 33.49% of all Southern Baptists in 1972, compared with 35.91% in 1917. In the order of the number of Southern Baptists living there in 1972, the several South Atlantic states contained the following percentages of Southern Baptists: North Carolina (8.67%), Georgia (8.62%), Florida (5.67%), South Carolina (5.00%), Virginia (4.48%), Maryland (.72%), and District of Columbia (.33%).

By 1972, 53.33% of all Southern Baptists lived in the eight South Central states of Kentucky, Tennessee, Alabama, Mississippi, Arkansas, Louisiana, Oklahoma, and Texas, compared with 54.14% in 1917. As in the case of the South Atlantic region, this drop in percentage of Southern Baptists did not take place because substantial growth was not experienced, but was the result of large numbers of Baptists in the new expansion areas in 1972. In the order of their Baptist strength, the South Central states in 1972 contained the following percentages of all Southern Baptists: Texas (16.29%), Tennessee (7.60%), Alabama (7.26%), Kentucky (5.67%), Oklahoma (4.77%), Mississippi (4.63%), Louisiana (4.06%), and Arkansas (3.04%).

The two states of the North Central region (Missouri and Illinois) contained 6.08% of all Southern Baptists in 1972, compared with 9.70% in 1917. Missouri had 4.43% of these in 1972, while Illinois had 1.65%.

New Mexico, the only Mountain region state with Baptists in 1917, contained .78% of all Southern Baptists in 1972, compared with .235% in 1917.

Although not the best way to describe advance, statistics were used to summarize the increase both in the enlistment of people and the enlargement of ministries in the older eighteen states during this period. A glance at the tables provided in the text of this chapter reveals the impressive nature of the growth experienced in the last fifty-five years. A cross section of the increasing importance of education, teaching, writing, laymen, and women may be glimpsed in a study of the leaders appearing in the *Encyclopedia of Southern Baptists* for the modern period. In the South Atlantic region, 172 names were shown as serving during this period. Of these, 130 were college trained, 64 were teachers (almost totally on a university or seminary level), 12 were authors, 2 were publishers, 19 were editors, 45 were laymen (including a governor and 2 United States senators), and 5 were women. Not many new schools were founded during this period, but the student enrollment in this region grew from approximately 8,300 in 1917 to 43,395 in 1972. In the South Central region, of the 394 names of persons active in this period, 247 had at least a college degree, 121 were teachers, 93 were authors, 38 were editors, 57 were laymen (including a United States senator), and 23 were women. The enrollment in Baptist schools in these eight states increased from approximately 9,886 in 1917 to 50,905 in 1972. In the North Central region, 22 persons were shown: 20 had at least a college degree, 10 were teachers, 1 was an author, 5 were editors, and 3 were laymen. In 1917 the statistics on enrollment in schools was not shown, but by 1972, there were 3,990 students in Missouri Baptist schools. Out of 7 persons named in the Mountain region (New Mexico only), 5 were university trained, 4 were teachers, 1 was a publisher, and 1 was a woman.

This story of the constituency would be incomplete unless the significant contributions made by the principal executive in each of the state bodies were noted. The executive secretaries in the various states in 1972 were as follows:

State	Executive Secretary
Alabama	George E. Bagley
Alaska	Troy Prince
Arizona	Roy F. Sutton
Arkansas	Charles H. Ashcraft
California	Robert D. Hughes
Colorado	Glen E. Braswell
District of Columbia	James A. Langley
Florida	Harold C. Bennett
Georgia	Searcy S. Garrison
Hawaii	Edmond Walker
Illinois	James H. Smith
Indiana	E. Harmon Moore
Kansas	James (Pat) McDaniel
Kentucky	Franklin Owen
Louisiana	Robert L. Lee
Maryland	Roy D. Gresham
Michigan	Robert Wilson
Mississippi	W. Douglas Hudgins
Missouri	Earl O. Harding
Montana-Wyoming-North Dakota- South Dakota	John P. Baker
New Mexico	R. Y. Bradford
New York	Paul S. James
North Carolina	Perry Crouch
Ohio	Ray E. Roberts
Oklahoma	Joe L. Ingram
Oregon-Washington	Dan C. Stringer, Jr.
Pennsylvania-New Jersey	G. W. Bullard
South Carolina	A. Harold Cole
Tennessee	Ralph E. Norton
Texas	T. A. Patterson
Utah-Idaho	Darwin E. Welsh
Virginia	Richard M. Stephenson
West Virginia	John I. Snedden

One of the most educational and unifying factors in Southern Baptist life has been the state paper. It provides information, inspiration, leadership, promotion, and editorial opinion. It would be difficult to overestimate the influence of the thirty-one papers that served the several state and regional bodies in 1972. The following table provides a summary of the outreach of these papers.

State Convention	Name of Paper	Editor	Circulation
Alabama	The Alabama Baptist	Hudson Baggett	150,000
Alaska	Alaska Baptist Messenger	J. Troy Prince	3,000
Arizona	Baptist Beacon	C. L. Pair	10,000
Arkansas	Arkansas Baptist Newsmagazine	J. E. Sneed	60,780
California	The California Southern Baptist	Donald T. McGregor	27,500
Colorado	Rocky Mountain Baptist	O. L. Bayless	10,500
D. C.	Capital Baptist	James O. Duncan	12,000
Florida	Florida Baptist Witness	Edgar R. Cooper	67,000
Georgia	The Christian Index	Jack U. Harwell	134,000
Hawaii	Hawaii Baptist	Edmond R. Walker	2,900
Illinois	Illinois Baptist	Robert J. Hastings	48,000
Indiana	Indiana Baptist	A. C. Shackleford	5,650
Kansas-Nebraska	Baptist Digest	Pat McDaniel	5,000
Kentucky	Western Recorder	C. R. Daley, Jr.	60,000
Louisiana	The Baptist Message	James F. Cole	56,500
Maryland	The Maryland Baptist	R. G. Puckett	18,000
Michigan	Michigan Baptist Advocate	Robert Wilson	4,500
Mississippi	The Baptist Record	Joe T. Odle	112,000
Missouri	Word and Way	W. Ross Edwards	65,000
New Mexico	Baptist New Mexican	C. Eugene Whitlow	15,000
North Carolina	Biblical Recorder	J. Marse Grant	102,554
Northwest	Pacific Coast Baptist	C. E. Boyle	5,600
Ohio	Ohio Baptist Messenger	L. H. Moore	10,350
Oklahoma	Baptist Messenger	Jack L. Gritz	86,500
Penn.-S. Jersey	The Pennsylvania-Jersey Baptist	G. W. Bullard	4,000
South Carolina	The Baptist Courier	John E. Roberts	113,000
Tennessee	Baptist and Reflector	James A. Lester	72,900
Texas	Baptist Standard	John J. Hurt	376,377
Utah-Idaho	Utah-Idaho Southern Baptist Witness	Darwin E. Welsh	2,400
Virginia	The Religious Herald	J. H. Pentecost	33,500
West Virginia	Southern Baptist in West Virginia	Francis R. Tallant	2,000

In the expansion areas of Southern Baptist life, there were fifteen state or regional bodies by 1972 (Alaska, Arizona, California, Colorado, Hawaii, Indiana, Kansas, Michigan, New York, Northern Plains, Northwest, Ohio, Pennsylvania-South Jersey, Utah-Idaho, and West Virginia). The New England region, with a population of 11,847,186, contained 31 Southern Baptist churches with 5,577 members, representing .046% of all Southern Baptists. The Middle Atlantic region, with a population of 37,152,813, contained 142 Southern Baptist churches with 22,693 members in 1972, representing .19% of all Southern Baptists. The two new states in the South Atlantic region (Delaware and West Virginia), with a population of 2,292,341, contained 62 Southern Baptist churches with 17,771 members, representing .15% of all Southern Baptists. The East North Central region, with a population of 29,138,742 (not counting Illinois), contained 801 Southern Baptist churches with 191,610 members, representing 1.59% of all Southern Baptists. The West North Central region, with a population of 11,646,240 (not counting Missouri), contained 256 Southern Baptist churches with 70,290 members (not counting Missouri, North Dakota, and South Dakota), representing .58% of all Southern Baptists. The Mountain region, with 7,267,585 population (not counting New Mexico) contained 537 Southern Baptist churches with 153,836 members (including North and South Dakota from the West North Central region but not New Mexico), representing 1.27% of all Southern Baptists. The Pacific region, with a population of 26,525,774, contained 1,193 Southern Baptist churches with 334,919 members (including Canadian churches affiliating with the Northwest Baptist Convention), representing 2.78% of all Southern Baptists. The grand total of churches in the new areas was 3,022 with 796,696 members, representing 6.60% of all Southern Baptists. These statistics may seem tedious in a day of small things, but they will be valuable in decades ahead as historians ponder the growth in the new areas.[87]

Although there has not been sufficient space in the description of the structures in the new expansion areas to spell out the organizational developments in detail, that material is readily available in the *Encyclopedia of Southern Baptists* (Volumes I-III). Typical Southern Baptist organizational patterns have been developed more or less fully in each state or regional body, ofttimes staffed by volunteer workers.

H. K. Neely is doubtless correct in naming the principal reasons for this rapid territorial expansion, as follows: geographical factors (involving expansion into additional southern states); economic, social, and military factors (involving the extensive mobility of Southern Baptists toward northern and western areas); personal factors (strong personalities who vitally influenced the new areas); and religious factors (doctrine, desire for unity of effort, southern denominational consciousness and program, the work of denominational agencies, and deep concern for both unenlisted and unsaved people.)[88]

A brief overall look at the entire constituency of the Southern Baptist Convention shows that Southern Baptists increased from work in 18 states, 909 associations, 24,883 churches, and 2,844,301 members in 1917 to activity in all 50 states of the Union through 33 states and regional bodies, 1,189 associations, 34,534 churches, and 12,067,284 members in 1972. The scope of this increase may be glimpsed by the fact that the population of the nation in a burgeoning period increased from 106,021,537 in 1920 to 203,184,772 in 1970, or an average annual growth of 1.83% in the fifty-year period, while Southern Baptists between 1917 and 1972 had an average annual constituency growth (including the slow increases in some of the new pioneer areas) of 5.90%, over three times the population rate. A chart in the Appendix will show the principal statistics for all Southern Baptists in 1972.

As a matter of fact, Southern Baptists outdistanced most other major denominations in their rate of growth. Roman Catholics have increased 3.84% annually since 1918; Protestant Episcopals, 3.57%; Missouri Synod Lutherans, 2.30%; United Methodists, 1.49%; and United Presbyterians, 1.29%. Of more immediate concern, during the latest seven years reported (from 1964 to 1971), Southern Baptists grew 11.6%; Roman Catholics, 6.0%; Missouri Synod Lutheran Church, 5.2%; Jewish congregations, 4.8%; The United Methodist Church, 2.0%; and most of the other major denominational bodies have lost in membership during the same period.[89]

Notes

1. *The Quarterly Review* (Nashville), Third Quarter, 1972, p. 83.
2. Baker, *The Story of the Sunday School Board,* p. 108.
3. *Ibid.,* p. 130.
4. The Cooperative Fund gifts are reported for the year ending December 31, 1971, since the 1972 figures, due to a change in the fiscal year by the Executive Committee, are for nine months only. It should be added that the sums shown for homes for children and the aged in all of the following charts represent only state appropriations in 1972 and do not include, for example, homes in the various states for the aged that were financed by residence fees, churches, private gifts, special offerings, and endowment. For these figures for 1972, see *The Quarterly Review* (Nashville), Third Quarter, 1973, pp. 68-69.
5. Statistics are for 1971 for the reason shown in #4.
6. See previous item.
7. See previous item.
8. Porter Routh, "Areas of Cooperation Between American and Southern Baptists," *Foundations,* July, 1961, p. 200.
9. Robert G. Torbet, "Historical Background of the Southern Baptist 'Invasion,' " *Foundations,* October, 1959, pp. 317-18.
10. Blake Smith, "The Southern Baptist 'Invasion': Right or Wrong?" *Foundations,* October, 1959, pp. 324-25.
11. See, for example, *Annual,* Southern Baptist Convention, 1909, p. 33.
12. For this story, see *Annual,* Baptist General Convention of Arizona, 1928, *passim.*
13. See *Annual,* Baptist Convention of New Mexico, 1923, *passim.*
14. *Annual,* Southern Baptist Convention, 1930, p. 303.
15. *Ibid.*
16. *Annual,* Northern Baptist Convention, 1932, pp. 243-44.
17. *Annual,* Southern Baptist Convention, 1933, p. 53.
18. *Ibid.,* 1946, p. 18.
19. *The Quarterly Review* (Nashville), Third Quarter, 1960, *passim.*
20. *Annual,* Southern Baptist Convention, 1851, p. 12.

21. Cox-Woolley, eds., *Encyclopedia*, I, p. 218.

22. See Floyd Looney, *History of California Southern Baptists* (Fresno: Board of Directors of the Southern Baptist General Convention of California, 1954), pp. 13-14; note also Cox-Woolley, eds., *Encyclopedia*, I, p. 218.

23. Looney, *op. cit.*, p. 19.

24. S. G. Posey, "Southern Baptist Pioneer Work in California," in *The Quarterly Review*, Third Quarter, 1955, pp. 7 f.

25. *Annual*, Southern Baptist General Convention of California, 1941, p. 11.

26. *Annual*, Southern Baptist Convention, 1942, p. 50.

27. *Ibid.*, 1944, pp. 50-52 and p. 128.

28. See William B. Lipphard's editorial, "Southern Baptist Infiltration into California," *Missions*, December, 1944, p. 499.

29. Porter Routh, *op. cit.*, p. 201.

30. See " 'Missions' in a Strange Mission," *Western Recorder* (Kentucky), May 27, 1943, p. 8.

31. See Baker, *Relations*, pp. 210-12.

32. *Ibid.*

33. *The Quarterly Review*, Third Quarter, 1960, *passim.*

34. Baker, *Relations*, p. 162.

35. *Annual*, Southern Baptist Convention, 1909, pp. 27-28.

36. For a good resumé of this story, see H. K. Neely, Jr., *The Territorial Expansion of the Southern Baptist Convention 1894-1959*, unpublished Th.D. dissertation, Southwestern Baptist Theological Seminary, Ft. Worth, Texas, 1963, pp. 203 ff.

37. *Annual*, Southern Baptist Convention, 1951, p. 36.

38. *Ibid.*, 1955, p. 210.

39. The principal sources for the brief resumés in these expansion states are Cox-Woolley, eds., *Encyclopedia*, III, *passim*, and a series of pamphlets issued by the Home Mission Board of the Southern Baptist Convention in July, 1966, describing the beginning of Southern Baptist activities in the new areas.

40. Cox-Woolley, eds., *Encyclopedia*, III, p. 1869.

41. *Ibid.*, p. 1868.

42. See *The Alabama Baptist*, April 21, 1960, p. 9.

43. *Ibid.*

44. Cox-Woolley, eds., *Encyclopedia*, III, p. 2046. See also Home Mission Board leaflet on West Virginia Southern Baptists.

45. *Ibid.*, II, 1027 f. See also Home Mission Board leaflet on Ohio.

46. See *The Quarterly Review*, Third Quarter, 1955, p. 13.

47. *Minutes of the State Convention of Baptists in Ohio*, 1956, p. 25.

48. *Ibid.*, 1954, p. 10.

49. Cox-Woolley, eds., *Encyclopedia*, III, p. 1776.

50. *Annual*, State Convention of Baptists in Indiana, 1959, p. 16.

51. See *The Illinois Baptist*, March 5, 1958, p. 1.

52. Cox-Woolley, eds., *Encyclopedia*, III, pp. 1834 ff.

53. There are slight differences in the information given in Cox-Woolley, eds., *Encyclopedia*, III, p. 1835 and *ibid.*, p. 1839.

54. Pamphlet of Home Mission Board on Wisconsin Baptists.

55. Pamphlet of Home Mission Board on Minnesota Baptists.

56. Pamphlet of Home Mission Board on Iowa Baptists.

57. Cox-Woolley, eds., *Encyclopedia*, III, p. 1884.

58. See *Baptist Digest* (Kansas), July 20, 1957, p. 1.

59. Cox-Woolley, eds., *Encyclopedia*, III, p. 1662.

60. *Southern Baptist Beams* (former name of *Baptist Digest* of Kansas), April 12, 1951, p. 5.

61. Cox-Woolley, eds., *Encyclopedia*, I, pp. 718 f.

62. See *The Baptist Program* (Nashville), November, 1948, p. 4.

63. *Baptist Digest* (Kansas), July 20, 1957, p. 1.

64. *The Quarterly Review*, Third Quarter, 1955, p. 27.

65. Cox-Woolley, eds., *Encyclopedia*, III, pp. 1657-68.

66. See *The Rocky Mountain Baptist* (Colorado), November, 1954, pp. 1, 4.

67. *Ibid.,* p. 8.

68. *Annual,* Colorado Baptist General Convention, 1956, pp. 18-19.

69. See *Annual,* Baptist General Convention of Arizona, 1951, p. 19 and *ibid.,* 1952, pp. 18, 20, 80.

70. See *Arizona Baptist Beacon,* August 14, 1958, p. 4.

71. Baker, *Relations,* pp. 208-12.

72. *Annual,* Southern Baptist Convention, 1894, p. 27; and 1897, pp. 23-24.

73. *The Quarterly Review,* Third Quarter, 1955, p. 17.

74. *Annual,* Southern Baptist Convention, 1948, p. 44; and *ibid.,* 1949, p. 49.

75. *Pacific Coast Baptist,* November, 1953, p. 2.

76. *Annual,* Baptist General Convention of Oregon-Washington, 1953, p. 4.

77. *Annual,* Southern Baptist Convention, 1954, p. 53.

78. See *Arizona Baptist Beacon,* December 23, 1954, p. 5.

79. *Annual,* Southern Baptist Convention, 1957, pp. 50-51.

80. *Ibid.,* 1958, p. 215.

81. For this story, see Cox-Woolley, eds., *Encyclopedia,* I, p. 30.

82. *Alaska Baptist Messenger,* April, 1946, p. 1.

83. See Southern Baptist *Home Missions* (Atlanta), January, 1967, p. 11; also the *Texas Baptist Standard,* January 3, 1946, p. 13; and *Annual,* Southern Baptist Convention, 1948, p. 47.

84. *Annual,* Hawaii Baptist Convention, 1945, p. 36.

85. Cox-Woolley, eds., *Encyclopedia,* I, p. 603.

86. *Annual,* Hawaii Baptist Convention, 1959, pp. 24-25.

87. It should be remembered that statistics for many of these expansion areas are included in other state conventions with whom they are affiliated. Thus, the total churches and members in the older states added to the figures given for the expansion states will not equal the statistics shown later in this summary.

88. H. K. Neely, Jr., *op. cit.,* pp. 176-202.

89. *The Quarterly Review,* Third Quarter, 1973, p. 78.

16 The Maturing Convention

The Southern Baptist Convention developed maturity in the years between 1917 and 1972. For the first time Southern Baptists corporately came to grips with the early European and British scientific and social challenges to their faith and simultaneously confronted fundamentalism on their left and liberalism on their right. The "social gospel," conceived initially to be antithetical to the basic supernaturalism involved in individual conversion, was accepted in modified forms as the salting and illuminating of born-again people to bless the world about them. These events will be related in their chronological sequence in this chapter.

The fifty-five years that make up this modern era in the life of the Southern Baptist Convention fall naturally into two distinct periods. The first, from 1917 to 1942, began with World War I and was characterized by financial stringency and oppressive debt; the second, from 1942 to 1972, began with World War II and was characterized by economic inflation and revolutionary involvements. The principal events of each period will be discussed separately and chronologically. Then, to maintain the unity of the whole period, the contemporary structure and work of the Convention will be described, and reference made to the total growth.

Advance Despite Adversity (1917-42)

The period between the two World Wars has combined paradoxical elements. On the one hand, Southern Baptists have never known a period of greater financial crisis and continuing threats of bankruptcy. Conditions were so difficult that one prominent Southern Baptist writer called these "the dark ages" in Southern Baptist life. Yet, on the other hand, these very harsh years were among the most creative and progressive the Southern Baptist Convention ever experienced.

The principal events characterizing the history of the Convention between the wars were the struggle to carry on its ministry despite the severe and continuing financial crisis, the impact of the attacks of liberals, the attempts to revise the structure of the Convention in order to provide an effective vehicle for the work of the denomi-

392

nation, the response of Southern Baptists to ecumenical efforts, and the substantial growth effected in the midst of a complex and evolving culture.

Depression and the Work of the Convention. At the close of World War I on November 11, 1918, Southern Baptists shared with the entire nation the jubilant optimism of a challenging and an unhindered future, since the war to make the world safe for democracy had been won. Clearly the time was ripe for lengthening the cords of service. Inspired by the united military effort in World War I, the overwhelming success of mammoth financial campaigns by Red Cross and Community Chest leaders, and idealistic proposals from religious leaders of several denominations for spectacular campaigns in behalf of the cause of Christ, Southern Baptists enthusiastically heard suggestions from Rufus W. Weaver to raise $100,000,000 for Jesus in five years; from their Education Commission to raise $15,000,000 in five years for Christian education; and from their ministerial relief and annuity leaders calling for a $5,000,000 campaign for their work. In 1918 the Convention created a committee to make plans for raising vast sums to promote all benevolences through the cooperation of all of its constituency. During the following year, Southern Baptist leaders uniformly appealed for the adoption of a great and challenging program.

1. The Seventy-five Million Campaign. On the opening morning of the 1919 session of the Convention at Atlanta, Georgia, President J. B. Gambrell set the tone for what would follow. He said:

> It is my deep conviction that this Convention ought to adopt a program for work commensurate with the reasonable demands on us and summon ourselves and our people to a new demonstration of the value of orthodoxy in free action.
>
> It is, moreover, a conviction as deep as my soul that this Convention, representing the sentiments and convictions of millions of Christ's baptizied people, ought to send out to our fellow Baptists everywhere a rallying call to unite to make effective in all lands the unique message of Christ.[1]

Committees were appointed to translate this word into action. A committee on Financial Aspect of the Enlarged Program recommended that the Convention undertake to raise $75,000,000 during the next five years. As later modified, the plan called for the appointment of a commission of fifteen members to lay plans and launch the campaign.[2] George W. Truett of Texas was appointed chairman of the Financial Campaign Committee, together with one member from each state. Promptly this committee met with the Executive Committee and the executive secretaries of the general and state boards. The Sunday School Board, Nashville, provided headquarters for the campaign; L. R. Scarborough, president of Southwestern Seminary, became general director; and I. J. Van Ness was named treasurer. Quotas were established for each state, and the proceeds were budgeted for missions, education, ministerial relief, orphanages, and hospitals. The seven remaining months of 1919 were designated to promote some aspect of the campaign: preparation, information, intercession, enlistment, stewardship, and Victory Week in December.

In May, 1920, it was reported that $92,630,923 had been subscribed, and $12,237,827 had been paid, despite very adverse conditions such as a major coal strike, almost incessant rain during a period of seventy-five days in more than one-half of the territory of the Convention, and the shortness of time for preparation.[3] But dark days were in the offing. In the last half of 1920 the most severe depression since the 1890's struck the nation. Perhaps hardest hit was the farmer, the mainstay of Southern Baptist support, who was submerged in depression until the late 1930's. Seven million unemployed Americans walked the streets in 1921. National income fell from $75,000,000,000 in 1920 to $59,000,000,000 in 1921.[4] Southern Baptists, with 23,143 rural churches (out of a total of less than 26,000), were greatly hurt.[5]

As a consequence, the receipts for all causes—state and southwide—began declining sharply in the second year of the campaign. At the end of the five years, only $58,591,713.69 was raised, over $34,000,000 less than was pledged. However, state, home, and foreign mission programs had already been rapidly enlarged to take advantage of the funds that had been promised. By 1926 the Convention alone had a staggering debt of approximately $6,500,000, not to speak of the debts compounded in the states.

2. The Struggle for Financial Integrity. Depression continued to plague the agricultural and rural areas in the mid-twenties, adding to the burdens remaining from the Seventy-five Million Campaign. In his financial analysis in 1930 E. P. Aldredge remarked that the severe local and state needs were clearly reflected in the giving trends of the previous five years. Gifts to state convention objects rose from $3,568,483 in 1925 to $5,515,040 in 1929, while gifts to the southern body dropped from $4,686,952 in 1925 to $2,227,290 in 1929.[6] But the trials of Southern Baptists had just begun. The stock market crash of 1929 was preceded by a shocking theft from the Home Mission Board in 1928 by Clinton S. Carnes, treasurer for almost a decade, amounting to $909,461 in principal and interest. This board's debt promptly rose to $2,257,453,[7] and the severest part of the depression was yet to come. The plight of the Convention's two mission boards illustrated the grim prognosis for their future. When C. E. Maddry took office on January 1, 1933, the Foreign Mission Board owed $1,110,000 to four banks in Richmond, together with $249,000 additional debt incurred by the missionaries on the fields. The banks notified the board it must immediately pay the $67,000 interest due in 1933 and at least $150,000 on the principal. Maddry said that this would be disastrous to the foreign mission work, whose budget for the year was only $600,000. He reminded the bankers that in the ninety years of the board's history their institutions had not lost a cent in principal or interest, and pledged that they would ultimately receive all of their money if the board were permitted to use enough of its $600,000 budget to operate its foreign mission program. The bankers finally agreed, and Maddry was successful in maintaining a missionary staff on the field while striving to pay off these debts. In the six years before 1932, the board lost 127 missionaries, one fourth of its peak force up to that time. Beginning in 1933 the retrenchment on the mission fields stopped, and the number of missionaries slowly rose until the close of the period.[8]

Meanwhile, the Home Mission Board also secured a new leader in J. B. Lawrence. He set the tone for Southern Baptists. When the creditors demanded the more than two and one-quarter million dollars, he faced them with honesty and integrity. They were sympathetic and offered to discount the debts in substantial amounts if the board would pay them promptly. His reply was, "We do not desire to receive a discount on our just debts. We will pay them in full. Just give us a little time and you will not lose one dollar." As the long depression decade of the 1930's approached its close, the integrity of Lawrence and Southern Baptists had been so demonstrated that the banks holding mortgages on their property were eager to refinance their loans at better interest rates and lift the mortgages promptly.[9] The debts were not finally paid until 1943, but the outbreak of war in late 1941 broke the strength of the depression period.

One factor of great significance in this period was the substantial contribution of Woman's Missionary Union in helping to sustain the mission programs of the Convention. That story will be told in describing their activities during this period.

Of great importance also during these stressful times was the work of the Executive Committee. Its enlargement in 1927 came partly as a result of the evident need for effective leadership in financial matters and efficient operation. In 1929 the Executive Committee recommended a belt-tightening financial plan that greatly aided in conserving the fiscal resources of the Convention. Again in 1938 the Executive Committee proposed sweeping recommendations, embodying developments evolved during the darkest days of the depression, which aimed to acquaint the denomination with the business methods of the Convention and to maintain the highest efficiency in fiscal matters.[10]

Perhaps the most effective effort to meet the crisis of huge debts and mounting interest was the Baptist Hundred Thousand Club. There had been prior campaigns to raise funds, such as Honor Day, the Emergency Mission Relief Campaign, and the Crucible Service Campaign, and some of these had been effective. On April 12-13, 1933, the Executive Committee considered a number of plans for some practicable and continuing program to reduce the Convention's debts, and adopted the one proposed by Frank Tripp. It was approved by the Convention at Washington in 1933, and Tripp became the director of the movement. The plan was simple: each member of the Hundred Thousand Club pledged to give $1.00 per month over and above his regular gifts through his church.[11] The following chart shows the funds given year by year between 1933 and 1943 (when all debts on Convention agencies were completely paid).[12] These amounts do not represent the total proceeds from the Hundred Thousand Club, since the various state bodies shared in half of the receipts from 1937 on.[13]

1933	$ 37,588.28
1934	160,565.96
1935	198,372.31
1936	191,296.88
1937	191,500.00
1938	161,726.07
1939	159,447.96
1940	158,279.43
1941	261,143.63
1942	377,277.82
1943	730,624.02
Total	$2,627,822.36

The disbursement of these receipts shows the amount of indebtedness relieved for the several Southwide institutions by the campaign.[14]

Southern Baptist Convention Notes	$ 184,111.82
Foreign Mission Board	428,143.25
Home Mission Board	623,307.87
National Baptist Memorial	8,373.21
Southern Baptist Hospital	59,495.96
Education Board	43,483.68
Southern Baptist Theological Seminary	503,898.55
Southwestern Baptist Theological Seminary	489,712.67
Baptist Bible Institute	286,045.61
American Baptist Theological Seminary	1,249.74
Total Disbursements	$2,627,822.36

Theological Controversies. The 1920's brought to a climax for Southern Baptists their corporate reaction to some of the fierce theological confrontations experienced by other denominations earlier in the century. It will be recalled that Professor Crawford H. Toy of Southern Baptist Theological Seminary, who had studied under liberal European theological teachers in German universities in 1867-69, had been forced to resign in 1879 because he was teaching these views in his seminary classes.[15] Other Southern Baptist teachers and schools felt the impact of these new ideas and events.

> During the early years of the century, an increasing number of ministers and theological seminaries were accepting the critical approach to the Scriptures, together with a liberal theology which minimized or rejected the doctrine of the deity of Christ, weakened the orthodox teaching of depravity and sin, deplored the view of the atonement as divine satisfaction or vicarious substitution for the sinner, and particularly rejected belief in the visible return of Christ to establish his kingdom.[16]

1. The Liberal-Fundamentalist Encounter.   Among northern Baptists and in other denominations the opposition to this liberal theology was manifested in Bible conferences and pungent literary responses in the closing decades of the nineteenth century. The conservative movement secured its name and united its forces about 1910 when two wealthy laymen financed the publication of twelve small volumes or pamphlets entitled *The Fundamentals: A Testimony of the Truth.* These pamphlets brought the name "Fundamentalists" to those holding to such views and asserted the five basic doctrines that characterized the Fundamentalist movement: the virgin birth, the bodily resurrection of Christ and his followers, the verbal inspiration of the Scriptures, the substitutionary theory of the atonement, and the imminent, physical second coming of Christ in the millennial reign. Some of the contributors to this series were Southern Baptists, including Professors J. J. Reeve and C. B. Williams of Southwestern Baptist Theological Seminary, and E. Y. Mullins, president of Southern Baptist Theological Seminary. Robert G. Torbet wrote that most Baptists probably accepted the theological views set forth by the fundamentalists, but their rigid creedalism, rationalization of faith, and most of all, their harsh and militant spirit alienated many who were sympathetic with their conservative doctrinal stance.[17] The World's Christian Fundamentals Association was formed in 1919 with members from Presbyterians, Methodists, Disciples, and Baptists included in their number.[18]

Among Southern Baptists the leading fundamentalist figure was J. Frank Norris of Fort Worth, Texas. He participated in the World's Christian Fundamentals Conference of 1919, and helped form the Baptist Bible Union of America four years later. Because of the overwhelmingly conservative nature of Southern Baptists, he and his group found it difficult to establish doctrinal grounds for attacking the Convention and its agencies. Norris, however, used fundamentalism as a platform for personal controversy and to further his ambitions. Although he had previously exercised his considerable gifts in forwarding the organized work of Texas and Southern Baptists, he began during this period to use his newspaper to attack the Seventy-five Million Campaign, Baylor University, Southwestern Seminary, Texas Baptists, and the Southern Baptist Convention. He was expelled from Tarrant County Baptist Association in 1922 and 1924 and by the Baptist General Convention of Texas in 1923 and 1924. He continued to harrass the Southern Convention until his death in 1952.[19]

2. The Evolutionary Confrontation. Inspired by Charles Darwin's seminal work, *The Origin of the Species,* in 1859, many theories were developed during the following decades by scientists and liberal theologians tending to discredit the Genesis account of creation and advancing an evolutionary hypothesis to account for the existence and nature of man. Perhaps the climax to this tension between the two sides in this controversy occurred in the South with the passing of a statute on March 21, 1925, in Tennessee which forbade any educational institution supported by public funds "to teach the theory that denies the story of the divine creation of man as taught in the Bible." John T. Scopes, a biology teacher in Dayton, Tennessee, provided a test case and was brought to trial. This attracted worldwide attention, and although he was convicted, his sentence was set aside by the supreme court on a technicality. In the midst of these exciting events the Southern Baptist Convention met at Memphis, Tennessee, in 1925, and the question of evolution spilled over into the deliberations of the Convention. Already the Convention had spoken on the issue. In 1922 and again in 1923 E. Y. Mullins had decried the attacks upon religion because of discoveries or alleged discoveries in physical nature; the use of such sciences as psychology, biology, and geology to deny the supernatural in the Christian religion as if they were necessarily relevant; and the teaching of mere hypotheses as though they were facts.[20] The Convention adopted this statement as its views. However, at Memphis in 1925, growing out of the continuing agitation over the question of evolution, the Convention adopted a confession of faith, not, they said, as a final or infallible statement of belief, or an authoritative creed, or an attempt to hamper freedom of thought; but to serve as a consensus of opinion by this particular session to assist in the interpretation of the Scriptures.[21] It should be said that many Southern Baptist leaders balked at the adoption of a confession of this kind, either believing that it would accomplish little good or that a voluntary Convention composed of cooperating Baptists from autonomous churches should not properly adopt such confessions. Perhaps they recalled that the Northern Baptist Convention had declined to adopt a similar confession of faith in 1922.

The adoption of a confession of faith, however, did not bring an end to the discussion of evolution in the Convention. Many of the conservatives felt that the confession had not been clear and specific in its denunciation of the evolutionary hypothesis. In the 1926 Convention, George W. McDaniel, in concluding his presidential address, purposely headed off an impending controversial debate by asserting:

> This Convention accepts Genesis as teaching that man was the special creation of God, and rejects every theory, evolution or other, which teaches that man originated in, or came by way of, a lower animal ancestry.[22]

By previous arrangement a motion was promptly made to the effect that this statement be the sentiment of the Convention, "and that from this point on no further consideration be given to this subject, and that the Convention go forward with the consideration of the main kingdom causes to which God has set our hearts and hands." This was adopted. However, on the fourth day of the Convention, S. E. Tull introduced a resolution asking that all of the Convention's institutions, boards, missionary representatives be requested to acquiesce to McDaniel's statement. The resolution was adopted.[23]

A rather curious constitutional situation grew out of this last resolution. On November 10, 1926, the Baptist General Convention of Oklahoma voted to withhold undesignated funds of the Cooperative Program from Southern Baptist seminaries whose faculties refused to sign the McDaniel statement; they took the same action in 1927. The funds were released in 1928.

Meanwhile, however, the constitutional question had occupied the minds of Southern Baptist leaders. In 1927 the Convention instructed the Executive Committee to prepare a statement on the basis of cooperation between the Convention and state bodies. At two points, in particular, the committee was asked to clarify the relationship: a definition of the duties, functions, and limitations of state conventions and boards as collecting agencies for the Convention; and the safeguarding of Convention funds in the hands of state bodies. The latter point touched directly upon the action of the Oklahoma body and also upon the practice of other state bodies that had withheld funds for Convention-wide objects. In 1928 the Executive Committee presented a detailed statement on relations between the Convention and state bodies that has become the basis of their relations. The report began by noting that the Convention "is not an ecclesiastical body composed of churches, nor a federal body composed of state conventions." All cooperation with the Convention is on a voluntary basis, and churches, associations, unions, and conventions are self-determining in their own spheres and activities. The Convention totally disclaimed any authority over state bodies, but set out four principles in relation to its own identity. (1) The cooperative relations between the Convention and state bodies includes the recognition that the state boards are collecting agencies for southwide as well as state funds, although this relationship is simply a matter of convenience and economy and may be changed at any time. (2) Even though the state bodies handle first the funds collected for the southwide body, the Convention retains as "inalienable and inherent" the right of direct appeal to the churches for funds; and in matters other than raising money, the Convention retains complete control of its own affairs, with the right to fix its own objectives and to determine the amounts of money allocated to its various objects. (3) The power of appointing members of all committees and boards of the Convention resides in the Convention itself, although the Convention may, if it so desires, consult the state or territorial subdivisions in this matter. (4) Neither the Convention nor a state body may impose its will upon the other in any manner or degree at any time. The Convention "has no authority to allocate funds or to divert funds from any object included in a state budget. In like manner no state body has any authority to allocate funds to or divert them from any object included in the Southwide budget." [24] It will be observed that this last sentence dealt with the action taken by the Oklahoma convention in 1926.

Major Structural Revisions. In the midst of continuing financial crisis and substantial doctrinal confrontations, the Southern Baptist Convention experienced one of the most creative structural eras in its entire history. The body achieved in this period a new denominational solidarity, a convention-type financial program, an improved basis of representation, and a significant supplementary structure for decision-making.

1. A New Denominational Solidarity. The background of the first Executive Committee of 1917 was described in a previous chapter. This original committee of 1917 was not particularly imposing in its size or functions, but in its development it revolutionized the nature and operation of the Southern Baptist Convention and brought a denominational solidarity never achieved under the older society pattern. At the close of the last period, a limited Executive Committee of seven members was formed, but it quickly proved its value. In 1918 the committee was enlarged to twenty-four members (including one from each state), and in 1921 women were added to it.

Sensitiveness relative to centralization in the Convention began to disappear rapidly during the 1920's. The increasing financial stringency following the Seventy-five Million Campaign, the overwhelming number of committee reports in any annual session (there were fifty-four committee reports in 1925), the painfully visible evidence of disunity in the work of the increasing number of agencies of the Convention, and the recognized need for a Convention "watchdog" to maintain the integrity of the body brought the appointment of a Committee on Correlation in 1923 and a Committee on Business Efficiency in 1925. The latter committee made an intensive survey of the work of the Convention and were convinced

> that the constituency of this convention is becoming insistent that the work of the agencies of the convention shall be more closely correlated, and that the agencies themselves shall be brought into such relations with the convention as will guarantee in advance both efficiency of administration and prevention of incurring any indebtedness, except for current expenses between the meetings of the convention.[25]

As a result, the Executive Committee was given additional powers in 1926, and in 1927 its structure was strengthened substantially to provide it with strong organizational functions. It became the fiduciary, fiscal, and executive agency of the Convention in all of its affairs not specifically committed to some other board or agency. It represented a de facto year-round corporate voice for the Convention. New structural unity was achieved, and denominational solidarity was magnified more than simply benevolent activity. A more detailed story of the Executive Committee and its functions during the remainder of the period will be given later in this chapter.

2. A Convention-type Financial Program. A second congenital tension in the structure of the Southern Baptist Convention resulted from the continuance in 1845 of the old society plan of financing benevolent work by promoting designated giving to particular benevolences. It was too much to expect that the grand denominational scope of the preamble to the constitution, as reflected in Article V, would be immediately grasped in a single historical act. The gulf between the society concept of supporting only *designated* benevolences and the fully developed convention program of financing *all* benevolences was too wide to leap in a single bound. To be consistent with the convention ideal, it would have been necessary in 1845 to abandon designated giving to particular benevolences and, instead, to provide undesignated financial support to the Convention, which should in turn foster all the benevolences the Convention might wish to promote. Such a radical break with the familiar and successful traditional financial pattern, however, was unthinkable. There was no hint in the minutes of the new Convention, in the denominational newspaper accounts, or in the several reminiscences by actors in the drama that any other form of financing was even suggested.

This society pattern of financing that was imbedded into a convention-type structure proved to have numerous weaknesses. For one thing, there was a critical need for better support of the benevolences promoted by the Convention; i.e., foreign and home missions. The demise of the Bible Board and the first Sunday School Board for lack of finances illustrated this problem. Secondly, at almost each session of the Convention it was recognized that there were many additional areas of service that needed to be penetrated but could not be because of financial stress. Finally, the collection of funds under the old society philosophy was completely haphazard. Once or twice a year a church would be visited by a representative of one of the benevolences and an offering for that particular benevolence would be taken. The whims of the people and of nature itself were involved: a lengthy rainy season in a particular area when benevolent offerings were being taken could almost eliminate these gifts. Under such a procedure, there could be no systematic planning either by the benevolent boards or the Convention itself. It became necessary, for example, for the two mission boards to borrow money from banks month by month in anticipation of receipts that might or might not come in a special campaign during the ensuing year. After the turn of the century, in particular, many resolutions were passed and numerous committees were appointed at Convention sessions to correct the situation.

The financial success of the Sunday School Board after 1891 provided some assistance to the beleaguered Convention, while the organization of the first Executive Committee in 1917 brought increased efficiency in the handling of funds that were secured; but it became desperately clear that better financial methods both in securing and in handling funds were imperatively needed. It took a crisis to bring a change; that crisis was the Seventy-five Million Campaign. Although it precipitated a financial crisis, this campaign was not simply a failure. For one thing, it marked a period of greatly expanded receipts which were put to good use. Frank E. Burkhalter wrote:

> It should be remembered that the campaign did raise $58,000,000 in cash for Baptist missionary, educational, and benevolent causes. This was several times what the same people were giving previous to the campaign. In five years state and associational missions received $9,900,785 from the campaign. Home missions received $6,622,725, as compared with only $8,188,730 in the preceding 74 years of its history. Foreign missions received $11,615,327, as compared with about $12,500,000 in the preceding 74 years. Seminaries, schools, and colleges received $16,087,942, or nearly as much as in all their years preceding.[26]

Furthermore, the campaign lifted the sights of the Baptist people concerning their potential in missions and stewardship. For the first time, the average Southern Baptist was called upon to make a significant gift to missions and education. In addition, the emphasis on "calling out the called," which accompanied this campaign, brought many vocational workers into active Christian service during this period. Finally, the experience gained from this campaign caused the Convention to confront seriously for the first time the ambivalence in their structure relative to finances, and turned them in a new direction. "Budget" became a large word; improved methods of enlistment and stewardship promotion were developed; and the Convention adopted a financial program designed to provide undesignated gifts "for eliciting, combining and directing the energies of the whole denomination in one sacred effort."

The critical debt remaining from the Seventy-five Million Campaign forced the Convention to give immediate attention to financial methods. Studies of various sorts had been made and committees appointed for over a decade, but the combination of debt and depression in 1924 worked a change. A Conservation Commission had been named at the beginning of the Seventy-five Million Campaign to promote the collection of campaign pledges. In 1923 a new Committee on Future Program was appointed to plan for the direction to be taken after the close of the campaign. In 1924 this committee recommended that a simultaneous every-member canvass be made in every Baptist church in the South from November 30 to December 7, 1924, to cover budgeted denominational needs for 1925. An appeal was made for all Southern Baptists to adopt the biblical principles of stewardship and tithing, and systematic giving week-by-week, rather than to follow the older pattern of two huge financial campaigns each year for benevolent work.[27] In 1925 the committee recommended the adoption of this "Co-Operative Program" of Southern Baptists, urging

> that there be a general committee, with headquarters in Nashville, for the promotion of the Co-Operative Program, which shall hereafter be designated as the Commission on Co-Operative Program, consisting of seventeen members chosen from the South at large, together with the general secretaries, state secretaries, secretary of Laymen's Movement, president and secretary and three members of the Woman's Missionary Union, and presidents of the three Southwide educational institutions.[28]

This program was adopted, and J. E. Dillard was named chairman of the new commission, holding that office until his death. In 1927 the new structural form adopted by the Convention in 1917 (the Executive Committee) and the improved financial program adopted in 1925 (the Cooperative Program) were combined. The Executive Committee was enlarged and given widely expanded duties: to prepare a detailed, combined budget for consideration by the Convention each year, to act as agent of the Convention to conclude all agreements with cooperating state agencies for handling southwide funds, to recommend percentages of southwide funds to be allocated to each cause or agency, and to serve in general as the fiscal agency of the Convention.[29] A Promotional Committee for raising funds sought in the annual budgets was named, but in 1929 its work was assumed by the Executive Committee.

Essentially the Cooperative Program involved the relationship between the Convention and the several state bodies related to the Convention. Each state body prepared a budget for the work of the following year, including its own financial needs and a proposed percentage for Convention needs. The percentage of distributable funds retained by the state and those sent to the Convention differed in each state. Some divided on a 50-50 basis, some on a 60-40 basis, and some (particularly in new areas) on a 75-25 basis—75% for the state and 25% for the Convention.

> The Cooperative Program includes all distributable funds, all designated funds, and all special offerings, such as the Woman's Missionary Union Lottie Moon Offering for foreign missions, the Annie Armstrong Offering for home missions, offering for state missions, etc. In reality, all funds received for any cause included in the Cooperative Program, whether they be distributable, designated, or special funds, belong to the Cooperative Program. Designated funds and special offerings for a cause cannot be divided. They must go according to the wish of the donor.[30]

The significance of the adoption of the Cooperative Program in 1925 resides in its correction of the ambivalence in the financial methods carried over from the society plan in 1845 and its exploiting of the genius of the convention-type program. The Cooperative Program brought the goal of the original constitution of 1845 closer to realization; i.e., the formation of a body to carry on all types of benevolent work desired by its constituency. The old society type of designated financing only was replaced by one which allowed designation but provided support for all benevolences, whether popular or otherwise. By this plan, each state became an active participant in both fostering appeals for benevolent objects promoted by the Convention and in the financial well-being of the Convention itself. This fusion between the state programs and the Convention's activities brought a new denominational unity to Southern Baptists.

3. An Improved Basis of Representation. It will be recalled that the third congenital tension introduced into the structure of the Southern Baptist Convention from the society method in 1845 involved the financial basis of representation. The continuous agitation of this question brought no change during the previous period, but was discussed almost exhaustively until 1927, when a strong Committee on the Basis of Representation, headed by E. Y. Mullins, severely criticized the existing structure and functions. Two years later a memorial from the District of Columbia echoed these sentiments. A Committee on Changes in the Constitution brought an extensive report in 1931. Relative to the basis of representation, it recommended that Article III be changed at several points, but that the financial basis of representation be retained. When this item was presented to the Convention, E. C. Routh of Oklahoma offered a substitute article which was adopted, providing a modified church basis of representation.[31] As subsequently refined, this article said that the Convention shall consist of messengers who are members of missionary Baptist churches cooperating with the Convention on the basis of one messenger from each church in friendly cooperation and sympathetic with its purposes and work, and has during the fiscal year preceding been a bona fide contributor to the Convention's work; that one additional messenger may be elected from each church for every 250 members or for each $250 paid to the work of the Convention during the fiscal year preceding the annual meeting; that the maximum number of messengers from any church is ten, and each messenger must be a member of the church by which he is appointed.[32] It should be recalled that this was not the Landmark position of *delegated* church representation (asserted in the Hayden controversy in Texas and the Bogard controversy in Arkansas), but was a *designated* church representation. The Routh article conceived of general bodies as mass meetings of representative Baptists composed of messengers designated by the churches, but who did not officially represent their churches nor possess any delegated authority from the churches. According to this view, the authority of the Convention stemmed from fraternal and widespread denominational consensus, not from any projection of the authority of the churches. This will explain why the Convention could consistently and heatedly refuse the Landmark church basis of representation between 1900 and 1930, and then in 1931, adopt the substitute article of E. C. Routh.

It should be observed that this change increased the visibility of churches by using them to provide the distribution of messengers at the annual meeting, but this was not a church delegate base after the Landmark pattern. It gave additional messengers on a numerical basis for the larger churches; and it rewarded the churches by additional messengers when they increased their financial gifts to the Convention. Undue influence by large and wealthy churches was minimized by limiting the maximum number of messengers from any church. Thus, by 1931, the old society financial basis of representation was modified to provide denominational consensus with a wide base, while additional visibility and a sense of immediate participation were given to each affiliating Southern Baptist church.

4. A Supplementary Structure for Decision-Making. Closely related to the question of the basis of representation at the Convention was the problem of the size of the body. This Pandora's box doubtless had several bases: the increasing number of benevolences promoted by the Convention brought numerous adherents from each one to the general meeting; the rapid growth of the constituency between 1845 and the turn of the century tended to increase the size of the annual meeting; the opportunities for fellowship and information at the Convention were a drawing point; and the rapid development of transportation facilities, especially the railroads, made attendance much more convenient. One reason for the constant tampering with the basis of representation, as well as the numerous suggestions for changing it, had been the recognition that the annual meetings were becoming unwieldy in their size, particularly when important issues were being decided from the floor of the Convention. In 1891 the largest building in Birmingham, Alabama, was so crowded with messengers that the speaker had to be boosted through a window and led by a devious route to the platform because of the press of the crowd. The numerical basis of representation was suggested in 1891 and again in 1893 in a deliberate attempt to control the size of the body. In 1893 a large committee composed of some of the most important members of the Convention recommended that the basis of representation be changed either to a numerical basis or to a combined numerical-financial basis. The numerical plan suggested ten representatives from each cooperating state, plus one representative for each 4,000 white Baptist membership within these states, and one representative from each cooperating district association. In 1894, 1902, 1919, and numerous other times, the numerical basis was stoutly championed, particularly because "practically all of the State Conventions and other Baptist bodies have a numerical basis of representation."

The dilemma of the size of the body at its annual meeting was dramatically illustrated in 1920 when the Convention convened at Washington, D. C. Twenty-five years before, when the Convention had met there, the messengers had numbered 870; in 1920, the messengers numbered 8,359. J. R. Graves would have stirred uneasily in his resting place had he known that in the 1920 session his son-in-law, O. L. Hailey, presented a resolution bewailing the size of the meeting and asking that a committee be appointed to consider several matters including "the number of messengers who may be appointed from each State." At the 1927 meeting of the Convention, E. Y. Mullins headed a strong committee to study the basis of representation. His report to the Convention listed the weaknesses of the existing plan: the immensely enlarged membership: the difficulties of deliberation; the great increase in the number of reports (which in 1845, he said, consisted of two or three missionary subjects, but now involved reports by over fifty committees on a variety of subjects); the ignorance of the messengers concerning new policies recommended, due to the absence of advance knowledge; the shortness of the Convention period, covering from three to five days only; the preponderance of those coming from the locality near the meeting place of the Convention with a consequent lack of balanced judgment from all geographical sections in reaching important decisions; the danger of sectional initiative in introducing new measures which might be lacking in proper coordination with other interests and activities, etc. The principal remedy suggested by Mullins was to utilize a numerical basis of representation so that the Convention would consist of a few hundred messengers, with 1,000 as the maximum, and virtually empowering an enlarged Executive Committee, along with a small but authoritative triennial Convention, to operate the affairs of the body.[33]

The Convention, however, after considerable deliberation, turned away from the suggestion that its annual session should be arbitrarily diminished in size to a few hundred messengers or representatives. In so doing the Convention had almost exhausted the possibilities suggested for reducing the size of the annual gathering which had been put forward during the past half century. It had ruled out the strictly financial basis of representation, numerical representation, and "presbygational" representation on both an associational and state level. Instead, the Convention approached the problem obliquely. The main concern of the Convention in taking this new direction was to meet an immediate situation rather than to grapple with the many problems involved in the size of the annual gathering. In the constitutional revision of 1931, the Convention introduced a bylaw to put into their formal structure a principle that had been informally followed since the beginning days of the Convention. From the very first years after 1845, when important decisions were to be made, the Convention regularly appointed committees composed of one or more representatives from each state cooperating with the Convention, in order to insure widespread distribution in the makeup of the committee. In 1931 a small group of Baptists in Arizona had asked for the privilege of having representation from their state on the boards of the Convention. The Convention passed Bylaw 17 which formally defined how a state could secure representation on the boards and the executive committee of the Convention. This bylaw said:

Any state desiring representation on any board or the Executive

Committee of this Convention shall make formal application for the representation desired, stating the number of Baptists in the state who are co-operating with this Convention and the total amount of money given to the Convention objects the preceding year. The Convention shall then make such investigation as it may desire and shall upon the basis of the information obtained vote on the question of representation on each board and the Executive Committee upon which representation is sought and the question shall be decided by a majority vote.[34]

Some refinements have subsequently been made by this bylaw, which will be discussed later.

This action took care of the immediate petition of Arizona, but it did much more than that. By the formal adoption of the principle of state representation on boards, commissions, and standing committees of the Convention, an official substructure on a decision-making level had been provided. As early as 1909 it had been recognized that the character of the Convention was already being altered by the substructure of boards and committees. The *Religious Herald* of Virginia remarked in an editorial in that year:

It must be frankly admitted, however, that the real work of the Convention is no longer done by the Convention itself. It is practically impossible, with the present organization and methods, and in the physical conditions in which the Convention is frequently forced to meet, to deliberate about anything. So it has come to pass that debate is practically unknown and conference is out of the question. We are coming rapidly to the place, if we have not already reached it, when we must rely wholly upon the Boards and standing committees to do our thinking for us. This is to some extent both desirable and inevitable.[35]

The editor did express the wish, however, that the annual meeting could retain some of its deliberative element. This statement and wish foreshadowed the actual development put into formal articulation in 1931: an extensive system of boards, commissions, and committees to do most of the study and make recommendations to the annual meeting, which, in turn determines the principles of operation. Thus, instead of an intermittent tampering with the basis of representation as a means of securing smaller annual gatherings, the Convention chose to operate through a dual representation: one on a state basis being penultimate in authority, aristocratic in make-up, widely representative, consisting of state membership as trustees on boards, commissions, committees, and institutions; the other being the Convention session itself—ultimate in authority, democratic in make-up, totally available for members of all cooperating churches, and less representative because of the size and place of the annual meeting, economic conditions, the intensity of issues confronting the Convention, etc. A sweeping constitutional revision in 1946 confirmed this dual representation as the desired organizational structure and focused on safe-guarding the makeup of the trustees of these boards, commissions, committees, and institutions as important substructures of the Convention. The qualifications, election, and rotation of these representatives were carefully spelled out in the constitution and bylaws of the Convention. They were to be chosen specifically "to represent the constituency of the Convention, rather than the staff of the agency."

One can glimpse the values of this dual structure from the Convention reports of 1972. The trustees of the boards, commissions, committees, and institutions of the Convention included more than 1,000 separate leaders chosen from representative geographical areas in the life of the Convention. It is interesting to notice that the 1927 Mullins committee suggested that the annual session of the Convention should consist of only a few hundred messengers, and not over 1,000 as the maximum. Had the Convention actually set up such a limited basis for forming the annual meeting, the whole system of decision-making would have had serious deficiencies that do not appear in the present dual system. Many of the objections of the Mullins committee to the old system have been met by this dual structure of representation. Over a thousand leaders from widely separated parts of Convention territory have been provided with specific knowledge and information in depth, and acquired such expertise that they are capable of making intelligent decisions concerning the particular benevolence with which they are related. They usually have had at least one year to deliberate on the problems involved. They are unswayed by inflammatory demagoguery at the Convention. The large attendance from points near the meeting place and sectional initiative in presenting programs to the Convention are minimized by the catholic nature of the trustees of the boards, commissions, committees, and institutions, for they are representative of every state related to Convention life. The many values involved in messengers from each church being free to attend the Convention and vote have been conserved, and even deliberative functions on major matters are still exercised by the annual meeting, as everyone knows who attends the gatherings of the Convention with any regularity. On the other hand, it is likely that 95 percent of all deliberation is done by the penultimate dual structure composed of over 1,000 leaders. Committees have not supplanted the authoritative Convention, but have evolved into technical and deliberative subsections of Convention life to bring recommendations to the whole body, thus supplementing the Convention. This combined aristocratic-democratic structure has solved many of the problems involved in the size of the annual meetings of the Convention.

The Hospital Venture. A very significant healing ministry was undertaken by the Convention in the early years of this period. Before that time, the various states or communities supported denominational hospitals of various sorts, as previously described. In 1920 a tuberculosis sanitorium was opened at El Paso, Texas, under the supervision of the Home Mission Board, but this institution was a casualty of the severe depression in October, 1937.

In 1923, as the culmination of several years of study and deliberation, a Hospital Commission was created by the Convention to oversee the erection and administration of a hospital at New Orleans, Louisiana. In the following year the Convention affirmed the general policy that state Baptist bodies would ordinarily own and control Baptist hospitals, but that the sanitorium at El Paso and the New Orleans hospital should constitute exceptions to this policy. Louis J. Bristow was the first secretary-treasurer of this commission, and until his retirement on May 1, 1947, led in developing the Southern Baptist Hospital, New Orleans. He was succeeded by Frank Tripp, under whose leadership the Baptist Memorial Hospital, Jacksonville, Florida, was established in 1953. Tripp was followed by Raymond C. Wilson in 1953 as executive.

For over a generation the Convention carried on this important ministry which blessed thousands of people physically and spiritually. The story is telescoped here because in 1971 the Convention relinquished ownership and operation of the hospitals at New Orleans and Jacksonville, as will be mentioned hereafter.

The Ecumenical Movement. It will be recalled that W. W. Barnes felt that at the close of the previous period in 1917, Southern Baptists were not unfavorable toward the question of participating in ecumenical conferences with other evangelical denominations. However, he believed that two factors were instrumental in chilling their interest. For one thing, the efforts of the War Department of the United States to force Baptists into a "Protestant" category with all other non-Roman Catholic and non-Jewish bodies in the provision of religious services for Southern Baptists in army camps aroused the ire of many Southern Baptist leaders, and occasioned an angry response from J. B. Gambrell, then president of the Convention, at the session in 1919.[36] The other factor was the too-rapid effort to engage Southern Baptists in a gigantic financial campaign to foster a world interdenominational thrust about which many Southern Baptists had serious misgivings at several points.[37] Other elements undoubtedly entered into the unenthusiastic response of Southern Baptists to the whole ecumenical movement. Just at the time when renewed overtures were being made to Southern Baptists after World War I by ecumenical leaders, the Convention became actively involved in its own denominational challenge (the Seventy-five Million Campaign). The financial burdens that this campaign bequeathed for the next twenty years occupied the whole attention of the southern body. In 1932 the Convention declined to appoint delegates to the proposed World Conference on Faith and Order. In 1937, John R. Sampey, then president of the Convention, was asked by the Executive Committee to attend the Conference on Faith and Order at Edinburgh. When he was invited to speak at the plenary sessions of the conference, he bluntly asserted his doctrinal disagreement with what he had seen and heard, saying:

> I have the distinct impression that in the findings of the Conference, though we affirm more than once our belief in the Saviourhood of the Lord Jesus and his sole mediatorship, yet time and time again the church and the sacraments are thrust between the individual soul and the Saviour, as in some sense essential to his salvation.[38]

In 1940, in response to an invitation to join the World Council of Churches, the Convention replied through a committee headed by George W. Truett that the ecclesiological basis of the Convention would not permit it to become a member of the World Council, since the Convention could not authoritatively speak or act for the churches affiliating with it, as required by the structure of the world body. A few messengers dissented from this reply.[39]

In 1948 the Convention endorsed the new "Protestants and Other Americans United for the Separation of Church and State" and declined to send even an observer to the World Council of Churches meeting that year in Amsterdam. Many Convention sessions have specifically stated since that time that it would compromise Baptist principles to enter into organic connections with the National Council or World Council of Churches.[40] The increasing influence of the Eastern Orthodox Catholic Church and the closer relations of Roman Catholics since the meetings of New Delhi (1961) and Uppsala (1968) have also estranged Southern Baptists. Little interest has been shown in joining the Consultation on Church Union or the National Association of Evangelicals. The invitations extended by the Roman Catholic Church to come to its fold during Vatican Council II (1962-present) have not drawn Southern Baptist support.

Substantial Growth. There is probably truth in allegations of some writers that during the first half of the twentieth century Southern Baptists were so engrossed in evangelism and growth that they neglected the social aspects of the gospel.[41] The constituency of the Convention increased from 2,844,301 in 1917 to 5,367,129 in 1942, or a growth of 88.73% in this twenty-five-year period, an average rate of 3.55% each year. Sunday School enrollment increased from 1,835,811 in 1917 to 3,430,929 in 1942, an 86.83% growth or average annual rate of 3.47%. Total gifts increased from $15,346,158 in 1917 to $52,247,622, or 240.46%, an average annual growth rate of 9.62%.

These percentages are impressive in view of the large figures at the beginning of the period.

Expansion Amidst Revolution (1942-72)

In the final period of this story of Southern Baptist life, the Convention faced problems and tensions of a magnitude and an intensity never before experienced in its history. More than ever before Southern Baptists interacted explicitly with the political, social, economic, and ecclesiological currents about them. These currents have been very complex, and as always, Southern Baptists did not present a monolithic response to them. As a result, many of the issues have been divisive, a few of them have been critical, and some of them have been fruitless.

Practically every writer has described the years since 1942 as revolutionary. Perhaps this era commenced when the first atomic bomb was dropped on Hiroshima on August 6, 1945, to bring a rapid end to World War II. It has been characterized by the extensive growth of disaffection and cynicism toward authority; the eroding of traditional moral and social restraints; violent confrontations to correct real or fancied wrongs, end wars, stop discrimination, diminish pollution, and air many other grievances; the impassioned search for identity; and the development of remarkable scientific and medical exploits, ranging from putting a man on the moon to the transplanting of human hearts. Editorials in Baptist newspapers and even references in *Annuals* of the Southern Baptist Convention to the fast-moving events of these three decades testified that Southern Baptists in the modern era were no longer isolated from the most secular aspects of daily living. Less than a century before, the Convention had refused ever to hear a resolution on temperance in one of its sessions.[42] Now it interacted with almost everything. World War II (1941-45), the Korean War (1950-53), and the war in Southeast Asia (About 1964-73) affected the enrollment in the auxiliaries of the Convention and involved moral questions that Southern Baptists discussed extensively. They reacted to the formation of the United Nations in 1945; to the cold war with the Soviet Union after President Truman enunciated his position in 1947; to the appointment by Truman of a personal ambassador to the Vatican, the formation of the National Council of Churches, the renaming of northern Baptists (the American Baptist Convention), the declaration of the dogma on the assumption of Mary in 1950, and the somber take-over of China by the Communists in the same year; to the accelerating racial struggles of the 1950's and 1960's; to the launching of the first Soviet satellite to inaugurate the space race in 1957; to the Bay of Pigs fiasco by President Kennedy in 1961, and the war scare of 1962 when the Soviets were forced to withdraw their missiles from Cuba; to the terrible assassinations of the two Kennedys and Martin Luther King, Jr.; to the runaway inflation of the 1960's; and to the political scandals of the early 1970's.

Meanwhile, the Convention instituted challenging programs of advance for its constituency. Due to the exigencies of war, Convention sessions in 1943 and 1945 were not held. A generous offering for world relief was promoted in 1946; simultaneous evangelistic campaigns were held in 1950 west of the Mississippi River, and in the following year, east of the river; a Jubilee Advance was promoted between 1959 and 1964 in cooperation with other Baptist groups in America, commemorating the 150th anniversary of the first Baptist general body in America; participation in a North American Baptist Fellowship was begun in 1965; and in that same year approval was given to the Crusade of the Americas, a movement involving fellowship and joint evangelistic efforts by Baptists of North, Central, and South America with a widespread evangelistic thrust in 1969. The principal areas of Convention preoccupation during this period, however, involved its continuing growth (although, as pointed out, serious concern was felt in the 1960's because of decreases in enrollment in some of its schools and auxiliaries); its expanded geographical base to include all of the United States, as described in chapter 15; its vexing controversies; and its intensive study of its own structure as a means of providing a better vehicle for achieving its goals.

Continuing Growth. Between 1942 and 1972, the membership enrolled in churches affiliated with the Convention increased from 5,367,129 in 1942 to 12,067,284 in 1972, a total of 124.83% for this thirty-year period, or an average annual growth of 4.16%. Sunday School enrollment increased from 3,430,929 in 1942 to 7,177,651 in 1972, for a total growth of 109.20%, or an average annual rate of 3.64%. Training Union enrollment increased from 801,567 in 1942 to 2,044,445 in 1972, for a total growth of 155.05%, or an average annual rate of 5.17%. Vacation Bible School enrollment increased from 590,114 in 1942 to 3,240,514 in 1972, for a total growth of 449.13%, or an average annual rate of 14.97%. Woman's Missionary Union enrollment increased from 748,465 in 1942 to 1,125,641 in 1972, for a total growth of 50.39%, or an average annual rate of 1.68%. Brotherhood enrollment increased from 54,868 in 1942 to 454,272 in 1972, for a total growth of 727.94%, or an average annual rate of 24.26%. In addition, church music enrollment reached 1,173,004, the fastest-growing area of work. Total receipts were $52,247,622 in 1942, while they were $1,071,512,302 in 1972, an increase of 1,950.8%, or an average annual rate of 65.03%. The number of churches increased from 25,737 in 1942 to 34,534 in 1972, while baptisms in the year 1942 were 209,127 compared with 445,725 in 1972.

Enlarged Geographical Base. Along with this numerical increase has also come a startling geographical expansion by churches and other bodies affiliating with the Southern Baptist Convention. As described previously, the geographical base of the Southern Baptist Convention in 1845 was described as embracing "fourteen States, with an aggregate area of 955,664 square miles, and a population of about eight millions."[43] Between 1845 and 1942 (over ninety-five years), only six additional states were added to Convention affiliation—Arizona, California, Illinois, New Mexico, Oklahoma, and Texas. But in less than thirty years that followed, the Southern Baptist geographic base was expanded to include the other thirty states of the Union. Some implications of this vast increase will be suggested at the close of this chapter, but it might be remarked that some of the same types of problems experienced by the United States when they worked out their "manifest destiny" will probably face Southern Baptists in the not-too-distant future.

Vexing Controversies. In this period Southern Baptists have confronted more controversial issues than in any other generation in their history. Some of them sprang from the context of society about them; some from their conservative doctrinal stance; and some from unresolved areas of authority within their functioning structure. The most significant of these are summarized here.

1. Social Upheavals. The principal social problem affecting Southern Baptists has been racial. As mentioned previously, Southern Baptists, like all denominations, did little about the unsophisticated discrimination against the Negro before World War II. David Reimers remarked that until then "the basic approach of Protestantism to a solution to the race problem still consisted of evangelism and Negro education."[44] The many "pronouncements" on race relations by the several denominations in the 1930's were relatively harmless.[45] Reimers counted the resolution adopted in March, 1946, by the Federal Council of Churches of Christ as being a major step toward confronting the evils of racial discrimination. Segregation was denounced as unnecessary and undesirable and a violation of the gospel of love and human brotherhood. In Reimers' words, this was

> the first time in the history of American Protestantism that a major interdenominational group committed itself to fight the traditional practices of racism, practices that had existed since colonial times.[46]

The initial thrusts toward Southern Baptist participation in this spirit were spearheaded by the Christian Life Commission, referred to during the previous period. When the Supreme Court declared in 1954 that segregation of the races was unconstitutional, the Southern Baptist Convention under the leadership of its Christian Life Commission adopted a resolution reading in part as follows:

> 1. That we recognize the fact that this Supreme Court decision is in harmony with the constitutional guarantee of equal freedom to all citizens, and with the Christian principles of equal justice and love for all men.
>
> .　　.　　.　　.
>
> 5. That we urge Christian statesmen and leaders in our churches to use their leadership in positive thought and planning to the end that this crisis in our national history shall not be made the occasion for new and bitter prejudices, but a movement toward a united nation embodying and proclaiming a democracy that will commend freedom to all peoples.[47]

Despite vigorous attempts during the following several years to hobble the active efforts of the Christian Life Commission to implement this resolution, Southern Baptists made progress toward overcoming attitudes and customs held for more than a century. The assassination of Martin Luther King, Jr., in Memphis, Tennessee, on April 4, 1968, and subsequent violence, caused Convention leaders to draft "A Statement Concerning the Crisis in our Nation." Endorsed by executives of the Convention's agencies and most of the executives and editors of state Baptist bodies, the statement was presented to the 1968 Convention by the Executive Committee and adopted by a majority vote of approximately 73 percent. It was the strongest statement on racism ever adopted. It read in part:

> We are a nation that declares the equality and rights of persons irrespective of race. Yet, as a nation, we have allowed cultural patterns to persist that have deprived millions of black Americans, and other racial groups as well, of equality of recognition and opportunity in the areas of education, employment, citizenship, housing, and worship. Worse still, as a nation, we have condoned prejudices that have damaged the personhood of blacks and whites alike. We have seen a climate of racism and reactionism develop resulting in hostility, injustice, suspicion, faction, strife, and alarming potential for bitterness, division, destruction, and death.

It went on to review efforts made in the past in this area by Southern Baptists, recognized their responsibility in helping to create the critical situation, confessed that they had come far short of their privilege in Christian brotherhood, and committed themselves to action "to accept the full demands of the love and lordship of Christ in human relationships and urgent ministry."[48] This document, of course, could not immediately effect the wholesome improvements in race relations that it espoused, but by 1972, a greatly improved relationship between the races was evident to writers both within and without the Convention. Integration in church life was not uncommon, black ministers were pastors of white or integrated churches, many black churches were affiliated with white associations and state bodies, and some white churches were affiliated with black associations and state bodies.

It is rather interesting to notice that this problem, as well as many of the other areas of social concern, has greatly influenced the literature published by the Convention. The Home Mission Board monthly, in particular, has developed a radically different format in an effort to understand and interpret the social revolution and provide methods for meeting the new needs.

2. Doctrinal Controversies. Two principal doctrinal controversies flared in the 1960's and 1970's. Professor Ralph H. Elliott of Midwestern Baptist Theological Seminary wrote *The Message of Genesis*, which received "passionate criticism" because of its interpretation of the events of the first book of the Bible. At the meeting of the Convention in 1962, in the midst of heated debate, two resolutions were passed: one affirmed faith in the entire Bible as the authoritative, authentic, infallible Word of God, while the other opposed views which would undermine the historical accuracy and doctrinal integrity of the Bible. The trustees of Midwestern Seminary supported Elliott until he informed them that although Broadman Press had chosen not to reprint the book, he would turn to another publisher. They demanded that he assure them he would not seek another publisher. "Elliott held that such a statement would leave the impression that he was retracting what he had written, an impression he was unwilling to permit." On October 25, 1962, he was dismissed for insubordination.[49]

Growing directly out of this confrontation, a strong committee (composed of the presidents of the various state conventions and headed by the Southern Baptist Convention's president, Herschel H. Hobbs) was given the task of preparing a statement of Baptist faith and message. In the introduction, as was also true in the 1925 Memphis Articles, it was specifically stated that these statements of consensus "have never been regarded as complete, infallible statements of faith, nor as official creeds carrying mandatory authority." It was adopted at Kansas City in 1963.[50]

The other doctrinal controversy had different actors and a new stage, but the plot was the same. The Sunday School Board projected a twelve-volume set entitled *The Broadman Bible Commentary* in 1961. The first volume (including Genesis) was published in October, 1969, and promptly was attacked from many sides for its interpretation of some passages and events of Genesis. At the Denver meeting in 1970, in a stormy session, the Convention voted 5,394 to 2,170 to ask the Sunday School Board to withdraw this volume of the commentary from further distribution and to rewrite it with due consideration of the conservative viewpoint. Two months later the Board voted by a two-to-one margin to withdraw this volume from distribution and to rewrite it from a conservative viewpoint. A special committee of the Board recommended in January, 1971, that the same authors be asked to rewrite their material "with due consideration of the conservative viewpoint." This action did not please the conservatives, and by a bare majority the 1971 Convention session voted

> that the Sunday School Board be advised that the vote of the 1970 Convention regarding the rewriting of Volume 1 of *The Broadman Bible Commentary* has not been followed and that the Sunday School Board obtain another writer and proceed with the Commentary according to the vote of the 1970 Convention in Denver.[51]

The Board secured another writer for Genesis in compliance with this request but responded that it had felt that it was following the desires of the Convention in taking its prior action.[52]

These theological controversies showed the diversity of doctrine within the constituency of the Convention and raised a question concerning the competence of the structure to handle similar controversies in the future, as will be mentioned briefly hereafter. Walter B. Shurden is doubtless correct in noting that controversy among Baptists is inevitable, is painful but profitable, is often embodied in powerful personalities, and can never be absolutely settled because of the absence of monarchical authority.[53]

3. Ecclesiological Dilemmas. Since the earliest cries for separation of church and state by Baptists in England and the United States, the perplexing question continually has come—how separate can they be? A survey of the *Report from the Capital,* the informative news bulletin of the Baptist Joint Committee on Public Affairs, reveals the amazingly complex and extensive nature of church-state tensions. Among items involved since 1956 were the authority of school boards to prescribe or require prayer or devotions; the power of military leaders to prescribe worship and require attendance; tax exemption for houses of worship as a judicial issue; tax support for religious elementary and secondary schools; college dormitory loans to religious institutions from government credit agencies; loans to college students in religious institutions from public funds; the use of Peace Corps personnel in religious schools in foreign nations; exports of surplus food to feed needy populations; government food surpluses given to church youth camps; federal and state hospital grants for religiously owned hospitals; religious texts for public office and for candidates; and government rehabilitation contracts with church-related agencies.[54] The controversy over prayer in public schools (with many influential Southern Baptists on both sides of the issue) was particularly long and painful. Similarly, on the issue of federal aid to Baptist institutions, important Baptist names were found in each party to the discussion. Some state Baptist bodies refused to grant permission for their colleges to receive federal grants or loans, while others permitted this. Several hospitals were released from state convention control to permit them to accept such grants. The Southern Baptist Convention was affected by these developments, and in 1970 and 1971 two consecutive sessions voted to release the two hospitals at New Orleans, Louisiana, and Jacksonville, Florida, from Convention control and operation.[55]

One of the most perilous areas of church-state relations in its far-reaching significance for Southern Baptist life concerned decisions made by state courts in litigation over church property. The earliest state courts in the United States were forced to pioneer in litigation of this sort, since the principle of separation of church and state in the new nation confounded most precedents. The problem was twofold. First, in view of the principle of separation of church and state, to what extent do courts have jurisdiction in cases of church litigation? Second, granting such jurisdiction to some degree, what legal principle would apply to assure equity to the widely differing systems of ecclesiastical government found in American religious life?

Considerable care was given to the answer of the first question. The position finally established has been summed up by the Supreme Court of North Carolina, as follows:

> The legal or temporal tribunals of the State have no jurisdiction over, and no concern with, purely ecclesiastical questions and controversies, for there is a constitutional guarantee of freedom of religious profession and worship, as well as an equally firmly established separation of church and state, but the courts do have jurisdiction, as to civil, contract and property rights which are involved in, or arise from, a church controversy. . . . This principle may be tersely expressed by saying religious societies have double aspects, the one spiritual, with which legal courts have no concern, and the other temporal, which is subject to judicial control.[56]

The second problem involving the equitable principle of adjudication was given a forthright answer. In order to deal fairly with the various types of church government involved (from Roman Catholicism with its rigid episcopal control, to Quakers with practically none), it was determined that each religious denomination be a law to itself. Thus, in cases involving the Roman Catholic Church the secular courts would attempt to apply the principles of that Church to the litigation at hand. Were a Congregational church involved in litigation, Congregational ecclesiology would be followed. Examples of this may be seen in the case of Father Francis Fromm in the Fifth Circuit Court of Pennsylvania in 1798, where Roman Catholic principles were used to determine the verdict, and the famous Dedham case of 1820 in Massachusetts, where the Supreme Court followed the ecclesiology of the Congregational churches.

The development of these basic principles did not automatically solve the problem of the proper decision in church litigation. In addition to determining the facts in a controversy, it became necessary for a court to distinguish the dominant ecclesiological factor of the particular denomination involved in the litigation. In Baptist life this was not easy. What is the unifying or dominant principle of Baptist life—majority rule by the congregation, or is it adherence to traditional Baptist doctrine?

One of the first legal cases of this sort among American Baptists pointed to Baptist doctrine as the distinctive element in a Baptist church, taking precedence even over majority rule. In 1781 the First Baptist Church of Philadelphia was involved in a bitter controversy. Because of the shortage of Baptist ministers in America, the church had extended a call to Elhanan Winchester to become its pastor without first investigating his theological views. After assuming his office, Winchester began preaching the doctrines of Universalism which, to say the least, the Baptists in the church believed were detrimental to the dignity and work of Jesus Christ. The leaders in the church were troubled, but many people flocked to hear Winchester and throngs joined the church under his preaching.

In a long address, the church appealed to other Baptist churches to stand by it. The language was vigorous.

> The method taken by him, at first, to propagate this wicked tenent, was by "creeping into houses, and leading captive persons of weak capacities" wherein he met with too much encouragement. Alarmed at this authenticated report, he was, at different times, privately conversed with on the subject, by several of the members;—he did not presume to contradict it fully, and yet his confession was, by no means, satisfactory: Upon these occasions he would frequently intimate his intention of *going away,* provided the smallest division took place on his account; while at the same juncture, as opportunity served, he failed not to use arguments in order to gain proselytes. Such conduct gave an early disgust to several, who, leaving their seats among us, went elsewhere to worship God. . . . Ruin began to stare us in the face! Hereupon many of the brethren, in a church capacity, called upon Mr. Winchester; and, with affectionate concern, intreated him, in case he held so dangerous a sentiment, by no means to promulgate it as it was totally repugnant to our principles: He acknowledged his holding the sentiment, but promised he would not advance it in public, without the church's approbation. Contrary to *their* ecpectation *(sic),* and *his* verbal engagement, he not long after, at different times and sundry places, spake openly and explicitly thereupon, to the grief of some and injury of others, as numbers can testify.[57]

Finally, the deacons of the church demanded that Winchester resign for preaching false doctrine. He declined. When the quarrel was brought before the church in conference, a majority sustained Winchester. It appeared that the First Baptist Church of Philadelphia would now become the First Universalist Church of Philadelphia.

Winchester, it should be said, was one of the founders of the Universalist movement in both America and England.

The Universalist majority began litigation to secure control of the church property, but on July 9, 1784, the court held for the Baptist minority on the ground that it was "the rightful church." [58] Subsequent decisions of various state courts established the principle that

> . . . a majority in a Baptist church is supreme, or a "law unto itself," so long as it remains a Baptist church, or true to the fundamental usages, customs, doctrine, practice, and organization of Baptists. For instance, if a majority of a Baptist church should attempt to combine with a Methodist or Presbyterian church, or in any manner depart from the fundamental faiths, usages, and customs which are distinctively Baptist, and which mark out that denomination as a separate entity from all others, then, in such case, the majority could not take the church property with them for the reason that they would not be acting in accordance with distinctively Baptist principles. [59]

In the Philadelphia decision one can glimpse the element of trust (which secular courts hold sacred). Baptist money and life had been put into this property. The court viewed the contending parties, not as majority or minority, but simply as corporate litigants. The decision was reached, not by counting the number on each side, but through determining which party could be identified with the undivided church before there was disagreement or schism. Since the minority remained Baptist and the majority adopted Universalist views, the property was awarded to the Baptist minority.

Thus, this early case suggested the principle that the unifying or dominant element in Baptist life is not majority rule but the continuity of Baptist doctrine. This principle has been followed regularly in many state courts. In fact, the Supreme Court of Illinois in the old case of *Ferraria v. Vasconcellos* ruled that those who abandon "the tenets and doctrines" of a given "denomination" forfeit their rights to the use of the property "although but a single member adhere to the original faith and doctrine of the church." Before the year 1900 Baptist litigation in Texas followed this principle regularly. [60]

However, there has been another point of view expressed by courts in various states concerning the unifying or dominant principle in Baptist life. Instead of viewing *Baptist doctrine* as the major principle in a Baptist church, they have held that *Baptist church government* should take precedence. In a denomination in which the church congregation is the governing authority, say proponents of this view, the majority always rules, regardless of the nature of the disagreement. Thus, if 100 members out of 150 in a Baptist church vote to change *anything*—affiliation, liturgy, even doctrine itself—there can be no legal recourse by the minority to secure the property. This was the decision of the Supreme Court of Texas in 1900 in a case involving the First

Baptist Church of Paris, Texas. The majority had abandoned the doctrines and practices of the undivided church, but secured the property on the ground that it was the majority and that this alone justified any action that might be taken. One Baptist historian in Texas wrote that the adoption of this principle was a great "menace" to all Baptist churches.[61]

This dual interpretation of Baptist life has continued in the decisions of various state courts. Some award property to the majority without giving recognition to the "faithful minority." Others probe the practices and doctrines of the undivided church to determine which party remained true to the doctrines and practices followed before disagreement and schism.

It is evident that the dual application of Baptist principles discussed heretofore does not in itself constitute any danger to the independence of Baptist churches. Whether the majority rules or the faithful minority remaining Baptist secures the property, both principle and equity support the verdict. When the majority rules, little needs to be said concerning church autonomy. A church is free enough even to wrench itself away from Baptist doctrine!

More problems are involved, however, in awarding the property to the faithful minority. The basic principle is equitable. If a majority in a Baptist church should turn to Presbyterian views, it appears reasonable that the true Baptists in the minority should retain the property which has been accumulated by Baptists through the years. But what shall be done in the case of a Baptist church which has a schism and *both sides,* majority and minority, remain Baptist? How much deviation from the practices of the undivided church constitutes ground for awarding the property to the minority? Even this question can be answered satisfactorily when there has been a *radical* break with the past by the majority; but what if the majority should remain distinctively Baptist and make only *mild* alterations in its program?

It is at this point that the danger of appealing to a secular court is apparent. The court ostensibly rules only on property matters; yet to arrive at that decision a secular court (sometimes not Baptist, sometimes not Christian) must sift the religious beliefs and practices of the two parties in a Baptist church and determine the most sensitive and vital point of Baptist life: the being or essence of a true Baptist church. This means that a secular judge must do something which even the wisest Baptist, steeped in Baptist history and doctrine, could never do. He must decide which group in the schism constitutes the true church and which are "the Nicolaitans." The opening wedge comes in the adjudication of property rights; but property rights must necessarily involve the identification by a secular court of the true church of God! A difficult assignment, even for the angels.

One of the outstanding cases along this line involved the North Rocky Mount Baptist Church in North Carolina. On August 9, 1953, at a properly called business conference of the church, a vote was taken concerning whether to remain affiliated with the Southern Baptist Convention and its related state and associational bodies or to withdraw. A majority of 241 favored withdrawal under leadership of the pastor; 144 were opposed to withdrawal; while 200 abstained from voting. In a lengthy and bitter trial, both sides used various denominational leaders to testify about the "fundamental usages, customs, doctrine, practice, and organization of missionary Baptists." The superior court allowed this testimony and awarded the property to the minority. The majority appealed, insisting that withdrawal from the Southern Baptist Convention did not constitute any change in the fundamental usages, customs, doctrine, etc., of the church. The decision was upheld by the Supreme Court of North Carolina, but a wise and significant emendation was made. In essence, the supreme court said that all denominational testimony was to be eliminated; that denominational affiliation or the lack of it was not the principal issue in the case; and that the decision to uphold the superior court was not based upon whether the North Rocky Mount Baptist Church remained in or withdrew from affiliation with the Southern Baptist Convention and its related bodies. The decision, it was said, rested only upon changes in the local church in fundamental usages, customs, doctrines, etc., *without reference to denominational affiliation and based solely upon testimony from the local body.* This was a very significant clarification by able judges and followed the ancient and original principle.[62]

However, the very point emphasized in this North Carolina Supreme Court emendation has been ignored in other litigation. The First Baptist Church of Normal, Illinois, by majority vote, decided to leave the American Baptist Convention and join the Conservative Baptist Association of America. The Circuit Court of McLean County held for the majority, but the Appellate Court of the Third District of Illinois reversed this decision and said: "Severing relations with the American Baptist Convention was a distinct departure from the doctrines, beliefs, and practices theretofore followed by the congregation and appears to have been so understood by both groups."[63] A change in inter-Baptist denominational affiliation alone was the ground for awarding property to the minority!

Another case moved even further from the original principles. The First Baptist Church of Wichita, Kansas, in March, 1960, voted 1,074 to 235 to withdraw from affiliation with the American Baptist Convention, the Kansas Baptist Convention, and the Wichita Association of Baptist Churches. *The church gave no indication that it would affiliate with any other group thereafter.* Ten members of the minority brought suit, but the district court held for the majority. The supreme court reversed this decision. Now, the fact of the reversal by the supreme court is in itself not a matter of concern, for, as pointed out previously, the minority has often been awarded the property in church litigation.

But the ground of this reversal was radical. Its principle can destroy voluntary cooperation by Baptist churches which cherish their independence. The supreme court quoted an earlier opinion that

> repudiation by the defendants of the national, state and local associations maintained by the churches of the Baptist faith constituted a departure from the original principles, rules and practices of church government recognized by the united body prior to the occurrence of any schism therein.[64]

The supreme court then added: "We hold that not even in an autonomous Baptist church may the denomination of the church be changed by a mere majority vote." It should be noted that there was no evidence that this majority group planned to affiliate with any other general body. Subsequently, however, the majority constituted itself a distinct congregation on August 12, 1962, and voted to cooperate with the Southern Baptist Convention on November 11, 1962. It is now known as the Metropolitan Baptist Church. The withdrawal from a general body by a majority in a church evidently was considered grounds for awarding church property to the minority.

What does this decision mean? It means simply that in those states where this precedent is followed, the general denominational bodies (national, sectional, state, or district association) have an interest in the property of every Baptist church affiliated with them. Even a disavowal of this by the general bodies themselves (as is true in the constitution of the Kansas state body affiliated with the Southern Baptist Convention) probably could not, in the eyes of the courts, bind the minority in any local church. If one person desired to continue in the old affiliation, that one person could hold the property against the remainder of the church. Denominational affiliation within Baptist ranks has replaced fundamental doctrines and practices of the undivided church as the criterion for awarding church property to the minority in cases where this precedent is followed. In essence, this decision robs an autonomous church of its autonomy.

Structural Refinements. The historical summary of the agencies of the Convention in the next section of this chapter will describe most of the important changes and additions to the organizational structure, but a specific reference should be made to some of the basic conceptual patterns retained in the Convention structure during these years.

Increasingly the Executive Committee began to assume its proper function, and it has become the organizational pivot of Southern

Baptist Convention work. Mainly through its initiative, some procedural alterations have been made in the general structure: more laymen were included on the boards, commissions, and committees (1958, 1961); two consecutive Conventions must vote before an agency is discontinued or the constitution is altered (1960, 1963); and more careful supervision of registration and voting with computer cards were introduced (1965). Two major constitutional revisions were made in 1946 and 1958. The constitution was entirely rewritten in 1946 (utilizing professional assistance in its study), and changes were made to clarify the meaning, eliminate unnecessary verbiage, use more constitutional rather than popular language, and make the document as accurate, precise, and concise as possible.[65]

Significantly, the extensive constitutional revision of 1946 explicitly approved the dual decision-making structure inaugurated formally in 1931 by refining the methodology for naming the trustees of the various boards, commissions, and committees. These were to be rotated regularly to provide wider representation. Another change attempted to decentralize the appointment of these trustees by providing that the Committee on Boards be elected from nominees chosen by a caucus of the messengers from each state in the Convention. After two years this plan was scrapped and the Committee on Boards was named by the Committee on Committees. Sensitive to the difference in the number of constituents in each state, the Convention voted that each state having 500,000 members should receive an additional member on each board, plus another one for each 250,000 members beyond the 500,000. In 1953 this same provision was extended to include membership on the Executive Committee, except that the first additional member was granted for 250,000 Baptists in a state instead of 500,000, and a total limit of five additional members was set. However, in 1967, an attempt to reduce the proportion of membership for trustees on all boards and agencies from smaller state conventions was voted down by the Convention.

The extensive 1958 changes in the constitution followed the appointment in 1956 of a Committee to Study the Total Baptist Program, headed by Douglas M. Branch. W. L. Howse judged one aspect of their work as "a major turning point in Southern Baptist life. It is doubtful whether the Convention at any time in its history has taken an action more far reaching than this"[66] He was referring to the correlation and coordination of Southern Baptist programs. He noted that since the opening of the present century there had been a striving to fulfill at least three basic needs of the Convention: (1) to define denominational programs better; (2) to correlate and coordinate denominational programming and long-range planning; and (3) to develop knowledge and skills in programming and long-range planning.

A recommendation in this area by the Total Study Committee urged that the Executive Committee should

> maintain an official organization manual defining the responsibilities of each agency of the Convention for conducting specific programs and for performing other functions. The manual shall cite the action of the Convention that assisted the programs and other functions to the agency. The Executive Committee shall present to the Convention recommendations required to clarify the responsibilities of the agencies for programs and other functions, to eliminate overlapping assignments or responsibility, and to authorize the assignment of new responsibilities for programs or functions to agencies.[67]

This was made a bylaw of the Convention in 1960.

Each agency of the Convention worked in its own area of program budgeting and moved toward correlating programs, curricula, and meetings of the various Southern Baptist Convention agencies affecting the local churches as the main center or basic unit of all programs.

> The Inter-Agency Council was enlarged and strengthened to provide the structure through which the Convention agencies could work to correlate their program efforts. Between 1960 and 1967 the Convention adopted a program statement for each agency, describing the work assigned to it. Agency programs were designed to prevent unnecessary overlapping of work, to lessen tensions between agencies, and to make possible a more objective study of budget needs.[68]

Another meaningful result of the Total Study Committee was the erection of a separate Southern Baptist Convention building in Nashville to house the Executive Committee and smaller agencies of the Convention. The Southern Baptist Convention Building was occupied in 1963 by the Executive Committee, Baptist Foundation, Stewardship Commission, Education Commission, and Christian Life Commission. The Seminary Extension offices were moved there from Jackson, Mississippi, the same year.

Also in 1958 a new bylaw pointed to the increasing desire by the Convention for wider representation in their trustees of boards and other agencies of the body by requiring that all Convention committees, boards, and commissions include both laymen and ordained persons, with neither contributing more than two thirds. In 1961 even more lay participation was structured: the Committee on Boards, Commissions, and Standing Committees was doubled in size to include two members from each state, one a layman. The first woman vice-president of the Convention was elected in 1963, Mrs. R. L. Mathis. In 1968 the Convention voted that young people should have broader participation in decision-making processes of Southern Baptists at all levels.[69]

It is worthy of notice that Southern Baptists made no basic alterations in the four significant structural concepts they had adopted between 1917 and 1942; namely, an Executive Committee to serve between sessions of the Convention, a Cooperative Program for financing all budgeted areas of work, a new widely-based plan of representation whose authority stemmed from consensus, and the formal articulation of a dual system of decision-making—trustees from states and the Convention sessions. Each of these has become a distinctive area of strength in the structure of the Convention. Hardly a session was held between 1967 and 1970, for example, that the messengers did not heartily praise the Cooperative Program as the best channel for supporting the work of the body. They reflected the flowery language of the 1939 Executive Committee report:

> The Cooperative Program is the greatest step forward in Kingdom finance Southern Baptists have ever taken. It was slow and gradual in its formation. It arose out of the desires and efforts of pastors and churches to find a plan whereby all worthy denominational causes might be cared for fully and fairly without conflicting with the necessary programs and work in the churches themselves. It is believed to be sane, scriptural, comprehensive, unifying, equitable, economical and thoroughly workable. It is based upon the assumption that all denominational causes will be included, that all agencies and institutions will co-operate in its promotion, that all pastors will represent and present all causes and seek to secure regular, proportionate and adequate support by putting on the Every Member Canvass every year. In this way all occasions for rivalries and conflicts and overlapping are removed, the offerings will come in regularly and each cause will receive and each contributing member will make fifty-two offerings a year instead of one. It is the best plan we know and it is hoped that it will increasingly receive the hearty and enthusiastic support of all our people.[70]

In 1956 the principles of cooperation between the state conventions and the Southern Baptist Convention relative to the Cooperative Program were reaffirmed (as set out in the 1934 and 1951 *Annuals*), with the added word that each state had the right to deduct or not to deduct any items from Cooperative Program receipts before setting the percentages of division. Cooperative Program undesignated receipts for Southern Baptist Convention causes had grown to $29,970,527 in 1971.[71]

The Developing Structure and Steady Progress of the Convention (1917-72)

In order to provide more unity in the description of the Convention and its various agencies in the period between 1917 and 1972, the chronological outline adopted for the first two general discussions will be supplemented by this section which will examine one by one the agencies of the Convention as they existed in 1972 and give a thumbnail sketch of their development from 1917 to 1972. They will be discussed in the order in which they appeared in the 1972 *Annual* of the Convention.

Executive Committee. This committee became the integrative element in the life of the Convention in a very short time after its founding in 1917, as described previously. In 1919 it was enlarged to include one member from each state and one from each of the boards of the Convention. In 1926 its duties were enlarged substantially. A Committee on Business Efficiency reported in 1927 some problems that demanded further enlargement of functions of the committee, including the preparation of a workable budget, raising sufficient money to care for the consolidated operating budget, allocation of funds, providing for the needs of the institutions of the Convention, paying off the indebtedness of the agencies of the Convention, and enlarging the work of the Convention's agencies.[72] New functional authority was given to the committee, including the assumption of the work of the Cooperative Program Commission. Its ministry and effectiveness have multiplied greatly since then.

This continuing executive body made its headquarters in Nashville, Tennessee, in 1927, and elected Austin Crouch to be its first secretary. He held that position until his retirement in 1946. Duke K. McCall served at this post from 1946 until 1951, when the present executive secretary-treasurer, Porter Routh, assumed leadership. The committee was reorganized in 1959 along the lines suggested by the Committee to Study the Total Program, and stewardship emphasis was placed under a separate commission. The Executive Committee's fourfold program, as formally stated and as approved by the Convention, was in 1971 service of general Convention administration, for which $204,599 was spent; service of general public relations, for which $181,182 was spent; service of Convention operations, for which $196,294 was spent; and the Baptist World Alliance, for which $112,000 was spent. The total operating budget of the committee in 1971 was $694,075.[73]

General Boards. The original Foreign and Home Mission Boards, supplemented by the second Sunday School Board in 1891, constituted the board structure of the Convention at the opening of this period in 1917. A fourth board, whose task was to provide ministerial relief and annuity programs, was added in 1918. The story of these four boards during the modern period will be sketched briefly.

1. Foreign Mission Board. The executive secretaries of the board during this period were J. F. Love (1915-28), T. B. Ray (1929-32), C. E. Maddry (1933-44), M. T. Rankin (1945-53), and Baker J. Cauthen (1954-present). Each made his own distinctive contribution to the foreign mission program. Before the financial disaster involved in the Seventy-five Million Campaign, Chile, Spain, Romania, and Palestine were entered as new fields during the term of J. F. Love. Because of heavy indebtedness, no more new fields were entered under T. B. Ray. Every resource was used to satisfy creditors and maintain the work on the existing fields. Reference has been made to the struggles of C. E. Maddry with debts, but Hungary and Yugoslavia were formally entered in 1935 and 1938, respectively. In 1943 Maddry had the satisfaction of announcing that "for the first time in a whole generation the Foreign Mission Board of the Southern Baptist Convention is out of debt." The administration of M. T. Rankin was characterized by a bold program of advance, presented to the Convention in 1948.[74] He led in the opening of new fields in Paraguay, Ghana, Guatemala, Lebanon, the Philippines, Switzerland, Taiwan, Costa Rica, Hong Kong, Thailand, Venezuela, Ecuador, Korea, Peru, Rhodesia, Singapore, the Bahamas, Indonesia, Malaysia, and Jordan. The administration of Baker J. Cauthen has continued this emphasis on advance. New fields have been opened in Gaza, Honduras, Kenya, Tanzania, East Pakistan, Portugal, Vietnam, Malawi, Zambia, France, Okinawa, Liberia (resumed), French West Indies, West Germany, Guam, Dominican Republic, Guyana, India, Tobago, Trinidad, Uranda, Iceland, Jamaica (resumed), Luxembourg, Togo, Yemen, Austria, Libya, Morocco, Bermuda, Ivory Coast, Turkey, Belgium, Botswana, Ethiopia, Angola, Iran, South West Africa, and Egypt. In 1971 the board reported 2,526 missionaries under assignment in 75 countries.

The sixfold program of this board, as approved by the Convention, included in 1972 the support of foreign missionaries, for which $22,423,972 was spent; evangelism and church development, for which $3,814,478 was spent; schools and student work, for which $2,483,950 was spent; publication work, for which $1,540,609 was spent; hospitals and medical care, for which $1,166,509 was spent; and benevolent ministries, for which $252,480 was spent.[75]

2. Home Mission Board. The executive secretaries of this board during the period were B. D. Gray (1903-28), J. B. Lawrence (1929-53), Courts Redford (1953-65), and Arthur B. Rutledge (1965-present). Under Gray the board had shown substantial progress in the fourteen years before this period, but the dire effects of the depression of the 1920's may be noted in the fact that missionaries under appointment dropped from 1,507 in 1917 to 765 in 1928. Although receipts increased from $474,375 in 1917 to $651,911 in 1928, the heavy debts on this agency cut radically into their work. Several new areas of service were inaugurated after 1917: good will center activity, the opening of the El Paso sanitarium, field work among the Jews, the rescue mission project in New Orleans, and the organization of the Department of Direct Missions. However, the Department of Evangelism was suspended in 1928 because of financial stringency. The tragic story of the defalcation of Clinton S. Carnes in 1928, involving almost a million dollars in principal and interest, has been told. Carnes was the only individual implicated, but because of the enormous loss, added to the existing crushing debt and his advancing years, Secretary Gray retired from office, honored and loved by his brethren. Carnes was apprehended and sent to the penitentiary.

After a brief interim in which Arch C. Cree of Georgia served most effectively, J. B. Lawrence came to the helm of this board. As pointed out previously, he set himself to preserving the integrity of the Convention by acknowledging and promising to pay every cent of indebtedness. His own account of this experience is typically low-key and unpretentious, but he served the Kingdom well. Significant events during his administration included the beginning of the publication of *Home Missions* in 1930, the Convention-wide promotion of schools of missions in 1932, restoration of the Department of Evangelism in 1936, the ministry which became Sellers Home and Adoption Center begun in 1937, the assignment of chaplaincy ministries by the Convention in 1941, the launching of the modern city-missions program in the same year, joint work with the American Baptist Home Mission Society in cooperative work with Negroes in 1942, establishment of the rural church program in 1943, and three meaningful expansion moves in 1944—beginning of western missions involvement, student summer missions initiated, and the establishment of a loan fund for churches in "pioneer" fields. In 1945 the board purchased its first office building for the central staff. Other striking achievements of the Lawrence administration included the beginning of correspondence Bible work, the initiation of a ministry to migrants, and the organization of the Department of Cooperative Missions in 1947; Southern Baptist Tentmakers' movement begun in 1951; the Long Range Rural Church Committee formed in 1952; and the Juvenile Rehabilitation Program initiated in 1953.[76] In the thirteen-year administration of Courts Redford the advances begun by Lawrence were continued. The modern "pioneer missions" program was established in 1954; the "Big Cities Program" was started in 1957; the In-Service Guidance ministry was begun in 1960, as were literacy missions. The first secretary of the hospital chaplaincy was employed in 1962, and in 1963 work in Puerto Rico was begun. It was during Redford's leadership that the total program study was made by the Convention, and reflecting recommendations from that source, in 1959 the entire staff was reorganized; new departments of missionary personnel and of survey and special studies were formed, and the first secretary of institutional and industrial chaplaincy was elected; and closer cooperation with the state conventions was inaugurated in order to develop a single uniform program of missions in the homeland.[77]

Additional ministries were begun under the secretaryship of Arthur B. Rutledge: the Christian Service Corps established, a Southern Baptist Race Relations Sunday established in collaboration with the Christian Life Commission, US-2 missions started, resort mission projects initiated, etc. But one of the principal thrusts of the period was the development of program statements and the establishment of long-range goals and guidelines in 1966-67. On June 30, 1971, the missionary force reached a high of 2,250. The report for 1972 named the twelve program assignments and the expenditures on each in that year, as follows: evangelism development ($744,465); chaplaincy ministries ($272,876); church loans ($1,433,742); new churches and church-type missions ($3,013,311); associational administration service ($249,598); pioneer missions ($6,416,653); rural-urban missions ($405,596); metropolitan missions ($904,792); language missions ($4,408,538); work with National Baptists ($851,088); Christian social ministries ($2,191,969); and work related to nonevangelicals ($284,369).[78]

3. Sunday School Board. This board has had but three executive-secretaries since 1917, as follows: I. J. Van Ness (1917-35), T. L. Holcomb (1935-53), and James L. Sullivan (1953-present). Under I. J. Van Ness, the board continued reorganizing its various functions systematically in an effort to meet the enlarging ministries it was fostering. Two of the important areas in this reorganization involved young people and students. It will be recalled that in 1895 the B.Y.P.U. had organized under the society program as an independent agency, calling itself an auxiliary to the Southern Baptist Convention. Year by year the ties between this body and the Convention became closer, as the Convention named the B.Y.P.U. executive committee annually and provided literature and financial assistance through the Sunday School Board. In 1918, upon the recommendation of a committee appointed to study the B.Y.P.U. movement, the Sunday School Board was "charged with the full work of fostering these organizations." [79] Reference has also been made previously to ministering among Baptist students away from home at college. The older Baptist Student Missionary Movement continued until 1920, when its work was discontinued in favor of the Convention program. After a short hiatus, an Inter-Board Commission, composed of board leaders of home and foreign mission, Sunday School, and education, together with the executive secretary of Woman's Missionary Union, met on April 15, 1921, and planned a joint program for college students. Frank H. Leavell was elected executive secretary, and was immediately effective in organizing and enlarging this "connecting link between the college and the local church in the college center. . . ." In 1928 the Convention established the student work as a department of the Sunday School Board, and Leavell was retained as its leader.

Along with these two new departments of work, the board during this period refashioned some of the older functions into more effective departmental structures and added such important programs as assistance in church architecture, age group departments, general religious book publishing (Broadman Press), and the Vacation Bible School.

The large debts left on the Convention and its agencies because of the Seventy-five Million Campaign did not directly affect the Sunday School Board since no receipts from the campaign were to be assigned to the board. However, the Sunday School Board was not unaffected by the heavy debts borne by the Convention and sister agencies. In addition, with the stock market collapse on October 24, 1929, the board found itself facing the same kind of stringent economic circumstances that every other business institution confronted. Its operating funds came from business sagacity in a competitive market, although, of course, it depended upon a loyal denomination to provide a virtual monopoly in its field of publications. For the first time in its history, the board reported receipts lower in 1929 than those of the previous year. Income for that year was shown as $1,870,653.97. Receipts dropped in 1933, the trough of the depression, but beginning in 1934 the upward trend continued throughout the remainder of the depression period.

In June, 1935, after the retirement of I. J. Van Ness, the new secretary was T. Luther Holcomb, who served until 1953. Holcomb's leadership during this period was characterized by an extensive reorganization of the board's structure, the inauguration of specialized campaigns to "carry from the steps of the Sunday School Board building to the last church all that we have come to know about Sunday school and Training Union methods," the initiation of new programs, and the achievement of splendid growth in every area. The reorganization brought up-to-date the structure of the board. The specialized campaigns began on November 26, 1935, with the adoption of a Five-Year Promotional Program "using the District Association as the major unit for promoting every phase of Sunday school and Baptist Training Union work." [80] A second four-year program of the same sort was begun at the close of the first campaign on December 31, 1940. In each instance, worthy goals were set and many of them exceeded in every area of the board's work. The statistical gains made during the first ten years of Holcomb's leadership were dwarfed by those of his last eight years of service because of the affluence after World War II. When he retired, his associates recounted total gains during his eighteen years of service: enrollment of Sunday Schools had almost doubled; enrollment in Training Union had almost trebled; enrollment in Vacation Bible Schools had increased from less than 150,000 to over 2,000,000; a new Convention-wide assembly was established at Glorieta, New Mexico; annual income had grown from about $1,600,000 to over $12,000,000; denominational contributions had increased from $431,000 to $1,585,000; and on and on.[81]

The first five years of the administration of James L. Sullivan can best be characterized by "evaluation, adjustment, and undergirding." They involved long-range planning, detailed analysis, organizational realignment, building of solid programs, and gearing the board for advance.[82] Since that time, the board has experienced

> the fuller definition of its purpose, the careful delineation of its programs, the coordination of its ministries, significant advancement along several fronts, the facing of some unprecedented problems, and the development of new plans for the 70's characterized by greater flexibility in the programs recommended to the churches.[83]

In 1960 the board was doing its work through eighteen major programs. Following the major study that developed from the Total Program Committee of the Convention, the board has delineated fifteen programs which were officially approved by the Southern Baptist Convention. These programs describe the contemporary work of the board, and the amount spent in 1972 for each program will suggest the extent of involvement: Book Store Operation ($19,942,627); Broadman Publishing ($4,516,643); Church Services and Materials Development ($16,805,790), including in its total—Church Music Promotion ($659,610), Church Training Development ($1,283,302), Sunday School Development ($2,296,297), Church Administration Development ($660,192), Church Architecture Development ($502,733), Church Library Development ($346,055), Church Recreation Development ($267,058), and National Student Ministries ($569,771); Conference Center Operation ($2,611,424); Sunday School Board General Management ($2,320,209); Cooperative Education and Promotion Work with State Conventions ($958,458); and Southern Baptist Convention Support ($326,389). Total revenue in 1972 was $44,852,153.[84]

4. Annuity Board. Southern Baptists were later than many denominations in providing some economic security for their aged ministers. In the earliest years, many Baptist ministers provided their own support by working at secular labor during the week, often receiving no remuneration at all for ministerial services. When they became disabled or too old to serve, they often spent their last days with relatives or, in some cases, with devoted church members whom they had served. In the nineteenth century, and particularly in the latter half, Baptists in many of the states of the South organized societies to provide relief for ministers and their widows in their last years. This was true in South Carolina (1813), Tennessee and Missouri (not long after the Civil War), Virginia (1872), Kentucky (1884), Texas (1887), and Maryland (1893).

In 1916 William Lunsford, pastor in Nashville, Tennessee, spoke to the pastor's conference on the need to give more attention to ministerial relief. Some at the conference were members of the Sunday School Board, and through their influence, this board agreed to set aside $100,000 to begin a program of ministerial relief with the understanding that the Southern Baptist Convention would give consideration to fostering this benevolence. Pursuant to this, the Convention in 1917 appointed a committee of twelve "to work out a just and equitable pension plan during the ensuing year. . . ." William Lunsford was named by this committee to formulate such a program, and in 1918, the Convention approved the commission's recommendation that "a Board of Ministerial Relief and Annuities" be established. It was located at Dallas, Texas, under the secretaryship of Lunsford. He designed the pioneer contracts for annuity plans and was zealous in the distribution of such relief funds as the Convention made available.

Lunsford was succeeded by T. J. Watts in 1927, who served for twenty years. It took a man of his optimism and enthusiasm to weather the difficult depression years. W. R. Alexander was secretary from 1942 to 1954, and helped build "the House of Security." R. Alton Reed, secretary from 1955 to 1972, displayed remarkable gifts as an administrator and financier. During his administration the title of the chief executive became president. Upon the retirement of Reed, Darold H. Morgan succeeded him on March 1, 1972.[85]

The approved programs of the board were retirement (for which $13,881,720 was spent in 1972) and relief (for which $171,581 was spent in 1972). Total revenue in 1972 was $55,629,430, while total funds of the board in 1972 were $336,439,081. In the retirement program, the board, under its agency plans, covered 69 educational institutions, 6 seminaries, 26 children's homes, 8 homes for the aged, 36 hospitals, 15 other agencies, and 33 state convention headquarters, making a total of 193 agency accounts. Under its supplemental plans, the Age Security Plan (Plan B) had 13,481 active members; the Variable Benefit Plan (Plan C) had 4,969 active members. In the relief program, there were 124 ministers and 274 widows on the relief roll, and a total amount spent on relief of $171,581. Because of the good experience in the inflated economy, additional payments were made beyond their contracts to annuitants as follows: a record 10% good experience credit was given January 1, 1973, to members of several plans; a 6% permanent increase was funded in January, 1973;

and 16.67% dividend check was paid in December, 1972.[86]

Institutions. Under this category, the Convention's directory includes the six seminaries, the Seminary Extension Department, and the Southern Baptist Foundation.

1. Golden Gate Baptist Theological Seminary, Mill Valley, California. With the rapid growth of Southern Baptists in California, two southern pastors, Isam B. Hodges and Dallas G. Faulkner, led their churches to incorporate and elect trustees for the Golden Gate Baptist Theological Seminary on July 12, 1944. With Hodges as president, the school opened in Oakland that fall, and was immediately promised prayerful and moral support from the Golden Gate Baptist Association. The first session enrolled seven students. The Southern Baptist General Convention of California voted to assume ownership and control of the school in November, 1945, and in May, 1946, B. O. Herring became the seminary's second president. He and a part-time secretary were the only salaried employees. The first class of seventeen was graduated in 1949. In May, 1950, the Southern Baptist Convention voted to sponsor the seminary, and on January 1, 1951, began its support. Following the resignation of Herring, the trustees elected Harold K. Graves to be president on May 13, 1952. In 1959 the seminary moved to a new campus on Strawberry Point in Marin County. The Convention has approved the twofold program statement of the seminary: training in theology (for which $438,748 was spent in 1972), and training in religious education and music (for which $197,119 was spent in 1972). Total enrollment in 1972 was 317, with 16 faculty members and 15 administrative and maintenance employees.[87]

2. Midwestern Baptist Theological Seminary, Kansas City, Missouri. As G. Hugh Wamble has pointed out, this school was one of the products of the rapid growth of Southern Baptists in the 1940's and 1950's. In 1956 a committee from the Southern Baptist Convention was invited to confer with Central Baptist Seminary in Kansas City, Kansas (which served both Northern and Southern Baptist churches) concerning the possibility of giving financial aid to that school. From these conferences the Convention set out two principles: (1) No funds would be allocated to any agency or institution for which the Convention did not elect trustees or directors. (2) The Convention would not enter into joint ownership, support, and administration of any new theological institution with any other Baptist body.[88] The first of these principles not only eliminated financial support of Central seminary but also affected the Woman's Training School at Louisville, as will be seen. On May 29, 1957, at the committee's recommendation, the Convention voted to locate a new seminary at Kansas City, Missouri, called Midwestern Baptist Theological Seminary, and in October the new trustees elected Millard J. Berquist as president. He was succeeded in 1973 by Milton Ferguson. A beautiful campus of over 200 acres was secured about six miles directly north of downtown Kansas City. The enrollment during the first year (1958-59) was 151; by 1972 it had increased to 347. The first faculty numbered four, together with the president and a librarian; in 1972 it had increased to nineteen. Program expenditures in 1972 were $525,553 for leadership training in theology, and $148,233 for leadership training in religious education.[89]

3. New Orleans Baptist Theological Seminary (initially, Baptist Bible Institute), New Orleans, Louisiana. The initiative that led to the founding of this school was taken in 1914 by P. I. Lipsey, editor of the Mississippi *Baptist Record,* when he wrote concerning the need for a Baptist school in New Orleans. During the 1915 meeting of the Southern Baptist Convention at Houston, Texas, a group of leaders discussed the advisability of such a school, and concluded by asking the state bodies in Louisiana and Mississippi, along with the Home Mission Board of the Convention, to appoint a committee to forward the project. The joint committee of nine met in February, 1916, in New Orleans, and made plans for establishing the school. The Southern Baptist Convention was invited to meet in New Orleans in 1917, and M. E. Dodd presented the project at that time. The Convention adopted a committee report endorsing the movement and requested

> the Home Mission Board and the Sunday School Board to join with the other interested bodies in founding the institution proposed (the Missionary Training School), in safeguarding the denomination's interests in the same and in making it effective in the work for which it is created.[90]

The school was chartered on October 8, 1917, and opened in September, 1918, sponsored by the Louisiana and Mississippi state bodies, but in 1925 the institution was accepted by the Southern Baptist Convention. Six presidents have served the institution (whose name was changed from Baptist Bible Institute to New Orleans Baptist Theological Seminary in 1946). There were B. H. DeMent (1917-27), W. W. Hamilton (1927-42), Duke McCall (1943-46), Roland Q. Leavell (1946-58), H. Leo Eddleman (1959-70), and Grady C. Cothen (1971-present). The enrollment during the first year was less than 100, but by 1972, 720 students were in attendance. The original faculty of six full-time teachers in 1918 has increased to thirty-eight in 1972. The three programs of the school approved by the Convention are leadership education in theology (for which $633,092 was spent in 1972), in religious education (for which $318,592 was spent in 1972), and in music (for which $164,886 was spent in 1972).[91]

4. Southeastern Baptist Theological Seminary, Wake Forest, North

Carolina. The obvious need for a seminary in the Southeast led to the appointment of committees for study and recommendation in 1947 and 1949 by the Southern Baptist Convention. In 1950 the Convention adopted a report calling for the sponsorship of Golden Gate seminary in Berkeley, California, and for the opening of a new seminary at Wake Forest, North Carolina. An offer to buy the old campus of Wake Forest College for $1,600,000 was also approved. Southeastern Baptist Theological Seminary opened in September, 1951, with the enrollment of eighty-five students and five faculty members (including the first president, Sydnor L. Stealey). By 1972 the enrollment was 699 with 25 faculty. Stealey served until 1956, when he was succeeded by O. T. Binkley (1956-present). The threefold program approved by the Convention involved leadership training in theology (for which $756,470 was spent in 1972), leadership training in religious education (for which $110,561 was spent in 1972), and leadership training in music (for which $19,397 was spent in 1972).[92]

5. *Southern Baptist Theological Seminary, Louisville, Kentucky.* It will be recalled that this first institution of Southern Baptists for theological education was developed on a society basis. For several reasons there was opposition in 1845 to conducting this benevolence through a board of the Convention.[93] Consequently, the Education Convention (on the society pattern) organized the seminary apart from the structure of the Southern Baptist Convention. The charter gave control of the body to the board of trustees, whose membership was constituted from designated states, members at large, and additional state representation when financial gifts from a state amounted to $100,000 in the aggregate. The initial board of trustees was named by the Education Convention, and the charter called them "self-perpetuating." The charter, however, voluntarily related the institution to the Southern Baptist Convention by providing that the trustees might fill vacancies or add other members through the nomination by the Convention of not less than three persons for each vacancy; and further that

> said nomination (is) to be made by the Southern Baptist Convention, at the session of that body next ensuing after such vacancy shall take place, or new appointment shall be required; *provided,* that should the Convention fail to nominate, as above, then the Board may proceed to an election without such nomination.[94]

This meant, of course, that should the Convention decline or fail to nominate trustees at the next session after a vacancy should take place, the board would be self-perpetuating; also, that the nomination by the Convention did not bind the board to elect one of its nominations. The Convention willingly accepted this relationship and permitted the seminary's leadership to appeal for offerings at the regular sessions of its body.

This oldest seminary of Southern Baptists became more closely related to the Convention during this period. Several events combined during the closing years of the presidency of E. Y. Mullins (1899-1928) to tie this school closer to the Convention: the stormy evolutionary controversy, the financial recession of the 1920's with the heavy debts left after the Seventy-five Million Campaign, the detailed study of both the New Orleans and the Fort Worth seminaries when they were accepted by the Convention in 1925, and specifically, the efforts to move the seminary to a new home from its crowded downtown quarters during which the trustees asked the Convention to provide $2,000,000 for buildings on the proposed new campus.[95] The Convention and the seminary appointed committees to discuss this request, resulting in a question about the control over the school by the Convention. In 1927 the seminary's committee presented a report which served to bring the school more completely under the control of the Convention: the original statement that the trustees of the board are "self-perpetuating" was stricken out, "thus putting beyond question the absolute right of the Convention in the nomination of trustees, regardless of invitation thereto from the Seminary Board"; the number of nominations by the Convention for vacancies was reduced from three to two for each vacancy, making it "but one-half a step from direct election"; the unlimited membership of the trustees was eliminated by providing for two from each state and nine members at large; the financial board was reorganized to bring it under the direct control of the trustees and the executive committee of the school; and the executive committee of the trustees was given enlarged powers. These changes "will adequately protect the interests of the Convention and assure the direct control of the institution through the trustees, whose terms expire from time to time and the nomination of whose successors are entirely in the hands of the Convention." [96]

After the death of Mullins, John R. Sampey succeeded him in May, 1929, and served until his retirement in 1942. Ellis A. Fuller (1942-50) was stricken in office, and he was followed by Duke K. McCall (1951-present). The enrollment during this period has increased from 383 in 1917 to 1,326 in 1972, while the faculty has grown from 12 to 54 during the same period. In 1972 the school spent $1,365,276 on their program of leadership training in theology, $282,712 on their program of leadership training in religious education, and $391,790 on their program of leadership training in church music.[97]

6. *Southwestern Baptist Theological Seminary, Fort Worth, Texas.* This school also became more closely related to the Convention during the present period. Before 1925, the Baptist General Convention of Texas was the principal sponsor, aided by ten additional

state bodies who appointed trustees and provided some support. In 1923 the trustees approached the Southern Baptist Convention with the proposal to transfer to it the ownership and control of the school. The formal offer was made at the 1924 session, and the transaction was completed in 1925.

Presidents of this seminary have been L. R. Scarborough (1914-42), E. D. Head (1942-53), J. Howard Williams (1953-58), and Robert E. Naylor (1958-present). Student enrollment has increased from 337 to 1917 to 2,406 in 1972, while the faculty has grown from 8 to 75. In their program of leadership training in theology this school spent $1,292,042 in 1972; in their program of leadership training in religious education they spent $493,887; while in their program of leadership training in church music they spent $393,549.[98]

7. *Seminary Extension Department, Nashville, Tennessee.* This department was established originally by representatives from the several seminaries in December, 1950, and named R. Lee Gallman as its first director, with headquarters at Jackson, Mississippi. At first only correspondence work was projected, and during the first year a total of 600 persons were enrolled. Extension centers were soon provided for class study in various parts of the South. Although the department was initially planned to serve ministers unable to secure seminary training, the majority of those enrolled now are laymen and women, while some seminary alumni use this means for refresher work. The directors of the department have been Lee Gallman (1951-60), Ralph A. Herring (1961-68), and Raymond M. Rigdon (1969-present). During 1972, course enrollments reached 6,998. A total of 215 seminary extension centers operated in 28 states and 4 foreign countries.[99]

8. *Southern Baptist Foundation, Nashville, Tennessee.* Before 1927, the Convention had no adequate method of handling occasional bequests and endowments that were given to it. In that year the Executive Committee was made the "fiduciary agency" of the Convention and assumed responsibility for such funds. The need for a separate agency became increasingly obvious, and after preliminary experimentation within the Executive Committee, a separate board of directors was provided in a new charter on February 26, 1947. This agency became responsible for the custody, investment, and administration of permanent funds entrusted to it by the Convention "or any of its agencies, or any causes controlled, fostered, or officially sanctioned by it" and for the solicitation of gifts to be added to those funds.[100] Its twofold program, as approved by the Convention, consists of fund management and informational and consultative services. The first executive-secretary of the foundation was Charles H. Bolton (1949-53), and succeeding him have been T. L. Holcomb (1953-56), J. W. Storer (1956-67), and Kendall Berry (1967-present), the first

layman to serve in this office. Trust funds in 1972 amounted to $13,884,232, while earnings totaled $653,303 during this year.[101]

Commissions of the Convention. In 1972 the Convention utilized seven commissions as agencies for handling specific functions of its work. As pointed out, a Hospital Commission, whose history began in 1923 to sponsor first a hospital at New Orleans and then one at Jacksonville, Florida, was phased out in 1971.

1. American Baptist Seminary Commission, Nashville, Tennessee. The first efforts of the Convention to cooperate with Negroes in establishing a seminary to train their ministers were thwarted by a serious division in the ranks of Negro Baptists and the confusion arising from American participation in World War I. The National Baptist Convention, Inc., one of the two parties in a schism, expressed their desire to work with the Convention in establishing a seminary. A commission was appointed by the Convention, and in 1919 O. L. Hailey was named its general secretary for the Convention. The agreement provided for two governing bodies, one to hold and control the property, the other to organize and conduct the affairs of the seminary. The Holding Board consisted of twelve members, eight to be elected by the Southern Baptist Convention and four by the National Baptist Convention, Inc. The Board of Directors, on the other hand, consisted of thirty-six members, twenty-four elected by the National Baptist Convention, Inc. and twelve by the Southern Baptist Convention. Each of these two boards elected its own officers, although the president of the Board of Directors was to be a member of the national convention, while the secretary of the body would be a southern convention paid officer. The president of the seminary was always to be a member of the national convention. This plan was modified slightly as experience dictated. The seminary, located on land adjacent to Roger Williams University, Nashville, Tennessee, opened October 1, 1924, with twenty-eight ministerial students and two women studying missions. The first president was S. E. Griggs, while the faculty consisted of William T. Amiger, dean and acting president initially, J. H. Garnett, and O. L. Hailey. Buildings for the school were provided by the southern convention, while the furnishings were supplied by the national convention.

This school experienced critical days in the early 1930's. Professors J. H. Garnett (later dean and acting president) and James C. Miles helped save the seminary by their sacrificial service. Following the death of O. L. Hailey in 1934, the general secretaries named by the Convention were E. P. Alldredge (1934-49), L. S. Sedberry (1949-61), Rabun L. Brantley (1961-70), and Ben C. Fisher (1970-present). Brantley and Fisher have been the executive secretaries of the Education Commission of the Southern Baptist Convention and in that capacity have been asked to represent Southern Baptists in the joint program with the National Baptist Convention, Inc. Revenues of the school in 1972 totaled $73,902, and the student body numbered over 100.[102]

2. Brotherhood Commission, Memphis, Tennessee. It will be recalled that this men's program was first known as the Laymen's Missionary Movement, headed by J. T. Henderson, its first executive secretary named in 1908. Until 1926 Henderson was largely responsible for organizing the work in the various states, educating the constituency in the new activity, and inspiring men to unite in the task. In that year, additional staff and a change of name forwarded the movement: it became known as the Baptist Brotherhood of the South, and the name marked the widening of the goals of the body from missions only to "the entire denominational program." [103] In 1938 Henderson resigned, and Lawson H. Cooke became the new executive, moving the headquarters to Memphis, Tennessee. In 1950 the name of the body was changed again, this time to the Brotherhood Commission of the Southern Baptist Convention. George W. Schroeder succeeded Cooke in 1951 and served until 1970, when Glendon McCullough followed him as executive secretary-treasurer.

Increasingly after the retirement of Henderson the Brotherhood movement was integrated into Convention activity and organization. No statistics on the number of men enrolled are available until 1942, when 54,868 were reported. A significant change took place in 1954 when the Royal Ambassador movement, which had been founded and sponsored by Woman's Missionary Union, was transferred to the Brotherhood Commission, and Edward Hurt, Jr., was elected associate secretary in charge of Royal Ambassador work. The three programs approved by the Convention for this commission are Brotherhood, Royal Ambassadors, and supporting services (distribution of periodicals and merchandise). Program expenditures in 1972 for these programs were $188,213, $282,319, and $607,099, respectively. Enrollment in 1972 was reported to be 454,272.[104]

3. Christian Life Commission, Nashville, Tennessee. The Social Service Commission established in 1913 laid the groundwork for larger service in the future by vigorously educating the constituency and informing the Convention relative to the evils of the liquor traffic, poor law enforcement, the growing crime wave, divorce, the motion picture, the justified unrest among minority groups, injustices in industrial relations, disregard for Sunday observance, obscene literature, and race-track gambling. Between 1921 and 1932 they urged in almost every report to the Convention that a competent leader be secured to lead this area of work for the Convention. Steps were taken to create an agency of social research in connection with the commission but without success.

The year 1946 marked the beginning of a new era by this commission. In its reports to the Convention it confronted the growing problem of racial understanding and entered actively into efforts to promote the Christian viewpoint in the matter. In addition, the commission requested that the Executive Committee be asked to study their agency and make recommendations relative to its work. In response, that committee defined the field of the commission's work and suggested the employment of qualified personnel for its leadership. Hugh A. Brimm became the first executive secretary-treasurer in 1948. He served until 1953 when A. C. Miller succeeded him. Miller resigned in 1960 and was followed by Foy D. Valentine (1960-present). From 1958 to the present this commission has been under attack from some segments of the Convention because of its forthright and courageous confrontation of contemporary injustices, particularly in the area of race.[105] The program approved by the Convention for this agency is Christian morality development (for which $153,062.13 was spent in 1972).[106]

4. Education Commission, Nashville, Tennessee. After some experimentation between 1915 and 1928, this commission was permanently established in the latter year.[107] Until 1951 its work was conducted on a voluntary basis by Charles D. Johnson, its chairman, and Spright Dowell, its secretary-treasurer. In 1951 an office was established in Nashville, Tennessee, and the first executive secretary, R. Orin Cornett, was named.[108] He was succeeded in 1959 by Rabun L. Brantley, and upon Brantley's retirement, Ben C. Fisher assumed the office in 1970. The fourfold program of this commission approved by the Convention is education leadership and coordination (for which $41,305 was spent in 1972), school and college studies and surveys (for which $16,730 was spent in 1972), teacher-personnel recruitment and placement service (for which $20,704 was spent in 1972), and student recruitment (for which $24,907 was spent in 1972).[109]

5. Historical Commission, Nashville, Tennessee. Prior to 1936 the historical interest of most Southern Baptists was sporadic and small. In 1921 the Convention appointed a committee on the preservation of Baptist history, but it died with its chairman, A. J. Holt, in 1933 after accomplishing little. The present Historical Commission stemmed from a similar committee appointed in 1936, led by W. O. Carver as its chairman. A Southern Baptist Historical Society was organized on May 13, 1938. On December 12, 1945, the Executive Committee was asked to transfer the committee's work to the Historical Society, and this was done in 1947. The society served as the history agency of the Convention until August 24, 1951, when the present Historical Commission was chartered, after which the society became an auxiliary to the commission. Norman W. Cox, the first secretary of the commission, assumed the office on February 15, 1951. After his retirement in 1959, Davis C. Woolley succeeded him, and after Woolley's untimely death in 1971, Lynn E. May, Jr., took the place of leadership. The two programs of this commission, as approved by the Convention, are the recording, procuring, and preserving of historical materials (for which $54,157 was spent in 1972) and the utilization of historical materials (for which $81,236 was spent in 1972).[110]

6. *Radio and Television Commission, Fort Worth, Texas.* With the growing use of radio in the 1930's, S. F. Lowe urged the Convention to explore the possibilities of this field for projecting the Baptist message. With Lowe as head of a radio committee, the Convention slowly moved into the broadcasting area, beginning the *Baptist Hour* on January 5, 1941. Lowe was employed as full-time director in 1942. With the cooperation of the Home Mission Board, the *Good News Hour* was inaugurated in January, 1946, but it was taken over by the *Baptist Hour* in 1953 after the resignation of J. B. Lawrence, the principal speaker on the program. Following the death of Lowe in 1952, Paul M. Stevens (1953-present) became director, who recom- mended that the agency be known as the Radio and Television Commission, and this was approved. In June, 1955, the commission was moved from Atlanta, Georgia, where it had been domiciled, to Fort Worth, Texas. The increasing scope of the ministry of this agency may be glimpsed in the fact that in 1969 the commission originated a broadcast somewhere in the world on the average of every three minutes during the year, for a total of 152,022 separate broadcasts.[111] The four programs approved for this agency by the Convention are preaching on radio and television (for which $970,701 was spent in 1972); audience building (for which $554,556 was spent in 1972); inquiry and counseling (for which $94,393 was spent during 1972); and technical assistance to agencies, churches, and individuals (for which $104,306 was spent during 1972).[112]

7. *Stewardship Commission, Nashville, Tennessee.* This agency was created upon recommendation of the Committee to Study the Total Southern Baptist Program, which was approved in 1958 and 1959 by the Convention. It became operative January 1, 1961, with Merrill D. Moore as executive director-treasurer. The stewardship promotion program of the Executive Committee was turned to this new commission. Its total program, approved by the Convention, included Cooperative Program promotion (for which $63,256 was spent in 1972); stewardship development (for which $64,639 was spent in 1972); endowment and capital giving service (for which $109,597 was spent in 1972); and publication and fund raising services (for which $283,134 was spent in 1972).[113]

Two Standing Committees. The two regular standing committees of the Convention for many years have been the Denominational Calendar Committee and the Baptist Joint Committee on Public Affairs.

1. Committee on Denominational Calendar. In 1933 the Executive Committee recommended that all Cooperative Program causes be given calendar time as a means of keeping the people informed. The following year the Executive Committee adopted a calendar to emphasize home and foreign missions the first quarter; hospitals and education in the states in the second quarter; seminaries and Relief and Annuity Board in the third quarter; and state missions, orphanages, and state papers in the fourth quarter.[114] In 1937 the Executive Committee recommended that the Convention name a Calendar Committee, and this was approved. In 1948 the Calendar Committee began the projecting of the calendar beyond the one year, and now the committee generally keeps five years ahead of the current year in its calendar projection. The members of this committee, composed of six persons in 1972, are nominated by the Committee on Committees, according to Bylaw 7.

2. Baptist Joint Committee on Public Affairs, Washington, D. C. In 1936 the Convention changed the name of a special committee on chaplains of Army and Navy to the Committee on Public Relations, and in 1939 this committee became a standing committee to act jointly with the Northern Baptist Convention on matters of public relations. In 1950 the name was changed to the Committee on Public Affairs, J. M. Dawson having been appointed as first executive director of this joint committee in 1946. At his retirement in 1953, he was succeeded by C. Emmanuel Carlson (1954-72), then by James E. Wood, Jr. The Southern Baptist Convention elects fifteen members annually to serve on this committee, and these are merged with similar committees from other Baptist bodies to form the joint committee. In 1972 nine Baptist denominations were members of this committee, as follows: American Baptist Convention, Baptist Federation of Canada, Baptist General Conference, National Baptist Convention of America, National Baptist Convention, U.S.A., Inc., North American Baptist General Conference, Progressive National Baptist Convention, Inc., Seventh Day Baptist General Conference, and the Southern Baptist Convention. The committee is authorized "to act in the field of public affairs whenever the interests or rights of the cooperating conventions" are affected by governmental activity.[115] The approved programs of activity for this agency are public affairs study and research (for which $30,804 was spent in 1972); church-state public relations (for which $12,967 was spent in 1972); public affairs information (for which $36,506 was spent in 1972); and correlation of Baptist influence in the field of church-state relations (for which $24,827 was spent in 1972).[116]

Three Associated Organizations. The three groups listed in 1972 under this category in the organizational structure of the Convention were Woman's Missionary Union, Baptist World Alliance, and American Bible Society.

1. Woman's Missionary Union, Birmingham, Alabama. At the opening of this period, the Union formally listed four fundamentals of their work: mission study, stewardship, community missions, and prayer. Detailed reports on the carrying out of these significant thrusts make inspiring reading, but special attention must be given to the relationship of the Union to the boards and institutions of the Convention during the very difficult days between 1917 and 1942, as well as the more affluent period that has followed. The offering at Christmas each year for foreign missions, named in 1918 the Lottie Moon Christmas Offering, along with the regular offerings of the women, were credited by foreign mission leaders as "saving the cause" during the dark days of depression. In 1972 increasing year by year, the Lottie Moon offering totaled $17,785,413.[117] In 1934 at the very depth of the depression, the week of self-denial offering for home missions took the name Annie Armstrong Offering for Home Missions. It, too, along with the regular offerings of the women, provided much-needed help for the home board in the critical days of the 1930's. In 1972 the Annie W. Armstrong offering was $6,059,703.[118] Woman's Missionary Union in the period under study also cooperated with the Home Mission Board in its church building and loan fund, with the Sunday School Board in distribution of the Bible, and with the Annuity Board in its provision for aged ministers.[119]

Developing from the bylaw adopted by the Convention in connection with negotiations with Central Baptist Seminary, Kansas City, Kansas, in 1956 to the effect that the Convention would allocate no funds for any institution for which the Convention did not elect trustees, Woman's Missionary Union in 1957 transferred Carver School of Missions and Social Work and their good will center property to the Convention in separate transactions. The latter was transferred to the Home Mission Board of the Convention, who agreed to continue the work of the center, which had been established partly by a trust fund. The Carver school property was merged with the Southern Baptist Theological Seminary, whose campus it adjoined, on August 1, 1963. Ten years later it was proposed that the property be utilized for the Boyce School of Christian Ministry, with a Bible-college division for ministers with limited formal education and a division for continuing education for seminary-trained ministers.[120]

The executive secretaries during this period have been Kathleen

Mallory (1912-48) and Alma Hunt (1948-present), while the presidents have been Mrs. W. C. James (1915-25), Mrs. W. J. Cox (1925-33), Mrs. Frank W. Armstrong (1933-45), Mrs. George W. Martin (1946-56), Mrs. R. L. Mathis (1956-63), Mrs. Robert Fling (1963-69), and the second term of Mrs. Mathis (1969-present). The twofold program of this auxiliary approved by the Convention is Woman's Missionary Union promotion and supporting services for the program of Woman's Missionary Union promotion.

2. Baptist World Alliance, Washington, D. C. Southern Baptists cordially related to the alliance during this period, despite the efforts of some English leaders to use the sessions to forward the ecumenical movement (particularly at the 1947 and 1950 meetings). When cooperation in the Baptist Jubilee Advance (1959-64) caused leaders in the several Baptist organizations in North America to desire a continuing cooperative relationship, the jubilee central committee formally suggested to the Baptist World Alliance that a North American Baptist Fellowship be established "in order to conserve the gains and values which have resulted from the Baptist Jubilee Advance and to increase opportunities for fellowship and for sharing mutual concerns." [121] As a result the alliance appointed a committee to study the matter and in 1964 proposed a structure titled the North American Baptist Fellowship. By 1966 six bodies of Baptists in North America had agreed to participate—the American Baptist Convention, the Baptist Federation of Canada, the National Baptist Convention of Mexico, the Progressive National Baptist Convention, Inc., the Seventh Day Baptist General Conference, and the Southern Baptist Convention. The general committee of the body meets annually, and may arrange occasional continental fellowship meetings.

In its relationship with Southern Baptists, the Baptist World Alliance has an eightfold approved program, as follows: communication (on which $59,270 was spent in 1972); relief and rehabilitation (on which $211,975 was spent in 1972); religious liberty and human rights (on which $5,600 was spent in 1972); study and research (on which $10,820 was spent in 1972); worldwide conferences (on which $14,980 was spent in 1972); regional consultation and cooperation (on which $16,270 was spent in 1972); evangelism and reconciliation (on which $18,015 was spent in 1972); and lay development (on which $28,733 was spent in 1972). [122]

The first general secretary of the alliance was J. H. Rushbrooke (1928-39), although J. H. Shakespeare practically functioned as such from 1905-25. Since Rushbrooke, the general secretaries have been W. O. Lewis (1939-48), Arnold T. Ohrn (1948-60), Josef F. Nordenhaug (1960-69), and Robert S. Denny (1969-present).

3. American Bible Society, New York, New York. After the Bible translation controversy about the middle of the nineteenth century and the subsequent use of their own agencies for Bible distribution, Southern Baptists had only occasional relations with the American Bible Society, the interdenominational body founded in 1816. However, in 1935 the Convention officially established contact with this society, and since that time each annual report of the Convention has contained reports from the society. Since 1966, Southern Baptists have given over $200,000 each year to the work of the society, and in 1971 their gifts totaling $240,249 exceeded those of any other denomination contributing to the society.

Overview of the Convention (1845-1972)

The Southern Baptist Convention has had 128 years of history since May 10, 1845, when it adopted a provisional constitution. Although it was structurally afflicted with several congenital tensions through the inclusion of some older society-type characteristics in the convention-type body it adopted, it has creatively faced and corrected these and developed a structure that has exploited the kind of organization deliberately chosen by its founders. It has grown from 9 state bodies, 213 associations, 4,395 churches, and 365,346 members in 1845 to 33 state or regional bodies (covering all 50 states), 1,189 associations, 34,354 churches, and 12,067,284 members in 1972. This represents an overall increase of 11,701,938 members in 128 years—a whopping 3203% growth from the original number in 1845, or an average net accretion over 128 years of 91,421 new members each year. The bulk of this increase has come in the modern period (from 1917 to 1972). It required 28 years for the Convention to reach the 1,000,000 mark in membership (1873); 34 more years to reach the 2,000,000 mark (1907); 13 more years to reach the 3,000,000 mark (1920); 12 more years to reach the 4,000,000 mark (1932); 8 more years to reach the 5,000,000 mark (1940); 6 more years to reach the 6,000,000 mark (1946); 4 more years to reach the 7,000,000 mark (1950); 4 more years to reach the 8,000,000 mark (1954); 4 more years to reach the 9,000,000 mark (1958); 4 more years to reach the 10,000,000 mark (1962); 5 more years to reach the 11,000,000 mark (1967); and 5 more years to reach the 12,000,000 mark (1972). The same is true concerning baptisms each year. Between 1902 and 1920, the number hovered in the 100,000 figure; with the exception of the severe depression years of 1926-30, the figure rose to about 200,000 annually until 1948; between 1948 and 1970, the number remained around 300,000 or 400,000; and in the last two years it has been over 400,000 (with a new high of 445,725 in 1972).

What have been the reasons for this remarkable growth? Only some generalities may be suggested, since the causative factors are imbedded in the whole fabric of Southern Baptist life. Perhaps the following reasons have been significant. (1) The simple biblical emphasis and democratic ecclesiology. Baptists helped the South to be called "the Bible belt." This basic biblicism and the democratic government were appealing to the people of the frontier, and Baptist growth was quite evident in the receding West before 1890. (2) The numerous self-sustaining ministry. Particularly in the nineteenth century, when monarchical-type denominations were suffering for the lack of qualified ministers, Baptists neglected all qualifications except that a man have a sense of divine calling for witnessing. Many such men provided their own support by "tent-making" of various kinds. (3) Identification with the culture-patterns of its environment. Like some other denominations in the South before its extensive expansion, Southern Baptists were viewed as a "people's church" in the sense that they reflected the views (as well as the prejudices) of the culture about them. It will be interesting for future historians to see how expansion beyond the southern geographical area will affect growth in the new regions. (4) Evangelistic zeal. Baptist growth must come by individual conversion of a person who has reached the age of making up his own mind. Babies are not added to their membership automatically by a sociological sacrament. While great emphasis has been given throughout each entire year to winning persons to follow Christ, Southern Baptists have continued to hold "revival" or "protracted" meetings for the specific purpose of making a special effort to reach the unsaved and unenlisted. Many other denominations have ceased this practice, but the evangelistic zeal of Southern Baptists has used it as another means of intensive witnessing. (5) Individual leadership. All along the course of American Baptist history there have been dominant leaders who have caught the imagination and loyalty of many followers. Sometimes they have challenged the multitudes simply by their courage and steadfastness under persecution; sometimes it has involved their effective preaching; sometimes, their organizational and methodological genius. Every region and every organization of Baptists could boast of its giants in almost every period of history. It would be unfair and impossible to illustrate such leadership in a few sentences. (6) The structure of the Convention. In its maturity, the Convention has so modified its structure as to encourage local, associational, and state cooperation (cooperation was made an article of the 1925 confession of faith adopted by the Convention), engendered a strong denominational consciousness, and set challenging goals for the constituency. The great thrust of the twentieth century has been spearheaded by the several boards. The Foreign Mission Board has lifted the vision of Southern Baptists to cause them to confront a needy world; the Home Mission Board has planted gospel seed over all the homeland; the Sunday School Board has provided superb leadership in the very areas of enlistment and methodology that led to church growth; the Annuity Board has given assurance to Southern Baptist leadership for their twilight years; and the other auxiliary bodies like Woman's Missionary Union and Brotherhood have emphasized specialized ministries. The centripetal nature of the Convention has drawn all basic benevolences into its orbit, and in so doing has tapped the genius of the grass roots of the denomination. (7) The absence of a significant schism. Before the organization of the Convention in 1845, Campbellism and Hardshellism made substantial inroads into the ranks of Southern Baptists, but since that time the excisions from cooperation with the Convention have been relatively few. (8) Emphasis on education. Although many Southern Baptist pastors are warmhearted, God-called men who serve despite lacking the opportunity of securing formal education, recent figures supplied by the Research Services Department of the Sunday School Board show that of 30,500 Southern Baptist pastors, 62.30% had college educations or beyond. Of this 62.30%, 5,100 pastors had 17-18 years of education (16.72%), 4,100 pastors had 19 years of education (13.44%), while 5,300 pastors had 20 or more years of education (17.38%). Those who had a college education only numbered 4,500 (14.75%). Of the remaining 38%, 6,000 pastors (19.67%) had 13-15 years of education, 3,000 pastors (9.84%) had 12 years of education (high school), while 2,500 pastors (8.20%) had less than 12 years of education.

The emphasis Southern Baptists are making on education may be glimpsed by the fact that in 1971 the Convention allocated 12.42% of its undesignated Cooperative Program receipts to theological education, amounting to $6,674,347.[123] There were 227 seminary professors and 5,815 students in the seminaries in 1972. In addition, in 1972 state Baptist colleges enrolled 96,336 students, while Bible school enrollment was 1,019. The several states appropriated over $23,000,000 for their Baptist schools (including designated gifts) in 1972. This increasing educational emphasis by Southern Baptists has been an important factor in their continuing growth.

The controversies in Southern Baptist life have demonstrated that the denomination has no monolithic doctrinal stance. Some areas accept alien immersion and open communion, while others reject them; some form close relations with ecumenical bodies, while others refuse; some cling to Landmark views, while others heatedly decry them. Walter Shurden has rendered a good service by showing that diversity in belief on peripheral doctrines is an integral part of Southern Baptist life, for this denomination has no monarchical head to forbid dissent or enforce uniformity. Most Southern Baptists agree on a basically conservative interpretation of the Scriptures.

A word should be added relative to some of the sensitive points and strengths of the Convention structure from a contemporary perspective. One of the sensitive facets of all Baptist life is the area of decision-making. The constitutional revision of 1931 by the Southern Baptist Convention formally provided a structure for representatives from various states to serve as trustees on decision-making boards, commissions, committees (the Executive Committee in particular), and other institutions and agencies. Although not specifically spelled out, it is evident that the annual sessions themselves no longer have immediate sovereignty over these boards, commissions, committees, and institutions, but only mediately control them through these trustees.[124] Ultimate sovereignty, of course, resides in the Convention, in that over a period of years it could replace all of the trustees of any agency with persons who agree with the decisions of the Convention. The method by which such ultimate sovereignty can be exercised is important. Trustees are nominated to the Convention by the Committee on Boards, Commissions, and Standing Committees, which is named by the Committee on Committees. This important committee is appointed by the president of the Convention, in conference with the two vice-presidents. Other methods of naming the Committee on Committees have been tried in recognition of the tremendous power exercised at this point by a majority of the three elected officials of the Convention, but no satisfactory alternative has been found to relate the two decision-making areas of the Convention. The qualifications of trustees have been carefully safeguarded in the bylaws. Recognizing the danger of "informal authority" described in the thorough study of the American Baptist Convention by Paul M. Harrison, the bylaws specifically state that those nominated "should represent the constituency of the Convention, rather than the staff of the agency." This would forbid the Committee on Boards, Commissions, and Standing Committees from approaching the institution or agency either formally or informally to see if a prospective trustee would be satisfactory to the institution or agency. That practice would strike a serious blow at one of the most sensitive areas of Convention decision-making, in that it would virtually give the institution or agency head immense personal power through control of the trustees.

Another sensitive area of Convention life involves the confidence of the constituency in the policy-making processes of the Convention and its agencies. There have been numerous instances of alienation between the "floor" and the "platform," much of which is the fault of neither. It was this sense of alienation by large segments of the constituency that led to substantial schisms in northern Baptist life in the 1940's and 1950's.[125] Sometimes this alienation comes from a misunderstanding of how the agencies of the Convention operate (as in the case of the controversy over the rewriting of Volume I of *The Broadman Bible Commentary*);[126] sometimes it springs from efforts to protect different facets of Baptist ideals (freedom of thought or orthodoxy, as in the case of the Ralph Elliott controversy); sometimes it occurs when deep convictions are confronted with what appears to be compromise (as in the case of the rejection of the initial presentation of the North American Baptist Fellowship in 1964). Every effort should be made to avoid such alienation by informing the constituency when Convention processes are misunderstood or issues are clouded. Furthermore, the very appearance of monolithic consensus by the "platform" as over against the "floor" should be avoided. In this connection, the Inter-Agency Council has sometimes been misunderstood. Instead of a coordinating body to prevent overlapping of functions and programs by all of the agencies of the Convention, it has occasionally been viewed as a means of securing "platform" consensus, particularly since its activity is reviewed by no decision-making or policy-making body, and it is not responsible to the Executive Committee or to the Convention itself.[127] It is quite possible that the Inter-Agency Council should be responsible to the Executive Committee in compliance with Bylaw 9(e).

The Convention itself, as a decision-making body, still has many problems. Choosing to continue giving all affiliating local congregations a sense of participation through representation in its annual sessions, it has refused to follow the example of the American Baptist Convention which has changed to a numerical type of representation in regional conventions that ignores the local congregations. Problems arising out of maintaining the local congregations as the base for representation are legion. For one thing, the size of the annual sessions will continue to make it difficult to find cities with adequate facilities to entertain the Convention. If each cooperating church had sent but one messenger in 1973, the attendance would have been 34,534. The place of meeting still substantially influences voting at the sessions, particularly when the Convention meets in one of the peripheral cities of the nation. The sectional impulses from the new expansion areas already have had influence upon the Convention's deliberations. Furthermore, the small percentage of the total constituency that meets annually deeply affects the representative nature of the general body. At the 1963 meeting in Kansas City, for example, only 6,643 of the 32,351 affiliating churches sent messengers. Only 12,971 were registered out of approximately 10,500,000 members. Not only so, but many who do attend an annual session of the Convention often are a different group than those who attended the previous year. This results in still more dependence upon a small group of leaders for charting the course of the Convention.

On the positive side, many worthy aspects of the Convention's structure could be listed. Its system of checks and balances in its constitution and bylaws is clearly stated and provides consistent and rational guidance for the orderly operation of the complex machinery involved in such a large enterprise. Lay persons are given a significant place on all important agencies, and the "floor" at the Convention sessions must be heard on debatable issues. The Executive Committee has functioned well in the duties assigned to it. It is difficult now to conceive how the Convention operated before this pivotal committee was formed in 1917 and strengthened in 1927. This committee, along with the Cooperative Program of 1925, has revolutionized the operation of the Convention.

From this rapid survey of the life of the Convention and its constituency comes the impression that three factors have developed the effectiveness of the Southern Baptist Convention in the past and still characterize the body: first, the continuing self-study of the structure and its functions in the light of contemporary changing needs; second, the willingness to change when that is advisable; and third, the capacity to distinguish between essentials and nonessentials and to respect diversity in love. These factors can keep the Convention responsive and effective in its service to Southern Baptists.

Notes

1. *Annual,* Southern Baptist Convention, 1919, p. 23.
2. *Ibid.,* 1919, p. 122.
3. George W. McDaniel, *The Southwestern Evangel* (Ft. Worth), pp. 89-91.
4. O. T. Barck and N. M. Blake, *Since 1900* (New York: The Macmillan Co., 1947), p. 393.
5. See *Southern Baptist Handbook* (Nashville), 1929, p. 57.
6. *Ibid.,* 1930, p. 100.
7. Rutledge, *op. cit.,* p. 56.
8. Cauthen, *op. cit.,* pp. 39-41.
9. *Annual,* Southern Baptist Convention, 1942, pp. 64-65.
10. *Ibid.,* 1929, p. 73; and *ibid.,* 1939, pp. 41-43.
11. *Ibid.,* 1933, p. 57.
12. *Ibid.,* 1944, p. 38.
13. *Ibid.,* 1937, p. 35.
14. *Ibid.,* 1944, p. 39.
15. Baker, *Source Book,* pp. 168-172 has the document.
16. Cox-Woolley, eds., *Encyclopedia,* I, p. 516.
17. Torbet, *op. cit.,* p. 427.
18. For old but still valuable books on this subject, see S. G. Cole, *The History of Fundamentalism* (London: Archon Books, 1931), and Norman F. Furniss, *The Fundamentalist Controversy 1918-1931* (New Haven: Yale University Press, 1954).
19. See a critical description of Norris' disruptive tactics in Baker, *Source Book,* pp. 196-97.
20. *Annual,* Southern Baptist Convention, 1923, p. 19.
21. *Ibid.,* 1925, p. 76. The document is in Baker, *Source Book,* pp. 200 ff.
22. *Annual,* Southern Baptist Convention, 1926, p. 18.
23. *Ibid.,* 1926, p. 98.

24. *Ibid.*, 1928, pp. 32-33.

25. *Ibid.*, 1926, p. 19.

26. Cox-Woolley, eds., *Encyclopedia,* II, p. 1197.

27. *Annual,* Southern Baptist Convention, 1924, pp. 65-68.

28. *Ibid.*, 1925, p. 36.

29. *Ibid.*, 1927, pp. 12 ff.

30. Cox-Woolley, eds., *Encyclopedia,* I, p. 323.

31. *Annual,* Southern Baptist Convention, 1931, p. 44.

32. *Ibid.*, 1972, p. 30.

33. *Ibid.*, 1926, pp. 32 ff.

34. *Ibid.*, 1931, p. 102.

35. See *Religious Herald* (Virginia), May 20, 1909, p. 10, col. 1. See also *Annual,* Southern Baptist Convention, 1912, pp. 77-78.

36. *Annual,* Southern Baptist Convention, 1919, pp. 19-23.

37. Barnes, *The Southern Baptist Convention,* p. 282.

38. See *Memoirs of John R. Sampey* (Nashville: Broadman Press, 1947), pp. 251-52.

39. *Annual,* Southern Baptist Convention, 1940, p, 99,

40. Cox-Woolley, eds., *Encyclopedia,* I, p. 321.

41. Eighmy, *op. cit.,* esp. p. xii of Preface and *passim.*

42. Barnes, *The Southern Baptist Convention,* p. 246.

43. Baker, *Source Book,* pp. 125-26.

44. Reimers, *op. cit.,* p. 95.

45. *Ibid.,* p. 96.

46. *Ibid.,* pp. 112-13.

47. *Annual,* Southern Baptist Convention, 1954, p. 56.

48. For the full document, see Cox-Woolley, eds., *Encyclopedia,* III, pp. 1668-69.

49. For this story in detail, see G. Hugh Wamble, "Midwestern Baptist Theological Seminary," in Cox-Woolley, eds., *Encyclopedia,* III, pp. 1841-42.

50. For the entire confession, see Baker, *Source Book,* pp. 205-11.

51. *Annual,* Southern Baptist Convention, 1971, p. 71.

52. See James L. Sullivan, "Compliance or Defiance?" in *Facts and Trends* (Gomer R. Lesch, ed., published monthly by the Sunday School Board, Nashville, Tennessee), pp. 2-3.

53. Walter B. Shurden, *Not a Silent People: Controversies That Have Shaped Southern Baptists* (Nashville: Broadman Press, 1972), pp. 122-127.

54. Cox-Woolley, eds., *Encyclopedia,* III, p. 1926.

55. For the specific actions in 1970 and 1971, see *Annual,* Southern Baptist Convention, 1970, pp. 65-66; and *ibid.,* 1971, p. 55.

56. Supreme Court of North Carolina, *Reid v. Johnston,* 241 N. C. 201, 85 S. E. 2d 114 (1954).

57. *Address from the Baptist Church in Philadelphia, to their Sister Churches of the Same Denomination, through the Confederated States of North America* (Philadelphia: Printed by Robert Atkin, at Pope's Head, 1781), np.

58. See William W. Keen, ed., *The Bi-Centennial Celebration of the Founding of the First Baptist Church of the City of Philadelphia* (Philadelphia: American Baptist Publication Society, 1899), pp. 66-69.

59. Supreme Court of North Carolina, *Dix v. Pruitt,* 192 N. C. 829, 135 S. E. 851 (1926).

60. B. F. Fuller, *History of Texas Baptists* (Louisville: Baptist Book Concern, 1900), pp. 431-466. See Supreme Court of Illinois, *Ferraria v. Vasconcelles* (sic) 23 Ill. 456 (1860); *Ferraria v. Vasconcellos,* 31 Ill. 25 (1863).

61. Fuller, *op. cit.,* p. 465.

62. *Reid v. Johnston, op. cit.*

63. *Sorrenson v. Logan,* 32 Ill. App. 2d 294.

64. Supreme Court of Kansas, *Huber v. Thorn,* 371 P2d 1943 (1962).

65. *Annual,* Southern Baptist Convention, 1946, p. 66.

66. Cox-Woolley, eds., *Encyclopedia,* III, p. 1918.

67. *Ibid.*

68. *Ibid.,* pp. 1965-66.

69. *Ibid.,* p. 1967.

70. *Annual,* Southern Baptist Convention, 1939, pp. 28-29.

71. The statistics of the Executive Committee for 1972 covered only nine months, due to a change in fiscal year, so this is the closest relevant figure.

72. Cox-Woolley, eds., *Encyclopedia,* I, pp. 429-30.

73. *Annual,* Southern Baptist Convention, 1972, p. 100. See Footnote #71.

74. See J. B. Weatherspoon, *M. Theron Rankin: Apostle of Advance* (Nashville: Broadman Press, 1958), and B. J. Cauthen, *op. cit.,* pp. 48-58.

75. *Book of Reports,* Southern Baptist Convention, 1973, p. 6.

76. Rutledge, *op. cit.,* pp. 237-38.

77. *Ibid.,* p. 238.

78. *Book of Reports,* Southern Baptist Convention, 1973, p. 8.

79. *Annual,* Southern Baptist Convention, 1918, p. 72.

80. For more detail, see Baker, *The Story of the Sunday School Board,* pp. 131 ff.

81. *Annual,* Southern Baptist Convention, 1953, p. 315.

82. *Ibid.,* 1958, p. 249.

83. Cox-Woolley, eds., *Encyclopedia,* III, p. 2,000.

84. *Book of Reports,* Southern Baptist Convention, 1973, pp. 8-10.

85. For the full story of this Board, see Robert A. Baker, *The Thirteenth Check* (Nashville: Broadman Press, 1968).

86. *Book of Reports,* Southern Baptist Convention, 1973, pp. 11, 100-101.

87. *Ibid.,* pp. 11, 15.

88. Cox-Woolley, eds., *Encyclopedia,* III, p. 1840.

89. *Book of Reports,* Southern Baptist Convention, 1973, pp. 12, 15.

90. *Annual,* Southern Baptist Convention, 1917, p. 81.

91. *Book of Reports,* Southern Baptist Convention, 1973, pp. 12, 15.

92. *Ibid.,* pp. 13, 15.

93. See, for example, *Religious Herald* (Virginia), March 15, 1849, p. 3, col. 1. Note also Barnes, *The Southern Baptist Convention,* pp. 127 ff.

94. *Charters and Fundamental Articles of The Southern Baptist Theological Seminary, Louisville, Kentucky* (published by the Board, Louisville, 1910), p. 15.

95. *Annual,* Southern Baptist Convention, 1924, pp. 47 ff.

96. *Ibid.,* 1927, p. 55.

97. *Book of Reports,* Southern Baptist Convention, 1973, pp. 14-15.

98. *Ibid.,* pp. 14-15.

99. *Ibid.,* p. 118.

100. Cox-Woolley, eds., *Encyclopedia,* II, p. 1263.

101. *Book of Reports,* Southern Baptist Convention, 1973, p. 119.

102. *Ibid.,* p. 16.

103. Cox-Woolley, eds., *Encyclopedia,* I, p. 198.

104. *Book of Reports,* Southern Baptist Convention, 1973, p. 39.

'05. Cox-Woolley, eds., *Encyclopedia,* III, p. 1968.

'6. *Book of Reports,* Southern Baptist Convention, 1973, p. 17.
Annual, Southern Baptist Convention, 1928, p. 377.
Cox-Woolley, eds., *Encyclopedia,* I, pp. 392-94.
. *Book of Reports,* Southern Baptist Convention, 1973, p. 18.
.0. *Ibid.,* p. 18.

111. Cox-Woolley, eds., *Encyclopedia,* III, p. 1933.

112. *Book of Reports,* Southern Baptist Convention, 1973, pp. 18-19.

113. *Ibid.,* pp. 19-20.

114. Cox-Woolley, eds., *Encyclopedia,* I, p. 217.

115. *Annual,* Southern Baptist Convention, 1972, p. 247.

116. *Book of Reports,* Southern Baptist Convention, 1973, p. 21.

117. *Ibid.,* p. 6.

118. *Ibid.,* p. 8.

119. Cox-Woolley, eds., *Encyclopedia,* III, pp. 1515-27.

120. *The Tie* (Louisville, Kentucky), May-June, 1973, p. 3.

121. Cox-Woolley, eds., *Encyclopedia,* III, p. 1873.

122. *Book of Reports,* Southern Baptist Convention, 1973, pp. 21-22.

123. Statistics for 1972 are not available, since the Executive Committee changed its fiscal year in 1972.

124. See Article VII of the Convention's constitution.

125. See Bruce L. Shelley, *Conservative Baptists* (Denver: Conservative Baptist Theological Seminary, 1960), pp. 13-15.

126. See James L. Sullivan, "Compliance or Defiance," *Facts and Trends* (Nashville: Sunday School Board, Nov., 1971), pp. 2-3.

127. Cox-Woolley, eds., *Encyclopedia,* III, pp. 1780-81.

APPENDIXES

Appendix A—Statistics

One of the weaknesses of many Southern Baptist histories is that the area of statistics is treated lightly. This is understandable. Statistics even in the state histories are sometimes provided only intermittently, and in some cases different state historians disagree over the right statistics to use.

Yet statistics can be quite valuable in a historical study. Not only can they reveal growth, but as well they can tell the rate of growth, the areas of greatest growth, and sometimes suggest reasons for growth in some areas and not in others. In addition, when it is possible to get relatively reliable statistics for Baptist growth, these can be compared with accurate population statistics after 1790 to provide a yardstick for measuring growth and add a new factor—population shifts. Comparison with the rate of growth of other denominations also is helpful in assizing the significance of the growth. Statistics properly used can even speak of the character of the people: despite serious difficulties, percentages of growth achieved can reflect a missionary spirit that overwhelms difficulties.

The first relatively accurate statistics both for Baptists and for the entire population became available about 1790. In that year the first United States census occurred, and each decennium thereafter the very best possible statistics were gathered. The general outline of this study divides American Baptists after 1790 into chronological periods breaking in 1814, 1845, 1860, 1877, 1917, and 1972. It seemed advisable, then, to secure Southern Baptist statistics for 1790 and for each of these chronological periods thereafter. This was not an easy task. Ideally, the best statistics would have been gathered and collated by one author, thus guaranteeing an evenhanded treatment in this sensitive area. It was not possible to find such an ideal situation. The alternative was to locate trustworthy statistics gathered by several authors. Uniformity in methodology for gathering and collating the statistics from all the states involving Southern Baptists was important. It was also important that the compiler be an accurate and careful **455** person and one not given to inflating statistics. In addition, the sources used by such a person should be meticulously examined in order to ascertain how recently before publication he had secured the information included in his summaries. Finally, the statistics gathered by such a person should be compared with the statistics gathered by historians in each of the states involved in his compilation to determine, if possible, if there were substantial deviations between his figures and those of the state historians.

With these factors in mind, the search for proper statistics was begun. Fortunately, Baptist statistics for 1790 were carefully gathered by John Asplund, a meticulous Swede who had worked as a commercial bookkeeper in America. He showed good sources for his information. He admitted that he might have missed some Baptist in America, but a comparison of his figures and sources with those of state historians makes it clear that he could not be accused of inflating statistics in any way. As a result, his statistics were used as the starting point in 1790.

Statistics for 1814 were more difficult. David Benedict published his history in 1813, which, of course, is one year before the date desired. However, in scrutinizing his work it is apparent that he used figures for the year 1813 at times in his compilations, although it is likely that 1812 figures were more often used. In the absence of other sources, however, and since the growth of Baptists during the War of 1812 and shortly thereafter was undoubtedly quite slow, it was felt best to use Benedict for this second date. As a matter of fact, any inaccuracies involved in the use of statistics for a year or two earlier than 1814 would be a common pattern for all states, and would not therefore affect any particular state more than another; while the method of computation (using the average annual percentage of growth during a period as long as that between 1814 and 1845) would diminish the percentage of inaccuracy to almost nothing. Furthermore, the figures for each state are continued period by period until the accurate figures of modern days are used, which ultimately evens up any slight inaccuracies for a single period.

There were several choices of statistics for 1845. Benedict revised his history in 1848, and many of his statistics were secured in 1845. On the other hand, many were not, and his figures seemed to be inflated far beyond even some of the state figures given for 1845. The *American Baptist Year Book* regularly showed the source of its annual statistics for this period. However, the sources usually ran several years behind the report of a given year. For example, in 1845 the *Year Book* reported statistics from 207 associations in the southern states. Of these, only 3 associations reported for 1844, 154 were for 1843, 40 for 1842, 5 for 1841, 3 for 1840, and 2 for 1839. This would mean that the figures in the 1845 *Year Book* represented the situation in 1842-43. In the 1846 *Year Book*, which is the one used for the official statistics in the *Encyclopedia of Southern Baptists*, only 2 associations reported for 1845, 153 for 1844, 42 for 1843; 10 for 1842, 2 for 1841, and 3 for 1840. This would average the approximate date for the statistics as between 1843 and 1844. The 1847 *Year Book* reflected more accurately the 1845 statistics: in the reports from 205 associations in the South, 84 were for 1846, 67 for 1845, 43 for 1844, 9 for 1843, and 2 for 1842. Since the *Year Book's* figures for 1847 reflect sources dating about 1845 as a whole, since the state figures that are available show much larger statistics for 1845 than those of the *Year Book* in 1847, and since David Benedict shows a much larger figure in each instance, I have concluded that the proper figures to be used for Southern Baptists in 1845 are those found in the 1847 *Year Book*.

The figures to use for 1860 were determined in this same way. Those shown in the 1862 *Year Book* were gathered from records dating about 1860 on the average, and these figures are used in this study.

The 1877 figure for Southern Baptists presented problems. The *Year Book* for 1878 had statistics collected for approximately 1877, but the statistics included both Negro and white churches in the southern states. These statistics were used in the *Encyclopedia of Southern Baptists*, but do not reflect the actual situation. The excision of Negroes from the white churches in the South began even before the close of civil war, and most of the Negroes had their own churches, unrelated to the Southern Baptist Convention, long before 1877. Since the 1878 statistics in the *Year Book* listed the Negro Baptist churches and associations separately in each state, I went through the reports state by state and culled out those churches and members that were identified as being Negro in the 1878 *Year Book*. I am convinced that this has produced the most accurate list possible of Baptists in the South related to the Southern Baptist Convention. There were a few Negroes still in integrated Southern Baptist churches in 1877, and these, of course, are included as a part of Baptists in the Southern Baptist Convention in that year.

The 1917 figures were easily secured from the 1918 Southern Baptist Convention *Annual*. The final figures shown for 1972 were also readily available from the same source.

Appendix B

HISTORICAL TABLE
Of the Southern Baptist Convention Since Its Organization

Date	Place of Meeting	Registration	Presidents	Secretaries	Preachers
1845	Augusta, Georgia	236	William B. Johnson, S.C.	Jesse Hartwell, Ala.; James C. Crane, Va.	Richard Fuller, Md.
1846	Richmond, Virginia	162	William B. Johnson, S.C.	Jesse Hartwell, Ala.; James C. Crane, Va.	W. B. Johnson, S.C.
1849	Charleston, South Carolina	103	William B. Johnson, S.C.	James C. Crane, Va.; Basil Manly, Jr., Ala.	J. B. Jeter, Va.; J. L. Reynolds, S. C.
1851	Nashville, Tennessee	124	R. B. C. Howell, Va.	James C. Crane, Va.; William Carey Crane, Miss.	R. B. C. Howell, Va.; S. Baker, Ky.
1853	Baltimore, Maryland	154	R. B. C. Howell, Va.	H. K. Ellyson, Va.; William Carey Crane, Miss.	A. D. Sears, Ky.
1855	Montgomery, Alabama	235	R. B. C. Howell, Va.	William Carey Crane, Miss.; James M. Watts, Ala.	William Carey Crane, Miss.
1857	Louisville, Kentucky	184	R. B. C. Howell, Va.	William Carey Crane, Miss.; George B. Taylor, Md.	Duncan R. Campbell, Ky.
1859	Richmond, Virginia	580	Richard Fuller, Md.	William Carey Crane, Miss.; George B. Taylor, Md.	William H. McIntosh, Ala.
1861	Savannah, Georgia	177	Richard Fuller, Md.	William Carey Crane, Miss.; George B. Taylor, Va.	J. L. Burrows, Va.
1863	Augusta, Georgia	181	P. H. Mell, Ga.	George B. Taylor, Va.; Sylvanus Landrum, Ga.	Richard Fuller, Md.
1866	Russellville, Kentucky	244	P. H. Mell, Ga.	George B. Taylor, Va.; W. Pope Yeamann, Ky.	W. T. Brantley, Md.
1867	Memphis, Tennessee	250	P. H. Mell, Ga.	A. Fuller Crane, Md.; A. P. Abell, Va.	T. E. Skinner, Tenn.
1868	Baltimore, Maryland	327	P. H. Mell, Ga.	A. P. Abell, Va.; A. F. Crane, Md.	E. T. Winkler, S.C.
1869	Macon, Georgia	266	P. H. Mell, Ga.	J. Russell Hawkins, Ky.; E. C. Williams, Md.	J. L. Burrows, Va.
1870	Louisville, Kentucky	399	P. H. Mell, Ga.	E. Calvin Williams, Md.; Truman S. Sumner, Ala.	William Williams, S. C.
1871	St. Louis, Missouri	360	P. H. Mell, Ga.	E. M. Williams, Md.; T. S. Sumner, Ala.	E. M. Williams, Md.
1872	Raleigh, North Carolina	304	James P. Boyce, S. C.	M. B. Wharton, Ky.; W. O. Tugale, Ga.	T. G. Jones, Tenn.
1873	Mobile, Alabama	289	James P. Boyce, Ky.	G. R. McCall, Ga.; W. O. Tugale, Ga.	E. G. Taylor, La.
1874	Jefferson, Texas	222	James P. Boyce, Ky.	W. O. Tugale, Ga.; G. R. McCall, Ga.	T. H. Pritchard, N. C.
1875	Charleston, South Carolina	302	James P. Boyce, Ky.	C. C. Bitting, Va.; E. Calvin Williams, Md.	George C. Lorimer, Mass.
1876	Richmond, Virginia	289	James P. Boyce, Ky.	O. F. Gregory, Ala.; W. E. Tanner, Va.	Henry McDonald, Ky.
1877	New Orleans, Louisiana	164	James P. Boyce, Ky.	C. E. W. Dobbe, Ky.; W. E. Tanner, Va.	B. H. Carroll, Texas
1878	Nashville, Tennessee	253	James P. Boyce, Ky.	C. E. W. Dobbe, Ky.; W. E. Tanner, Va.	J. C. Furman, S.C.
1879	Atlanta, Georgia	313	P. H. Mell, Ga.	C. E. W. Dobbe, Ky.; O. F. Gregory, S.C.	P. H. Mell, Ga.
1880	Lexington, Kentucky	360	P. H. Mell, Ga.	C. E. W. Dobbe, Ky.; Lansing Burrows, Ky.	Sylvanus Landrum, Ga.
1881	Columbus, Mississippi	335	P. H. Mell, Ga.	Lansing Burrows, Ky.; O. F. Gregory, Md.	T. T. Eaton, Ky.
1882	Greenville, South Carolina	237	P. H. Mell, Ga.	Lansing Burrows, Ky.; O. F. Gregory, N. C.	John A. Broadus, Ky.
1883	Waco, Texas	612	P. H. Mell, Ga.	Lansing Burrows, Ga.; O. F. Gregory, Md.	Lansing Burrows, Ga.
1884	Baltimore, Maryland	637	P. H. Mell, Ga.	Lansing Burrows, Ga.; O. F. Gregory, Md.	J. L. M. Curry, Va.; J. L. Burrows
1885	Augusta, Georgia	528	P. H. Mell, Ga.	Lansing Burrows, Ga.; O. F. Gregory, La.	J. B. Hawthorne, Ga.
1886	Montgomery, Alabama	488	P. H. Mell, Ga.	Lansing Burrows, Ga.; O. F. Gregory, Md.	George Cooper, Va.
1887	Louisville, Kentucky	589	James P. Boyce, Ky.	Lansing Burrows, Ga.; O. F. Gregory, Md.	Francis M. Ellis, Md.
1888	Richmond, Virginia	835	Jonathan Haralson, Ala.	Lansing Burrows, Ga.; O. F. Gregory, Md.	J. P. Greene, Mo.
1889	Memphis, Tennessee	706	Jonathan Haralson, Ala.	Lansing Burrows, Ga.; O. F. Gregory, Md.	J. W. Carter, N. C.
1890	Fort Worth, Texas	901	Jonathan Haralson, Ala.	Lansing Burrows, Ga.; O. F. Gregory, Md.	Carter H. Jones, Tenn.
1891	Birmingham, Alabama	915	Jonathan Haralson, Ala.	Lansing Burrows, Ga.; O. F. Gregory, Md.	J. B. Gambrell, Miss.
1892	Atlanta, Georgia	978	Jonathan Haralson, Ala.	Lansing Burrows, Ga.; O. F. Gregory, Md.	W. E. Hatcher, Va.
1893	Nashville, Tennessee	818	Jonathan Haralson, Ala.	Lansing Burrows, Ga.; O. F. Gregory, Md.	W. E. Hatcher, Va.
1894	Dallas, Texas	772	Jonathan Haralson, Ala.	Lansing Burrows, Ga.; O. F. Gregory, Md.	F. H. Kerfoot, Ky.
1895	Washington, District of Columbia	870	Jonathan Haralson, Ala.	Lansing Burrows, Ga.; O. F. Gregory, Md.	Geo. B. Eager, Ala.; W. H. Whitsitt, Ky.
1896	Chattanooga, Tennessee	819	Jonathan Haralson, Ala.	Lansing Burrows, Ga.; O. F. Gregory, Md.	Chas. A. Stakely, D. C.
1897	Wilmington, North Carolina	724	Jonathan Haralson, Ala.	Lansing Burrows, Ga.; O. F. Gregory, Md.	R. A. Venable, Miss.
1898	Norfolk, Virginia	857	Jonathan Haralson, Ala.	Lansing Burrows, Ga.; O. F. Gregory, Md.	B. L. Whitman, D. C.
1899	Louisville, Kentucky	869	W. J. Northen, Ga.	Lansing Burrows, Ga.; O. F. Gregory, Md.	Geo. W. Truett, Texas
1900	**Hot Springs, Arkansas**	**646**	**W. J. Northen, Ga.**	**Lansing Burrows, Tenn.; O. F. Gregory, Md.**	**J. J. Taylor, Va.**
1901	**New Orleans, Louisiana**	**787**	**W. J. Northen, Ga.**	**Lansing Burrows, Tenn.; O. F. Gregory, Md.**	**E. Y. Mullins, Ky.**
1902	**Asheville, North Carolina**	**1,093**	**James P. Eagle, Ark.**	**Lansing Burrows, Tenn.; O. F. Gregory, Md.**	**W. J. McConnell, Ga.**
1903	**Savannah, Georgia**	**1,136**	**James P. Eagle, Ark.**	**Lansing Burrows, Tenn.; O. F. Gregory, Ala.**	**W. J. Williamson, Mo.**
1904	**Nashville, Tennessee**	**1,095**	**James P. Eagle, Ark.**	**Lansing Burrows, Tenn.; O. F. Gregory, Ala.**	**W. W. Landrum, Ga.**
1905	**Kansas City, Missouri**	**816**	**E. W. Stephens, Mo.**	**Lansing Burrows, Tenn.; O. F. Gregory, Ala.**	**W. H. Felix, Ky.**
1906	**Chattanooga, Tennessee**	**1,461**	**E. W. Stephens, Mo.**	**Lansing Burrows, Tenn.; O. F. Gregory, Va.**	**W. R. L. Smith, Ala.**
1907	**Richmond, Virginia**	**1,411**	**E. W. Stephens, Mo.**	**Lansing Burrows, Tenn.; O. F. Gregory, Va.**	**A. J. Dickinson, Ala.**
1908	**Hot Springs, Arkansas**	**1,258**	**Joshua Levering, Md.**	**Lansing Burrows, Tenn.; O. F. Gregory, Va.**	**Henry W. Battle, N. C.**
1909	**Louisville, Kentucky**	**1,547**	**Joshua Levering, Md.**	**Lansing Burrows, Ga.; O. F. Gregory, Va.**	**Edwin C. Dargan, Ga.**

Year	Place	Number	President	Recording Secretaries	Convention Sermon
1910	Baltimore, Maryland	1,641	Joshua Levering, Md.	Landing Burrows, Ga.; O. F. Gregory, Va.	K. L. Pickard, Ga.
1911	Jacksonville, Florida	1,658	Edwin C. Dargan, Ga.	Landing Burrows, Ga.; O. F. Gregory, Va.	C. S. Gardner, Ky.
1912	Oklahoma City, Oklahoma	1,223	Edwin C. Dargan, Ga.	Landing Burrows, Ga.; O. F. Gregory, Md.	Z. T. Cody, S. C.
1913	Saint Louis, Missouri	1,403	Edwin C. Dargan, Ga.	Landing Burrows, Ga.; O. F. Gregory, Md.	T. W. O'Kelley, N. C.
1914	Nashville, Tennessee	1,930	Landing Burrows, Ga.	O. F. Gregory, Md.; Hight C Moore, N.C.	Geo. W. McDaniel, Va.
1915	Houston, Texas	1,408	Landing Burrows, Ga.	O. F. Gregory, Md.; Hight C Moore, N.C.	J. W. Porter, Ky.
1916	Asheville, North Carolina	2,125	Landing Burrows, Ga.	O. F. Gregory, Md.; Hight C Moore, N.C.	Chas. W. Daniel, Ga.
1917	New Orleans, Louisiana	1,683	J. B. Gambell, Texas	O. F. Gregory, Md.; Hight C Moore, N.C.	C. V. Edwards, Mo.
1918	Hot Springs, Arkansas	2,043	J. B. Gambell, Texas	O. F. Gregory, Md.; Hight C Moore, Tenn.	W. H. Geistweit, Mo.
1919	Atlanta, Georgia	4,224	J. B. Gambell, Texas	Hight C Moore, Tenn.; J. Henry Burnett, Ga.	M. E. Dodd, La.
1920	Washington, District of Columbia	8,359	J. B. Gambell, Texas	Hight C Moore, Tenn.; J. Henry Burnett, Ga.	Jno. E. White, S. C.
1921	Chattanooga, Tennessee	4,773	E. Y. Mullins, Ky.	Hight C Moore, Tenn.; J. Henry Burnett, Ga.	H. L. Winburn, Ark.
1922	Jacksonville, Florida	4,193	E. Y. Mullins, Ky.	Hight C Moore, Tenn.; J. Henry Burnett, Ga.	S. J. Porter, Okla.
1923	Kansas City, Missouri	4,273	E. Y. Mullins, Ky.	Hight C Moore, Tenn.; J. Henry Burnett, Ga.	R. G. Bowers, Tex.
1924	Atlanta, Georgia	5,632	Geo. W. McDaniel, Va.	Hight C Moore, Tenn.; J. Henry Burnett, Ga.	F. F. Gibson, Ky.
1925	Memphis, Tennessee	5,600	Geo. W. McDaniel, Va.	Hight C Moore, Tenn.; J. Henry Burnett, Ga.	Len G. Broughton, Fla.
1926	Houston, Texas	4,268	Geo. W. McDaniel, Va.	Hight C Moore, Tenn.; J. Henry Burnett, Ga.	F. F. Brown, Tenn.
1927	Louisville, Kentucky	4,454	Geo. W. Truett, Texas	Hight C Moore, Tenn.; J. Henry Burnett, Ga.	Wallace Bassett, Texas
1928	Chattanooga, Tennessee	3,999	Geo. W. Truett, Texas	Hight C Moore, Tenn.; J. Henry Burnett, Ga.	J. R. Hobbs, Ala.
1929	Memphis, Tennessee	3,940	Geo. W. Truett, Texas	Hight C Moore, Tenn.; J. Henry Burnett, Ga.	W. L. Ball, S. C.
1930	New Orleans, Louisiana	3,193	W. J. McGlothlin, S.C.	Hight C Moore, Tenn.; J. Henry Burnett, Tenn.	Robt. G. Lee, Tenn.
1931	Birmingham, Alabama	3,194	W. J. McGlothlin, S.C.	Hight C Moore, Tenn.; J. Henry Burnett, Tenn.	John W. Phillips, Va.
1932	St. Petersburg, Florida	2,178	W. J. McGlothlin, S.C.	Hight C Moore, Tenn.; J. Henry Burnett, Tenn.	W. Marshall Craig, Texas
1933	Washington, District of Columbia	2,705	F. F. Brown, Tenn.	Hight C Moore, Tenn.; J. Henry Burnett, Tenn.	J. L. White, Fla.
1934	Fort Worth, Texas	4,435	M. E. Dodd, La.	Hight C Moore, Tenn.; J. Henry Burnett, Tenn.	T. L. Holcomb, Okla.
1935	Memphis, Tennessee	4,268	M. E. Dodd, La.	Hight C Moore, Tenn.; J. Henry Burnett, Tenn.	J. B. Weatherspoon, Ky
1936	Saint Louis, Missouri	3,702	John R. Sampey, Ky.	Hight C Moore, Tenn.; J. Henry Burnett, Tenn.	John A. Huff, La.
1937	Louisville, Kentucky	4,807	John R. Sampey, Ky.	Hight C Moore, Tenn.; J. Henry Burnett, Tenn.	Solon B. Cousins, Ark.
1938	Richmond, Virginia	5,786	John R. Sampey, Ky.	Hight C Moore, Tenn.; J. Henry Burnett, Tenn.	E. P. J. Garrott, Ark.
1939	Oklahoma City, Oklahoma	4,868	L. R. Scarborough, Texas	Hight C Moore, Tenn.; J. Henry Burnett, Tenn.	Perry F. Webb, Texas
1940	Baltimore, Maryland	5,876	L. R. Scarborough, Texas	Hight C Moore, Tenn.; J. Henry Burnett, N.C.	W. R. White, Oklahoma
1941	Birmingham, Alabama	5,694	W. W. Hamilton, La.	Hight C Moore, Tenn.; J. Henry Burnett, N.C.	J. Clyde Turner, N. C.
1942	San Antonio, Texas	4,301	Pat M. Neff, Texas	Hight C Moore, Tenn.; J. Henry Burnett, N.C.	Ellis A. Fuller, Ga.
1944	Atlanta, Georgia	4,771	Pat M. Neff, Texas	Hight C Moore, N.C.; J. Henry Burnett, N.C.	John H. Buchanan, Al
1946	Miami, Florida	7,973	Pat M. Neff, Texas	Hight C Moore, N.C.; J. Henry Burnett, N.C.	J. W. Storer, Okla.
1947	St. Louis, Missouri	8,508	Louie D. Newton, Georgia	Porter Routh, Tenn.; Joe W. Burton, Tenn.	W. A. Criswell, Texas
1948	Memphis, Tennessee	8,843	Louie D. Newton, Georgia	Porter Routh, Tenn.; Joe W. Burton, Tenn.	W. R. Pettigrew, Kentucky
1949	Oklahoma City, Oklahoma	9,393	Robert G. Lee, Tennessee	Porter Routh, Tenn.; Joe W. Burton, Tenn.	Norman W. Cox, Mississippi
1950	Chicago, Illinois	8,151	Robert G. Lee, Tennessee	Porter Routh, Tenn.; Joe W. Burton, Tenn.	R. C. Campbell, North Carolina
1951	San Francisco, California	6,493	Robert G. Lee, Tennessee	Porter Routh, Tenn.; Joe W. Burton, Tenn.	C. Roy Angell, Florida
1952	Miami, Florida	10,960	J. D. Grey, La.	George B. Fraser, D. C.; Joe W. Burton, Tenn.	Ramsey Pollard, Tenn.
1953	Houston, Texas	12,976	J. D. Grey, La.	Joe W. Burton, Tenn.	J. H. Landes, Texas
1954	St. Louis, Missouri	10,962	J. W. Storer, Oklahoma	James W. Merritt, Ga.; Joe W. Burton, Tenn.	Slater A. Murphy, Tenn.
1955	Miami, Florida	10,837	J. W. Storer, Oklahoma	James W. Merritt, Ga.; Joe W. Burton, Tenn.	Monroe F. Swilley, Ga.
1956	Kansas City, Missouri	12,254	C. C. Warren, N.C.	James W. Merritt, Ga.; Joe W. Burton, Tenn.	Harry P. Stagg, N. Mex.
1957	Chicago, Illinois	9,109	C. C. Warren, N.C.	James W. Merritt, Ga.; Joe W. Burton, Tenn.	Herschel H. Hobbs, Oklahoma
1958	Houston, Texas	11,965	Brooks Hays, Arkansas	James W. Merritt, Ga.; Joe W. Burton, Tenn.	Robert E. Naylor, Texas
1959	Louisville, Kentucky	13,612	Brooks Hays, Arkansas	James W. Merritt, Ga.; Joe W. Burton, Tenn.	R. Paul Caudill, Tenn.
1960	Miami Beach, Florida	13,143	Ramsey Pollard, Tennessee	James W. Merritt, Ga.; Joe W. Burton, Tenn.	Ralph A. Herring, N. C.
1961	St. Louis, Missouri	11,143	Ramsey Pollard, Tennessee	James W. Merritt, Ga.; Joe W. Burton, Tenn.	A. B. Van Arsdale, Ala.
1962	San Francisco, California	9,396	Herschel H. Hobbs, Oklahoma	James W. Merritt, Ga.; Joe W. Burton, Tenn.	H. Franklin Paschall, Tenn.
1963	Kansas City, Missouri	12,971	Herschel H. Hobbs, Oklahoma	James W. Merritt, Ga.; Joe W. Burton, Tenn.	Carl Bates, N. C.
1964	Atlantic City, New Jersey	13,136	Herschel H. Hobbs, Oklahoma	James W. Merritt, Ga.; Joe W. Burton, Tenn.	Enoch C. Brown, S. C.
1965	Dallas, Texas	16,053	K. Owen White, Texas	Clifton J. Allen, Tenn.; W. Fred Kendall, Tenn.	John H. Haldeman, Florida
1966	Detroit, Michigan	10,414	Wayne Dehoney, Tennessee	Clifton J. Allen, Tenn.; W. Fred Kendall, Tenn.	Ray E. Roberts, Ohio
1967	Miami Beach, Florida	14,794	Wayne Dehoney, Tennessee	Clifton J. Allen, Tenn.; W. Fred Kendall, Tenn.	Landrum P. Leavell, II, Texas
1968	Houston, Texas	15,071	H. Franklin Paschall, Tennessee	Clifton J. Allen, Tenn.; W. Fred Kendall, Tenn.	W. Douglas Hudgins, Mississippi
1969	New Orleans, Louisiana	16,678	H. Franklin Paschall, Tennessee	Clifton J. Allen, Tenn.; W. Fred Kendall, Tenn.	Scott L. Tatum, Louisiana
1970	Denver, Colorado	13,692	W. A. Criswell, Texas	Clifton J. Allen, Tenn.; W. Fred Kendall, Tenn.	Grady C. Cothen, Oklahoma
1971	St. Louis, Missouri	13,716	W. A. Criswell, Texas	Clifton J. Allen, Tenn.; W. Fred Kendall, Tenn.	John R. Claypool, Kentucky
1972	Philadelphia, Pennsylvania,	13,163	Carl E. Bates, N. C.	Clifton J. Allen, Tenn.; W. Fred Kendall, Tenn.	E. Hermond Westmoreland, Texas

Appendix C

SUMMARY OF CHURCHES BY STATE CONVENTIONS—1972 *

SBC and State Conventions	Associations	Churches	Baptism	Additions by Letter	Resident Members	Total Membership	SS Ongoing Enrolment	VBS Enrolment	Training Union Ongoing Enrolment	WMU[2] Ongoing Enrolment	Brotherhood Ongoing Enrolment	Church Music Ongoing Enrolment	Value Church Property	Total Receipts[3]	Total Mission Expenditure
SBC	1,189	34,534	445,725	518,419	8,784,699	12,067,284	7,177,651	3,240,514	2,044,445	1,125,641	454,272	1,173,004	$4,601,622,835	$1,071,512,302	$174,772,885
Alabama	75	2,950	32,265	35,526	646,188	876,237	516,821	232,873	221,991	85,073	42,451	94,471	322,358,743	74,537,554	11,516,723
Alaska	4	37	773	864	6,801	12,961	7,355	4,629	2,835	1,016	371	840	7,609,322	1,397,110	260,279
Arizona	15	232	4,792	5,672	52,426	78,187	49,911	47,168	14,936	6,148	2,767	6,148	31,500,014	6,749,552	1,080,420
Arkansas	44	1,192	14,551	17,796	251,747	367,020	212,555	92,414	84,772	17,184	9,324	31,183	126,828,907	31,672,637	6,048,726
California	34	890	14,747	15,890	181,221	267,745	156,545	82,221	46,808	17,204	7,034	22,604	115,148,623	23,133,920	2,757,815
Colorado	10	129	2,980	3,994	29,204	43,102	27,049	19,516	8,516	3,002	1,642	4,711	16,993,508	4,323,470	578,855
District of Columbia	1	62	1,406	1,896	34,095	39,766	19,105	8,003	2,517	3,552	688	3,100	33,699,592	5,741,728	650,104
Florida	47	1,481	30,908	36,794	497,899	684,747	414,699	163,593	116,911	54,256	24,204	72,138	274,821,685	67,589,889	10,016,081
Georgia	93	2,930	33,175	40,975	786,816	1,039,953	586,954	264,743	171,301	105,365	50,638	108,228	411,976,577	90,628,635	13,810,611
Hawaii	6	32	498	814	5,762	9,572	7,274	2,827	1,506	890	165	957	7,668,354	1,405,253	208,377
Illinois	35	889	9,073	7,237	140,040	199,016	135,661	74,833	34,890	17,310	6,611	15,577	73,347,798	17,481,691	2,603,141
Indiana	14	232	4,150	2,963	49,241	59,234	45,026	28,627	11,578	5,882	2,544	5,327	20,670,504	5,611,190	785,266
Kansas	13	198	3,105	3,754	40,201	57,666	38,519	21,914	11,703	5,021	2,016	5,932	21,361,997	5,303,752	867,760
Kentucky	80	2,201	22,084	19,494	492,009	684,246	364,200	170,870	71,328	51,428	17,095	50,376	215,918,031	47,658,277	7,833,021
Louisiana	51	1,309	17,527	23,316	354,999	489,727	269,813	124,927	116,693	36,144	14,062	48,145	183,230,714	44,312,134	7,073,140
Maryland	14	254	4,547	4,000	67,686	86,442	62,467	38,513	11,650	9,582	3,840	8,566	47,030,051	9,870,462	1,618,219
Michigan	13	169	2,286	1,896	29,824	37,384	27,312	17,207	7,470	3,552	1,686	3,865	17,865,886	3,733,774	538,214
Mississippi	76	1,885	19,178	25,796	405,419	558,742	311,475	134,041	124,632	47,554	19,786	65,182	199,885,942	50,596,007	7,857,271
Missouri	79	1,826	20,277	20,686	383,689	534,106	330,920	158,654	92,107	57,336	19,268	47,067	189,089,916	45,944,724	8,362,447
New Mexico	16	250	4,052	5,546	58,573	94,089	49,702	27,055	16,271	5,716	3,229	7,150	31,502,732	7,832,330	1,244,291
New York	6	85	1,028	1,466	10,107	12,874	10,661	15,938	2,757	2,075	782	1,990	8,409,788	2,650,181	470,169
North Carolina	80	3,461	31,978	30,647	815,371	1,046,302	693,176	284,350	119,230	136,768	50,824	125,676	441,039,174	98,921,298	15,683,929
Northern Plains	14	83	1,078	1,352	8,831	14,247	10,231	11,722	3,382	1,555	562	1,317	5,811,240	1,542,412	274,765
Northwest	22	234	2,874	2,724	31,215	44,641	32,408	23,081	10,834	3,597	1,119	3,532	20,737,776	4,498,421	736,197
Ohio	17	381	7,505	5,667	77,277	91,540	72,484	54,234	18,955	9,234	4,246	9,947	42,338,293	9,644,670	1,671,177
Oklahoma	41	1,386	21,586	25,060	371,275	575,747	312,505	119,940	99,021	36,830	18,184	42,875	172,672,042	42,919,893	7,339,317
Penn.-South Jersey	3	57	915	831	7,768	9,819	7,168	9,018	2,392	1,613	705	1,314	4,436,500	1,549,962	444,432
South Carolina	43	1,605	19,477	21,897	478,924	603,815	407,267	169,590	117,178	95,621	40,217	72,927	277,765,218	64,845,866	10,531,961
Tennessee	68	2,722	32,185	33,178	695,429	917,579	524,962	222,953	163,218	72,039	27,910	81,945	325,280,031	75,166,553	12,091,786
Texas	118	3,845	67,180	103,577	1,326,017	1,965,831	1,097,342	476,338	289,828	133,444	60,322	173,580	694,494,114	172,466,560	31,074,678
Utah-Idaho	8	62	570	978	6,503	9,916	6,416	5,223	2,111	1,085	405	781	3,404,100	835,437	148,489
Virginia	43	1,411	16,081	16,094	430,659	540,705	358,711	144,649	41,852	84,568	18,974	54,070	252,454,993	49,718,892	8,419,135
West Virginia	6	54	894	545	11,483	14,626	9,113	8,132	1,512	1,809	600	1,483	4,270,450	1,228,468	176,089
Miscellaneous								594							

[1]Includes 421 "nonreporting" churches. "Nonreporting" refers to those still affiliated with the Convention but who have not submitted a report for three or more years.
[2]Includes Campus and Hospital BYW as well as church statistics.
[3]Includes small amounts of income from fees, rentals, etc.

*Chart from *The Quarterly Review* (Nashville), Third Quarter, 1973, p. 9. Used by permission.

Appendix D —Educational Institutions*

SEMINARIES, ACADEMIES, BIBLE SCHOOLS—1972-1973

NAME	LOCATION	PRESIDENT	Accreditation	Faculty Including Administrative Officers	Enrolment Fall, 1972 Reg.	Enrolment Fall, 1972 Total	Enrolment Total 1972-1973 Reg.	Enrolment Total 1972-1973 Total	Graduate Students Enrolled	Graduated Sept. 1971-Aug. 1972	Graduated Since Founding	Ministerial Students	Home and Foreign Mission Volunteers	Church Education Volunteers	Church Music Volunteers	Other Church Vocation Volunteers	Volumes in Library Excluding Public Documents
Seminaries																	
American Baptist Theological Seminary[2][4]	Nashville, Tennessee	Charles E. Boddie	St.[1]	14	70	93	110	110		8	472	70		25			11,600
Golden Gate Baptist Theological Seminary	Mill Valley, California	Harold K. Graves	R.[3]	27	262	278	306	316	33	71	1,278	230	37	71		7	79,422
Midwestern Baptist Theological Seminary	Kansas City, Missouri	Milton Ferguson	R.[3]	24	234	272	346	347	33	66	620	216	38	24	6		59,775
New Orleans Baptist Theological Seminary	New Orleans, Louisiana	Grady C. Cothen	R.[3]	45	598	598	782	782	100	196	5,686	480	98	220	50		123,300
Southeastern Baptist Theological Seminary	Wake Forest, N.C.	Olin T. Binkley	R.[3]	38	581	581	693	694	94	110	2,700	633	11	49			96,667
Southern Baptist Theological Seminary	Louisville, Kentucky	Duke K. McCall	R.[3]	72	1,129	1,197	1,323	1,419	1,206	323	11,485	904	75	248	171		204,534
Southwestern Baptist Theological Seminary	Fort Worth, Texas	Robert E. Naylor	R.[3]	86	2,019	2,138	2,406	2,406	243	457	13,651	1,510	342	643	253		372,000
American Seminary Extension Center						850		850									
Seminary Extension Dept., S.B.C.					4,748	4,748											
Totals—Seminaries				306	4,893	10,755	5,966	11,672	1,709	1,231	35,892	4,043	601	1,280	480	7	947,298
Academies																	
Acadia Baptist Academy	Eunice, Louisiana	G. L. Higgins, Jr.	St.[1]	9	110	111	126	*126		28	815					1	5,183
Fork Union Mil. Academy	Fork Union, Virginia	Kenneth T. Whitescarver	R.St.	66	601	601	616	616		91	4,545				2	3	10,605
Hargrave Mil. Academy	Chatham, Virginia	Verron T. Lankford	R.St.	54	402	402	514	514		111	3,104				2	5	12,328
Harrison-Chilhowee Baptist Academy	Seymour, Tennessee	Hubert B. Smothers	St.[1]	17	169	170	293	293		42	1,895	16					5,700
Oak Hill Academy	Mouth of Wilson, Va.	Robert B. Isner	St.[1]	21	186	186	268	268		25	1,734						3,962
Oneida Baptist Institute	Oneida, Kentucky	Barclay Moore	St.[1]	17	180	180	176	176		66	1,700						7,208
San Marcos Bapt. Academy	San Marcos, Texas	Jack E. Byrom	R.St.	46	420	420	505	505		12	3,020	10		4			12,500
Valley Baptist Academy	Harlingen, Texas	H. E. Gary		12	167	167	172	172			275						4,000
Totals—Academies				242	2,235	2,237	2,670	2,676		375	17,088	29		4			61,486
Bible Schools																	
Baptist Bible Institute	Graceville, Florida	James E. Southerland	St.[1]	16	385	395	444	456		64	594	285		85		9	20,346
Clear Creek Baptist School	Pineville, Kentucky	D. M. Aldridge		12	174	174	174	174		34	541	100	15		74		10,000
Fruitland Baptist Bible Institute	Hendersonville, N.C.	E. Gary Harthcock		14	212	212	286	286		56	743	286					8,956
Mexican Baptist Bible Institute	San Antonio, Texas	H. B. Ramsour, Jr.		9	93	93	103	103		7	112	58	45				9,000
Totals—Bible Schools				51	864	874	1,007	1,019		161	1,990	729	60	85	74	1	48,302

[1]Accreditation by regional association is indicated by R. Accreditation by state department of education (or state university) is indicated by St.
[2]Supported jointly with National Baptist Convention, U.S.A. Incorporated
[3]Member, American Association of Theological Schools, on accredited list. Also accredited by the American Association of Schools of Religious Education.
[4]Accredited by Association of Bible Colleges.

*Charts from *The Quarterly Review* (Nashville), Third Quarter, 1973, pp. 58-60. Used by permission.

SENIOR COLLEGES AND UNIVERSITIES—1972-1973

NAME	LOCATION	PRESIDENT	Accreditation	Faculty Including Administrative Officers	Enrolment Fall, 1972		Enrolment Total 1972-73		Graduate Students Enrolled	Graduated Sept. 1971-Aug. 1972	Graduated Since Founding	Ministerial Students	Home and Foreign Mission Volunteers	Church Education Volunteers	Church Music Volunteers	Other Church Vocation Volunteers	Volumes in Library Excluding Public Documents
					Reg.	Total	Reg.	Total									
Averett College	Danville, Virginia	Conwell A. Anderson	R., St.	71	842	986	876	1,176		211	4,449	20		2	2	2	42,278
Bapt. Col. at Charleston	Charleston, S.C.	John A. Hamrick	R., St.	92	1,841	1,920	1,966	2,141		358	1,297	10	3	4	3		53,900
Baylor University	Waco, Texas	Abner V. McCall	R., St.	375	7,643	8,084	9,519	9,925	529	1,587	47,429	237	178	43	159	512	619,927
Belmont College	Nashville, Tenn.	Herbert C. Gabhart	R., St.	68	892	930	1,150	1,150		178	1,862	62	35	5	25		53,000
Blue Mountain Col.[2]	Blue Mtn., Miss.	E. Harold Fisher	R., St.	37	273	281	368	477		90	3,624	63		27	7	10	33,183
California Bapt. Col.	Riverside, Calif.	James R. Staples	R., St.	33	609	662	716	842		123	1,153	120	45	28	76	60	102,700
Campbell College	Bue's Creek, N.C.	Norman A. Wiggins	R., St.	120	2,156	2,344	3,061	3,246		599	10,901	96	5	16	17	64	107,240
Campbellsville College	Campbellsville, Ky.	William R. Davenport	R., St.	53	736	743	893	893		180	1,689	78	16	16	23	43	64,128
Carson Newman Col.	Jefferson City, Tenn.	John A. Fincher	R., St.	137	1,679	1,880	1,920	1,950		387	8,446	231	80	124	169	20	107,720
Cumberland College	Williamsburg, Ky.	J. M. Boswell	R., St.	98	1,751	1,751	2,176	2,176		420	6,749	81	35	52	60	16	62,908
Dallas Baptist College	Dallas, Texas	Charles P. Pitts	R., St.	77	1,395	1,475	1,794	1,814		187	545	200	6	15	8	47	77,228
East Texas Bapt. Col.	Marshall, Texas	Howard C. Bennett	R., St.	54	740	742	742	880		115	2,365	182	33	45	16	48	75,000
Furman University	Greenville, S.C.	Gordon W. Blackwell	R., St.	147	2,425	2,425	2,269	3,490	81	386	13,521	99	53	53	57	7	195,500
Gardner-Webb College	Boiling Springs, N.C.	E. Eugene Poston	R., St.	105	1,528	1,567	1,828	1,854		349	4,151	161	15	10	44		66,321
Georgetown College	Georgetown, Ky.	Robert L. Mills	R., St.	84	1,261	1,261	1,261	1,391	150	217	7,576	30	15	8	5	25	100,000
Grand Canyon College	Phoenix, Arizona	William R. Hintze, Actg.	R., St.	38	615	772	777	1,223		115	1,351	112	12	11	20	65	63,675
Hardin-Simmons Univ.	Abilene, Texas	Elwin L. Skiles	R., St.	102	1,552	1,624	2,300	2,426	276	336	11,581	114	5	5	35		166,180
Houston Baptist College	Houston, Texas	William H. Hinton	R., St.	90	1,092	1,143	1,459	1,515		187	738	60	8	5	10		63,000
Howard Payne College	Brownwood, Texas	Roger L. Brooks	R., St.	88	1,475	1,573	1,665	1,735	10	213	7,971	201	9	5		307	89,000
Judson College[1]	Marion, Ala.	N. H. McCrummen	R., St.	38	330	407	383	439		77	3,474	84	5	18	11	44	43,556
Louisiana College	Pineville, La.	G. Earl Guinn	R., St.	59	863	925	878	1,297		163	5,082	34	12	2	9	5	74,723
Mars Hill College	Mars Hill, N.C.	Fred B. Bentley	R., St.	110			1,780	1,804		285	9,398	7	8	11	25	4	80,000
Mary Hardin-Baylor Col.	Belton, Texas	Bobby E. Parker	R., St.	75	851	1,158	1,237	1,446		239	4,936	10	8	8			67,123
Mercer University	Macon, Georgia	Rufus Carrollton Harris	R., St.	173	2,305	2,326	2,782	2,818	61	451	14,674	21	8	8	8	8	180,000
Mercer Univ. at Atla.	Atlanta, Georgia	Rufus Carrollton Harris	R., St.	29	439	447	595	656		39	45			19	10	2	39,638
Meredith College[2]	Raleigh, N.C.	John E. Weems	R., St.	84	1,259	1,500	1,295	1,456		226	6,394		43		81	26	61,298
Mississippi College	Clinton Mississippi	W. Lewis Nobles	R., St.	123	2,373	2,430	2,270	3,420	526	622	13,192	155	30	22	52	70	134,000
Mo. Bapt. Col.-St. Louis	St. Louis, Missouri	Frank B. Kellogg	R., St.	40	442	483	483	563				70			40		20,261
Mobile College	Mobile, Alabama	William K. Weaver, Jr.	R., St.	46	494	629	551	887		92	436	94	120	10			37,063
Oklahoma Bapt. Univ.	Shawnee, Okla.	William G. Tanner	R., St.	133	1,701	1,707	1,916	1,922		230	6,272	289		24	34	7	95,000
Ouachita Bapt. Univ.	Arkadelphia, Ark.	Daniel R. Grant	R., St.	102	1,468	1,507	1,560	1,860	45	217	6,770	123	18		10	20	84,244
Palm Beach Atlantic Col.	W. Palm Beach, Fla.	Warner Earle Fusselle	R., St.	38	346	363	386	386		54	54	72	6	8	7		31,000
Richmond, Univ. of	Richmond, Virginia	E. Bruce Heilman	R., St.	235	4,550	5,150	4,359	6,699	482	618	17,554	24				21	188,000

NAME	LOCATION	PRESIDENT	Accreditation	Faculty, incl. Admin. Officers	Enrol. Fall 1972 Reg.	Enrol. Fall 1972 Total	Enrol. Total 1972-73 Reg.	Enrol. Total 1972-73 Total		Graduated Sept. 1971-Aug. 1972	Graduated Since Founding	Ministerial Students	Home & Foreign Mission Vol.	Church Education Vol.	Church Music Vol.	Other Church Vocation Vol.	Volumes in Library Excluding Public Documents
Samford University	Birmingham, Ala.	Leslie S. Wright	R., St.	162	2,867	5,027	3,062	5,222	201	611	13,987	193	28	50	92	92	192,891
Shorter College	Rome, Georgia	Randall H. Minor	R., St.	55	501	537	543	590		120	3,300	28	10	3	27	9	60,000
Southwest Baptist Col.	Bolivar, Missouri	James L. Sells	R., St.	62	1,152	1,171	1,379	1,379		205	3,813	197	42		16	44	70,000
Stetson University	DeLand, Florida	John E. Johns	R., St.	139	2,789	2,998	3,014	3,771	216	623	12,470	45	3		24	17	215,529
Tift College[2]	Forsyth, Georgia	Robert W. Jackson	R., St.	36	405	657	581	839		105	3,702		3	1	3	4	46,634
Union University	Jackson, Tennessee	Robert E. Craig	R., St.	62	815	946	950	1,131		164	11,541	85	22	17	32	23	55,815
Va. Intermont Col.[2]	Bristol, Virginia	Floyd V. Turner	R., St.	52	564	589	578	606		153	6,354						49,322
Wake Forest Univ.	Winston-Salem, N.C.	James Ralph Scales	R., St.	504	4,013	4,050	4,756	4,756	786	767	19,843	36	12	12	3	3	439,209
Wayland Bapt. Col.	Plainview, Texas	Roy C. McClung	R., St.	52	927	934	1,222	1,229		88	1,863	132	35	6	35		61,000
William Carey College	Hattiesburg, Miss.	J. Ralph Noonkester	R., St.	68	835	1,002	1,138	1,397		244	3,157	107	2	25	27	29	76,000
William Jewell College	Liberty, Missouri	Thomas S. Field	R., St.	81	1,185	1,205	1,160	1,236	—	191	6,734	36	4	9	7	5	112,128
Totals—Senior Colleges				4,427	55,483	71,839	75,698	88,113	3,363	12,822	312,442	4,000	928	730	1,221	1,659	4,657,322

¹Accreditation by regional association is indicated by R. Accreditation by state department of education (or state university) is indicated by St.
²Colleges for women.

JUNIOR COLLEGES—1972-1973

NAME	LOCATION	PRESIDENT	Accreditation	Faculty, including Administrative Officers	Enrolment Fall, 1972 Reg.	Enrolment Fall, 1972 Total	Enrolment Total 1972-1973 Reg.	Enrolment Total 1972-1973 Total	Graduated Sept. 1971-Aug. 1972	Graduated Since Founding	Ministerial Students	Home and Foreign Mission Volunteers	Church Education Volunteers	Church Music Volunteers	Other Church Vocation Volunteers	Volumes in Library Excluding Public Documents
Anderson College	Anderson, S.C.	J. Cordell Maddox	R., St.[1]	48	1,044	1,044	1,331	1,331	194	3,740	54	3		5		16,207
Bluefield College	Bluefield, Virginia	Charles L. Tyer	R., St.	27	260	354	270	275	89	3,098	10			8	8	25,533
Brewton-Parker Col.	Mt. Vernon, Georgia	J. Theodore Phillips	R., St.	33	512	512	512	762	108	5,037	25	2				17,466
Chowan College	Murfreesboro, N.C.	Bruce E. Whitaker	R., St.	87	1,194	1,239	1,504	1,504	298	3,462	20	3	3	4	5	43,825
Clarke College	Newton, Mississippi	W. Lowrey Compere	R., St.	20	199	335	226	320	88	4,365	90	3		20	17	16,000
Missouri Baptist College	Hannibal, Missouri	Frank B. Kellogg	R., St.	30	386	418	465	465	108	3,802	22	5	4	1	13	21,025
N. Greenville College	Tigerville, S.C.	Harold E. Lindsey	R., St.	35	601	638	533	533	133	3,044	45	2		3		25,076
Southern Baptist College	Walnut Ridge, Arkansas	H. E. Williams	R., St.	30	525	570	765	765	43	1,529	35	1	5	10		32,242
Truett-McConnell College	Cleveland, Georgia	Ronald E. Weitman	R., St.	28	266	309	348	417	44	1,362	12		1	1		18,000
Wingate College	Wingate, N.C.	Budd E. Smith	R., St.	84	1,536	1,560	1,794	1,851	600	37,163	22	4	17	17	5	57,000
Totals—Junior Colleges				422	6,523	6,988	7,748	8,223	1,805	66,602	335	23	25	68	48	272,374

¹Accreditation by regional association is indicated by R. Accreditation by state department of education (or state university) is indicated by St.

BIBLIOGRAPHY

The following is a select bibliography to direct attention to the principal materials used in the preparation of this book. Hundreds of other books, particularly in the area of biography, could have been included. All thirty-one of the Baptist state papers have been read extensively. *The Commission* (Richmond), *Home Missions* (Atlanta), and *Facts and Trends* (Nashville) and their predecessors, along with other periodicals and pamphlets from agencies of the Convention, have been used. Journals like the *Review and Expositor* (Louisville), *Southwestern Journal of Theology* (Fort Worth), *Foundations* (Rochester, New York), *Church History* (Berne, Indiana), and several journals now extinct have contributed. All state Baptist histories have been examined. The principal source has been the *Annuals* of the Southern Baptist Convention from 1845 to the present. These have been supplemented by *The Quarterly Review* (Nashville) and the *Southern Baptist Handbook* (Nashville). The minutes of the state conventions have been scanned and in some cases researched thoroughly. The following additional books have helped.

American Baptist Year Book. Philadelphia: American Baptist Publication Society, 1847, 1862, and 1878.

ASPLUND, JOHN (ed.). *The Annual Register of the Baptist Denomination in North America* (1791-96). Copies on file at Southwestern Baptist Theological Seminary, Fort Worth, Texas.

BAILEY, KENNETH K. *Southern White Protestantism in the Twentieth Century*. New York: Harper and Row, 1964.

BAKER, ROBERT A. *A Baptist Source Book, with Particular Reference to Southern Baptists*. Nashville: Broadman Press, 1966.

_____. *Relations Between Northern and Southern Baptists*. Fort Worth: 2nd edition, Marvin D. Evans Printing Company, 1954.

_____. *The Blossoming Desert: A Concise History of Texas Baptists*. Waco: Word Books, 1970.

_____. *The First Southern Baptists*. Nashville: Broadman Press, 1966.

_____. *The Story of the Sunday School Board*. Nashville: Convention Press, 1966.

_____. *The Thirteenth Check—The Jubilee History of the Annuity Board of the Southern Baptist Convention 1918-68*. Nashville: Broadman Press, 1968.

Baptist Missionary Magazine (Boston) under various titles, 1803-1909.

Baptist World Congress Proceedings (since 1905).

BARCK, OSCAR THEODORE and BLAKE, NELSON MANFRED. *Since 1900*. New York: The Macmillan Company, 1952.

BARNES, GILBERT H. *The Anti-Slavery Impulse (1830-1844)*. New York: Appleton-Century-Crofts, Inc., 1933.

BARNES, W. W. *The Southern Baptist Convention 1845-1953*. Nashville: Broadman Press, 1954.

BENEDICT, DAVID. *A General History of the Baptist Denomination in America, and Other Parts of the World.* Boston: Lincoln and Edmands, 1813—in two volumes.

———. *Fifty Years Among the Baptists.* New York: Sheldon and Company, 1859.

BROADUS, JOHN A. *Memoir of James Petigru Boyce.* Nashville: Sunday School Board, 1927.

BURKITT, LEMUEL, and READ, JESSE. *A Concise History of the Kehukee Baptist Association.* Halifax: A. Hodge, 1803.

BURROUGHS, PRINCE E. *Fifty Fruitful Years.* Nashville: Baptist Sunday School Board, 1941.

BURTON, JOE W. *Epochs of Home Missions.* Atlanta: Home Mission Board, 1945.

CAMPBELL, JESSE H. *Georgia Baptists: Historical and Biographical.* Macon: J. W. Burke and Company, rev. 1874.

CAREY, S. P. *William Carey.* Philadelphia: The Judson Press, 1923.

CARLETON, WILLIAM A. *"Not Yours But You"—The Life of Joseph Samuel Murrow.* Unpublished Th.D. dissertation, Southwestern Baptist Theological Seminary, Fort Worth, Texas, 1945.

CARROLL, B. H., JR. *The Genesis of American Anti-Missionism.* Louisville: Baptist Book Concern, 1902.

CARROLL, J. M. *A History of Texas Baptists.* Dallas: Baptist Standard Publishing Co., 1923.

CAUTHEN, BAKER JAMES. *Advance: A History of Southern Baptist Foreign Missions.* Nashville: Broadman Press, 1970.

CHRISTIAN, JOHN T. *History of Baptists of Louisiana.* Shreveport: Louisiana Baptist Convention, 1923.

COLE, STEWART G. *History of Fundamentalism.* New York: Richard R. Smith, Inc., 1931.

COOK, HARVEY T. *A Biography of Richard Furman.* Greenville: Baptist Courier, 1915.

COX, NORMAN W. (ed.). *Encyclopedia of Southern Baptists,* Vols. I and II. Nashville: Broadman Press, 1958; Davis C. Woolley, (ed.). Vol. III. Nashville: Broadman Press, 1971.

COX, MRS. W. J. *Following in His Train.* Nashville: Broadman Press, 1938.

COX, F. A. and HOBY, J. *The Baptists in America.* New York: Leavitt, Lord and Co., 1836.

DAGG, J. L. *A Treatise on Church Order.* Charleston, S. C.: Southern Baptist Publication Society, 1858.

DAVIS, J. *History of the Welsh Baptists.* Pittsburgh: D. M. Hogan, 1835.

EATON, W. H. *Historical Sketch of the Massachusetts Baptist Missionary Society and Convention, 1802-1902.* Boston: Massachusetts Baptist Convention, 1903.

EDWARDS, MORGAN. *Materials Toward a History of American Baptists.* Of the twelve-volume work projected, only four have been published (Philadelphia 1770-1792). Manuscript volumes are on microfilm at the Southern Baptist Historical Commission, Nashville, Tennessee.

EIGHMY, JOHN LEE. *Churches in Cultural Captivity.* Knoxville: University of Tennessee Press, 1972.

ESTEP, W. R. *Baptists and Christian Unity.* Nashville: Broadman Press, 1966.

FROST, J. M. *The Sunday School Board, Southern Baptist Convention, Its History and Work.* Nashville: Sunday School Board, 1914.

FULLER, B. F. *History of Texas Baptists.* Louisville: Baptist Book Concern, 1900.

FULLER, RICHARD and WAYLAND, FRANCIS. *Domestic Slavery Considered As a Scriptural Institution.* New York: Lewis Colby, 1845.

FURMAN, WOOD. *A History of the Charleston Association of Baptist Churches in the State of South Carolina.* Charleston: J. Hoff, 1811.

FURNISS, NORMAN F. *The Fundamentalist Controversy 1918-1931.* New Haven: Yale University Press, 1954.

GATES, ERRETT. *The Early Relation and Separation of Baptists and Disciples.* Chicago: R. R. Donnelly and Sons, 1904.

GEWEHR, WESLEY M. *The Great Awakening in Virginia, 1740-1790.* Durham: Duke University Press, 1930.

GILLETTE, A. D. (ed.). *Century Minutes of the Philadelphia Baptist Association, 1707-1807.* Philadelphia: American Baptist Publication Society, 1851.

GOEN, C. C. *Revivalism and Separatism in New England, 1740-1800.* New Haven: Yale University Press, 1962.

GRAVES, J. R. *Old Landmarkism—What Is It?* Memphis: Baptist Book House, Graves, Mahaffy and Co., 1880.

GRIME, J. H. *History of Middle-Tennessee Baptists.* Nashville: Baptist and Reflector, 1902.

GUILD, REUBEN A. *Chaplain Smith and the Baptists.* Philadelphia: American Baptist Publication Society, 1885.

HARRISON, PAUL M. *Authority and Power in the Free Church Tradition: A Social Case Study of the American Baptist Convention.* Princeton: Princeton University Press, 1959.

HASSELL, C. B. *History of the Church of God from the Creation to A.D. 1885,* rev. by Sylvester Hassell. Middletown, New York: Gilbert Beebe's Sons, 1886.

HOLCOMBE, HOSEA. *Baptists in Alabama.* Philadelphia: King and Beard, 1840.

HOVEY, ALVAH. *A Memoir of the Life and Times of the Reverend Isaac Backus.* Boston: Gould and Lincoln, 1859.

HUDSON, WINTHROP S. (ed.). *Baptist Concepts of the Church.* Philadelphia: The Judson Press, 1959.

HUGGINS, M. A. *A History of North Carolina Baptists 1727-1932.* Raleigh: General Board, North Carolina Baptist State Convention, 1967.

JERNEGAN, MARCUS W. *The American Colonies 1492-1750.* New York: F. Unger Pub. Co., 1959.

JETER, J. B. *The Recollections of a Long Life.* Richmond: Religious Herald Co., 1891.

JOINER, E. E. *A History of Florida Baptists.* Jacksonville: Florida Baptist Convention, 1972.

JONES, J. WILLIAM. *Christ in the Camp.* Richmond: B. F. Johnson, 1887.

LATOURETTE, KENNETH SCOTT. *The Nineteenth Century Outside Europe,* Volume III in series, *Christianity in a Revolutionary Age.* New York: Harper & Brothers, 1961.

LITTLE, LEWIS P. *Imprisoned Preachers and Religious Liberty in Virginia.* Lynchburg: J. P. Bell Co., 1938.

LOONEY, FLOYD. *History of California Southern Baptists.* Fresno: Board of Directors of The Southern Baptist General Convention of California, 1954.

LUMPKIN, WILLIAM L. *Baptist Foundations in the South.* Nashville: Broadman Press, 1961.

KEEN, WILLIAM W. (ed.). *The Bi-Centennial Celebration of the Founding of the First Baptist Church of the City of Philadelphia, 1698-1898.* Philadelphia: American Baptist Publication Society, 1899.

KING, JOE M. *History of South Carolina Baptists.* Columbia: General Board of the South Carolina Baptist Convention, 1964.

McGLOTHLIN, W. J. *Baptist Confessions of Faith.* Philadelphia: American Baptist Publication Society, 1911.

McLEMORE, R. A. *A History of Mississippi Baptists, 1780-1970.* Jackson: Mississippi Baptist Convention Board, 1971.

MANSCHRECK, CLYDE L. (ed.). *A History of Christianity* (Vol. 2, *Reformation to the Present*). Englewood Cliffs, New Jersey: Prentice-Hall, Inc., 1964.

MASTERS, FRANK M. *A History of Baptists in Kentucky.* Louisville: Kentucky Baptist Historical Society, 1953.

MAY, LYNN E., JR. *The First Baptist Church of Nashville, Tennessee 1820-1970.* Nashville: First Baptist Church, 1970.

MERRIAM, EDMUND F. *A History of American Baptist Missions.* Philadelphia: American Baptist Publication Society, 1900.

MOREHOUSE, HENRY L. *Baptist Home Missions in America 1832-1882.* New York: American Baptist Home Mission Society, 1883.

MUELLER, WILLIAM A. *A History of Southern Baptist Theological Seminary.* Nashville: Broadman Press, 1959.

NEELY, H. K., JR. *The Territorial Expansion of the Southern Baptist Convention 1894-1959.* Unpublished Th.D. dissertation, Southwestern Baptist Theological Seminary, Fort Worth, Texas, 1963.

NEWMAN, A. H. (ed.). *A Century of Baptist Achievement.* Philadelphia: American Baptist Publication Society, 1901.

———. *A History of Baptist Churches in the United States.* Philadelphia: American Baptist Publication Society, 1898.

OWENS, LOULIE LATIMER. *Saints of Clay—The Shaping of South Carolina Baptists.* Columbia: The South Carolina Baptist Convention, 1971.

PASCHAL, GEORGE W. *History of North Carolina Baptists.* Raleigh: General Board, North Carolina Baptist State Convention, two volumes, 1930, 1955.

PATTERSON, W. MORGAN. *Baptist Successionism—A Critical View.* Valley Forge: The Judson Press, 1969.

REIMERS, DAVID M. *White Protestantism and the Negro.* New York: Oxford University Press, 1965.

RIPPON, JOHN (ed.). *Baptist Annual Register.* London: 1790-1802.

ROBERTSON, A. T. *Life and Letters of John Albert Broadus.* Philadelphia: American Baptist Publication Society, 1901.

ROGERS, J. S. *History of Arkansas Baptists.* Little Rock: Executive Board of Arkansas Baptist State Convention, 1948.

RUTLEDGE, ARTHUR B. *Mission to America.* Nashville: Broadman Press, 1969.

RYLAND, GARNETT. *The Baptists of Virginia 1699-1926.* Richmond: The Virginia Baptist Board of Missions and Education, 1955.

SAMPEY, JOHN R. *Memoirs of John R. Sampey.* Nashville: Broadman Press, 1947.

SEMPLE, ROBERT B. *A History of the Rise and Progress of the Baptists in Virginia,* rev. by G. W. Beals. Philadelphia: American Baptist Publication Society, 1894.

SHEETS, HENRY. *Who Are Primitive Baptists?* Raleigh: Edwards and Broughton Printing Co., c1908.

SHELLEY, BRUCE L. *Conservative Baptists: A Story of Twentieth-Century Dissent.* Denver: Conservative Baptist Theological Seminary, 1960.

SHURDEN, WALTER B. *Not a Silent People: Controversies That Have Shaped Southern Baptists.* Nashville: Broadman Press, 1972.

SMITH, J. A. *Memoir of Nathaniel Colver.* Boston: George A. Foxcroft, Jr., 1875.

SPAIN, RUFUS B. *At Ease in Zion—Social History of Southern Baptists 1865-1900.* Nashville: Vanderbilt University Press, 1961, 1967.

ST. AMANT, C. PENROSE. *Short History of Louisiana Baptists.* Nashville: Broadman Press, 1948.

STRIPLING, PAUL W. *The Negro Excision from Baptist Churches in Texas 1861-1870.* Unpublished Th.D. dissertation, Southwestern Baptist Theological Seminary, Fort Worth, 1967.

SWEET, W. W. (ed.). *Religion on the American Frontier,* 4 vols. Vol. I, *The Baptists, 1783-1830.* New York: Henry Holt and Co., 1931.

TAYLOR, JAMES B. *Memoir of Luther Rice.* Baltimore: Armstrong and Berry, 2nd ed., 1841.

TAYLOR, JOHN. *A History of Ten Baptist Churches.* Frankfort, Ky.: J. H. Holeman, 1823.

THOM, WILLIAM T. *The Struggle for Religious Freedom in Virginia: the Baptists.* Baltimore: The Johns Hopkins University Press, 1900.

TORBET, ROBERT G. *A History of the Baptists.* Valley Forge: The Judson Press, 1950, 1963.

TOWNSEND, LEAH. *South Carolina Baptists, 1670-1805.* Florence, S.C.: Florence Printing Co., 1935.

TULL, JAMES E. *A Study of Southern Baptist Landmarkism in the Light of Historical Baptist Ecclesiology.* Privately published Ph.D. dissertation, Columbia University, New York, 1960.

TURNER, FREDERICK JACKSON. *The Rise of the New West 1819-1829.* New York: Harper and Brothers, 1906.

———. *The United States 1830-1850.* New York: P. Smith, 1950.

VAIL, ALBERT L. *The Morning Hour of American Baptist Missions.* Philadelphia: American Baptist Publication Society, 1907.

———. *Baptists Mobilized for Missions.* Philadelphia: American Baptist Publication Society, 1911.

VEDDER, H. C. *A Short History of the Baptists.* Philadelphia: American Baptist Publication Society, 1927.

WATTS, JOSEPH T. *The Rise and Progress of Maryland Baptists.* Baltimore: State Mission Board, c1951.

WAYLAND, FRANCIS. *Notes on the Principles and Practices of Baptist Churches.* Boston: Gould and Lincoln, 1856.

WHITE, CHARLES L. *A Century of Faith.* Philadelphia: The Judson Press, 1932.

WHITSITT, WILLIAM H. *A Question in Baptist History.* Louisville: Dearing, 1896.

WOODSON, HORTENSE. *Giant in the Land.* Nashville: Broadman Press, 1950.

WRIGHT, STEPHEN. *History of the Shaftsbury Baptist Association from 1781 to 1853.* Troy, N. Y.: A. G. Johnson, 1853.

YEAMAN, W. POPE. *History of the Missouri Baptist General Association.* Columbia: E. W. Stephens Press, 1899.

INDEX

471

345-47
United Society for the Spread of the
Gospel, 143
University of Richmond (see Richmond
College), 126, 184
Utah-Idaho Southern Baptist
Convention, 379-80
Utah Southern Baptists, 379-80

Valentine, Foy D., 441
Van Ness, I. J., 430
Vardeman, Jeremiah, 143
Vaughn, Ashley, 140
Vermont Southern Baptists, 366
Virginia, 37-38, 60-61
Virginia Baptist Education Society, 125,
146, 200
Virginia Baptist Foreign Mission
Society, 159
Virginia Baptists, 37-38, 43-45, 52-54,
64-73, 78-81, 122-26, 183-84
Virginia Baptists, call of, 159
Virginia, General Association of Baptists
of, 72-73

Wake Forest College, 128, 146
Walker, Arthur L., 367
Walker, Edmond, 384
Walker, Joseph, 206
Waller, John, 64-67, 80
Waller, John L., 135, 190, 197, 212-14
Ward, William, 106
Warren, E. W., 291
Washington conference, 266-67
Washington, George, 73
Washington Southern Baptists, 381-83
Watson, L. A., 383
Watts, T. J., 433
Wayland, Francis, 110-11, 158
Welch, James E., 110, 115
Welsh, Darwin E., 380
Welsh Neck church, 36-37
West North Central Region, 374-75
West Virginia Convention of Southern
Baptists, 371
West Virginia Southern Baptists, 370-71
Western Baptist Education Society, 200
Western Baptist Theological Institute,
200
Westmoreland, N. J., 377
Westward expansion after the
Revolution, 86-87
Whitefield, George, 47-48
Whitsitt controversy, 281
Whitsitt, William H., 303
Wicker, Maurice F., 380
Wichita, Kansas, First Baptist Church,
422-23

William Jewell College, 221
Williams, J. Howard, 438
Williams, Robert, 45-46
Williams, Roger, 21
Willingham, R. J., 288-89
Willis, Joseph, 141
Winchester, Elhanan, 419-21
Winkler, E. T., 262
Wisconsin Southern Baptists, 374
Wolfe, M. H., 312
Woman's Missionary Union, 297-99,
395, 444-45
Women in mission work, 247-48
Wood, James E., Jr., 443
Woolley, Davis C., 442
World Council of Churches, 411
World's Christian Fundamentals
Conference, 397
Wyoming Southern Baptists, 377-78

Yates, Matthew T., 205, 228-29
Youth enlistment, 299-300